31472400301226

AUG 1 1 2017

D1120106

the unbeatable Squirrel Girl

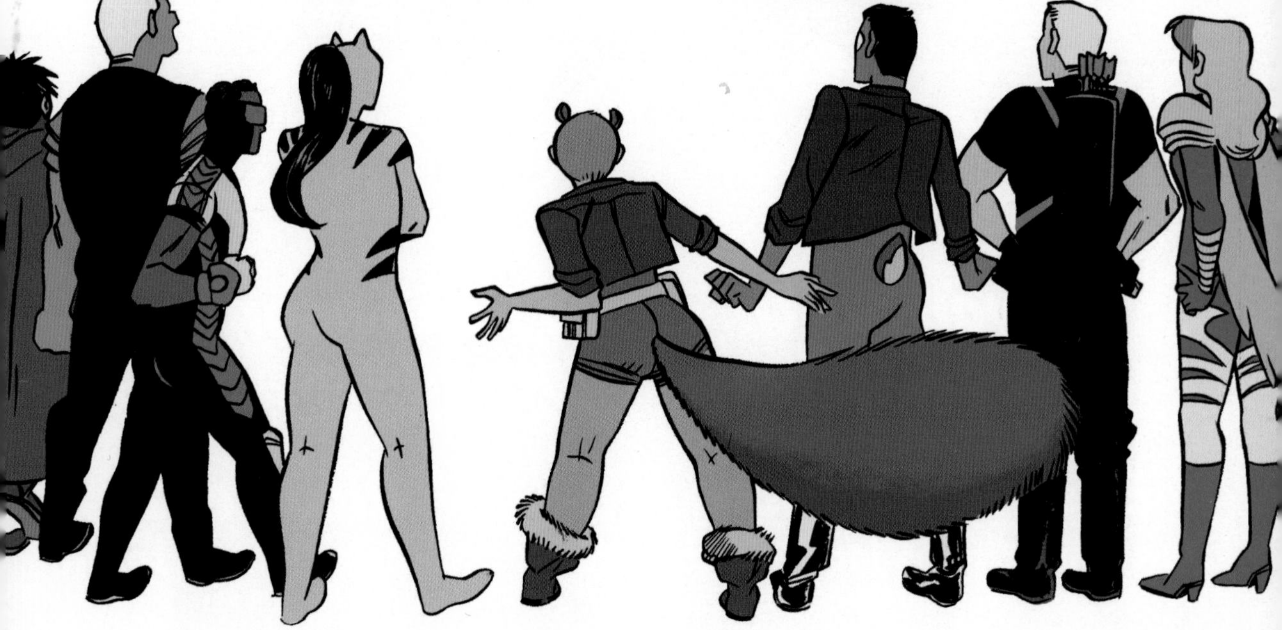

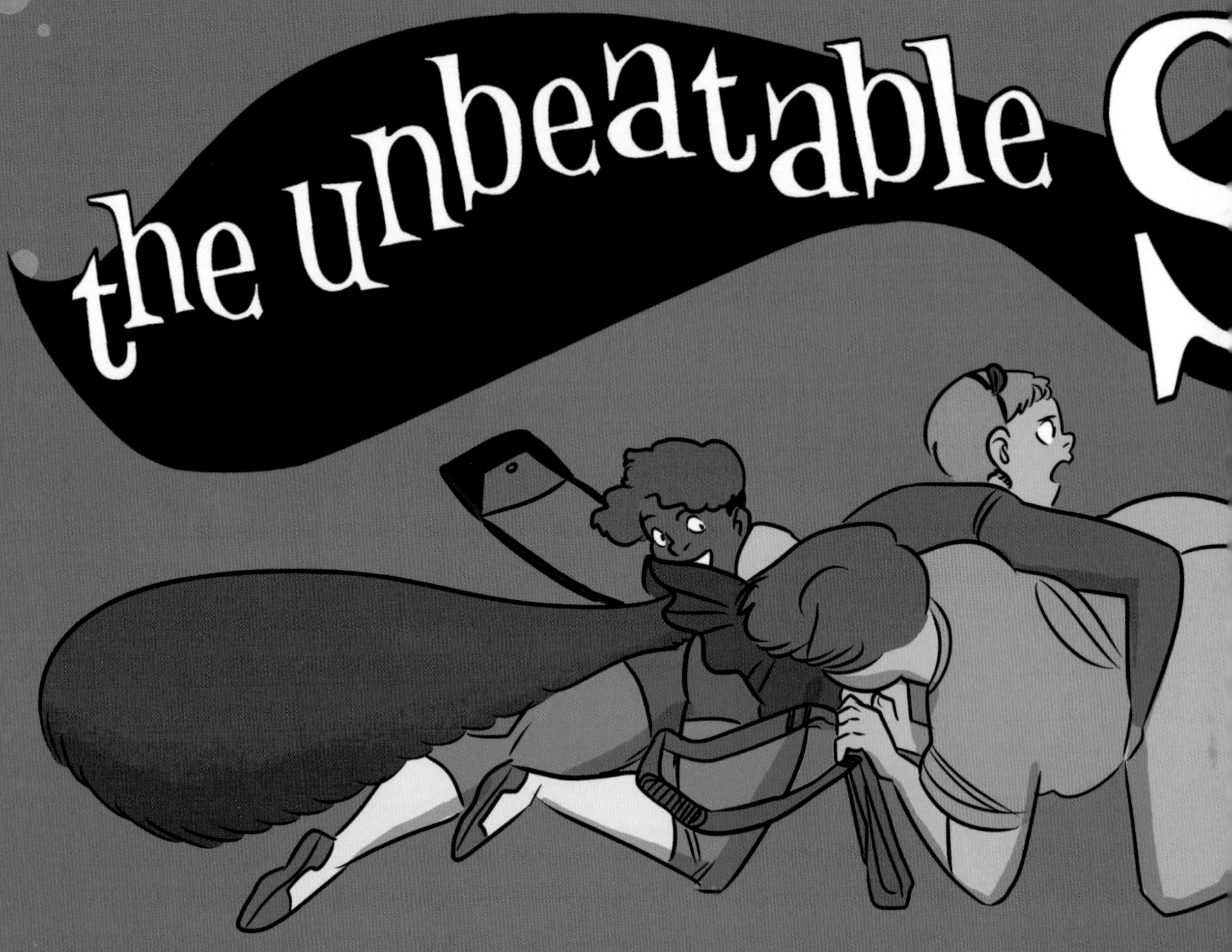
the unbeatable

Ryan North
WITH **Chip Zdarsky** (#6)
WRITERS

Erica Henderson (#1-10)
& **Jacob Chabot** (#11)
PENCILERS

Erica Henderson (#1-8),
Tom Fowler (#9-10) & **Jacob Chabot** (#11)
INKERS

Rico Renzi
WITH **Erica Henderson** (#7)
COLOR ART

COLLECTION EDITOR: **JENNIFER GRÜNWALD**
ASSISTANT EDITOR: **CAITLIN O'CONNELL**
ASSOCIATE MANAGING EDITOR: **KATERI WOODY**
EDITOR, SPECIAL PROJECTS: **MARK D. BEAZLEY**
VP PRODUCTION & SPECIAL PROJECTS: **JEFF YOUNGQUIST**
SVP PRINT, SALES & MARKETING: **DAVID GABRIEL**
BOOK DESIGNER: **JAY BOWEN**

EDITOR IN CHIEF: **AXEL ALONSO**
CHIEF CREATIVE OFFICER: **JOE QUESADA**
PUBLISHER: **DAN BUCKLEY**
EXECUTIVE PRODUCER: **ALAN FINE**

THE UNBEATABLE SQUIRREL GIRL VOL. 2. Contains material originally published in magazine form as THE UNBEATABLE SQUIRREL GIRL #1-11 and HOWARD THE DUCK #6. First printing 2017. ISBN# 978-1-302-90373-2. Published by MARVEL WORLDWIDE, INC., a subsidiary of MARVEL ENTERTAINMENT, LLC. OFFICE OF PUBLICATION: 135 West 50th Street, New York, NY 10020. **Printed in China.** ALAN FINE, President, Marvel Entertainment; DAN BUCKLEY, President, TV, Publishing & Brand Management; JOE QUESADA, Chief Creative Officer; TOM BREVOORT, SVP of Publishing; DAVID BOGART, SVP of Business Affairs & Operations, Publishing & Partnership; C.B. CEBULSKI, VP of Brand Management & Development, Asia; DAVID GABRIEL, SVP of Sales & Marketing, Publishing; JEFF YOUNGQUIST, VP of Production & Special Projects; DAN CARR, Executive Director of Publishing Technology; ALEX MORALES, Director of Publishing Operations; SUSAN CRESPI, Production Manager; STAN LEE, Chairman Emeritus. For information regarding advertising in Marvel Comics or on Marvel.com, please contact Vit DeBellis, Integrated Sales Manager, at vdebellis@marvel.com. For Marvel subscription inquiries, please call 888-511-5480. **Manufactured between 12/30/2016 and 3/13/2017 by R.R. DONNELLEY ASIA PRINTING SOLUTIONS, CHINA.**

10 9 8 7 6 5 4 3 2 1

quirrel Girl

Joe Morris (#1), **Matt Digges** (#2), **David Robbins** (#2), **Chip Zdarsky** (#2 & #6),
Doc Shaner (#3), **Joey Ellis** (#7), **Chris Schweizer** (#8) & **Brandon Lamb** (#9)
TRADING CARD ART

Joe Quinones
#6 VAN ART

Andy Hirsch
#8 1918 SEQUENCE ART

David Malki
#9 "MOLE MAN'S DEAL..."

Kyle Starks
#10 FLASHBACK ART

Erica Henderson
#11 FINAL PANEL ART

VC's Clayton Cowles (#1-2, #4)
& **Travis Lanham** (#3, #5-11)
LETTERERS

Erica Henderson
WITH **Joe Quinones** (#6)
COVER ARTISTS

Howard the Duck #6

WRITERS: **CHIP ZDARSKY** WITH **RYAN NORTH**
PENCILER: **JOE QUINONES**
INKERS: **JOE RIVERA, MARC DEERING & JOE QUINONES**

COLORISTS: **JOE QUINONES & JORDAN GIBSON**
LETTERER: **VC'S TRAVIS LANHAM**
COVER ART: **JOE QUINONES** WITH **ERICA HENDERSON**

Chris Robinson & **Charles Beacham**
ASSISTANT EDITORS

Wil Moss
EDITOR

Tom Brevoort
EXECUTIVE EDITOR

SPECIAL THANKS TO CK RUSSELL, DYLAN TODD, MICHAEL WIGGAM & CASSIE KELLY

1

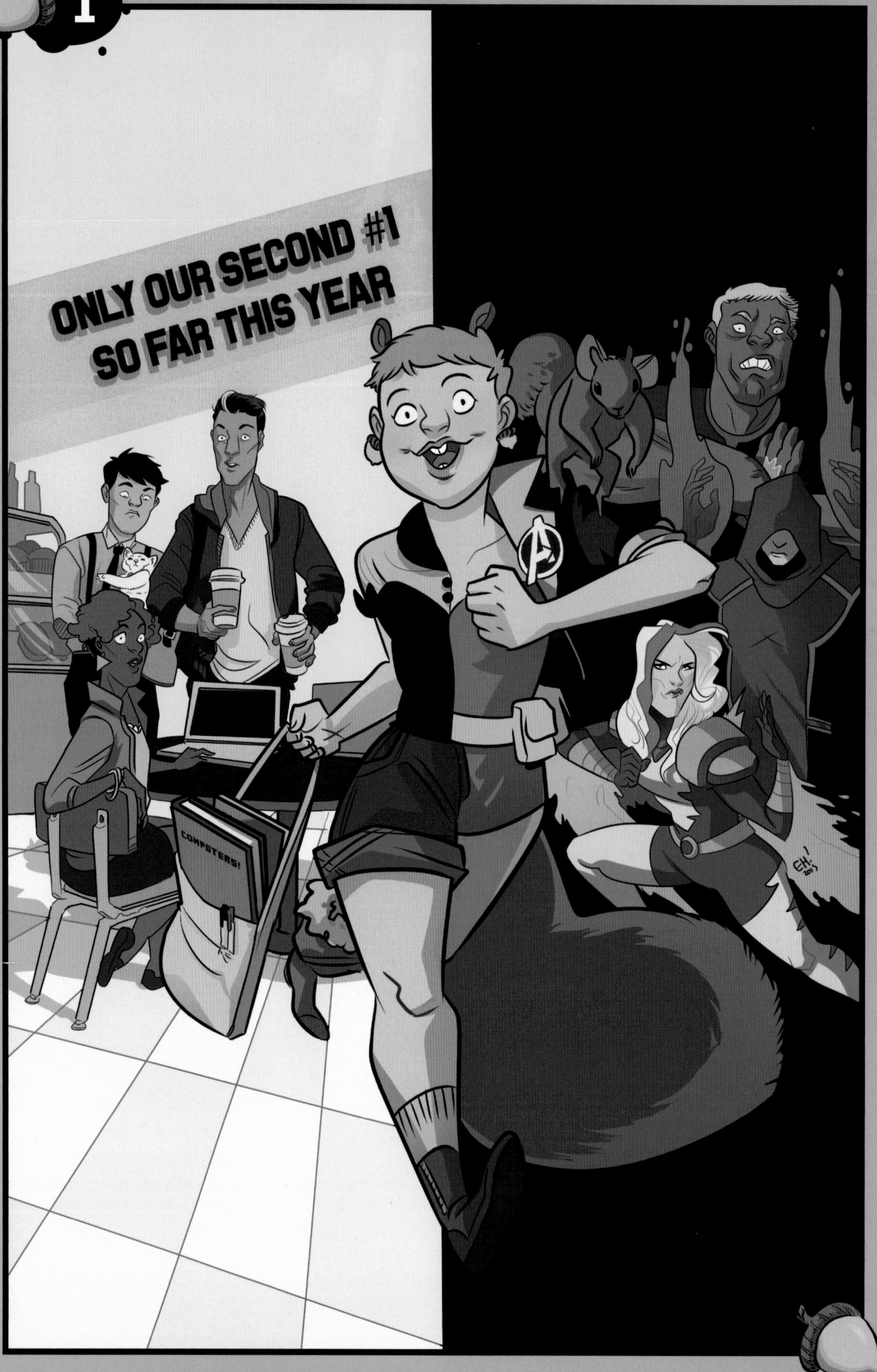
ONLY OUR SECOND #1
SO FAR THIS YEAR
COMPUTERS!

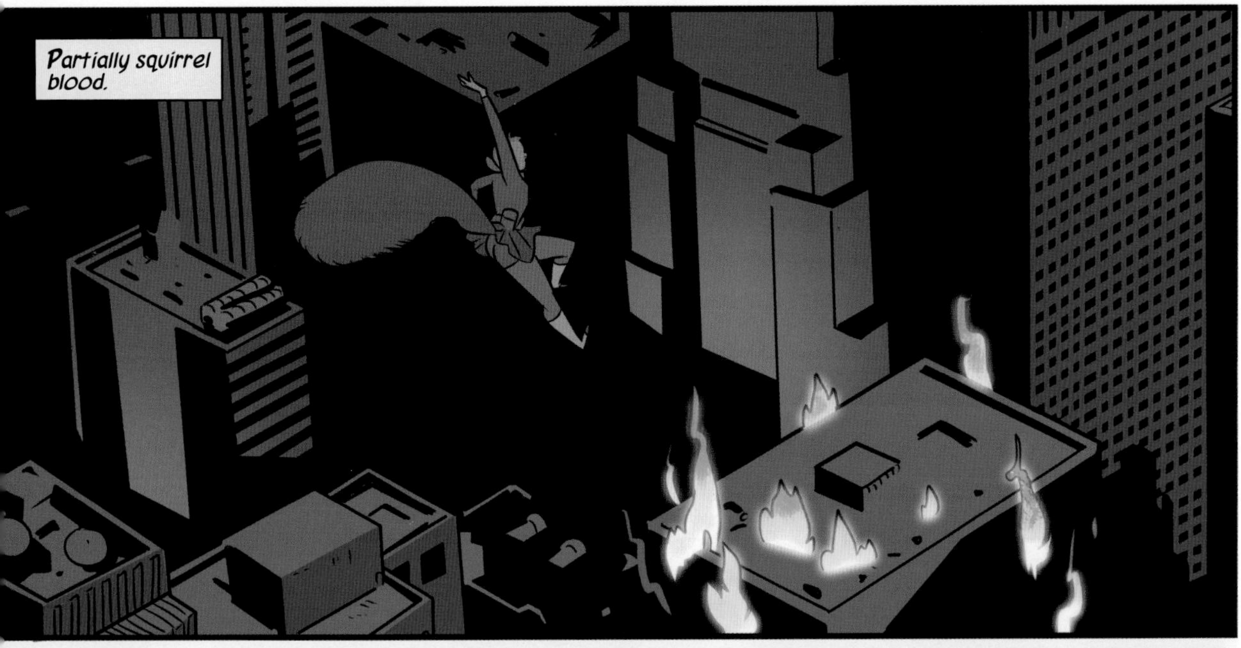
Partially squirrel blood.

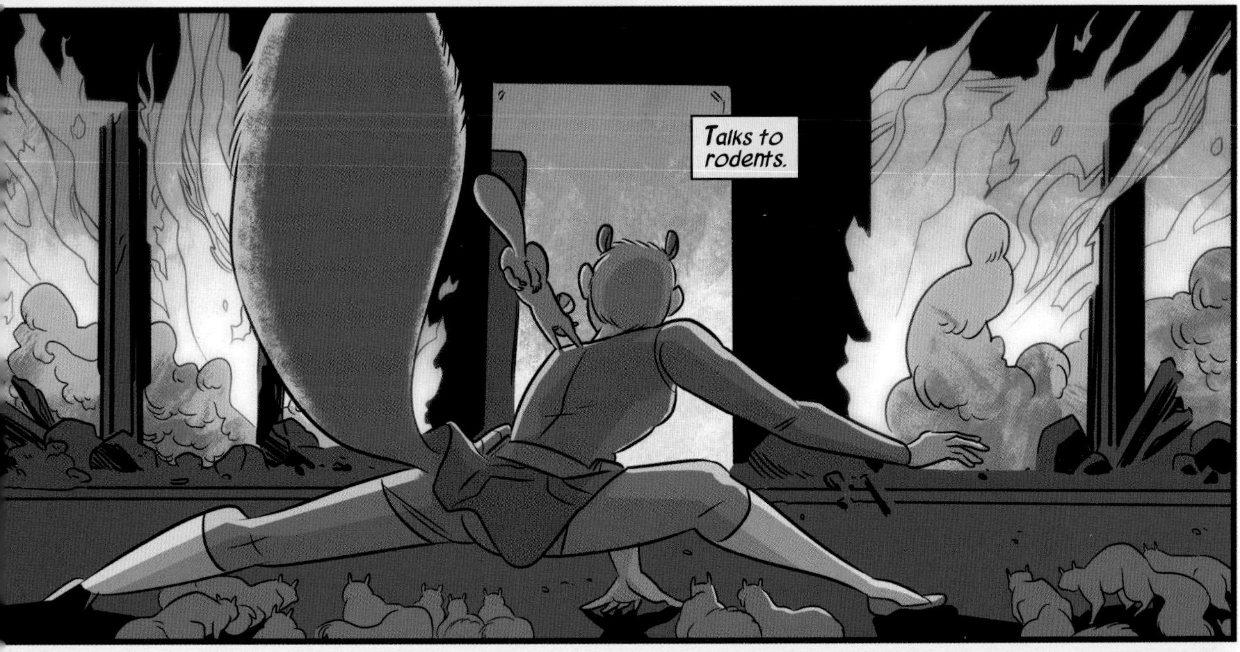
Talks to rodents.

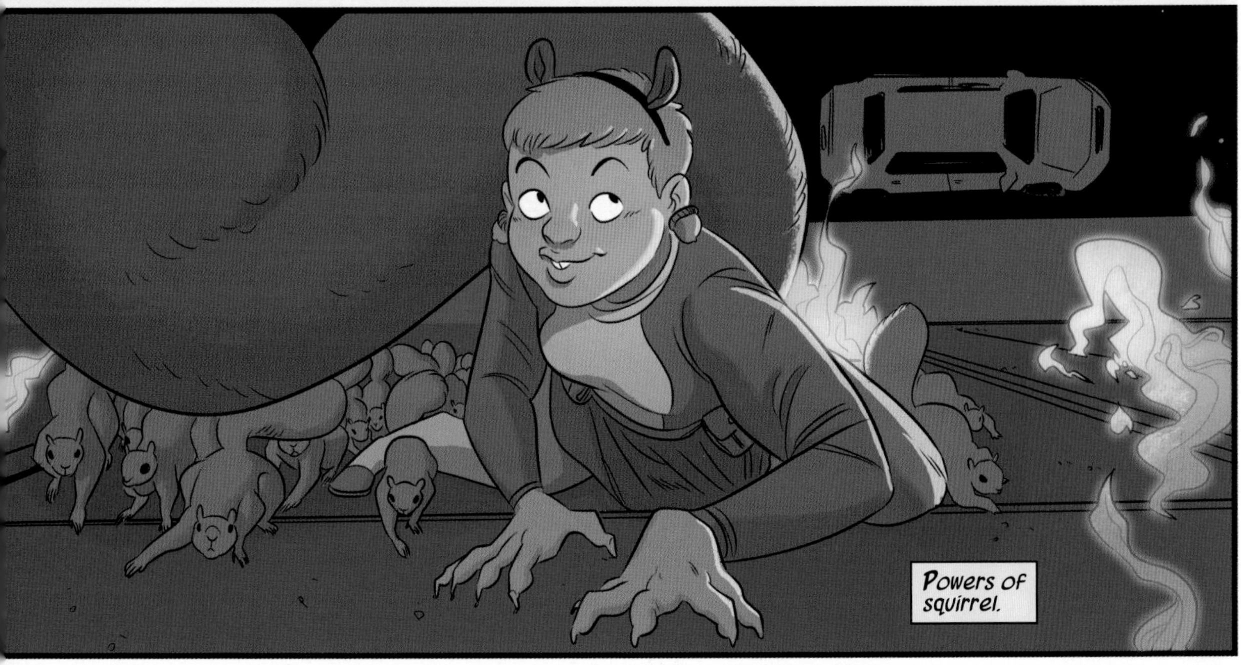
Powers of squirrel.

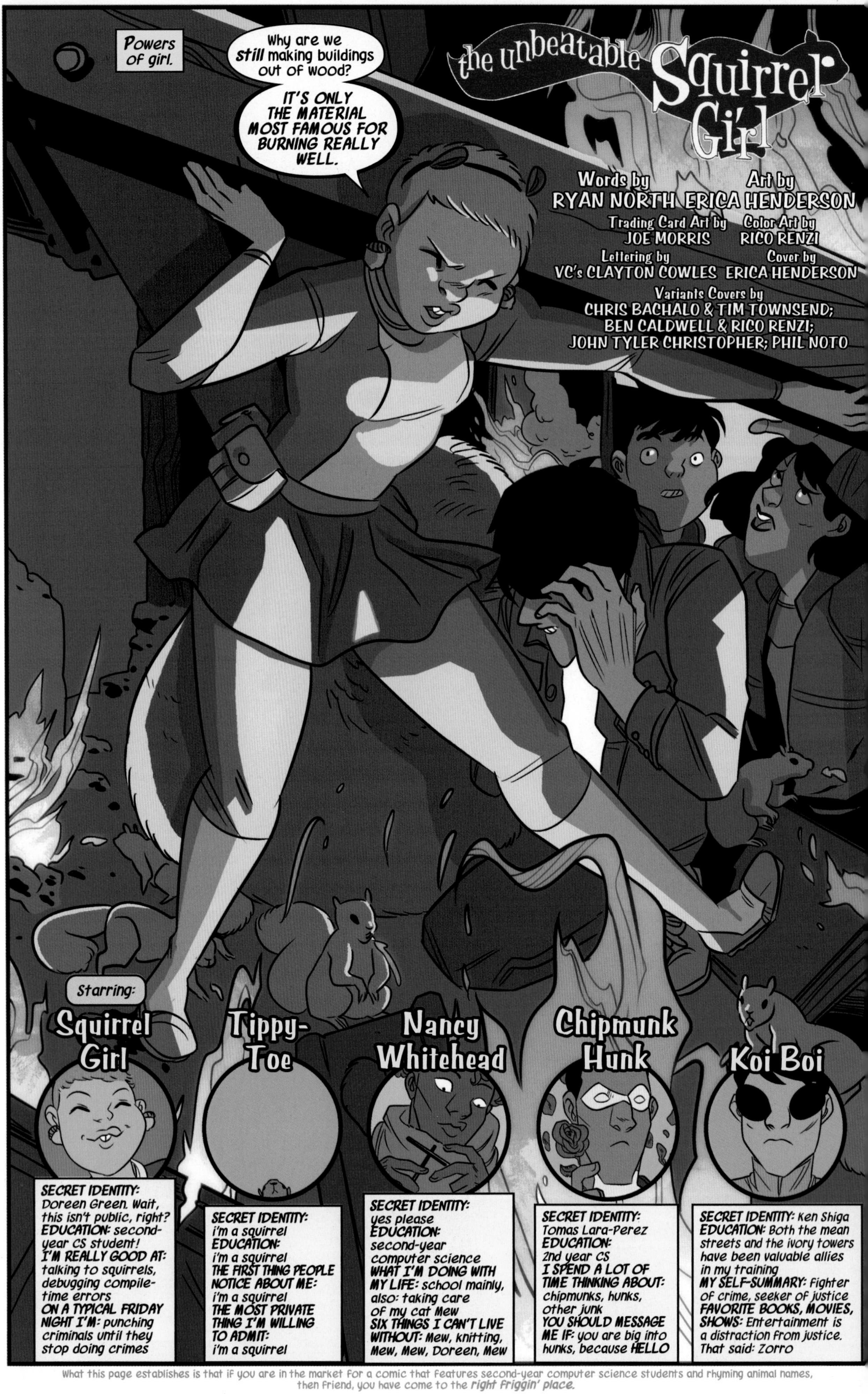

Powers of girl.
Why are we *still* making buildings out of wood?
IT'S ONLY THE MATERIAL MOST FAMOUS FOR BURNING REALLY WELL.
the unbeatable Squirrel Girl
Words by RYAN NORTH
Art by ERICA HENDERSON
Trading Card Art by JOE MORRIS
Color Art by RICO RENZI
Lettering by VC's CLAYTON COWLES
Cover by ERICA HENDERSON
Variants Covers by CHRIS BACHALO & TIM TOWNSEND; BEN CALDWELL & RICO RENZI; JOHN TYLER CHRISTOPHER; PHIL NOTO
Starring:
Squirrel Girl
Tippy-Toe
Nancy Whitehead
Chipmunk Hunk
Koi Boi
SECRET IDENTITY: Doreen Green. Wait, this isn't public, right? EDUCATION: second-year CS student! I'M REALLY GOOD AT: talking to squirrels, debugging compile-time errors ON A TYPICAL FRIDAY NIGHT I'M: punching criminals until they stop doing crimes
SECRET IDENTITY: i'm a squirrel EDUCATION: i'm a squirrel THE FIRST THING PEOPLE NOTICE ABOUT ME: i'm a squirrel THE MOST PRIVATE THING I'M WILLING TO ADMIT: i'm a squirrel
SECRET IDENTITY: yes please EDUCATION: second-year computer science WHAT I'M DOING WITH MY LIFE: school mainly, also: taking care of my cat Mew SIX THINGS I CAN'T LIVE WITHOUT: Mew, knitting, Mew, Mew, Doreen, Mew
SECRET IDENTITY: Tomas Lara-Perez EDUCATION: 2nd year CS I SPEND A LOT OF TIME THINKING ABOUT: chipmunks, hunks, other junk YOU SHOULD MESSAGE ME IF: you are big into hunks, because HELLO
SECRET IDENTITY: Ken Shiga EDUCATION: Both the mean streets and the ivory towers have been valuable allies in my training MY SELF-SUMMARY: Fighter of crime, seeker of justice FAVORITE BOOKS, MOVIES, SHOWS: Entertainment is a distraction from justice. That said: Zorro

What this page establishes is that if you are in the market for a comic that features second-year computer science students and rhyming animal names, then friend, you have come to the *right friggin' place.*

Hi, I'm Squirrel Girl!

Uh...I'm Corey, this is Emily and our little Joey. You're a... super hero?

HI SQUIRREL GIRL!!

I sure am! And Tippy-Toe over there is too. Plus there's Koi Boi and Chipmunk Hunk, but they're rescuing the floor beneath us.

Anyway, let's get you guys up on my shoulders and get everyone out of here, huh?

Chhhk!

Um...

Pardon me for asking, but how do squirrels fight fire?

Oh, hah hah!

Not super effectively, actually??

They carried up a little water in their mouths, but that only bought us, like, a few seconds tops.

Hey Joey, you like jumping off things?

I love jumping off things!!

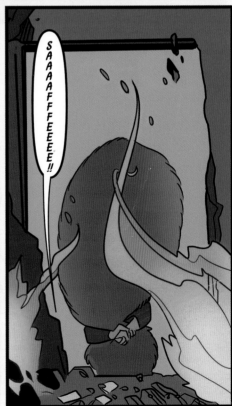

SAAAAFFFEEEE!!

Perfect. Then grab my tail!

Wait wait wait, what? Stop! You can't--this isn't--

YAAAY!!

I was gonna say the mom is being a drag here for not assuming this is safe, but Squirrel Girl never actually told her that "leaping hecka far" is one of her powers, so-- good work, mom. You are a sensible mom, and you only want the best for your child...

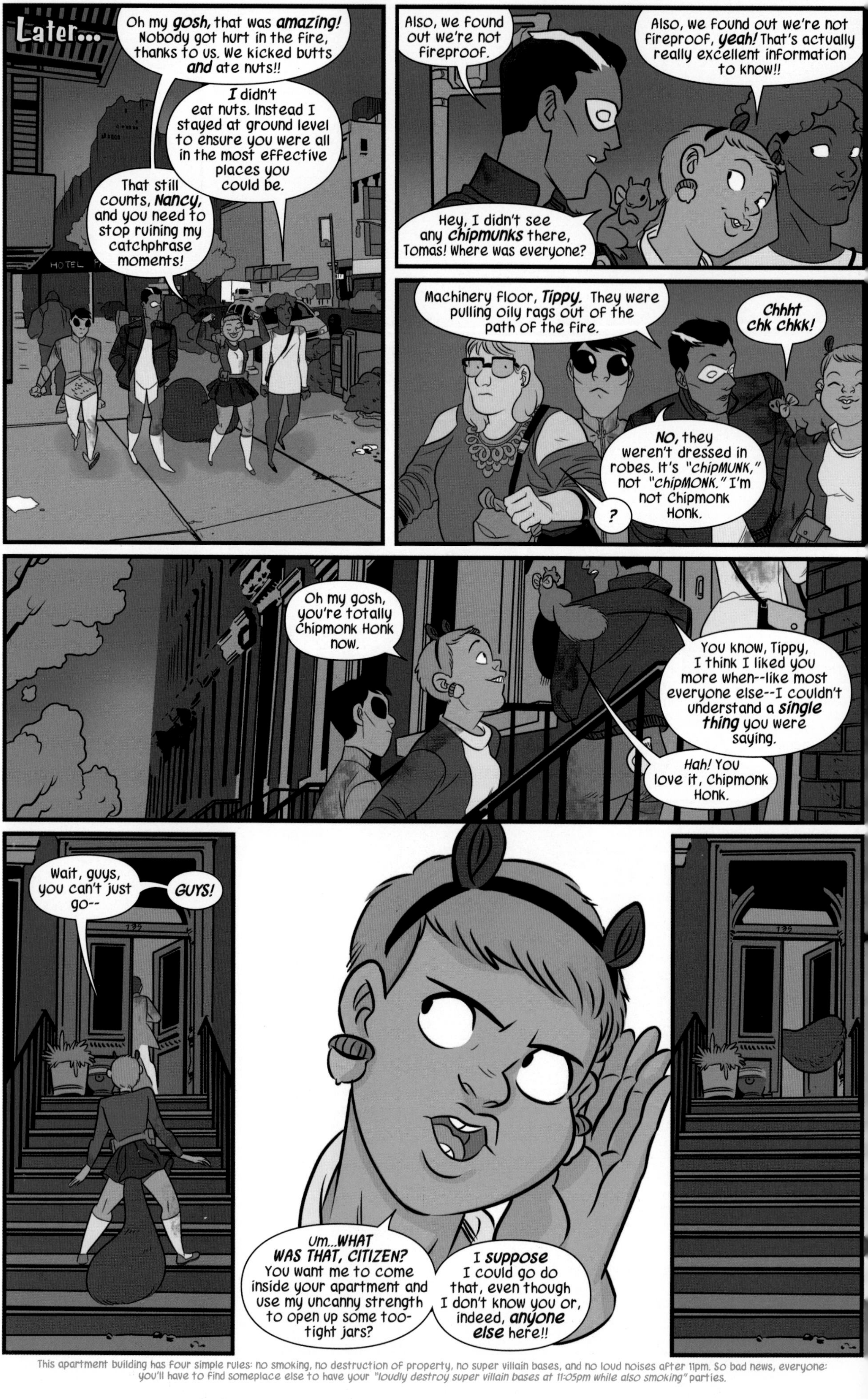
Later...
Oh my gosh, that was amazing! Nobody got hurt in the fire, thanks to us. We kicked butts and ate nuts!!
I didn't eat nuts. Instead I stayed at ground level to ensure you were all in the most effective places you could be.
That still counts, Nancy, and you need to stop ruining my catchphrase moments!
HOTEL
Also, we found out we're not fireproof.
Also, we found out we're not fireproof, yeah! That's actually really excellent information to know!!
Hey, I didn't see any chipmunks there, Tomas! Where was everyone?
Machinery floor, Tippy. They were pulling oily rags out of the path of the fire.
Chhht chk chkk!
No, they weren't dressed in robes. It's "chipMUNK," not "chipMONK." I'm not Chipmonk Honk.
?
Oh my gosh, you're totally Chipmonk Honk now.
You know, Tippy, I think I liked you more when--like most everyone else--I couldn't understand a single thing you were saying.
Hah! You love it, Chipmonk Honk.
Wait, guys, you can't just go--
GUYS!
Um...WHAT WAS THAT, CITIZEN? You want me to come inside your apartment and use my uncanny strength to open up some too-tight jars?
I suppose I could go do that, even though I don't know you or, indeed, anyone else here!!

This apartment building has four simple rules: no smoking, no destruction of property, no super villain bases, and no loud noises after 11pm. So bad news, everyone: you'll have to find someplace else to have your *"loudly destroy super villain bases at 11:05pm while also smoking"* parties.

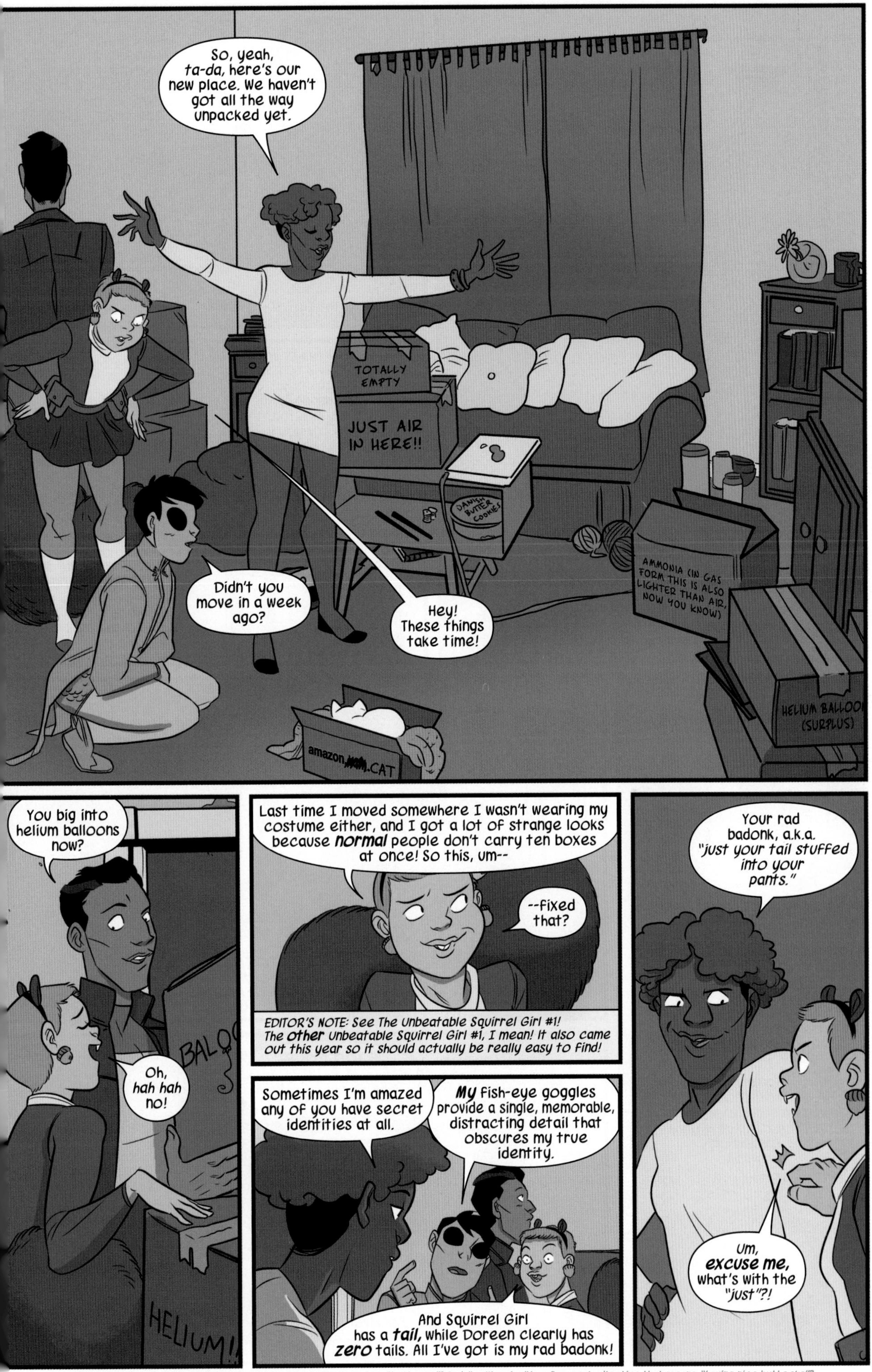
So, yeah, ta-da, here's our new place. We haven't got all the way unpacked yet.
TOTALLY EMPTY
JUST AIR IN HERE!!
DANISH BUTTER COOKIES
AMMONIA (IN GAS FORM THIS IS ALSO LIGHTER THAN AIR, NOW YOU KNOW)
(SURPLUS)
Didn't you move in a week ago?
Hey! These things take time!
You big into helium balloons now?
Oh, hah hah no!
HELIUM!!
Last time I moved somewhere I wasn't wearing my costume either, and I got a lot of strange looks because *normal* people don't carry ten boxes at once! So this, um--
--fixed that?
EDITOR'S NOTE: See The Unbeatable Squirrel Girl #1! The *other* Unbeatable Squirrel Girl #1, I mean! It also came out this year so it should actually be really easy to find!
Sometimes I'm amazed any of you have secret identities at all.
My fish-eye goggles provide a single, memorable, distracting detail that obscures my true identity.
And Squirrel Girl has a *tail,* while Doreen clearly has *zero* tails. All I've got is my rad badonk!
Your rad badonk, a.k.a. "just your tail stuffed into your pants."
Um, *excuse me,* what's with the "just"?!

DID YOU KNOW: *"badonk"* is slang for *"butt"*? And *"butt"* is slang for *"buttocks"*? And *"callipygian"* is a for-real adjective that means *"having nice buttocks"*? Look at you, just trying to relax with a talking squirrel comic and instead learning how to say *"My word, what a callipygian badonk!"*

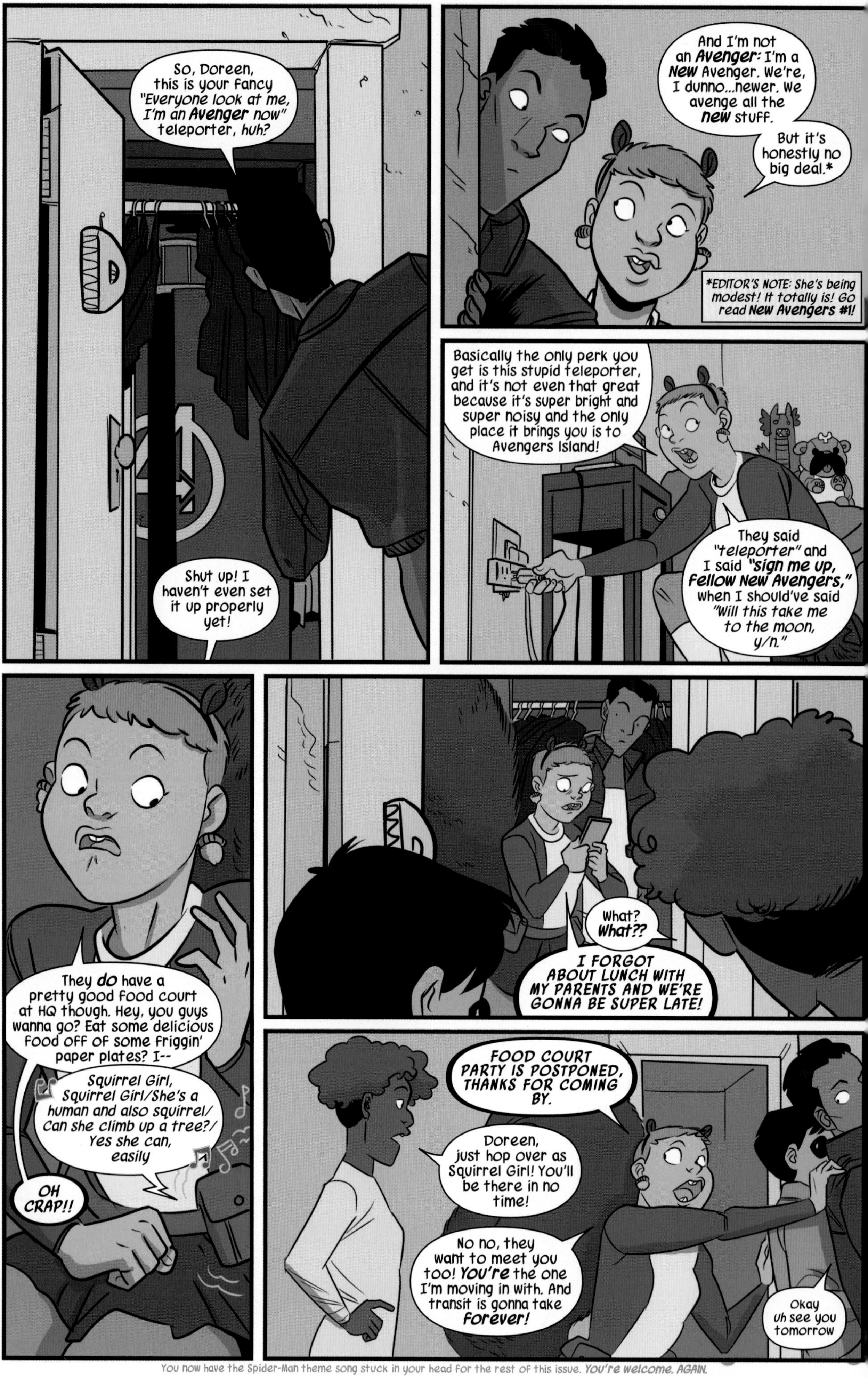
So, Doreen, this is your fancy "Everyone look at me, I'm an Avenger now" teleporter, huh?
Shut up! I haven't even set it up properly yet!
And I'm not an Avenger: I'm a New Avenger. We're, I dunno...newer. We avenge all the new stuff.
But it's honestly no big deal.*
*EDITOR'S NOTE: She's being modest! It totally is! Go read New Avengers #1!
Basically the only perk you get is this stupid teleporter, and it's not even that great because it's super bright and super noisy and the only place it brings you is to Avengers Island!
They said "teleporter" and I said "sign me up, fellow New Avengers," when I should've said "Will this take me to the moon, y/n."
They do have a pretty good food court at HQ though. Hey, you guys wanna go? Eat some delicious food off of some friggin' paper plates? I--
Squirrel Girl, Squirrel Girl/She's a human and also squirrel/ Can she climb up a tree?/ Yes she can, easily
OH CRAP!!
What? What??
I FORGOT ABOUT LUNCH WITH MY PARENTS AND WE'RE GONNA BE SUPER LATE!
FOOD COURT PARTY IS POSTPONED, THANKS FOR COMING BY.
Doreen, just hop over as Squirrel Girl! You'll be there in no time!
No no, they want to meet you too! You're the one I'm moving in with. And transit is gonna take forever!
Okay uh see you tomorrow

You now have the Spider-Man theme song stuck in your head for the rest of this issue. *You're welcome. AGAIN.*

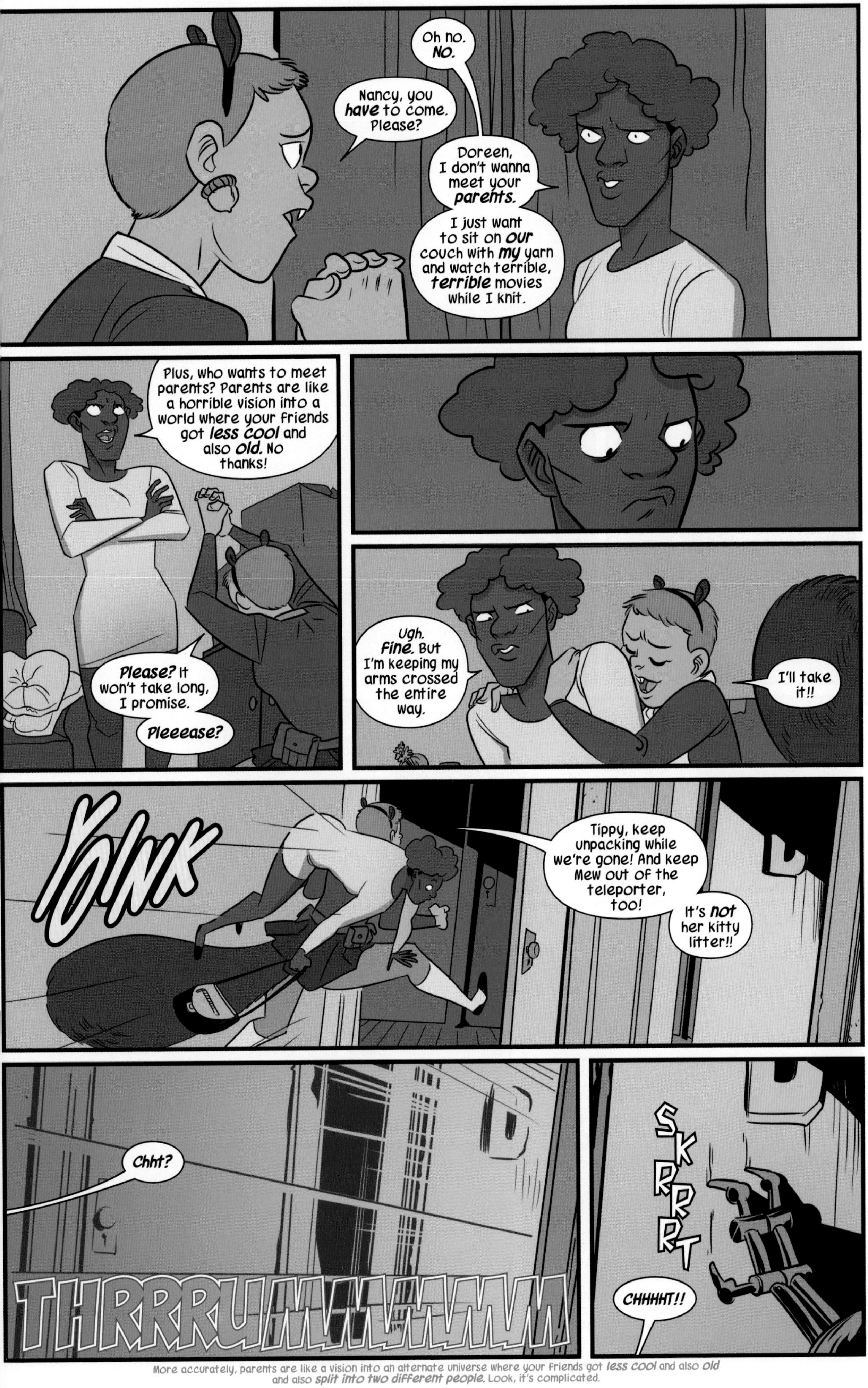
Nancy, you **have** to come. Please?
Oh no. **NO.**
Doreen, I don't wanna meet your **parents.**
I just want to sit on **our** couch with **my** yarn and watch terrible, **terrible** movies while I knit.
Plus, who wants to meet parents? Parents are like a horrible vision into a world where your friends got **less cool** and also **old.** No thanks!
Please? It won't take long, I promise.
Pleeease?
Ugh. **Fine.** But I'm keeping my arms crossed the entire way.
I'll take it!!
YOINK
Tippy, keep unpacking while we're gone! And keep Mew out of the teleporter, too!
It's **not** her kitty litter!!
Chht?
THRRRUMMMMMMMM
SKRRRT
CHHHHT!!

More accurately, parents are like a vision into an alternate universe where your friends got *less cool* and also *old* and also *split into two different people.* Look, it's complicated.

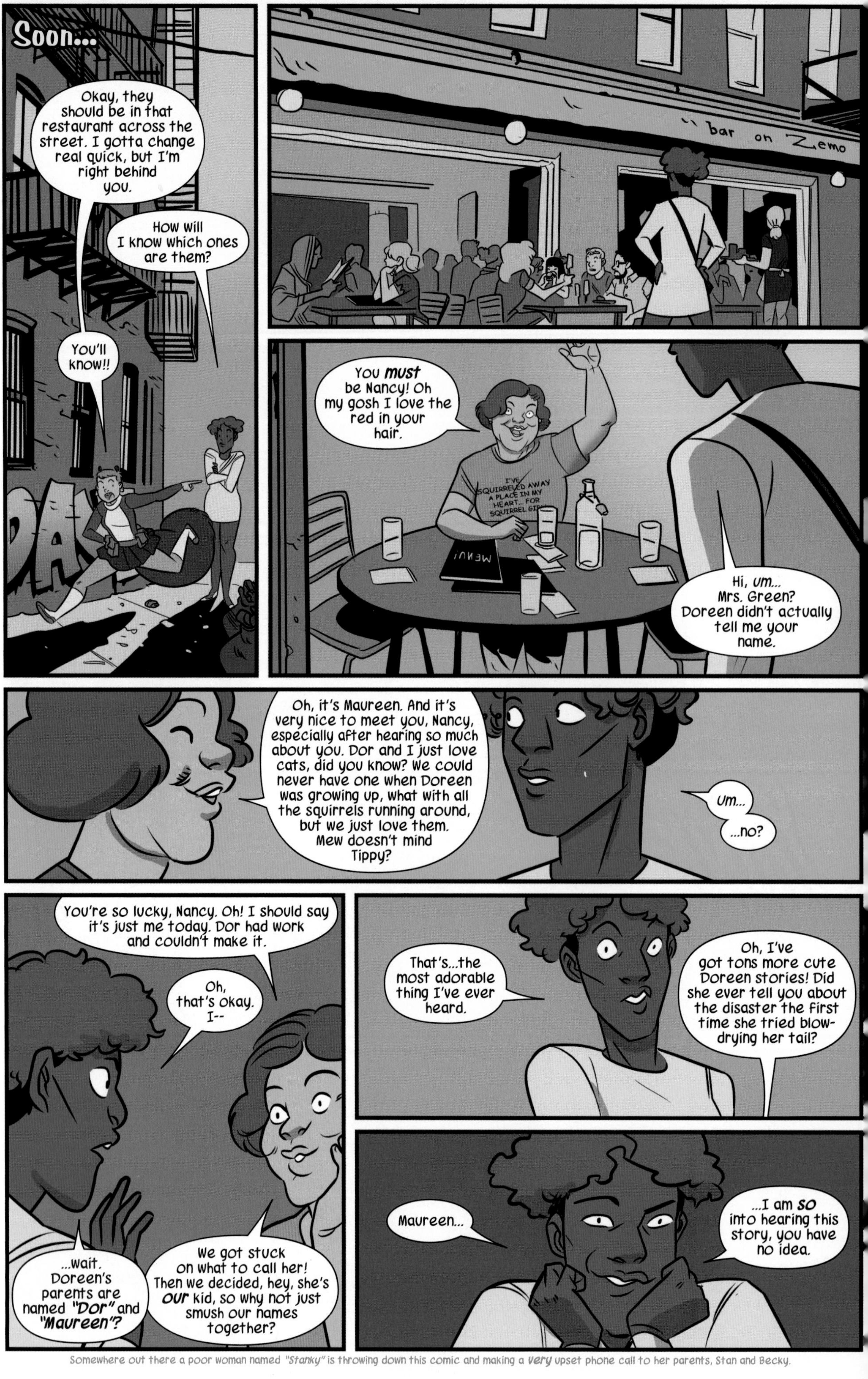
Soon...
Okay, they should be in that restaurant across the street. I gotta change real quick, but I'm right behind you.
How will I know which ones are them?
You'll know!!
bar on Zemo
You **must** be Nancy! Oh my gosh I love the red in your hair.
I'VE SQUIRRELED AWAY A PLACE IN MY HEART... FOR SQUIRREL GIRL
MENU
Hi, *um*... Mrs. Green? Doreen didn't actually tell me your name.
Oh, it's Maureen. And it's very nice to meet you, Nancy, especially after hearing so much about you. Dor and I just love cats, did you know? We could never have one when Doreen was growing up, what with all the squirrels running around, but we just love them. Mew doesn't mind Tippy?
Um...
...no?
You're so lucky, Nancy. Oh! I should say it's just me today. Dor had work and couldn't make it.
Oh, that's okay. I--
...wait. Doreen's parents are named **"Dor"** and **"Maureen"**?
We got stuck on what to call her! Then we decided, hey, she's **our** kid, so why not just smush our names together?
That's...the most adorable thing I've ever heard.
Oh, I've got tons more cute Doreen stories! Did she ever tell you about the disaster the first time she tried blow-drying her tail?
Maureen...
...I am **so** into hearing this story, you have no idea.

Somewhere out there a poor woman named *"Stanky"* is throwing down this comic and making a ***very*** upset phone call to her parents, Stan and Becky.

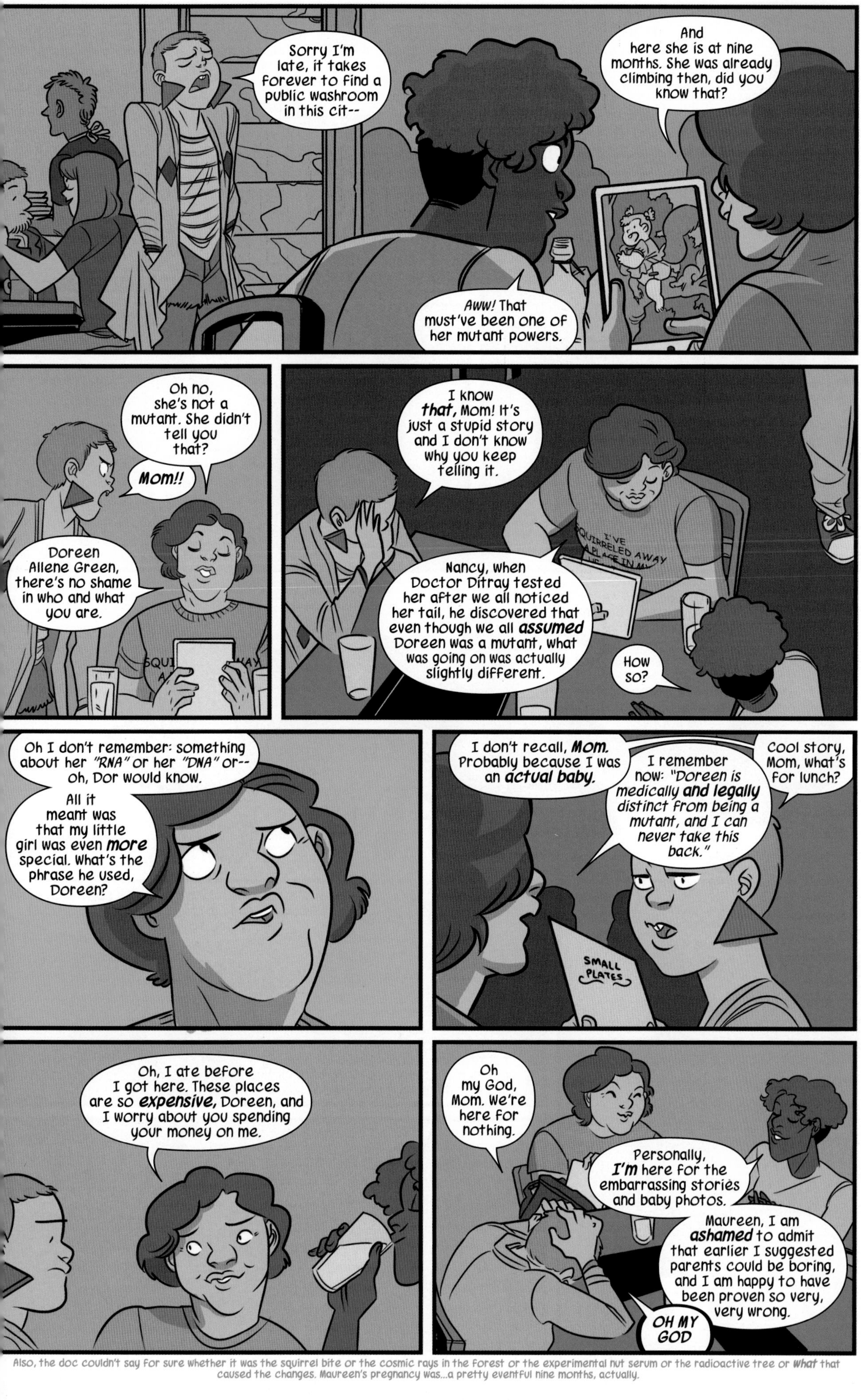
Sorry I'm late, it takes forever to find a public washroom in this cit--
And here she is at nine months. She was already climbing then, did you know that?
Aww! That must've been one of her mutant powers.
Oh no, she's not a mutant. She didn't tell you that?
Mom!!
Doreen Allene Green, there's no shame in who and what you are.
I know ***that,*** Mom! It's just a stupid story and I don't know why you keep telling it.
Nancy, when Doctor Ditray tested her after we all noticed her tail, he discovered that even though we all ***assumed*** Doreen was a mutant, what was going on was actually slightly different.
How so?
Oh I don't remember: something about her *"RNA"* or her *"DNA"* or-- oh, Dor would know.
All it meant was that my little girl was even ***more*** special. What's the phrase he used, Doreen?
I don't recall, ***Mom.*** Probably because I was an ***actual baby.***
I remember now: *"Doreen is medically **and legally** distinct from being a mutant, and I can never take this back."*
Cool story, Mom, what's for lunch?
SMALL PLATES
Oh, I ate before I got here. These places are so ***expensive,*** Doreen, and I worry about you spending your money on me.
Oh my God, Mom. We're here for nothing.
Personally, ***I'm*** here for the embarrassing stories and baby photos.
Maureen, I am ***ashamed*** to admit that earlier I suggested parents could be boring, and I am happy to have been proven so very, very wrong.
OH MY GOD

Also, the doc couldn't say for sure whether it was the squirrel bite or the cosmic rays in the forest or the experimental nut serum or the radioactive tree or *what* that caused the changes. Maureen's pregnancy was...a pretty eventful nine months, actually.

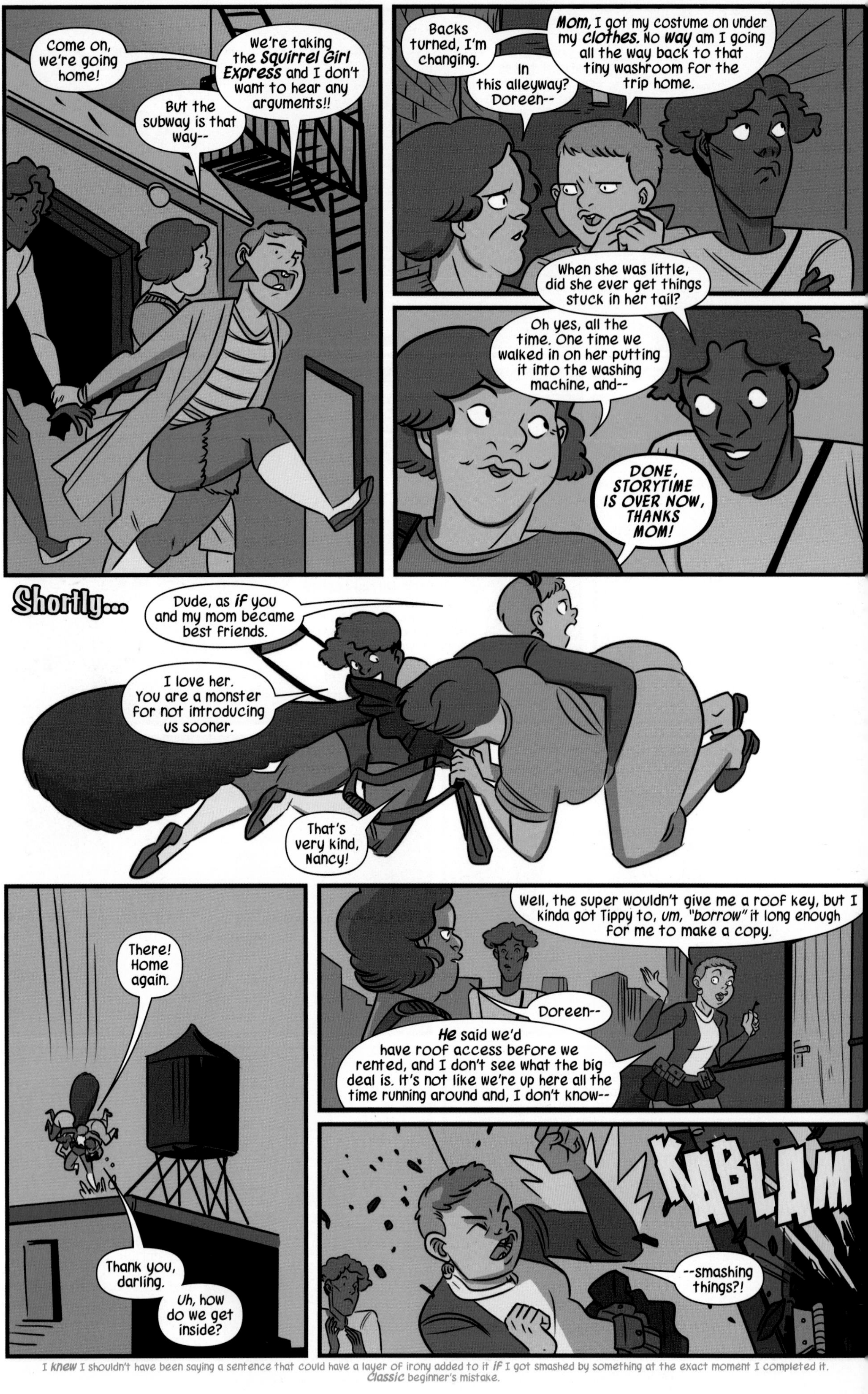
Come on, we're going home!
We're taking the Squirrel Girl Express and I don't want to hear any arguments!!
But the subway is that way--
Backs turned, I'm changing.
In this alleyway? Doreen--
Mom, I got my costume on under my clothes. No way am I going all the way back to that tiny washroom for the trip home.
When she was little, did she ever get things stuck in her tail?
Oh yes, all the time. One time we walked in on her putting it into the washing machine, and--
DONE, STORYTIME IS OVER NOW, THANKS MOM!
Shortly...
Dude, as if you and my mom became best friends.
I love her. You are a monster for not introducing us sooner.
That's very kind, Nancy!
There! Home again.
Thank you, darling.
Uh, how do we get inside?
Well, the super wouldn't give me a roof key, but I kinda got Tippy to, um, "borrow" it long enough for me to make a copy.
Doreen--
He said we'd have roof access before we rented, and I don't see what the big deal is. It's not like we're up here all the time running around and, I don't know--
KABLAM
--smashing things?!

I *knew* I shouldn't have been saying a sentence that could have a layer of irony added to it *if* I got smashed by something at the exact moment I completed it. *Classic* beginner's mistake.

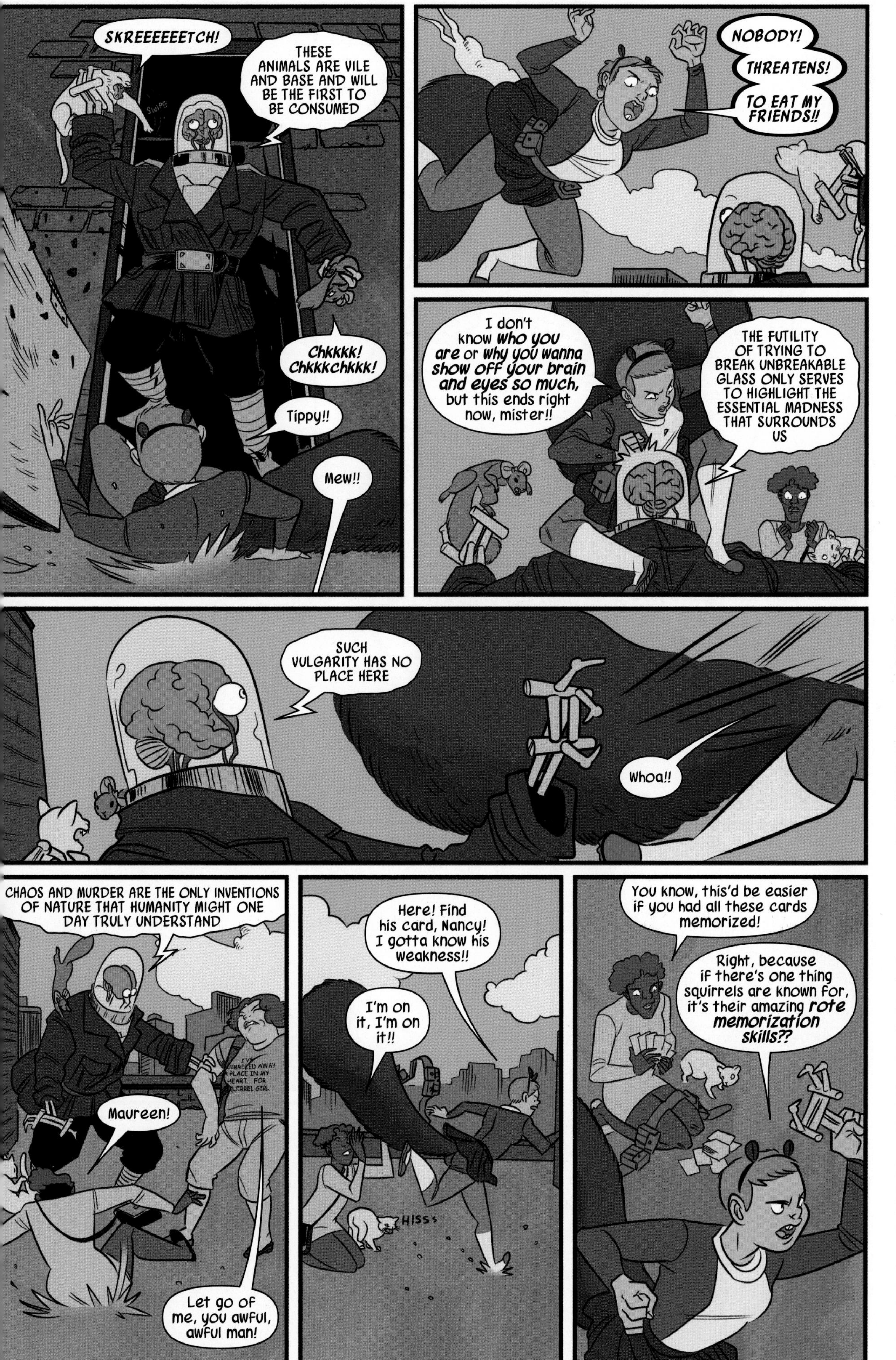
SKREEEEEEETCH!
THESE ANIMALS ARE VILE AND BASE AND WILL BE THE FIRST TO BE CONSUMED
Chkkkk! Chkkkchkkk!
Tippy!!
Mew!!
NOBODY!
THREATENS!
TO EAT MY FRIENDS!!
I don't know who you are or why you wanna show off your brain and eyes so much, but this ends right now, mister!!
THE FUTILITY OF TRYING TO BREAK UNBREAKABLE GLASS ONLY SERVES TO HIGHLIGHT THE ESSENTIAL MADNESS THAT SURROUNDS US
SUCH VULGARITY HAS NO PLACE HERE
Whoa!!
CHAOS AND MURDER ARE THE ONLY INVENTIONS OF NATURE THAT HUMANITY MIGHT ONE DAY TRULY UNDERSTAND
Maureen!
Let go of me, you awful, awful man!
Here! Find his card, Nancy! I gotta know his weakness!!
I'm on it, I'm on it!!
HISSS
You know, this'd be easier if you had all these cards memorized!
Right, because if there's one thing squirrels are known for, it's their amazing rote memorization skills??

Actually, some tree species rely on squirrels stealing their nuts, burying them, and then completely forgetting where they're buried! This allows the trees to spread far and wide. THERE: now you know some squirrel facts ***and*** some "fancy words for butts" facts! I'd ***sincerely*** like to see each issue of *The Amazing Spider-Man* do ***that.***

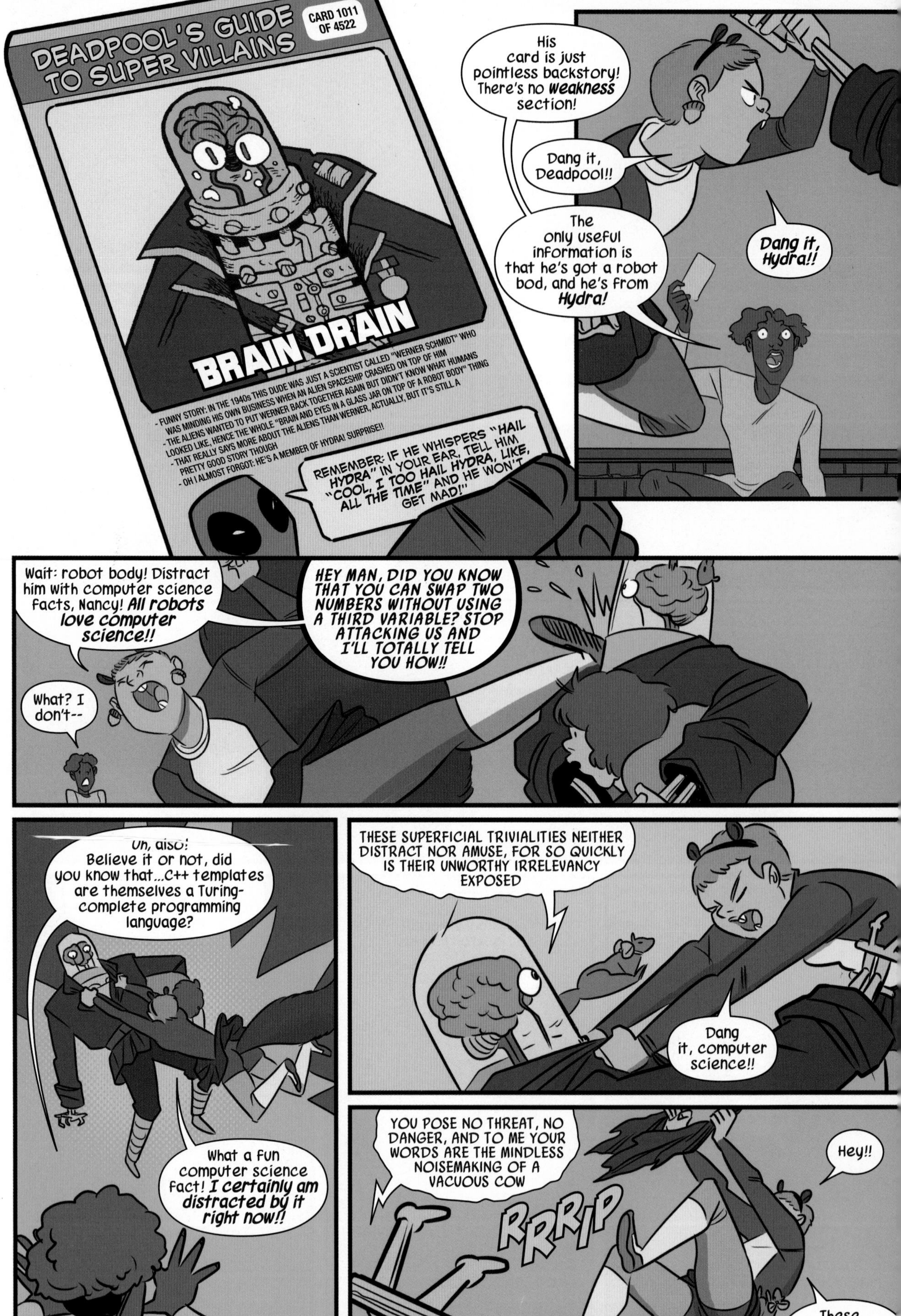
DEADPOOL'S GUIDE TO SUPER VILLAINS
CARD 1011 OF 4522
BRAIN DRAIN
- FUNNY STORY: IN THE 1940s THIS DUDE WAS JUST A SCIENTIST CALLED "WERNER SCHMIDT" WHO WAS MINDING HIS OWN BUSINESS WHEN AN ALIEN SPACESHIP CRASHED ON TOP OF HIM
- THE ALIENS WANTED TO PUT WERNER BACK TOGETHER AGAIN BUT DIDN'T KNOW WHAT HUMANS LOOKED LIKE, HENCE THE WHOLE "BRAIN AND EYES IN A GLASS JAR ON TOP OF A ROBOT BODY" THING
- THAT REALLY SAYS MORE ABOUT THE ALIENS THAN WERNER, ACTUALLY, BUT IT'S STILL A PRETTY GOOD STORY THOUGH
- OH I ALMOST FORGOT: HE'S A MEMBER OF HYDRA! SURPRISE!!
REMEMBER: IF HE WHISPERS "HAIL HYDRA" IN YOUR EAR, TELL HIM "COOL, I TOO HAIL HYDRA, LIKE, ALL THE TIME" AND HE WON'T GET MAD!"
His card is just pointless backstory! There's no *weakness* section!
Dang it, Deadpool!!
The only useful information is that he's got a robot bod, and he's from *Hydra!*
Dang it, Hydra!!
Wait: robot body! Distract him with computer science facts, Nancy! *All robots love computer science!!*
HEY MAN, DID YOU KNOW THAT YOU CAN SWAP TWO NUMBERS WITHOUT USING A THIRD VARIABLE? STOP ATTACKING US AND I'LL TOTALLY TELL YOU HOW!!
What? I don't--
Uh, also! Believe it or not, did you know that...C++ templates are themselves a Turing-complete programming language?
What a fun computer science fact! *I certainly am distracted by it right now!!*
THESE SUPERFICIAL TRIVIALITIES NEITHER DISTRACT NOR AMUSE, FOR SO QUICKLY IS THEIR UNWORTHY IRRELEVANCY EXPOSED
Dang it, computer science!!
YOU POSE NO THREAT, NO DANGER, AND TO ME YOUR WORDS ARE THE MINDLESS NOISEMAKING OF A VACUOUS COW
RRRIP
Hey!!
These disses are actually getting *mega* unkind??

Also if you wanted to say *"mindless noisemaking of a chattering squirrel,"* that would be a more on-point insult. I'm Squirrel Girl, not Lady Cattle Battle. Although, actually, she sounds pretty great and I am interested in hearing more about her powers *and* lifestyle choices.

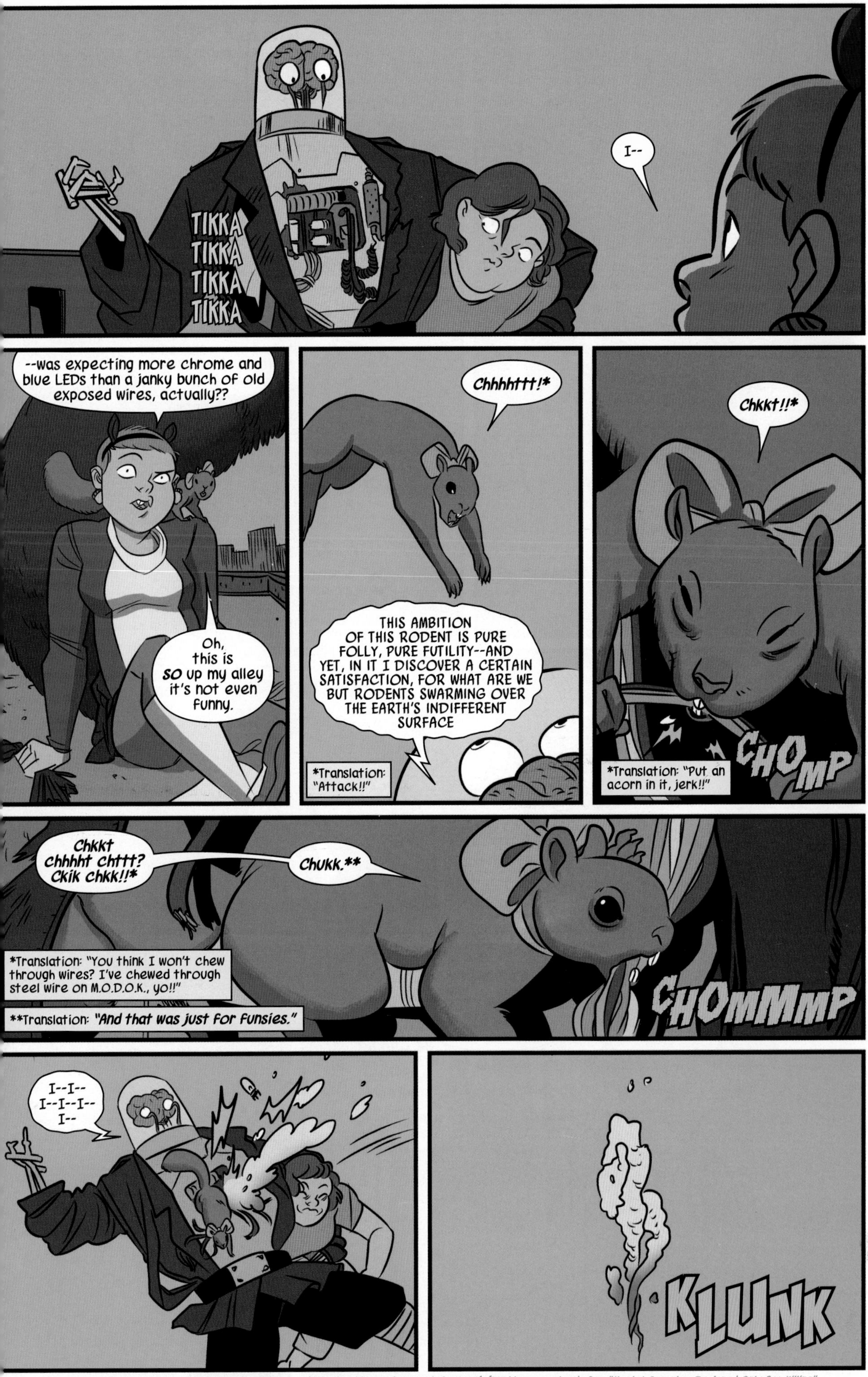
TIKKA
TIKKA
TIKKA
TIKKA
I--
--was expecting more chrome and blue LEDs than a janky bunch of old exposed wires, actually??
Oh, this is SO up my alley it's not even funny.
Chhhhttt!*
THIS AMBITION OF THIS RODENT IS PURE FOLLY, PURE FUTILITY--AND YET, IN IT I DISCOVER A CERTAIN SATISFACTION, FOR WHAT ARE WE BUT RODENTS SWARMING OVER THE EARTH'S INDIFFERENT SURFACE
*Translation: "Attack!!"
Chkkt!!*
*Translation: "Put an acorn in it, jerk!!"
CHOMP
Chkkt chhhht chttt? Ckik chkk!!*
Chukk.**
*Translation: "You think I won't chew through wires? I've chewed through steel wire on M.O.D.O.K., yo!!"
**Translation: "And that was just for funsies."
CHOMMMMP
I--I--
I--I--I--
I--
KLUNK

If you're wondering who M.O.D.O.K. is, he's a giant head who has his own hover chair. He *claims* his name stands for *"Mental Organism Designed Only For Killing"* but he has ***never*** denied the allegations that his name ***actually*** stands for *"Mental Organism Delivering* ***Outstanding*** *Kissing"*

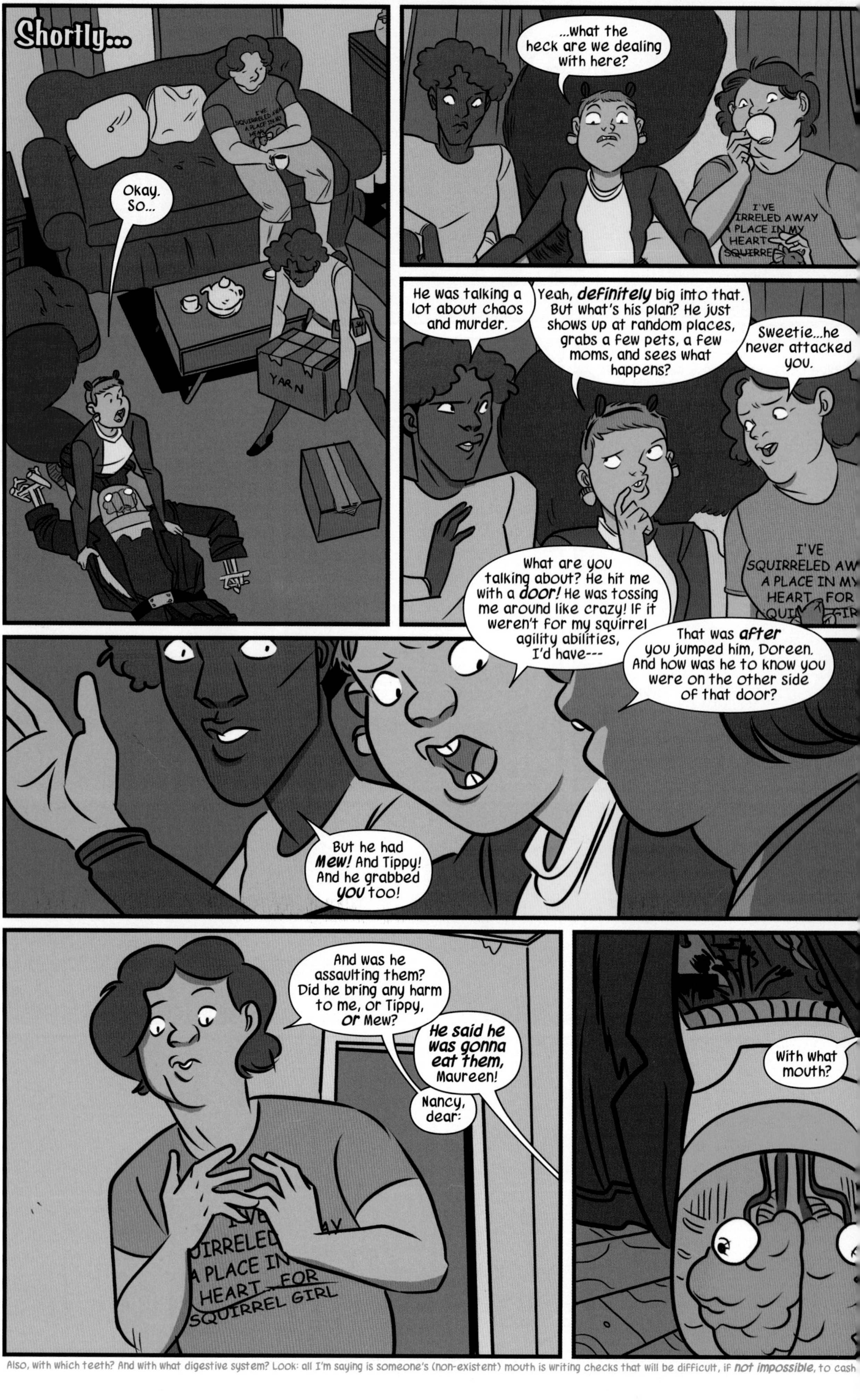
Shortly...
Okay. So...
YARN
...what the heck are we dealing with here?
He was talking a lot about chaos and murder.
Yeah, definitely big into that. But what's his plan? He just shows up at random places, grabs a few pets, a few moms, and sees what happens?
Sweetie...he never attacked you.
What are you talking about? He hit me with a door! He was tossing me around like crazy! If it weren't for my squirrel agility abilities, I'd have---
That was after you jumped him, Doreen. And how was he to know you were on the other side of that door?
But he had Mew! And Tippy! And he grabbed you too!
And was he assaulting them? Did he bring any harm to me, or Tippy, or Mew?
He said he was gonna eat them, Maureen!
Nancy, dear:
With what mouth?

Also, with which teeth? And with what digestive system? Look: all I'm saying is someone's (non-existent) mouth is writing checks that will be difficult, if *not impossible*, to cash

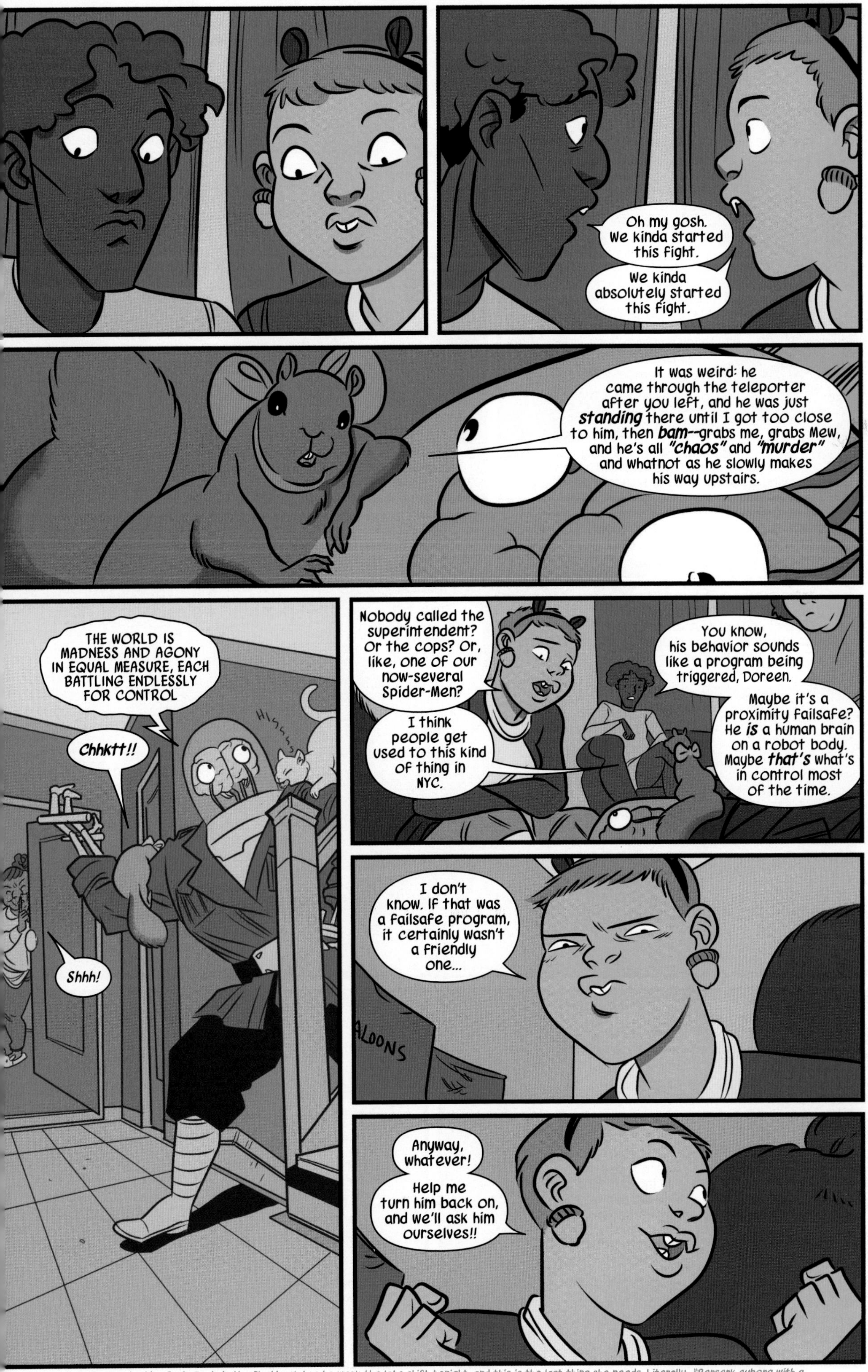
Oh my gosh. We kinda started this fight.
We kinda absolutely started this fight.
It was weird: he came through the teleporter after you left, and he was just *standing* there until I got too close to him, then *bam*--grabs me, grabs Mew, and he's all *"chaos"* and *"murder"* and whatnot as he slowly makes his way upstairs.
THE WORLD IS MADNESS AND AGONY IN EQUAL MEASURE, EACH BATTLING ENDLESSLY FOR CONTROL
Chhktt!!
Shhh!
Nobody called the superintendent? Or the cops? Or, like, one of our now-several Spider-Men?
I think people get used to this kind of thing in NYC.
You know, his behavior sounds like a program being triggered, Doreen.
Maybe it's a proximity failsafe? He *is* a human brain on a robot body. Maybe *that's* what's in control most of the time.
I don't know. If that was a failsafe program, it certainly wasn't a friendly one...
Anyway, whatever!
Help me turn him back on, and we'll ask him ourselves!!

That person shushing Brain Drain in the flashback has to work the late shift tonight, and this is the last thing she needs. Literally. *"Berserk cyborg with a human brain carrying screaming animals and shouting about madness"* is actually written at the very bottom of her list of *"things I need right now."*

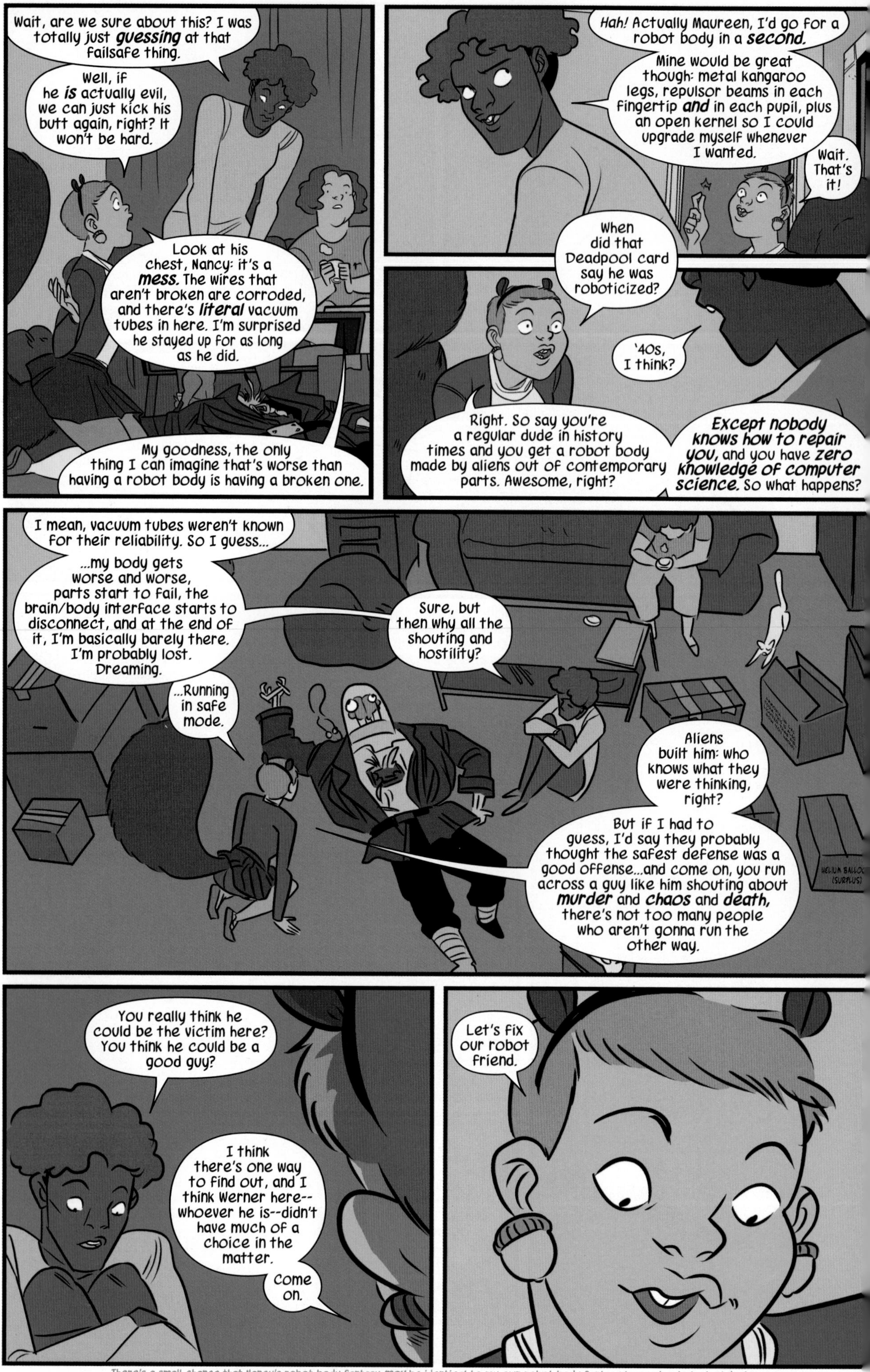
Wait, are we sure about this? I was totally just guessing at that failsafe thing.
Well, if he is actually evil, we can just kick his butt again, right? It won't be hard.
Look at his chest, Nancy: it's a mess. The wires that aren't broken are corroded, and there's literal vacuum tubes in here. I'm surprised he stayed up for as long as he did.
My goodness, the only thing I can imagine that's worse than having a robot body is having a broken one.
Hah! Actually Maureen, I'd go for a robot body in a second.
Mine would be great though: metal kangaroo legs, repulsor beams in each fingertip and in each pupil, plus an open kernel so I could upgrade myself whenever I wanted.
Wait. That's it!
When did that Deadpool card say he was roboticized?
'40s, I think?
Right. So say you're a regular dude in history times and you get a robot body made by aliens out of contemporary parts. Awesome, right?
Except nobody knows how to repair you, and you have zero knowledge of computer science. So what happens?
I mean, vacuum tubes weren't known for their reliability. So I guess...
...my body gets worse and worse, parts start to fail, the brain/body interface starts to disconnect, and at the end of it, I'm basically barely there. I'm probably lost. Dreaming.
...Running in safe mode.
Sure, but then why all the shouting and hostility?
Aliens built him: who knows what they were thinking, right?
But if I had to guess, I'd say they probably thought the safest defense was a good offense...and come on, you run across a guy like him shouting about murder and chaos and death, there's not too many people who aren't gonna run the other way.
HELIUM BALLO
(SURPLUS)
You really think he could be the victim here? You think he could be a good guy?
I think there's one way to find out, and I think Werner here--whoever he is--didn't have much of a choice in the matter.
Come on.
Let's fix our robot friend.

There's a small chance that Nancy's robot body fantasy *may* be identical to my own robot body fantasy/spec sheets/actual designs that I've written up and carry with me everywhere and think about all the time.

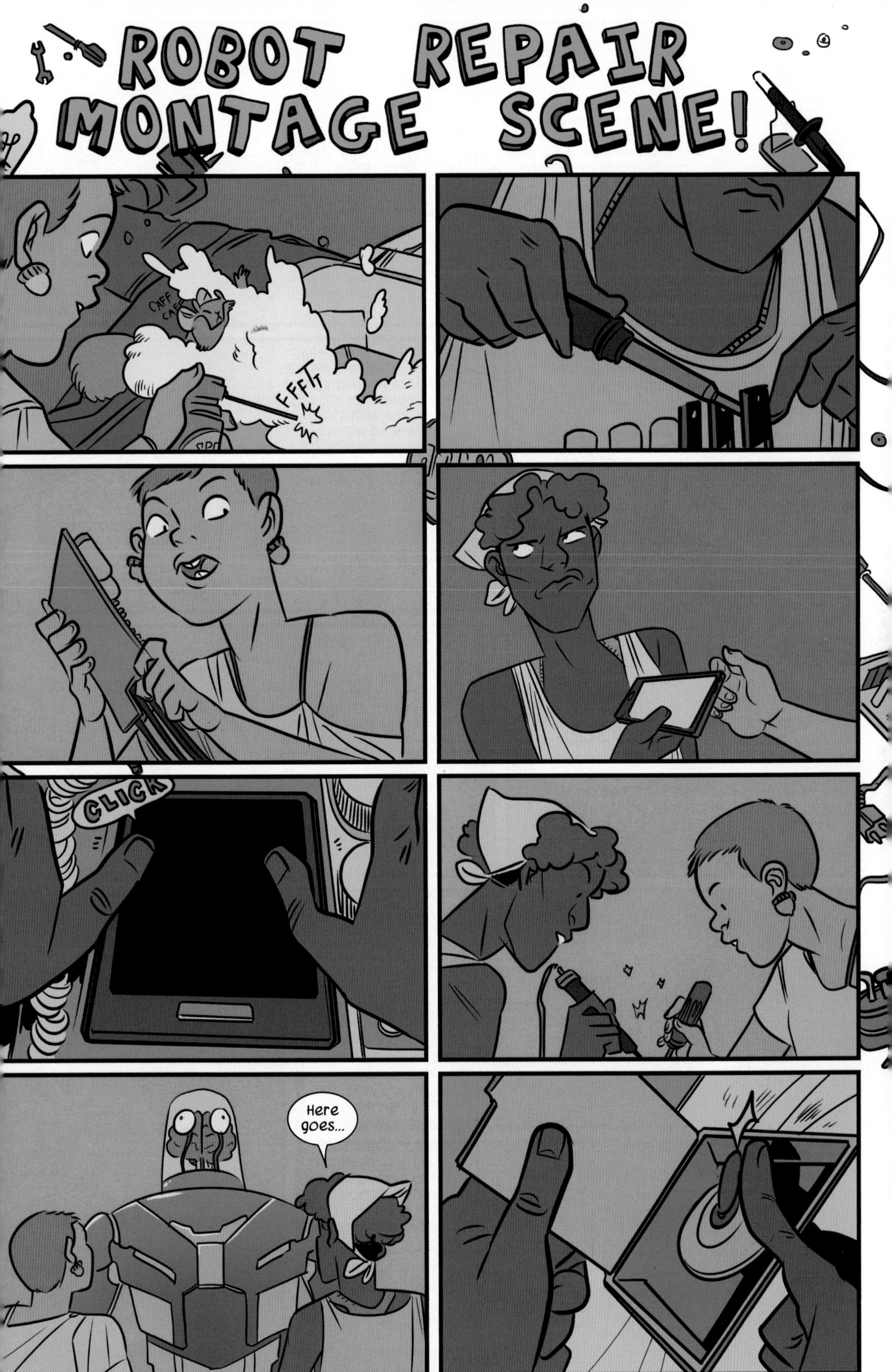
ROBOT REPAIR MONTAGE SCENE!
FFFTT
CLICK
Here goes...

That *"robot repair montage"* header stops you from wondering why everyone in the comic stopped talking, and also from wondering why you can hear awesome pump-up robot repair montage music in your head whenever you look at this page and concentrate really hard!

And so after the Canadian tundra released its frozen grasp upon me, I tried to direct myself elsewhere--but like the dreamer who is unaware of the dream, my moments of lucidity were all too brief.

So you *wanted* to come to NYC?

Not at first, but eventually I heard from others that you have a way of...helping. Hippo the Hippo speaks very highly of you.

No way! You know Hippo? How is he?

He destroys the unwanted detritus of civilization, and in doing so, at last finds a way to participate within it.

Oh nice, so the demolition job's working out great!!

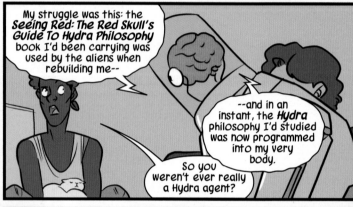

My struggle was this: the *Seeing Red: The Red Skull's Guide To Hydra Philosophy* book I'd been carrying was used by the aliens when rebuilding me--

--and in an instant, the *Hydra* philosophy I'd studied was now programmed into my very body.

So you weren't ever really a Hydra agent?

No. I must admit I was.

But unlike all the others, I was unable to change or atone, for while my mind grew, my body continued as always, its self-defense protocols and self-defense nihilist rants at odds with my new purpose.

"I could change, but my actions could not, and so was taken from me the greatest kindness life offers: the ability to learn from our mistakes and to not repeat them.

"Do you remember the person you were ten, even five years ago?

Yes.

No. Absolutely not.

"Could you imagine being forced to be that person forever?"

3...2...1... HAPPY NEW YEAR'S!!

Other books in that series include *Well 'Read': The Hydra Essays Of The Red Skull*, *Paint The Town Red: The Red Skull's Guide To Small-Town Infiltration*, and *Bone Appetite: The Red Skull's Favorite* and *Most Evil Recipes*.

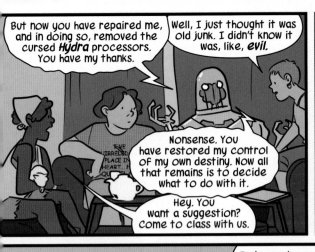

But now you have repaired me, and in doing so, removed the cursed *Hydra* processors. You have my thanks.

Well, I just thought it was old junk. I didn't know it was, like, *evil.*

Nonsense. You have restored my control of my own destiny. Now all that remains is to decide what to do with it.

Hey. You want a suggestion? Come to class with us.

You've been out of the loop for half a century: there's tons of new things you can learn about.

I have been meaning to make a study of how civilization's false veneer of decency is spread all too thin across the face of a monstrously indifferent universe.

That...or *instead,* computer science!

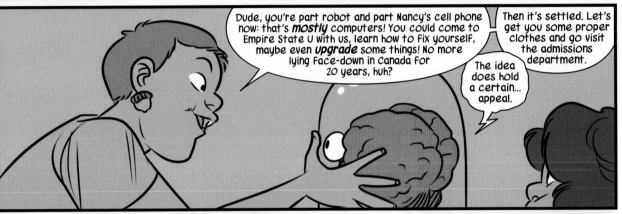

Dude, you're part robot and part Nancy's cell phone now: that's *mostly* computers! You could come to Empire State U with us, learn how to fix yourself, maybe even *upgrade* some things! No more lying face-down in Canada for 20 years, huh?

Then it's settled. Let's get you some proper clothes and go visit the admissions department.

The idea does hold a certain... appeal.

And So...

"Sorry I can't find your son's application on file" doesn't solve my problem, *does it,* mister?? *Well!* I guess you'll just have to let him audit courses for *free* until you find it, *HUH?*

Yes ma'am that is allowable ma'am please stop yelling ma'am

I love you, Mom.

Um...I kinda love you too, actually.

I don't like to do that often, but you deserve a chance, Mr. Drain.

I look forward to earning this trust placed in me today.

In addition, I am also looking forward to "achieving consistency across distributed database systems."

Oh man, don't get your hopes up on that. Turns out they don't even *start* on that till *third* year!

Total ripoff!!

Doreen and Nancy don't keep any clothes that fit weird giant robot men in their house, so they had to make do. Personally, I think they did a terrific job!

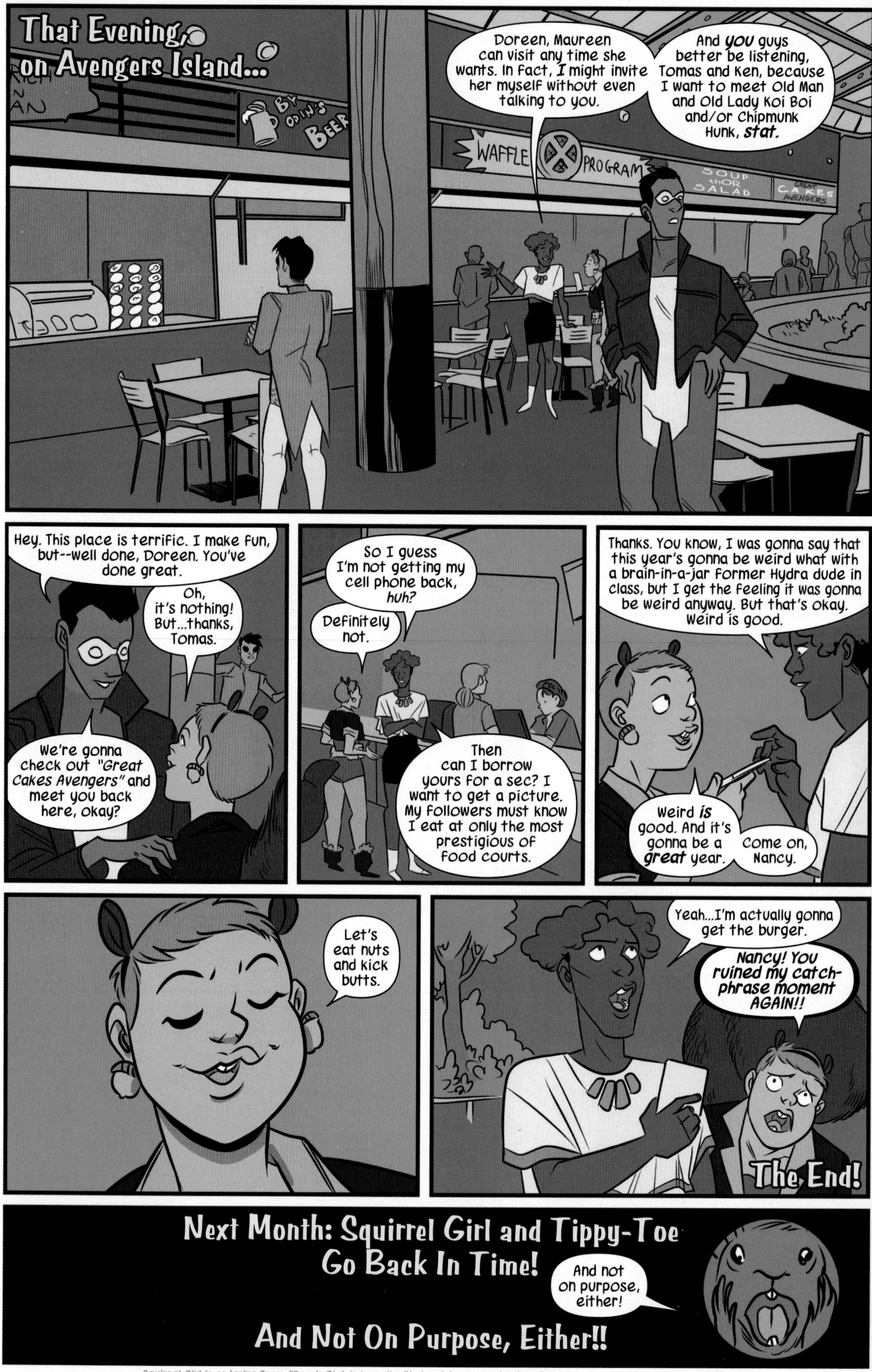
That Evening, on Avengers Island...
By Odin's Beer
Waffle Program
Soup thor Salad
Great Cakes Avengers
Doreen, Maureen can visit any time she wants. In fact, *I* might invite her myself without even talking to you.
And ***you*** guys better be listening, Tomas and Ken, because I want to meet Old Man and Old Lady Koi Boi and/or Chipmunk Hunk, ***stat.***
Hey. This place is terrific. I make fun, but--well done, Doreen. You've done great.
Oh, it's nothing! But...thanks, Tomas.
We're gonna check out *"Great Cakes Avengers"* and meet you back here, okay?
So I guess I'm not getting my cell phone back, *huh?*
Definitely not.
Then can I borrow yours for a sec? I want to get a picture. My followers must know I eat at only the most prestigious of food courts.
Thanks. You know, I was gonna say that this year's gonna be weird what with a brain-in-a-jar former Hydra dude in class, but I get the feeling it was gonna be weird anyway. But that's okay. Weird is good.
Weird ***is*** good. And it's gonna be a ***great*** year.
Come on, Nancy.
Let's eat nuts and kick butts.
Yeah...I'm actually gonna get the burger.
Nancy! You ruined my catch-phrase moment AGAIN!!
The End!
Next Month: Squirrel Girl and Tippy-Toe Go Back In Time!
And not on purpose, either!
And Not On Purpose, Either!!

Squirrel Girl is ordering from *"Foods Rich In Iron, Man"* but not because she likes Tony. Iron is a very important nutrient!

Letters From Nuts

Ryan!

Erica!

Send letters to mheroes@marvel.com or 135 W 50th St, 7th Floor, New York, NY 10020 (Please mark "OKAY TO PRINT")

And we're back! MISSED YOU GUYS!!!

Dear Ryan & Erica,
Hello I am 7. I know that I'm way too little for squirrel comics! But I can't help it!!!! Plus I am the greatest reader in my class! This is my favorite Halloween picture, it is of me dressed up as Squirrel Girl last year! I also love it when new Squirrel Girl comics come out! Keep up the good work!!!!!!!!

Tilly,
Twin Falls ID.

RYAN: Hey Tilly, nobody is too little for Squirrel Girl comics! Here are the rules for reading our comics:
1) You must be able to read.
2) Actually no, it's fine if you don't know how to read, as long as you know someone else who does.
3) You should probably learn to read though, honestly it helps out a lot.
So since you're ALREADY the greatest reader in your class, you definitely meet all the criteria to read our comics, and I'm really glad you do because that costume is terrific! Also I think Spider-Man borrowed your van without asking.
ERICA: *INCOHERENT SQUEALING*

Dear Ryan and Erica,
I am so far loving Squirrel Girl she's so kooky and fun but I'm worried, does she have back up trading cards? What if she loses them?!

Evie Gaffney

E: It's rough! They only sell them in sealed packs and you have to HOPE that the one you're missing is in there but it's probably not. There's also a pretty big market for them online, but do you really want to pay between 20 and 200 dollars for ONE card?

Great Odin's Ravens!
I literally CROWED with delight when Odinson busted out the Wabanaki origin for Ratatoskr in issue 7! Really, take a bow, because you nailed it. Charles G. Leland would be proud (Who's he? Look it up!). Erica, your flashback panels on that page are gorgeous, too. I just wish the text boxes didn't cover so much of them up! If this issue gets another printing later (like pretty much all the others), Wil has GOT to use those panels

for the cover. They're just too beautiful to be covered up! If this is what the bestiary you'd mentioned looks like, I want more!

Darryl Etheridge
St. Catharines, ON

R: Haha, I actually cut those text boxes down when I saw Erica's art because I felt bad covering them up too! They were TOO GOOD.
E: Fun fact about when I was drawing those boxes: If you do a Google search for viking art or norse art you get a lot of modern fan art or people's tree tattoos. Look up the Viking Art Museum! It's great!

I initially picked up SQUIRREL GIRL to browse at the letter column, since there was a mention in SILK #2 of a fan mail competition between the editors of both books. I flipped through the rest of the issue and it looked interesting enough to take home. My main thought was that it would possibly be a comic that my daughters would like.
Here we are over half a dozen issues later and I came to a realization the other evening. While telling some buddies at my local comic book shop about THE UNBEATABLE SQUIRREL GIRL series, a light bulb popped up and exploded over my head. I blurted out, "It's hands down my favorite Marvel book being published right now."
So there it is. My most beloved Marvel comic is SQUIRREL GIRL. If you had told me that I would be feeling that way prior to actually reading the stories, I wouldn't have believed it. Not with all of the other classic characters I grew up with and collected throughout the years...but Doreen just happens to be the bomb.
Erica's artwork is perfect for this series. It works so well with the style of writing provided by Ryan. Speaking of which, another thing I have said more than once to other people is, "It's hilarious. The writing is intimidatingly funny. I don't think I could ever come up with something as comical and amusing as SQUIRREL GIRL." (Feel free to use that as a back cover blurb on a trade paperback.)

Darrick Patrick
Dayton, Ohio

R: I love hearing about people picking up this book saying "Squirrel Girl?! PFFT" and then putting it down saying "Squirrel Girl! HECK YES." Thank you, Darrick!

Dear Erica and Ryan (or Ryan and Erica. Have a knife fight for top billing?),
As a long-time comic fan, I've always had a vague knowledge of Squirrel Girl as a character who started out as a joke and went on to have a life of her own, if only as a tool for writers to literally do what they want because they're the writers and shut up. I'm cool with that, because the idea of some girl with strange, seemingly almost useful powers that was destroying the most powerful beings in the universe amused me. Then I had a friend strongly recommend your run on the series and I said, "Okay, it's a new #1 and I'm looking for something to fill my subscription roster." Well, I wasn't expecting this. This Squirrel Girl

is as Unbeatable as you claim, but not as a show of the writer's power, but because she uses her wits to come up with long-term solutions to the problems she faces, and that's refreshing. It's become one of my most-looked-forward-to comics since #1. Keep up the great work, guys!
I love it so much that I went out and made a genderbent cosplay (which was long before Squirrel Earl) called High-Flying Squirrel Guy, AKA Frederick Reddington III, AKA Fred Red. The photos included are the earliest incarnation that was made in a few nights for a photoshoot, but I'm continuing to improve it! He's going to have more of a flying squirrel / aviation motif. Hope you guys like it!

Computer science student, cosplayer, and Squirrel
Girl fan,

David "Rookie" Railey, Auburn, AL

P.S. Pretty sure I fell in love when she said she wanted to study computer science...

R: David, the aviator glasses are an amazing touch, and I hereby declare Squirrel Guy to be MEGA SWEET. Nicely done!! Also, Erica, I checked my pocket and only brought a pack of gum and some lint to this knife fight.
E: OH MY GOD I LOVE IT. Love it so much. Ryan, I was just putting up pictures before I sat down to answer letters so I have a hammer in reach. Sorry, buddy.

Okay, that's all the room we have for this month, folks. Don't forget to check out our production blog at unbeatablesquirrelgirl.tumblr.com and we'll see you next month for #2!

Chris Robinson	Wil Moss	Tom Brevoort	Axel Alonso	Joe Quesada	Dan Buckley	Alan Fine
asst. editor	editor	executive editor	editor in chief	chief creative officer	publisher	exec. producer

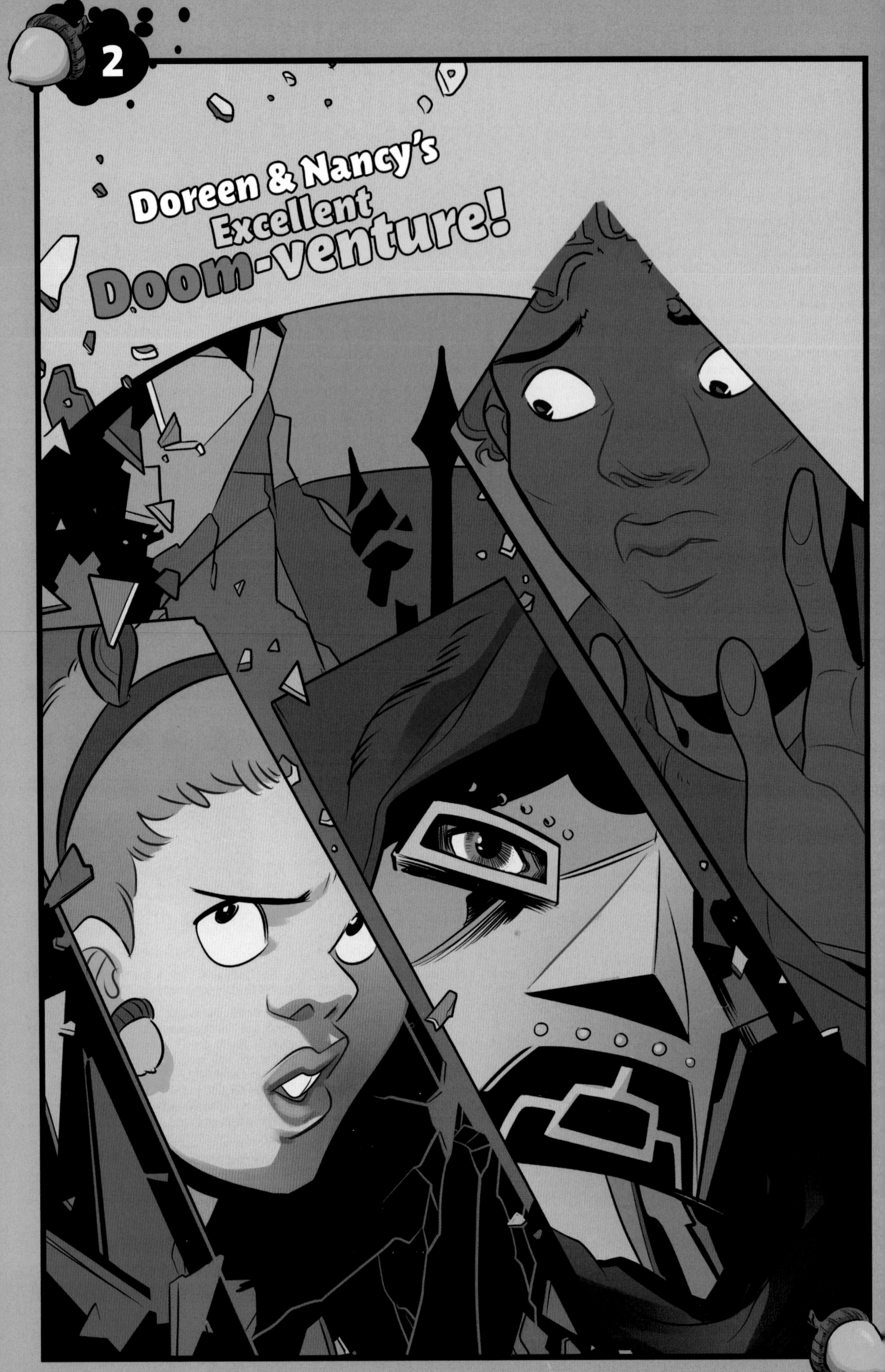
2
Doreen & Nancy's
Excellent
Doom-venture!

Doreen Green isn't just a second-year computer science student: she secretly also has all the powers of both squirrel and girl! She uses her amazing abilities to fight crime *and* be as awesome as possible. You know her as...The Unbeatable Squirrel Girl! Find out what she's been up to, with...

Squirrel Girl *in a nutshell*

search! 🔍

#TIMEforachange

#aheadofherTIME

#theresaTIMEandaplace

#thirdTIMEisthecharm

#anywayyesthisissueisabouttimetravel

#surprise

Ryan North - writer
Erica Henderson - artist
Matt Digges, David Robbins, Chip Zdarsky - trading card artists
Rico Renzi - color artist
VC's Clayton Cowles - letterer
Erica Henderson - cover artist
Brittney L. Williams - variant cover artist
Special Thanks to Lissa Pattillo and Nick Russell
Chris Robinson - asst. editor
Wil Moss - editor
Tom Brevoort - executive editor
Axel Alonso - editor in chief
Joe Quesada - chief creative officer
Dan Buckley - publisher
Alan Fine - exec. producer

Squirrel Girl! @unbeatablesg
Philosophers are always like "whoa I'm gonna a blow your mind what if we're just brains in jars and reality is fake whoaaaa"!

Squirrel Girl! @unbeatablesg
But check this: what if we're just brains in jars on SUPERPOWERED ROBOT BODIES? Oh snap! Did philosophy just get...SUPER AWESOME??

Squirrel Girl! @unbeatablesg
Anyway this is all to say I fought a brain in a jar on a robot bod and it was rad and his name is Werner and we're friends now, nbd

Squirrel Girl! @unbeatablesg
@starkmantony hey Tony I had a great idea! What if instead of wearing Iron Man suits, you put your brain in a jar and armored THAT instead?

Squirrel Girl! @unbeatablesg
@starkmantony you'd save mega $$$ on iron suits for sure PLUS it would give your enemies a smaller target to hit (tactical advantage)

Squirrel Girl! @unbeatablesg
@starkmantony instead of "Iron Man" we could call you "Iron MIND," and you'd float around the city solving math puzzles

Tony Stark @starkmantony ✓
@unbeatablesg Squirrel Girl, don't you have a crime to fight somewhere? Anywhere?

Squirrel Girl! @unbeatablesg
@starkmantony yes

Squirrel Girl! @unbeatablesg
@starkmantony for example, i'm currently fighting the crime of you not calling yourself "Iron Mind" and solving brain teasers

Nancy W. @sewwiththeflo
How attractive is it to be in your early 20s and running a blog for your cat? Because I'm seriously considering it.

Nancy W. @sewwiththeflo
And by "how attractive" I don't mean, like, "attractive to guys." I mean "how instantly appealing is that idea." Answer? Extremely.

Squirrel Girl! @unbeatablesg
@sewwiththeflo NEVER CHANGE <3

Nancy W. @sewwiththeflo
@unbeatablesg I'm gonna post Cat Thor fics too, and I'm working on one featuring Lokitten (v mischievous kitten)

Squirrel Girl! @unbeatablesg
@sewwiththeflo omg!! WE HAVE TO SEND THEM TO LOKI

Squirrel Girl! @unbeatablesg
@starkmantony TONY DO YOU HAVE A WAY TO EMAIL ASGARD

Squirrel Girl! @unbeatablesg
@starkmantony TONY

Squirrel Girl! @unbeatablesg
@starkmantony TONY

Squirrel Girl! @unbeatablesg
@starkmantony TONY

Squirrel Girl! @unbeatablesg
@starkmantony TONY WHY DOES IT SAY I'M BLOCKED

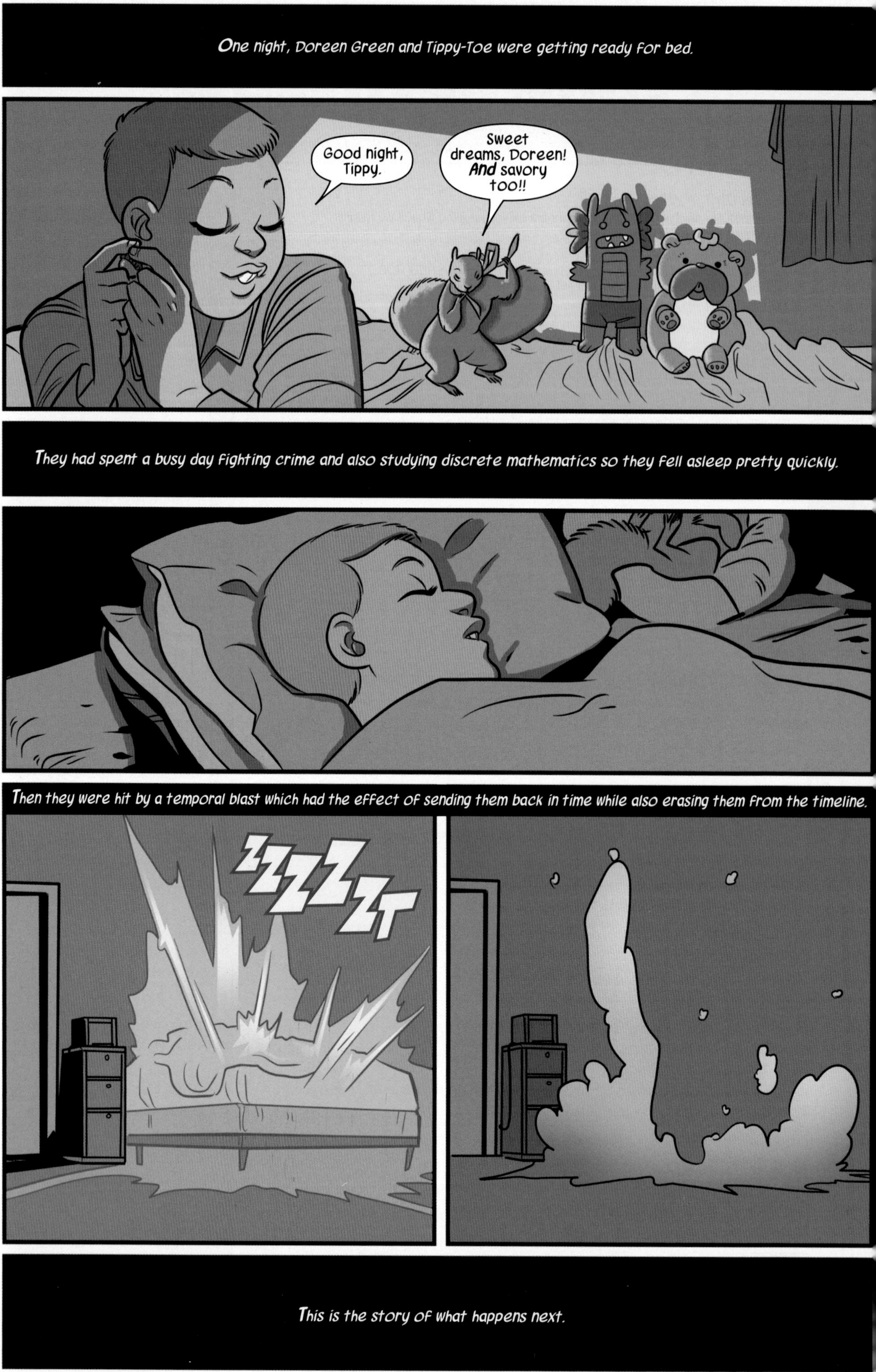
One night, Doreen Green and Tippy-Toe were getting ready for bed.
Good night, Tippy.
Sweet dreams, Doreen! And savory too!!
They had spent a busy day fighting crime and also studying discrete mathematics so they fell asleep pretty quickly.
Then they were hit by a temporal blast which had the effect of sending them back in time while also erasing them from the timeline.
ZZZZZZT
This is the story of what happens next.

See that? Other comics will make you read ***a whole miniseries*** just to see their heroes get sent back in time and also erased from the timeline. We did it on our very first page! How's ***that*** taste, all other comics?

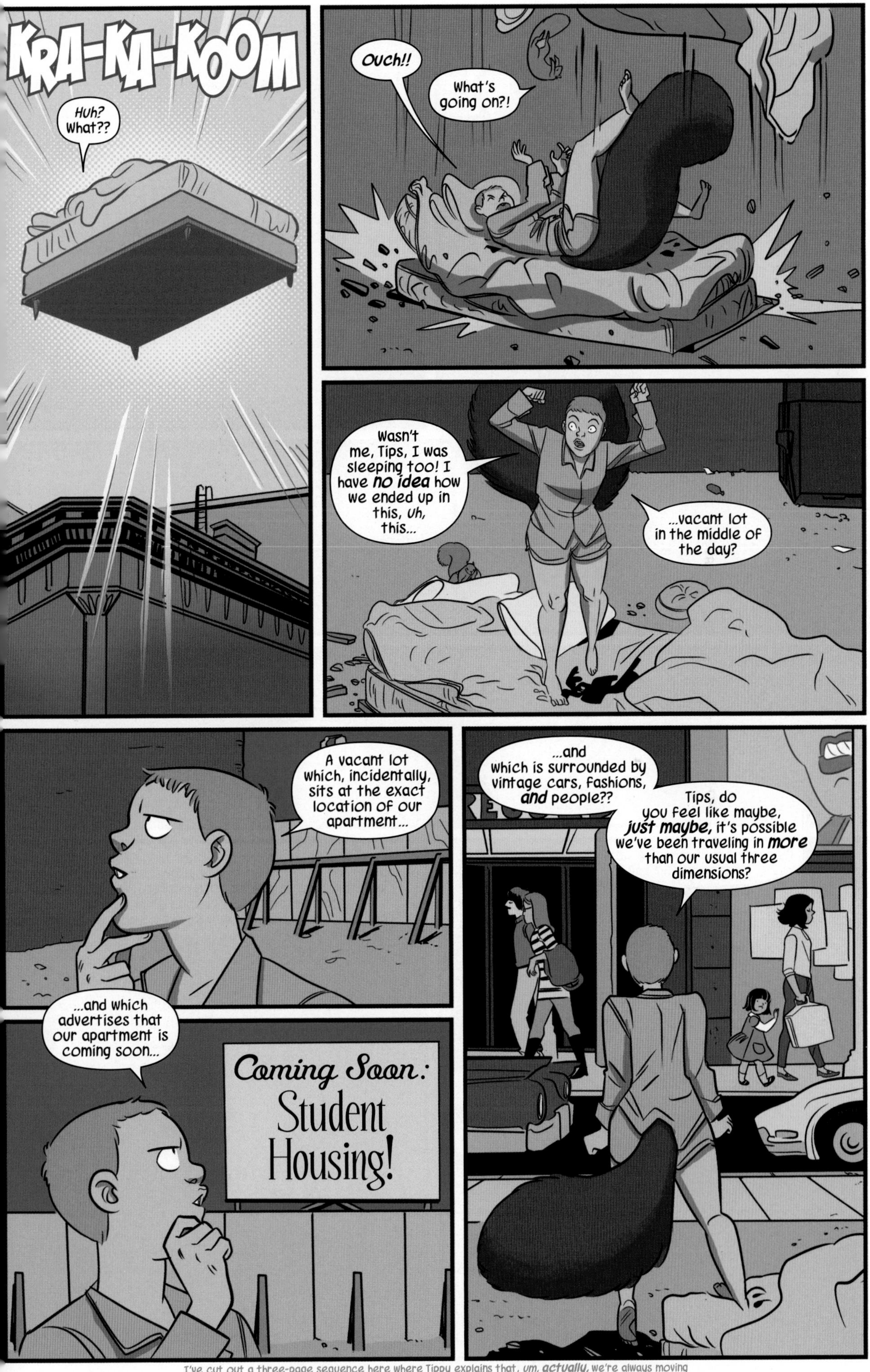
KRA-KA-KOOM
Huh? What??
Ouch!!
What's going on?!
Wasn't me, Tips, I was sleeping too! I have **no idea** how we ended up in this, uh, this...
...vacant lot in the middle of the day?
A vacant lot which, incidentally, sits at the exact location of our apartment...
...and which advertises that our apartment is coming soon...
Coming Soon:
Student Housing!
...and which is surrounded by vintage cars, fashions, **and** people??
Tips, do you feel like maybe, ***just maybe,*** it's possible we've been traveling in ***more*** than our usual three dimensions?

I've cut out a three-page sequence here where Tippy explains that, *um,* ***actually,*** we're always moving through the fourth dimension (time) too. Come on, Tippy. Don't be that gal.

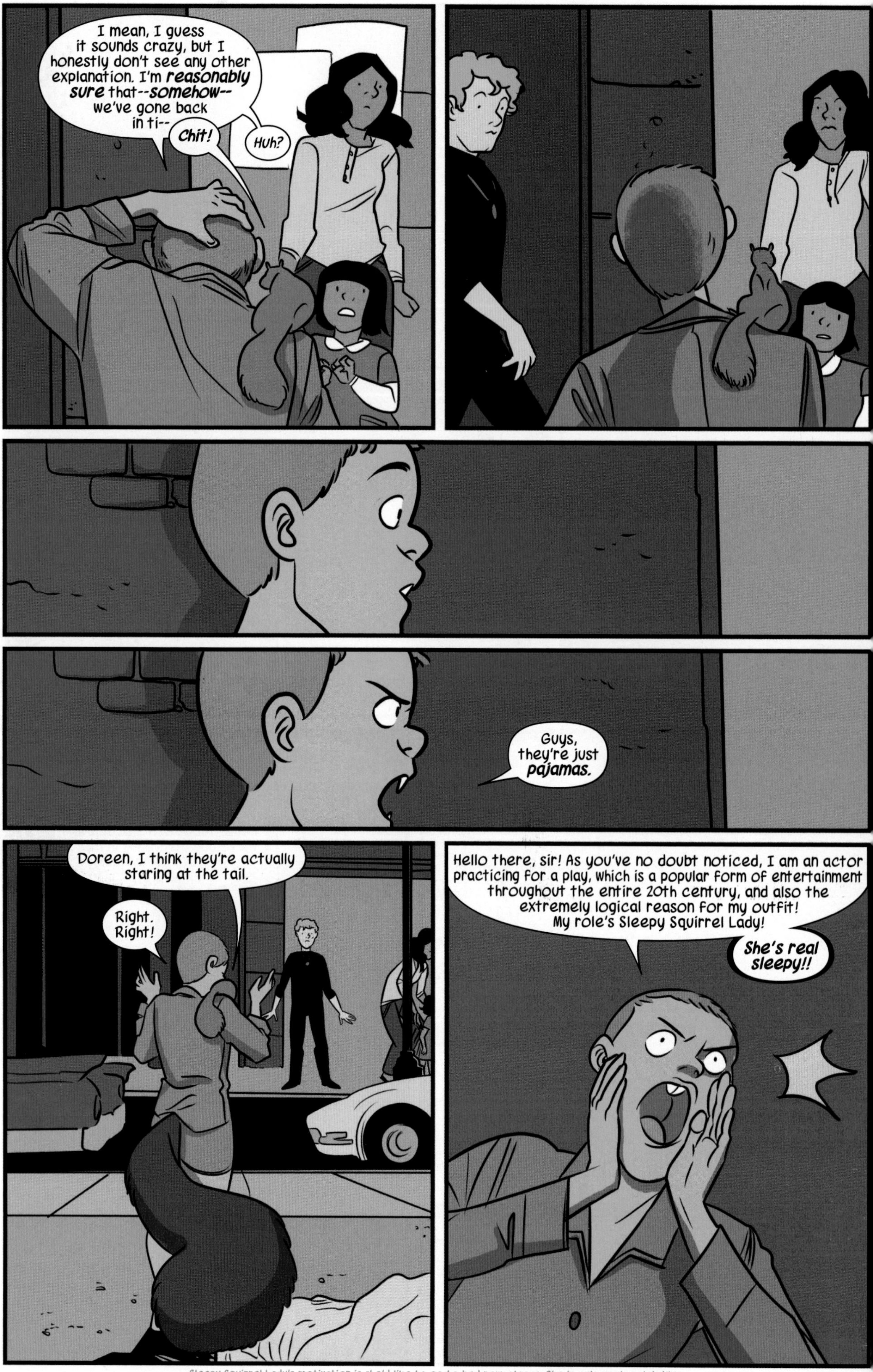
I mean, I guess it sounds crazy, but I honestly don't see any other explanation. I'm **reasonably sure** that--**somehow**--we've gone back in ti--
Chit!
Huh?
Guys, they're just **pajamas.**
Doreen, I think they're actually staring at the tail.
Right. Right!
Hello there, sir! As you've no doubt noticed, I am an actor practicing for a play, which is a popular form of entertainment throughout the entire 20th century, and also the extremely logical reason for my outfit! My role's Sleepy Squirrel Lady!
She's real sleepy!!

Sleepy Squirrel Lady's motivation is she'd like to go to bed now, please. She is extremely relatable.

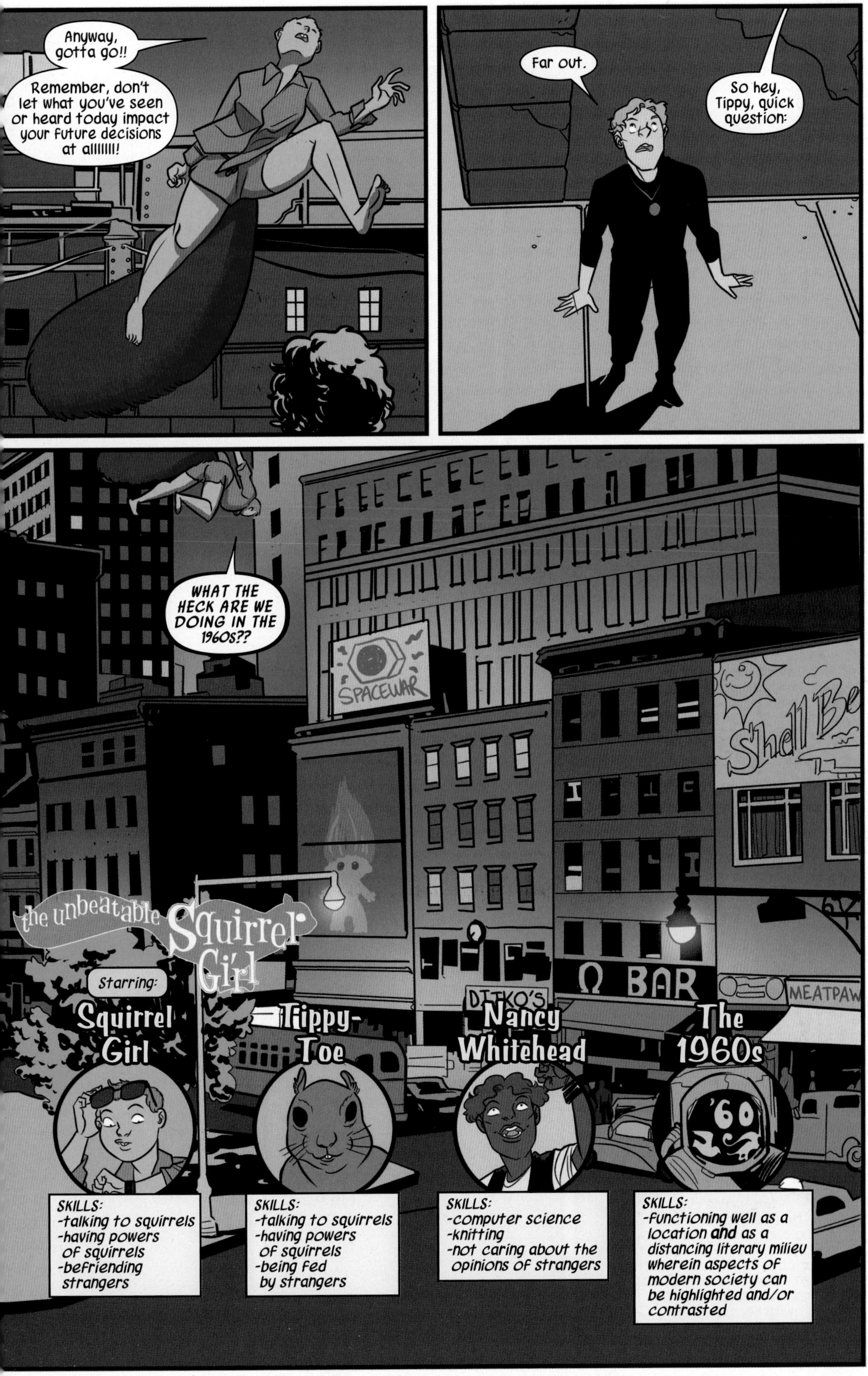
Anyway, gotta go!!
Remember, don't let what you've seen or heard today impact your future decisions at allllll!
Far out.
So hey, Tippy, quick question:
WHAT THE HECK ARE WE DOING IN THE 1960s??
SPACEWAR
Ω BAR
DITKO'S
MEATPAW
the unbeatable Squirrel Girl
Starring:
Squirrel Girl
SKILLS:
-talking to squirrels
-having powers of squirrels
-befriending strangers
Tippy-Toe
SKILLS:
-talking to squirrels
-having powers of squirrels
-being fed by strangers
Nancy Whitehead
SKILLS:
-computer science
-knitting
-not caring about the opinions of strangers
The 1960s
'60
SKILLS:
-functioning well as a location and as a distancing literary milieu wherein aspects of modern society can be highlighted and/or contrasted

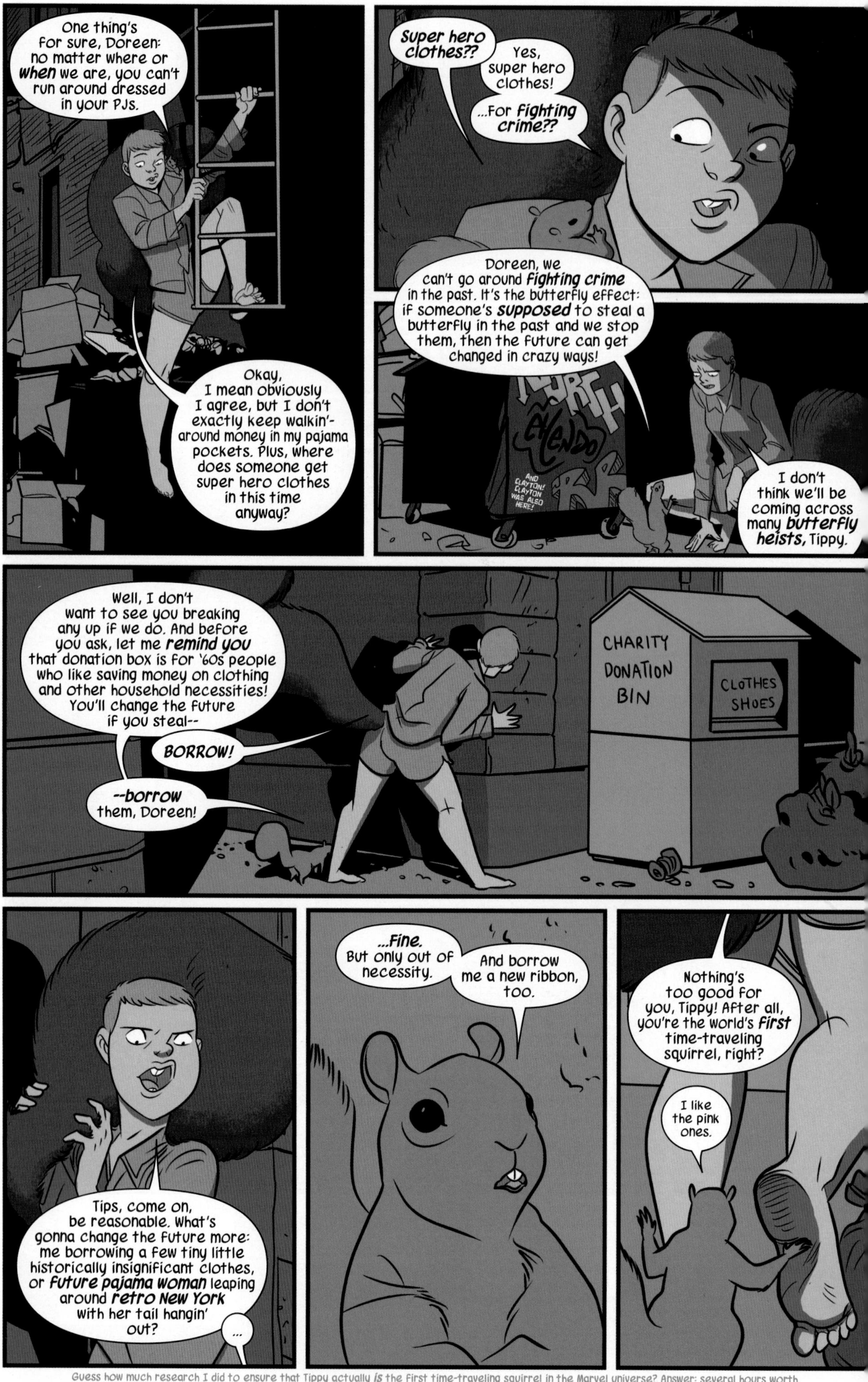
One thing's for sure, Doreen: no matter where or *when* we are, you can't run around dressed in your PJs.
Okay, I mean obviously I agree, but I don't exactly keep walkin'-around money in my pajama pockets. Plus, where does someone get super hero clothes in this time anyway?
Super hero clothes??
Yes, super hero clothes!
...For ***fighting crime??***
Doreen, we can't go around ***fighting crime*** in the past. It's the butterfly effect: if someone's ***supposed*** to steal a butterfly in the past and we stop them, then the future can get changed in crazy ways!
AND CLAYTON! CLAYTON WAS ALSO HERE!
I don't think we'll be coming across many ***butterfly heists,*** Tippy.
Well, I don't want to see you breaking any up if we do. And before you ask, let me ***remind you*** that donation box is for '60s people who like saving money on clothing and other household necessities! You'll change the future if you steal--
BORROW!
--borrow them, Doreen!
CHARITY DONATION BIN
CLOTHES SHOES
Tips, come on, be reasonable. What's gonna change the future more: me borrowing a few tiny little historically insignificant clothes, or ***future pajama woman*** leaping around ***retro New York*** with her tail hangin' out?
...
...Fine. But only out of necessity.
And borrow me a new ribbon, too.
Nothing's too good for you, Tippy! After all, you're the world's ***first*** time-traveling squirrel, right?
I like the pink ones.

Guess how much research I did to ensure that Tippy actually *is* the first time-traveling squirrel in the Marvel universe? Answer: several hours worth. But *"research"* actually means *"sitting around reading other comics,"* so it's actually no big deal!

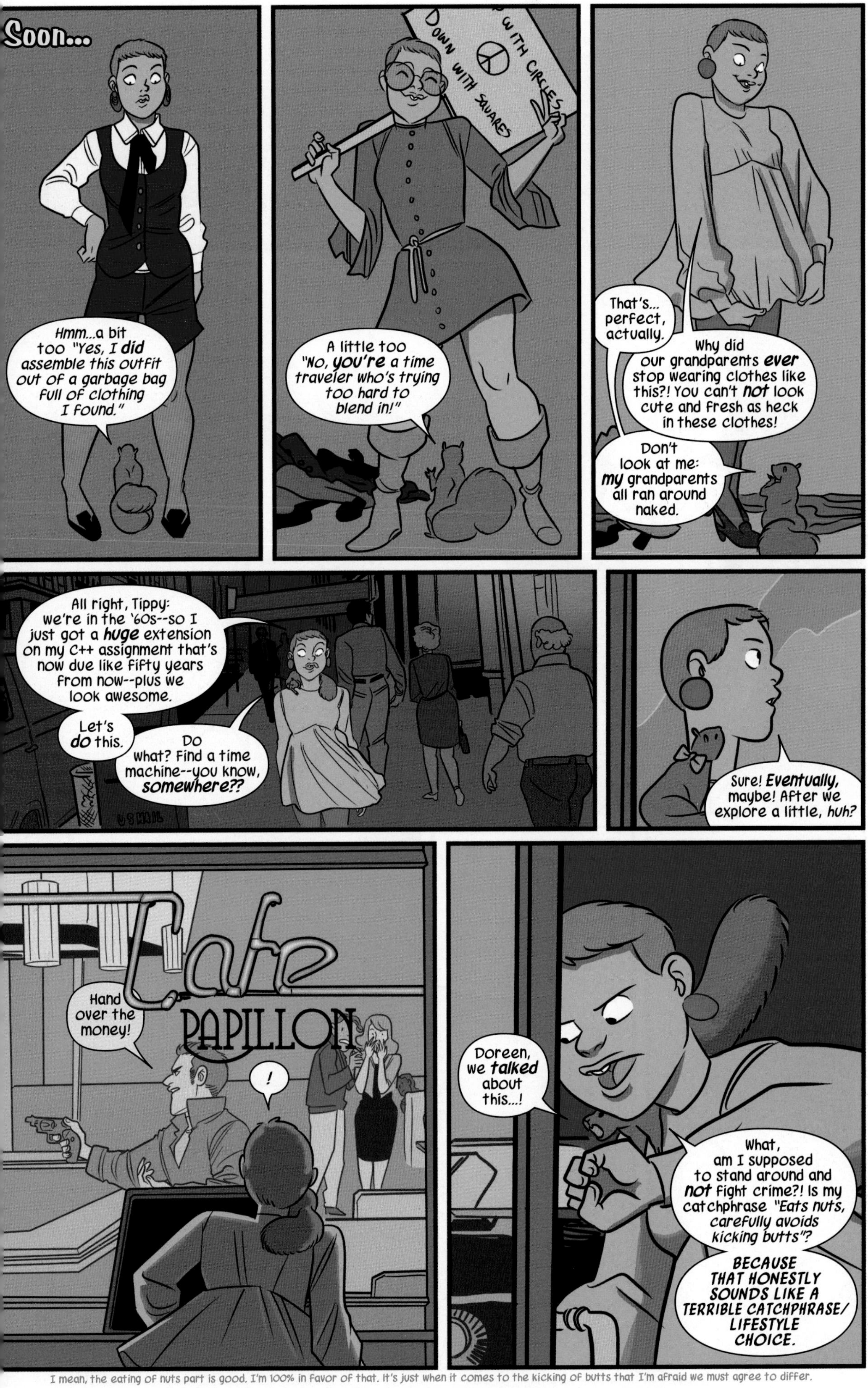

Soon...
Hmm...a bit too "Yes, I did assemble this outfit out of a garbage bag full of clothing I found."
WITH CIRCLES
DOWN WITH SQUARES
A little too "No, you're a time traveler who's trying too hard to blend in!"
That's... perfect, actually.
Why did our grandparents ever stop wearing clothes like this?! You can't not look cute and fresh as heck in these clothes!
Don't look at me: my grandparents all ran around naked.
All right, Tippy: we're in the '60s--so I just got a huge extension on my C++ assignment that's now due like fifty years from now--plus we look awesome.
Let's do this.
Do what? Find a time machine--you know, somewhere??
U S MAIL
Sure! Eventually, maybe! After we explore a little, huh?
Cafe
PAPILLON
Hand over the money!
!
Doreen, we talked about this...!
What, am I supposed to stand around and not fight crime?! Is my catchphrase "Eats nuts, carefully avoids kicking butts"?
BECAUSE THAT HONESTLY SOUNDS LIKE A TERRIBLE CATCHPHRASE/ LIFESTYLE CHOICE.

I mean, the eating of nuts part is good. I'm 100% in favor of that. It's just when it comes to the kicking of butts that I'm afraid we must agree to differ.

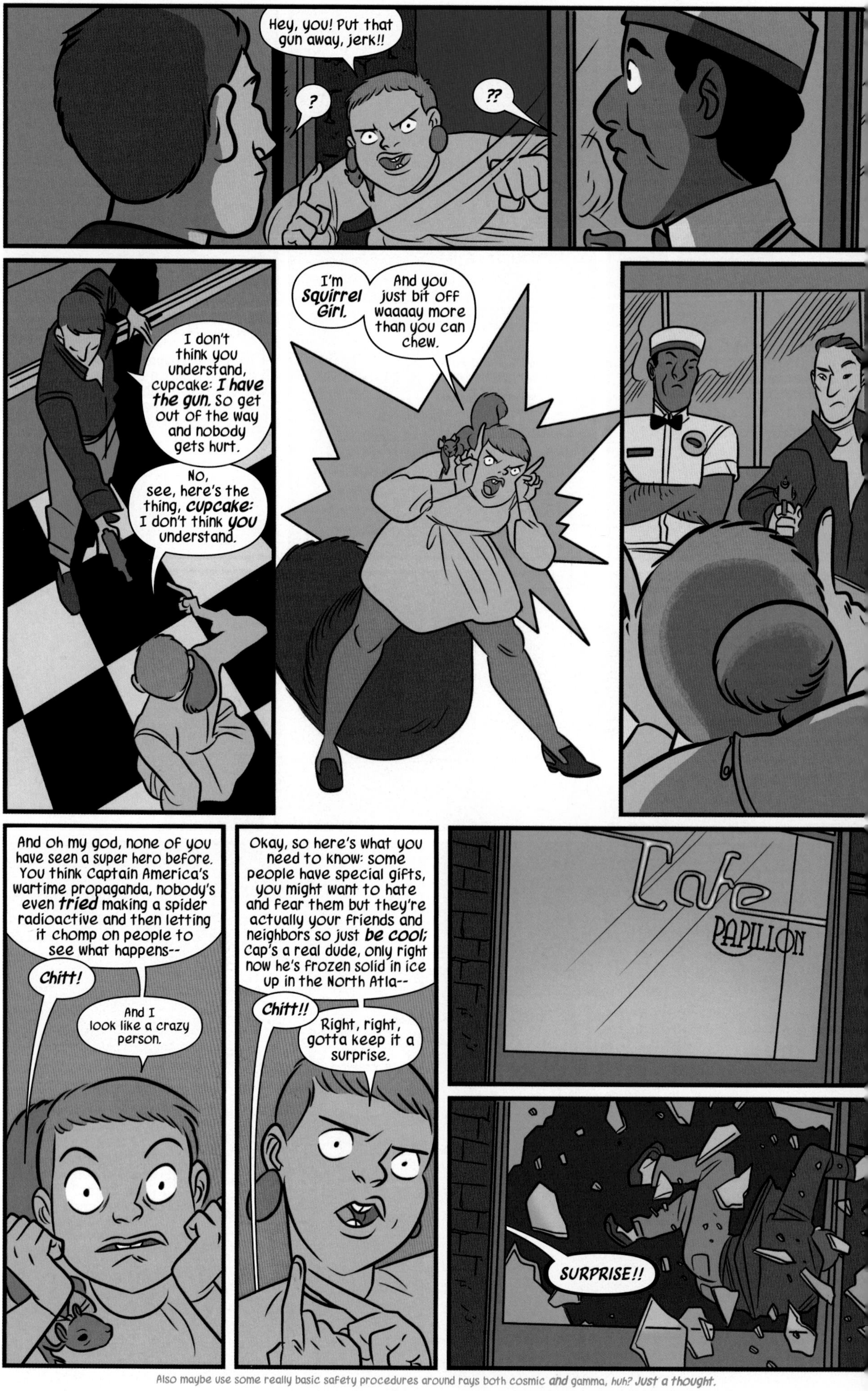
Hey, you! Put that gun away, jerk!!
?
??
I don't think you understand, cupcake: I have the gun. So get out of the way and nobody gets hurt.
No, see, here's the thing, cupcake: I don't think you understand.
I'm Squirrel Girl.
And you just bit off waaaay more than you can chew.
And oh my god, none of you have seen a super hero before. You think Captain America's wartime propaganda, nobody's even tried making a spider radioactive and then letting it chomp on people to see what happens--
Chitt!
And I look like a crazy person.
Okay, so here's what you need to know: some people have special gifts, you might want to hate and fear them but they're actually your friends and neighbors so just be cool; Cap's a real dude, only right now he's frozen solid in ice up in the North Atla--
Chitt!!
Right, right, gotta keep it a surprise.
Cafe
PAPILLON
SURPRISE!!

Also maybe use some really basic safety procedures around rays both cosmic *and* gamma, *huh?* ***Just a thought.***

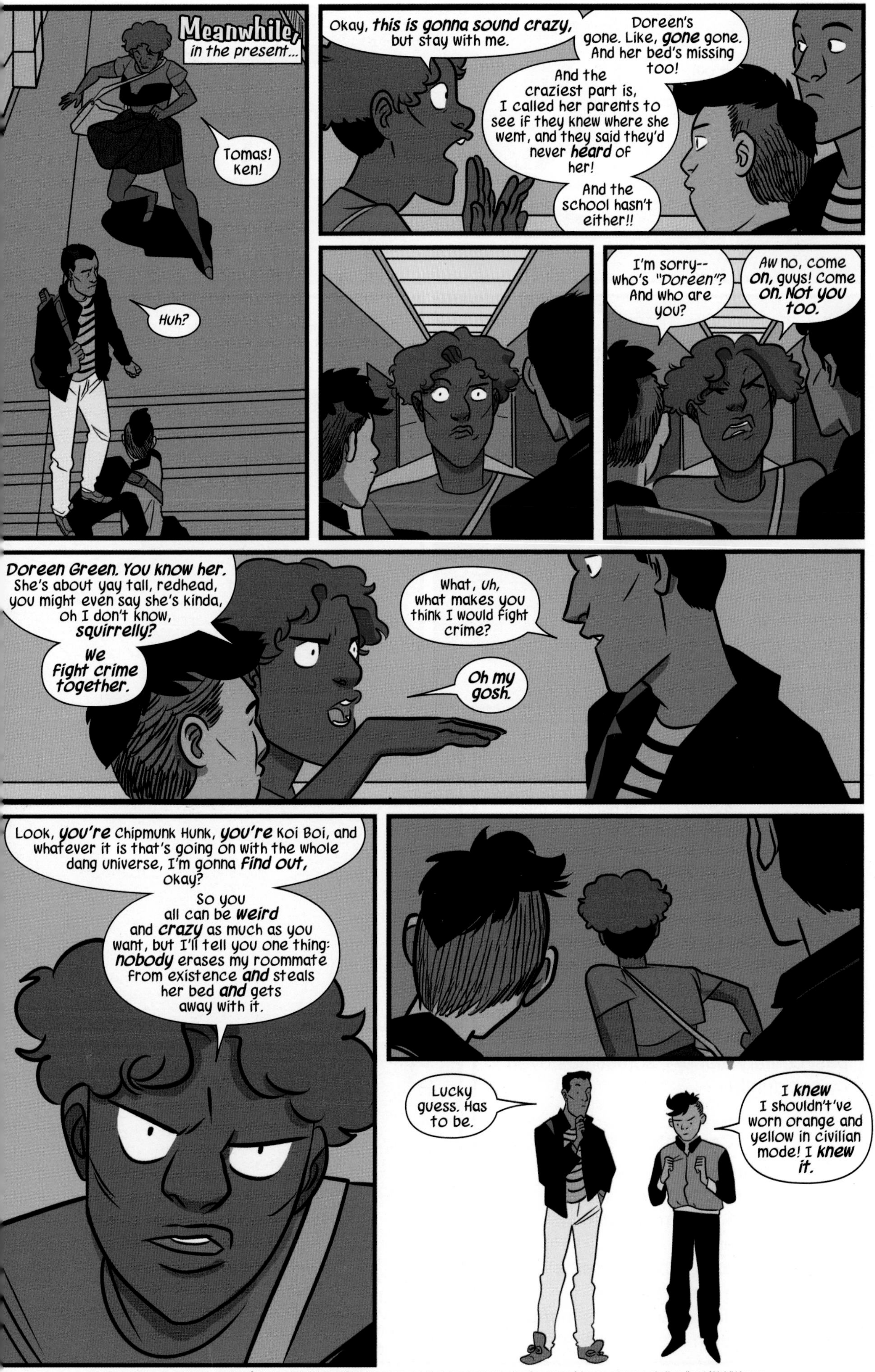

Meanwhile, in the present...
Tomas! Ken!
Huh?
Okay, this is gonna sound crazy, but stay with me.
Doreen's gone. Like, gone gone. And her bed's missing too!
And the craziest part is, I called her parents to see if they knew where she went, and they said they'd never heard of her!
And the school hasn't either!!
I'm sorry-- who's "Doreen"? And who are you?
Aw no, come on, guys! Come on. Not you too.
Doreen Green. You know her. She's about yay tall, redhead, you might even say she's kinda, oh I don't know, squirrelly?
We fight crime together.
What, uh, what makes you think I would fight crime?
Oh my gosh.
Look, you're Chipmunk Hunk, you're Koi Boi, and whatever it is that's going on with the whole dang universe, I'm gonna find out, okay?
So you all can be weird and crazy as much as you want, but I'll tell you one thing: nobody erases my roommate from existence and steals her bed and gets away with it.
Lucky guess. Has to be.
I knew I shouldn't've worn orange and yellow in civilian mode! I knew it.

I just love these colors *so much*. Honestly, it's really lucky for me that my powers also happened to go along a similar *"goldfish"* theme.

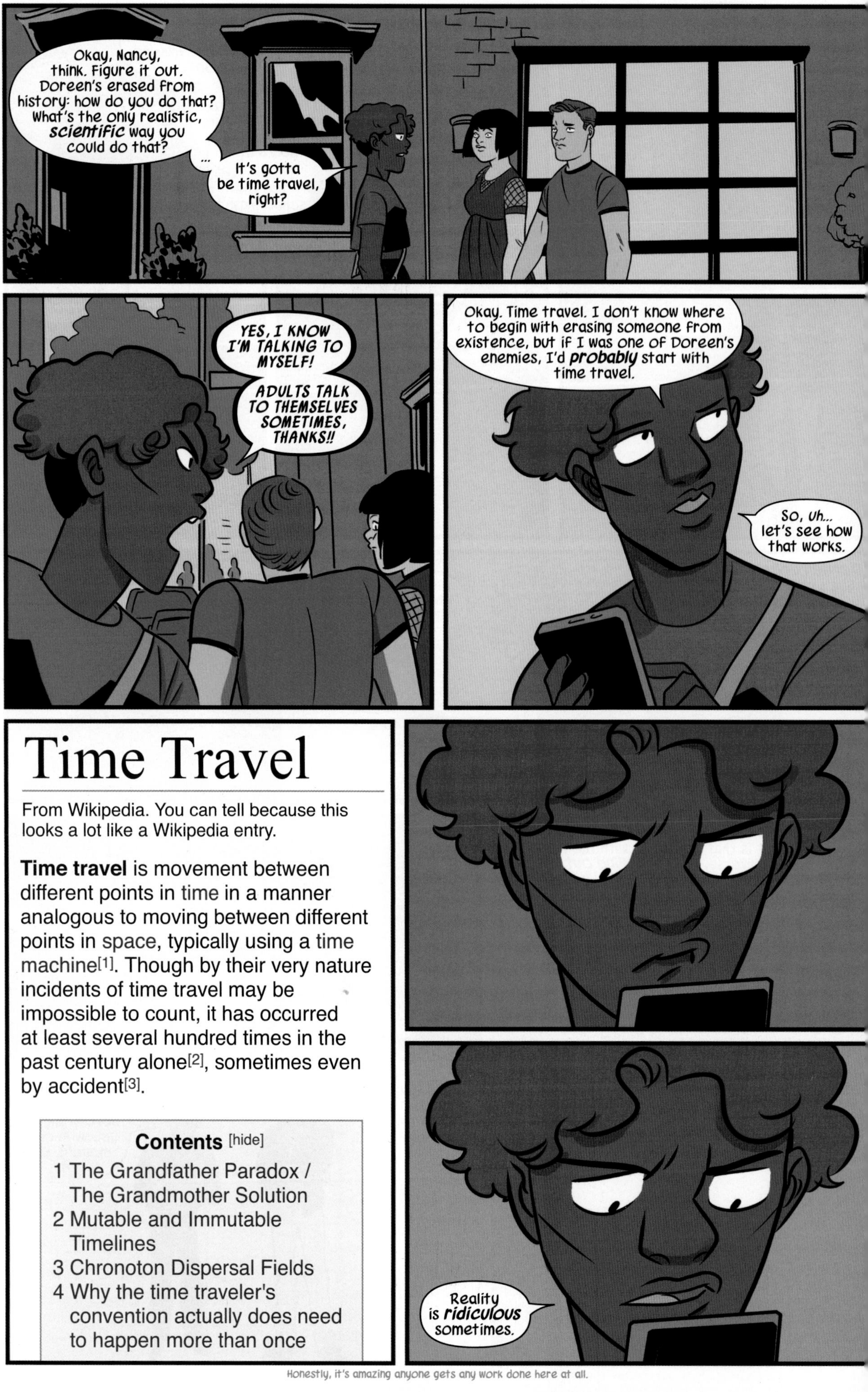
Okay, Nancy, think. Figure it out. Doreen's erased from history: how do you do that? What's the only realistic, scientific way you could do that?
...
It's gotta be time travel, right?
YES, I KNOW I'M TALKING TO MYSELF!
ADULTS TALK TO THEMSELVES SOMETIMES, THANKS!!
Okay. Time travel. I don't know where to begin with erasing someone from existence, but if I was one of Doreen's enemies, I'd probably start with time travel.
So, uh... let's see how that works.
Time Travel
From Wikipedia. You can tell because this looks a lot like a Wikipedia entry.
Time travel is movement between different points in time in a manner analogous to moving between different points in space, typically using a time machine[1]. Though by their very nature incidents of time travel may be impossible to count, it has occurred at least several hundred times in the past century alone[2], sometimes even by accident[3].
Contents [hide]
1 The Grandfather Paradox / The Grandmother Solution
2 Mutable and Immutable Timelines
3 Chronoton Dispersal Fields
4 Why the time traveler's convention actually does need to happen more than once
Reality is ridiculous sometimes.

Honestly, it's amazing anyone gets any work done here at all.

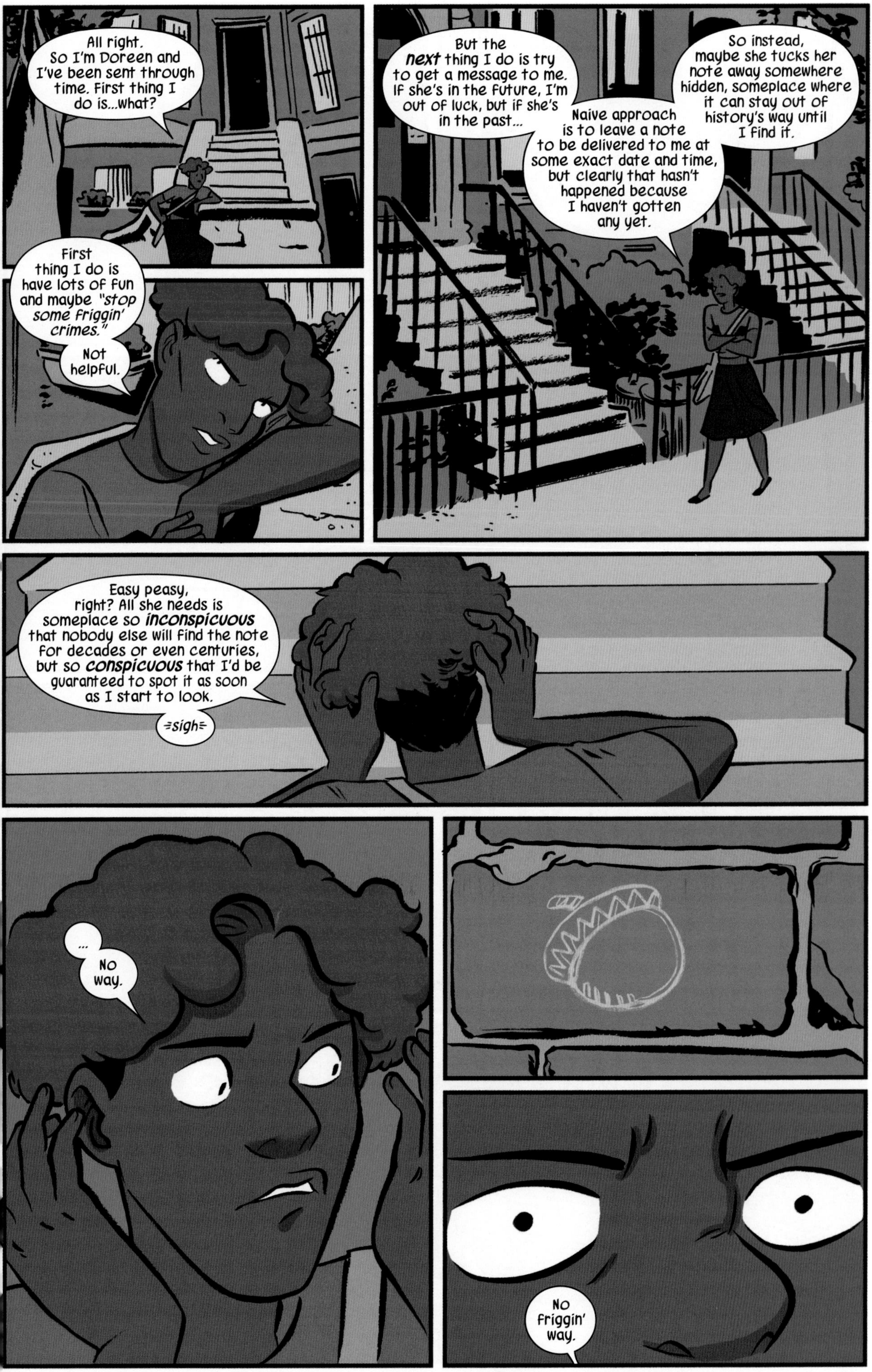
All right. So I'm Doreen and I've been sent through time. First thing I do is...what?
First thing I do is have lots of fun and maybe "stop some friggin' crimes."
Not helpful.
But the next thing I do is try to get a message to me. If she's in the future, I'm out of luck, but if she's in the past...
Naive approach is to leave a note to be delivered to me at some exact date and time, but clearly that hasn't happened because I haven't gotten any yet.
So instead, maybe she tucks her note away somewhere hidden, someplace where it can stay out of history's way until I find it.
Easy peasy, right? All she needs is someplace so inconspicuous that nobody else will find the note for decades or even centuries, but so conspicuous that I'd be guaranteed to spot it as soon as I start to look.
=sigh=
... No way.
No friggin' way.

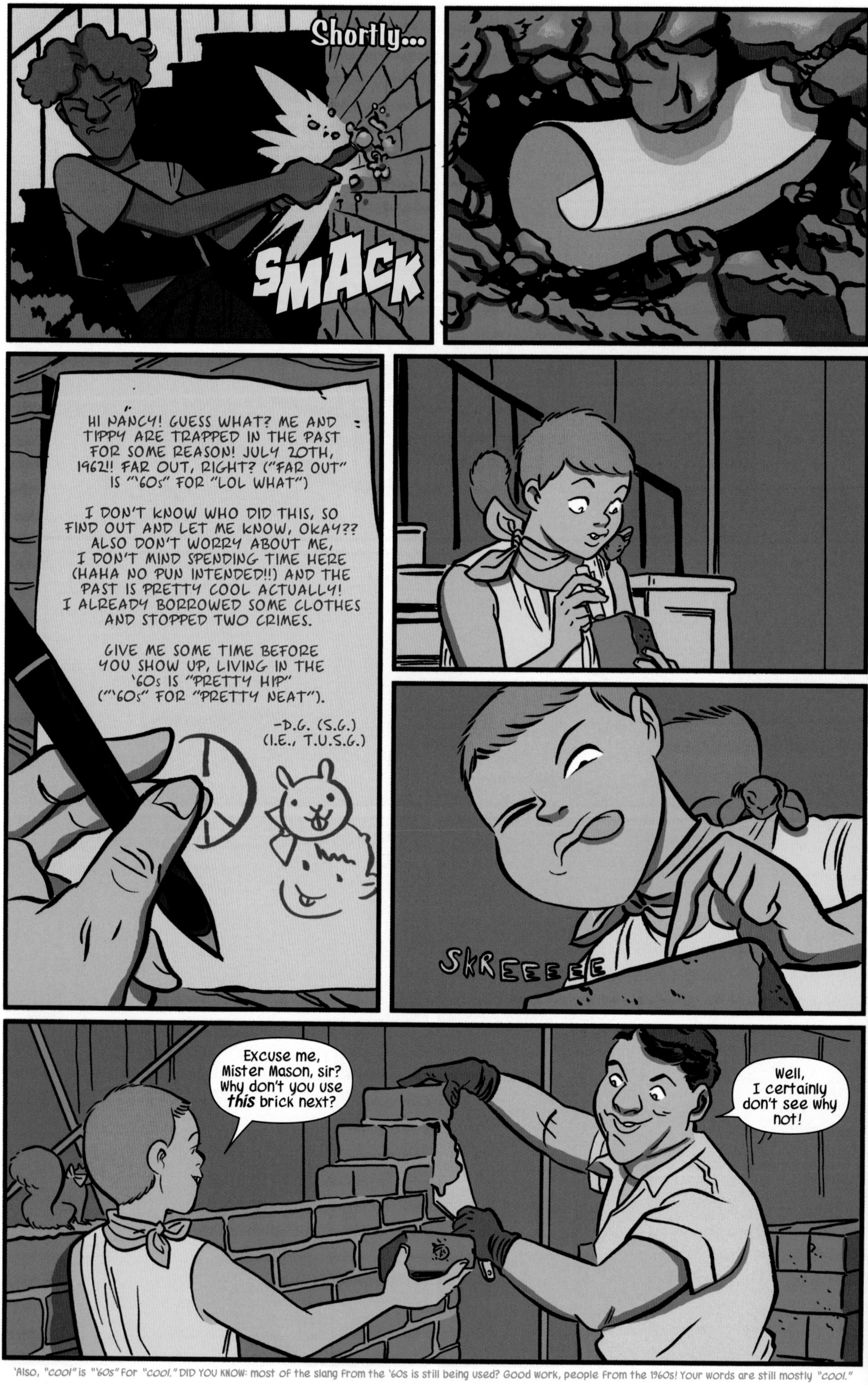
Shortly...
SMACK
HI NANCY! GUESS WHAT? ME AND TIPPY ARE TRAPPED IN THE PAST FOR SOME REASON! JULY 20TH, 1962!! FAR OUT, RIGHT? ("FAR OUT" IS "'60s" FOR "LOL WHAT")
I DON'T KNOW WHO DID THIS, SO FIND OUT AND LET ME KNOW, OKAY?? ALSO DON'T WORRY ABOUT ME, I DON'T MIND SPENDING TIME HERE (HAHA NO PUN INTENDED!!) AND THE PAST IS PRETTY COOL ACTUALLY! I ALREADY BORROWED SOME CLOTHES AND STOPPED TWO CRIMES.
GIVE ME SOME TIME BEFORE YOU SHOW UP, LIVING IN THE '60s IS "PRETTY HIP" ("'60s" FOR "PRETTY NEAT").
-D.G. (S.G.) (I.E., T.U.S.G.)
SKREEEEEE
Excuse me, Mister Mason, sir? Why don't you use *this* brick next?
Well, I certainly don't see why not!

'Also, "*cool*" is "'60s" for "*cool*." DID YOU KNOW: most of the slang from the '60s is still being used? Good work, people from the 1960s! Your words are still mostly "*cool*."

Okay, talking to the future is taken care of! Now all I need is a job and an apartment, huh?

But what if Nancy never finds your note?

Then I'll send another one, no biggie! We're the ones in the past, yo. We can just keep sending notes till one gets through!

Worst case, old lady me gets to cool student Nancy the slow way, tells her to come back and rescue me back when I was cool too, and--

And young you gets rescued so old you never existed to tell Nancy to rescue you, and you've got a *paradox*, Doreen!

Pfft. If paradoxes really tore apart the fabric of the universe they would've done it *long ago*, and--

--what?!

--ook me a minute before I realized earbuds aren't gonna exist for like thirty years or whatever, so I know this is gonna sound weird but I was just wondering, are you from what people *here* would think is the future but to us is just the boring ol' present?

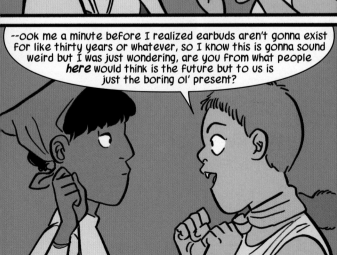

Oh, *thank god.* I was beginning to think I was *crazy.*

I was also beginning to think maybe I should've put a few more songs on this before I was involuntarily blasted back in time, but hey, hindsight's always 20/20, even in the '60s.

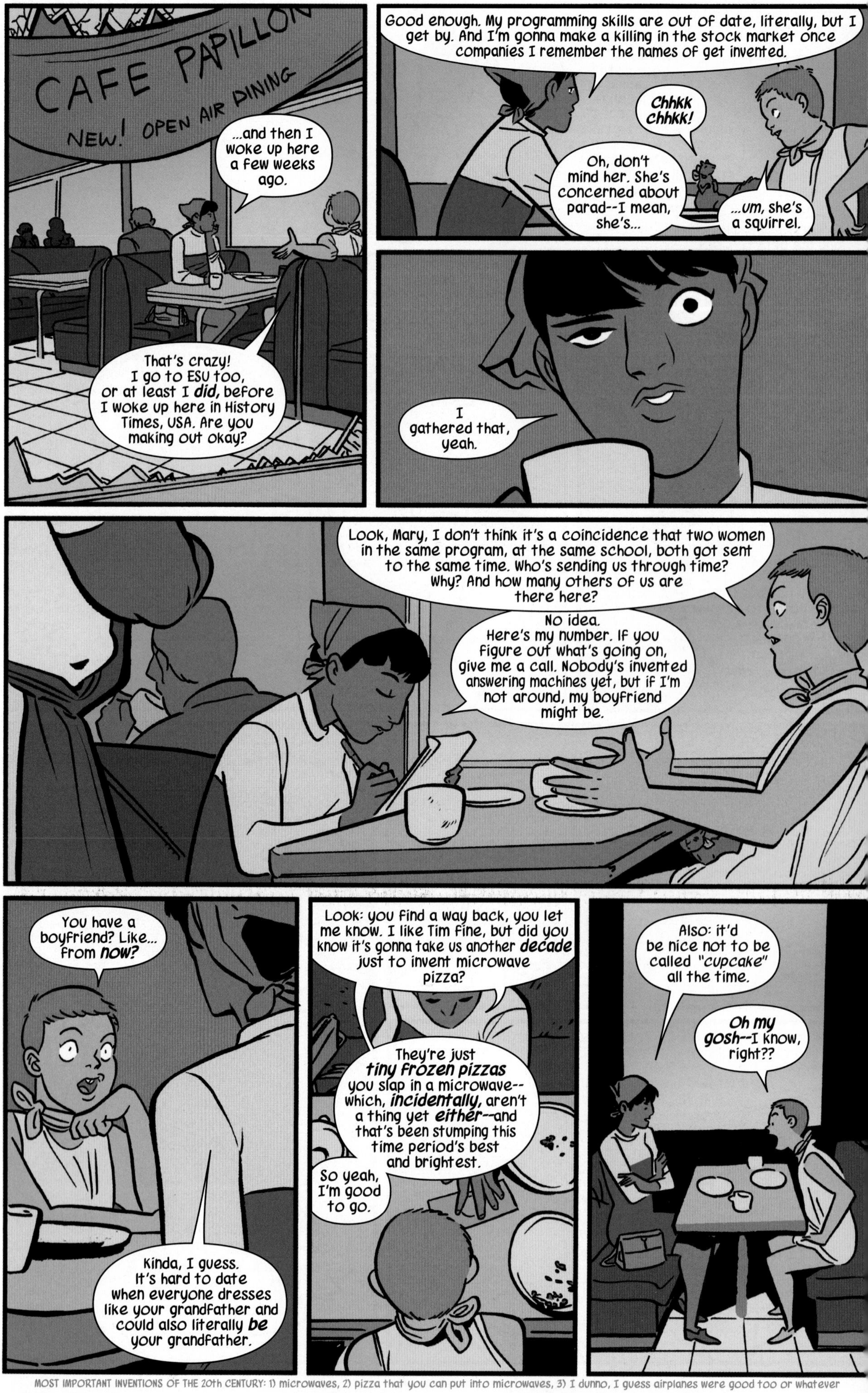
CAFE PAPILLON
NEW! OPEN AIR DINING
...and then I woke up here a few weeks ago.
That's crazy! I go to ESU too, or at least I *did*, before I woke up here in History Times, USA. Are you making out okay?
Good enough. My programming skills are out of date, literally, but I get by. And I'm gonna make a killing in the stock market once companies I remember the names of get invented.
Chhkk chhkk!
Oh, don't mind her. She's concerned about parad--I mean, she's...
...um, she's a squirrel.
I gathered that, yeah.
Look, Mary, I don't think it's a coincidence that two women in the same program, at the same school, both got sent to the same time. Who's sending us through time? Why? And how many others of us are there here?
No idea. Here's my number. If you figure out what's going on, give me a call. Nobody's invented answering machines yet, but if I'm not around, my boyfriend might be.
You have a boyfriend? Like... from *now?*
Kinda, I guess. It's hard to date when everyone dresses like your grandfather and could also literally *be* your grandfather.
Look: you find a way back, you let me know. I like Tim fine, but did you know it's gonna take us another *decade* just to invent microwave pizza?
They're just *tiny frozen pizzas* you slap in a microwave--which, *incidentally,* aren't a thing yet *either*--and that's been stumping this time period's best and brightest.
So yeah, I'm good to go.
Also: it'd be nice not to be called "*cupcake*" all the time.
Oh my gosh--I know, right??

MOST IMPORTANT INVENTIONS OF THE 20th CENTURY: 1) microwaves, 2) pizza that you can put into microwaves, 3) I dunno, I guess airplanes were good too or whatever

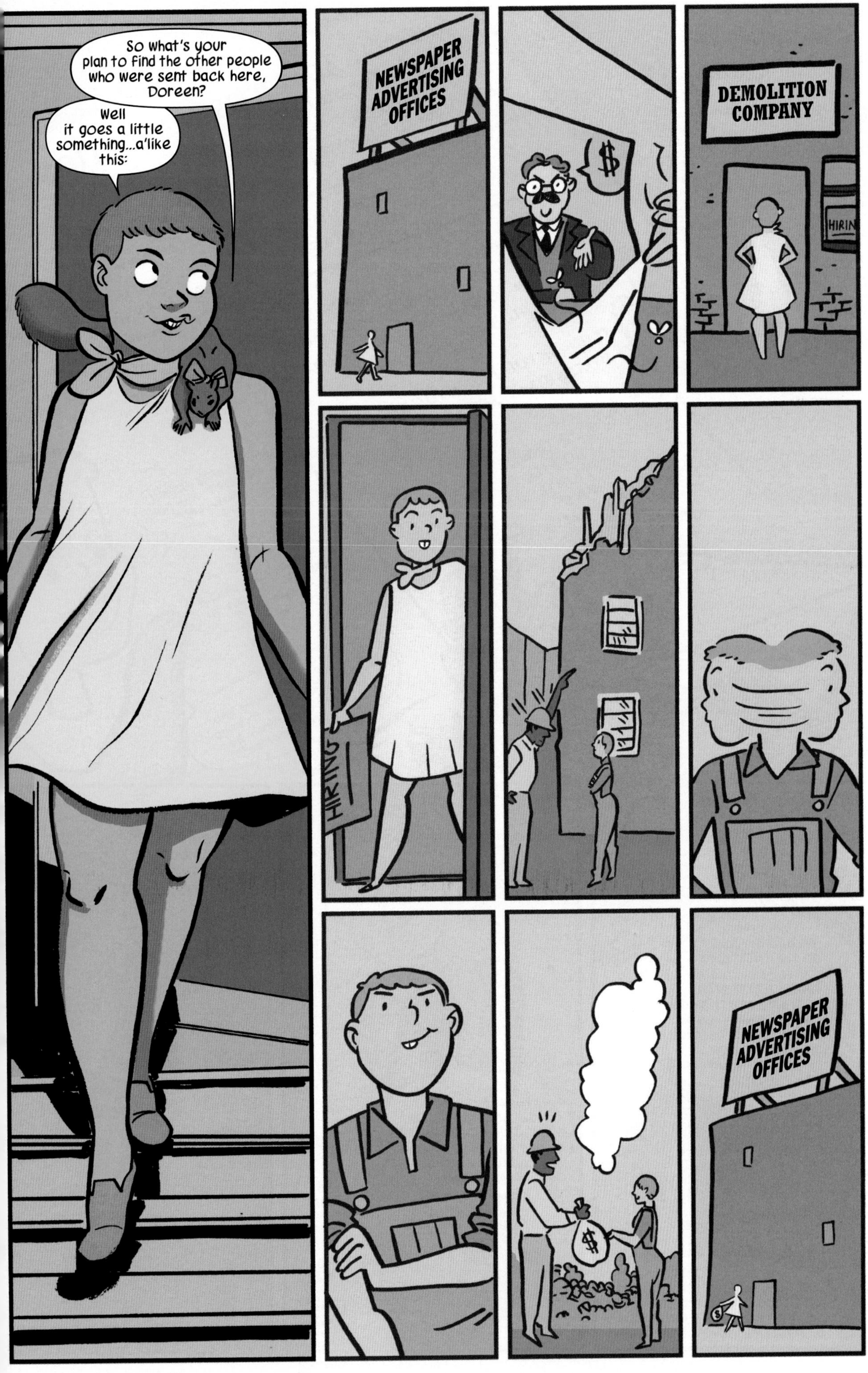
So what's your plan to find the other people who were sent back here, Doreen?
Well it goes a little something...a'like this:
NEWSPAPER ADVERTISING OFFICES
$
DEMOLITION COMPANY
HIRIN
HIRING
$
NEWSPAPER ADVERTISING OFFICES

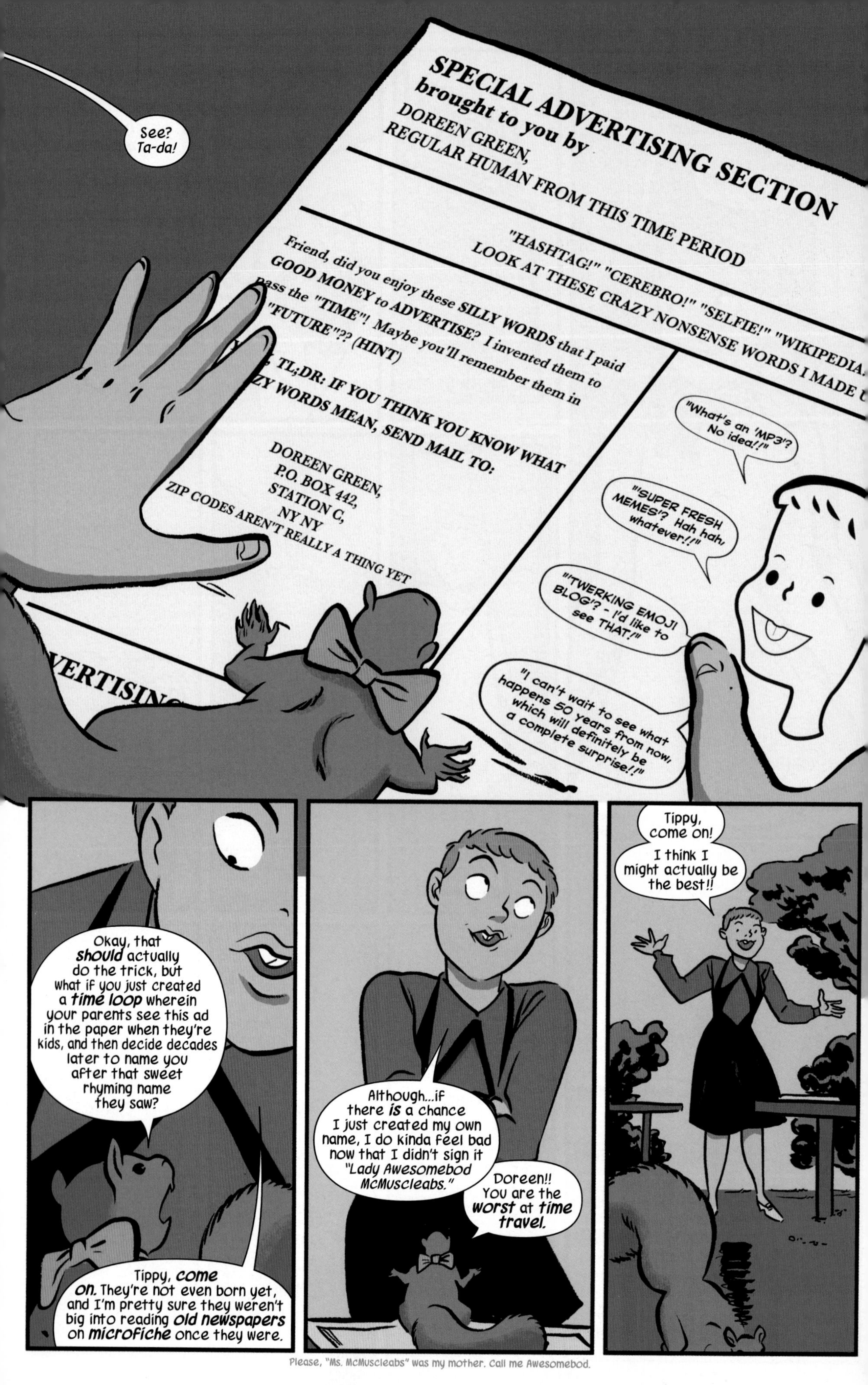
See? Ta-da!
SPECIAL ADVERTISING SECTION
brought to you by
DOREEN GREEN,
REGULAR HUMAN FROM THIS TIME PERIOD
"HASHTAG!" "CEREBRO!" "SELFIE!" "WIKIPEDIA
LOOK AT THESE CRAZY NONSENSE WORDS I MADE U
Friend, did you enjoy these SILLY WORDS that I paid GOOD MONEY to ADVERTISE? I invented them to pass the "TIME"! Maybe you'll remember them in "FUTURE"?? (HINT)
TL;DR: IF YOU THINK YOU KNOW WHAT ZY WORDS MEAN, SEND MAIL TO:
DOREEN GREEN,
P.O. BOX 442,
STATION C,
NY NY
ZIP CODES AREN'T REALLY A THING YET
"What's an 'MP3'? No idea!!"
"SUPER FRESH MEMES'? Hah hah, whatever!!"
"TWERKING EMOJI BLOG'? - I'd like to see THAT!"
"I can't wait to see what happens 50 years from now, which will definitely be a complete surprise!!"
VERTISIN
Okay, that should actually do the trick, but what if you just created a time loop wherein your parents see this ad in the paper when they're kids, and then decide decades later to name you after that sweet rhyming name they saw?
Tippy, come on. They're not even born yet, and I'm pretty sure they weren't big into reading old newspapers on microfiche once they were.
Although...if there is a chance I just created my own name, I do kinda feel bad now that I didn't sign it "Lady Awesomebod McMuscleabs."
Doreen!! You are the worst at time travel.
Tippy, come on!
I think I might actually be the best!!

Please, "Ms. McMuscleabs" was my mother. Call me Awesomebod.

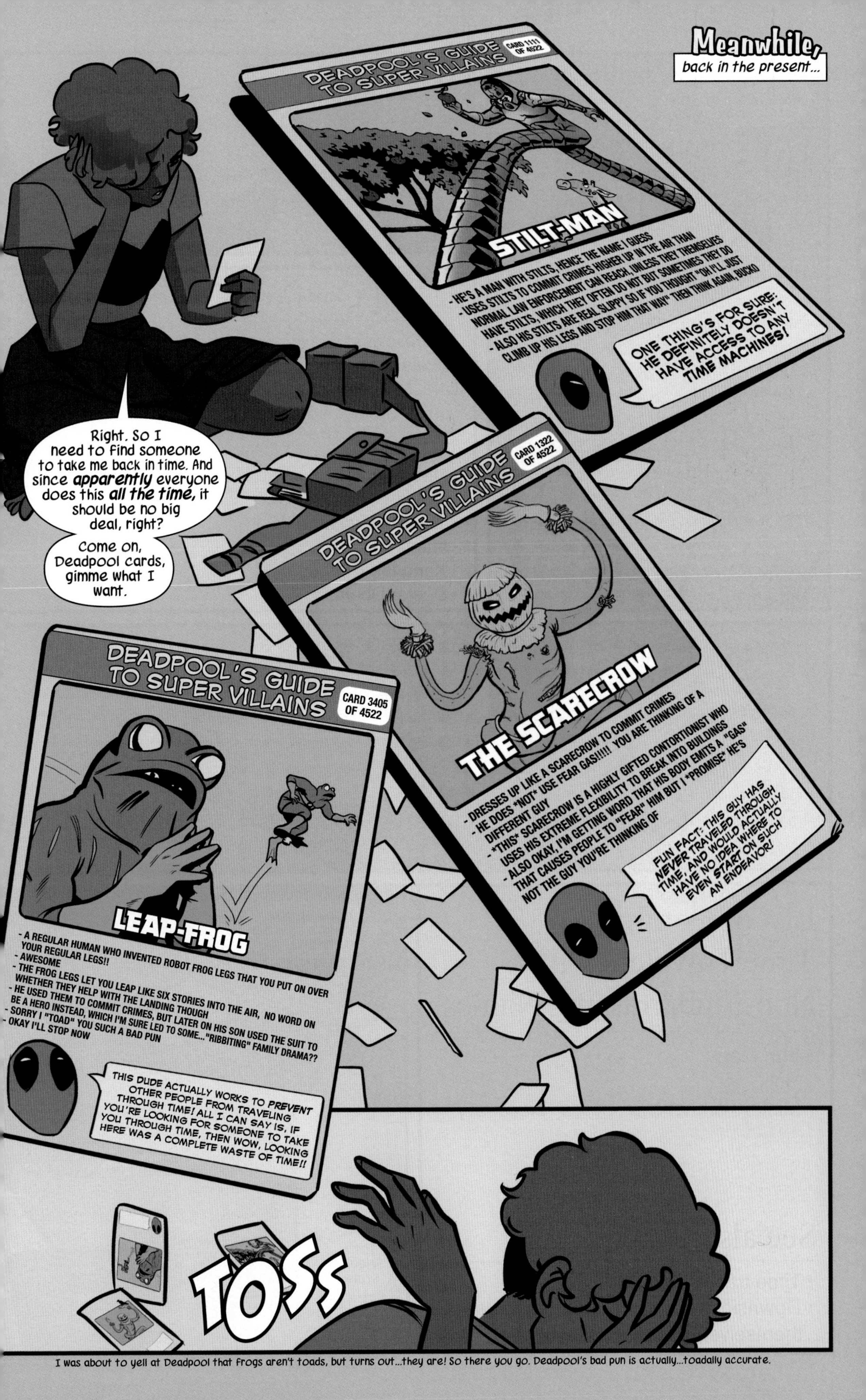
Meanwhile, back in the present...
DEADPOOL'S GUIDE TO SUPER VILLAINS
CARD 1111 OF 4522
STILT-MAN
- HE'S A MAN WITH STILTS, HENCE THE NAME I GUESS
- USES STILTS TO COMMIT CRIMES HIGHER UP IN THE AIR THAN NORMAL LAW ENFORCEMENT CAN REACH, UNLESS THEY THEMSELVES HAVE STILTS, WHICH THEY OFTEN DO NOT BUT SOMETIMES THEY DO
- ALSO HIS STILTS ARE REAL SLIPPY SO IF YOU THOUGHT "OH I'LL JUST CLIMB UP HIS LEGS AND STOP HIM THAT WAY" THEN THINK AGAIN, BUCKO
ONE THING'S FOR SURE: HE DEFINITELY DOESN'T HAVE ACCESS TO ANY TIME MACHINES!
Right. So I need to find someone to take me back in time. And since apparently everyone does this all the time, it should be no big deal, right?
Come on, Deadpool cards, gimme what I want.
DEADPOOL'S GUIDE TO SUPER VILLAINS
CARD 1322 OF 4522
THE SCARECROW
- DRESSES UP LIKE A SCARECROW TO COMMIT CRIMES
- HE DOES *NOT* USE FEAR GAS!!!!! YOU ARE THINKING OF A DIFFERENT GUY
- *THIS* SCARECROW IS A HIGHLY GIFTED CONTORTIONIST WHO USES HIS EXTREME FLEXIBILITY TO BREAK INTO BUILDINGS
- ALSO OKAY, I'M GETTING WORD THAT HIS BODY EMITS A "GAS" THAT CAUSES PEOPLE TO "FEAR" HIM BUT I *PROMISE* HE'S NOT THE GUY YOU'RE THINKING OF
FUN FACT: THIS GUY HAS NEVER TRAVELED THROUGH TIME, AND WOULD ACTUALLY HAVE NO IDEA WHERE TO EVEN START ON SUCH AN ENDEAVOR!
DEADPOOL'S GUIDE TO SUPER VILLAINS
CARD 3405 OF 4522
LEAP-FROG
- A REGULAR HUMAN WHO INVENTED ROBOT FROG LEGS THAT YOU PUT ON OVER YOUR REGULAR LEGS!!
- AWESOME
- THE FROG LEGS LET YOU LEAP LIKE SIX STORIES INTO THE AIR, NO WORD ON WHETHER THEY HELP WITH THE LANDING THOUGH
- HE USED THEM TO COMMIT CRIMES, BUT LATER ON HIS SON USED THE SUIT TO BE A HERO INSTEAD, WHICH I'M SURE LED TO SOME... "RIBBITING" FAMILY DRAMA??
- SORRY I "TOAD" YOU SUCH A BAD PUN
- OKAY I'LL STOP NOW
THIS DUDE ACTUALLY WORKS TO PREVENT OTHER PEOPLE FROM TRAVELING THROUGH TIME! ALL I CAN SAY IS, IF YOU'RE LOOKING FOR SOMEONE TO TAKE YOU THROUGH TIME, THEN WOW, LOOKING HERE WAS A COMPLETE WASTE OF TIME!!
TOSS

I was about to yell at Deadpool that frogs aren't toads, but turns out...they are! So there you go. Deadpool's bad pun is actually...toadally accurate.

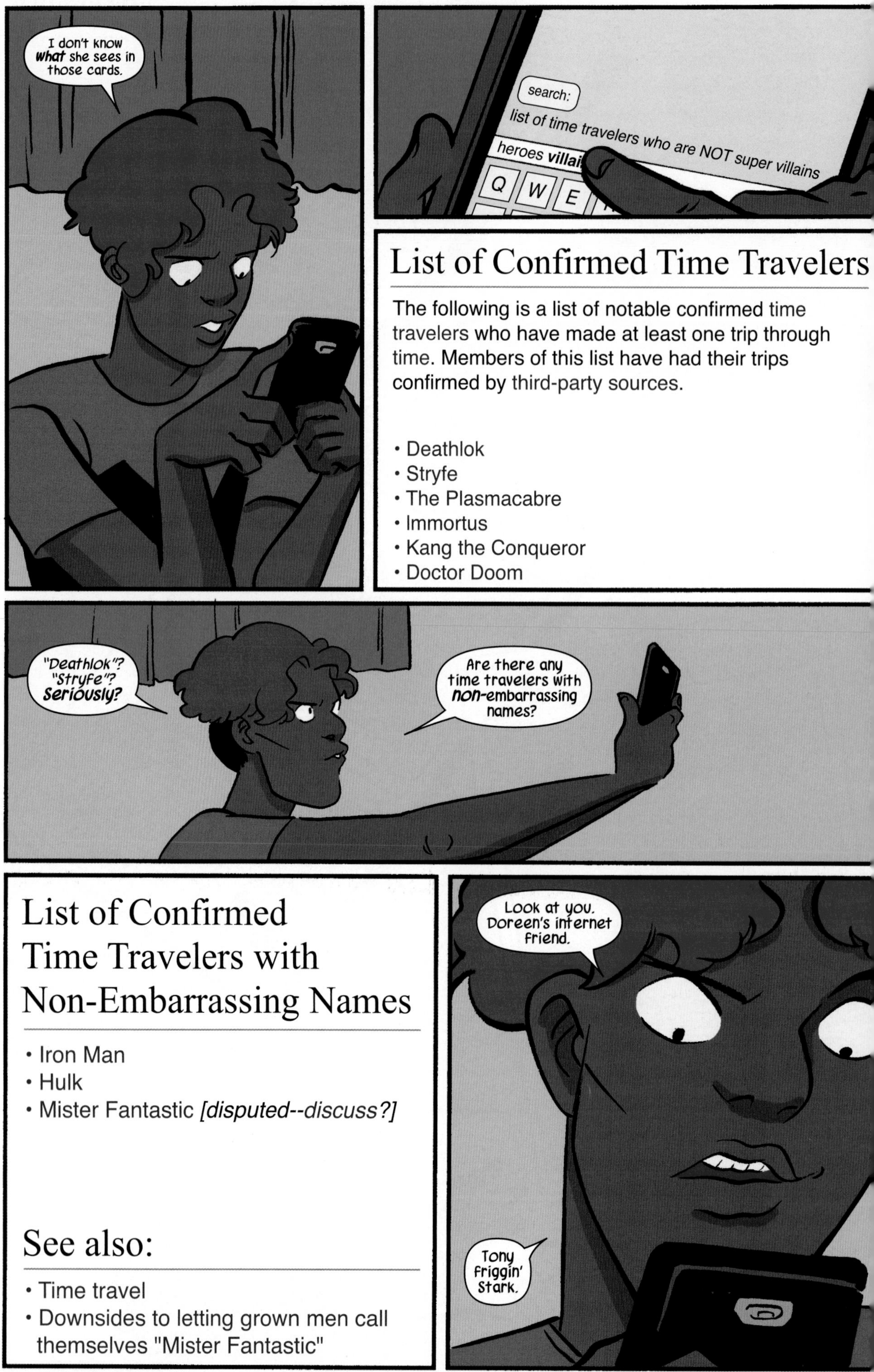

I don't know *what* she sees in those cards.
search:
list of time travelers who are NOT super villains
heroes villai
Q W E
List of Confirmed Time Travelers
The following is a list of notable confirmed time travelers who have made at least one trip through time. Members of this list have had their trips confirmed by third-party sources.
• Deathlok
• Stryfe
• The Plasmacabre
• Immortus
• Kang the Conqueror
• Doctor Doom
"Deathlok"? "Stryfe"? *Seriously?*
Are there any time travelers with *non*-embarrassing names?
List of Confirmed Time Travelers with Non-Embarrassing Names
• Iron Man
• Hulk
• Mister Fantastic *[disputed--discuss?]*
See also:
• Time travel
• Downsides to letting grown men call themselves "Mister Fantastic"
Look at you, Doreen's internet friend.
Tony friggin' Stark.

Please, "Mister Fantastic" was my father. Call me...actually, no, "Mister Fantastic" is fine, and on second thought that's absolutely a name I would like everyone to know me by

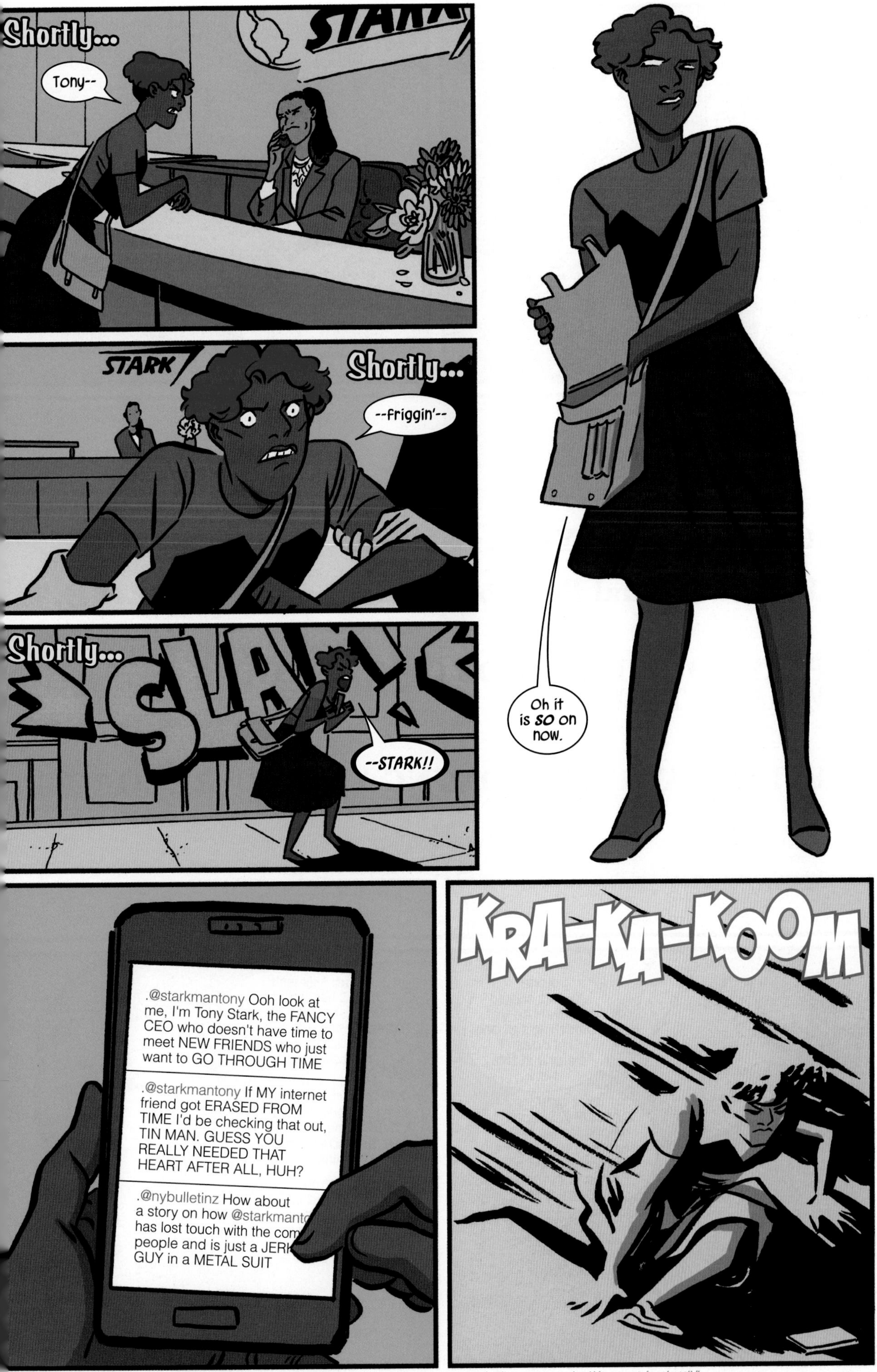

STARK
Shortly...
Tony--
STARK
Shortly...
--friggin'--
Shortly...
--STARK!!
Oh it is SO on now.
.@starkmantony Ooh look at me, I'm Tony Stark, the FANCY CEO who doesn't have time to meet NEW FRIENDS who just want to GO THROUGH TIME
.@starkmantony If MY internet friend got ERASED FROM TIME I'd be checking that out, TIN MAN. GUESS YOU REALLY NEEDED THAT HEART AFTER ALL, HUH?
.@nybulletinz How about a story on how @starkmanto has lost touch with the com people and is just a JERK GUY in a METAL SUIT
KRA-KA-KOOM

Tony's gonna check his mentions later on and be like, "Wow I don't even know who this person is, oh well."

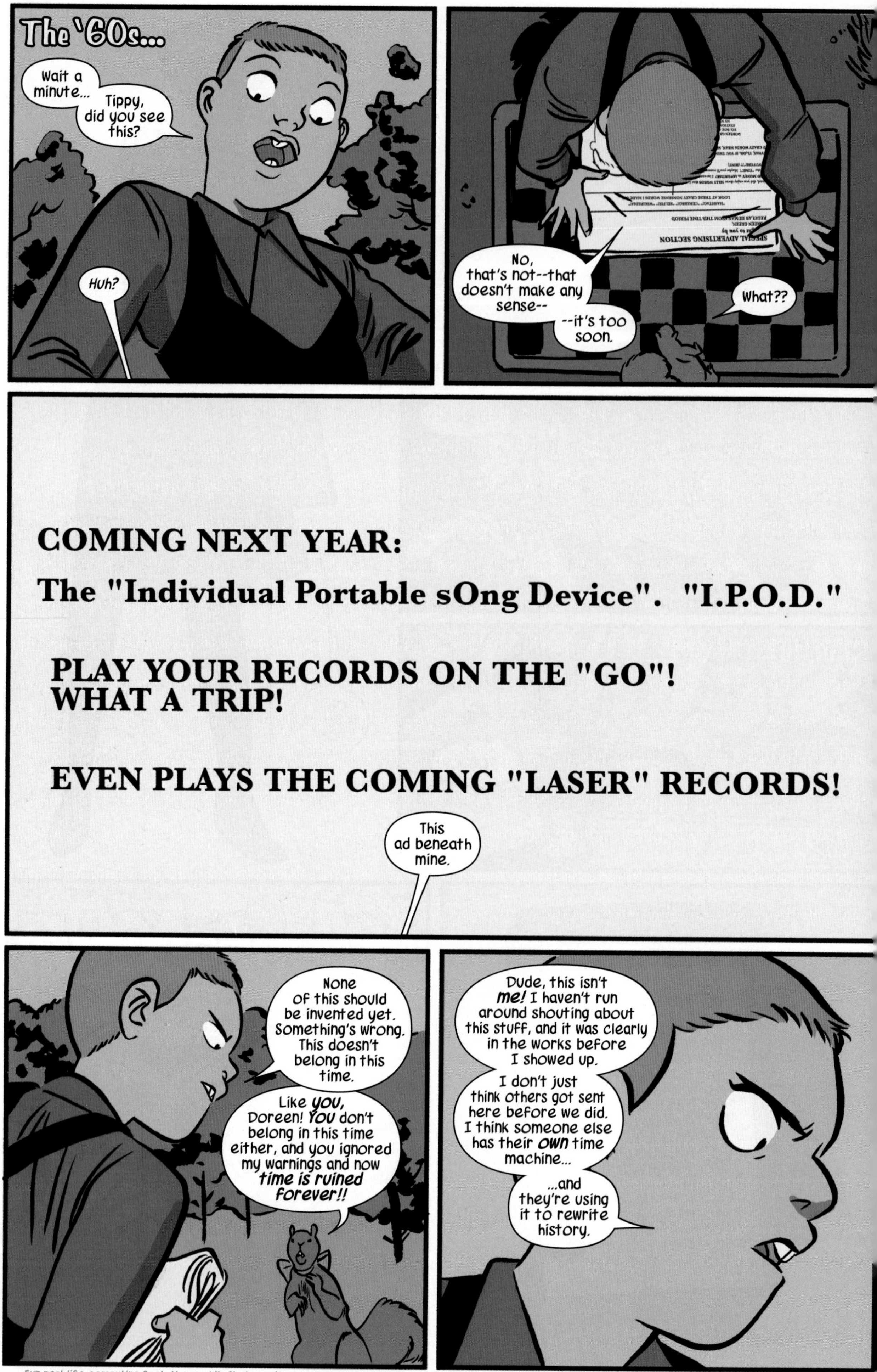
The '60s...
Wait a minute... Tippy, did you see this?
Huh?
No, that's not--that doesn't make any sense--
--it's too soon.
What??
SPECIAL ADVERTISING SECTION
COMING NEXT YEAR:
The "Individual Portable sOng Device". "I.P.O.D."
PLAY YOUR RECORDS ON THE "GO"! WHAT A TRIP!
EVEN PLAYS THE COMING "LASER" RECORDS!
This ad beneath mine.
None of this should be invented yet. Something's wrong. This doesn't belong in this time.
Like *YOU*, Doreen! *YOU* don't belong in this time either, and you ignored my warnings and now *time is ruined forever!!*
Dude, this isn't *me!* I haven't run around shouting about this stuff, and it was clearly in the works before I showed up.
I don't just think others got sent here before we did. I think someone else has their *OWN* time machine...
...and they're using it to rewrite history.

Fun real-life computing fact: the world's first word processor--a program that turned $100,000 worth of bleeding-edge 1960s computational machinery into what was effectively just an expensive typewriter--was named, appropriately enough, *"Expensive Typewriter."*

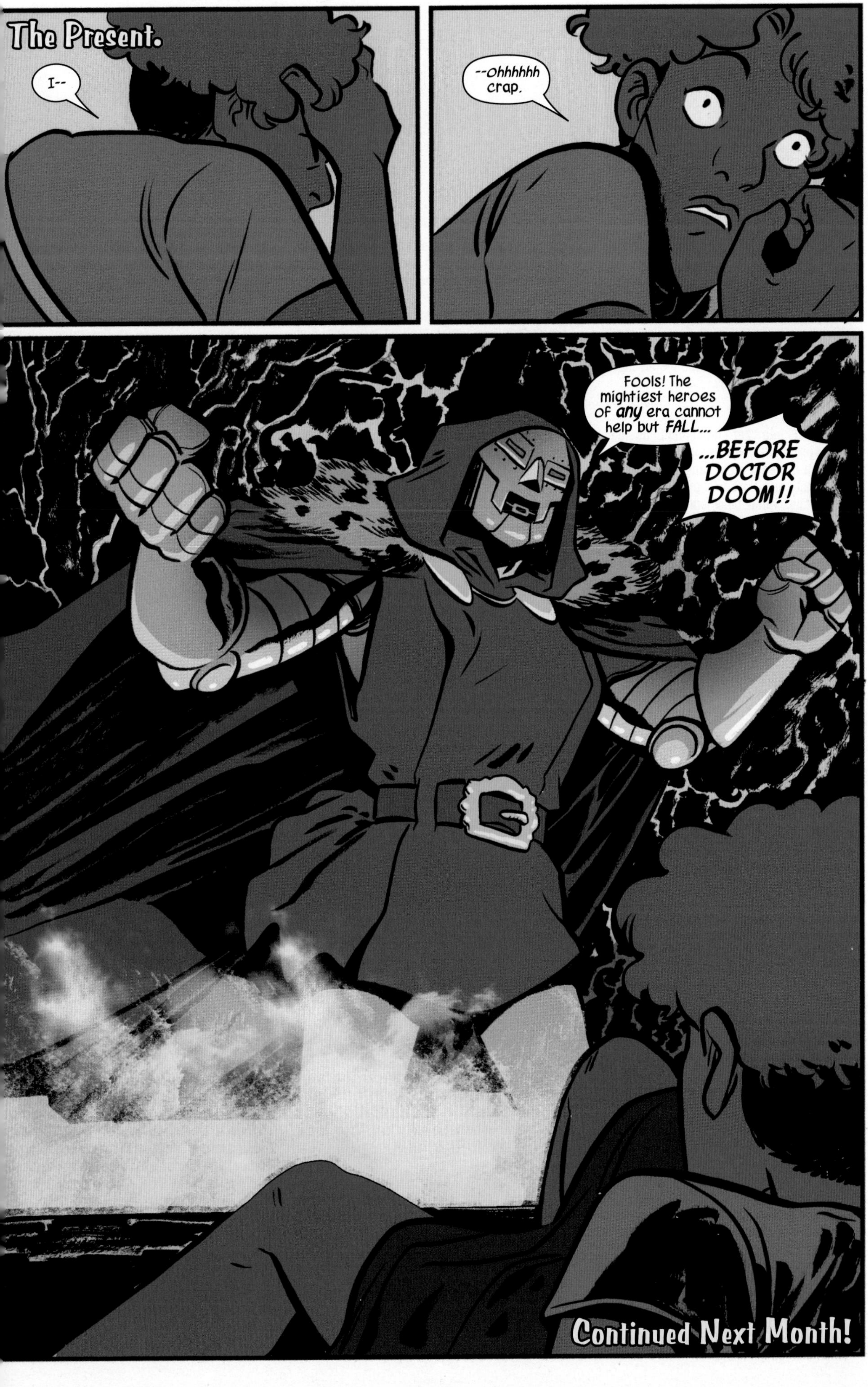
The Present.
I--
--Ohhhhhh crap.
Fools! The mightiest heroes of any era cannot help but FALL...
...BEFORE DOCTOR DOOM!!
Continued Next Month!

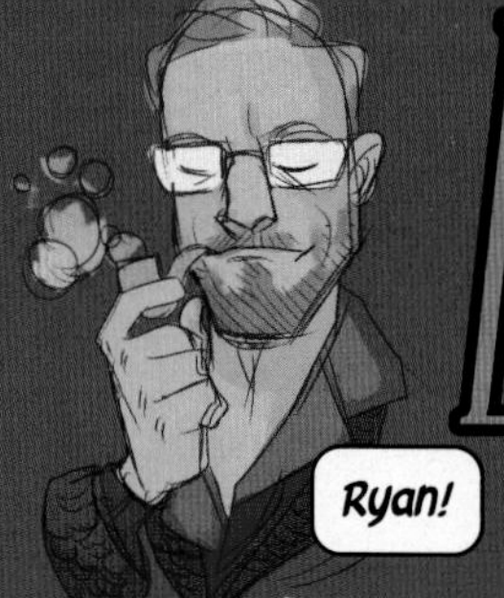
Ryan!

Letters From Nuts

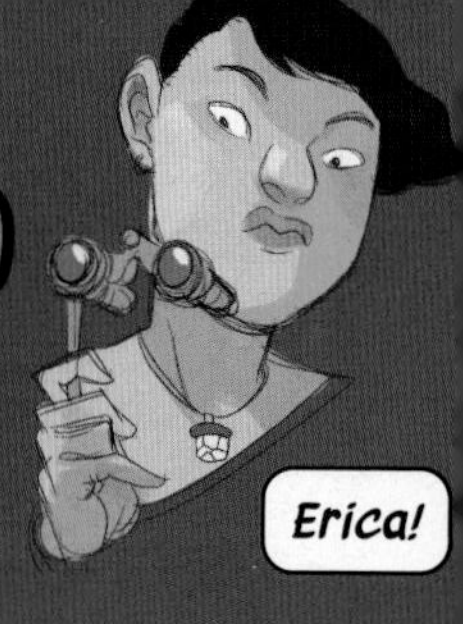
Erica!

Send letters to mheroes@marvel.com or 135 W 50th St, 7th Floor, New York, NY 10020 (Please mark "OKAY TO PRINT

Hey everybody! No time for a fancy intro--let's dive right in!

Q: You know how the movement of a squirrel is very jerky? Since it is hard to show movement in comics, I was wondering if Doreen is jerky like a squirrel when she moves (proportional speed)? Erica's pencils give me the feeling that Doreen has a lot of energy.

Benjamin J.

RYAN: I see her movement as being more quick than jerky! Squirrels can also be indecisive (at least when caught in the middle of the road) and Doreen's pretty good at not changing her mind back and forth over and over, so while I think it's good that she's got PARTIALLY squirrel blood, I'm glad it's not 100%. Hence her slogan, "50% Squirrel, 100% Girl!"

ERICA: I don't think she's that jerky. Unless she hasn't gotten enough sleep. Crimefighting and being a full time student makes for a difficult work-life balance, guys! Stay hydrated!

P.S. Squirrels run in a jerky zigzag to confuse predators. And the twitchy tail is to silently warn others of danger.

Hey everyone! I had heard about squirrel girl before but I didn't know much about her. When I saw this on marvel unlimited, I decided "what the heck, I'll read". Great decision on my part if I do say so my self. I absolutely love her! She's awesome as a super hero and she's awesome as a person. The way she's drawn makes her look so adorable! I have a few questions.

1. What's the point of having a secret identity if she doesn't wear a mask? Not hating though 2. How did she get her powers? (Is her tail real?) 3. How did she and Tippy meet?

Love the comic! Keep up the good work!

Harley Massey
Harlingen, Texas

R: Thanks Harley! Really stoked you like the comic. I read it on Marvel Unlimited too and even commented there saying "I'm the guy who wrote this comic and I give it FIVE STARS" but I don't think anyone reads the comments there, so now I'm mentioning it here in the letters page because I crave attention.

1) As she says, the most identifying feature of Squirrel Girl is her tail, and Doreen Green CLEARLY has zero tails. That's a pretty good alibi, if you ask me!

2) This is touched on a bit in our new #1 issue last month (which is kind of unfair for me to say, because you wrote this before that issue was out! HOW COULD YOU HAVE KNOWN?) so I'm in the position of answering a question you may already know the answer to! Anyway, for anyone who isn't us, the answer to "how did she get her powers" is "over time, I guess".

E: 1) As someone who grew up watching *Sailor Moon*, I have no problem with this. Also what Ryan said.

3) In a tree.

The other day, my wife and I were sitting out on the porch enjoying a sunny afternoon. My wife was telling me of how she almost ran her vehicle off of the road in order to avoid a squirrel that had charged out of the woods and into the direct path of her car. I quipped, "Perhaps the squirrel had intended to cause you to wreck. Maybe it was an incarnation of Ratatoskr bringing both life and destruction." Naturally, she asked for clarification. "Ratatoskr is a squirrel from Norse mythology that represents the continual cycle of rebirth. It travels up and down the world tree as a sort of messenger." Of course, she had to validate this for herself, and was promptly viewing the Wikipedia page on her phone . "How did you know this?" she asked, continuing to read. "I am well-learned, Jeanie. I am working on my Master's degree, after all," I responded.

Suddenly, I was the smartest man in the world, and she gave me that look that at once conveyed respect, love, and "hey handsome." Unfortunately, my feeling of pride could not last. Since Ratatoskr hasn't really made its mark on popular culture, Wikipedia finds it necessary to mention that the Marvel comic, The Unbeatable Squirrel Girl, makes reference to the demigod in issues 7 and 8. That beautiful look on my wife's face suddenly morphed into an expression that I still do not understand. Was it surprise? Was it confusion? I may never know, but what I do know is that your comic has taught me much that I can use to impress individuals who are not as quite as inquisitive of my lovely wife. Touché, Wikipedia. Touché, indeed.

Adam Felty
Virginia

P.S. Did you know that the English word "squirrel" comes from the Greek word "skiouros"? It means "shadow-tailed," which gives me an unbeatable story idea. What about you? Trust me, Greek is part of my major... but I found this online!

R: Wikipedia, you could've had Adam's back and made him look really smart in front of a loved one!! INSTEAD you outed him as ... a reader of quality comics entertainment from which he learns about the world around him, allowing him to apply that knowledge as situations warrant? That's still a pretty great person to be, actually. Tell your wife that yo comic book said you're a good guy who i probably still worth marrying!

E: Here are more squirrel facts to dazz your friends and loved ones with and to mak your enemies cower at the might of you intellect: 1. Did you know that a squirrel' rear feet can turn 180 degrees? It's how the climb down trees! 2. There are 265 specie of squirrel worldwide, 44 of which are flyin squirrels. 3. The squirrel is the Nativ American symbol for preparation, trust an thriftiness. 4. Squirrels were introduced int major urban parks by PEOPLE. In the 1870 they were one of several animals introduce into places like Central Park to create mo of a natural atmosphere. They were a symbo of rural life, but also diurnal animals tha coexist well with humans. 5. Squirrels ar opportunistic omnivores and a diet of most nuts is actually bad for them because nuts ar fairly fatty.

Greetings squirrel squad,

I was singing the Squirrel Girl theme song o my way to work earlier today (as I'm sure mos of us do) and I couldn't help but wonder abou one of the lines; "Like a human squirrel sh enjoys fighting crime" Does this mean that a is characteristic of human squirrels Squirrel Gi enjoys fighting crime? Or is it that she enjoy fighting crime in a human squirrel like way? O is she like a human squirrel and also unrelate to that she enjoys fighting crime? I suppose if was that last one it would say who rather tha she. However all three options are well withi the plausible range given the context. Thi problem has really been gnawing at me so I' much appreciate if you could clear it up for me I also had a question regarding the Deadpoo super villain cards. There are over 4,000 card how is Squirrel Girl able to carry and quickl retrieve the correct card so quickly? Does sh have squirrel hoarding powers?

Thanks in advance for your answers an thanks also for writing such a great comic.

J

R: I like the implication that ALL huma squirrels would enjoy fighting crime, so that' the one I'm going with! But you could als change it to "Like a human girl she enjoy fighting crime" and it still scans, and as I hav not met any human girls who have specificall told me that they DON'T enjoy fighting crime we're probably good.

And as for Squirrel Girl having over 400 cards to carry around, that is absolutely use of her super squirrel hoarding powers which makes total scientific sense and has no problems associated with it whatsoever!

See y'all next month!

Attention, Squirrel Scouts! Make sure to check out our production blog, **unbeatablesquirrelgirl.tumblr.com**, where we post behind-the-scenes stuff on how the book gets made, along with all sorts of cool things *you* make: fanart, cosplay, whatever!

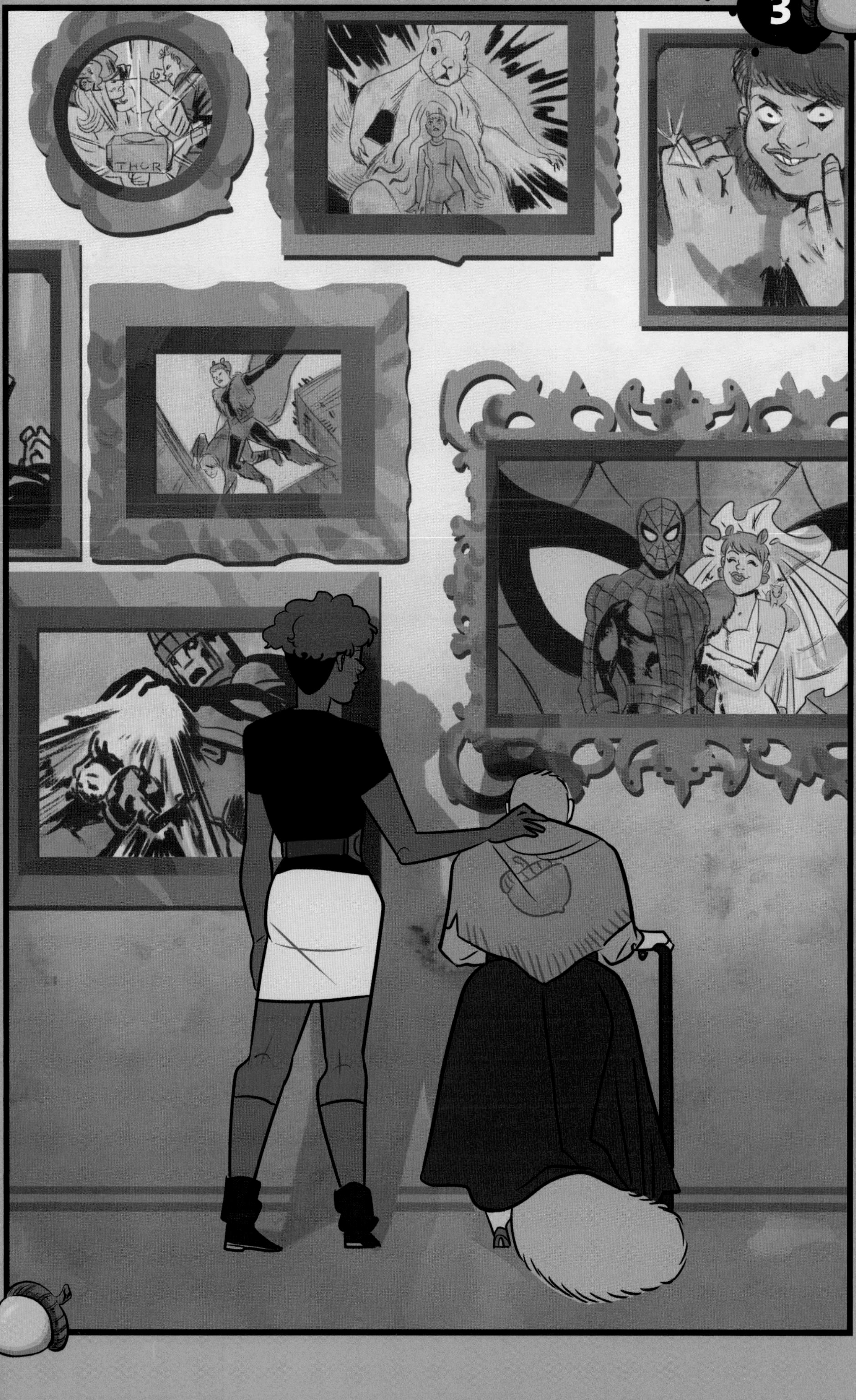
THOR

*Doreen Green isn't just a second-year computer science student: she secretly also has all the powers of both squirrel and girl! She uses her amazing abilities to fight crime **and** be as awesome as possible. You know her as...**The Unbeatable Squirrel Girl**! Find out what she's been up to, with...*

Squirrel Girl in a nutshell

Nancy W. @sewwiththeflo
Nobody believes me, but before this morning Mew and I had a roommate. Then she got erased from time, and now nobody remembers her but me.

Nancy W. @sewwiththeflo
And she was AWESOME and SWEET and SMART and GOOD AT FIGHTS ACTUALLY, and it sucks without her.

Nancy W. @sewwiththeflo
RT if your roommate got erased from time and nobody remembers her.

Nancy W. @sewwiththeflo
See? That's proof she's gone, right there. She would've AT LEAST faved that.

Tony Stark @starkmantony
Do you ever get the sense that the universe is missing something? Like there's something that should be there and just--isn't.

Nancy W. @sewwiththeflo
@starkmantony Whoa whoa whoa--you remember her too? I thought I was the only one!

Tony Stark @starkmantony
Like you woke up today and even though you could SWEAR everything was the same, you still feel like something very important is absent...

Nancy W. @sewwiththeflo
@starkmantony Yes! Doreen!!

Tony Stark @starkmantony
...and while though some part of you knows that thing--whatever it was--might've been kind of a pain sometimes, you still miss it?

Nancy W. @sewwiththeflo
@starkmantony You and her do have a special relationship. Thank you! I felt like I was going crazy. So what's our next move, Tony?

Tony Stark @starkmantony
Because I too had that feeling...UNTIL I tried the new consumer-level #IronManicure home beauty treatment kit, available TODAY!

Tony Stark @starkmantony
Your hands are too precious for just any manicure kit. Take the Stark #IronManicure Challenge: satisfaction guaranteed or your money back!

Tony Stark @starkmantony
You'll feel like a Stark with our red-and-gold nail file, clipper, and angled cuticle nipper. All thanks to the new #IronManicure kit!

Nancy W. @sewwiththeflo
@starkmantony blocked

HULK @HULKYSMASHY
@starkmantony HULK WONDERS IF MANICURE KIT COMES IN GREEN AND PURPLE BECAUSE HULK THINK THOSE COLORS ARE MUCH PRETTIER

Nancy W. @sewwiththeflo
So here I am, minding my own business, when there's a huge blast of sound and light and I get knocked over. Guess who did it?

Nancy W. @sewwiththeflo
Doctor Doom. Doctor DOOM, friends and neighbors. Ruler of Latveria, ambassador, metal-suit wearer. Big as life.

Nancy W. @sewwiththeflo
So yeah anyway I should really get off my phone now because he's RIGHT HERE

search!

#doctordoom
#wikipedia
#doomipedia
#timetravel
#rhymetravel
#thymetravel

Ryan North - writer
Erica Henderson - artist
Doc Shaner - trading card artist
Rico Renzi - color artist
Travis Lanham - guest letterer
Erica Henderson - cover artist
John Tyler Christopher; Matt Waite - variant cover artists

Special Thanks to **Lissa Pattillo, CK Russell,** and **Michael Wiggam**

Chris Robinson - asst. editor
Wil Moss - editor
Tom Brevoort - executive editor
Axel Alonso - editor in chief
Joe Quesada - chief creative officer
Dan Buckley - publisher
Alan Fine - exec. producer

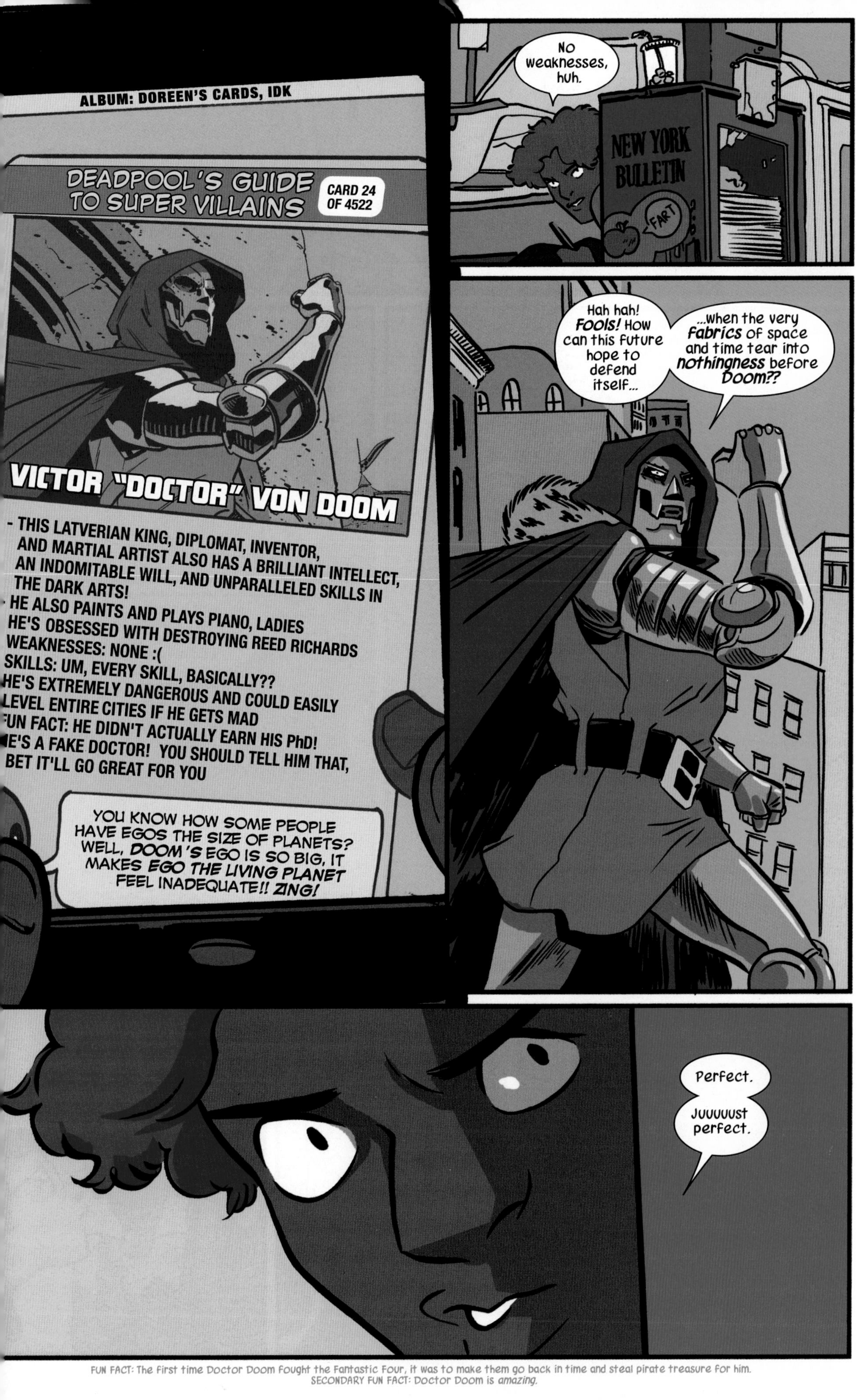
ALBUM: DOREEN'S CARDS, IDK
DEADPOOL'S GUIDE TO SUPER VILLAINS
CARD 24 OF 4522
VICTOR "DOCTOR" VON DOOM
- THIS LATVERIAN KING, DIPLOMAT, INVENTOR, AND MARTIAL ARTIST ALSO HAS A BRILLIANT INTELLECT, AN INDOMITABLE WILL, AND UNPARALLELED SKILLS IN THE DARK ARTS!
HE ALSO PAINTS AND PLAYS PIANO, LADIES
HE'S OBSESSED WITH DESTROYING REED RICHARDS
WEAKNESSES: NONE :(
SKILLS: UM, EVERY SKILL, BASICALLY??
HE'S EXTREMELY DANGEROUS AND COULD EASILY LEVEL ENTIRE CITIES IF HE GETS MAD
UN FACT: HE DIDN'T ACTUALLY EARN HIS PhD!
E'S A FAKE DOCTOR! YOU SHOULD TELL HIM THAT, BET IT'LL GO GREAT FOR YOU
YOU KNOW HOW SOME PEOPLE HAVE EGOS THE SIZE OF PLANETS? WELL, DOOM'S EGO IS SO BIG, IT MAKES EGO THE LIVING PLANET FEEL INADEQUATE!! ZING!
No weaknesses, huh.
NEW YORK BULLETIN
FART
Hah hah! Fools! How can this future hope to defend itself...
...when the very fabrics of space and time tear into nothingness before Doom??
Perfect.
Juuuuust perfect.

FUN FACT: The first time Doctor Doom fought the Fantastic Four, it was to make them go back in time and steal pirate treasure for him.
SECONDARY FUN FACT: Doctor Doom is *amazing.*

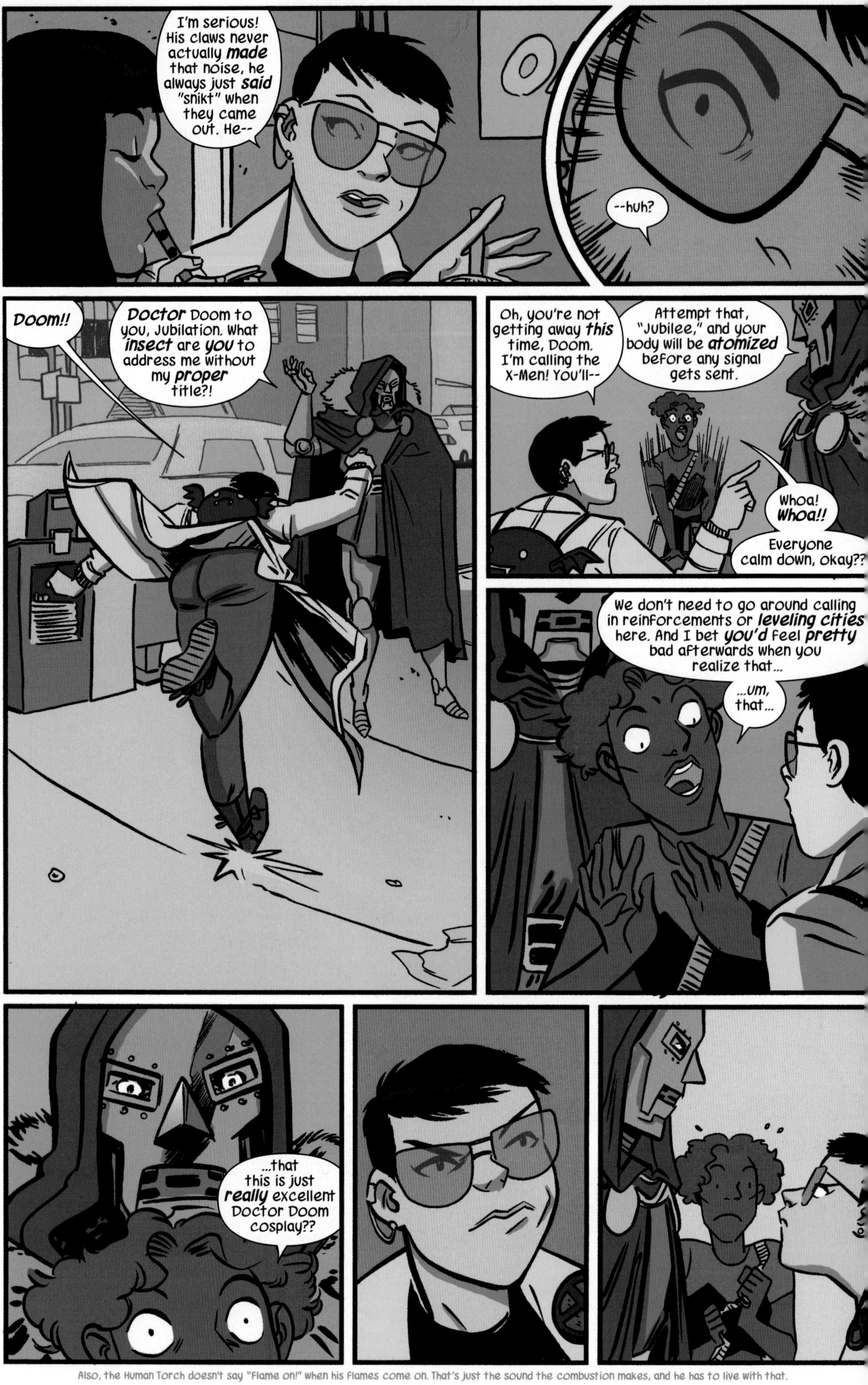
I'm serious! His claws never actually made that noise, he always just said "snikt" when they came out. He--
--huh?
Doom!!
Doctor Doom to you, Jubilation. What insect are you to address me without my proper title?!
Oh, you're not getting away this time, Doom. I'm calling the X-Men! You'll--
Attempt that, "Jubilee," and your body will be atomized before any signal gets sent.
Whoa! Whoa!!
Everyone calm down, okay??
We don't need to go around calling in reinforcements or leveling cities here. And I bet you'd feel pretty bad afterwards when you realize that...
...um, that...
...that this is just really excellent Doctor Doom cosplay??

Also, the Human Torch doesn't say "Flame on!" when his flames come on. That's just the sound the combustion makes, and he has to live with that.

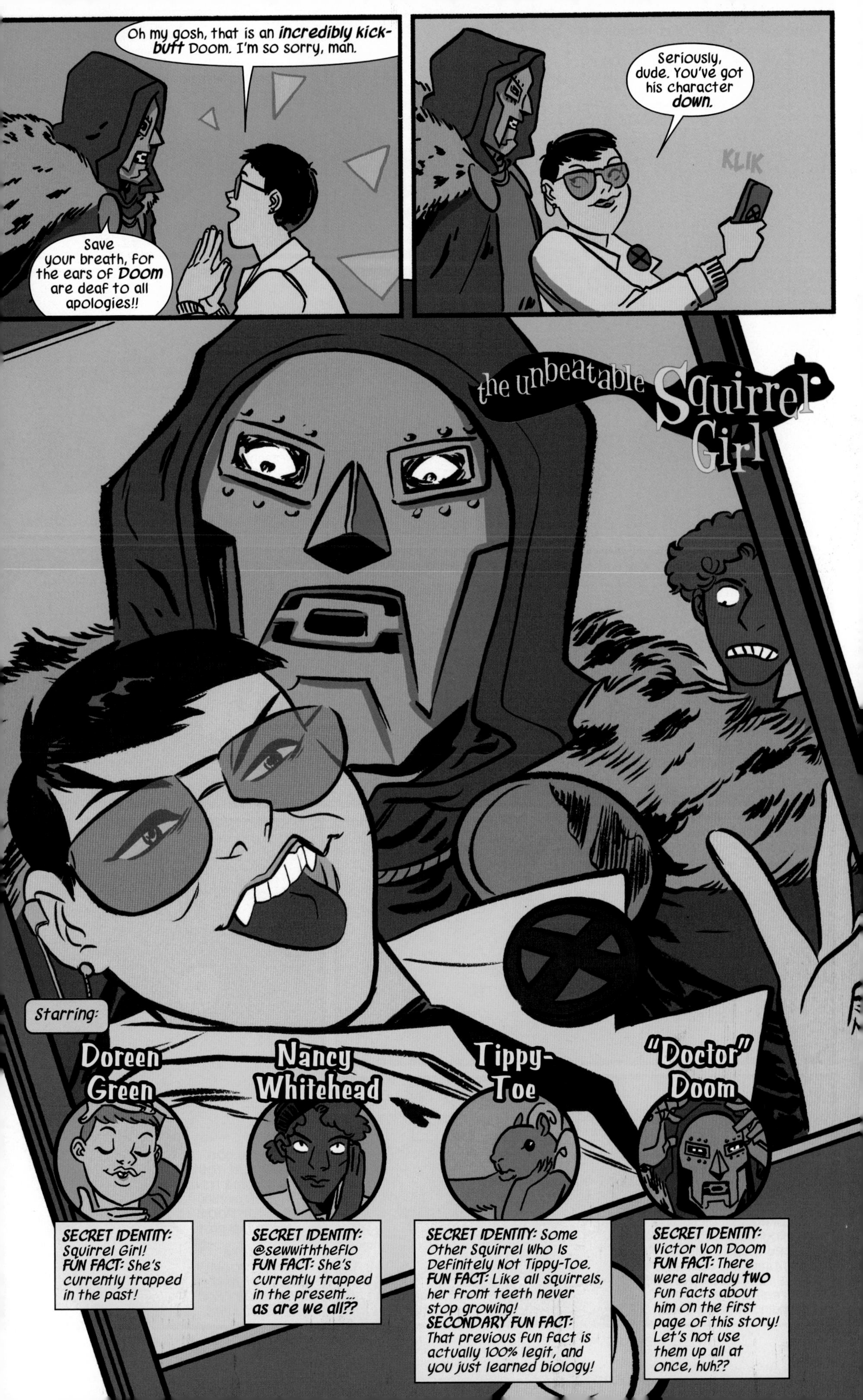

Oh my gosh, that is an *incredibly kick-butt* Doom. I'm so sorry, man.
Save your breath, for the ears of *DOOM* are deaf to all apologies!!
Seriously, dude. You've got his character *down.*
KLIK
the unbeatable Squirrel Girl
Starring:
Doreen Green
Nancy Whitehead
Tippy-Toe
"Doctor" Doom
SECRET IDENTITY: Squirrel Girl! **FUN FACT:** She's currently trapped in the past!
SECRET IDENTITY: @sewwiththeflo **FUN FACT:** She's currently trapped in the present... **as are we all??**
SECRET IDENTITY: Some Other Squirrel Who Is Definitely Not Tippy-Toe. **FUN FACT:** Like all squirrels, her front teeth never stop growing! **SECONDARY FUN FACT:** That previous fun fact is actually 100% legit, and you just learned biology!
SECRET IDENTITY: Victor Von Doom **FUN FACT:** There were already **TWO** fun facts about him on the first page of this story! Let's not use them up all at once, huh??

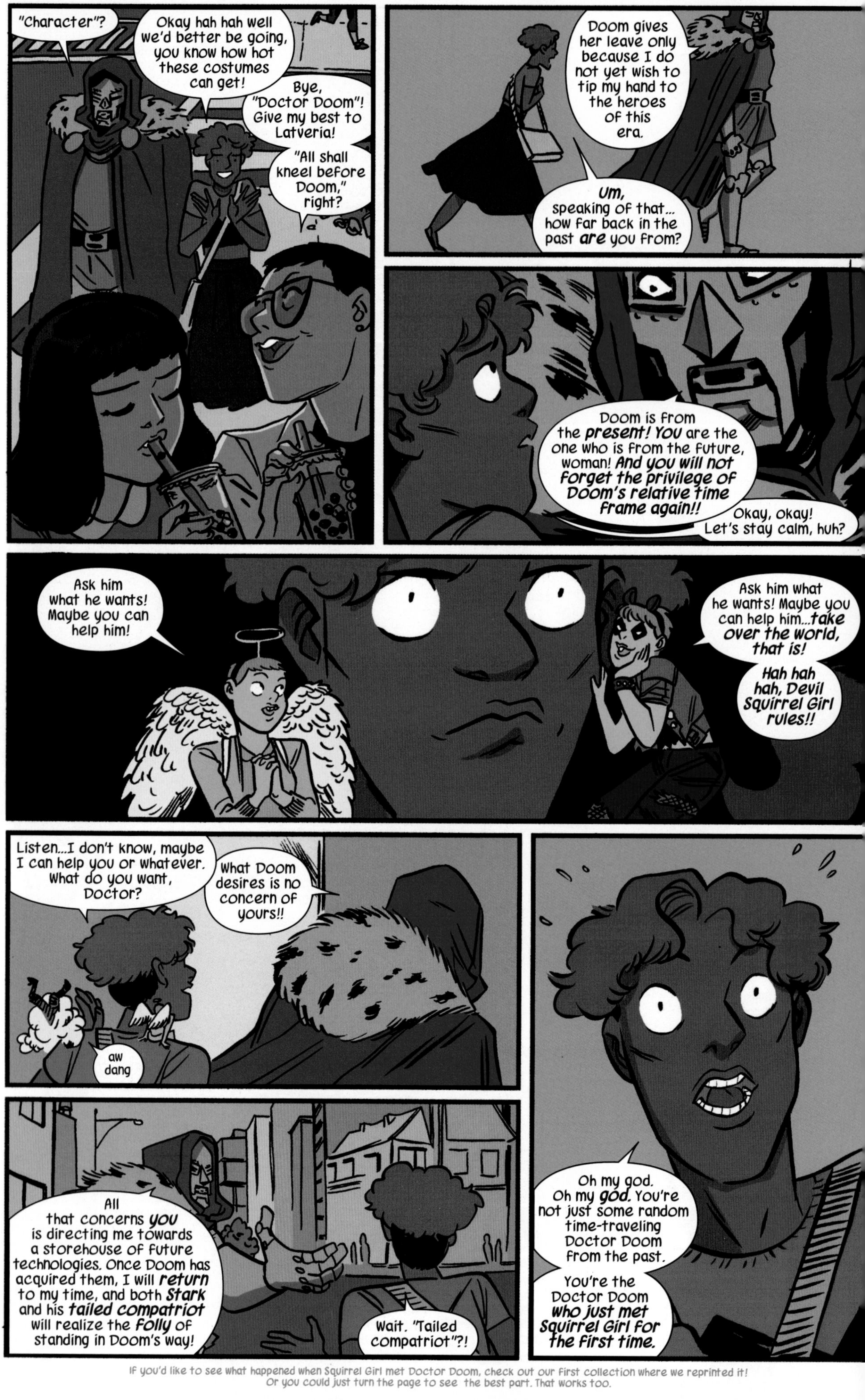
"Character"?
Okay hah hah well we'd better be going, you know how hot these costumes can get!
Bye, "Doctor Doom"! Give my best to Latveria!
"All shall kneel before Doom," right?
Doom gives her leave only because I do not yet wish to tip my hand to the heroes of this era.
Um, speaking of that... how far back in the past are you from?
Doom is from the present! You are the one who is from the future, woman! And you will not forget the privilege of Doom's relative time frame again!!
Okay, okay! Let's stay calm, huh?
Ask him what he wants! Maybe you can help him!
Ask him what he wants! Maybe you can help him...take over the world, that is!
Hah hah hah, Devil Squirrel Girl rules!!
Listen...I don't know, maybe I can help you or whatever. What do you want, Doctor?
What Doom desires is no concern of yours!!
aw dang
All that concerns you is directing me towards a storehouse of future technologies. Once Doom has acquired them, I will return to my time, and both Stark and his tailed compatriot will realize the folly of standing in Doom's way!
Wait. "Tailed compatriot"?!
Oh my god. Oh my god. You're not just some random time-traveling Doctor Doom from the past.
You're the Doctor Doom who just met Squirrel Girl for the first time.

If you'd like to see what happened when Squirrel Girl met Doctor Doom, check out our first collection where we reprinted it! Or you could just turn the page to see the best part. That works too.

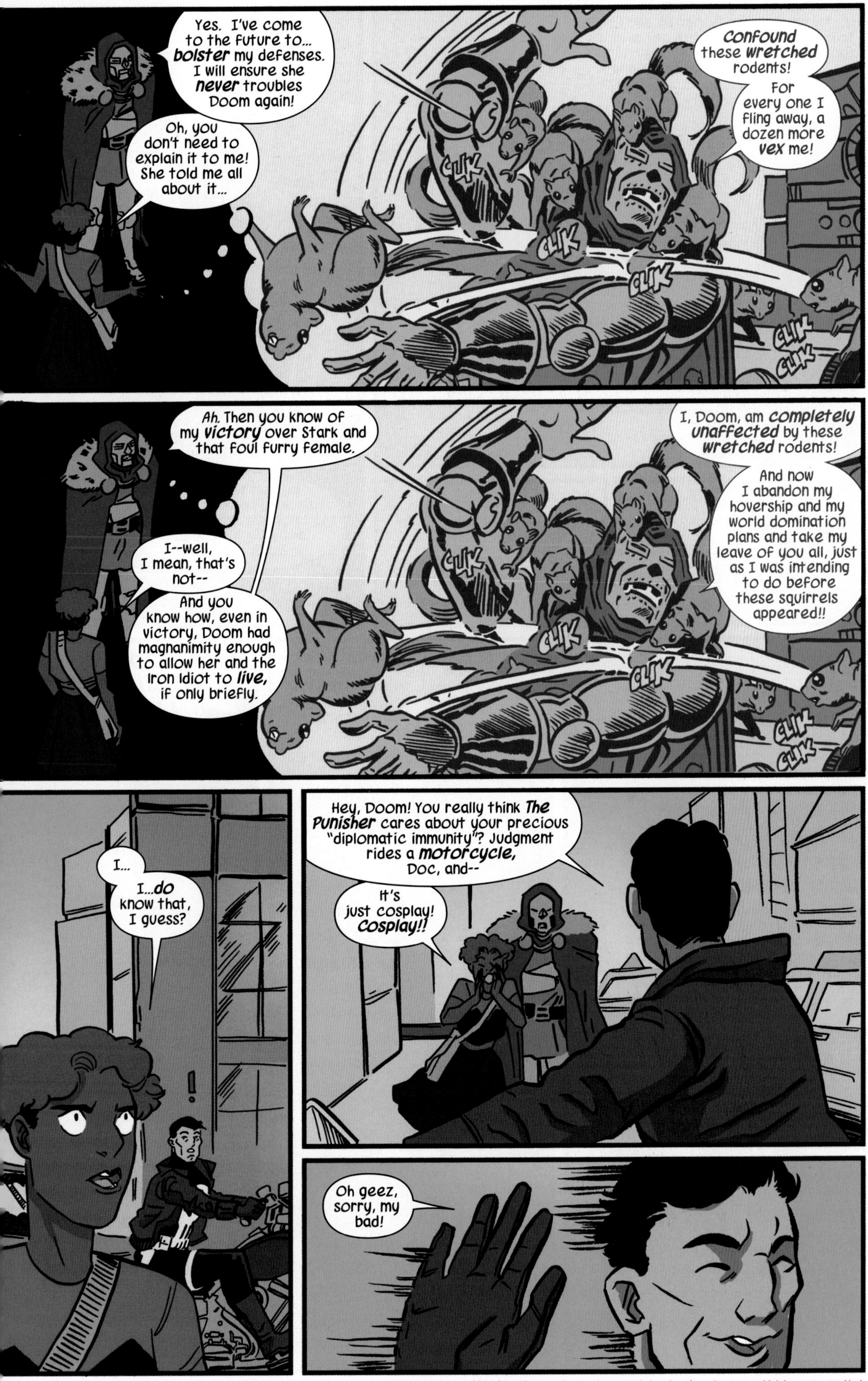
Yes. I've come to the future to... bolster my defenses. I will ensure she never troubles Doom again!
Oh, you don't need to explain it to me! She told me all about it...
Confound these wretched rodents!
For every one I fling away, a dozen more vex me!
CLIK
CLIK
CLIK
CLIK
CLIK
Ah. Then you know of my victory over Stark and that foul furry female.
I, Doom, am completely unaffected by these wretched rodents!
And now I abandon my hovership and my world domination plans and take my leave of you all, just as I was intending to do before these squirrels appeared!!
I--well, I mean, that's not--
And you know how, even in victory, Doom had magnanimity enough to allow her and the Iron Idiot to live, if only briefly.
CLIK
CLIK
CLIK
CLIK
CLIK
I...
I...do know that, I guess?
!
Hey, Doom! You really think The Punisher cares about your precious "diplomatic immunity"? Judgment rides a motorcycle, Doc, and--
It's just cosplay! Cosplay!!
Oh geez, sorry, my bad!

hat guy's The Punisher! Like all men who take themselves extremely seriously, he likes to spend his downtime sewing cartoon skeleton heads onto every shirt he owns, so that way everyone can tell right away how extremely serious he is.

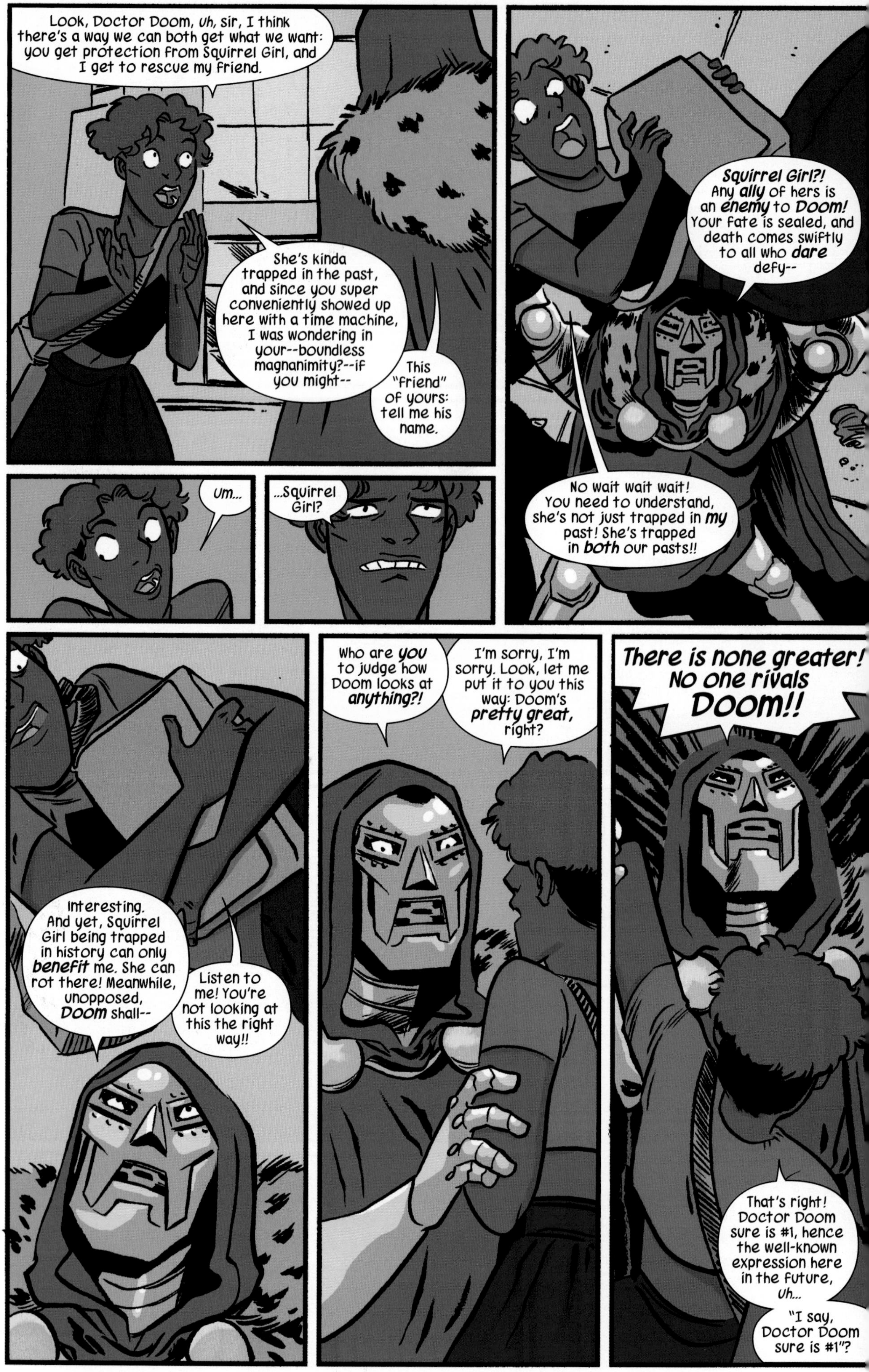
Look, Doctor Doom, uh, sir, I think there's a way we can both get what we want: you get protection from Squirrel Girl, and I get to rescue my friend.
She's kinda trapped in the past, and since you super conveniently showed up here with a time machine, I was wondering in your--boundless magnanimity?--if you might--
This "friend" of yours: tell me his name.
Um...
...Squirrel Girl?
Squirrel Girl?! Any ally of hers is an enemy to Doom! Your fate is sealed, and death comes swiftly to all who dare defy--
No wait wait wait! You need to understand, she's not just trapped in my past! She's trapped in both our pasts!!
Interesting. And yet, Squirrel Girl being trapped in history can only benefit me. She can rot there! Meanwhile, unopposed, Doom shall--
Listen to me! You're not looking at this the right way!!
Who are you to judge how Doom looks at anything?!
I'm sorry, I'm sorry. Look, let me put it to you this way: Doom's pretty great, right?
There is none greater! No one rivals Doom!!
That's right! Doctor Doom sure is #1, hence the well-known expression here in the future, uh...
"I say, Doctor Doom sure is #1"?
Doctor Doom's plan here is to just pick Nancy up and throw her into the sun. As far as plans go, it's...pretty credible for him, actually.

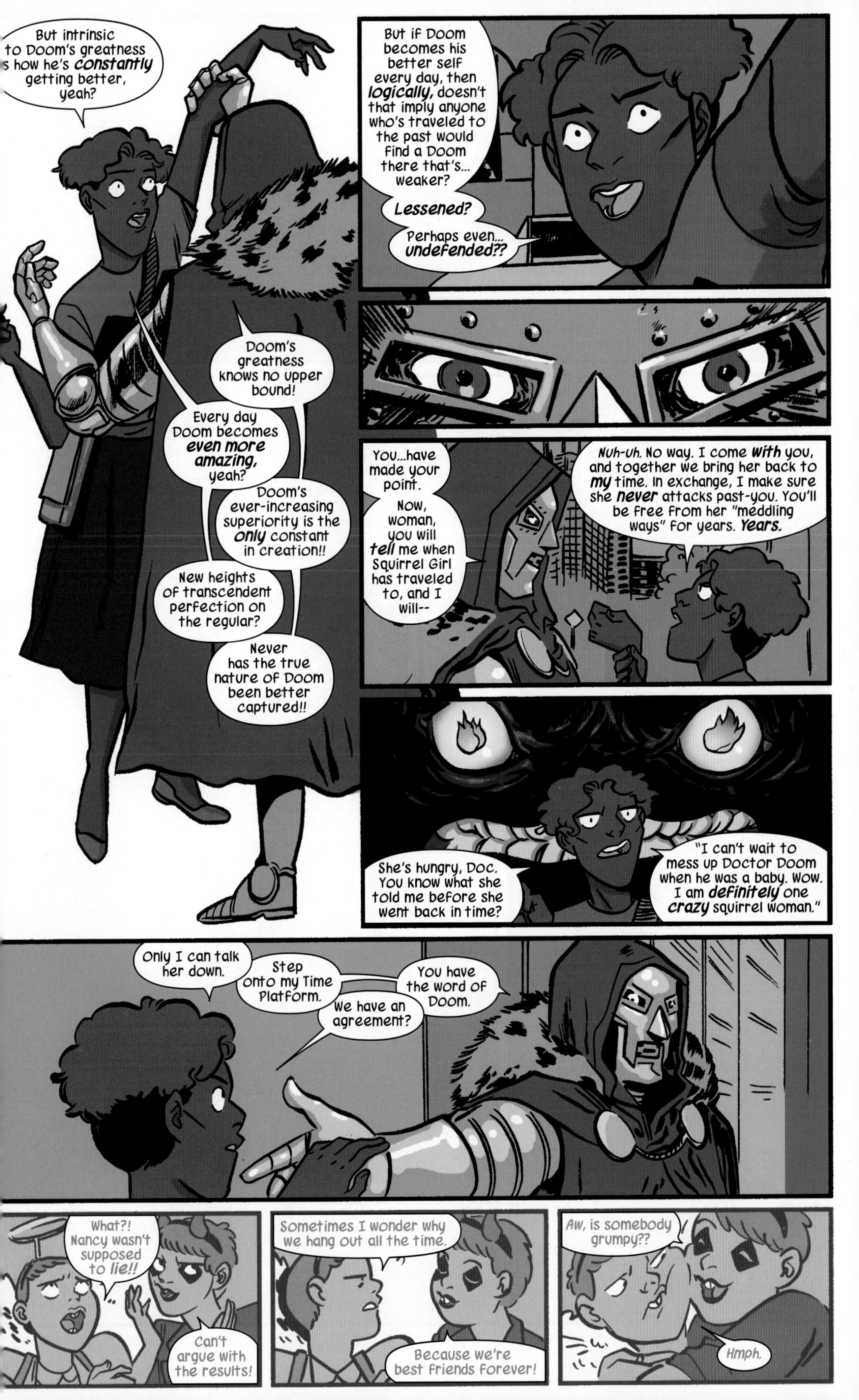
But intrinsic to Doom's greatness is how he's *constantly* getting better, yeah?
Doom's greatness knows no upper bound!
Every day Doom becomes *even more amazing,* yeah?
Doom's ever-increasing superiority is the *only* constant in creation!!
New heights of transcendent perfection on the regular?
Never has the true nature of Doom been better captured!!
But if Doom becomes his better self every day, then *logically,* doesn't that imply anyone who's traveled to the past would find a Doom there that's... weaker?
Lessened?
Perhaps even... *undefended??*
You...have made your point.
Now, woman, you will *tell* me when Squirrel Girl has traveled to, and I will--
Nuh-uh. No way. I come *with* you, and together we bring her back to *my* time. In exchange, I make sure she *never* attacks past-you. You'll be free from her "meddling ways" for years. *Years.*
She's hungry, Doc. You know what she told me before she went back in time?
"I can't wait to mess up Doctor Doom when he was a baby. Wow. I am *definitely* one *crazy* squirrel woman."
Only I can talk her down.
Step onto my Time Platform.
We have an agreement?
You have the word of Doom.
What?! Nancy wasn't supposed to *lie!!*
Can't argue with the results!
Sometimes I wonder why we hang out all the time.
Because we're best friends forever!
Aw, is somebody grumpy??
Hmph.

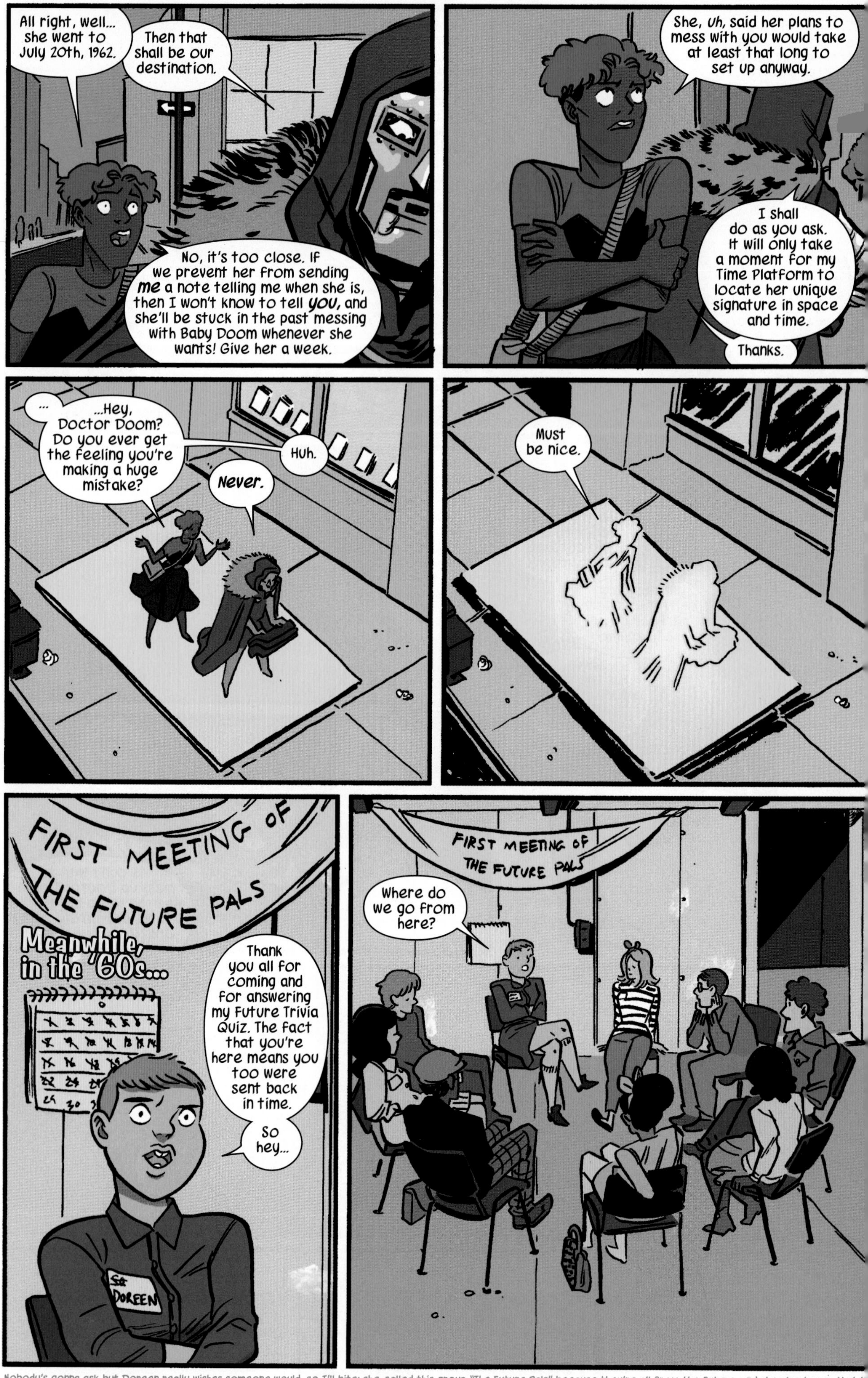
All right, well... she went to July 20th, 1962.
Then that shall be our destination.
No, it's too close. If we prevent her from sending *me* a note telling me when she is, then I won't know to tell *YOU*, and she'll be stuck in the past messing with Baby Doom whenever she wants! Give her a week.
She, *uh*, said her plans to mess with you would take at least that long to set up anyway.
I shall do as you ask. It will only take a moment for my Time Platform to locate her unique signature in space and time.
Thanks.
...
...Hey, Doctor Doom? Do you ever get the feeling you're making a huge mistake?
Huh.
Never.
Must be nice.
FIRST MEETING OF THE FUTURE PALS
Meanwhile, in the '60s...
Thank you all for coming and for answering my Future Trivia Quiz. The fact that you're here means you too were sent back in time.
So hey...
DOREEN
FIRST MEETING OF THE FUTURE PALS
Where do we go from here?

Nobody's gonna ask but Doreen really wishes someone would, so I'll bite: she called this group "The Future Pals" because they're all from the future, and she also hopes that i time they'll all become pals. ***Pretty adorable, Doreen.***

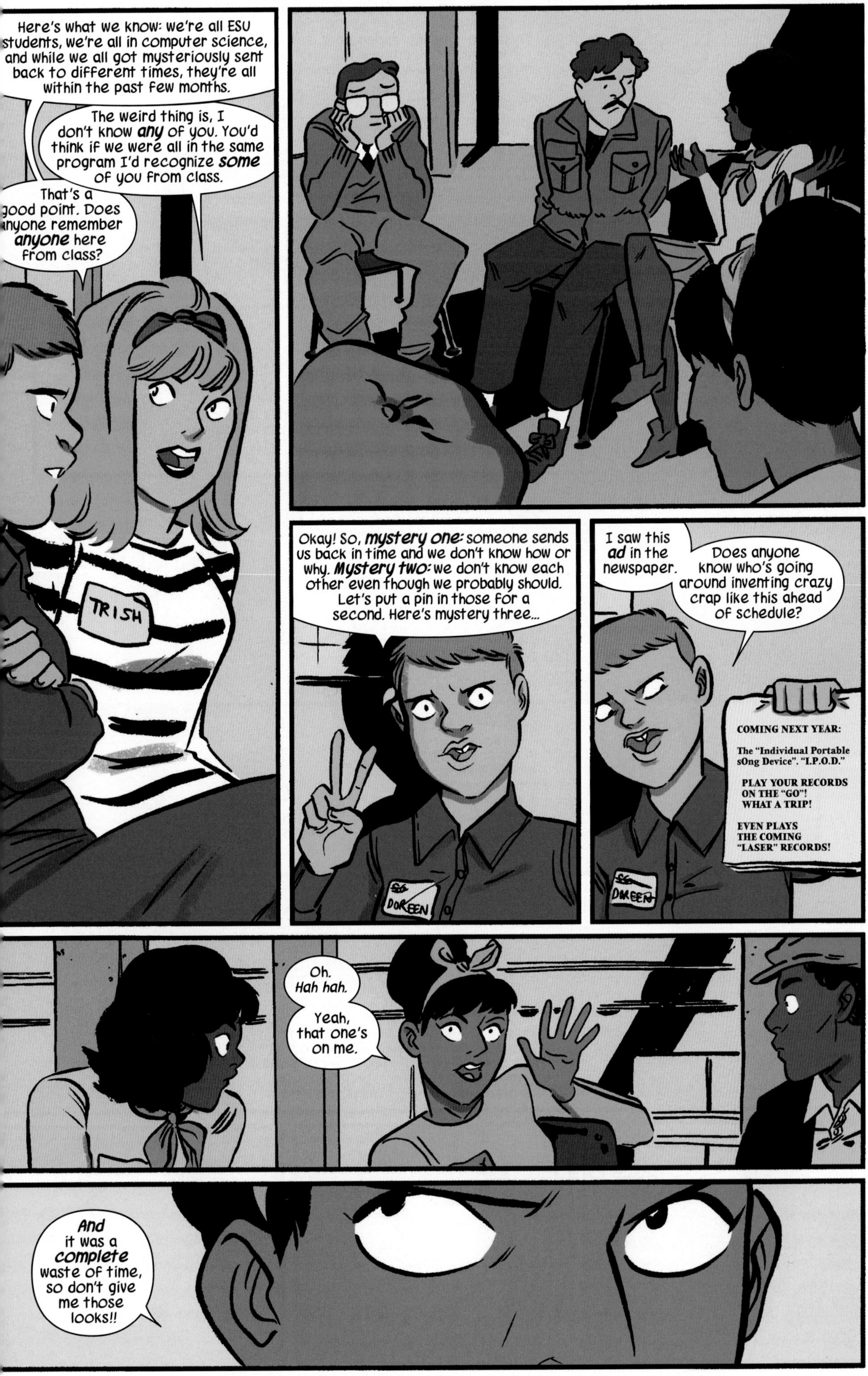
Here's what we know: we're all ESU students, we're all in computer science, and while we all got mysteriously sent back to different times, they're all within the past few months.
The weird thing is, I don't know any of you. You'd think if we were all in the same program I'd recognize some of you from class.
That's a good point. Does anyone remember anyone here from class?
TRISH
Okay! So, mystery one: someone sends us back in time and we don't know how or why. Mystery two: we don't know each other even though we probably should. Let's put a pin in those for a second. Here's mystery three...
DOREEN
I saw this ad in the newspaper.
Does anyone know who's going around inventing crazy crap like this ahead of schedule?
COMING NEXT YEAR:
The "Individual Portable sOng Device". "I.P.O.D."
PLAY YOUR RECORDS ON THE "GO"! WHAT A TRIP!
EVEN PLAYS THE COMING "LASER" RECORDS!
DOREEN
Oh. Hah hah.
Yeah, that one's on me.
And it was a complete waste of time, so don't give me those looks!!

It was also a complete waste of my hard-earned "Sixties Buxx," or as they're known in this time period: "dollars."

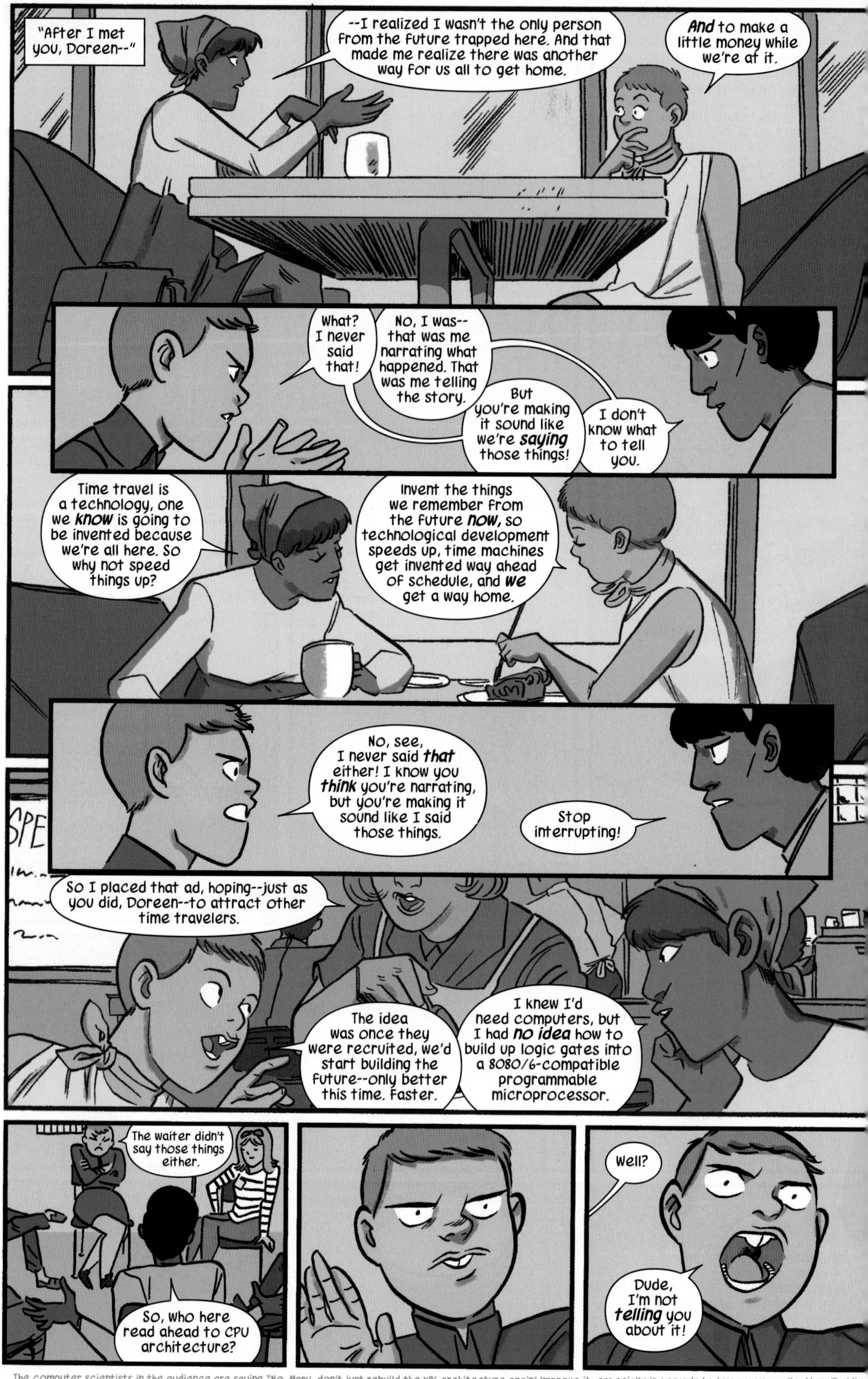

"After I met you, Doreen--"
--I realized I wasn't the only person from the future trapped here. And that made me realize there was another way for us all to get home.
And to make a little money while we're at it.
What? I never said that!
No, I was-- that was me narrating what happened. That was me telling the story.
But you're making it sound like we're saying those things!
I don't know what to tell you.
Time travel is a technology, one we know is going to be invented because we're all here. So why not speed things up?
Invent the things we remember from the future now, so technological development speeds up, time machines get invented way ahead of schedule, and we get a way home.
No, see, I never said that either! I know you think you're narrating, but you're making it sound like I said those things.
Stop interrupting!
So I placed that ad, hoping--just as you did, Doreen--to attract other time travelers.
The idea was once they were recruited, we'd start building the future--only better this time. Faster.
I knew I'd need computers, but I had no idea how to build up logic gates into a 8080/6-compatible programmable microprocessor.
The waiter didn't say those things either.
So, who here read ahead to CPU architecture?
Well?
Dude, I'm not telling you about it!

The computer scientists in the audience are saying "No, Mary, don't just rebuild the x86 architecture again! Improve it, especially in regards to low-power applications!" while the non-computer scientists in the audience are saying "Eh, computers gonna compute."

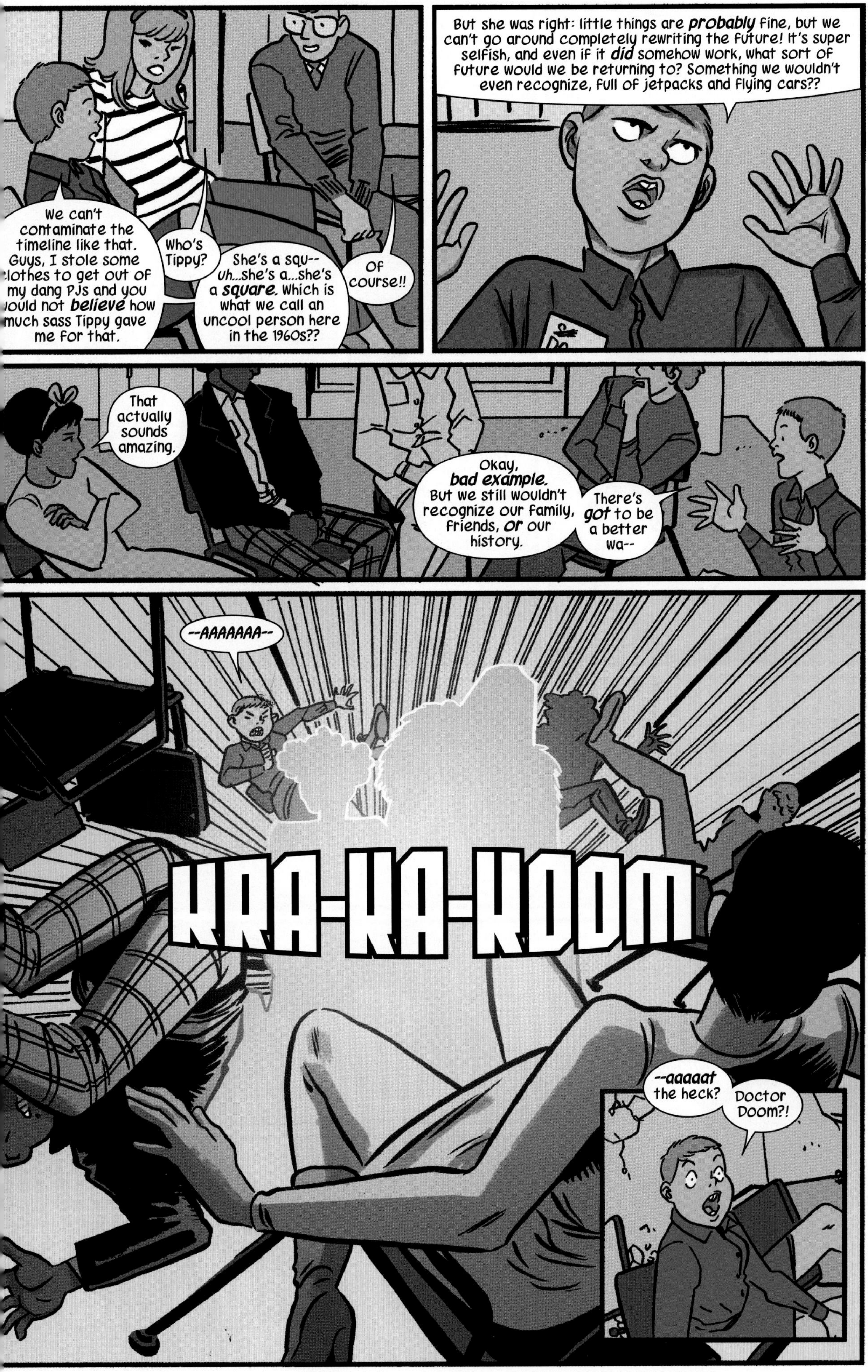

We can't contaminate the timeline like that. Guys, I stole some lothes to get out of my dang PJs and you vould not believe how much sass Tippy gave me for that.
Who's Tippy?
She's a squ-- uh...she's a...she's a square. Which is what we call an uncool person here in the 1960s??
Of course!!
But she was right: little things are probably fine, but we can't go around completely rewriting the future! It's super selfish, and even if it did somehow work, what sort of future would we be returning to? Something we wouldn't even recognize, full of jetpacks and flying cars??
That actually sounds amazing.
...
Okay, bad example. But we still wouldn't recognize our family, friends, or our history.
...
There's got to be a better wa--
--AAAAAAA--
KRA-KA-KOOM
--aaaaat the heck?
Doctor Doom?!

Doctor Doom, you're not even *close* to the better way I was talking about before your perfectly timed entrance!!

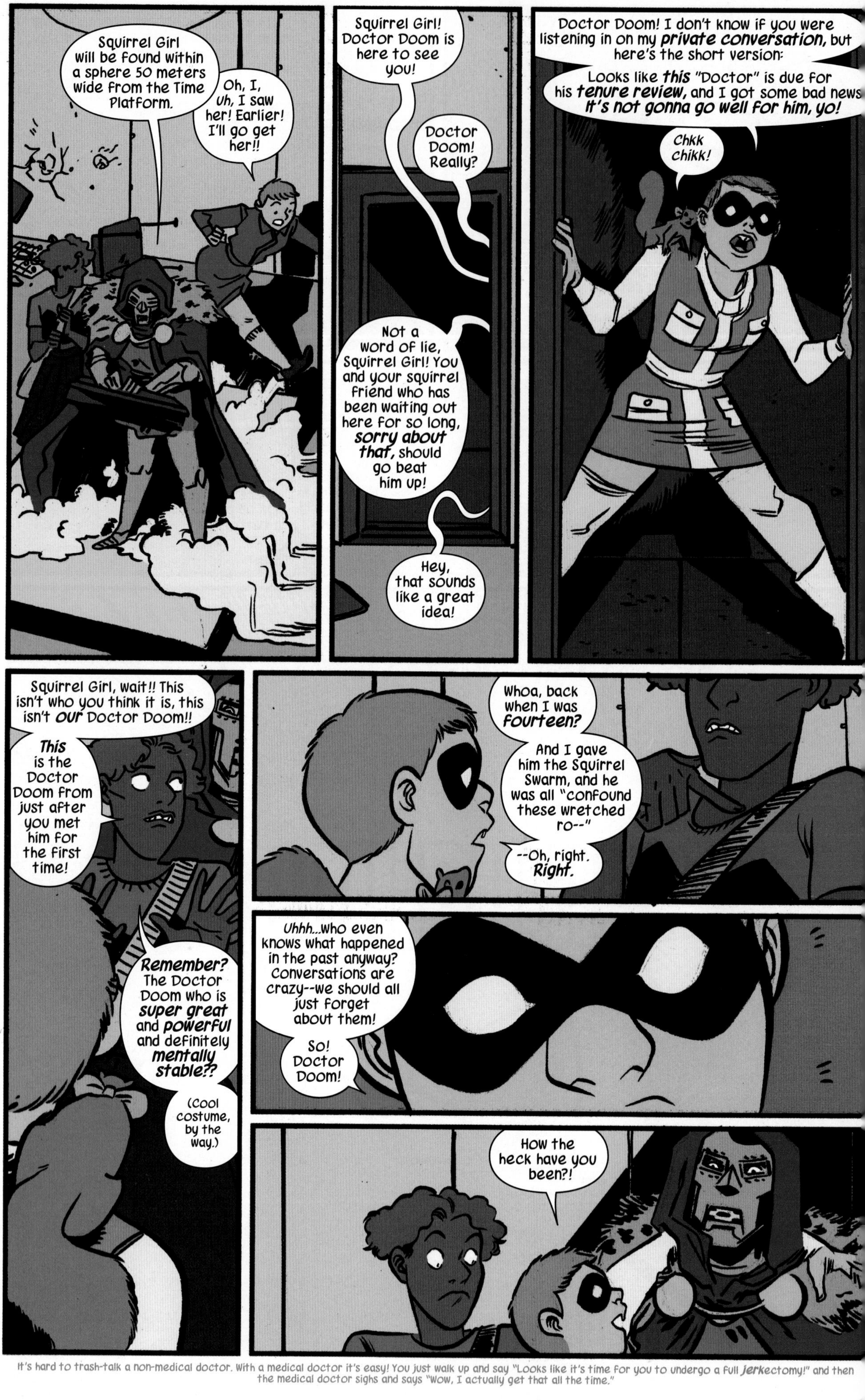
Squirrel Girl will be found within a sphere 50 meters wide from the Time Platform.
Oh, I, uh, I saw her! Earlier! I'll go get her!!
Squirrel Girl! Doctor Doom is here to see you!
Doctor Doom! Really?
Not a word of lie, Squirrel Girl! You and your squirrel friend who has been waiting out here for so long, sorry about that, should go beat him up!
Hey, that sounds like a great idea!
Doctor Doom! I don't know if you were listening in on my private conversation, but here's the short version:
Looks like this "Doctor" is due for his tenure review, and I got some bad news: It's not gonna go well for him, yo!
Chkk chikk!
Squirrel Girl, wait!! This isn't who you think it is, this isn't our Doctor Doom!!
This is the Doctor Doom from just after you met him for the first time!
Remember? The Doctor Doom who is super great and powerful and definitely mentally stable??
(Cool costume, by the way.)
Whoa, back when I was fourteen?
And I gave him the Squirrel Swarm, and he was all "confound these wretched ro--"
--Oh, right. Right.
Uhhh...who even knows what happened in the past anyway? Conversations are crazy--we should all just forget about them!
So! Doctor Doom!
How the heck have you been?!

It's hard to trash-talk a non-medical doctor. With a medical doctor it's easy! You just walk up and say "Looks like it's time for you to undergo a full *jerkectomy!*" and then the medical doctor sighs and says "Wow, I actually get that all the time."

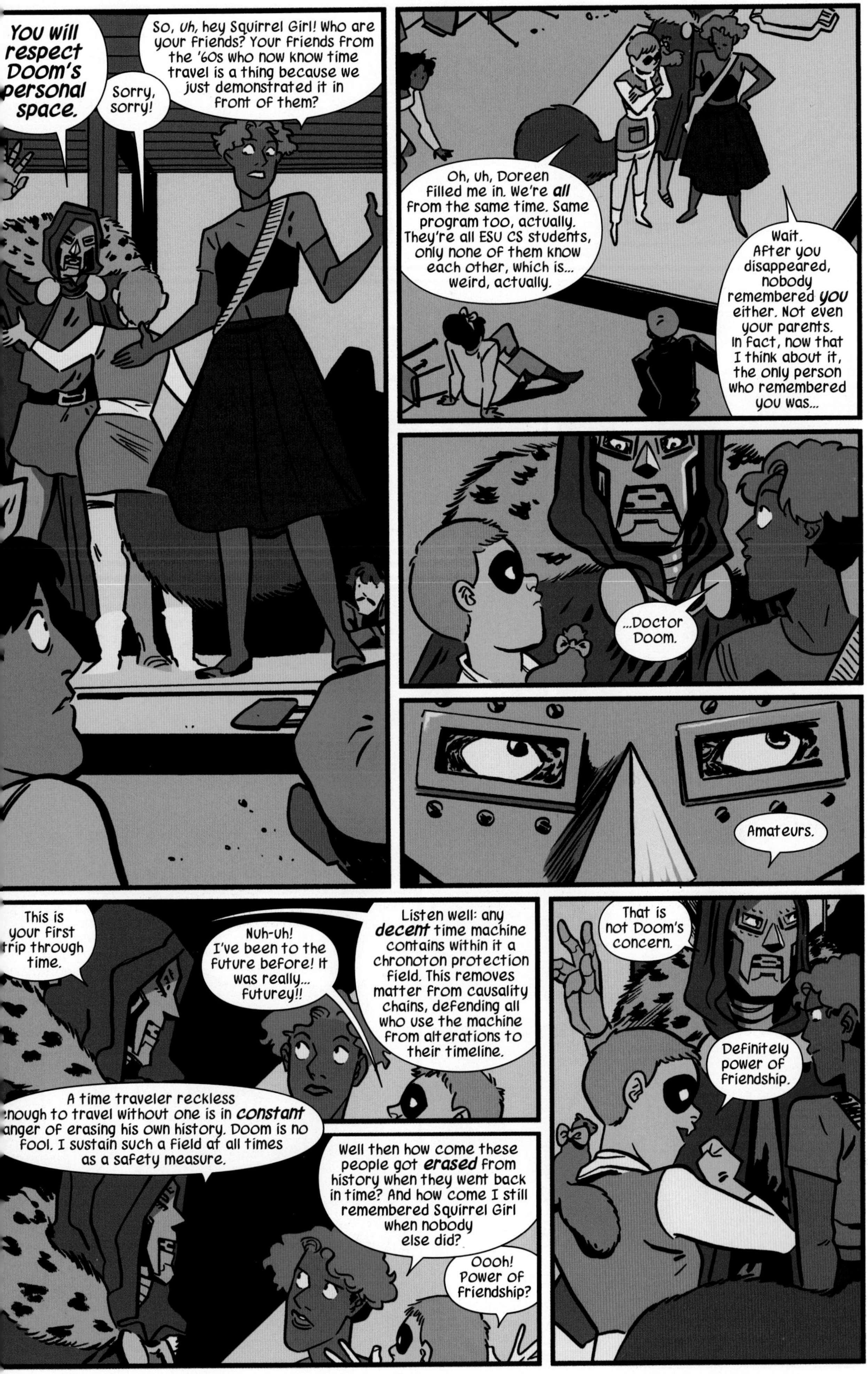
You will respect Doom's personal space.
Sorry, sorry!
So, uh, hey Squirrel Girl! Who are your friends? Your friends from the '60s who now know time travel is a thing because we just demonstrated it in front of them?
Oh, uh, Doreen filled me in. We're *all* from the same time. Same program too, actually. They're all ESU CS students, only none of them know each other, which is... weird, actually.
Wait. After you disappeared, nobody remembered *you* either. Not even your parents. In fact, now that I think about it, the only person who remembered you was...
...Doctor Doom.
Amateurs.
This is your first trip through time.
Nuh-uh! I've been to the future before! It was really... futurey!!
Listen well: any *decent* time machine contains within it a chronoton protection field. This removes matter from causality chains, defending all who use the machine from alterations to their timeline.
A time traveler reckless nough to travel without one is in *constant* anger of erasing his own history. Doom is no fool. I sustain such a field at all times as a safety measure.
Well then how come these people got *erased* from history when they went back in time? And how come I still remembered Squirrel Girl when nobody else did?
Oooh! Power of friendship?
That is not Doom's concern.
Definitely power of friendship.

Come on, Squirrel Girl. What about a man who wears a metal suit ***all the time*** made you think "now ***here*** is a guy who likes to be touched unexpectedly"?

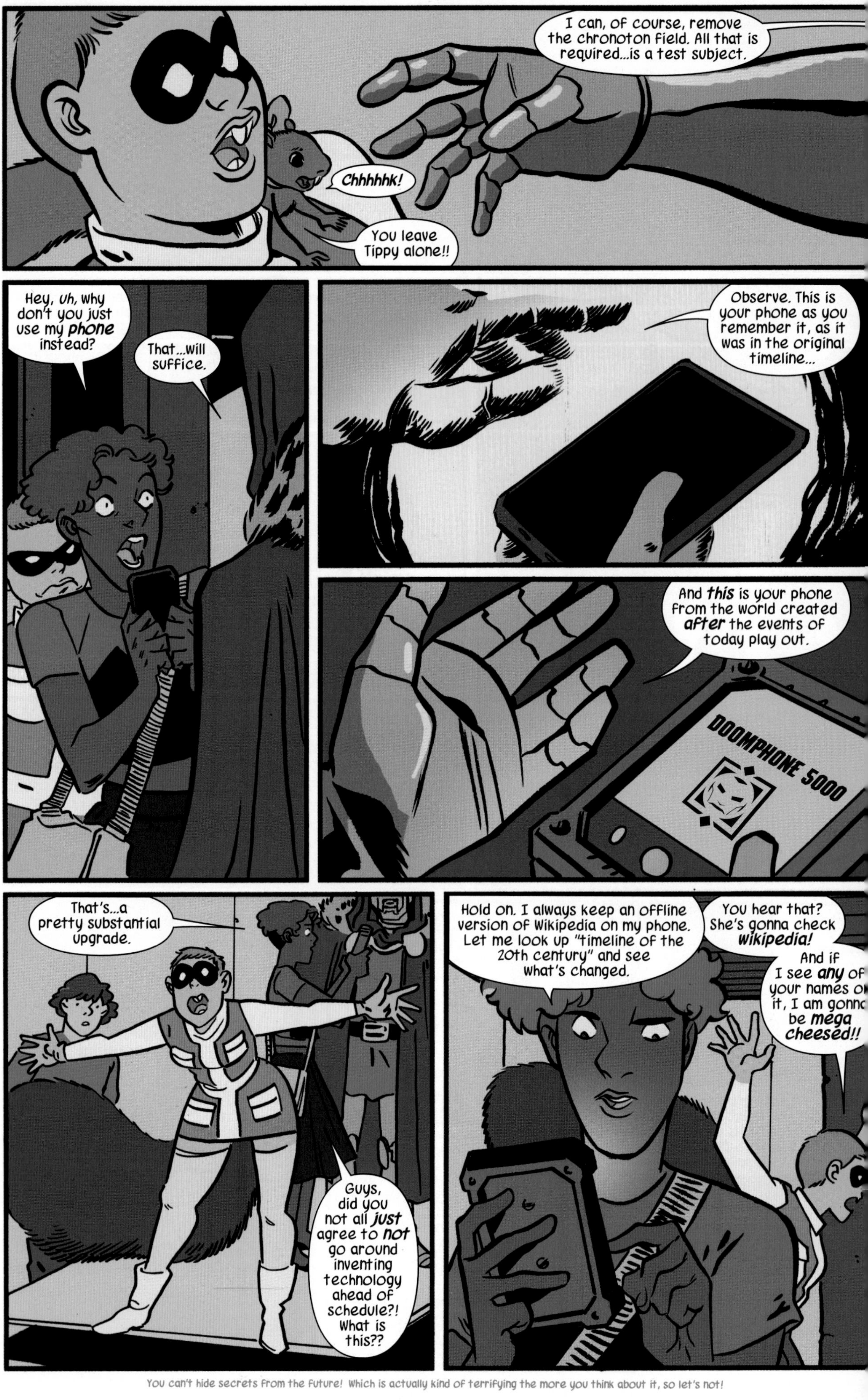
I can, of course, remove the chronoton field. All that is required...is a test subject.
Chhhhhk!
You leave Tippy alone!!
Hey, uh, why don't you just use my phone instead?
That...will suffice.
Observe. This is your phone as you remember it, as it was in the original timeline...
And this is your phone from the world created after the events of today play out.
DOOMPHONE 5000
That's...a pretty substantial upgrade.
Guys, did you not all just agree to not go around inventing technology ahead of schedule?! What is this??
Hold on. I always keep an offline version of Wikipedia on my phone. Let me look up "timeline of the 20th century" and see what's changed.
You hear that? She's gonna check wikipedia!
And if I see any of your names o it, I am gonn be mega cheesed!!

You can't hide secrets from the future! Which is actually kind of terrifying the more you think about it, so let's not!

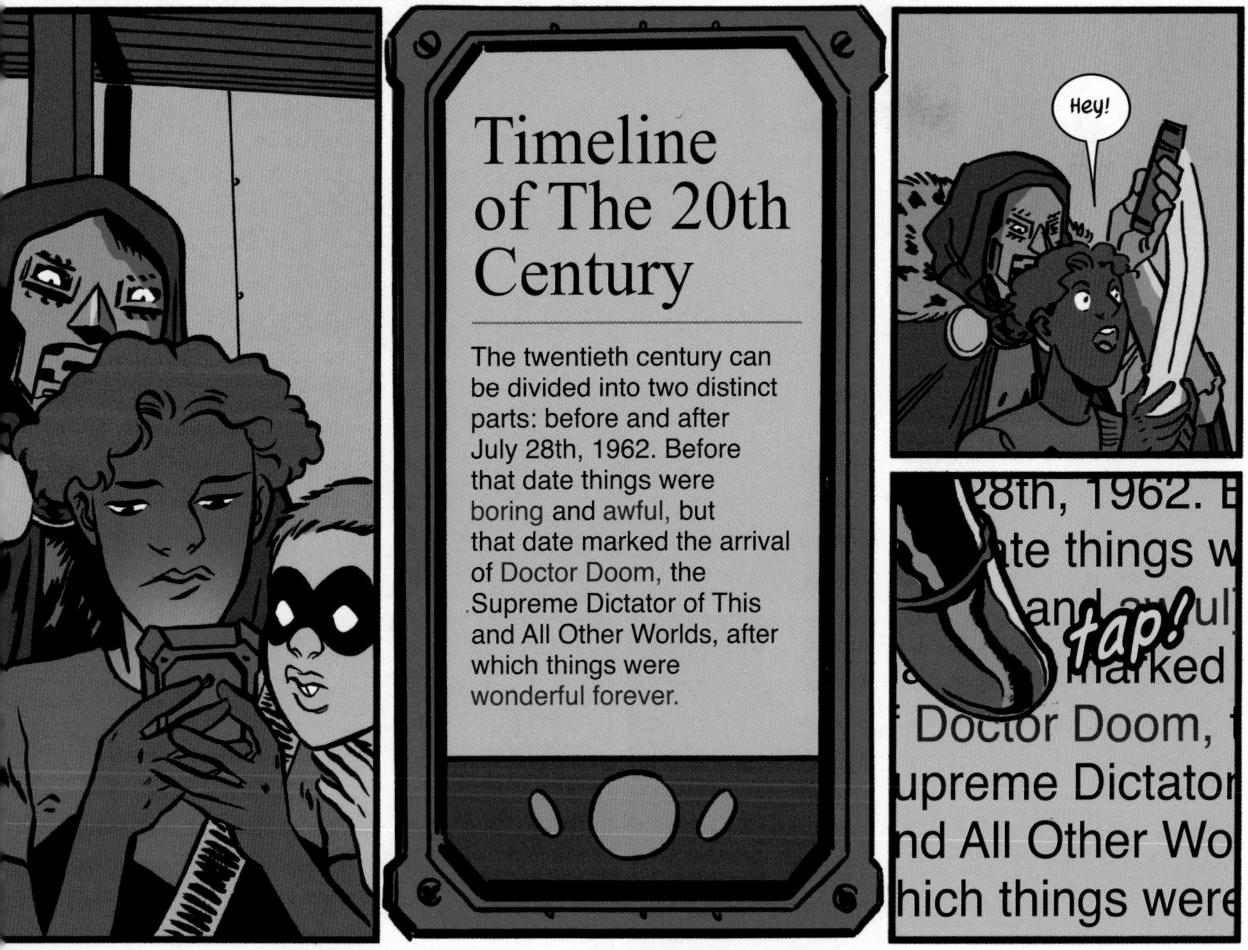
Timeline of The 20th Century
The twentieth century can be divided into two distinct parts: before and after July 28th, 1962. Before that date things were boring and awful, but that date marked the arrival of Doctor Doom, the Supreme Dictator of This and All Other Worlds, after which things were wonderful forever.
Hey!
tap!

Doctor Victor Von Doom, PhD, is a beloved benevolent dictator, scientist, inventor, sorcerer supreme, genius, and artist who appeared under mysterious circumstances on Planet Doom (formerly "Earth") on July 28th, 1962. He quickly took over the world, issuing many decrees for reasons known only to His Supreme Greatness, including specifying that Reed Richards and his closest three associates be kept out of space, alternate dimensions, and cinemas; that otherwise-unremarkable student Peter Parker under no circumstances be allowed near spiders; that all gamma ray testing be immediately suspended; among others. His rule is notable for having been absolutely perfect in every way.

Contents [hide]

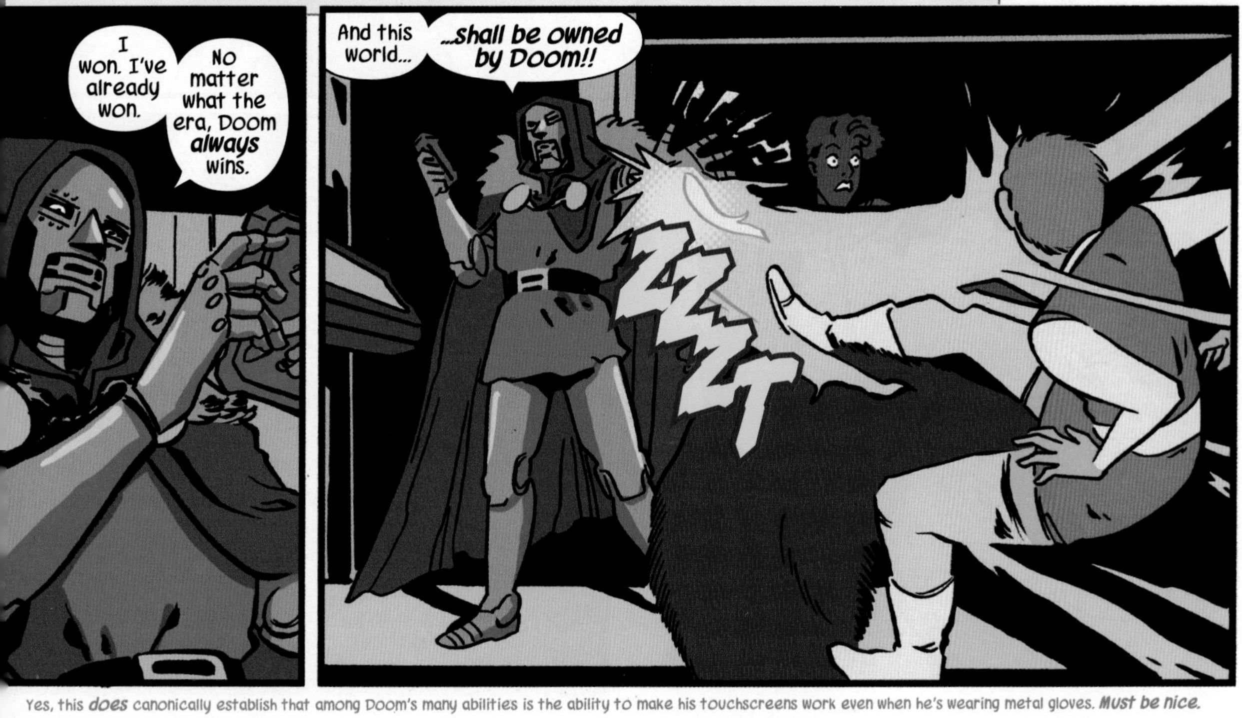
I won. I've already won.
No matter what the era, Doom *always* wins.
And this world...
...shall be owned by Doom!!
ZZZT

Yes, this *does* canonically establish that among Doom's many abilities is the ability to make his touchscreens work even when he's wearing metal gloves. ***Must be nice.***

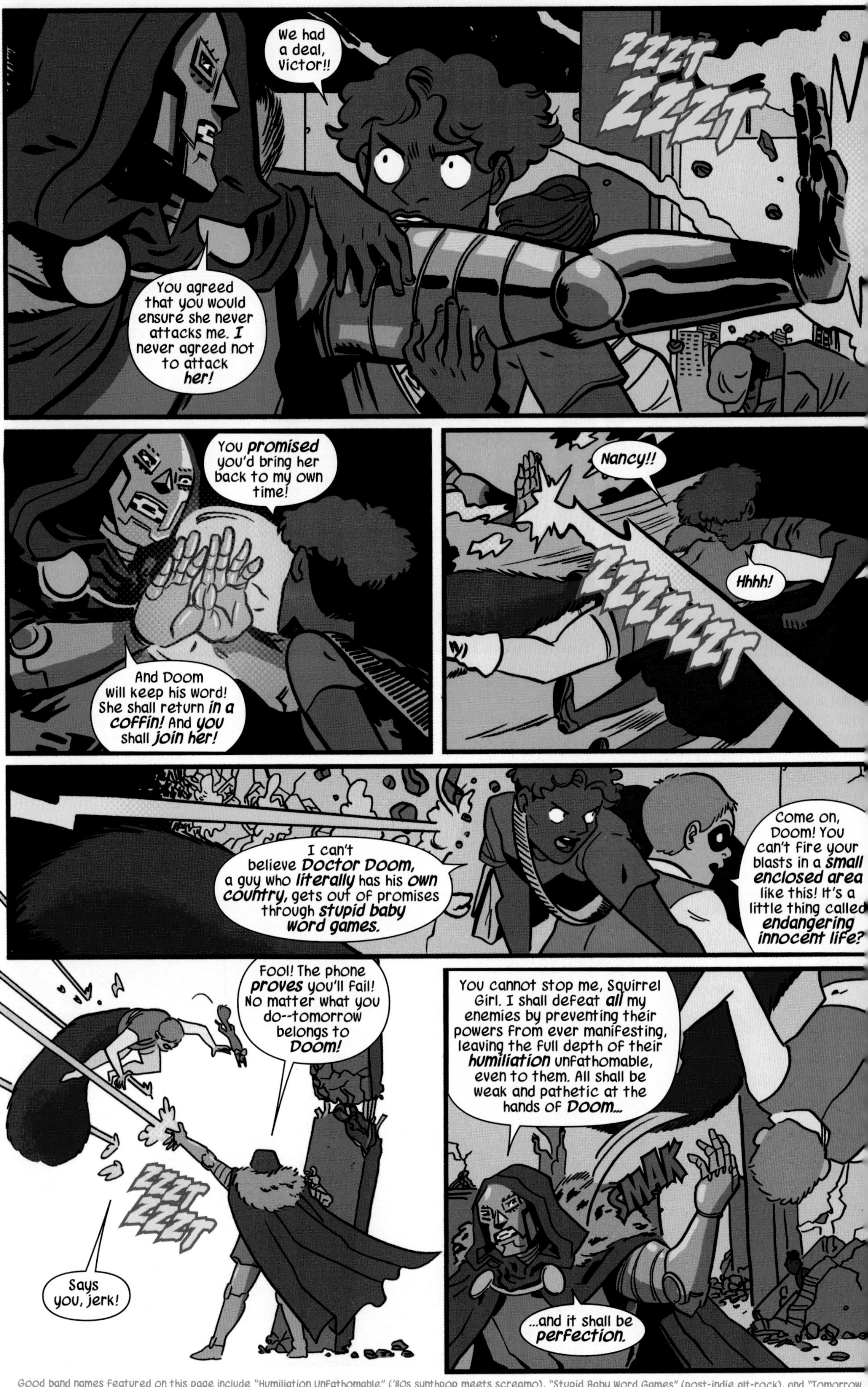
We had a deal, Victor!!
ZZZT ZZZT
You agreed that you would ensure she never attacks me. *I* never agreed not to attack *her!*
You *promised* you'd bring her back to my own time!
And Doom will keep his word! She shall return *in a coffin!* And *you* shall *join her!*
Nancy!!
ZZZZZZZT
Hhhh!
I can't believe *Doctor Doom,* a guy who *literally* has his *own country,* gets out of promises through *stupid baby word games.*
Come on, Doom! You can't fire your blasts in a *small enclosed area* like this! It's a little thing called *endangering innocent life?*
Fool! The phone *proves* you'll fail! No matter what you do--tomorrow belongs to *DOOM!*
ZZZT ZZZT
Says you, jerk!
You cannot stop me, Squirrel Girl. I shall defeat *all* my enemies by preventing their powers from ever manifesting, leaving the full depth of their *humiliation* unfathomable, even to them. All shall be weak and pathetic at the hands of *DOOM...*
SMAK
...and it shall be *perfection.*

Good band names featured on this page include "Humiliation Unfathomable" ('80s synthpop meets screamo), "Stupid Baby Word Games" (post-indie alt-rock), and "Tomorrow Belongs To Doom" (death metal, obvs).

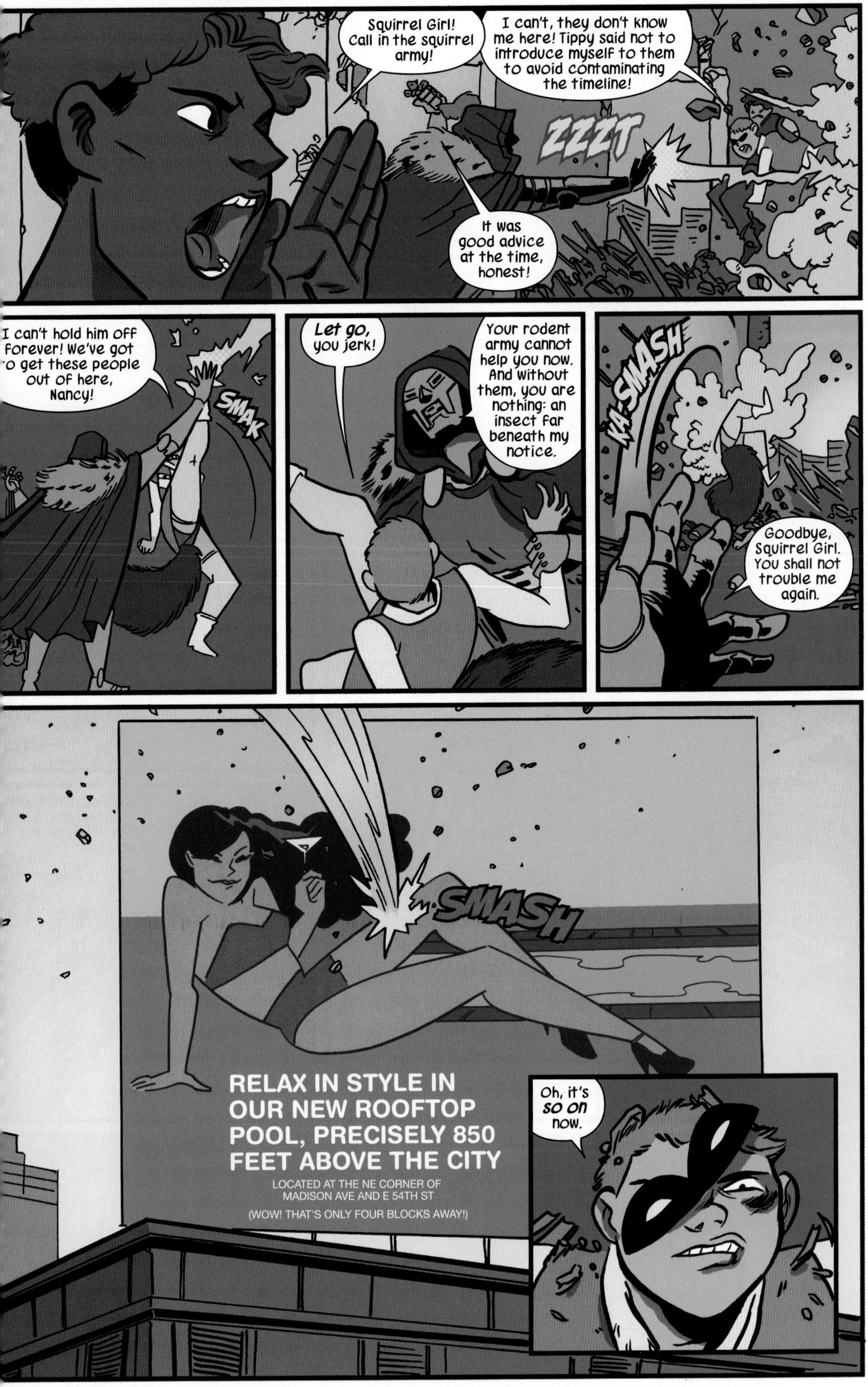
Squirrel Girl! Call in the squirrel army!
I can't, they don't know me here! Tippy said not to introduce myself to them to avoid contaminating the timeline!
ZZZT
It was good advice at the time, honest!
I can't hold him off forever! We've got to get these people out of here, Nancy!
SMAK
Let go, you jerk!
Your rodent army cannot help you now. And without them, you are nothing: an insect far beneath my notice.
KA-SMASH
Goodbye, Squirrel Girl. You shall not trouble me again.
SMASH
RELAX IN STYLE IN OUR NEW ROOFTOP POOL, PRECISELY 850 FEET ABOVE THE CITY
LOCATED AT THE NE CORNER OF MADISON AVE AND E 54TH ST
(WOW! THAT'S ONLY FOUR BLOCKS AWAY!)
Oh, it's *so on* now.

Meanwhile, some poor billboard repairman who was five minutes away from clocking off for the day is looking up at that sign and sighing deeply.

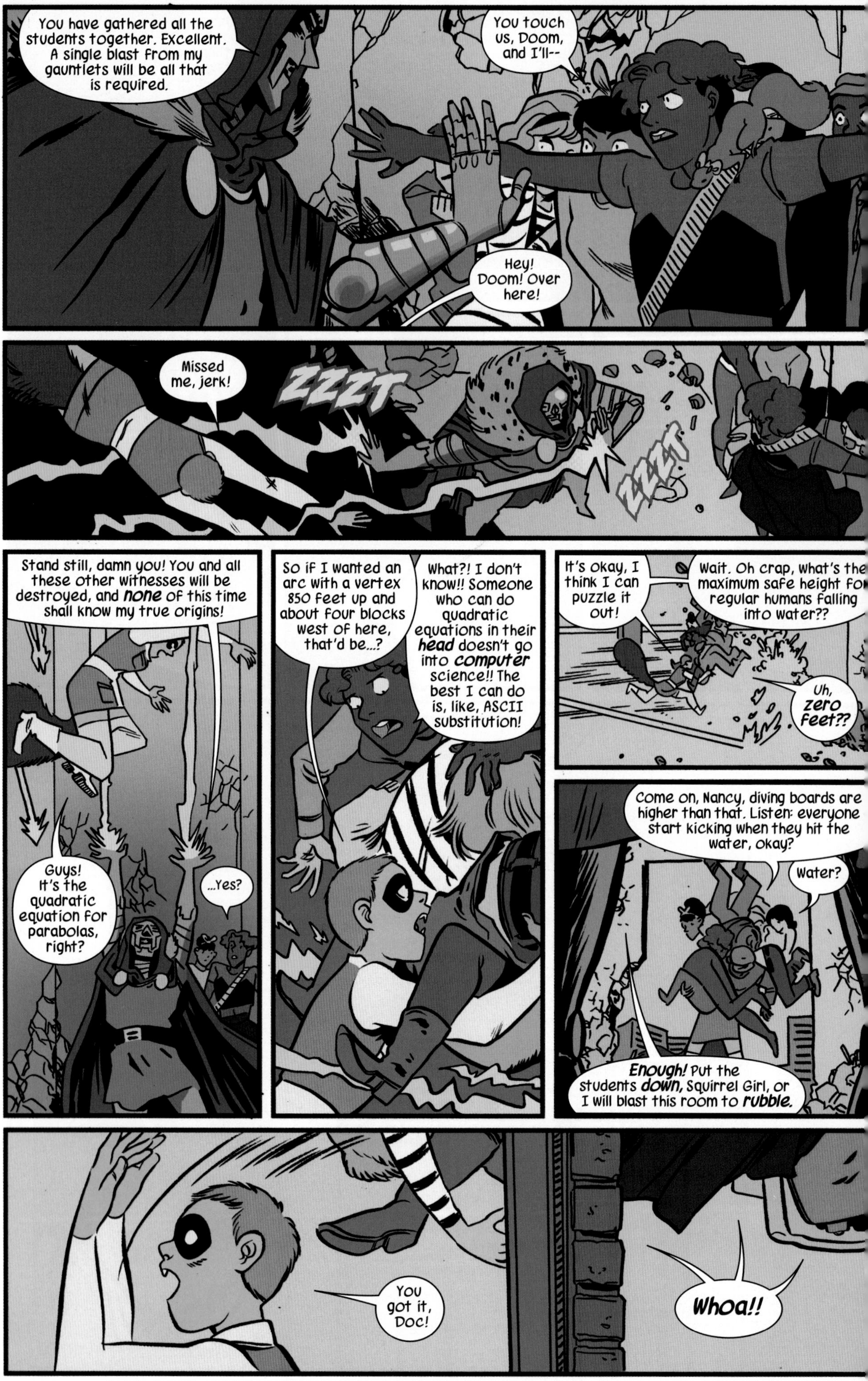

You have gathered all the students together. Excellent. A single blast from my gauntlets will be all that is required.
You touch us, Doom, and I'll--
Hey! Doom! Over here!
Missed me, jerk!
ZZZT
ZZZT
Stand still, damn you! You and all these other witnesses will be destroyed, and none of this time shall know my true origins!
Guys! It's the quadratic equation for parabolas, right?
...Yes?
So if I wanted an arc with a vertex 850 feet up and about four blocks west of here, that'd be...?
What?! I don't know!! Someone who can do quadratic equations in their head doesn't go into computer science!! The best I can do is, like, ASCII substitution!
It's okay, I think I can puzzle it out!
Wait. Oh crap, what's the maximum safe height fo regular humans falling into water??
Uh, zero feet??
Come on, Nancy, diving boards are higher than that. Listen: everyone start kicking when they hit the water, okay?
Water?
Enough! Put the students down, Squirrel Girl, or I will blast this room to rubble.
You got it, Doc!
Whoa!!

The trick to solving a quadratic equation in your head is factoring. I say this as someone who solves quadratic equations in his head ***all the time,*** and definitely not as someone who quickly looked up "secret to solve quadratic equation in your head" + "its an emergency."

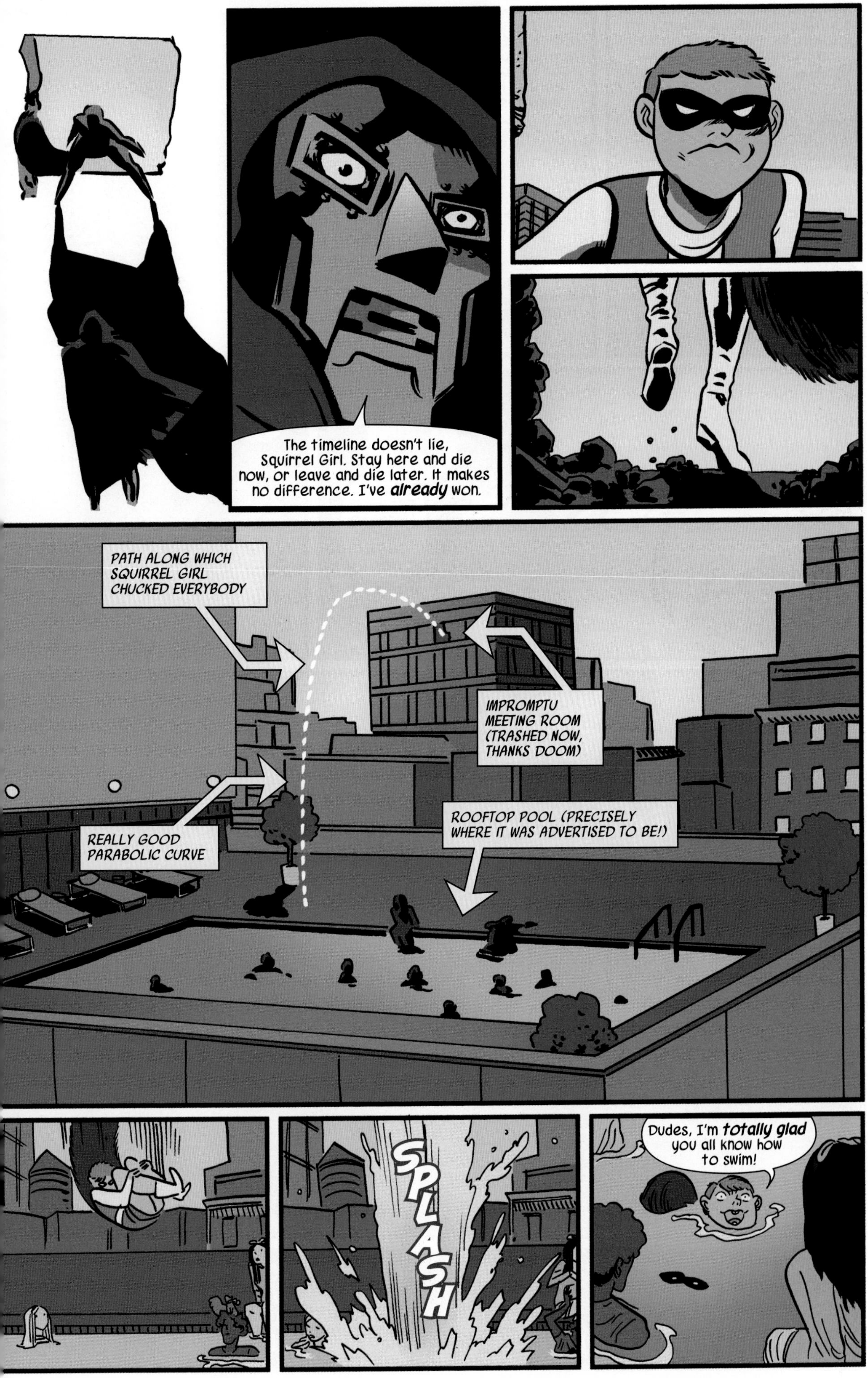

The timeline doesn't lie, Squirrel Girl. Stay here and die now, or leave and die later. It makes no difference. I've ***already*** won.
PATH ALONG WHICH SQUIRREL GIRL CHUCKED EVERYBODY
IMPROMPTU MEETING ROOM (TRASHED NOW, THANKS DOOM)
REALLY GOOD PARABOLIC CURVE
ROOFTOP POOL (PRECISELY WHERE IT WAS ADVERTISED TO BE!)
SPLASH
Dudes, I'm ***totally glad*** you all know how to swim!

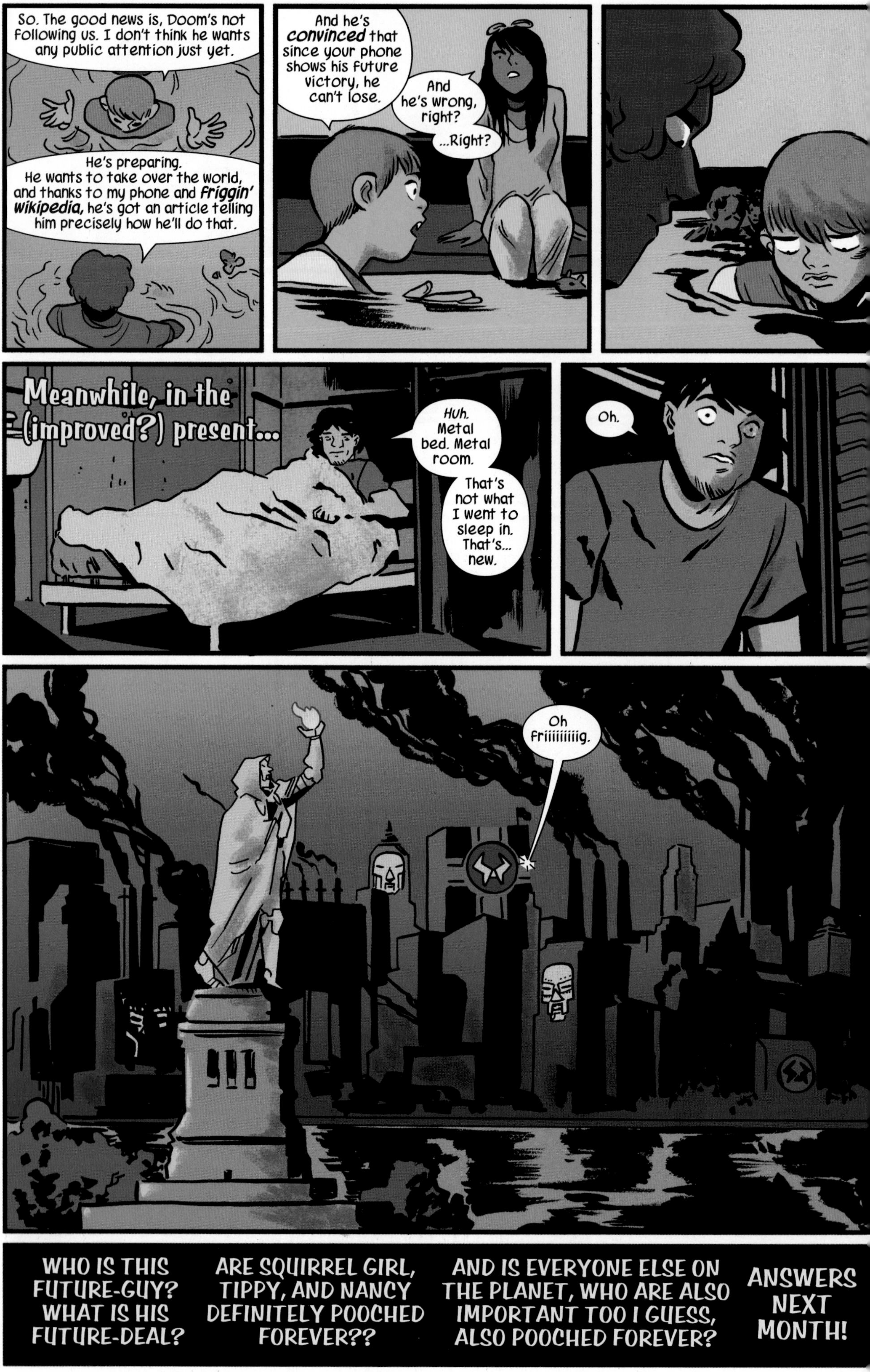
So. The good news is, Doom's not following us. I don't think he wants any public attention just yet.
He's preparing. He wants to take over the world, and thanks to my phone and *friggin' wikipedia,* he's got an article telling him precisely how he'll do that.
And he's *convinced* that since your phone shows his future victory, he can't lose.
And he's wrong, right?
...Right?
Meanwhile, in the (improved?) present...
Huh. Metal bed. Metal room.
That's not what I went to sleep in. That's... new.
Oh.
Oh Friiiiiiiig.
WHO IS THIS FUTURE-GUY? WHAT IS HIS FUTURE-DEAL?
ARE SQUIRREL GIRL, TIPPY, AND NANCY DEFINITELY POOCHED FOREVER??
AND IS EVERYONE ELSE ON THE PLANET, WHO ARE ALSO IMPORTANT TOO I GUESS, ALSO POOCHED FOREVER?
ANSWERS NEXT MONTH!

Ryan!

Letters From Nuts

Erica!

Send letters to mheroes@marvel.com or 135 W 50th St, 7th Floor, New York, NY 10020 (Please mark "OKAY TO PRINT")

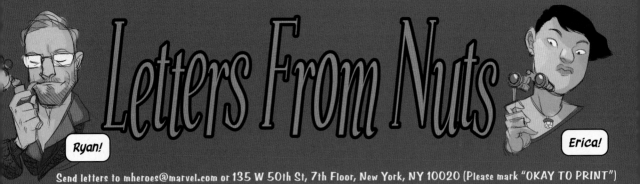

Hey squirrel dudes, it's Drew. Have you ever thought of giving Squirrel Girl an alternative monicker? Batman has "The Dark Knight". Superman is "The Man of Steel". Captain America is "The First Avenger". I've got a great one for Squirrel Girl! You better sit down for this... The Supreme Sciuridae!

If I ever saw that printed I would just die. Keep up the GREAT work! I am in love with this current Squirrel Girl series! You can really tell that everyone that works on it is passionate and committed.

Andrew Torres

RYAN: Hey Drew! I am the guy who writes a comic called The Unbeatable Squirrel Girl and I can't spell sciuridae without double-checking it, so we MIGHT hold off on it until I can spell it reliably. But you are correct (both about that being a cool monicker AND that everyone who works on this book really loves it!).

Neko always enjoys reading the newest issue of Squirrel Girl but after issue #8 came out she new exactly what she wanted to be for Halloween. CAT THOR!

She is still disappointed that I won't let her carry around a hammer to wack the shins of people who annoy her (mainly me) but otherwise this is "the best Halloween ever" her words.

Kelsey B

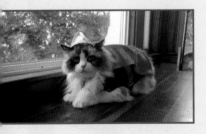

R: NEKO IS ADORABLE. I now want to see tons of photos of catsplay, which is a word I just made up that means cosplay for cats. I am 100% certain that all cats will be big into this and see no possible downsides.

ERICA: When I first read this I completely missed that Neko is Japanese for cat (thanks, three years of high school Japanese) and expected to see a child in an outfit. ANYWAY, where did you find this beautiful cat that didn't try to eat you alive for putting it in clothes? I need deets. Does Neko have siblings? Can I have one?

Hi Ryan and Erica!

I have been a lifelong comics fan and I'm being completely honest when I say that your Squirrel Girl run is one of the best I've ever read, so hats off to you!

Perhaps more importantly however is your accomplishment in getting my wonderful girlfriend into reading comics! I must say I was a tad tentative introducing comics to her, but your writing and your art have absolutely hooked her! We read every issue together and it's one of our favourite things to do.

I hope to be reading Squirrel Girl with her for years to come, keep up your amazing work!

Sam and Catherine
England

PS Who do you think would win in a lip-sync battle between Squirrel Girl, Devil Dinosaur and Ms Marvel?

R: Hooray for being people's gateway comic, that's what I say! More precisely, what I've often said during talks and on panels is comics is a medium, not a genre, and like all mediums can be used to tell all sorts of stories, and then I go on to say if the only movies you ever saw were romantic comedies and you didn't like romantic comedies, you might be forgiven for saying 'wow I guess I just don't like movies' and then proceed to draw an analogy involving the types of comics people THINK they know compared to the full spectrum of amazingness that comics ACTUALLY ARE and comparing that to that person who thinks they hate movies because they've only ever seen one small slice of what movies can be. ANYWAY, this is all to say: thanks, and I'm super glad she likes comics now!

Also, in a lip-sync battle I would have to give it to Devil Dinosaur, because he is an actual dinosaur, and I have it on good authority that dinosaurs can spit rhymes like CRAZY.

E: Ryan has pretty well covered the first half of the question. If you want some non-super hero comic recommendations that are women-friendly, I have them! Tweet at me: @ericafails.

To answer the second part of your letter, I would also have to go with Devil Dinosaur, but for a different reason. As someone who studied animation, it's a lot easier to match mouth movements on something that doesn't really have a wide range of mouth movements. So he can match himself up faster and easier since he doesn't have to worry about his mouth looking like the wrong word.

Hi, my name is Isla. I am 6 years old and I really like Squirrel Girl.

Here is a picture of me and my sister. We dressed up on Halloween. I was Squirrel Girl and my sister was Tippy Toe. Since Squirrel Girl keeps Deadpool villain cards in her utility belt, I made some out of paper and put them in my utility belt.

Thank you. I hope you keep making Squirrel Girl.

Isla

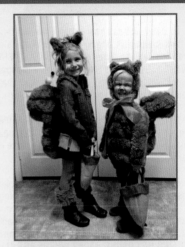

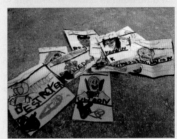

R: Isla, I hope so too! Here is the thing about you and your sister's costumes: THEY ARE AMAZING, and I can't get over your Deadpool villain cards. You've made some that we haven't even gotten to in the comics yet! SO GOOD. Thank you for reading our comics, and for sharing your costumes with us! I'm old enough that I get to give out candy on Hallowe'en, so this year at my house I was giving out chocolate bars AND issues of Squirrel Girl. If I'd seen you I would've given you the entire bowl of candy!!

E: AHHH. You guys look so goooood! I want to know how you decided who would be Squirrel Girl and who would be Tippy. Ryan, I guess we'll have to put all those bad guys in the book so that these cards are accurate.

Dear Ryan and Erica,

My dog Sawyer and I love Squirrel Girl so much that we decided to dress like Doreen Green and Tippy-Toe for Halloween. It was so much fun to walk down the street and hear people shout out "Hey! Squirrel Girl!"I am 11 years old and have read every issue of your comic. I really like Chipmunk Hunk and Nancy Whitehead. I love Squirrel Girl so much that I have a big poster of her in my room.

I have included a picture so that you can see how great we looked.

Squirrel Girl Forever!

Love, Olivia G.

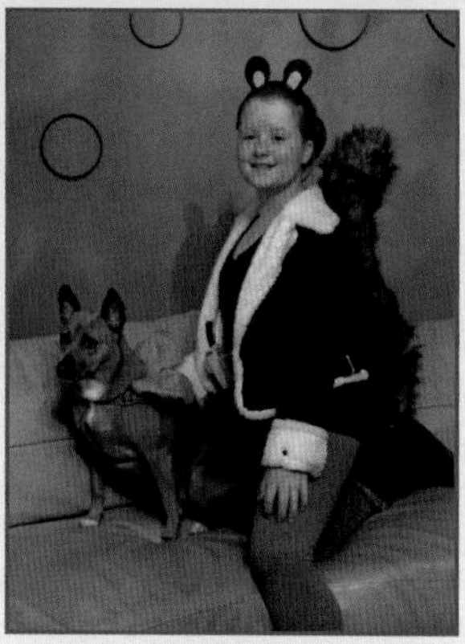

R: Can I just say how happy I am that this letters column is chock full of both people dressing up as Squirrel Girl AND THEIR PETS? Because I am extremely happy. Thank you, Olivia! I'm super stoked that people recognized you too: word of Squirrel Girl is spreading!

Nancy Whitehead is a favourite of mine too, and I really want to see more of Chipmunk Hunk. These time travel shenanigans make it hard but we'll see him soon, I promise!

E: Listen, all of you made a big mistake posting your cute animals because I'm going to come and steal them. I don't care that my apartment doesn't allow dogs. Stealing them all. Yeah, Ryan, where's Chipmunk Hunk? WHEN'S HE COMING BACK? WHERE ARE ALL THE HUNKS?

Ryan, Erica, et al,

Congrats on another #1! I was super-pleased to hear how Hippo the Hippo is doing. Frankly, if you went all-in on Hippo the Hippo referencing and had him move in downstairs from Doreen and Nancy I'd be at least a thousand percent into that. Hippo would be a great nutty neighbor. Like a 3000 lb Fred Mertz. In a year choked with good comics USG is my favorite by (squirrel) leaps and (squirrel) bounds.

Questions:

When Doreen talks about nuts does she mean botanical nuts, culinary nuts, or both?

Which C compiler does Nancy prefer? CMake? gcc? Borland? (Visual Studio is not up for consideration as Nancy is not evil)

Regards,
Gary

R: Haha, yes! LET US TALK ABOUT C COMPILERS. Nancy uses gcc for day-to-day compilation, but has messed around with Borland Turbo C in order to get some classic games running. As for nuts, it really depends on the context, but I'd guess it's usually culinary. Erica? You are the nut expert here and know where to buy acorn flour, so I defer to you.

E: Ryan, I only know where to buy acorn flour because it's the main ingredient in a popular Korean dish and there's a Korean market down the street. For the most part, she's going to be talking about nuts she can eat. They're a decently large part of her diet (along with beans and yogurt and seeds) because they're rich in protein, and Ryan and I agreed early on that someone who is aware of animal sentience has to be a vegetarian.

Dear Ryan and Erica,

I am a cranky middle-aged male comicreader and devoted fan of The Unbeatable Squirrel Girl. Her light-hearted but respectful interaction with deep Marvel mythology is a comfort to those of us who have given up our dreams of ever visiting the moon of Titan IRL. Bookssuch asyours and Ant-Man allow us to look back momentarily like Camus' Sisyphus and say, "It wasn't entirely a waste of time." In fact mybiggestanxietyover a post-Secret Wars cosmosis the effect it will have on Doreen's adventures. I want to be clear, I harbor no prejudice against female Thors. I simply fear change. (Those darn kids with their texting and their Ultimate Universes!) The appeal of the book depends so much on long, long-established canon. What happens after the shake-up? Any arboreal species will tell you it's difficult and dangerous to scamper up a tree that has no roots. On the other hand, at the risk of sounding pessimistic if her purpose is to puncture pretentious and pervasive pomposity (sorry, it was Stan who learned me how to talk good) we may need her now more than ever.

Chip Karpus
Elyria, Ohio

P.S. Attached are photos of a colony of white squirrels that live in the town square in Oberlin, Ohio and have been adopted as unofficial mascots of the college. Coincidentally about 60 miles up the road a much larger army of mutant black squirrels has overtaken the campus of Kent State, descendants supposedly of a couple of lab specimens released by a megalomaniacal zoology professor in an attempt (not making any of this up) to give visual distinction to the landscape. Only the Celestials know what would happen if they ever got together.

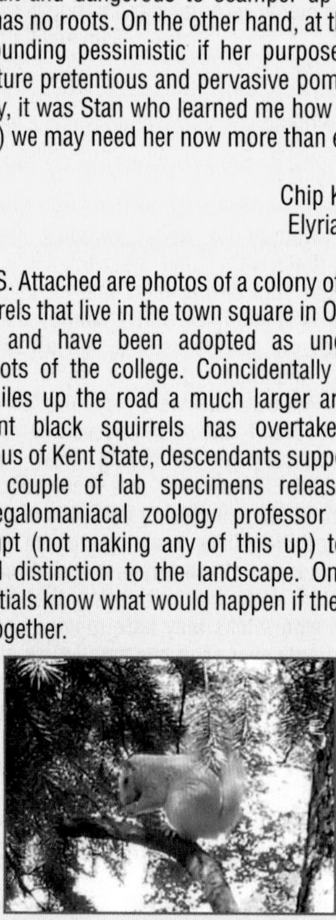

R: White squirrel COLONY? That's amazing. I live in Toronto and we have a famous white squirrel that always hangs out in the same park, so spotting that is always a thrill. I can't imagine what it's like having a colony nearby!

Your zoology prof introducing squirrels is not the first time that's happened, actually. They weren't always common in cities: in fact, in 1856 the sight of a squirrel it was an escaped pet - was so unusual that the New York Daily Times reported a crowd of hundreds gathering to watch it. But by the 1870s it was a full-on fad to introduce squirrels to city parks in America, with the idea that it gave a touch of the country to city-dwellers, which would help maintain their health and sanity. And the fact they were super cute, super trusting, and willing to take food from people's outstretched hands didn't hurt! Along with squirrels, there were experiments in introducing peacocks and deer, but those weren't nearly as successful.

Please send me updates if the white and black squirrels ever cross over; the Celestials are horrible at email.

E: WAIT. RYAN. Did we discuss the 1870s introduction of squirrels into American parks in part due to their docile nature and in part to create a more rural atmosphere, or did we just do the same research into the history of squirrels in Central Park? There's also a white squirrel in my city that everyone freaks out over. And yeah, we're going to be needing photos of those giant black squirrels.

Hey Squirrel Girl Squad!

I have always read comics to my daughter Nova. Even when I was pregnant with her. When she was two, she developed her first favorite which was The Amazing Spider-Man. At three she had a heart-wrenching breakdown in the back of the car, sobbing hysterically that when she grew up she wanted to be Spider-Man but she couldn't be Spider-Man because she was a girl. Despite our best efforts and gender neutral parenting tactics, we could not console her. I am a Ms Marvel fan and had been reading the current story arc so I pulled all the issues and read those to her, but they didn't really capture her interest. Around this time, Thor #1 came out and while her eyes lit up at the sight of a female Thor, she couldn't really follow the story. A few months passed, and my friend suggested we pick up The Unbeatable Squirrel Girl and generously donated the first four issues. Man was she hooked. When the time came to pick out a Halloween costume, it was no contest. Eat nuts and kick butts all day long.

Thank you for providing a role model for our little girl. Thank you for having my back when I told her girls can be awesome superheroes too. Thank you for the laughs. Even though working with faux fur was a battle in itself.

Mary

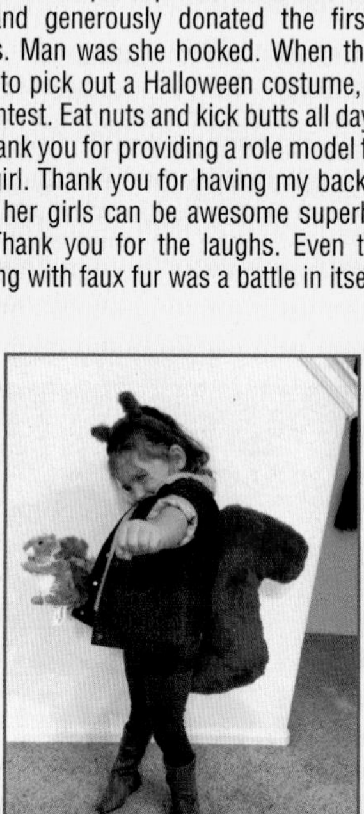

R: Mary, thank you for this. Sometimes people think making a comic about a lady who can talk to squirrels is a pretty silly way to spend your time, but letters like this and experiences like what your daughter had - are so important. So important! I'm so glad your daughter found Squirrel Girl. And her costume is top notch, so all those struggles with faux fur were worth it. Tell her she leaves no nut uneaten and no butt un-kicked!

Okay, see y'all next month! Keep writing!

Attention, Squirrel Scouts! Make sure to check out our production blog, **unbeatablesquirrelgirl.tumblr.com**, where we post behind-the-scenes stuff on how the book gets made, along with all sorts of cool things *you* make: fanart, cosplay, whatever!

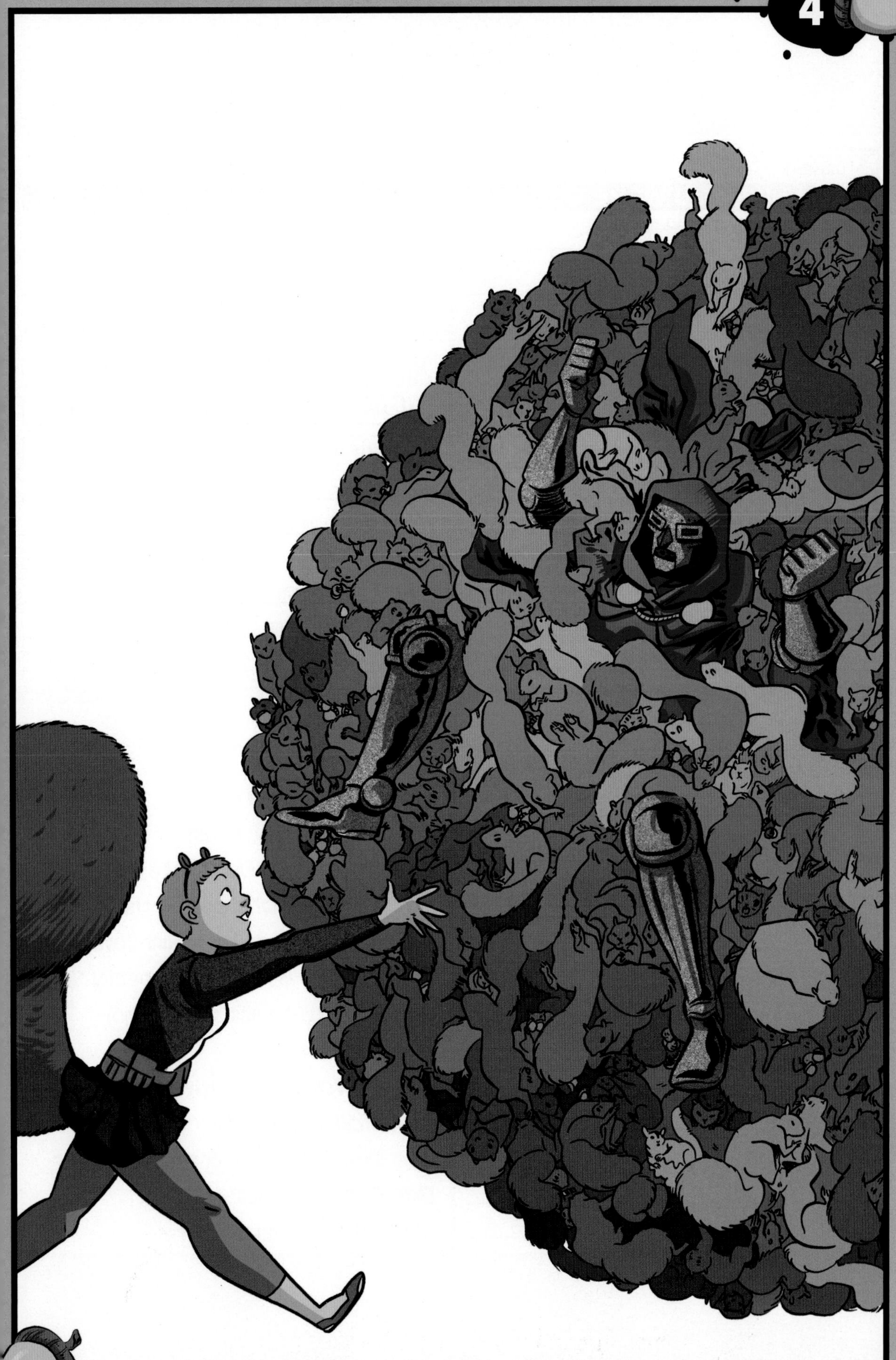

*Doreen Green isn't just a second-year computer science student: she secretly also has all the powers of both squirrel and girl! She uses her amazing abilities to fight crime **and** be as awesome as possible. You know her as...**The Unbeatable Squirrel Girl!** Find out what she's been up to, with...*

Squirrel Girl in a nutshell

[X] URGENT

WHILE YOU WERE OUT

To: The United Nations

From: Squirrel Girl

Of: ~~The Future~~ The Present

[X] TELEPHONED [ ] PLEASE CALL
[ ] CAME TO SEE YOU [ ] WILL CALL AGAIN
[X] WANTS TO SEE YOU [ ] RETURNED YOUR CALL

Message: You guys, Doctor Doom came back to the ***sixties*** (which is ***now***) (obviously) and is going to take over the world TOMORROW unless we stop him, but he's got ***Future Wikipedia*** that already shows he's gonna win so I'm not really sure what to do, if you have any idea I'm all ears (not a pun even though I wear a second set of ears for fashion reasons)

[ ] URGENT

WHILE YOU WERE OUT

To: Nancy Whitehead

From: Squirrel Girl

Of: The apartment we share because we're roommates

[X] TELEPHONED [ ] PLEASE CALL
[ ] CAME TO SEE YOU [X] WILL CALL AGAIN
[ ] WANTS TO SEE YOU [ ] RETURNED YOUR CALL

Message: Nancy it was super cool that you came back in time to rescue me and all these other CS students trapped here!! ps I know you don't have a phone, will you write me back on one of these notes because I've got like a thousand of them [ ]yes [ ]no

[ ] URGENT

WHILE YOU WERE OUT

To: Mr. and Mrs. Stark

From: Squirrel Girl

Of: The Iron Man Fandom

[ ] TELEPHONED [ ] PLEASE CALL
[X] CAME TO SEE YOU [ ] WILL CALL AGAIN
[ ] WANTS TO SEE YOU [ ] RETURNED YOUR CALL

Message: hey you don't know me but I just wanted to say the two of you should definitely have a baby in a few decades and name him Tony!! okay, thank me later

Ryan North Writer
Erica Henderson Artist
Rico Renzi Color Artist
VC's Clayton Cowles Letterer
Erica Henderson Cover Artist
John Tyler Christopher Variant Cover Artist
CK Russell & Lissa Pattillo Special Thanks
Chris Robinson Assistant Editor
Wil Moss Editor
Tom Brevoort Executive Editor
Axel Alonso Editor In Chief
Joe Quesada Chief Creative Officer
Dan Buckley Publisher
Alan Fine Exec. Producer

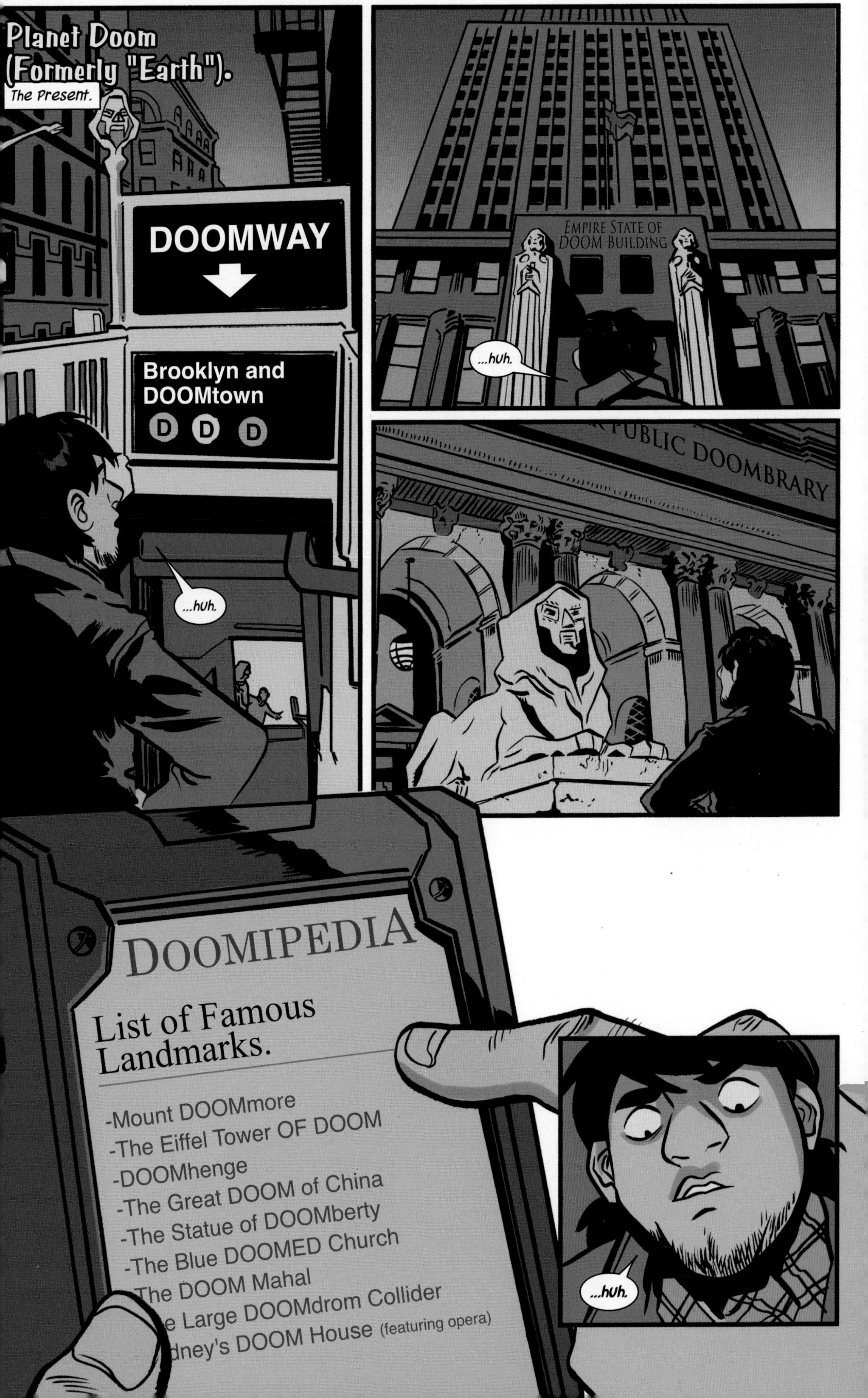
Planet Doom (Formerly "Earth").
The Present.
DOOMWAY
Brooklyn and DOOMtown
D D D
...huh.
EMPIRE STATE OF DOOM BUILDING
...huh.
PUBLIC DOOMBRARY
DOOMIPEDIA
List of Famous Landmarks.
-Mount DOOMmore
-The Eiffel Tower OF DOOM
-DOOMhenge
-The Great DOOM of China
-The Statue of DOOMberty
-The Blue DOOMED Church
The DOOM Mahal
e Large DOOMdrom Collider
dney's DOOM House (featuring opera)
...huh.

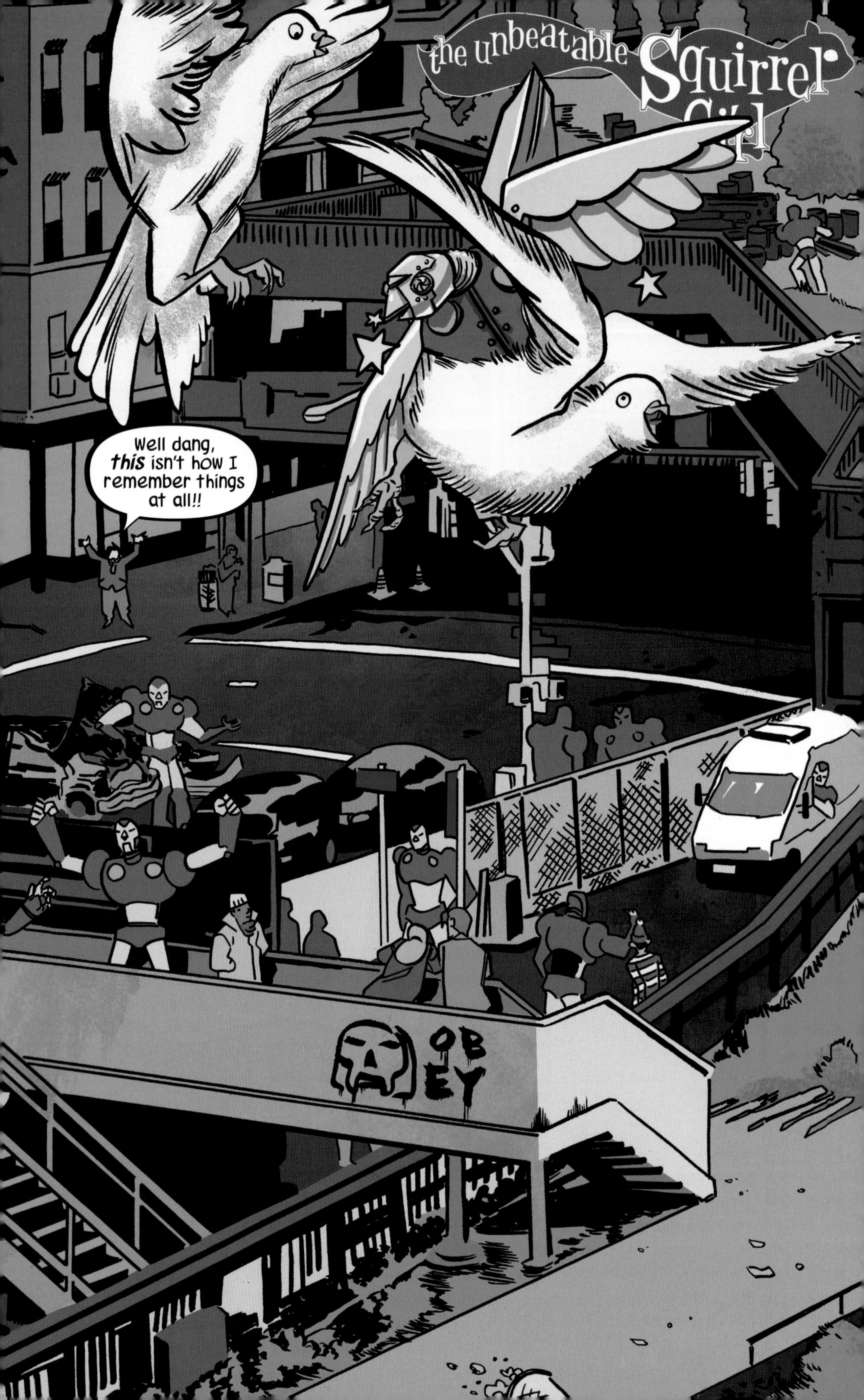
the unbeatable Squirrel Girl
Well dang, this isn't how I remember things at all!!
OBEY

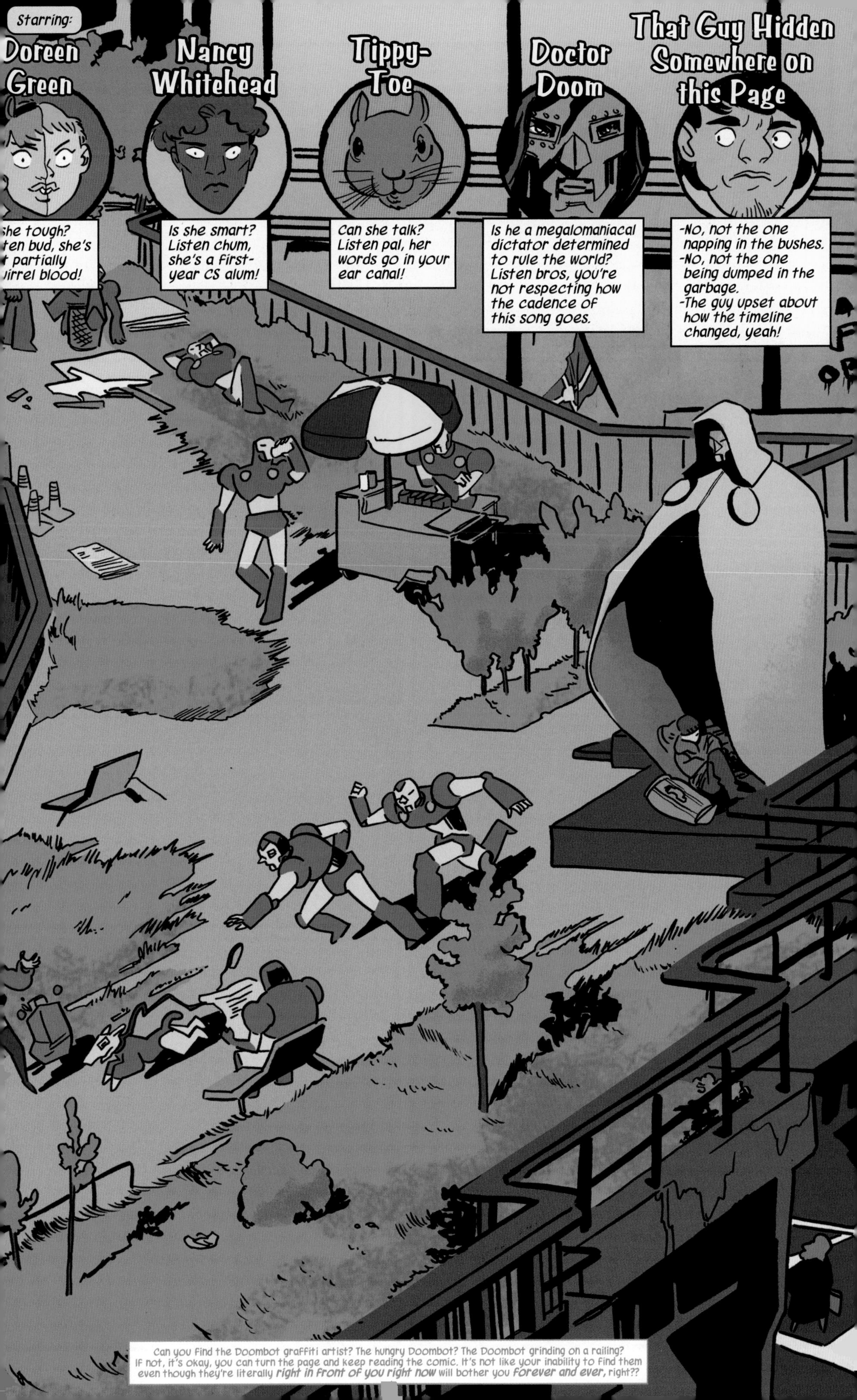
Starring:
Doreen Green
Nancy Whitehead
Tippy-Toe
Doctor Doom
That Guy Hidden Somewhere on this Page
she tough? ten bud, she's partially uirrel blood!
Is she smart? Listen chum, she's a first-year CS alum!
Can she talk? Listen pal, her words go in your ear canal!
Is he a megalomaniacal dictator determined to rule the world? Listen bros, you're not respecting how the cadence of this song goes.
-No, not the one napping in the bushes. -No, not the one being dumped in the garbage. -The guy upset about how the timeline changed, yeah!
Can you find the Doombot graffiti artist? The hungry Doombot? The Doombot grinding on a railing? If not, it's okay, you can turn the page and keep reading the comic. It's not like your inability to find them even though they're literally right in front of you right now will bother you forever and ever, right??

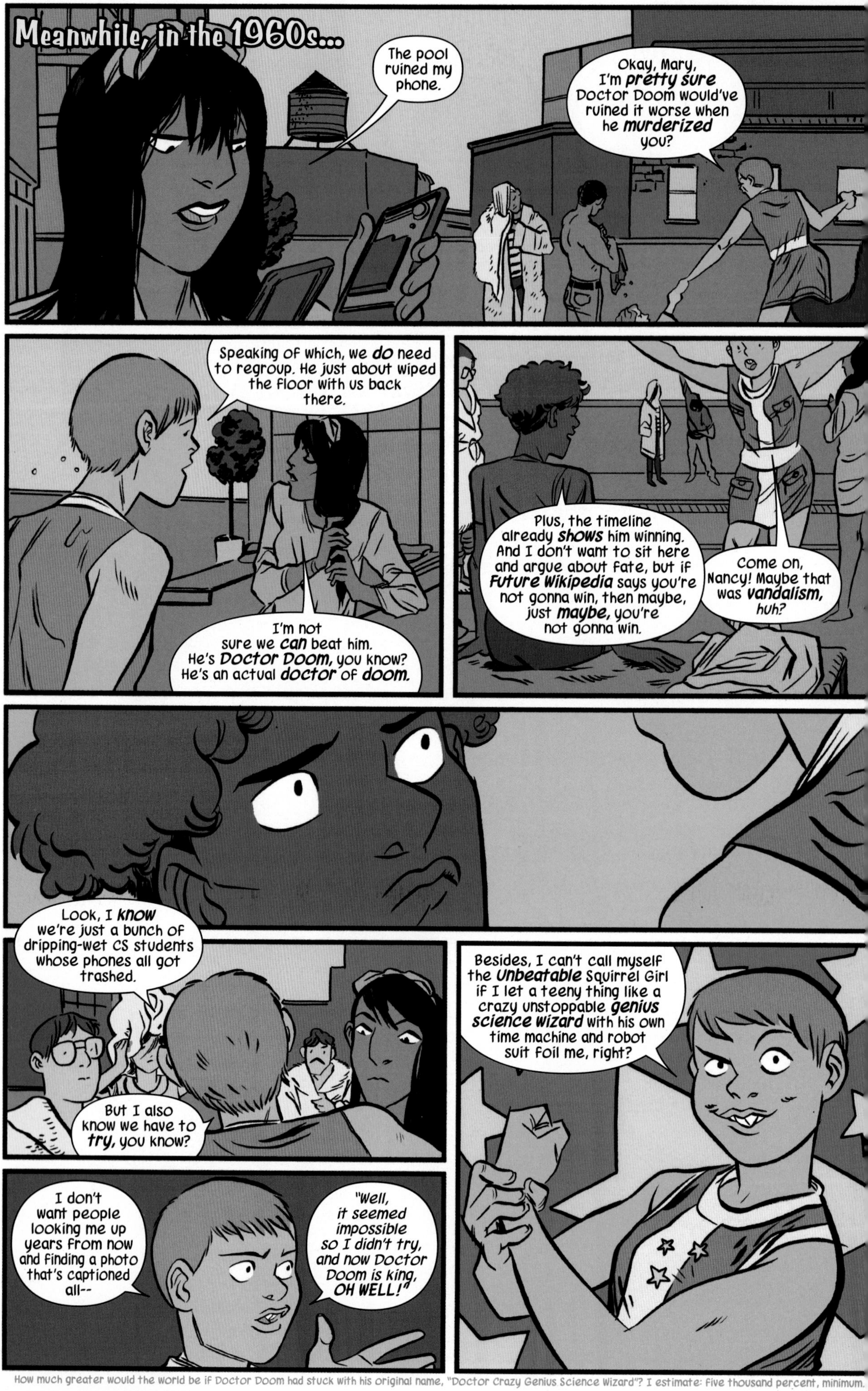
Meanwhile, in the 1960s...
The pool ruined my phone.
Okay, Mary, I'm pretty sure Doctor Doom would've ruined it worse when he murderized you?
Speaking of which, we do need to regroup. He just about wiped the floor with us back there.
I'm not sure we can beat him. He's Doctor Doom, you know? He's an actual doctor of doom.
Plus, the timeline already shows him winning. And I don't want to sit here and argue about fate, but if Future Wikipedia says you're not gonna win, then maybe, just maybe, you're not gonna win.
Come on, Nancy! Maybe that was vandalism, huh?
Look, I know we're just a bunch of dripping-wet CS students whose phones all got trashed.
But I also know we have to try, you know?
I don't want people looking me up years from now and finding a photo that's captioned all--
"Well, it seemed impossible so I didn't try, and now Doctor Doom is king, OH WELL!"
Besides, I can't call myself the Unbeatable Squirrel Girl if I let a teeny thing like a crazy unstoppable genius science wizard with his own time machine and robot suit foil me, right?

How much greater would the world be if Doctor Doom had stuck with his original name, "Doctor Crazy Genius Science Wizard"? I estimate: five thousand percent, minimum.

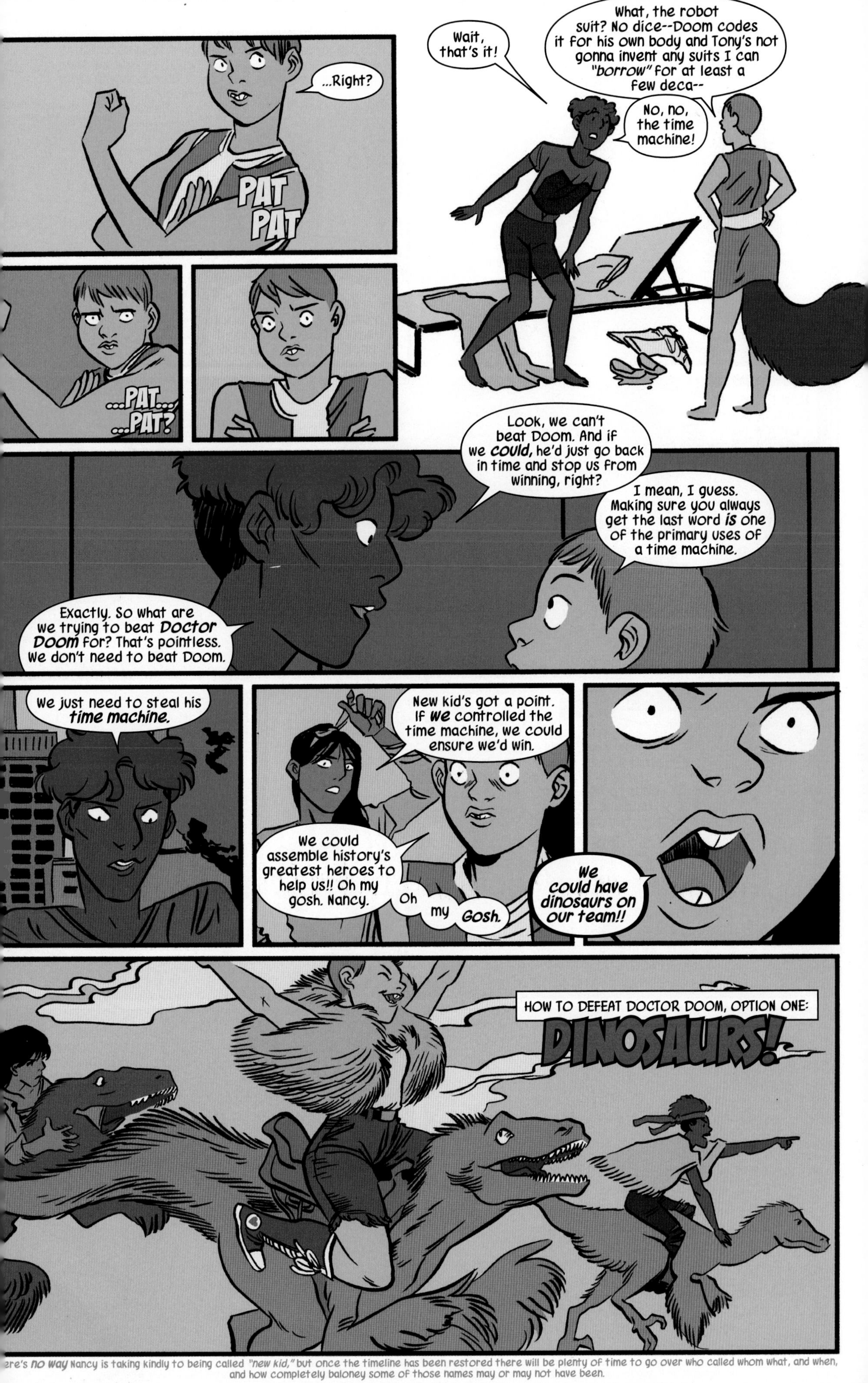
...Right?
PAT PAT
...PAT... ...PAT?
Wait, that's it!
What, the robot suit? No dice--Doom codes it for his own body and Tony's not gonna invent any suits I can "borrow" for at least a few deca--
No, no, the time machine!
Look, we can't beat Doom. And if we could, he'd just go back in time and stop us from winning, right?
I mean, I guess. Making sure you always get the last word is one of the primary uses of a time machine.
Exactly. So what are we trying to beat Doctor Doom for? That's pointless. We don't need to beat Doom.
We just need to steal his time machine.
New kid's got a point. If we controlled the time machine, we could ensure we'd win.
We could assemble history's greatest heroes to help us!! Oh my gosh. Nancy.
Oh my Gosh.
We could have dinosaurs on our team!!
HOW TO DEFEAT DOCTOR DOOM, OPTION ONE:
DINOSAURS!

ere's *no way* Nancy is taking kindly to being called *"new kid,"* but once the timeline has been restored there will be plenty of time to go over who called whom what, and when, and how completely baloney some of those names may or may not have been.

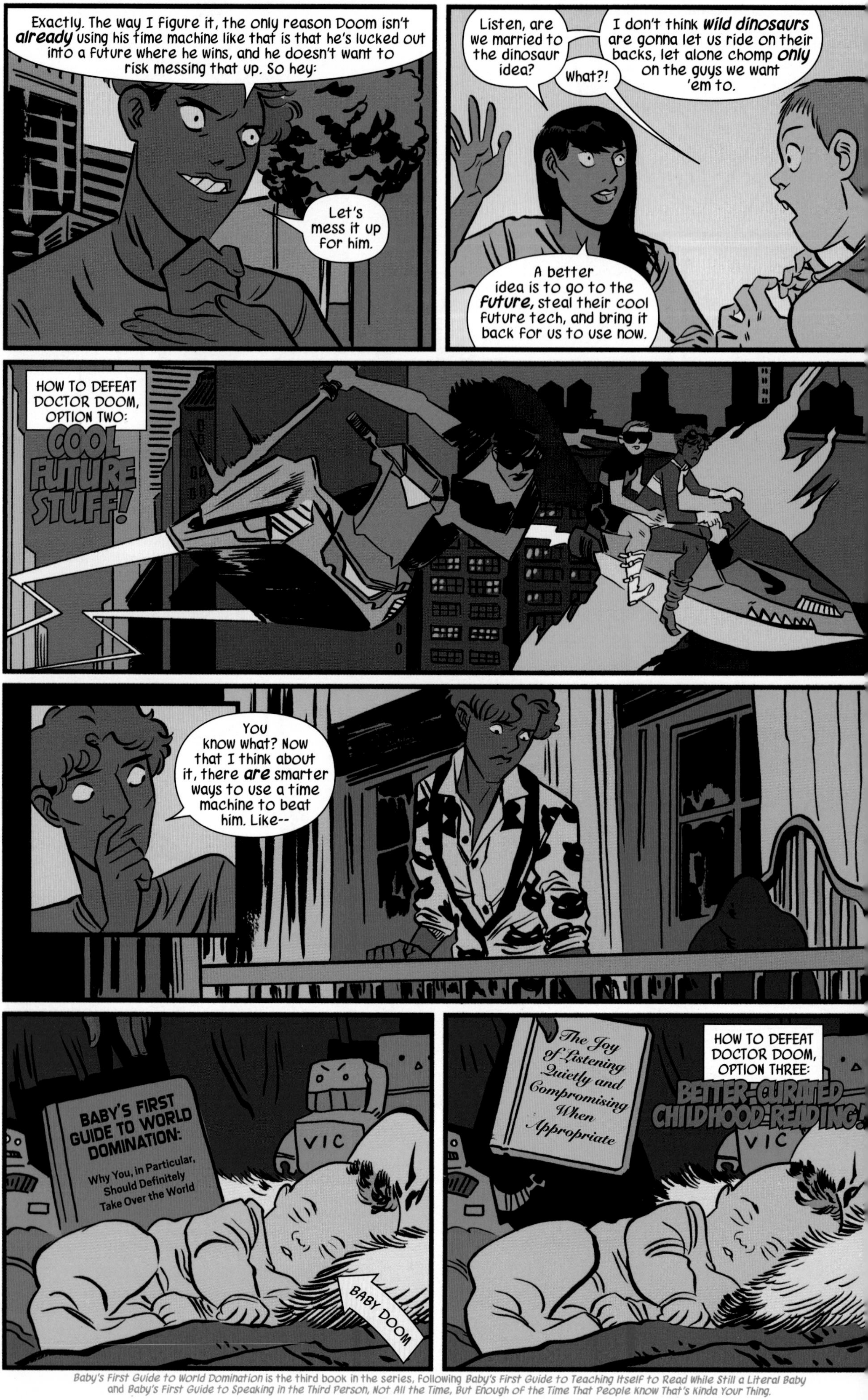
Exactly. The way I figure it, the only reason Doom isn't **already** using his time machine like that is that he's lucked out into a future where he wins, and he doesn't want to risk messing that up. So hey:
Let's mess it up for him.
Listen, are we married to the dinosaur idea?
What?!
I don't think **wild dinosaurs** are gonna let us ride on their backs, let alone chomp **only** on the guys we want 'em to.
A better idea is to go to the **future,** steal their cool future tech, and bring it back for us to use now.
HOW TO DEFEAT DOCTOR DOOM, OPTION TWO:
COOL FUTURE STUFF!
You know what? Now that I think about it, there **are** smarter ways to use a time machine to beat him. Like--
BABY'S FIRST GUIDE TO WORLD DOMINATION:
Why You, in Particular, Should Definitely Take Over the World
VIC
BABY DOOM
The Joy of Listening Quietly and Compromising When Appropriate
HOW TO DEFEAT DOCTOR DOOM, OPTION THREE:
BETTER-CURATED CHILDHOOD READING!
VIC

Baby's First Guide to World Domination is the third book in the series, following *Baby's First Guide to Teaching Itself to Read While Still a Literal Baby* and *Baby's First Guide to Speaking in the Third Person, Not All the Time, But Enough of the Time That People Know That's Kinda Your Thing.*

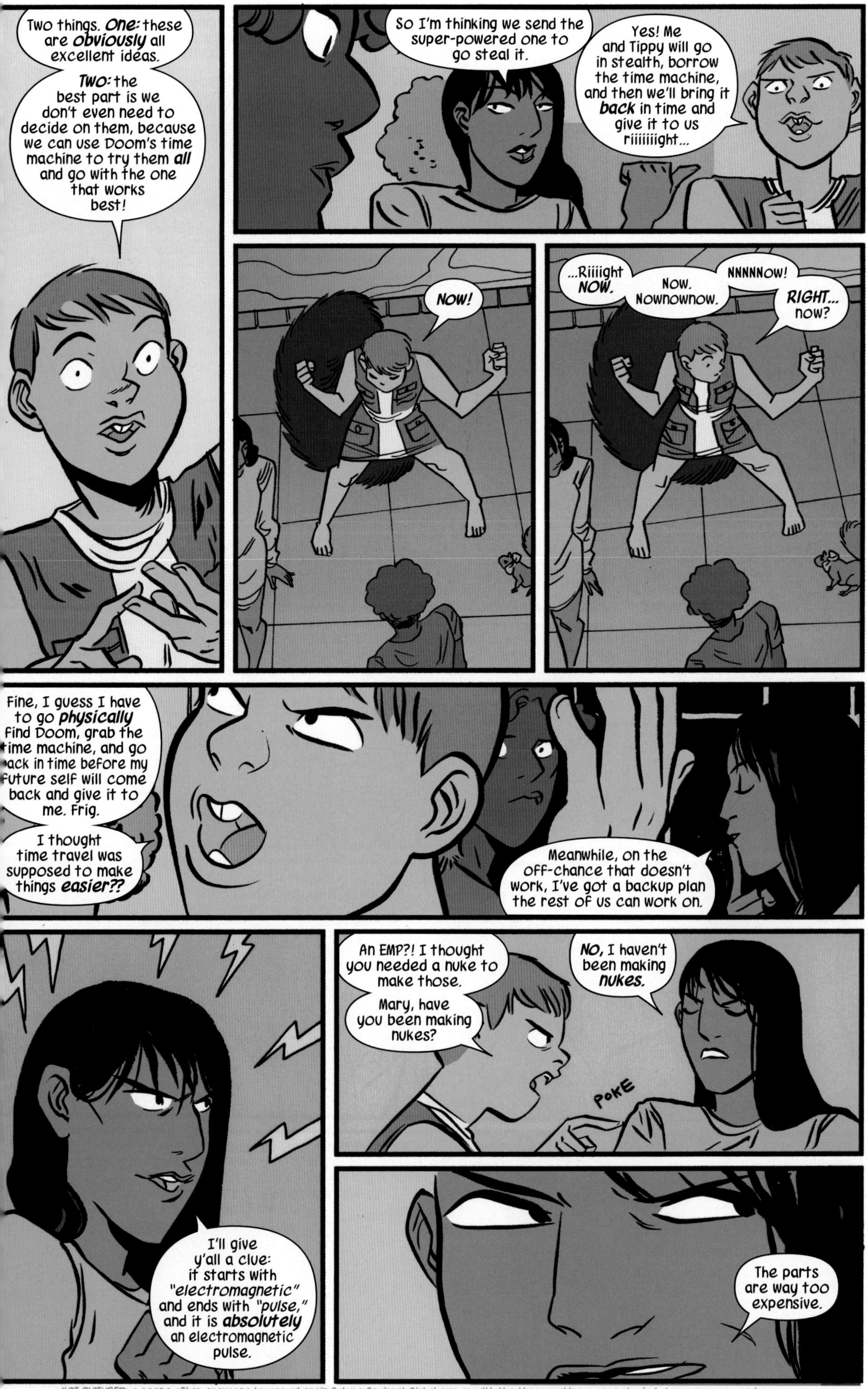

Two things. One: these are obviously all excellent ideas.
Two: the best part is we don't even need to decide on them, because we can use Doom's time machine to try them all and go with the one that works best!
So I'm thinking we send the super-powered one to go steal it.
Yes! Me and Tippy will go in stealth, borrow the time machine, and then we'll bring it back in time and give it to us riiiiiiight...
NOW!
...Riiiight NOW.
Now. Nownownow.
NNNNNow!
RIGHT... now?
Fine, I guess I have to go physically find Doom, grab the time machine, and go back in time before my future self will come back and give it to me. Frig.
I thought time travel was supposed to make things easier??
Meanwhile, on the off-chance that doesn't work, I've got a backup plan the rest of us can work on.
I'll give y'all a clue: it starts with "electromagnetic" and ends with "pulse," and it is absolutely an electromagnetic pulse.
An EMP?! I thought you needed a nuke to make those.
Mary, have you been making nukes?
NO, I haven't been making nukes.
POKE
The parts are way too expensive.

NOT PICTURED: a scene after everyone leaves, wherein Future Squirrel Girl shows up with the time machine, sees nobody is here anymore, and says "Dang it, I really need to wear a watch with my costume because I have *no idea* what time it was I was talking about" and disappears again.

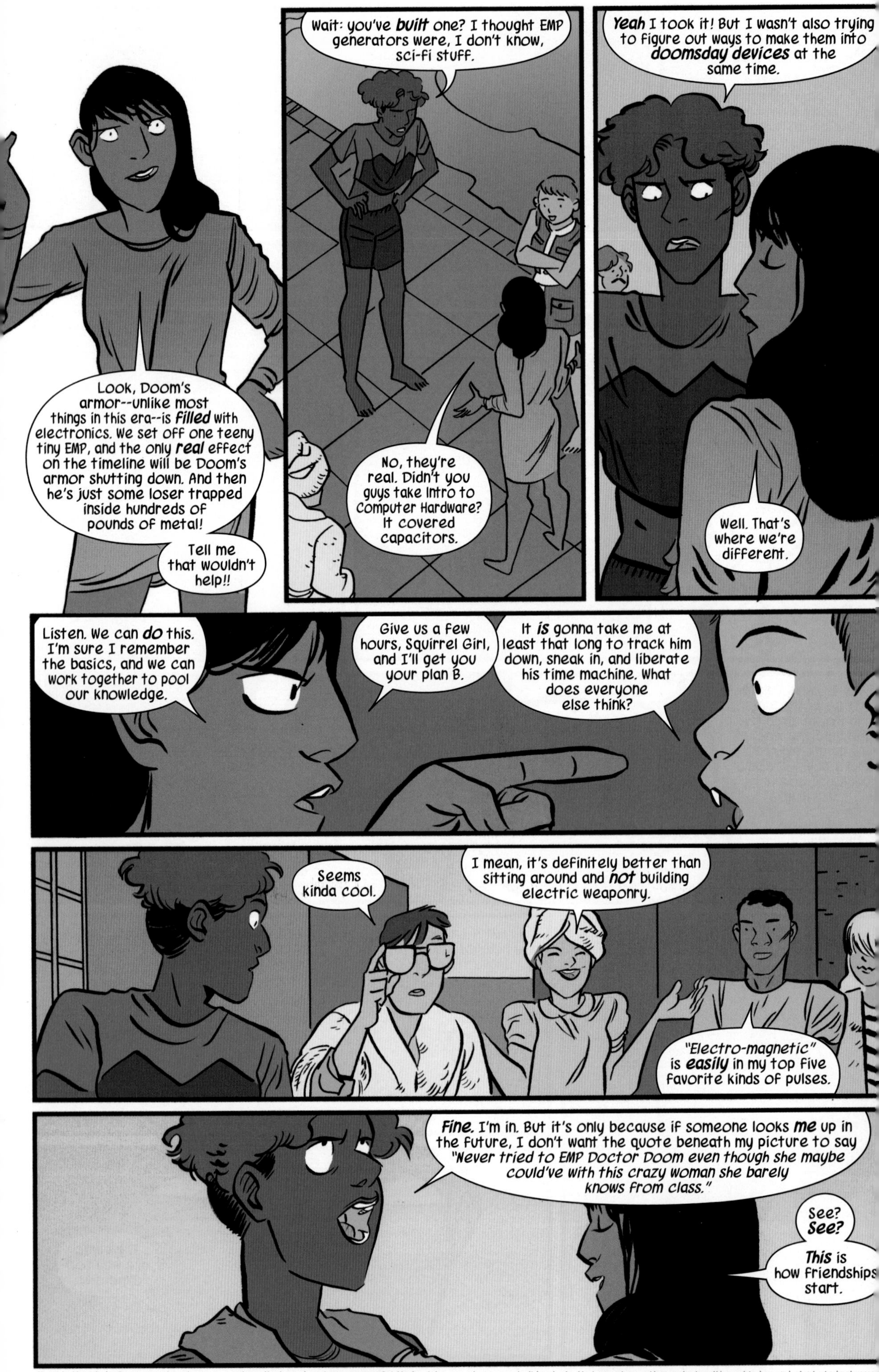
Look, Doom's armor--unlike most things in this era--is *filled* with electronics. We set off one teeny tiny EMP, and the only *real* effect on the timeline will be Doom's armor shutting down. And then he's just some loser trapped inside hundreds of pounds of metal!
Tell me that wouldn't help!!
Wait: you've *built* one? I thought EMP generators were, I don't know, sci-fi stuff.
No, they're real. Didn't you guys take Intro to Computer Hardware? It covered capacitors.
Yeah I took it! But I wasn't also trying to figure out ways to make them into *doomsday devices* at the same time.
Well. That's where we're different.
Listen. We can *do* this. I'm sure I remember the basics, and we can work together to pool our knowledge.
Give us a few hours, Squirrel Girl, and I'll get you your plan B.
It *is* gonna take me at least that long to track him down, sneak in, and liberate his time machine. What does everyone else think?
Seems kinda cool.
I mean, it's definitely better than sitting around and *not* building electric weaponry.
"Electro-magnetic" is *easily* in my top five favorite kinds of pulses.
Fine. I'm in. But it's only because if someone looks *me* up in the future, I don't want the quote beneath my picture to say *"Never tried to EMP Doctor Doom even though she maybe could've with this crazy woman she barely knows from class."*
See? *See?*
This is how friendships start.

Mary is the kind of person who chooses a university based on how successful their clubs are where you build robots that smash up other robots with sawblades and giant sledgehamm
Mary is the kind of person who has the right friggin' idea!!

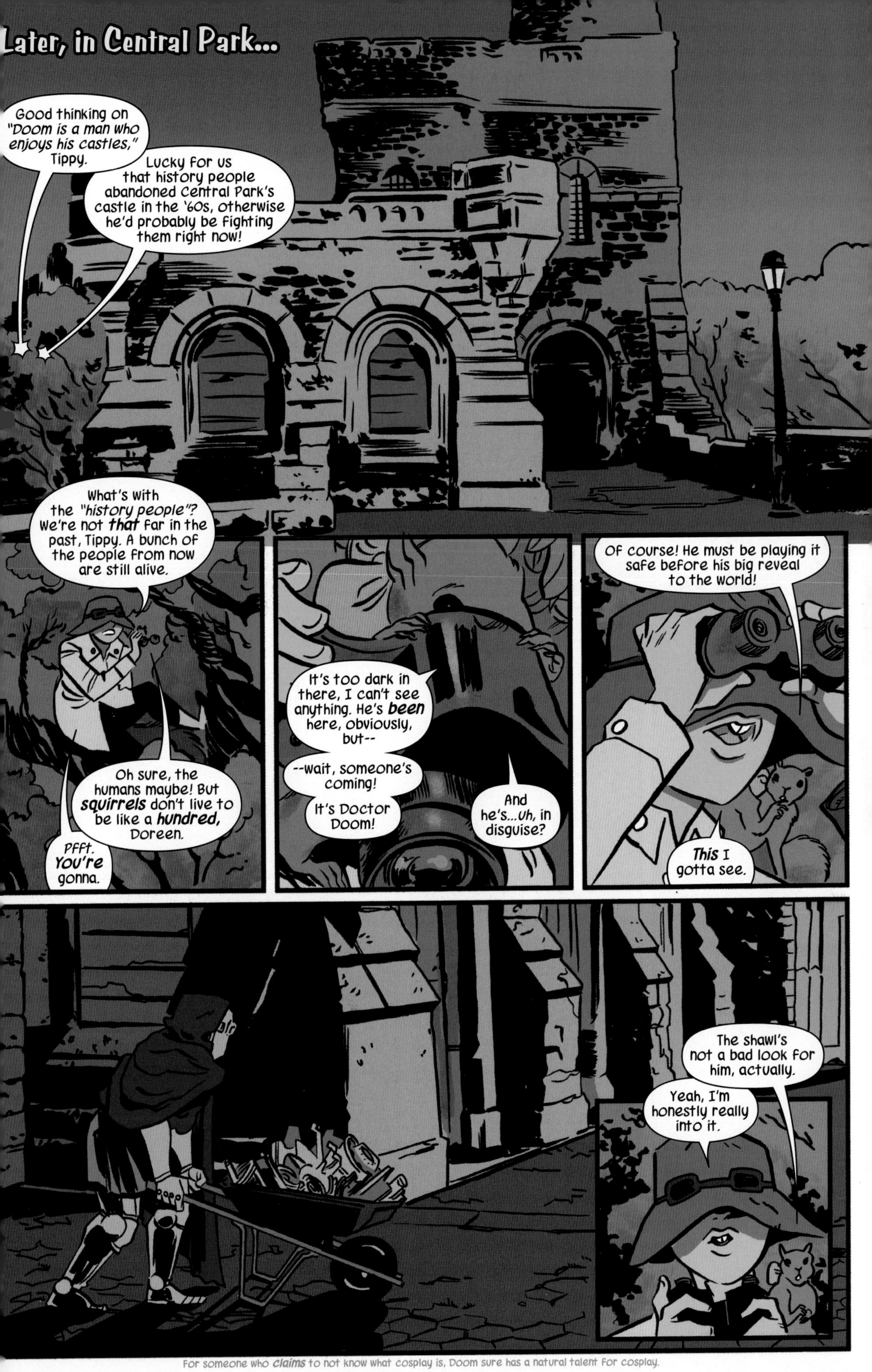
Later, in Central Park...
Good thinking on "Doom is a man who enjoys his castles," Tippy.
Lucky for us that history people abandoned Central Park's castle in the '60s, otherwise he'd probably be fighting them right now!
What's with the "history people"? We're not that far in the past, Tippy. A bunch of the people from now are still alive.
Oh sure, the humans maybe! But squirrels don't live to be like a hundred, Doreen.
Pfft. You're gonna.
It's too dark in there, I can't see anything. He's been here, obviously, but--
--wait, someone's coming!
It's Doctor Doom!
And he's...uh, in disguise?
Of course! He must be playing it safe before his big reveal to the world!
This I gotta see.
The shawl's not a bad look for him, actually.
Yeah, I'm honestly really into it.
For someone who *claims* to not know what cosplay is, Doom sure has a natural talent for cosplay.

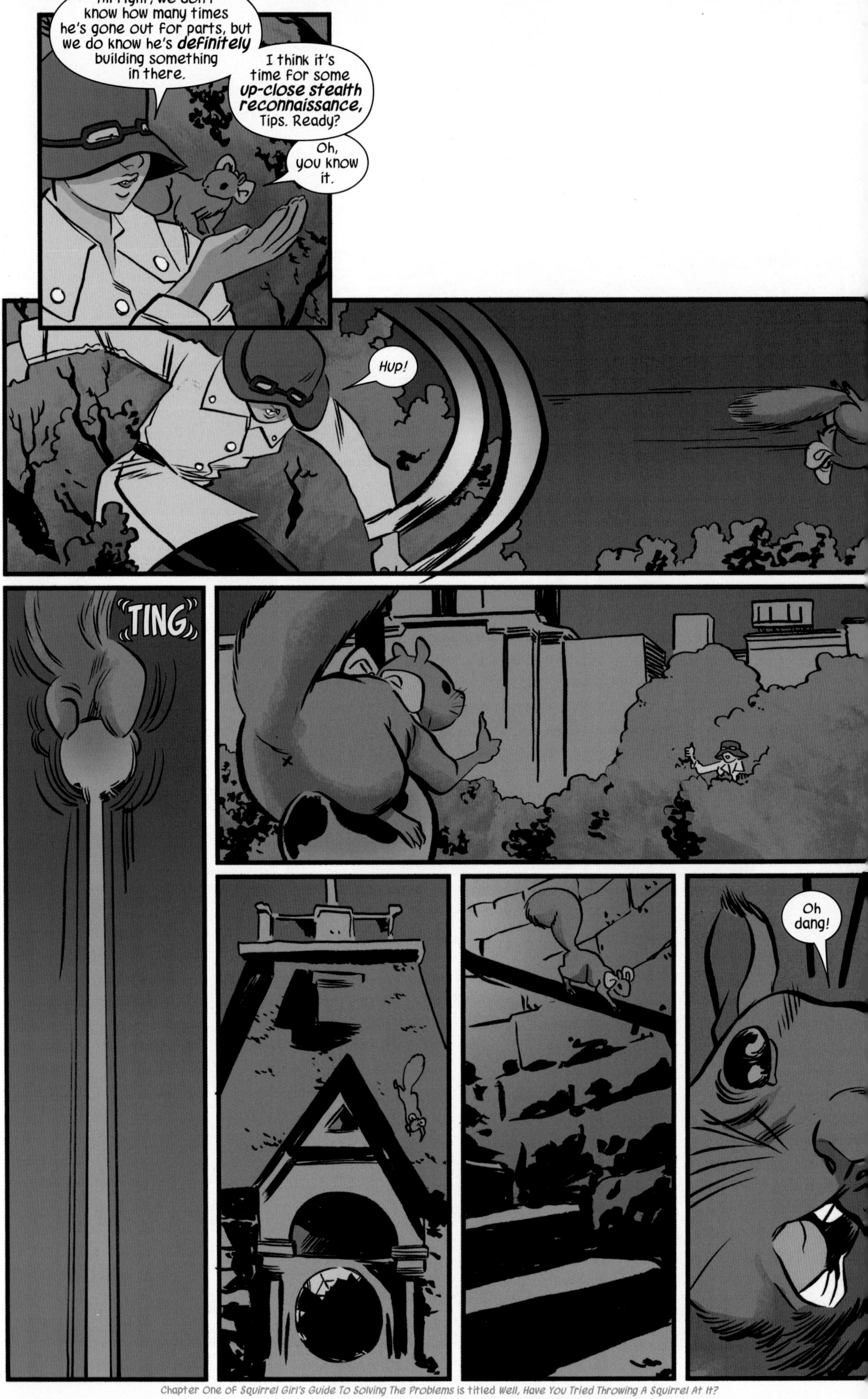
All right, we don't know how many times he's gone out for parts, but we do know he's definitely building something in there.
I think it's time for some up-close stealth reconnaissance, Tips. Ready?
Oh, you know it.
Hup!
TING
Oh dang!

Chapter One of Squirrel Girl's Guide To Solving The Problems is titled Well, Have You Tried Throwing A Squirrel At It?

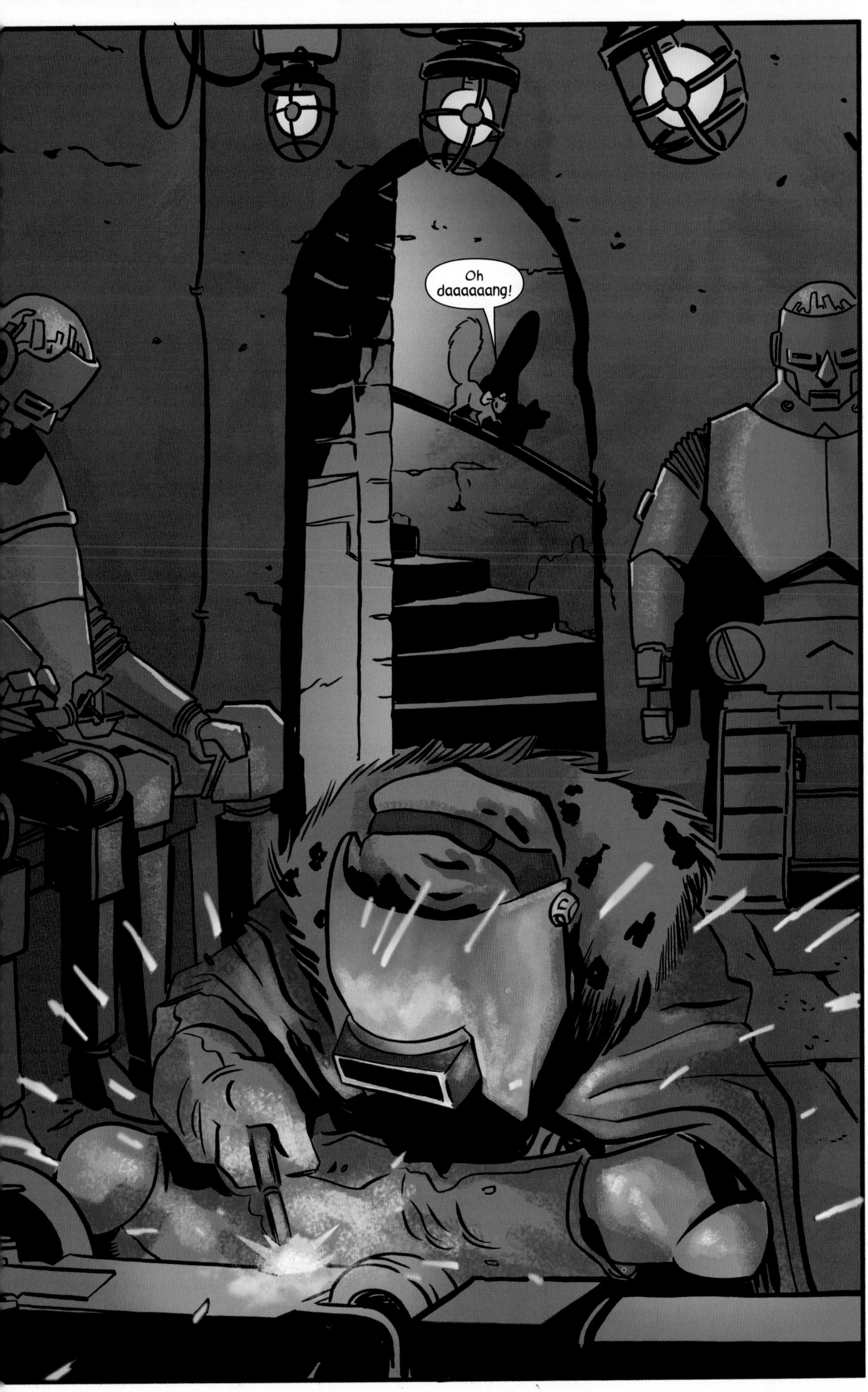
Oh daaaaaang!

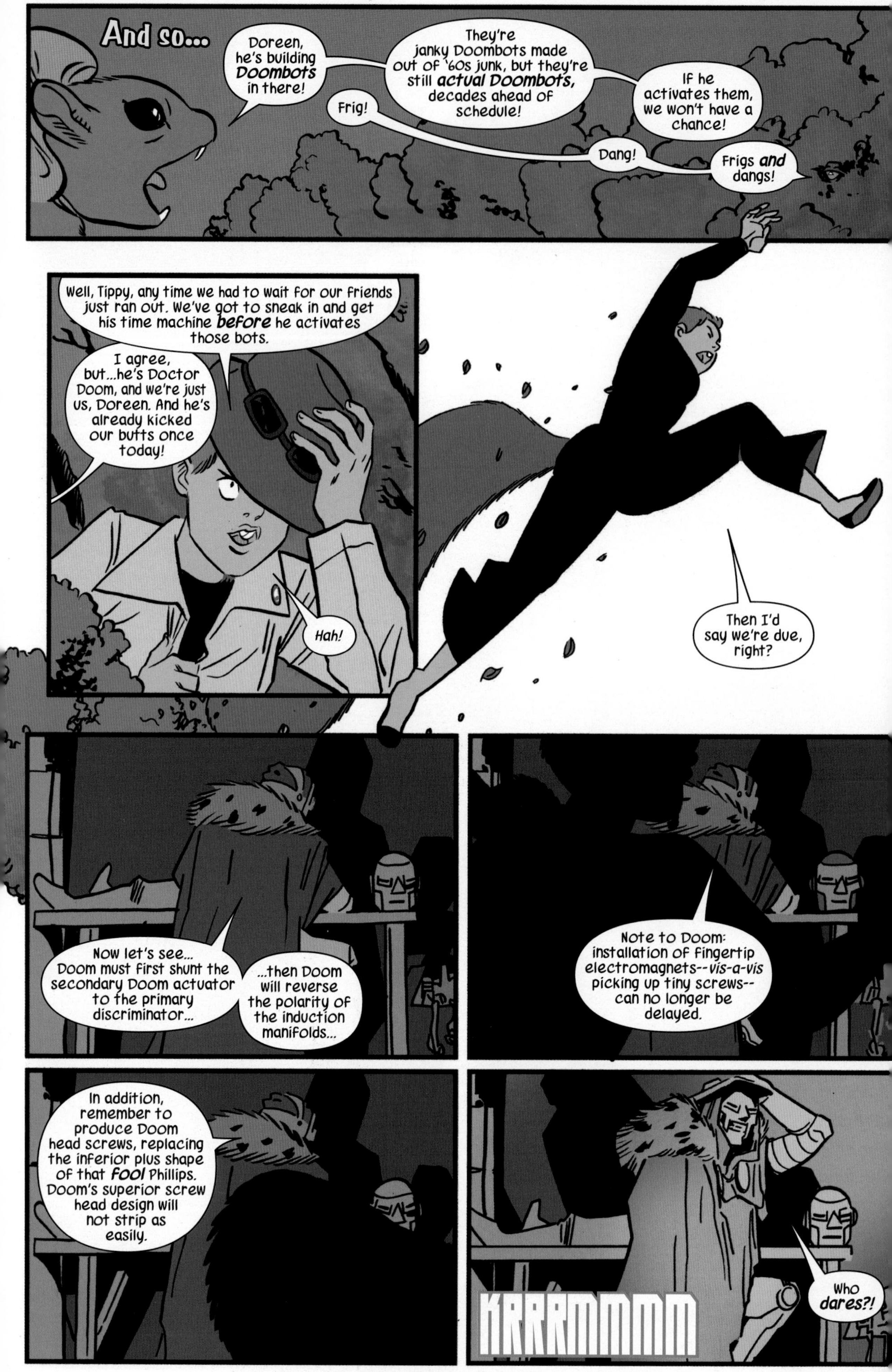
And so...
Doreen, he's building *Doombots* in there!
They're janky Doombots made out of '60s junk, but they're still *actual Doombots,* decades ahead of schedule!
If he activates them, we won't have a chance!
Frig!
Dang!
Frigs *and* dangs!
Well, Tippy, any time we had to wait for our friends just ran out. We've got to sneak in and get his time machine *before* he activates those bots.
I agree, but...he's Doctor Doom, and we're just us, Doreen. And he's already kicked our butts once today!
Hah!
Then I'd say we're due, right?
Now let's see... Doom must first shunt the secondary Doom actuator to the primary discriminator...
...then Doom will reverse the polarity of the induction manifolds...
Note to Doom: installation of fingertip electromagnets--*vis-a-vis* picking up tiny screws--can no longer be delayed.
In addition, remember to produce Doom head screws, replacing the inferior plus shape of that *fool* Phillips. Doom's superior screw head design will not strip as easily.
KRRRMMMM
Who *dares?!*

Anyone who works with screws for a living is remembering all the stripped screws in their past, nodding their head, and quietly whispering *"Today is the day I agree with Doctor Doom."*

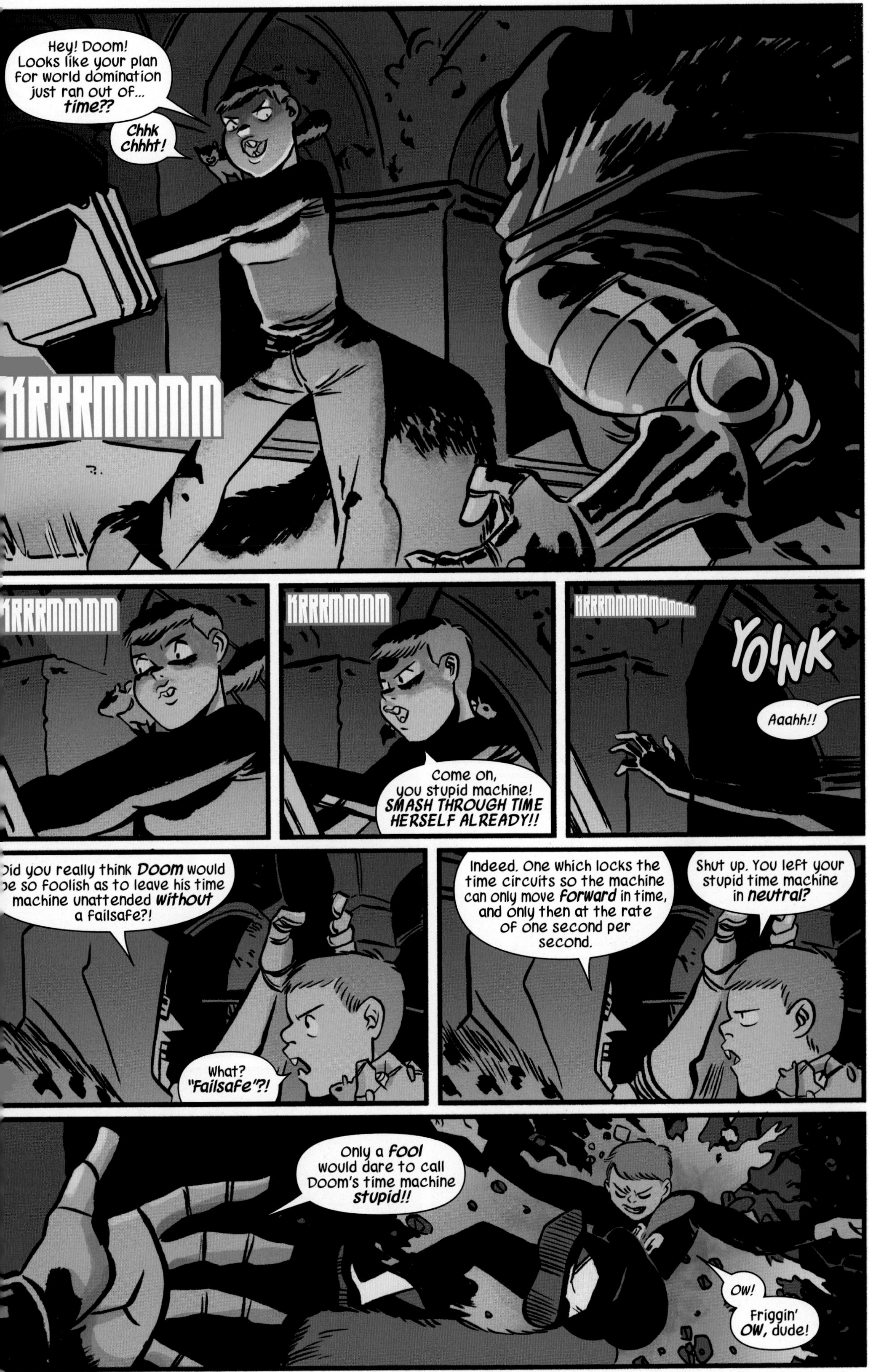
Hey! Doom! Looks like your plan for world domination just ran out of... time??
Chhk chhht!
KRRRMMMM
KRRRMMMM
KRRRMMMM
Come on, you stupid machine! SMASH THROUGH TIME HERSELF ALREADY!!
KRRRMMMMMmmmm
YOINK
Aaahh!!
Did you really think Doom would be so foolish as to leave his time machine unattended without a failsafe?!
What? "Failsafe"?!
Indeed. One which locks the time circuits so the machine can only move forward in time, and only then at the rate of one second per second.
Shut up. You left your stupid time machine in neutral?
Only a fool would dare to call Doom's time machine stupid!!
Ow! Friggin' OW, dude!

One second per second is a pretty popular speed to careen through time at. Why, I'd bet *money* it's the time travel that you're personally doing right now!!

Look. I don't **want** to fight you, Doom, and I'm guessing you don't want to fight me either.

Nothing would give me more pleasure.

...Okay.

Okay, fair enough. Let me rephrase that.

On the contrary.

I don't want **US** to fight, okay? And okay, **yes**, I was trying to steal your time machine just now, but only to end this **peacefully**, Doom!

There must be some way we can both get what we want!

Doom desires nothing less than world domination, and unless you wish for the same, there can be no common ground.

Come on, once I found common ground with **Galactus**. Galactus, dude! I'm sure there's **something** we can do here.

Hah. Galactus is **a child**, unable to focus on anything but his next meal.

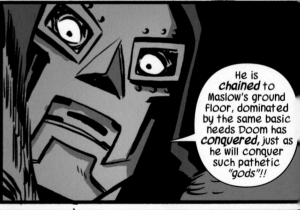

He is **chained** to Maslow's ground floor, dominated by the same basic needs Doom has **conquered**, just as he will conquer such pathetic "gods"!!

KRASH

Dude, did you just namecheck **Maslow's Hierarchy of Needs** in a friggin' **fistfight?**

IF you don't know it, Maslow's Hierarchy of Needs basically says "yo, ain't nobody self-actualizing their bad selves if they're friggin' hungry or sad or whatever," only Maslow didn't say "yo" or "friggin'" nearly as much in his book as I did in my summary of it here (his loss).

I'm... sincerely impressed, actually??

Doom conquers all psychological theory as readily as he will conquer this planet.

For Doom--

--conquers--

--all.

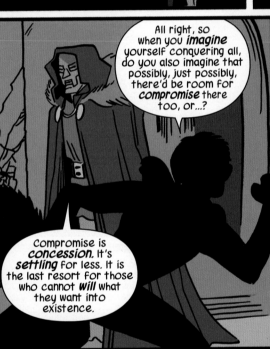

All right, so when you *imagine* yourself conquering all, do you also imagine that possibly, just possibly, there'd be room for *compromise* there too, or...?

Compromise is *concession*. It's *settling* for less. It is the last resort for those who cannot *will* what they want into existence.

Compromise is for the *weak!*

You--

--you put on a good show, Victor. Talking like a monster, acting monstrous, dressing up as scary as you can.

But I got some bad news for you:

I don't *believe* in monsters.

Beneath that cold metal mask, you're still human. Human like me.

I believe you'll listen to reason.

And I don't believe humans stop *being* human even when they pretend they're monsters.

Then you will die.

Okay, dude, I'm trying here, but you're *really* not making this easy!!

You put on a good show, Victor. Talking like a monster, acting monstrous, gluing purple fur on your armor, juggling, spinning plates, doing jazz hands constantly. It's an impressive, extremely confusing show.

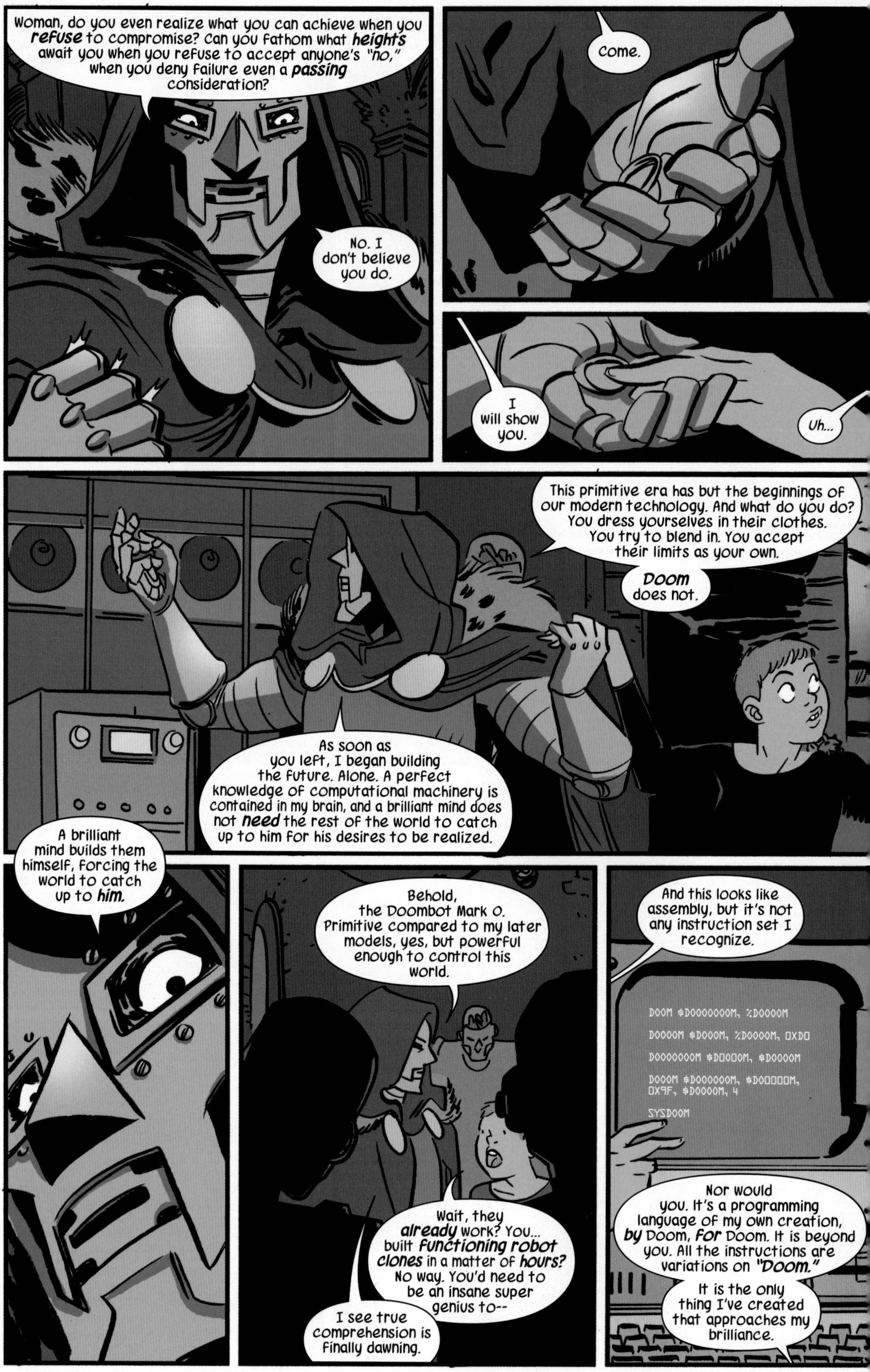
Woman, do you even realize what you can achieve when you *refuse* to compromise? Can you fathom what *heights* await you when you refuse to accept anyone's *"no,"* when you deny failure even a *passing* consideration?
No. I don't believe you do.
Come.
I will show you.
Uh...
This primitive era has but the beginnings of our modern technology. And what do you do? You dress yourselves in their clothes. You try to blend in. You accept their limits as your own.
Doom does not.
As soon as you left, I began building the future. Alone. A perfect knowledge of computational machinery is contained in my brain, and a brilliant mind does not *need* the rest of the world to catch up to him for his desires to be realized.
A brilliant mind builds them himself, forcing the world to catch up to *him.*
Behold, the Doombot Mark 0. Primitive compared to my later models, yes, but powerful enough to control this world.
Wait, they *already* work? You... built *functioning robot clones* in a matter of *hours?* No way. You'd need to be an insane super genius to--
I see true comprehension is finally dawning.
And this looks like assembly, but it's not any instruction set I recognize.
DOOM $DOOOOOOOM, %DOOOOM
DOOOOM $DOOOM, %DOOOOM, 0XD0
DOOOOOOOM $D0O0OM, $DOOOOM
DOOOM $DOOOOOOM, $DO0000M,
0X9F, $DOOOOM, 4
SYSDOOM
Nor would you. It's a programming language of my own creation, *by* Doom, *for* Doom. It is beyond you. All the instructions are variations on *"Doom."*
It is the only thing I've created that approaches my brilliance.

It's a good language because it reminds me of myself. And doom in general too. So, that's two reasons.

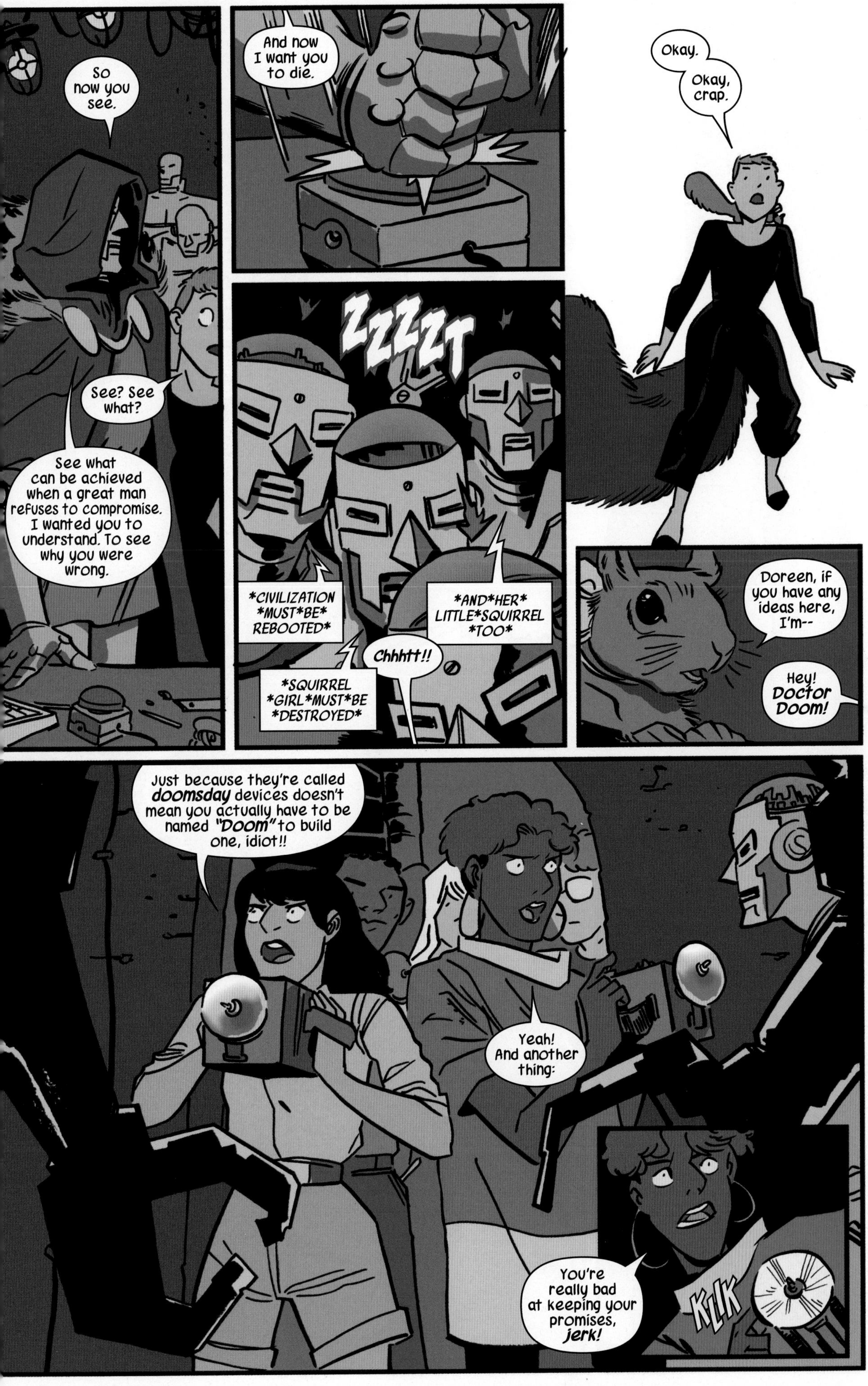
So now you see.
And now I want you to die.
Okay.
Okay, crap.
See? See what?
See what can be achieved when a great man refuses to compromise. I wanted you to understand. To see why you were wrong.
ZZZZT
*CIVILIZATION *MUST*BE* REBOOTED*
*AND*HER* LITTLE*SQUIRREL *TOO*
Chhhtt!!
*SQUIRREL *GIRL*MUST*BE *DESTROYED*
Doreen, if you have any ideas here, I'm--
Hey! Doctor Doom!
Just because they're called doomsday devices doesn't mean you actually have to be named "Doom" to build one, idiot!!
Yeah! And another thing:
You're really bad at keeping your promises, jerk!
KLIK

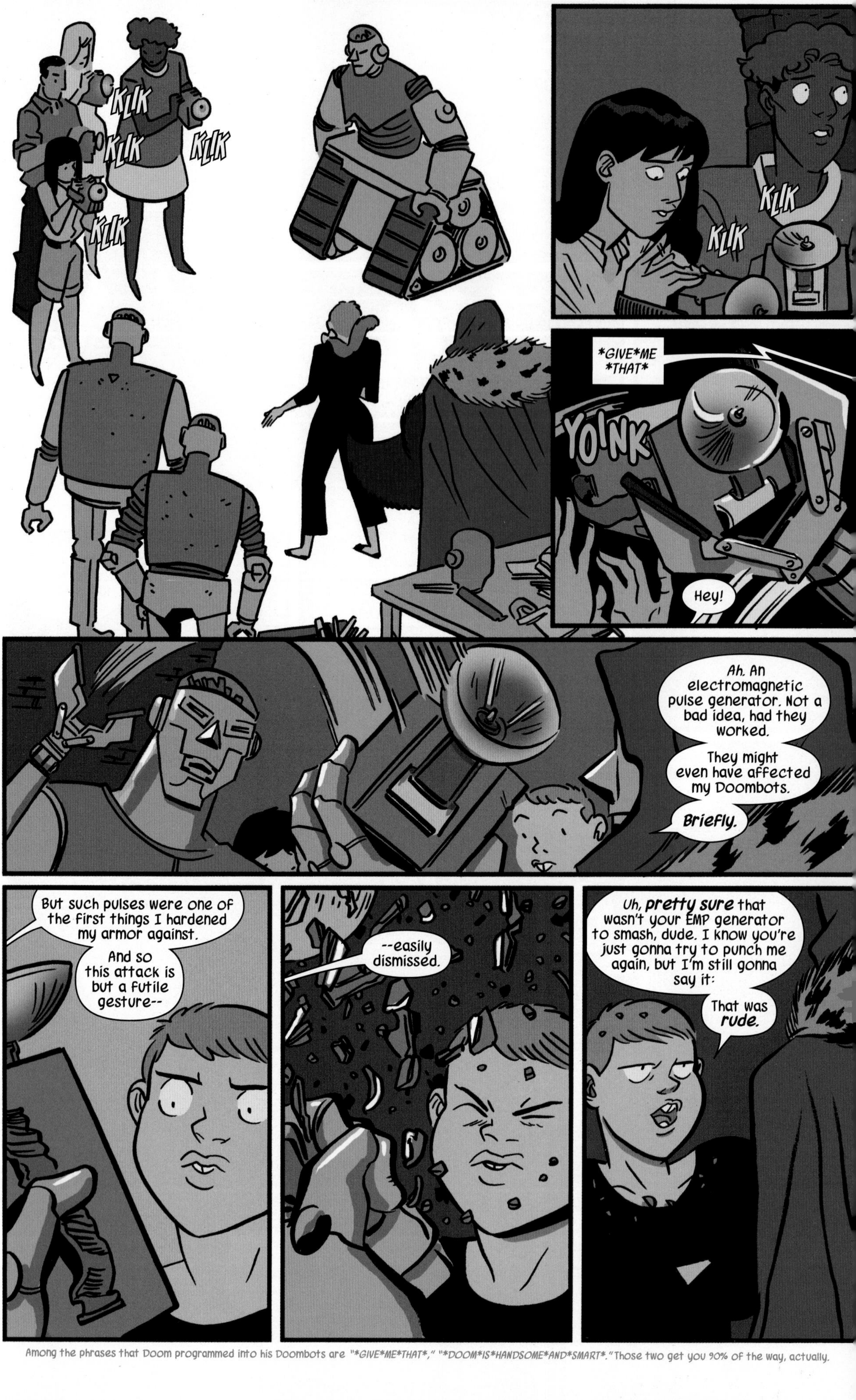
KLIK
KLIK
KLIK
KLIK
KLIK
KLIK
*GIVE*ME *THAT*
YOINK
Hey!
Ah. An electromagnetic pulse generator. Not a bad idea, had they worked.
They might even have affected my Doombots.
Briefly.
But such pulses were one of the first things I hardened my armor against.
And so this attack is but a futile gesture--
--easily dismissed.
Uh, pretty sure that wasn't your EMP generator to smash, dude. I know you're just gonna try to punch me again, but I'm still gonna say it:
That was rude.

Among the phrases that Doom programmed into his Doombots are "*GIVE*ME*THAT*," "*DOOM*IS*HANDSOME*AND*SMART*." Those two get you 90% of the way, actually.

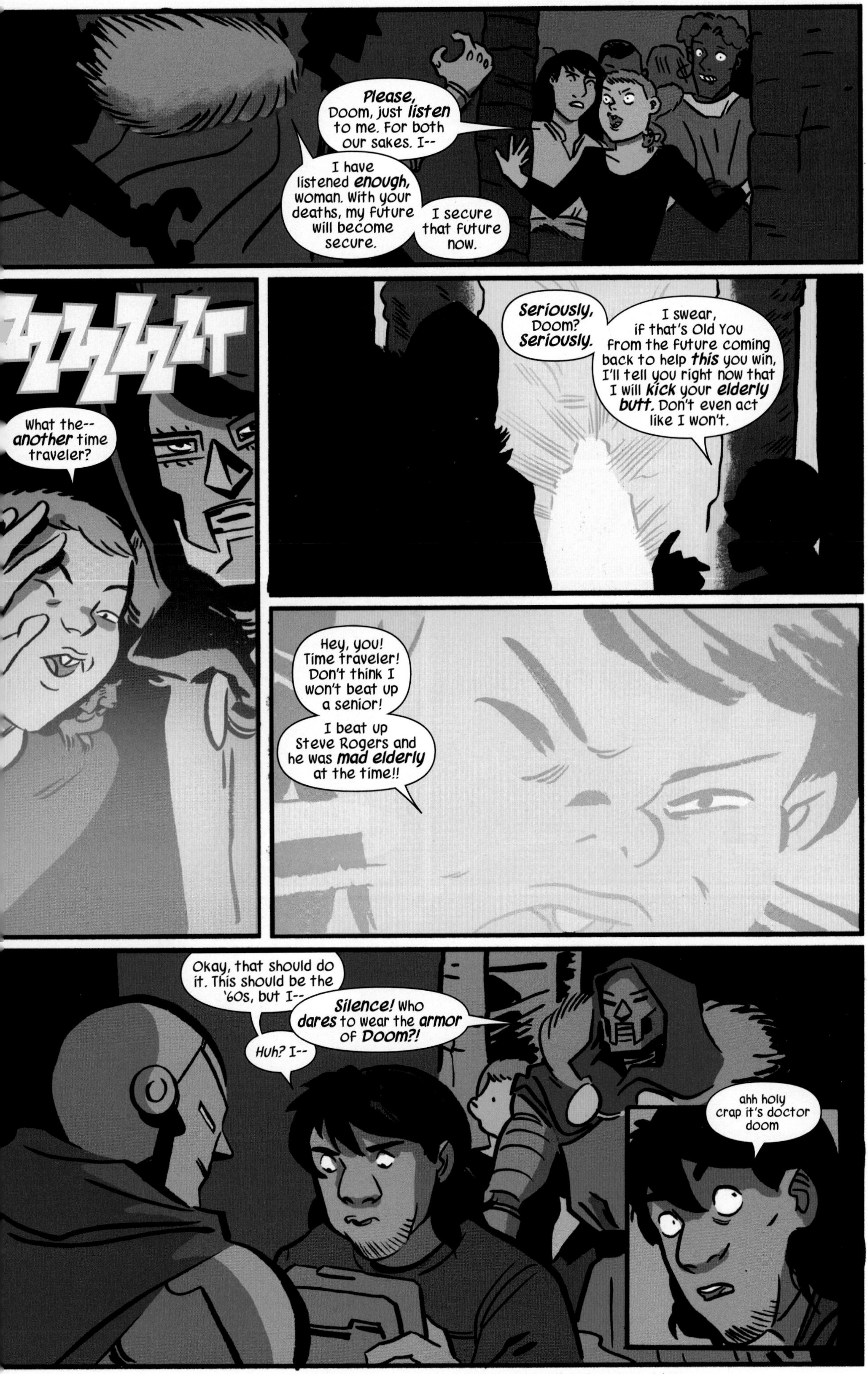

Please, Doom, just listen to me. For both our sakes. I--
I have listened enough, woman. With your deaths, my future will become secure.
I secure that future now.
ZZZZZZZT
What the-- another time traveler?
Seriously, Doom? Seriously.
I swear, if that's Old You from the future coming back to help this you win, I'll tell you right now that I will kick your elderly butt. Don't even act like I won't.
Hey, you! Time traveler! Don't think I won't beat up a senior!
I beat up Steve Rogers and he was mad elderly at the time!!
Okay, that should do it. This should be the '60s, but I--
Silence! Who dares to wear the armor of Doom?!
Huh? I--
ahh holy crap it's doctor doom

Later on, when I apologized for beating him up, Steve Rogers called me "son." Steve Rogers, man. I dunno.

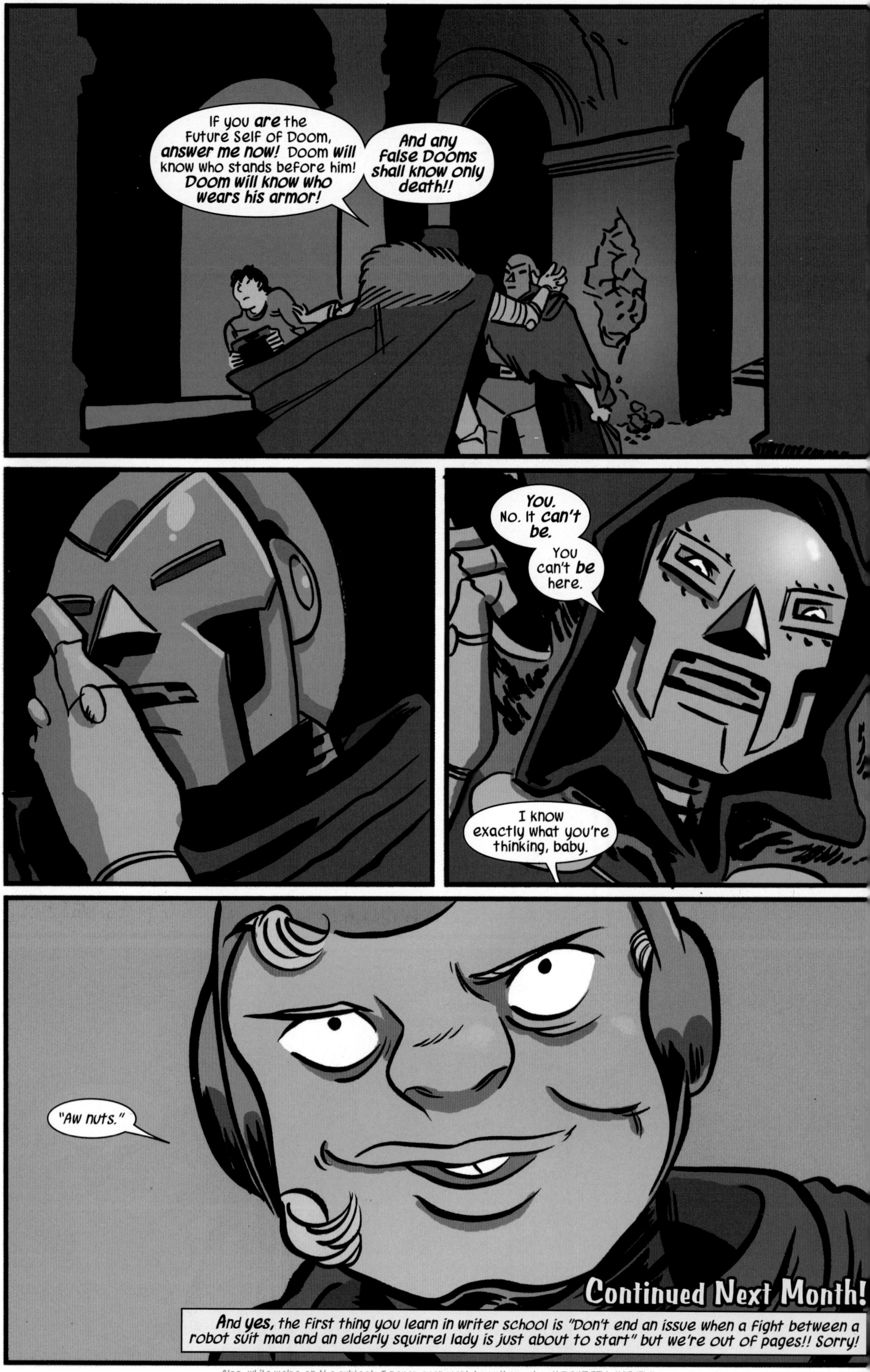
If you are the Future Self of Doom, answer me now! Doom will know who stands before him! Doom will know who wears his armor!
And any false Dooms shall know only death!!
YOU. No. It can't be.
You can't be here.
I know exactly what you're thinking, baby.
"Aw nuts."
Continued Next Month!
And yes, the first thing you learn in writer school is "Don't end an issue when a fight between a robot suit man and an elderly squirrel lady is just about to start" but we're out of pages!! Sorry!

Also, while we're on the subject: I never even went to writer school! DON'T TELL MARVEL!!

Ryan!

Letters From Nuts

Erica!

Send letters to mheroes@marvel.com or 135 W 50th St, 7th Floor, New York, NY 10020 (Please mark "OKAY TO PRINT")

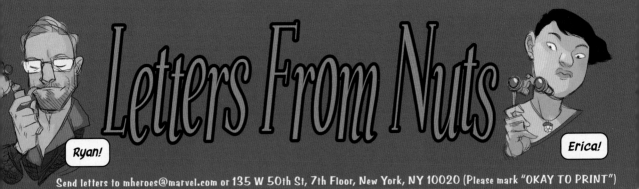

Dear Squirrel Girl Family,

I'm pretty sure I am Squirrel Girl. My ame isn't Doreen, but I do go to school for ngineering (pretty close to CS) in Boston (a ig city like New York). I also have a friend hat loves cats, and also crochets (which is ust like knitting). However, her cat's name is rape, not Mew. While my squirrel skillz have ot shown themselves yet, I'm sure they will oon. I'll just keep waiting and hanging out at he park with my squirrel friends. I think I've igured out how to say acorn.

Anyways, I just read the second, second ssue of the Unbeatable Squirrel Girl and I have o say I thoroughly enjoyed it. I especially liked he clothes Doreen ended up choosing to help er blend in to the '60s (one of my personal avorite decades, I'm listening to Jimi Hendrix s I write this, great choice). She will be my ashion inspiration this weekend for sure!

So I was wondering if you know what kind f music Doreen jams to? I think that would be n important clue to really reveal if I am in fact quirrel Girl or not.

I've attached an image of myself and my earless sidekick, Tippy-Toe.

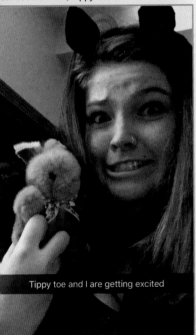

Tippy toe and I are getting excited

Best,
Squirrel Girl... I mean, Emily

RYAN: This is a great costume, dang! So great. I am also big into the idea that you're living the SG lifestyle so completely that really our comic is just Emily fan fiction. For music, Erica and I actually make a playlist that's half music we listen to and half music Doreen does: if you look up "Music to Marvel By: Squirrel Girl" you will find it! I warn you: it contains only the tightest of jams and the sickest of beats. FUN FACT: this story was originally going to have SG be sent back to the 1950s, but Erica pointed out that a) everyone goes to the '50s, and b) the '60s had way more fun fashions anyway. And she was correct! Also the '60s ended up working a lot better for the story anyway, so GOOD WORK, ERICA. Good work spotting my bad ideas and making them good.

ERICA: Ryan, everyone does the '50s. Like EVERYONE. I know you wanted to do Back To The Future, but we're not meeting anyone's grandparents so we can go to ANY TIME WE WANT.

Hello all,

It both makes me lol and makes me sad that the cover says 'Only our second #1 this year!'...

But I digress. I'm writing because I just have to ask:

When Brain Drain says "And so after the Canadian tundra released its frozen grasp up on me," is that a reference to his appearances in Alpha Flight?

Because that would be so so so cool to me.

Mik Bennett
Canberra, Australia

R: Yep! I wanted to work in this dude's history, even if I was retroconning it I MEAN FIXING IT at the same time.

Dear Ryan and Erica,

Congratulations on surviving Secret Wars! I'll admit that I was a bit worried about how Squirrel Girl and her friends would fare in the "All-New, All Different" era of Marvel Comics, but after reading The Unbeatable Squirrel Girl #1 No. 2, I'm glad to see that this corner of the Marvel Universe hasn't changed too much. Squirrel Girl is still the funniest, most optimistic, most butt-kicking and nut-eating comic on the market today!

I've been a fan since Issue #1 No. 1. I love how Doreen uses her wits and her charming personality to defeat the bad guys. I mean, this is the hero who literally defeated Galactus by using the Power of Friendship—and it was awesome! And speaking of friends, I love how Nancy and Doreen are super tight. No matter what super villain or complex algorithm Squirrel Girl finds herself up against, Nancy, Mew, and Nancy's knitting needles have got her back. I can't wait to see what kinds of shenanigans they'll get into next! It was great to see Nancy get her moment in the spotlight in Asgard. Will we get to see another Nancy-centric issue again soon? And what's the deal with Chipmunk Hunk? Do I sense a budding romance for our favorite squirrel-themed super hero?

By the way, speaking of Doreen and Nancy, I love their new haircuts! As always, Erica, you are knocking it out of the park with the artwork. And Ryan's jokes have had me busting a gut laughing in every single issue so far. As I keep telling all my comics-reading friends, "Hey, remember when comics were fun? Remember how great that was? Then you should be reading Squirrel Girl! Seriously!"

Keep on rockin' it, Squirrel Gang!

R Evans
Tacoma, WA

p.s. Nice leaning on the fourth wall re: Squirrel Girl's backstory. "Doreen is medically and legally distinct from being a mutant, and I can never take this back," eh? I see what you did there.

p.p.s. What are the odds of a Squirrel Girl/ Ms. Marvel team-up? Or even better: Squirrel Girl and Groot vs. the Termite-inator?

R: Aw thanks, man! This was super flattering to read. I really like Nancy too, and I think you were probably happy with how much Nancy there was in the last couple issues! There's less of her in this issue, but that's only because I didn't get your letter in time. So let's say that every scene that she DOESN'T appear in during this issue, it's only because she was just out of frame, only nobody comments on that for some reason. I'm sure that won't cause any continuity problems at all!

p.s.: The deal with Chipmunk Hunk is that he is a hunk who has all the powers of a chipmunk. I thought that was pretty clear??

Dear Ryan and Erica,

Your series has made Squirrel Girl my favorite hero of all time! I love that she is smart and powerful, but also goofy and sassy. The writing is snappy and hilarious, and makes me laugh out loud every issue. I adore your cute art style, especially the body diversity that shows up in the different characters. Can't wait to see more of Squirrel Girl and Tippy's adventures! I have included photos of me in my Unbeatable Squirrel Girl costume. And thank you guys so much for an Unbeatable Comic!

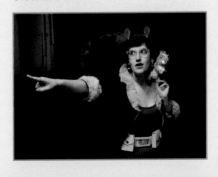

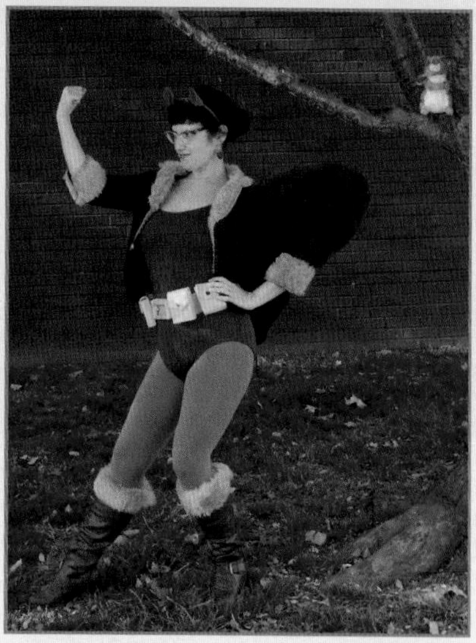

Sincerely,
Amanda Kindler

R: Amanda, your costume is spot-on! Amazing. I'm sincerely impressed! And now we've gone and given her a new costume, but it's our intention that she keeps them both around and uses them at different times and for different reasons: I figure that jacket probably gets hot if you do too much running around in it. Hey, does that jacket get hot if you do too much running around in it?

E: That jacket probably does get too hot. The new costume was based on tennis dresses that I saw at a sneaker store that was doing some big tennis-related promotion. And I liked the idea that it's this cute little girl dress but also 100% useful for running around in the heat.

Dear Ryan and Erica,

I just finished reading your new second issue, and it looks like Volume 2 of The Unbeatable Squirrel Girl is off and running. I look forward to seeing where your time travel story is headed; Dr. Doom has already appeared and I can only wonder if Doreen will become entangled in any of the timelines involving Kang / Rama-Tut / Immortus.

It was fun to see Doreen adjust to 1962. I've enclosed a Marvel Comics Group house ad from that year. As an old Silver Ager, I love how The Unbeatable Squirrel Girl logo uses a typeface virtually identical to that used on the Amazing Adult Fantasy and Fantastic Four comics of yesteryear. Who, pray tell, designed your logo? Please thank and congratulate him/her on my behalf.

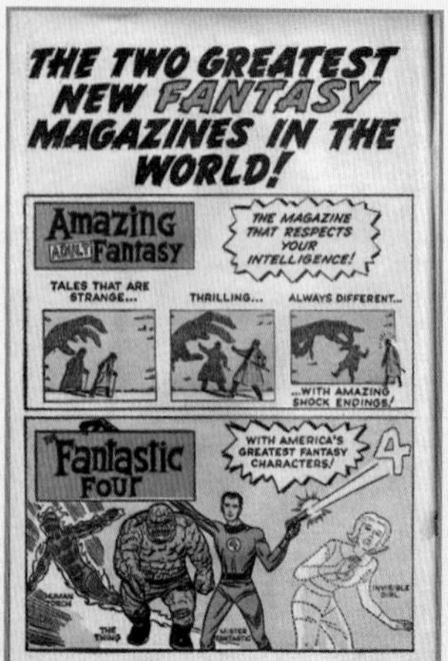
THE TWO GREATEST NEW FANTASY MAGAZINES IN THE WORLD!
Amazing Adult Fantasy
THE MAGAZINE THAT RESPECTS YOUR INTELLIGENCE!
TALES THAT ARE STRANGE...
THRILLING...
ALWAYS DIFFERENT...
...WITH AMAZING SHOCK ENDINGS!
The Fantastic Four
WITH AMERICA'S GREATEST FANTASY CHARACTERS!

Excelsior!

Charles Hoffman
Van Nuys, CA

R: Oh man, I never even realized the similar type treatment to Amazing ADULT Fantasy (what a title that was) but I hope we can carry on its tradition of being The Magazine That Respects Your Intelligence! Our logo was done by Mike Allred, who you don't need me to tell you is AMAZING, and whose work you can check out on SILVER SURFER AS WE SPEAK (ps: it's really good).

E: DON'T EVEN GET ME STARTED ON HOW BAD I WANT TO DRAW KANG.

Dear Ryan and Erica,

Hey guys! I'm loving the new series, and I'm trying to get some of my friends into it. The trouble is, they don't think Squirrel Girl is important enough to care about. Do you have any advice on how to change their minds?

Oscar Lee

R: Oh this is an easy one! Grab one of our issues and tape over its cover with a piece of paper upon which you have written "VERY IMPORTANT DOCUMENTS!!!!!!". They will be drawn to it like a moth to flame, or more appropriately, like a ground-dwelling squirrel to other ground-dwelling squirrels (ground-dwelling squirrels are generally social animals, while tree-dwelling squirrels are more solitary). P.S.: guess what? That was a very important squirrel fact that your friends who only care about important things should be made aware of!!

Hello, Team SG! I just wanted to say thank you for making such a wonderful comic. Doreen and Nancy are both so relatable and inspirational. Every single issue makes me laugh and smile, mostly from Ryan's dorky comments. Erica, I absolutely adore how you draw Doreen. She's not the overused stereotype of enormous breasts and unrealistic waistline. She looks like a realistic representation of a college student, and she helps me feel better about my own appearance. Keep up the great work, you two!

Sam
Colorado

R: Hey Sam, thanks! I think I've mentioned this before, but the character of SG really came into focus for me when Erica sent over her early sketches: they had such life and humor and confidence in them that I was like, oh, OKAY, I know who this person is! DONE. And I like how Erica draws different body types in our book because I think it's great when you can look inside a comic and see someone who looks like you. I'm glad you agree!

E: Thanks! It's not really something I thought about too much except that in most of her older appearances the joke was that she was the most unassuming and sometimes dorky looking character who nobody could think was UNBEATABLE. Also I just like when characters who are more physical are a little thicker--makes me think I can't take them out by sitting on them.

Dear Ryan and Erica.

The Unbeatable Squirrel Girl is the first comic that my 7 year old daughter Riley rea and every month we eagerly await the ne issue to read at bedtime. Riley is such a hug fan of Doreen that she dressed up as her fo Halloween. Here are some photos of her (wit Tippy-Toe)

Mike Davi

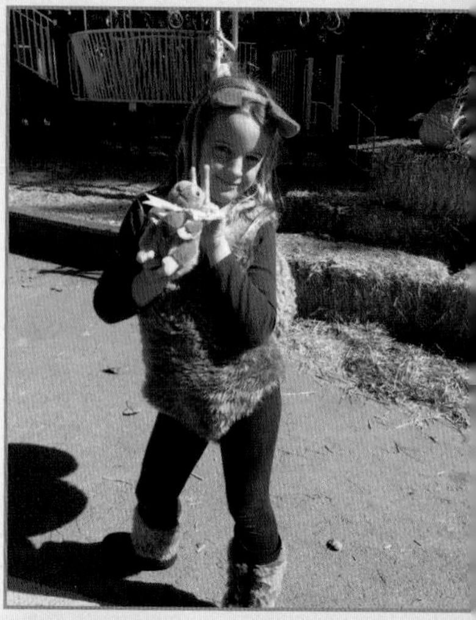

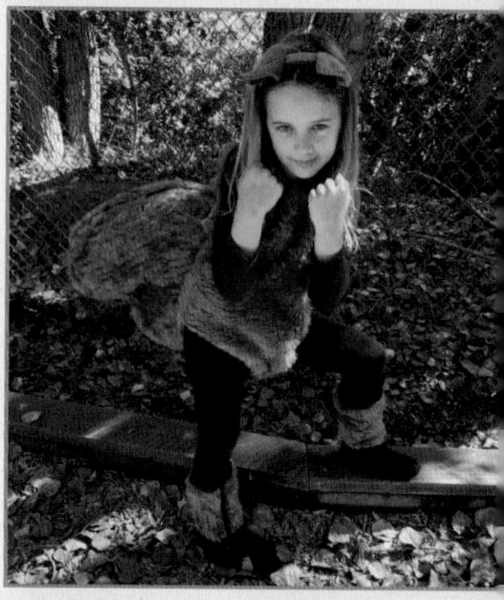

R: Riley, I'll tell you one thing: you costume is amazing and you've got the attitude down COLD. I hope you enjoyed this issue! Now since you read these at bedtime, I guess it's TIME FOR SLEEP. Here's a fun fact about sleep: we don't really know why it happens! Scientists think that maybe it helps our brains and/or bodies recharge and recover, but we can't yet say for sure. Basically, ask a scientist for the reason why people sleep, and they'll say "because they get real sleepy." Amazing!

Dear Ryan & Erica,

Thank you so much for your work on The Unbeatable Squirrel Girl! There's not a lot of books that I pick up on Wednesdays that my wife wants to read too. Now, we share the adventures of Doreen and the gang together. And we've become an even closer couple.

I can't remember where I heard it first, but I know there was talk sometime ago about Kristen Schaal being on the short list to portray SG in the MCU. Reading issue 1, all I could hear was her voice for Miss Green.

Ryan, did you have anyone in mind when pennig the script?

Erica, is Squirrel Girl's mug modeled after anyone in particular?

R & E, how would you guys feel about Kristen playing the role? Or whom else would

u cast if not her?
Thanks again for a wonderful read!

Take care,
Todd A. Davis
Greenville, SC
@MrToddADavis

R: I didn't have anyone in mind for SG when I was writing her, , but I can see Kristen Schaal being a good fit! I've also heard ople suggest Ellie Kemper in a sort of "Unbreakable Squirrel rl" pitch and I can totally see that too. ComicsAlliance suggested ae Whitman for Doreen and Vicky Jeudy for Nancy (and Eugene tz for Kraven) earlier this year and I was like, yes, yes, please. The bad news is we don't get to say who gets cast in movies (or en which characters show up in movies) but clearly SOMEONE es, and hopefully that person likes comics! HELLO, person who cides to put Squirrel Girl in a movie and who is reading this tters page right now! In my opinion, you should decide to do that ing you're currently considering!!

E: I didn't have anyone in mind when I started. Now, I'd like see Jennifer Lawrence in the role since she's known for being ofy, is an action hero and has those cheeks! She's also in the "if u think that's fat then I don't even know" category.

llege-Educated Squirrel Girl Folks,

I decided to give my Statistics class the included question on an signment I'll be handing out today. Surely, you all can determine e answers!

Stephen Davidson
Danville, VA

R: AMAZING. Also, if you are a student in Stephen's class who s picked up this comic to find out the correct answers (thank u! I hope you enjoyed it!), you should know that I'm not gonna st GIVE you them, but I'll remind you you're simply looking for e ratio of the standard deviation to the mean! No sweat!

E: I...went to art school.

Come back next month for #5, the exciting conclusion! (Old Lady Squirrel Girl is even more awesome than you're no doubt already imagining her to be!)

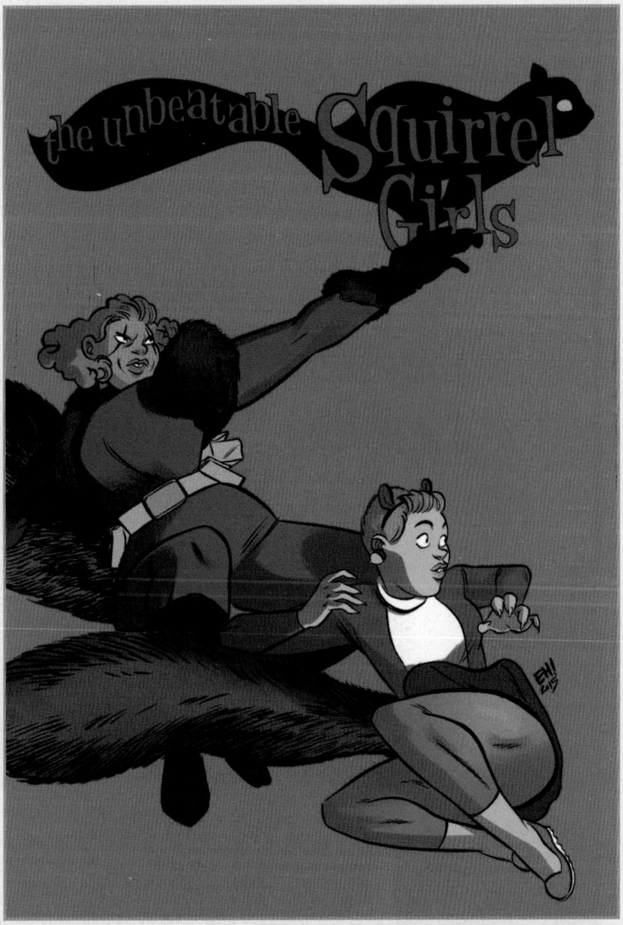

the unbeatable Squirrel Girls
EH! 2015

10. Squirrel Girl and her friends are preparing a huge Arbor Day celebration (like we all do) and they have decided to go out and collect nuts for the big bash rather than spend money buying them. They also hold a friendly competition to see who has more invitees show up at the party because all parties are in actuality a celebration of friendship. The below table lists how many nuts each party planner collects and how many invitees of each planner attends the party. Find the coefficient of variation of the number of collected nuts as well as for the number of attending invitees. Also, read THE UNBEATABLE SQUIRREL GIRL. Unless you hate art, fun, friendship, laughing, being entertained, and words.

Party Planner	Number of Nuts Collected	Number of Attending Invitees
Squirrel Girl – 50% squirrel, 100% girl	578	34
Tippy Toe – 100% squirrel	3,916	4
Nancy Whitehead – 100% girl	110	42
Koi Boi – 0% squirrel, 0% girl	6	2
Chipmunk Hunk – the rhyming squirrel names were taken	488	19

Attention, Squirrel Scouts! Make sure to check out our production blog, **nbeatablesquirrelgirl.tumblr.com**, where we post behind-the-scenes stuff on how the book gets made, along with all sorts of cool things *you* make: fanart, cosplay, whatever!

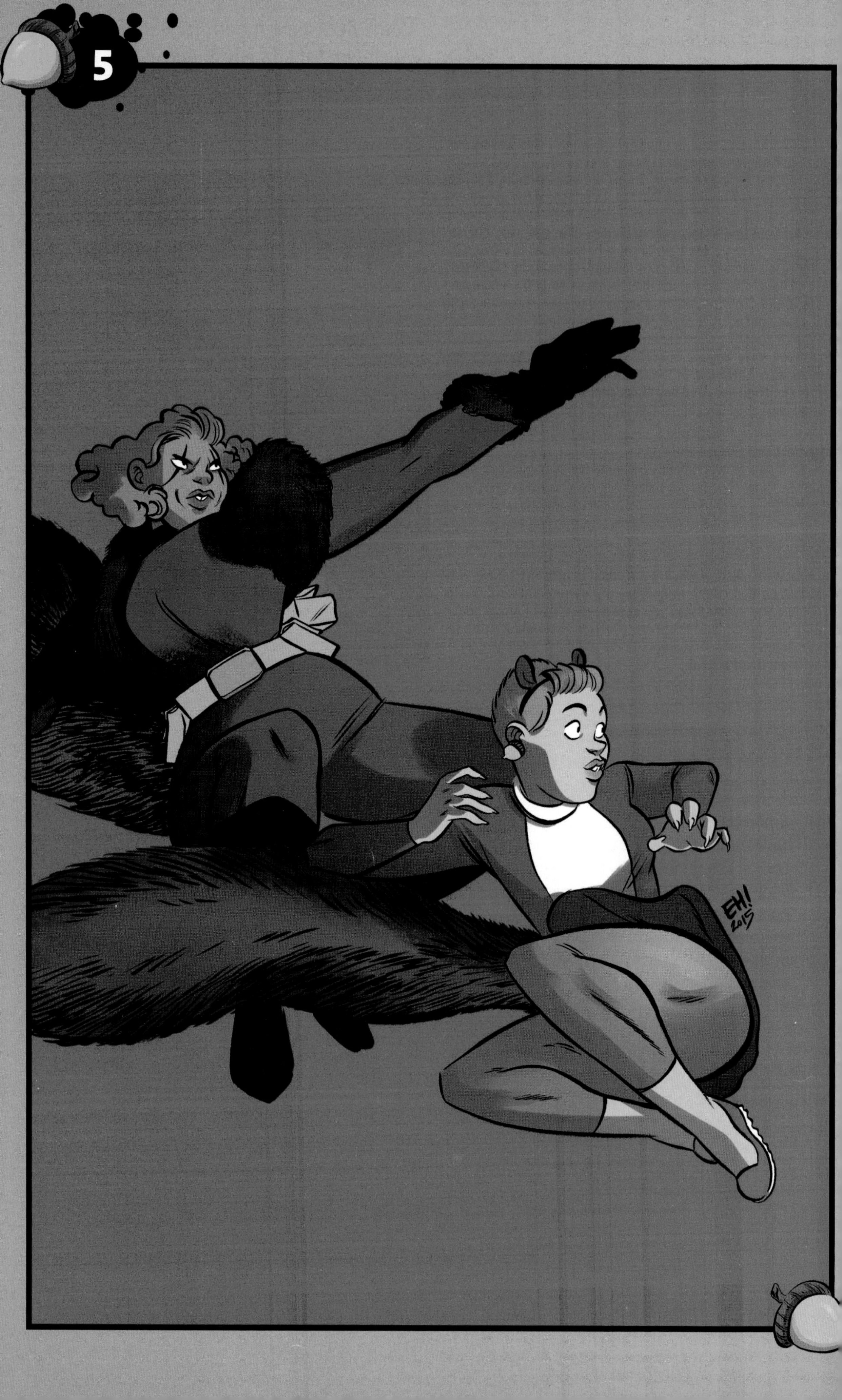
5
EH!
2015

Doreen Green isn't just a second-year computer science student: she secretly also has all the powers of both squirrel and girl! She uses her amazing abilities to fight crime **and** be as awesome as possible. You know her as...**The Unbeatable Squirrel Girl!** Find out what she's been up to, with...

Squirrel Girl in a nutshell

☒ URGENT

WHILE YOU WERE OUT

To **The United Nations**

From **Squirrel Girl**

Of **The East Coast Squirrel Girls**

☒ TELEPHONED ☐ PLEASE CALL
☐ CAME TO SEE YOU ☐ WILL CALL AGAIN
☒ WANTS TO SEE YOU ☐ RETURNED YOUR CALL

Message Um, I warned y'all that Doctor Doom came back in time to the '60s (ie: RIGHT NOW) and what did you do? NOTHING. So me and my friends ~~invented EMP generators~~ found some EMP generators lying around and tried to stop him, but it didn't work! SO THANKS FOR NOTHING, THE UNITED NATIONS!

☒ URGENT

WHILE YOU WERE OUT

To **The United Nations**

From **Squirrel Girl**

Of **The same woman who sent the last note**

☒ TELEPHONED ☒ PLEASE CALL
☐ CAME TO SEE YOU ☐ WILL CALL AGAIN
☐ WANTS TO SEE YOU ☐ RETURNED YOUR CALL

Message Oh and, AND, Doom also built DOOMBOTS (robot duplicates of himself) and programmed them using a weird "DOOMssembly" language he invented, so if we lose and he takes over the world then all I can tell you about it is that the commands are all variants of "DOOM" and it looks like a real pain to program in, tbh

---

☒ URGENT

WHILE YOU WERE OUT

To **The United Nations**

From **Squirrel Girl**

Of **how do you not know me yet, sheesh**

☐ TELEPHONED ☐ PLEASE CALL
☐ CAME TO SEE YOU ☐ WILL CALL AGAIN
☒ WANTS TO SEE YOU ☐ RETURNED YOUR CALL

Message Also this guy Cody came back in time from the future (ie: MY present) with an older me!! Haha YEP I'M FROM THE FUTURE and wasn't even born in the '60s!! I don't even mind telling you United Nations guys anymore, because nobody even READS these notes even though I put them up really nicely on your stupid bulletin board!!

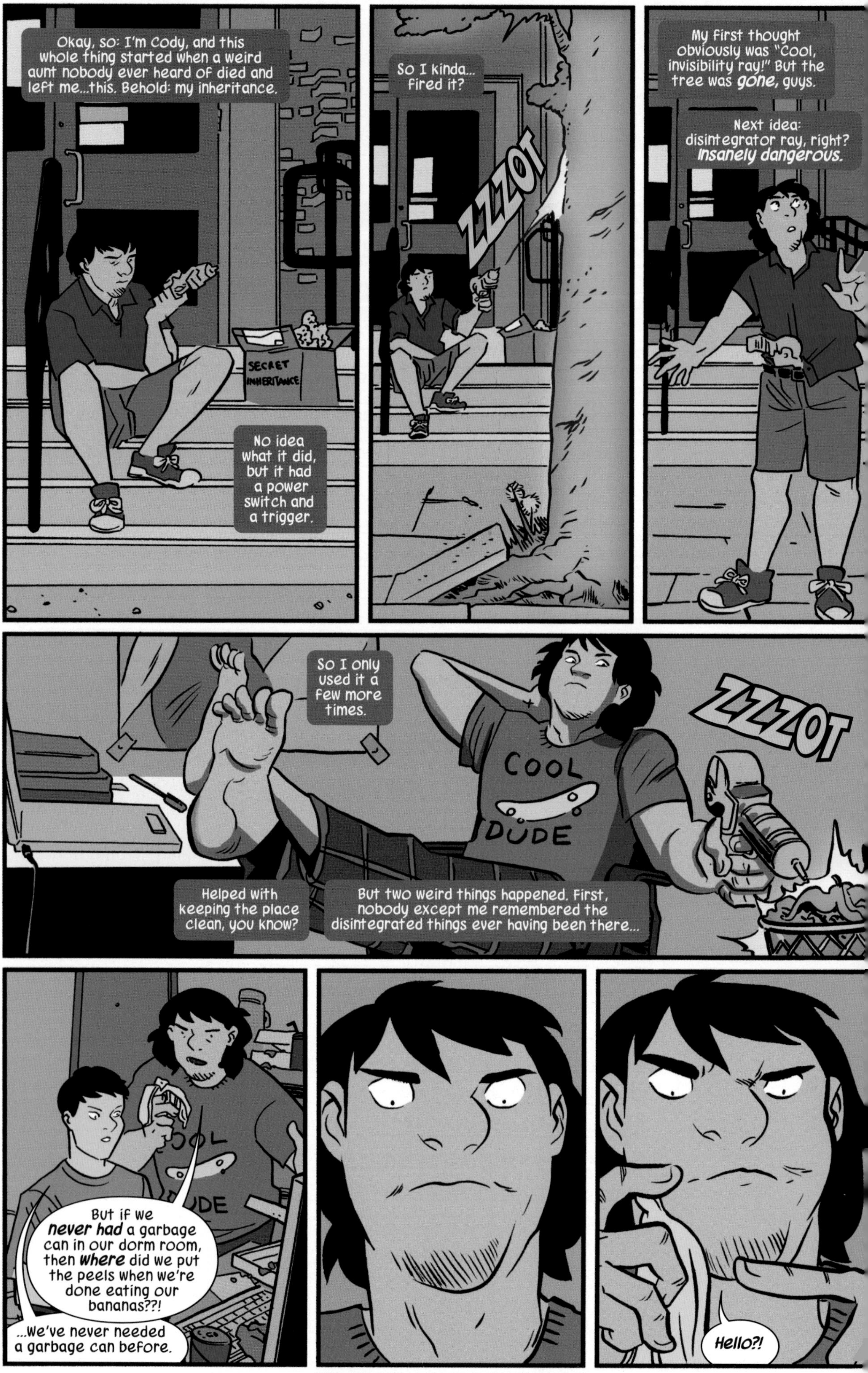
Okay, so: I'm Cody, and this whole thing started when a weird aunt nobody ever heard of died and left me...this. Behold: my inheritance.
SECRET INHERITANCE
No idea what it did, but it had a power switch and a trigger.
So I kinda... fired it?
ZZZOT
My first thought obviously was "Cool, invisibility ray!" But the tree was gone, guys.
Next idea: disintegrator ray, right? Insanely dangerous.
So I only used it a few more times.
ZZZOT
COOL DUDE
Helped with keeping the place clean, you know?
But two weird things happened. First, nobody except me remembered the disintegrated things ever having been there...
But if we never had a garbage can in our dorm room, then where did we put the peels when we're done eating our bananas??!
...We've never needed a garbage can before.
Hello?!

Weird aunts are the best aunts. You heard it here first!

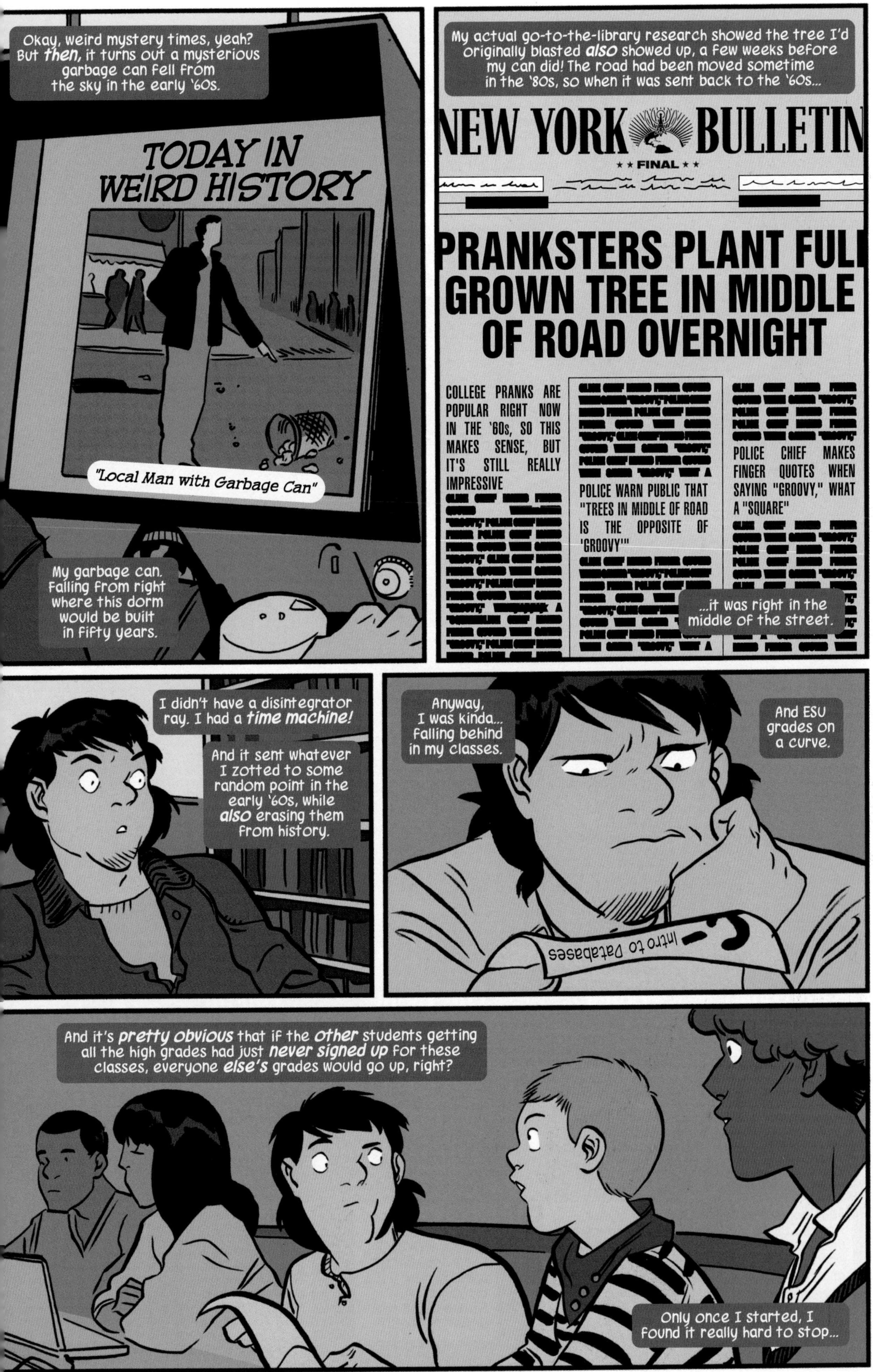
Okay, weird mystery times, yeah? But *then*, it turns out a mysterious garbage can fell from the sky in the early '60s.
TODAY IN WEIRD HISTORY
"Local Man with Garbage Can"
My garbage can. Falling from right where this dorm would be built in fifty years.
My actual go-to-the-library research showed the tree I'd originally blasted *also* showed up, a few weeks before my can did! The road had been moved sometime in the '80s, so when it was sent back to the '60s...
NEW YORK BULLETIN
★★ FINAL ★★
PRANKSTERS PLANT FULL GROWN TREE IN MIDDLE OF ROAD OVERNIGHT
COLLEGE PRANKS ARE POPULAR RIGHT NOW IN THE '60s, SO THIS MAKES SENSE, BUT IT'S STILL REALLY IMPRESSIVE
[redacted]
POLICE WARN PUBLIC THAT "TREES IN MIDDLE OF ROAD IS THE OPPOSITE OF 'GROOVY'"
[redacted]
POLICE CHIEF MAKES FINGER QUOTES WHEN SAYING "GROOVY," WHAT A "SQUARE"
[redacted]
...it was right in the middle of the street.
I didn't have a disintegrator ray. I had a *time machine!*
And it sent whatever I zotted to some random point in the early '60s, while *also* erasing them from history.
Anyway, I was kinda... falling behind in my classes.
And ESU grades on a curve.
Intro to Databases
And it's *pretty obvious* that if the *other* students getting all the high grades had just *never signed up* for these classes, everyone *else's* grades would go up, right?
Only once I started, I found it really hard to stop...

If you go back to Volume 1 Issue 7 of this book, you'll see Cody in class there, ***almost like we planned this all along!*** Yes, we truly are excellent comics professionals and ***definitely*** not making this up as we go along.

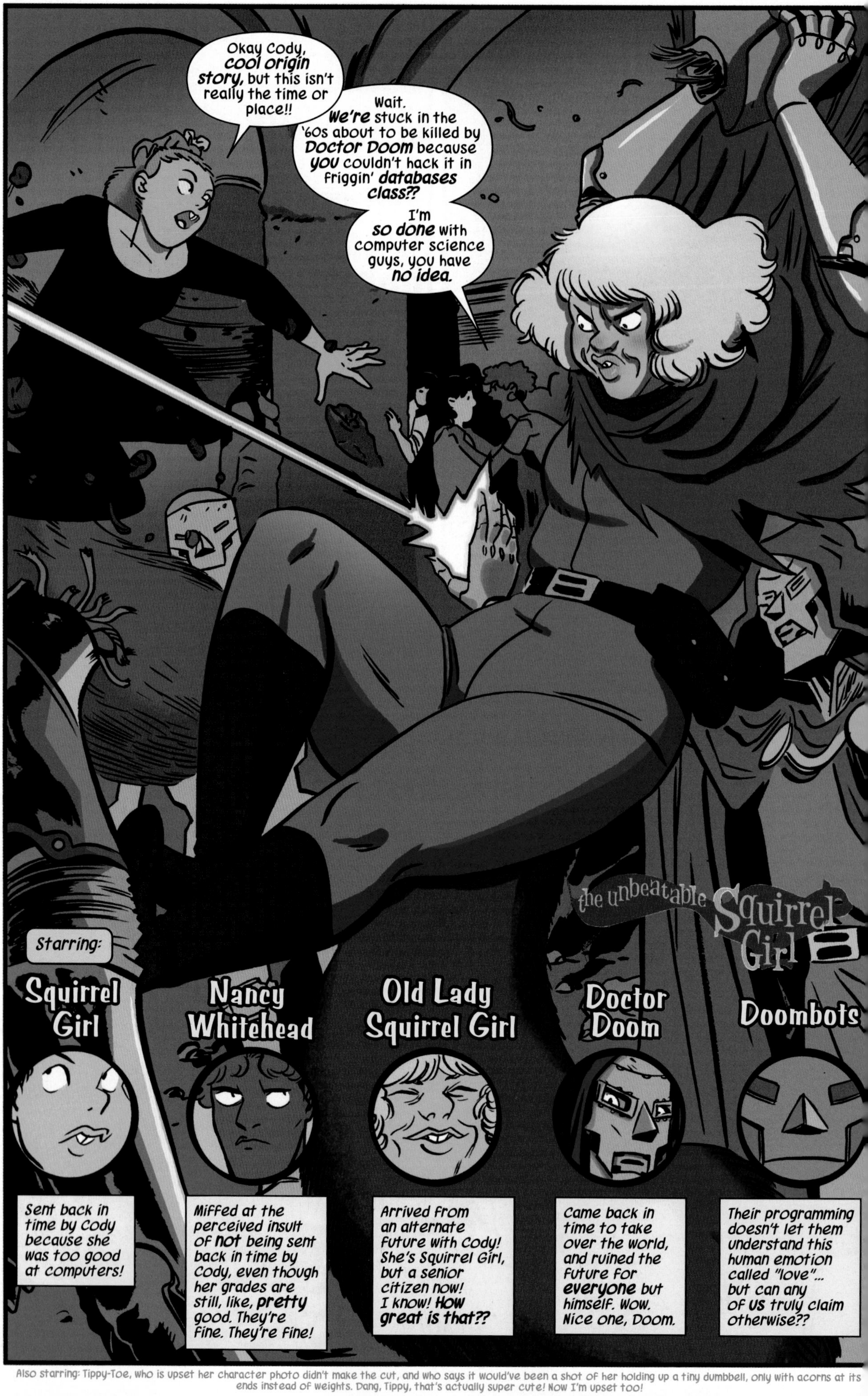
Okay Cody, cool origin story, but this isn't really the time or place!!
Wait. We're stuck in the '60s about to be killed by Doctor Doom because you couldn't hack it in friggin' databases class??
I'm so done with computer science guys, you have no idea.
the unbeatable Squirrel Girl
Starring:
Squirrel Girl
Sent back in time by Cody because she was too good at computers!
Nancy Whitehead
Miffed at the perceived insult of not being sent back in time by Cody, even though her grades are still, like, pretty good. They're fine. They're fine!
Old Lady Squirrel Girl
Arrived from an alternate future with Cody! She's Squirrel Girl, but a senior citizen now! I know! How great is that??
Doctor Doom
Came back in time to take over the world, and ruined the future for everyone but himself. Wow. Nice one, Doom.
Doombots
Their programming doesn't let them understand this human emotion called "love"... but can any of us truly claim otherwise??

Also starring: Tippy-Toe, who is upset her character photo didn't make the cut, and who says it would've been a shot of her holding up a tiny dumbbell, only with acorns at its ends instead of weights. Dang, Tippy, that's actually super cute! Now I'm upset too!

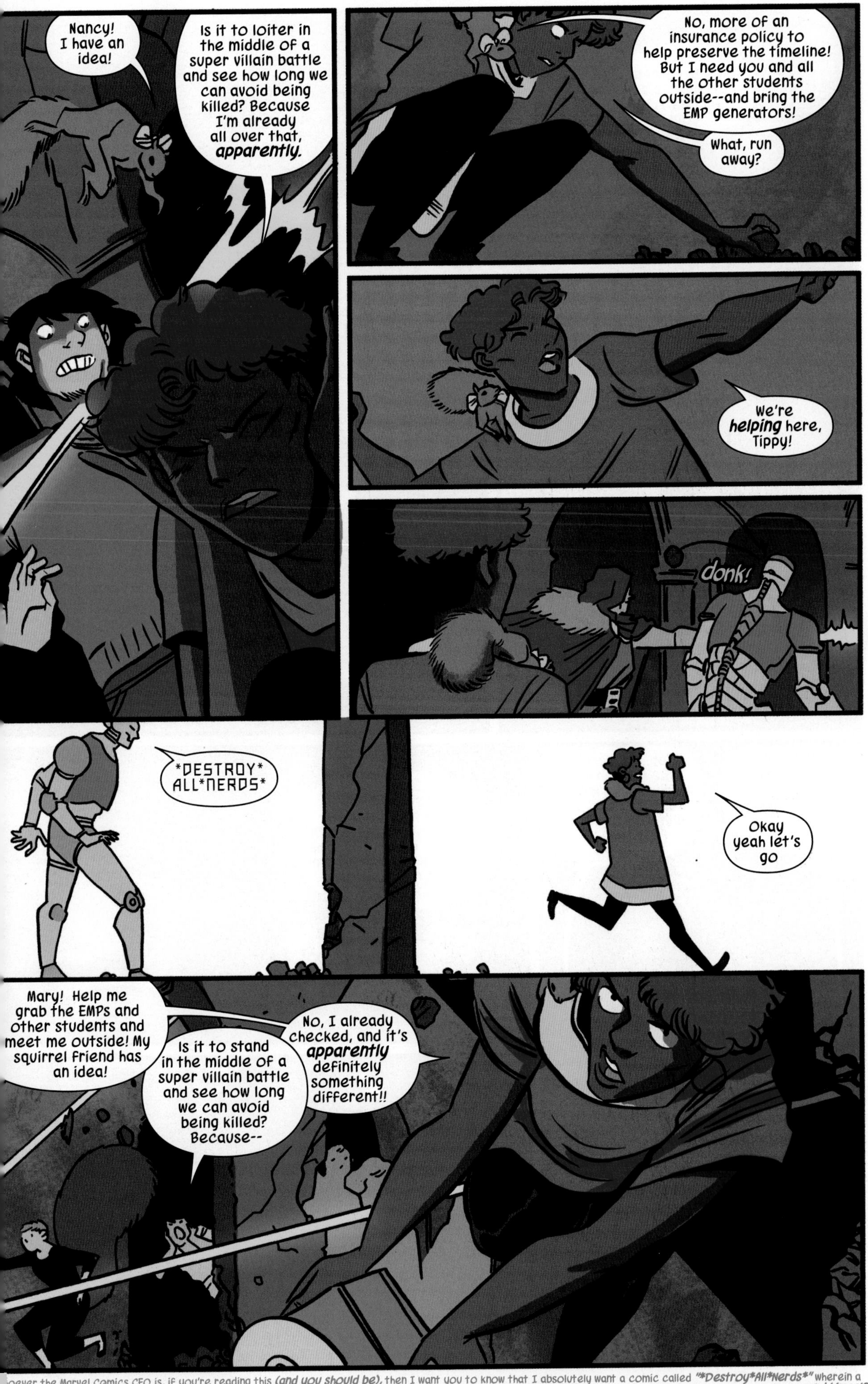
Nancy! I have an idea!
Is it to loiter in the middle of a super villain battle and see how long we can avoid being killed? Because I'm already all over that, *apparently.*
No, more of an insurance policy to help preserve the timeline! But I need you and all the other students outside--and bring the EMP generators!
What, run away?
We're *helping* here, Tippy!
donk!
DESTROY ALL*NERDS*
Okay yeah let's go
Mary! Help me grab the EMPs and other students and meet me outside! My squirrel friend has an idea!
Is it to stand in the middle of a super villain battle and see how long we can avoid being killed? Because--
No, I already checked, and it's *apparently* definitely something different!!

oever the Marvel Comics CEO is, if you're reading this *(and you should be)*, then I want you to know that I absolutely want a comic called *"*Destroy*All*Nerds*"* wherein a ue Doombot makes his way across 1960s America, accidentally gets involved in the space program, and in doing so learns a lot about love, life, computer science... ***and himself.***

Stand still, vile women! My Doombots and I will **destroy** you!

What's the matter, Doom? Is not being able to hit me and my elderly self getting a bit, oh I don't know...

...old??

SMAK

Whoa!

So real talk, Squirrel Girl to Squirrel Girl: you're **seriously** me from the future?

Yep. But here's the thing, it's a totally sucky future! I actually **lost** this fight with Doom the first time we did it.

Shut up. Just like Doomipedia said!

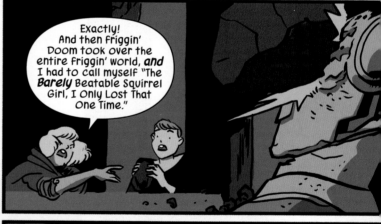

Exactly! And then friggin' Doom took over the entire friggin' world, **and** I had to call myself "The **Barely** Beatable Squirrel Girl, I Only Lost That One Time."

Ugh. Awful name.

Right?! **Super** messed up the cadence of the theme song.

Squirrel Girl, Squirrel Girl / Let's not beat / Squirrel Girl / Did she lose? / On-ly once / And it was / To a dunce / Hey there! Sick burns on Doctor Doom

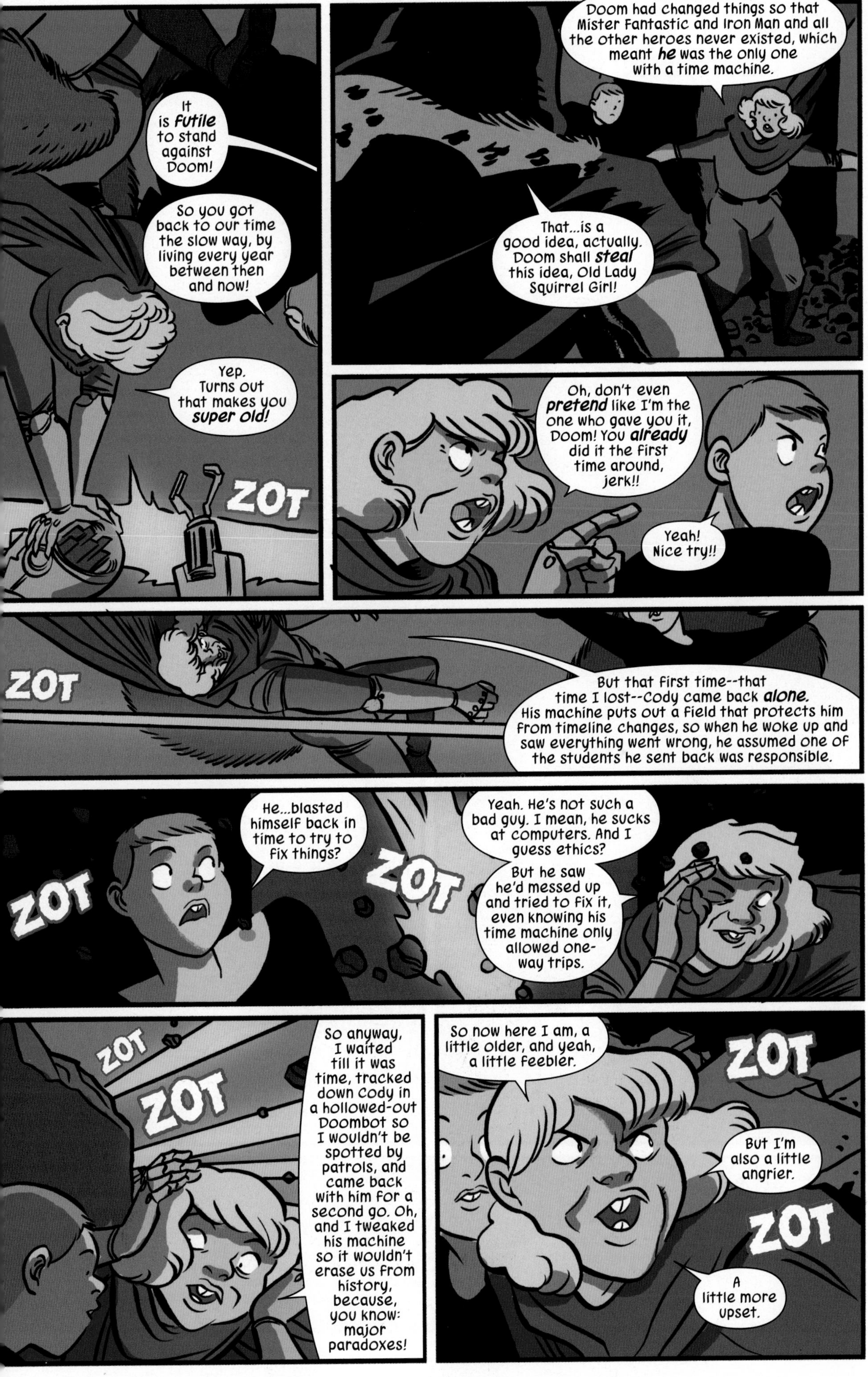
The catch was, Doom had changed things so that Mister Fantastic and Iron Man and all the other heroes never existed, which meant he was the only one with a time machine.
It is futile to stand against Doom!
So you got back to our time the slow way, by living every year between then and now!
That...is a good idea, actually. Doom shall steal this idea, Old Lady Squirrel Girl!
Yep. Turns out that makes you super old!
ZOT
Oh, don't even pretend like I'm the one who gave you it, Doom! You already did it the first time around, jerk!!
Yeah! Nice try!!
ZOT
But that first time--that time I lost--Cody came back alone. His machine puts out a field that protects him from timeline changes, so when he woke up and saw everything went wrong, he assumed one of the students he sent back was responsible.
ZOT
He...blasted himself back in time to try to fix things?
ZOT
Yeah. He's not such a bad guy. I mean, he sucks at computers. And I guess ethics?
But he saw he'd messed up and tried to fix it, even knowing his time machine only allowed one-way trips.
ZOT
ZOT
So anyway, I waited till it was time, tracked down Cody in a hollowed-out Doombot so I wouldn't be spotted by patrols, and came back with him for a second go. Oh, and I tweaked his machine so it wouldn't erase us from history, because, you know: major paradoxes!
So now here I am, a little older, and yeah, a little feebler.
ZOT
But I'm also a little angrier.
ZOT
A little more upset.

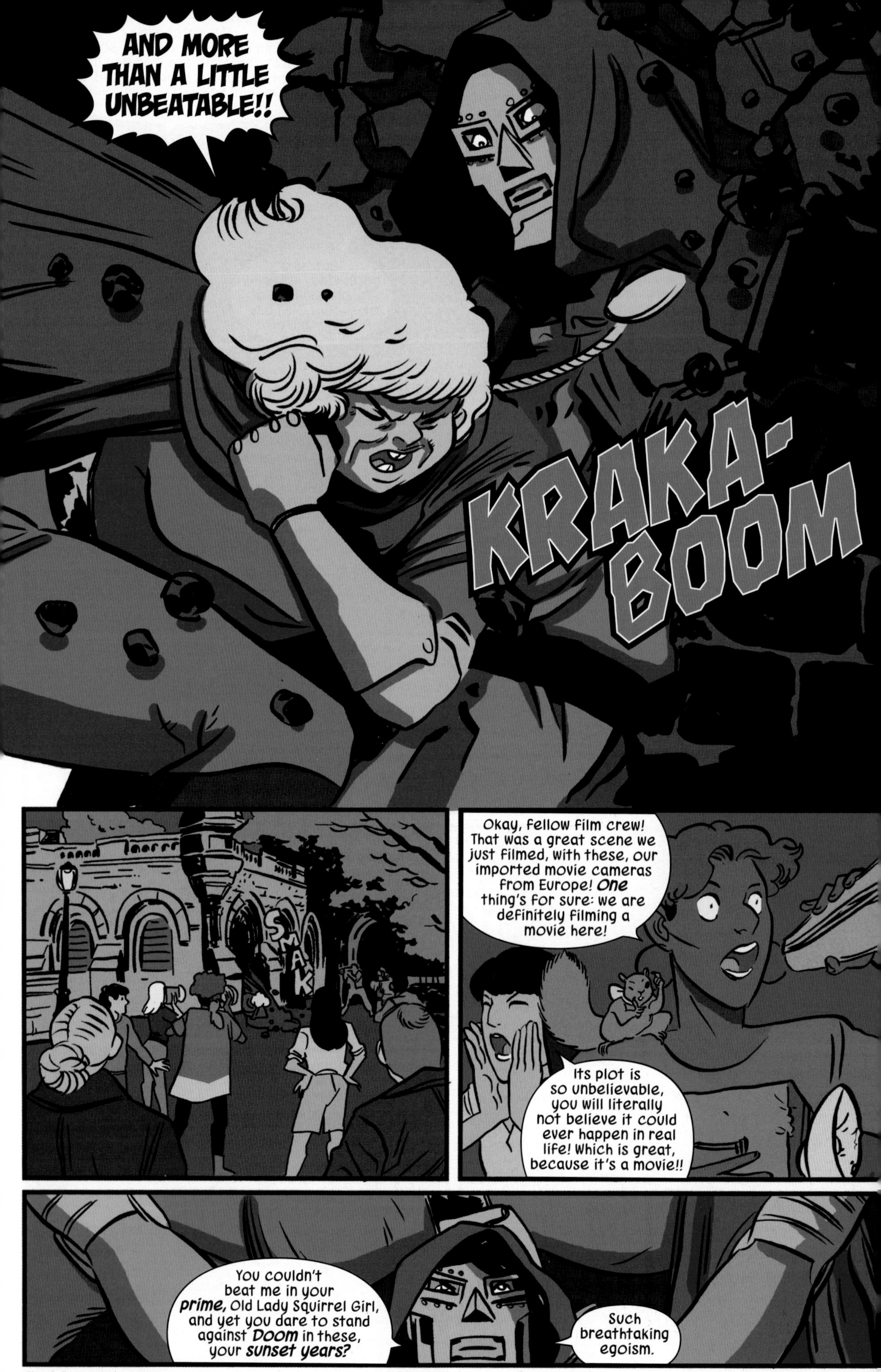
AND MORE THAN A LITTLE UNBEATABLE!!
KRAKA-BOOM
SMAK
Okay, fellow film crew! That was a great scene we just filmed, with these, our imported movie cameras from Europe! One thing's for sure: we are definitely filming a movie here!
Its plot is so unbelievable, you will literally not believe it could ever happen in real life! Which is great, because it's a movie!!
You couldn't beat me in your prime, Old Lady Squirrel Girl, and yet you dare to stand against Doom in these, your sunset years?
Such breathtaking egoism.

Tippy's "pretend we're filming a movie so nobody suspects we're from the future" plan is pretty good, especially when you consider that it was thought up by an actual squirre

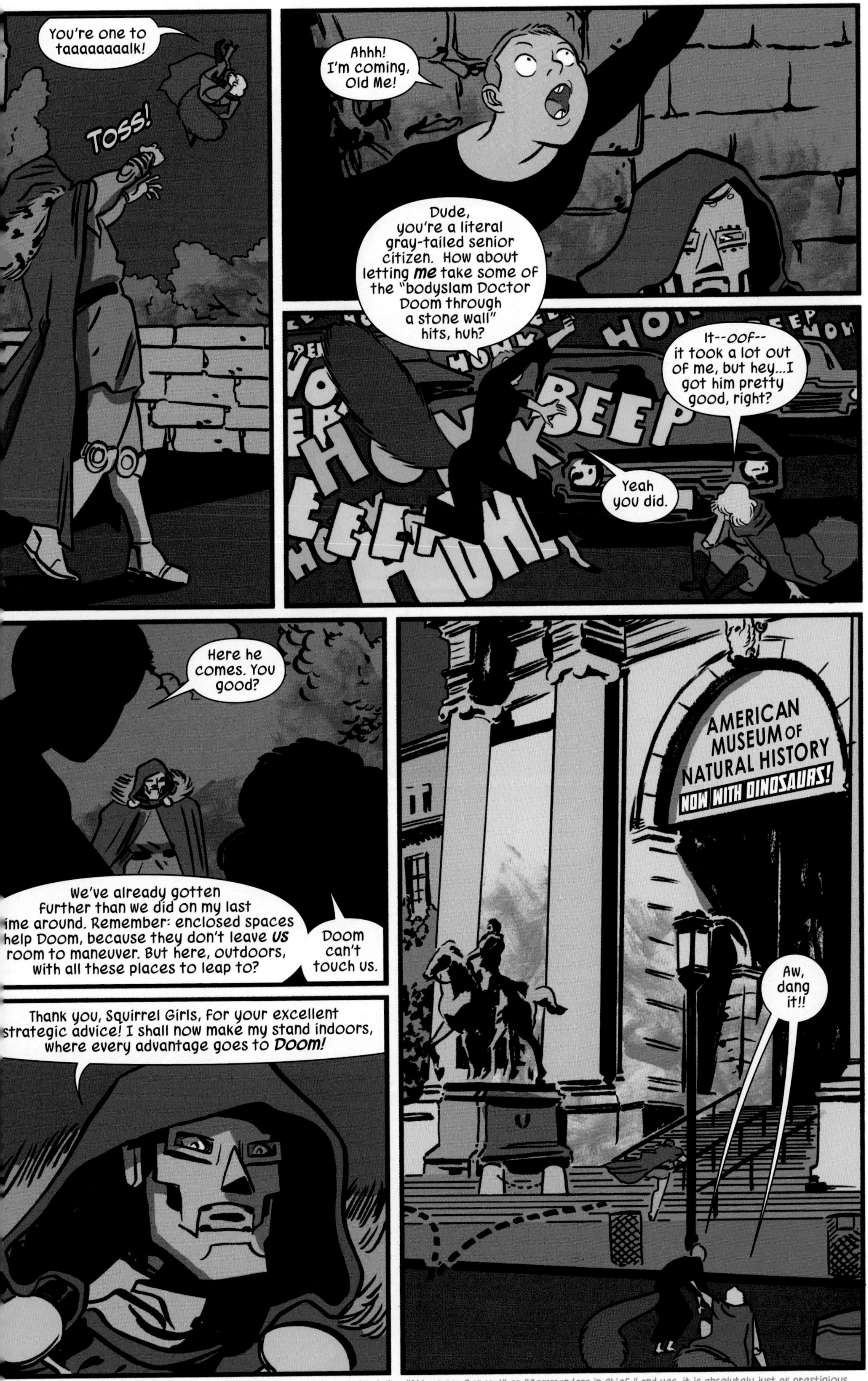
You're one to taaaaaaaalk!
TOSS!
Ahhh! I'm coming, Old Me!
Dude, you're a literal gray-tailed senior citizen. How about letting *me* take some of the "bodyslam Doctor Doom through a stone wall" hits, huh?
HONK
BEEP
It--OOF--it took a lot out of me, but hey...I got him pretty good, right?
Yeah you did.
Here he comes. You good?
We've already gotten further than we did on my last ime around. Remember: enclosed spaces help Doom, because they don't leave *US* room to maneuver. But here, outdoors, with all these places to leap to?
Doom can't touch us.
Thank you, Squirrel Girls, for your excellent strategic advice! I shall now make my stand indoors, where every advantage goes to *DOOM!*
AMERICAN MUSEUM OF NATURAL HISTORY
NOW WITH DINOSAURS!
Aw, dang it!!

Actually, the preferred pluralization is "Squirrels Girl." It's an internal plural, like "Attorneys General" or "Commanders in Chief," and yes, it is absolutely just as prestigious.

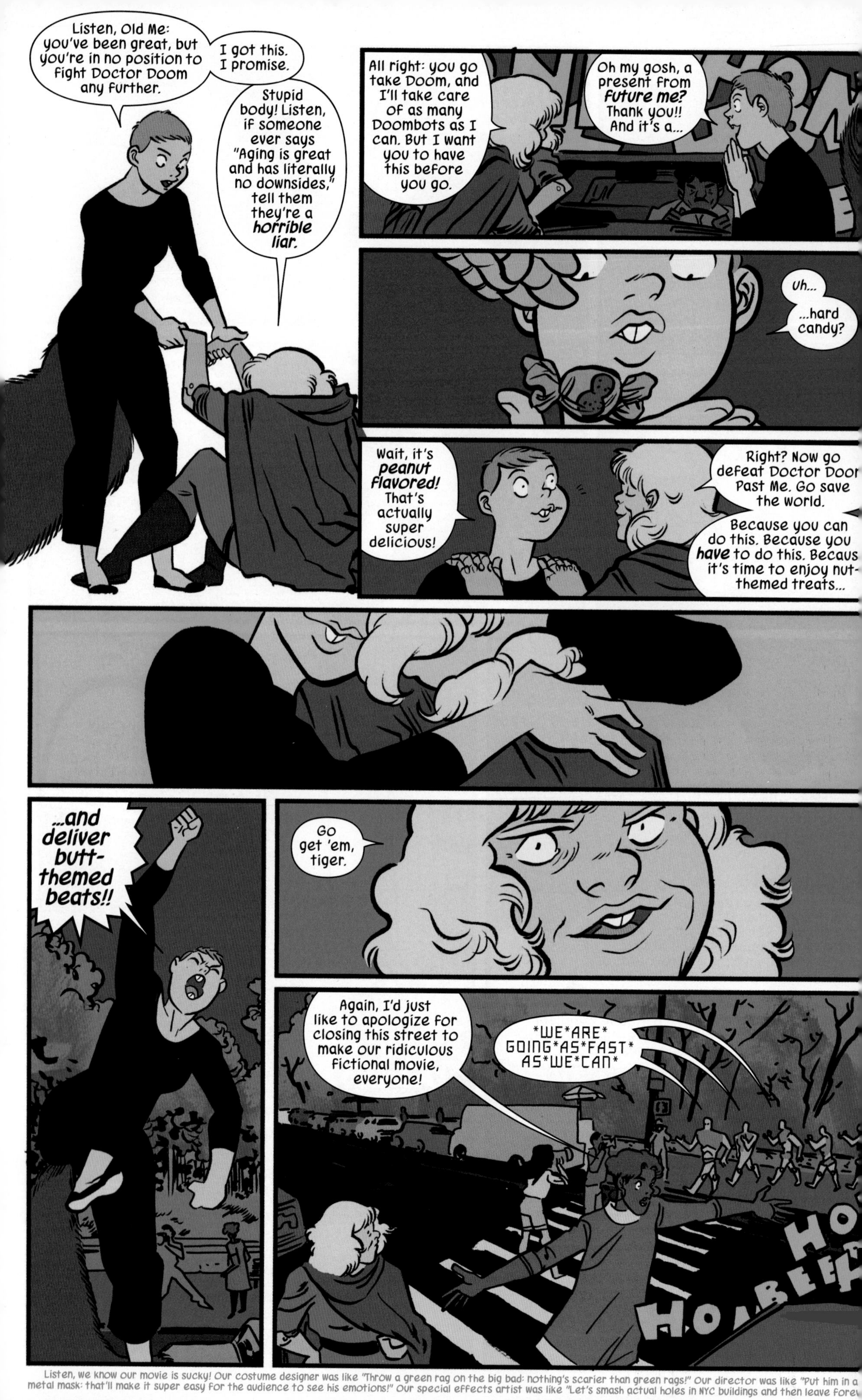
Listen, Old Me: you've been great, but you're in no position to fight Doctor Doom any further.
I got this. I promise.
Stupid body! Listen, if someone ever says "Aging is great and has literally no downsides," tell them they're a horrible liar.
All right: you go take Doom, and I'll take care of as many Doombots as I can. But I want you to have this before you go.
Oh my gosh, a present from future me? Thank you!! And it's a...
Uh...
...hard candy?
Wait, it's peanut flavored! That's actually super delicious!
Right? Now go defeat Doctor Doom Past Me. Go save the world.
Because you can do this. Because you have to do this. Becaus it's time to enjoy nut-themed treats...
...and deliver butt-themed beats!!
Go get 'em, tiger.
Again, I'd just like to apologize for closing this street to make our ridiculous fictional movie, everyone!
*WE*ARE* GOING*AS*FAST* AS*WE*CAN*

Listen, we know our movie is sucky! Our costume designer was like "Throw a green rag on the big bad: nothing's scarier than green rags!" Our director was like "Put him in a metal mask: that'll make it super easy for the audience to see his emotions!" Our special effects artist was like "Let's smash actual holes in NYC buildings and then leave forev

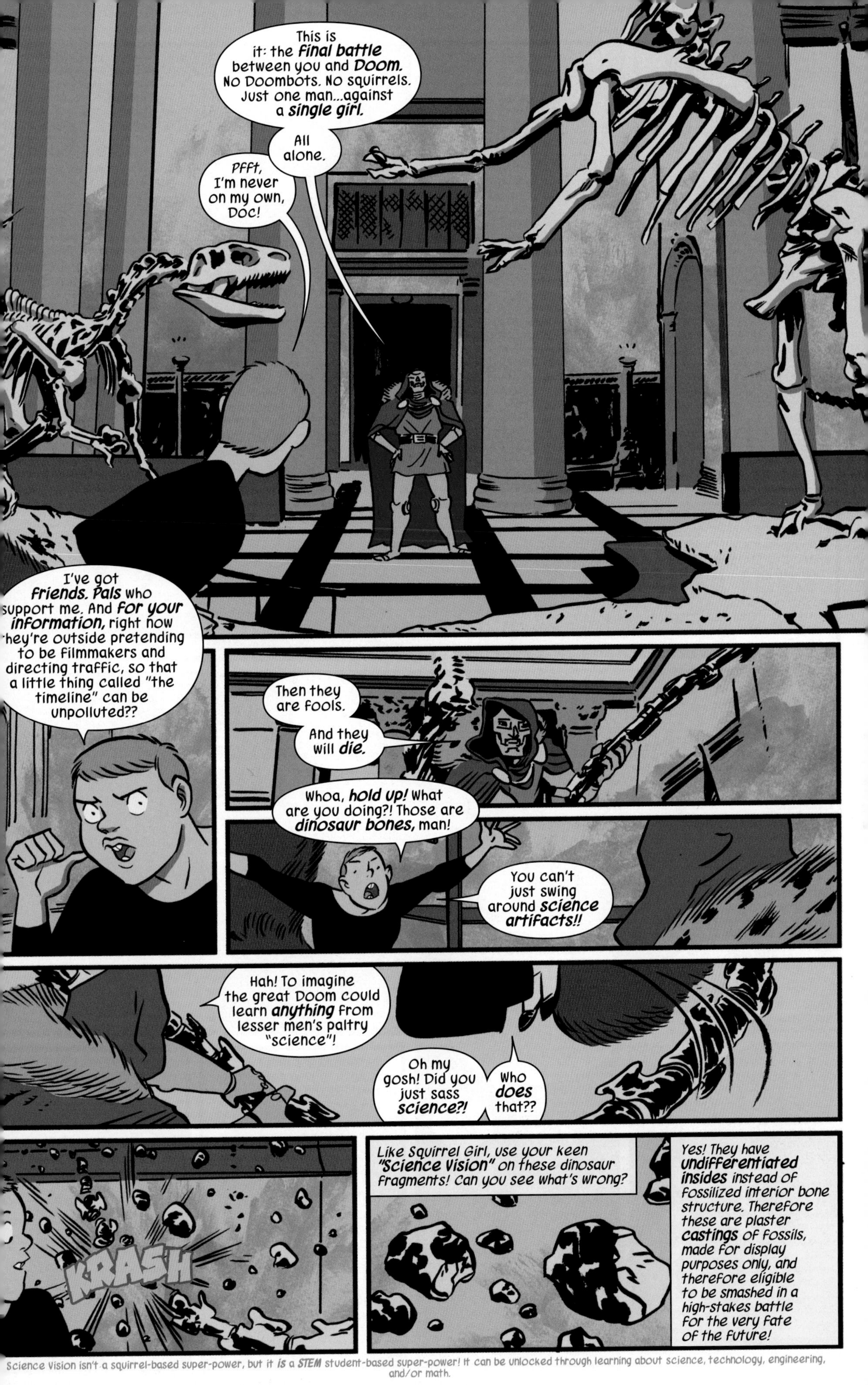

This is it: the final battle between you and Doom. No Doombots. No squirrels. Just one man...against a single girl.
All alone.
Pfft, I'm never on my own, Doc!
I've got friends. Pals who support me. And for your information, right now they're outside pretending to be filmmakers and directing traffic, so that a little thing called "the timeline" can be unpolluted??
Then they are fools.
And they will die.
Whoa, hold up! What are you doing?! Those are dinosaur bones, man!
You can't just swing around science artifacts!!
Hah! To imagine the great Doom could learn anything from lesser men's paltry "science"!
Oh my gosh! Did you just sass science?!
Who does that??
KRASH
Like Squirrel Girl, use your keen "Science Vision" on these dinosaur fragments! Can you see what's wrong?
Yes! They have undifferentiated insides instead of fossilized interior bone structure. Therefore these are plaster castings of fossils, made for display purposes only, and therefore eligible to be smashed in a high-stakes battle for the very fate of the future!

Science Vision isn't a squirrel-based super-power, but it *is* a *STEM* student-based super-power! It can be unlocked through learning about science, technology, engineering, and/or math.

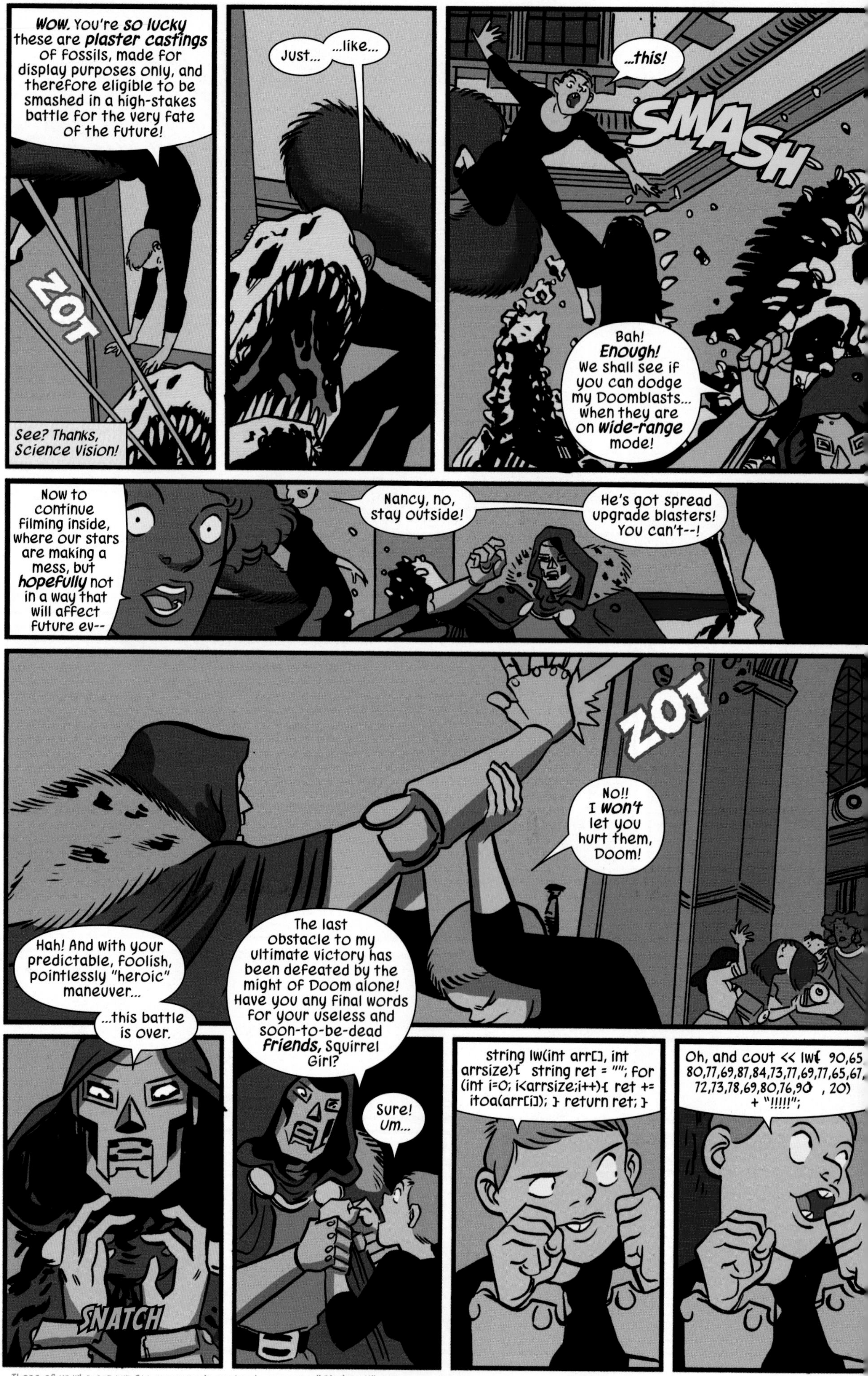
WOW. You're so lucky these are plaster castings of fossils, made for display purposes only, and therefore eligible to be smashed in a high-stakes battle for the very fate of the future!
ZOT
See? Thanks, Science Vision!
Just...
...like...
...this!
SMASH
Bah! Enough! We shall see if you can dodge my Doomblasts... when they are on wide-range mode!
Now to continue filming inside, where our stars are making a mess, but hopefully not in a way that will affect future ev--
Nancy, no, stay outside!
He's got spread upgrade blasters! You can't--!
ZOT
No!! I won't let you hurt them, Doom!
Hah! And with your predictable, foolish, pointlessly "heroic" maneuver...
...this battle is over.
SNATCH
The last obstacle to my ultimate victory has been defeated by the might of Doom alone! Have you any final words for your useless and soon-to-be-dead friends, Squirrel Girl?
Sure! Um...
string lw(int arr[], int arrsize){ string ret = ""; for (int i=0; i<arrsize;i++){ ret += itoa(arr[i]); } return ret; }
Oh, and cout << lw{ 90,65 80,77,69,87,84,73,77,69,77,65,67, 72,73,78,69,80,76,90} , 20) + "!!!!!";

Those of us who can run C++ programs in our heads are going *"Oh dang!!"* right now, while the rest of us are saying "Man, I could run that program in my head if I wanted to," looking around, and then quickly turning the page to see what happens.

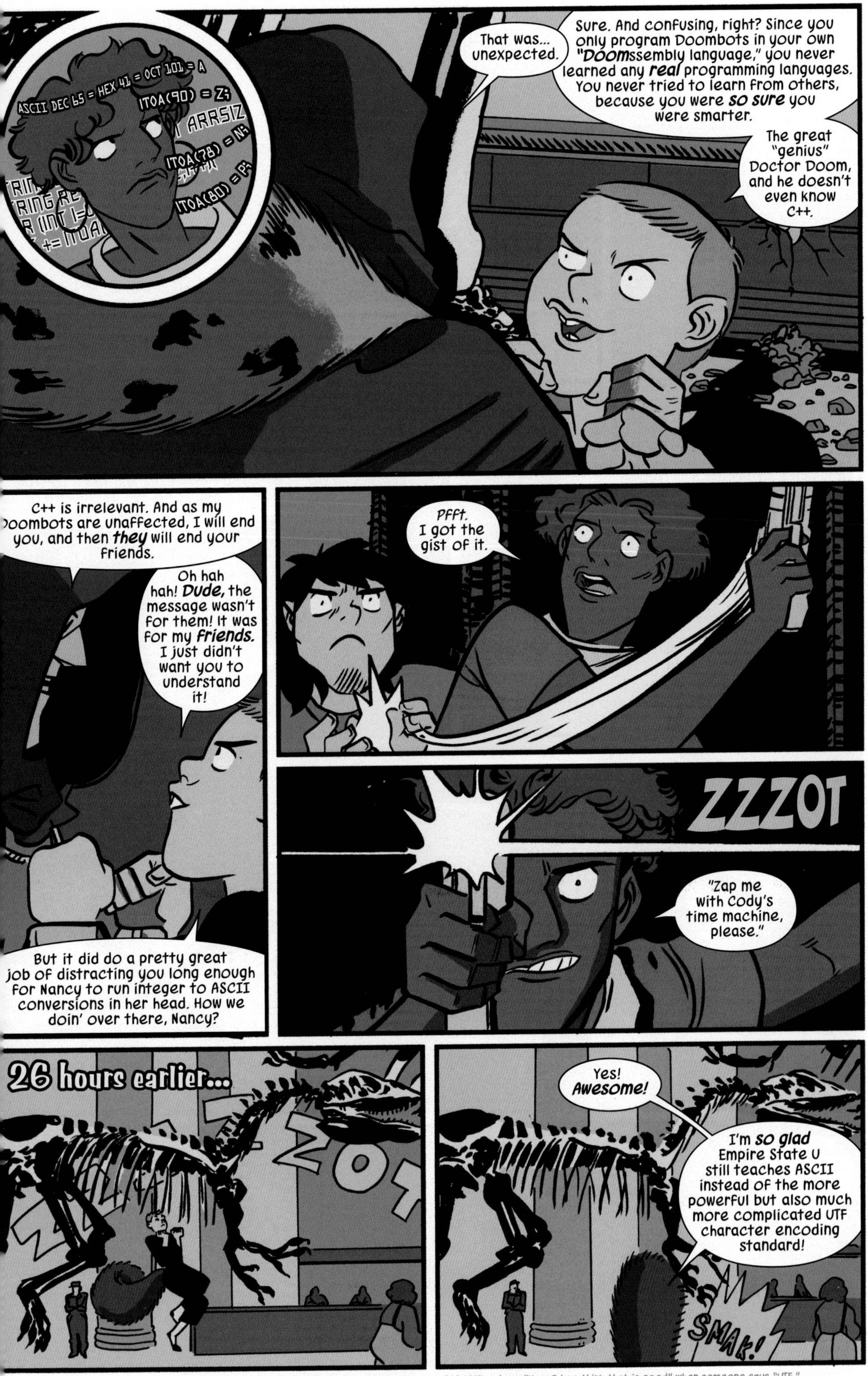
ASCII DEC 65 = HEX 41 = OCT 101 = A
ITOA(90) = Z;
ITOA(78) = N;
ITOA(80) = P;
That was... unexpected.
Sure. And confusing, right? Since you only program Doombots in your own "Doomssembly language," you never learned any real programming languages. You never tried to learn from others, because you were so sure you were smarter.
The great "genius" Doctor Doom, and he doesn't even know C++.
C++ is irrelevant. And as my Doombots are unaffected, I will end you, and then they will end your friends.
Oh hah hah! Dude, the message wasn't for them! It was for my friends. I just didn't want you to understand it!
But it did do a pretty great job of distracting you long enough for Nancy to run integer to ASCII conversions in her head. How we doin' over there, Nancy?
Pfft. I got the gist of it.
ZZZOT
"Zap me with Cody's time machine, please."
26 hours earlier...
ZOT
Yes! Awesome!
I'm so glad Empire State U still teaches ASCII instead of the more powerful but also much more complicated UTF character encoding standard!
SMAK!

Again, these are real computer science facts! Just scoff when someone says "ASCII" and say "Yes, I too think that is good" when someone says "UTF," and you will *absolutely* pass as a computer scientist.

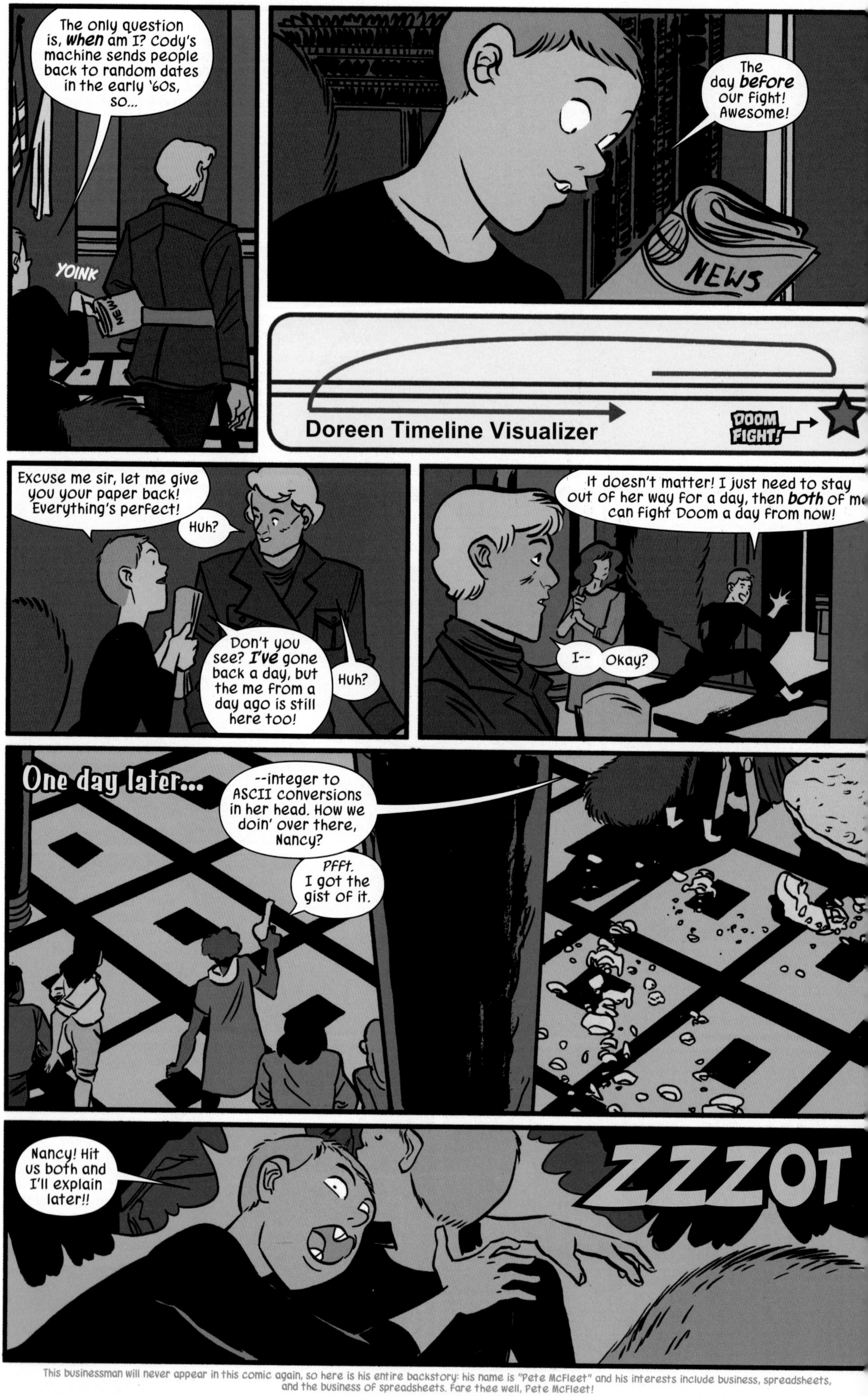
The only question is, *when* am I? Cody's machine sends people back to random dates in the early '60s, so...
YOINK
NEWS
The day *before* our fight! Awesome!
NEWS
Doreen Timeline Visualizer
DOOM FIGHT!
Excuse me sir, let me give you your paper back! Everything's perfect!
Huh?
Don't you see? *I've* gone back a day, but the me from a day ago is still here too!
Huh?
It doesn't matter! I just need to stay out of her way for a day, then *both* of me can fight Doom a day from now!
I--
Okay?
One day later...
--integer to ASCII conversions in her head. How we doin' over there, Nancy?
Pfft. I got the gist of it.
Nancy! Hit us both and I'll explain later!!
ZZZOT

This businessman will never appear in this comic again, so here is his entire backstory: his name is "Pete McFleet" and his interests include business, spreadsheets, and the business of spreadsheets. Fare thee well, Pete McFleet!

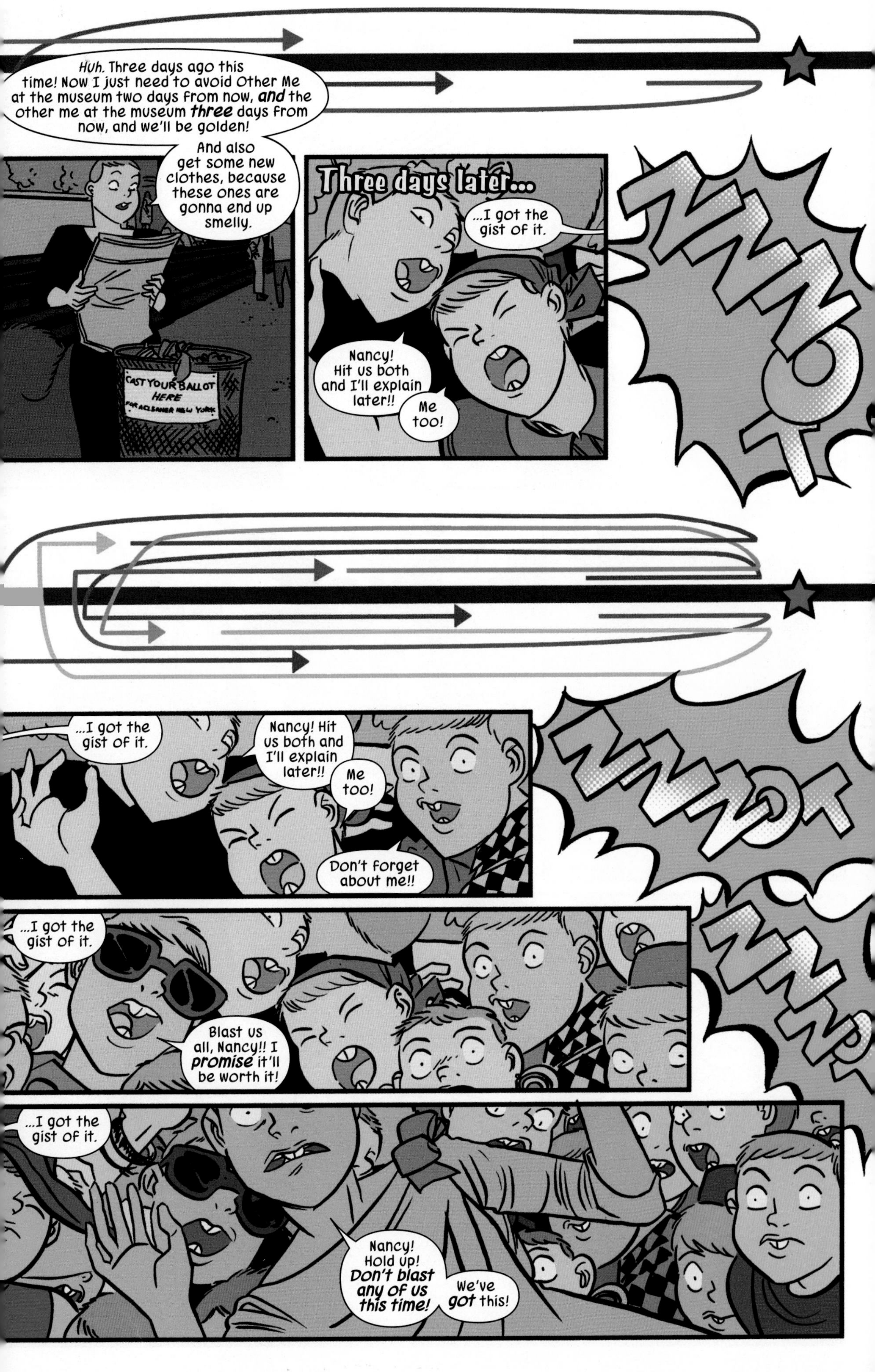
Huh. Three days ago this time! Now I just need to avoid Other Me at the museum two days from now, and the other me at the museum three days from now, and we'll be golden!
And also get some new clothes, because these ones are gonna end up smelly.
CAST YOUR BALLOT HERE FOR A CLEANER NEW YORK
Three days later...
...I got the gist of it.
Nancy! Hit us both and I'll explain later!!
Me too!
NNNOT
...I got the gist of it.
Nancy! Hit us both and I'll explain later!!
Me too!
Don't forget about me!!
NNNOT
...I got the gist of it.
Blast us all, Nancy!! I promise it'll be worth it!
NNNR
...I got the gist of it.
Nancy! Hold up! Don't blast any of us this time!
We've got this!

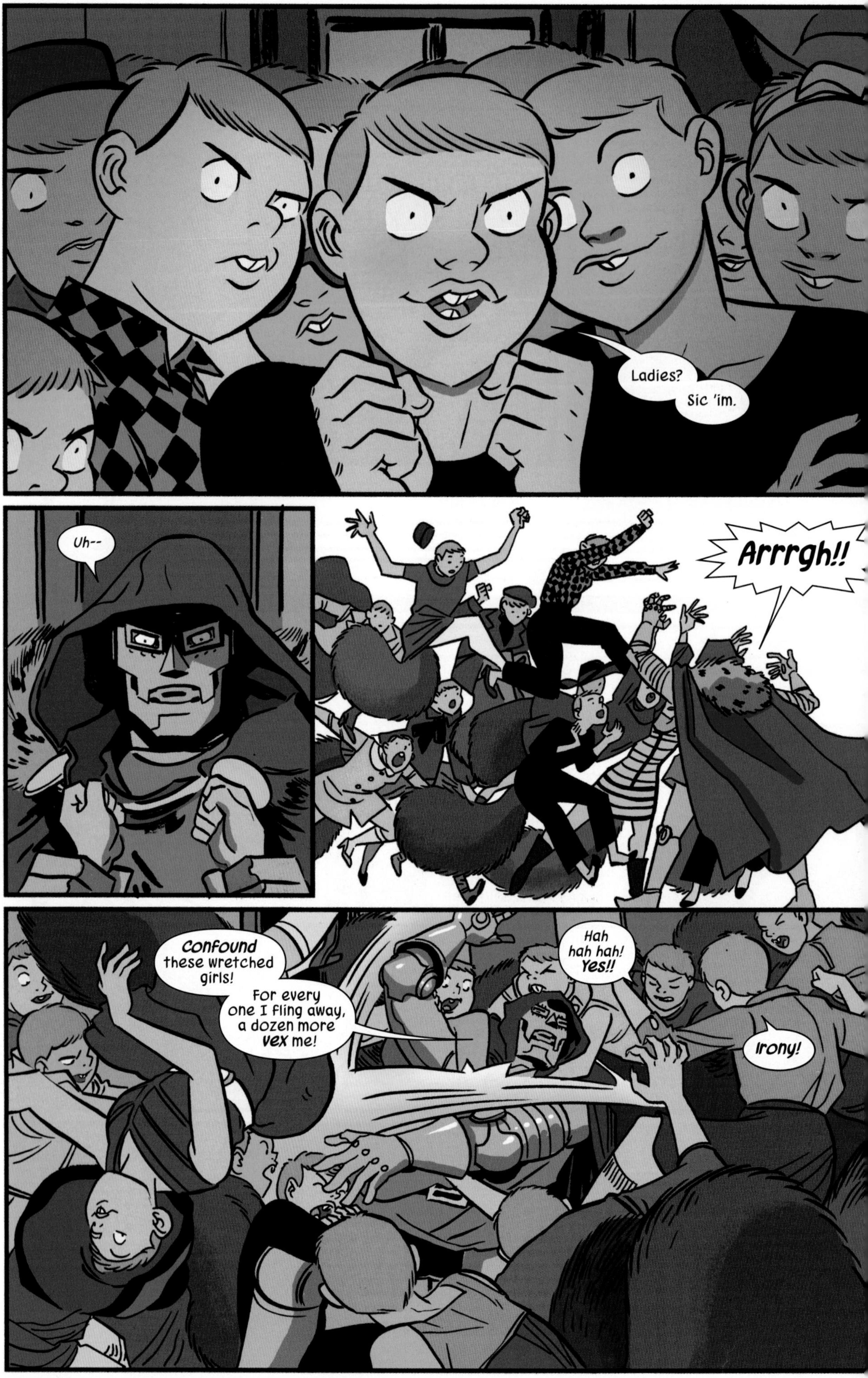
Ladies?
Sic 'im.
Uh--
Arrrgh!!
Confound these wretched girls!
For every one I fling away, a dozen more vex me!
Hah hah hah! Yes!!
Irony!

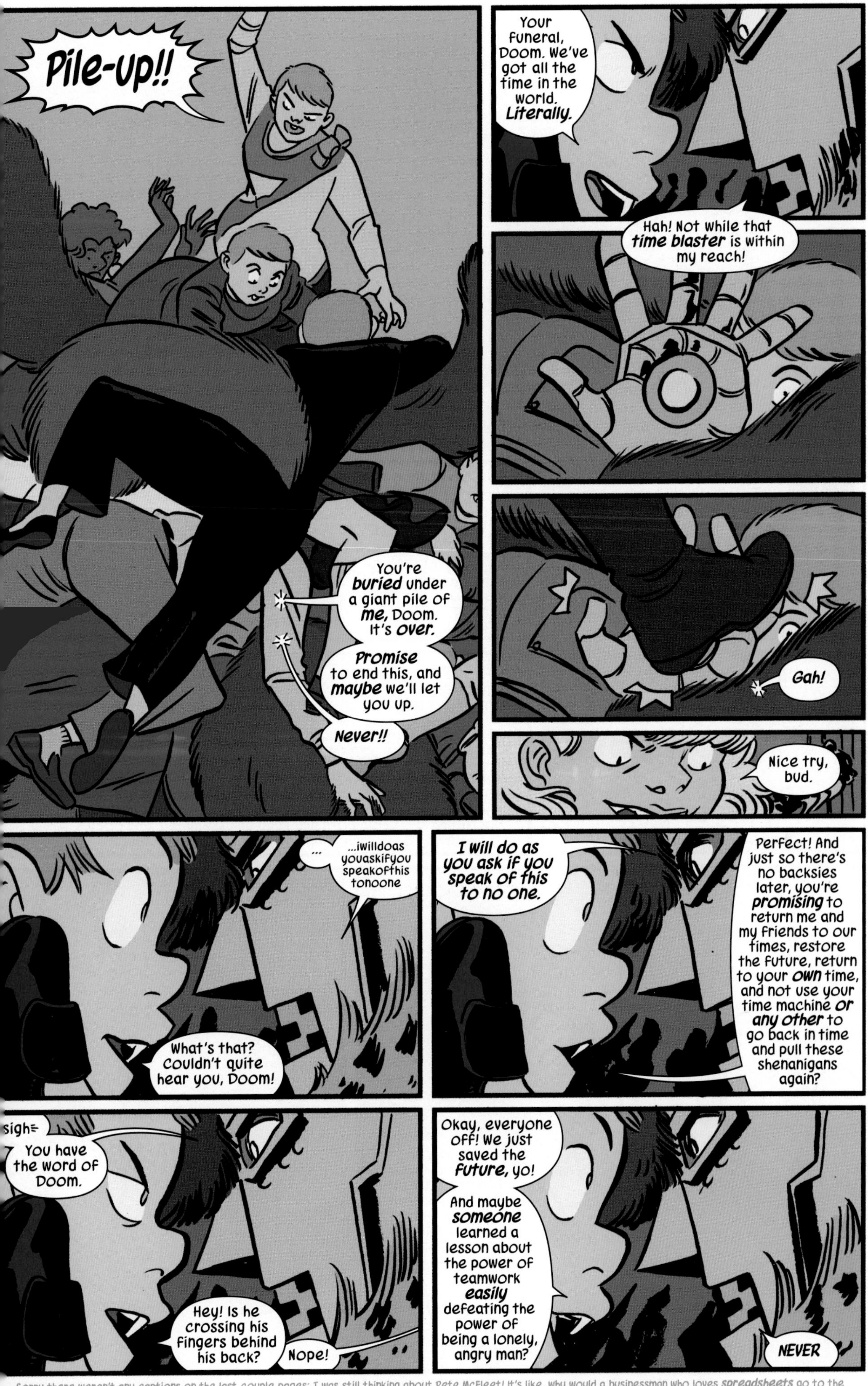
Pile-up!!
Your funeral, Doom. We've got all the time in the world. Literally.
Hah! Not while that time blaster is within my reach!
You're buried under a giant pile of me, Doom. It's over.
Promise to end this, and maybe we'll let you up.
Never!!
Gah!
Nice try, bud.
...
...iwilldoas youaskifyou speakofthis tonoone
What's that? Couldn't quite hear you, Doom!
I will do as you ask if you speak of this to no one.
Perfect! And just so there's no backsies later, you're promising to return me and my friends to our times, restore the future, return to your own time, and not use your time machine or any other to go back in time and pull these shenanigans again?
sigh
You have the word of Doom.
Hey! Is he crossing his fingers behind his back?
Nope!
Okay, everyone off! We just saved the future, yo!
And maybe someone learned a lesson about the power of teamwork easily defeating the power of being a lonely, angry man?
NEVER

Sorry there weren't any captions on the last couple pages: I was still thinking about Pete McFleet! It's like, why would a businessman who loves *spreadsheets* go to the dinosaur exhibit...in the middle of a workday? I'll tell you what I think: I think Pete's a mass of contradictions and untold nuance, and I think he feels things very deeply. I hope he's doing well.

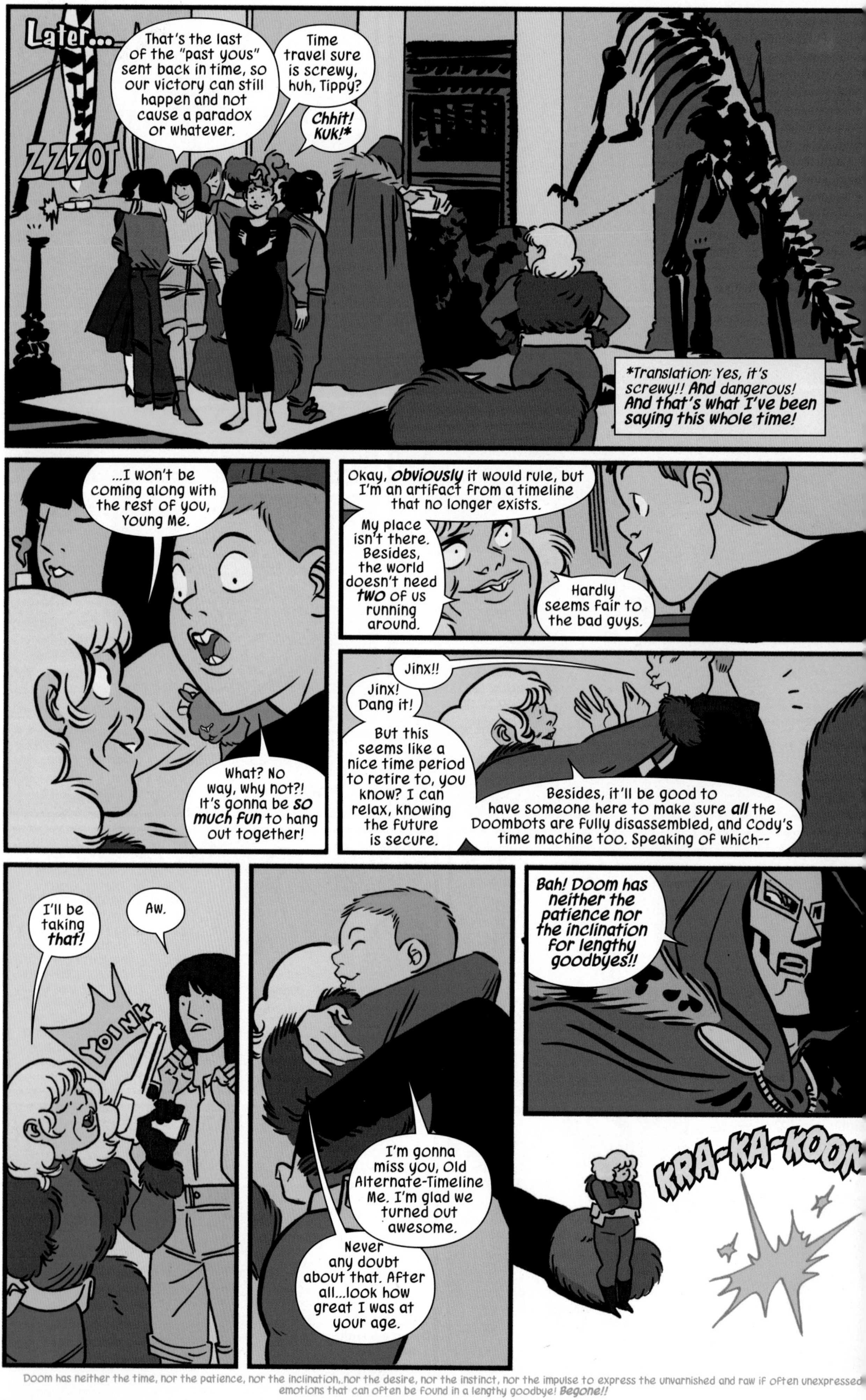
Later...
That's the last of the "past yous" sent back in time, so our victory can still happen and not cause a paradox or whatever.
Time travel sure is screwy, huh, Tippy?
Chhit! KUK!*
ZZZOT
*Translation: Yes, it's screwy!! And dangerous! And that's what I've been saying this whole time!
...I won't be coming along with the rest of you, Young Me.
What? No way, why not?! It's gonna be so much fun to hang out together!
Okay, obviously it would rule, but I'm an artifact from a timeline that no longer exists.
My place isn't there. Besides, the world doesn't need two of us running around.
Hardly seems fair to the bad guys.
Jinx!!
Jinx! Dang it!
But this seems like a nice time period to retire to, you know? I can relax, knowing the future is secure.
Besides, it'll be good to have someone here to make sure all the Doombots are fully disassembled, and Cody's time machine too. Speaking of which--
I'll be taking that!
Aw.
YOINK
I'm gonna miss you, Old Alternate-Timeline Me. I'm glad we turned out awesome.
Never any doubt about that. After all...look how great I was at your age.
Bah! Doom has neither the patience nor the inclination for lengthy goodbyes!!
KRA-KA-KOOM

Doom has neither the time, nor the patience, nor the inclination, nor the desire, nor the instinct, nor the impulse to express the unvarnished and raw if often unexpressed emotions that can often be found in a lengthy goodbye! *Begone!!*

And thus, the future was restored and all the students were dropped off back to their own times and everything was back to normal...

I have undone the alterations from the other time device, and your "friends" are no longer erased from the timeline.

What? Don't put "friends" in quotes! *Friendship is real,* yo, and it kicked *your* butt!

Doom shall put quotes around whatever he pleases.

Pfft.

Well, remember what you agreed to: *you can't change the past.* I'm still protected from timeline changes, so we'll know if you go back on your word!

Doom's word is bond. You have earned my respect today, Squirrel Girl. Very few in this universe can say that. It is all that protects you now.

Pray that you don't lose it.

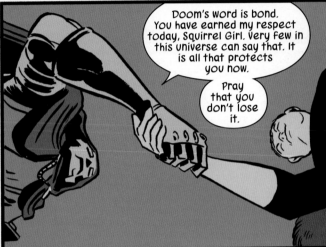

KRA-KA-KOOM

Oh crap: Doreen!! We forgot Doreen in the past!!

Huh? Uh...I mean, who?

Doreen Green! She was there at the start! She was the one who organized the first meeting for us all after spotting my earbuds!

Uh...

Come *on!* She was about your height? With your complexion? And your hair color? And a similar voice, actually? And she disappeared right around when you...

...when you showed up...

Oh my god I'm a complete idiot.

Whoever this "Doreen Green" is, she sounds *pretty amazing* and also very smart? Oh, and cute too. Listen, she sounds great.

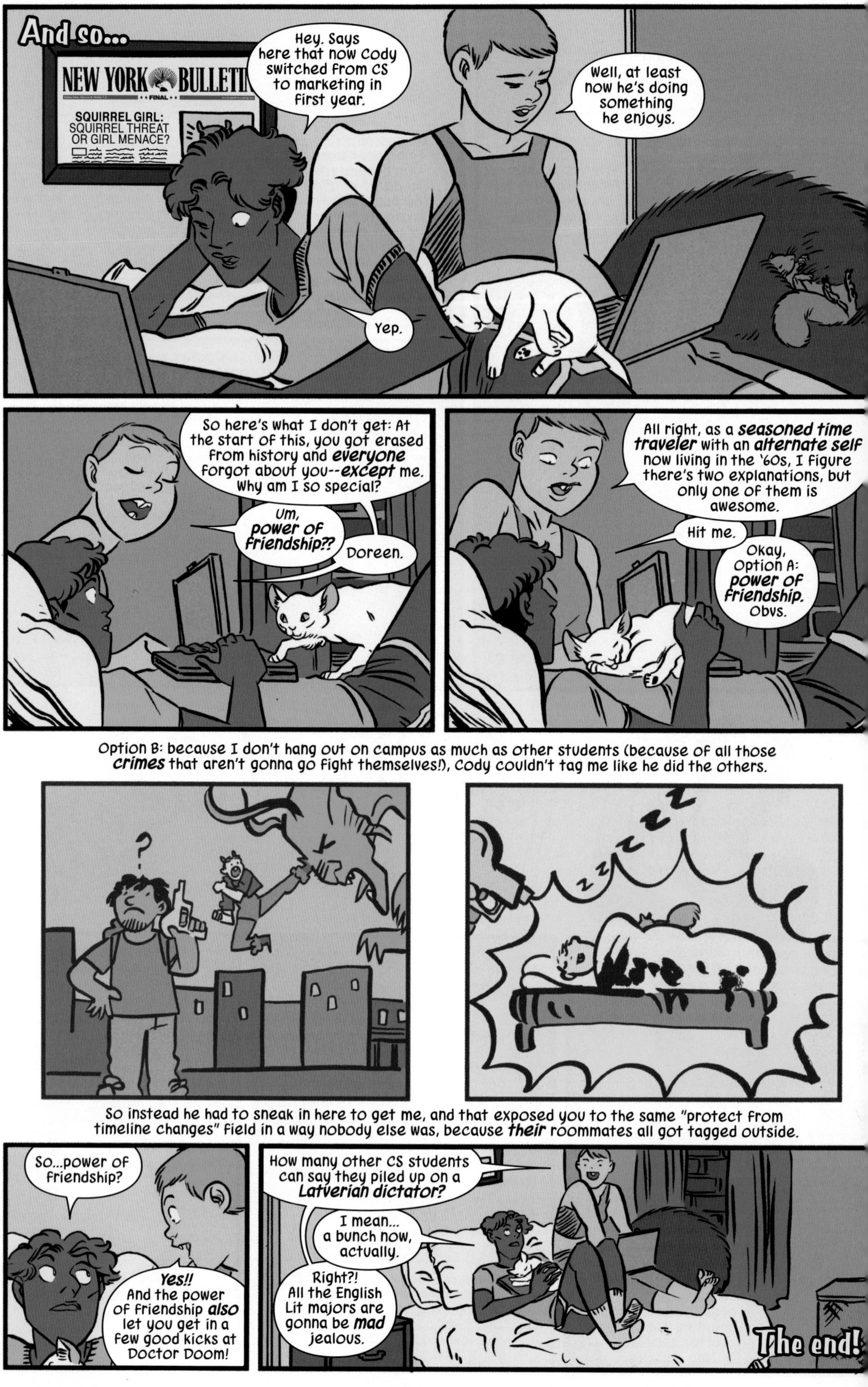
And so...
NEW YORK BULLETI
FINAL
SQUIRREL GIRL: SQUIRREL THREAT OR GIRL MENACE?
Hey. Says here that now Cody switched from CS to marketing in first year.
Well, at least now he's doing something he enjoys.
Yep.
So here's what I don't get: At the start of this, you got erased from history and everyone forgot about you--except me. Why am I so special?
Um, power of friendship??
Doreen.
All right, as a seasoned time traveler with an alternate self now living in the '60s, I figure there's two explanations, but only one of them is awesome.
Hit me.
Okay, Option A: power of friendship. Obvs.
Option B: because I don't hang out on campus as much as other students (because of all those crimes that aren't gonna go fight themselves!), Cody couldn't tag me like he did the others.
?
Z Z Z Z Z Z
So instead he had to sneak in here to get me, and that exposed you to the same "protect from timeline changes" field in a way nobody else was, because their roommates all got tagged outside.
So...power of friendship?
Yes!! And the power of friendship also let you get in a few good kicks at Doctor Doom!
How many other CS students can say they piled up on a Latverian dictator?
I mean... a bunch now, actually.
Right?! All the English Lit majors are gonna be mad jealous.
The end!

Letters From Nuts

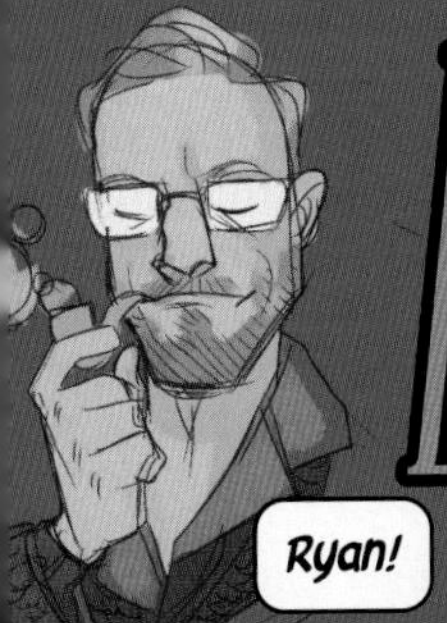

Ryan!

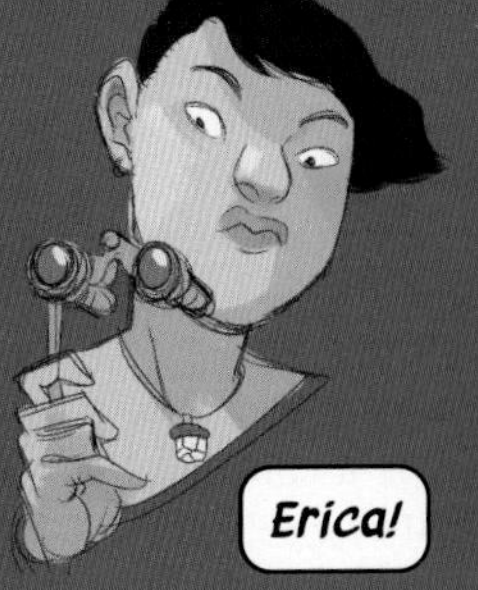

Erica!

Send letters to mheroes@marvel.com or 135 W 50th St, 7th Floor, New York, NY 10020 (Please mark "OKAY TO PRINT")

Dearest Squirrel Girl team,

I just wanted to drop you guys a line bout how amazing this series has been, rom issue 1. It can be difficult to find omics that read so well with my five-ear-old daughter, but you guys have nade it easy. Squirrel Girl has a proud, rominent place in her short box, and nuts" and "butts" a prominent place n her vocabulary, so thanks I guess? nyway, issue 4 in particular was a big hit vith her and the very next morning she nade me staple some paper together so he could start creating her own comics. o keep up the good work!

Cheers,
Alexander and Zoe Burns

PS: Zoe found Galactus to be "very illy," so maybe up your game in the illain department?

RYAN: Haha, that is amazing! MAZING. And I'm super glad we could nspire Zoe to make her own comics. omics is my favorite medium and the nore people playing in it the better! If ur legacy can be "got lots of people nto comics, while at the same time etting lots of people into the word butts,'" I will be a very happy man.

ERICA: From now on we will only stick o the very serious villains like Rhino, he Rhino. Also I am now working on vays to get more butts into this comic.

P.S. A friend of mine who just came ack from visiting family told me that n (adult) relative of hers only JUST earned that girls can read comics, so 'm glad we're getting the word out earlier now!

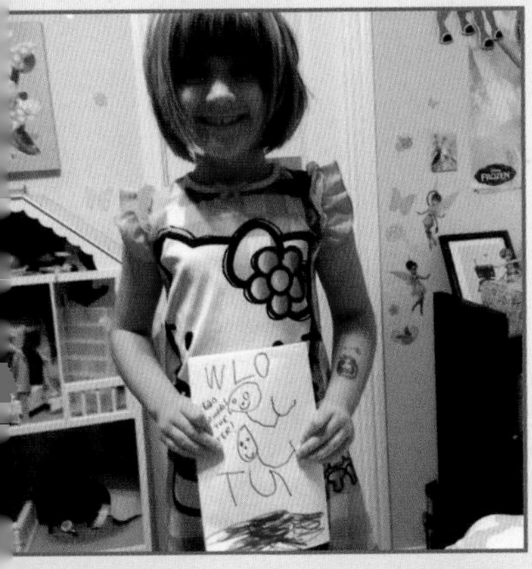

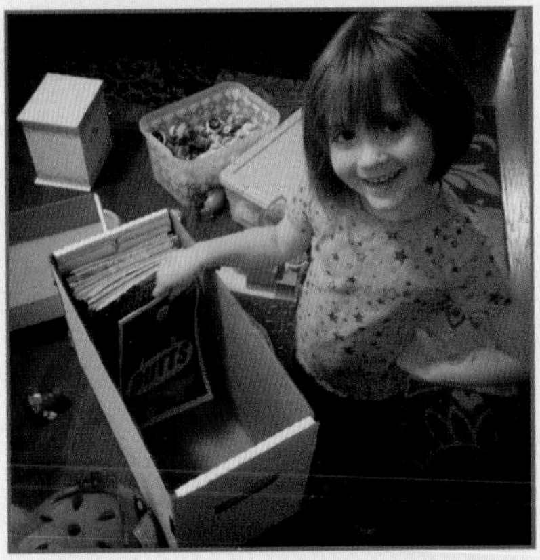

Hello,

I have been a fan of Squirrel Girl for a long time, and I love what you have done with the book. The writing, art, lettering, and coloring, it all matches the tone of the character wonderfully. Keep up the excellent work! Just some questions:

Will Monkey Joe ever make a return from the dead? Will Doreen ever check in with her former teammates in the GLA and see what they have been up to recently? Will she get new villains, maybe take on squirrel hunters? (Or would that be too serious? Maybe make it in tone with comics that took on political issues of the '60s and '70s, though, with a Doreen twist?)

Anyway, happy Squirrel Appreciation Day (Jan 21st), and thanks for the stories.

Paul

R: Guess who didn't know about Squirrel Appreciation Day until just recently, when January 21st rolled around? THIS GUY. We run Squirrel Girl's Twitter account, @unbeatablesg (also, yes, all those Twitter accounts in the recap pages are real, SURPRISE), and that day it was just a million people tagging her with photos of squirrels. It was... kinda the best??

Anyway, in answer to your questions, one of them at least is a yes! But... WHICH ONE?? It's probably the GLA one; Erica's big into seeing Flatman come back. She put a scarf in his likeness on the cover of issue 5 like it wasn't even a big deal!!

E: I learned about Squirrel Appreciation Day about two weeks prior to the 21st because of Cute Overload, may it rest in peace. Anyway, am I allowed to say this? I don't know, I didn't consult with anyone [It's fine, Erica, you can say anything you want! Go ahead! – Wil], but I'm going to pretty firmly say that Monkey Joe is staying the way he is [Wait, what?!? – Wil]. I think I've said it before, but even just going past the whole problem with bringing the dead back, I think as maybe the only super hero to stay dead (and he WAS a full card-carrying member of the GLA, so he's totes a real super hero), his death is the most poignant and important of any super hero. So to sum up, Monkey Joe > most other heroes.

Hey guys!

I can't really add anything on top of the praise I've been reading in your letters column but allow me to throw this out there: If ever there's a Squirrel Girl cartoon, I think Kristen Schaal should do the voice. I already hear her in my head whenever I read the comic, so why not make it official?

Keep up the solid work,

Vrej H.
Brossard, Quebec

R: Thank you! My typical go-to answer to "who should voice-act a character" is "Patrick Stewart" -- regardless of who the character is -- and I'm afraid I must stand firm on that choice here. Whenever you read the comic, please imagine Doreen using Patty Stew's stentorian tones. It is definitely a reasonable thing to do.

That said, Kristen Schaal would be a solid understudy!

E: My vote is Alison Brie. Her voice has such a good "friendly to angry" screaming transition. I think I had Schaal in mind for Tippy. I'm listening to Schaal's voice screeching about time

paradoxes right now, actually.

Dear Ryan and Erica,

My 10-year-old daughter has gone nuts for Squirrel Girl! She was just outside singing the Squirrel Girl theme song to a squirrel in the tree. It's great to have a comic that has hooked the whole family. Keep up the great work!

Here is a picture of her wearing her Squirrel Girl shirt, holding her Deadpool's Guide to Super Villains trading cards that she made herself, and her stuffed toy Tippy-Toe, and she is wearing a Squirrel Girl headband she also made herself.

Amy (and young Squirrel Girl superfan)

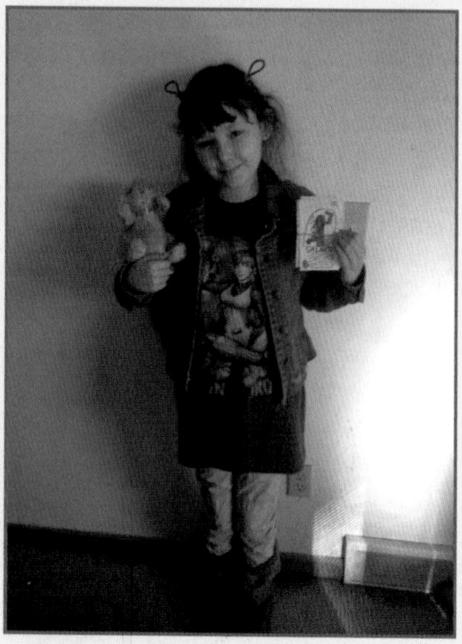

R: Amy, your daughter is SUPER GREAT, and I love her Deadpool cards. If Squirrel Girl got de-aged into a 10-year-old girl, I think your daughter would be a dead ringer for her! And yes, I know that this implies that a de-aged Doreen would go around wearing a Squirrel Girl t-shirt. I feel like that fits her personality -- kinda perfectly, actually??

E: I love this. This is great. Seeing people make their own Deadpool cards is one of my favorite things.

Dear Erica & Ryan,

I don't remember when or how I picked up the first issue of SQUIRREL GIRL, but I can tell you I've never put it down! Doreen's ability to defuse potential conflicts into friendship is the best ability (honestly, the Avengers are underutilizing her amazingness). Maybe Mr. Ultron could have been persuaded to value humanity by sharing some hearty laughs over a cup of tea and candied pecans (seriously, Avengers, a prerequisite Squirrel Essentials 101 course). With that being said, I wanted to thank your team and all my fellow fans of Squirrel Girl for ensuring her a place on comic store shelves. Doreen Green adds the much needed joy and sunshine into my otherwise exhausting graduate student life!!!

Forever A Squirrel Girl Fan,

Brandy Heath
Syracuse, NY

R: Aw, thank you, Brandy! I'm stoked that we can end out a column that has lots of "my child loves your comic!" letters with a "I am a grad student and I love your comic too!" letter. When I was a grad student I was not a particularly great grad student, because I spent most of my free time writing comics instead of researching the class-based productivity of light verb expressions like "take a walk" and "give a smile," like I was supposed to be doing. So I'm glad I can kinda make up for that by having our comics HELP you in your studies by giving you a break from your work!

P.S.: In case you're interested, turns out they ARE productive, and to find out more, look up "Computational Measures of the Acceptibility of Light Verb Constructions by Ryan North" to find my Masters thesis on the matter! It took me three years, so I am absolutely justified in giving it a shout out on the letters page of our talking squirrel comic.

E: I only have four years of higher education under my belt, which is probably okay considering I really only use my BFA in film to tweet about old movies that aren't very good. At any rate, I'm glad we can help you take a break. It'll make your work that much better! As a serial workaholic, I know what I'm talking about here!

Okay, everybody, thanks again for reading and writing in -- keep the letters and photos coming! And hey, come back next month for "Animal House" Part One, kicking off our two-part crossover with HOWARD THE DUCK! The creative team of HOWARD, writer Chip Zdarsky and artist Joe Quinones, will be joining us, and then we'll be joining them on HOWARD THE DUCK #6 a few weeks later!

Want some teases? Here you go: Learn the origin of Squirrel Girl's new costume! Witness the return of Kraven driving his new Kra-Van! And watch Doreen and Howard throw garbage at each other! It's truly gonna be a story for the ages!!!

USG#5 Michael Cho variant:

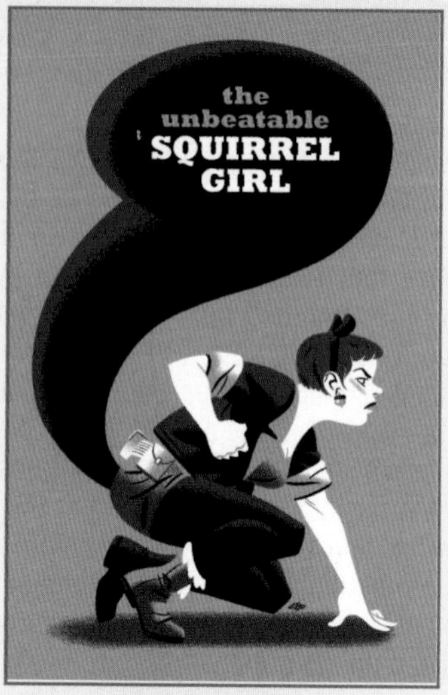
the unbeatable SQUIRREL GIRL

USG #6 cover:

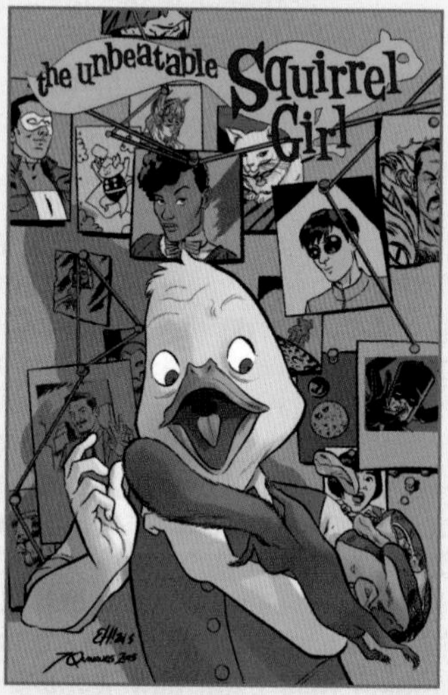
the unbeatable Squirrel Girl

Howard the Duck #6 cover:

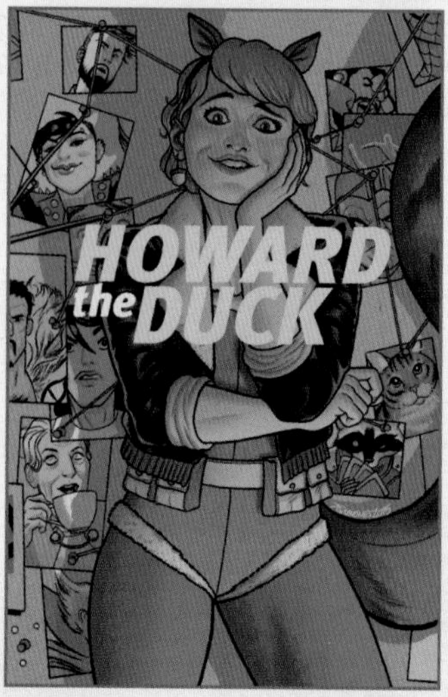
HOWARD the DUCK

Attention, Squirrel Scouts! Make sure to check out our production blog, **unbeatablesquirrelgirl.tumblr.com**, where we post behind-the-scenes stuff on how the book gets made, along with all sorts of cool things *you* make: fanart, cosplay, whatever!

Meanwhile, in the past...

To think that the great *Doctor Doom* could suffer *any* defeat at the claws of *Squirrel Girl* is too insulting-- too *ignominious*-- to consider!

All the better that, by the time this hour is out, it will *never* have taken place! For while Doom *did* make promises about his *own* time traveling...

...he made *no* such promises for his *Doombots!*

Come, Doombots, to my *time platform!* I shall send *you* back in time, where your new mission will be to *aid* your master in his battle against that vile woman!

Defeat the Squirrel Girl, or you shall *all* be reduced to debris, nothing more than worthless metal s--

--crap.

Squirrel Girl.

Blast you, Squirrel Girl!

Blaaast youuu, Squiiiirrél Giiiirl!

Blaaaaaaasssssssst youuuuuuuuuuuu!!

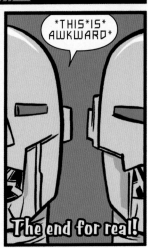

THIS *IS* AWKWARD*

The end for real!

Afterwards Old Lady Squirrel Girl lived happily ever after until she eventually died of old age, which is a pretty good way to go, assuming you have to. And in her will she left the time blaster to Cody, so everything would work out as it was supposed to! *Oh snap she was the weird aunt all along, oh snap!!*

6

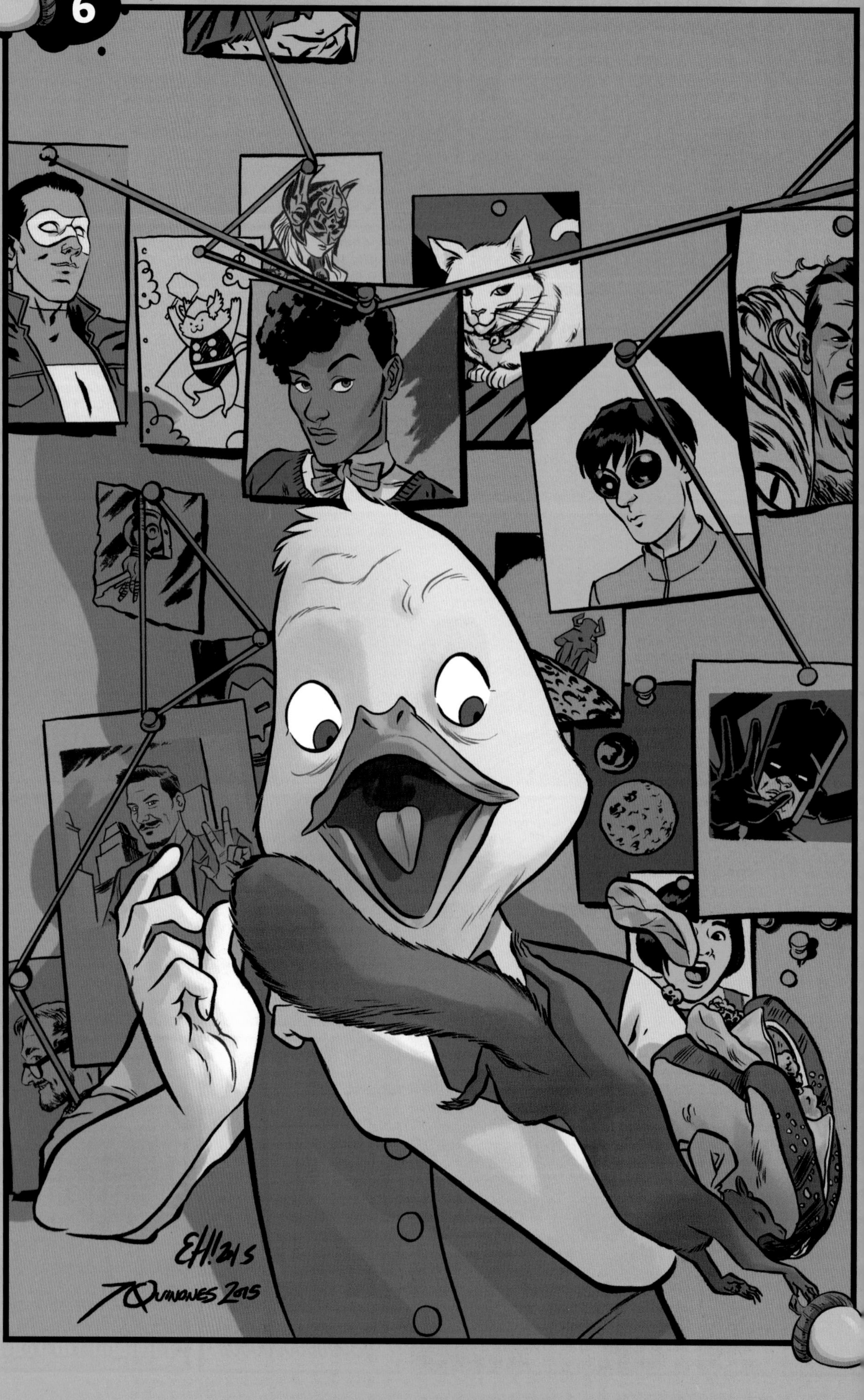
EH! 2015
QUINONES 2015

Doreen Green isn't just a first-year computer science student: she secretly also has all the powers of both squirrel and girl! She uses her amazing abilities to fight crime **and** be as awesome as possible. You know her as...**The Unbeatable Squirrel Girl!** Let's catch up with what she's been up to until now, with...

Squirrel Girl in a nutshell

Nancy W. @sewwiththeflo
That's right. You are reading the tweets of a first-year computer science GRADUATE, friends and neighbors. 2nd year, here I come.

Nancy W. @sewwiththeflo
But first: a summer break filled with knitting, Mew, knitting, Mew, movies, knitting, and Mew.

Squirrel Girl @unbeatablesg
@sewwiththeflo OMG Nancy that sounds super great!! make it a double

Nancy W. @sewwiththeflo
@unbeatablesg Yes! It sure does! Thank you for taking an INEXPLICABLE INTEREST IN ME, RANDOM SUPER HERO!!

Squirrel Girl @unbeatablesg
@starkmantony Hey Tony!! You don't have a secret identity--do you think that's something other super heroes should try? Seems easier tbh

Tony Stark @starkmantony
@unbeatablesg Who says I don't have a secret identity? ;P

Squirrel Girl @unbeatablesg
@starkmantony omg did you just type out a winky smiley with its tongue hanging out

Squirrel Girl @unbeatablesg
@starkmantony did a founding member of the avengers and platinum-elite ceo just send me a ;P

Tony Stark @starkmantony
@unbeatablesg No. Obviously I am too important a person to have done that. It must have been my secretary, who sent it by accident.

Squirrel Girl @unbeatablesg
@starkmantony your secretary. who handles chatting online for you. who reads your messages and then takes your dictated responses.

Tony Stark @starkmantony
@unbeatablesg Tell her yes, Jarvis, and let's leave it there. Stop typing, Jarvis. There's no reason for you to be typing. Jarvis.

Squirrel Girl @unbeatablesg
@starkmantony hahaha NICE TRY ;P ;P ;P

Howard The Duck @imhowatrd
thids siote is badf!!@ how comr thisd wax the onhyl namr lefy

Howard The Duck @imhowatrd
anf its hardf top tyhpe wi8tghy feqaythers anbyewayh!1 whyt wolujd anyon e ujse thyis stu[id sitew

Squirrel Girl @unbeatablesg
@imhowatrd You should talk to the Hulk! The fact that @HULKYSMASHY was the only name left for HIM just serves to increase his anger too!!

HULK @HULKYSMASHY
@unbeatablesg @imhowatrd HULK ALSO GET ANGRY THAT WE CAN SEND MAN TO MOON BUT SOMEHOW CAN'T FILTER OUT PEOPLE SASSING HULK ON THIS SITE??

HULK @HULKYSMASHY
@unbeatablesg @imhowatrd HULK DOESN'T NEED RANDOS TELLING HIM OFF!!!! HULK SMASH ENOUGH KEYBOARDS ALREADY!!!

HULK @HULKYSMASHY
@unbeatablesg @imhowatrd ARGH!! HJGIHBDA,N'K',KNGDS'HJRWPO98Y43POUEQ IU'

Squirrel Girl @unbeatablesg
@HULKYSMASHY @imhowatrd It's okay big guy! They don't know the REAL you, remember!!

Howard The Duck @imhowatrd
@unbeatablesg @HULKYSMASHY i donlt kmow anyt of youi perople

search!

#kraVAN

#kraVAN

#kraVAN

#kraVAN

#kraVAN

#kraVAN4life

Ryan North with
Chip Zdarsky - writers
Erica Henderson - artist
Chip again - trading card artist
Joe Quinones - van art, *uh,* artist
Rico Renzi - color artist
Travis Lanham - letterer & production
Erica Henderson with
Joe Quinones - cover artists
Erica Henderson with
Chip Zdarsky; Tradd Moore & Matthew Wilson;
Kamome Shirahama - variant cover artists
Chris Robinson - ex-asst. editor
Charles Beacham - new asst. editor
Wil Moss - editor
Tom Brevoort - executive editor
Axel Alonso - editor in chief
Joe Quesada - chief creative officer
Dan Buckley - publisher
Alan Fine - exec. producer

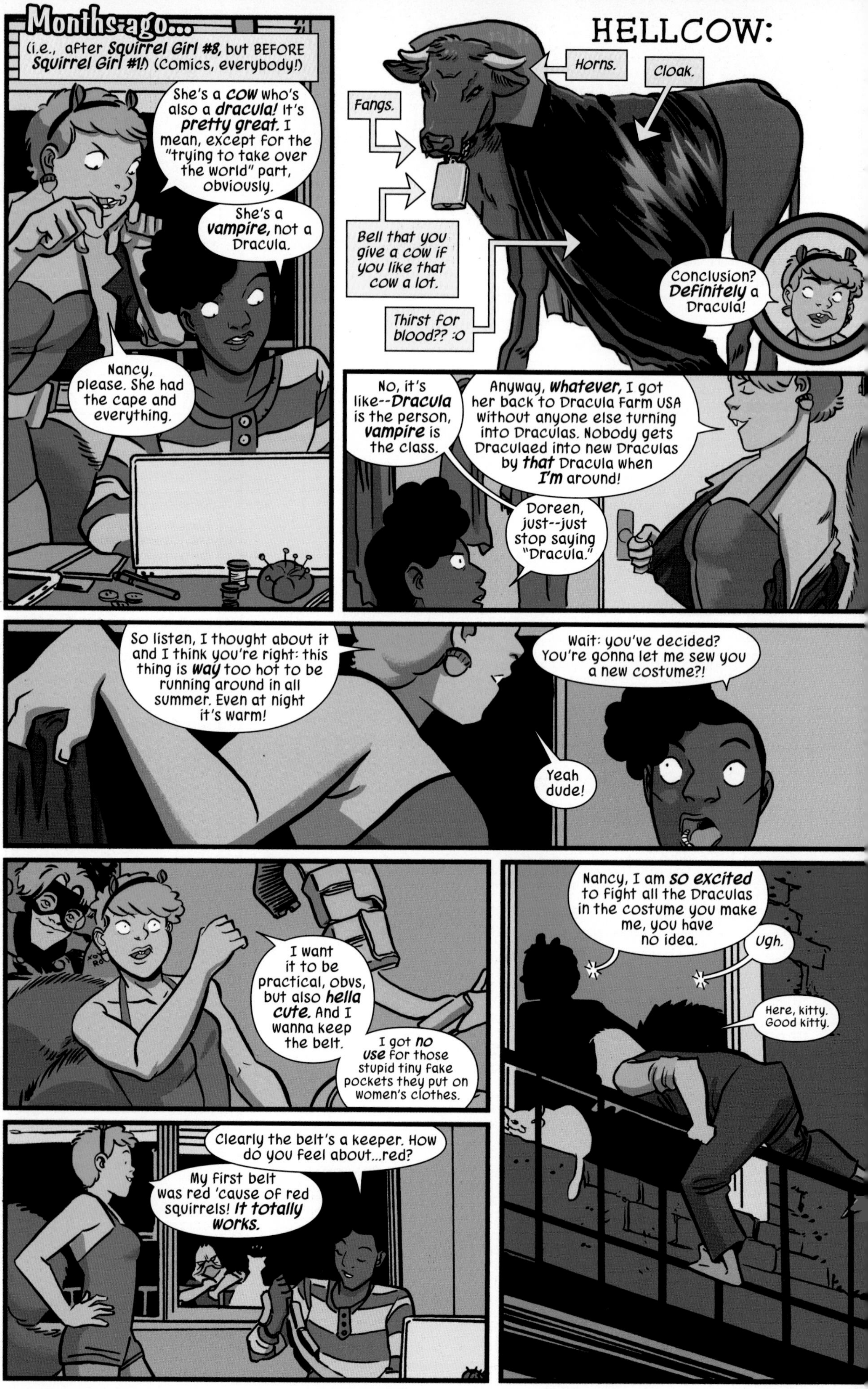

Months ago...
(i.e., after Squirrel Girl #8, but BEFORE Squirrel Girl #1!) (Comics, everybody!)
She's a cow who's also a dracula! It's pretty great. I mean, except for the "trying to take over the world" part, obviously.
She's a vampire, not a Dracula.
Nancy, please. She had the cape and everything.
HELLCOW:
Horns.
Cloak.
Fangs.
Bell that you give a cow if you like that cow a lot.
Thirst for blood?? :O
Conclusion? Definitely a Dracula!
No, it's like--Dracula is the person, vampire is the class.
Anyway, whatever, I got her back to Dracula Farm USA without anyone else turning into Draculas. Nobody gets Draculaed into new Draculas by that Dracula when I'm around!
Doreen, just--just stop saying "Dracula."
So listen, I thought about it and I think you're right: this thing is way too hot to be running around in all summer. Even at night it's warm!
Wait: you've decided? You're gonna let me sew you a new costume?!
Yeah dude!
I want it to be practical, obvs, but also hella cute. And I wanna keep the belt.
I got no use for those stupid tiny fake pockets they put on women's clothes.
Nancy, I am so excited to fight all the Draculas in the costume you make me, you have no idea.
Ugh.
Here, kitty. Good kitty.
Clearly the belt's a keeper. How do you feel about...red?
My first belt was red 'cause of red squirrels! It totally works.

Oh, and if it strikes terror into the cowardly and superstitious hearts of criminals, all the better! So to summarize: practical, cute, reduces criminals to a state of quivering and abject terror, useful pockets and/or belt. Got it, Chip?

Is this...do you do this in every issue? Does Marvel pay more for these?

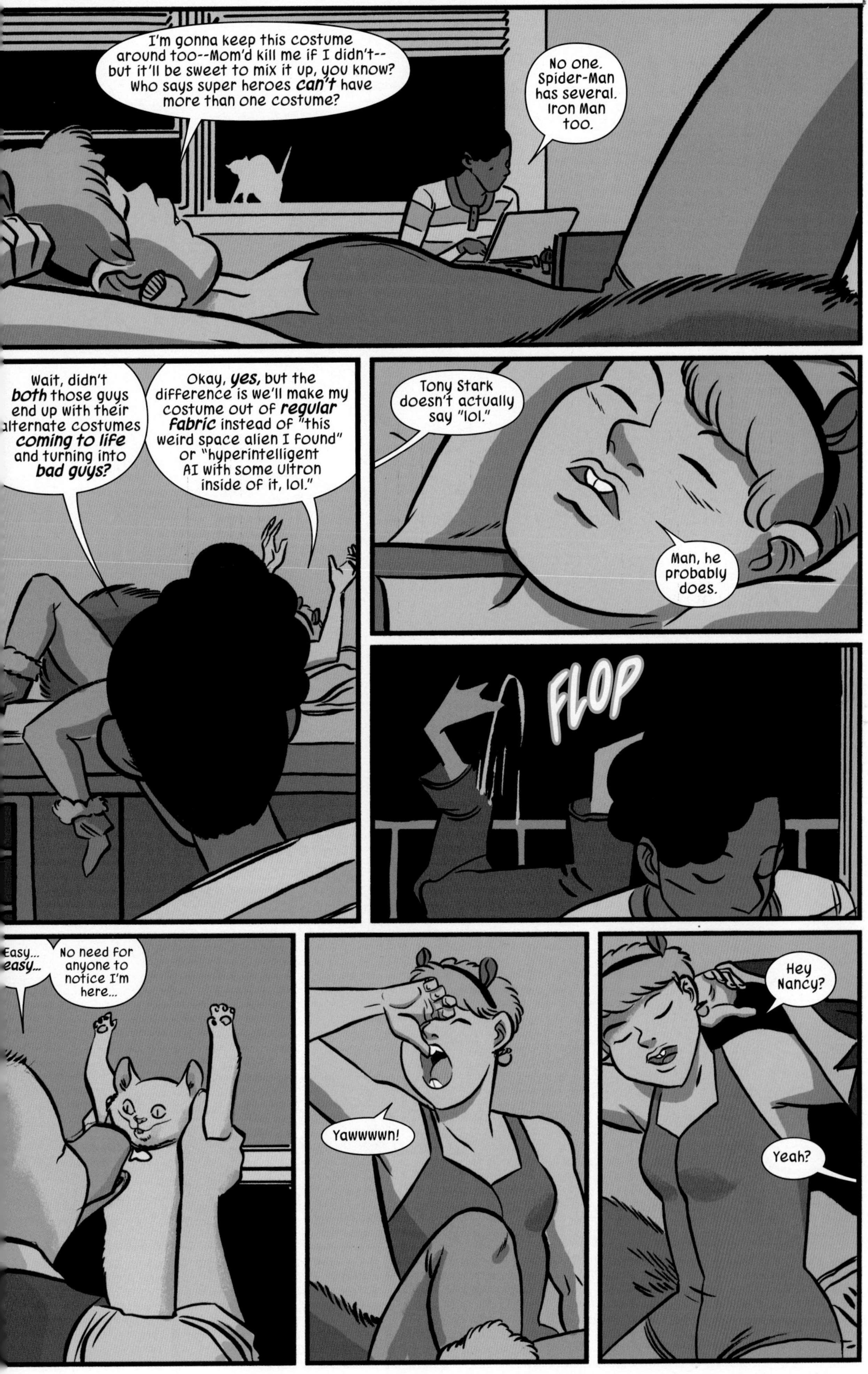

I'm gonna keep this costume around too--Mom'd kill me if I didn't--but it'll be sweet to mix it up, you know? Who says super heroes **can't** have more than one costume?
No one. Spider-Man has several. Iron Man too.
Wait, didn't **both** those guys end up with their alternate costumes **coming to life** and turning into **bad guys?**
Okay, **yes,** but the difference is we'll make my costume out of **regular fabric** instead of "this weird space alien I found" or "hyperintelligent AI with some Ultron inside of it, lol."
Tony Stark doesn't actually say "lol."
Man, he probably does.
FLOP
Easy... **easy...**
No need for anyone to notice I'm here...
Yawwwwn!
Hey Nancy?
Yeah?

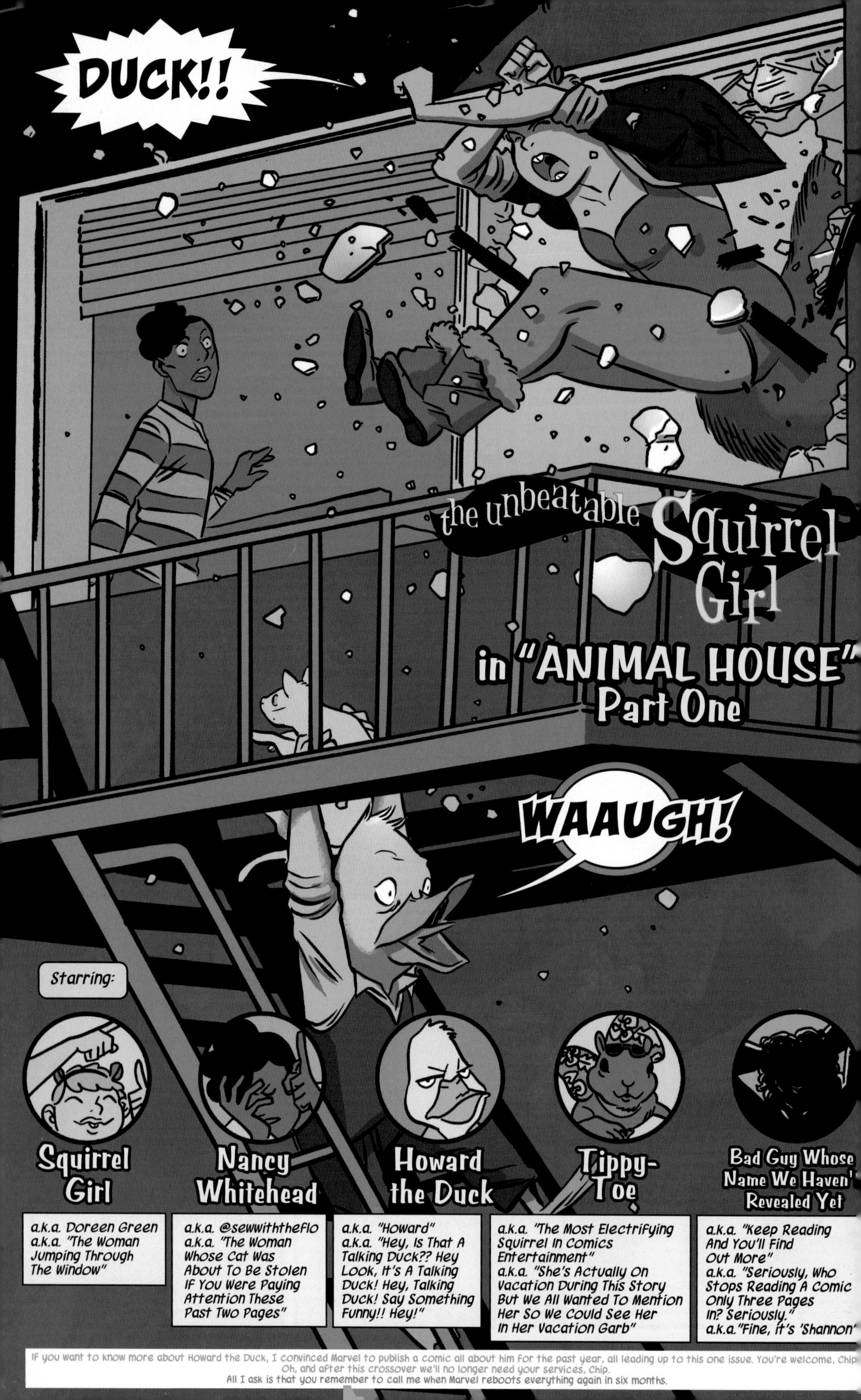
DUCK!!
the unbeatable Squirrel Girl
in "ANIMAL HOUSE" Part One
WAAUGH!
Starring:
Squirrel Girl
a.k.a. Doreen Green a.k.a. "The Woman Jumping Through The Window"
Nancy Whitehead
a.k.a. @sewwiththeflo a.k.a. "The Woman Whose Cat Was About To Be Stolen If You Were Paying Attention These Past Two Pages"
Howard the Duck
a.k.a. "Howard" a.k.a. "Hey, Is That A Talking Duck?? Hey Look, It's A Talking Duck! Hey, Talking Duck! Say Something Funny!! Hey!"
Tippy-Toe
a.k.a. "The Most Electrifying Squirrel In Comics Entertainment" a.k.a. "She's Actually On Vacation During This Story But We All Wanted To Mention Her So We Could See Her In Her Vacation Garb"
Bad Guy Whose Name We Haven't Revealed Yet
a.k.a. "Keep Reading And You'll Find Out More" a.k.a. "Seriously, Who Stops Reading A Comic Only Three Pages In? Seriously." a.k.a."Fine, it's 'Shannon'"
If you want to know more about Howard the Duck, I convinced Marvel to publish a comic all about him for the past year, all leading up to this one issue. You're welcome, Chip.
Oh, and after this crossover we'll no longer need your services, Chip.
All I ask is that you remember to call me when Marvel reboots everything again in six months.

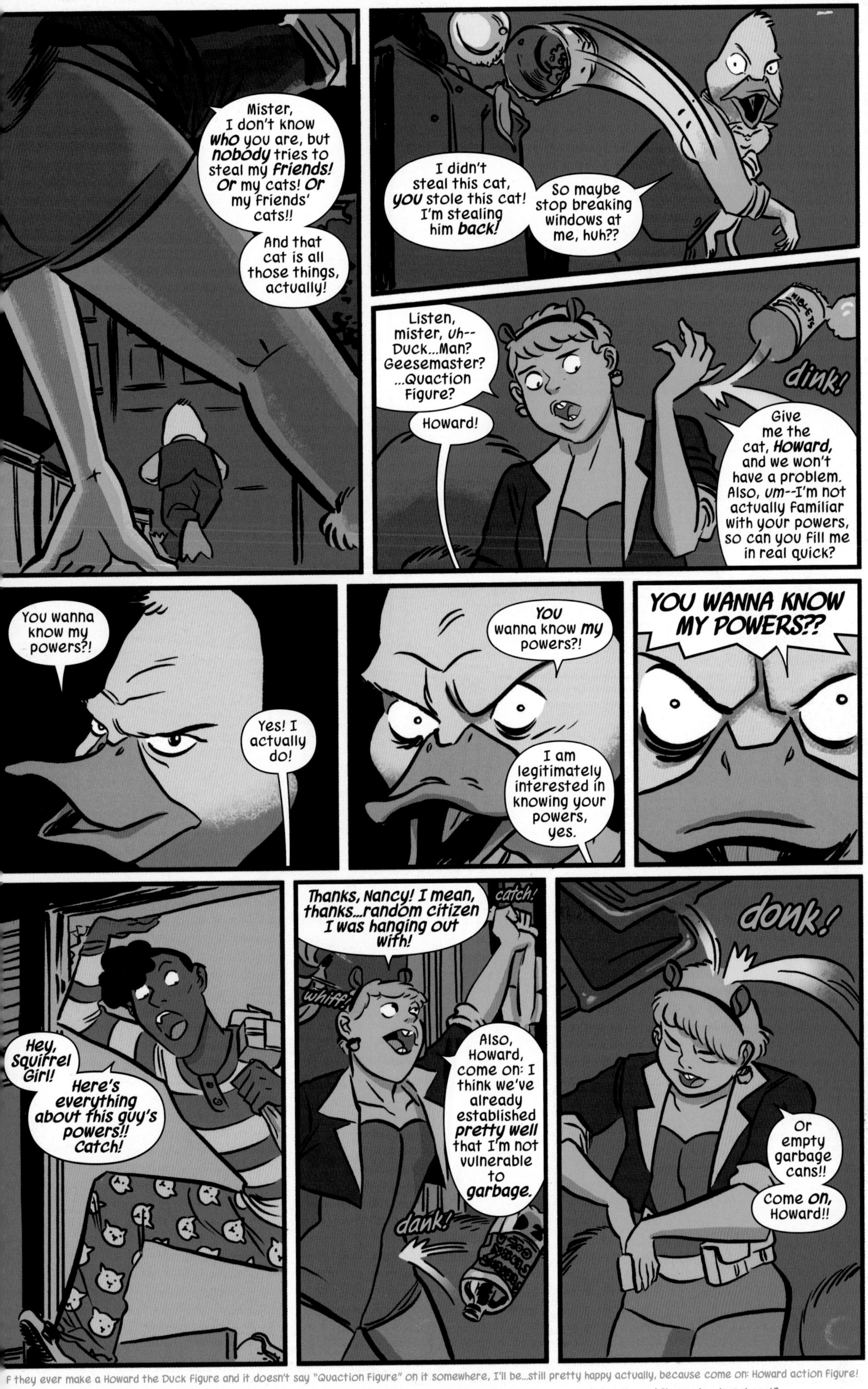
Mister, I don't know who you are, but nobody tries to steal my friends! Or my cats! Or my friends' cats!!
And that cat is all those things, actually!
I didn't steal this cat, you stole this cat! I'm stealing him back!
So maybe stop breaking windows at me, huh??
Listen, mister, uh-- Duck...Man? Geesemaster? ...Quaction Figure?
Howard!
dink!
Give me the cat, Howard, and we won't have a problem. Also, um--I'm not actually familiar with your powers, so can you fill me in real quick?
You wanna know my powers?!
Yes! I actually do!
You wanna know my powers?!
I am legitimately interested in knowing your powers, yes.
YOU WANNA KNOW MY POWERS??
Hey, Squirrel Girl!
Here's everything about this guy's powers!! Catch!
Thanks, Nancy! I mean, thanks...random citizen I was hanging out with!
catch!
whiff!
Also, Howard, come on: I think we've already established pretty well that I'm not vulnerable to garbage.
dank!
donk!
Or empty garbage cans!!
Come on, Howard!!

f they ever make a Howard the Duck figure and it doesn't say "Quaction Figure" on it somewhere, I'll be...still pretty happy actually, because come on: Howard action figure!
I hate paying the same amount for an action figure that's half the size of a normal figure. Can we make it two Howard figures in a trenchcoat?

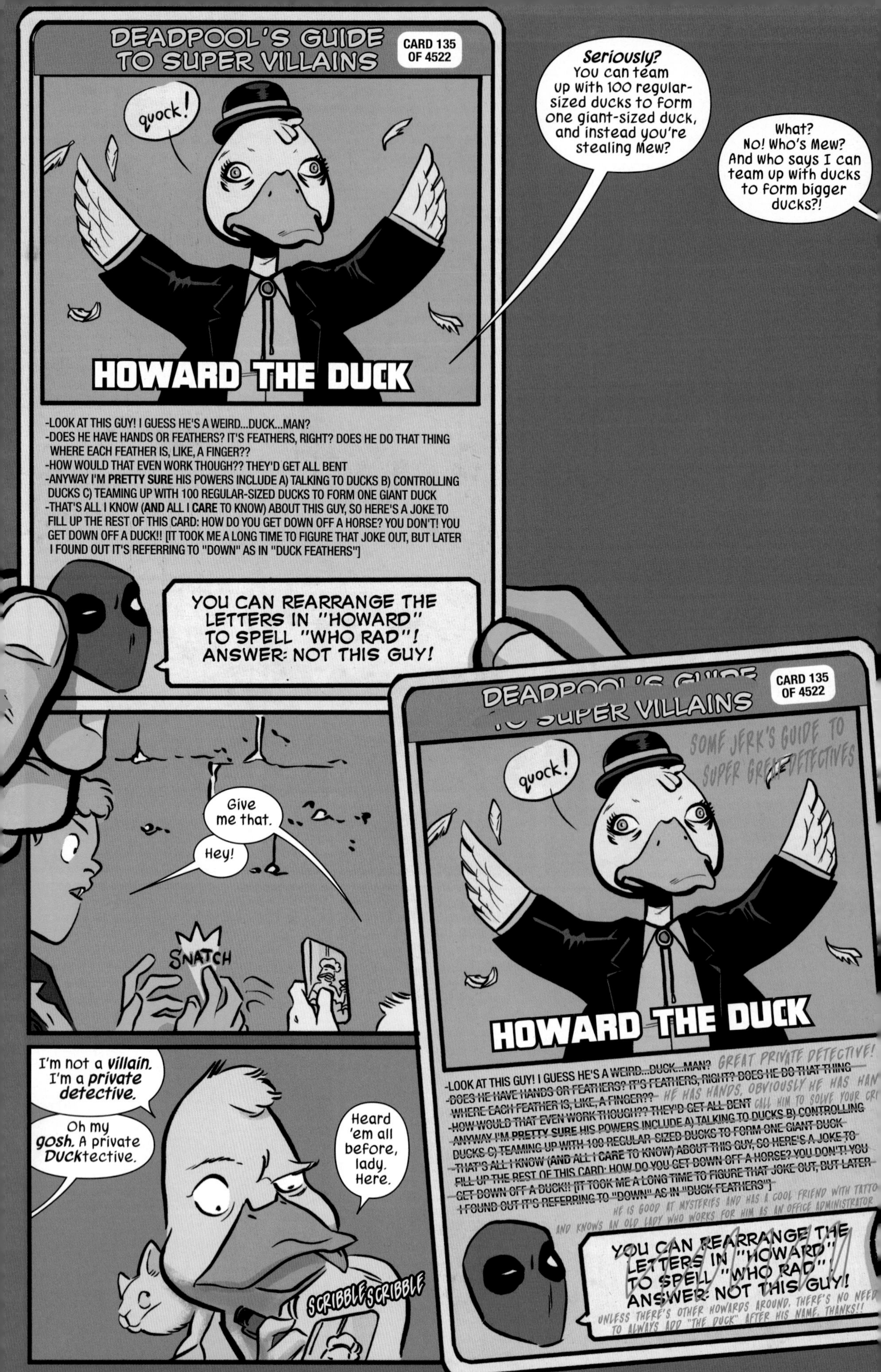
DEADPOOL'S GUIDE TO SUPER VILLAINS
CARD 135 OF 4522
quock!
HOWARD THE DUCK
-LOOK AT THIS GUY! I GUESS HE'S A WEIRD...DUCK...MAN?
-DOES HE HAVE HANDS OR FEATHERS? IT'S FEATHERS, RIGHT? DOES HE DO THAT THING WHERE EACH FEATHER IS, LIKE, A FINGER??
-HOW WOULD THAT EVEN WORK THOUGH?? THEY'D GET ALL BENT
-ANYWAY I'M PRETTY SURE HIS POWERS INCLUDE A) TALKING TO DUCKS B) CONTROLLING DUCKS C) TEAMING UP WITH 100 REGULAR-SIZED DUCKS TO FORM ONE GIANT DUCK
-THAT'S ALL I KNOW (AND ALL I CARE TO KNOW) ABOUT THIS GUY, SO HERE'S A JOKE TO FILL UP THE REST OF THIS CARD: HOW DO YOU GET DOWN OFF A HORSE? YOU DON'T! YOU GET DOWN OFF A DUCK!! [IT TOOK ME A LONG TIME TO FIGURE THAT JOKE OUT, BUT LATER I FOUND OUT IT'S REFERRING TO "DOWN" AS IN "DUCK FEATHERS"]
YOU CAN REARRANGE THE LETTERS IN "HOWARD" TO SPELL "WHO RAD"! ANSWER: NOT THIS GUY!
Seriously? You can team up with 100 regular-sized ducks to form one giant-sized duck, and instead you're stealing Mew?
What? No! Who's Mew? And who says I can team up with ducks to form bigger ducks?!
Give me that.
Hey!
SNATCH
I'm not a villain. I'm a private detective.
Oh my gosh. A private DUCKtective.
Heard 'em all before, lady. Here.
SCRIBBLE SCRIBBLE
DEADPOOL'S GUIDE TO SUPER VILLAINS
CARD 135 OF 4522
SOME JERK'S GUIDE TO SUPER GREAT DETECTIVES
quock!
HOWARD THE DUCK
-LOOK AT THIS GUY! I GUESS HE'S A WEIRD...DUCK...MAN? GREAT PRIVATE DETECTIVE!
-DOES HE HAVE HANDS OR FEATHERS? IT'S FEATHERS, RIGHT? DOES HE DO THAT THING WHERE EACH FEATHER IS, LIKE, A FINGER?? HE HAS HANDS, OBVIOUSLY HE HAS HAN
-HOW WOULD THAT EVEN WORK THOUGH?? THEY'D GET ALL BENT CALL HIM TO SOLVE YOUR CRI
-ANYWAY I'M PRETTY SURE HIS POWERS INCLUDE A) TALKING TO DUCKS B) CONTROLLING DUCKS C) TEAMING UP WITH 100 REGULAR-SIZED DUCKS TO FORM ONE GIANT DUCK
-THAT'S ALL I KNOW (AND ALL I CARE TO KNOW) ABOUT THIS GUY, SO HERE'S A JOKE TO FILL UP THE REST OF THIS CARD: HOW DO YOU GET DOWN OFF A HORSE? YOU DON'T! YOU GET DOWN OFF A DUCK!! [IT TOOK ME A LONG TIME TO FIGURE THAT JOKE OUT, BUT LATER I FOUND OUT IT'S REFERRING TO "DOWN" AS IN "DUCK FEATHERS"]
HE IS GOOD AT MYSTERIES AND HAS A COOL FRIEND WITH TATTO
AND KNOWS AN OLD LADY WHO WORKS FOR HIM AS AN OFFICE ADMINISTRATOR
YOU CAN REARRANGE THE LETTERS IN "HOWARD" TO SPELL "WHO RAD"! ANSWER: NOT THIS GUY!
UNLESS THERE'S OTHER HOWARDS AROUND, THERE'S NO NEED TO ALWAYS ADD "THE DUCK" AFTER HIS NAME. THANKS!!

If you're wondering why Howard's card is number 135, 135 is the sum of 40 plus 34 plus 61, and those numbers make up an ASCII-art duck. ***OBSERVE:*** ("=

("= ((ha ha see what i did there ha ha

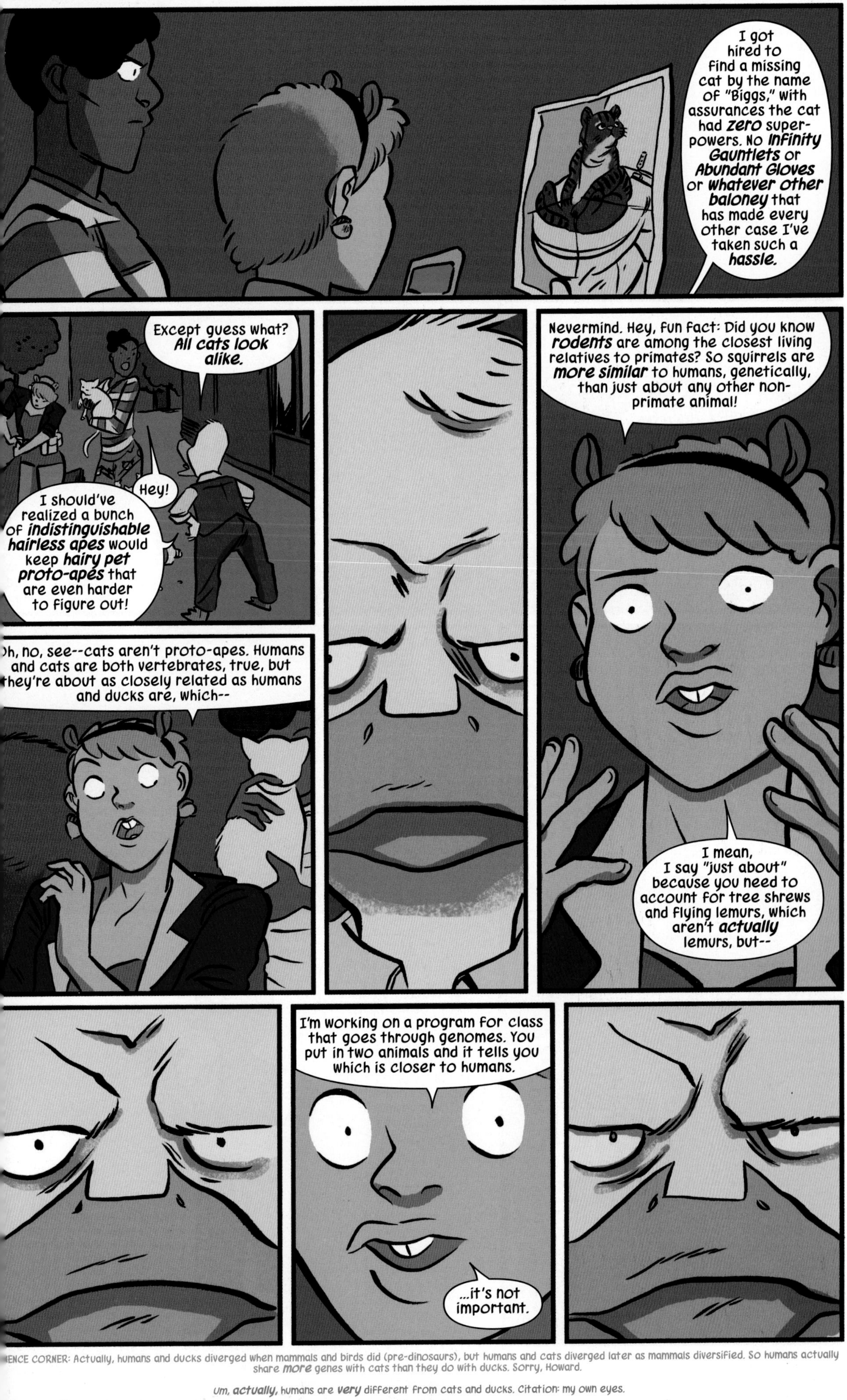
I got hired to find a missing cat by the name of "Biggs," with assurances the cat had *zero* super-powers. No *Infinity Gauntlets* or *Abundant Gloves* or *whatever other baloney* that has made every other case I've taken such a *hassle.*
Except guess what? *All cats look alike.*
Hey!
I should've realized a bunch of *indistinguishable hairless apes* would keep *hairy pet proto-apes* that are even harder to figure out!
h, no, see--cats aren't proto-apes. Humans and cats are both vertebrates, true, but hey're about as closely related as humans and ducks are, which--
Nevermind. Hey, fun fact: Did you know *rodents* are among the closest living relatives to primates? So squirrels are *more similar* to humans, genetically, than just about any other non-primate animal!
I mean, I say "just about" because you need to account for tree shrews and flying lemurs, which aren't *actually* lemurs, but--
I'm working on a program for class that goes through genomes. You put in two animals and it tells you which is closer to humans.
...it's not important.

ENCE CORNER: Actually, humans and ducks diverged when mammals and birds did (pre-dinosaurs), but humans and cats diverged later as mammals diversified. So humans actually share *more* genes with cats than they do with ducks. Sorry, Howard.

Um, *actually*, humans are *very* different from cats and ducks. Citation: my own eyes.

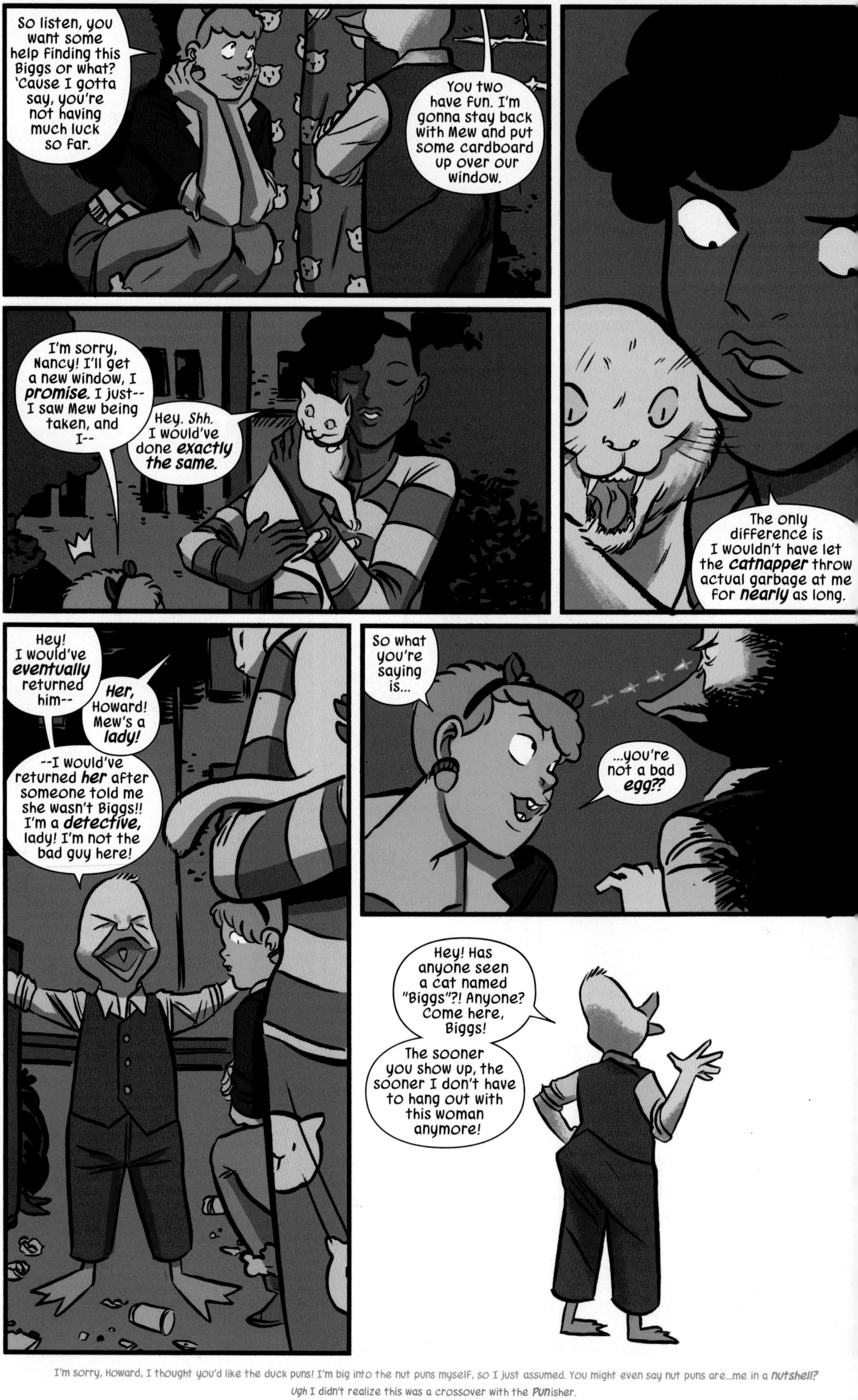
So listen, you want some help finding this Biggs or what? 'Cause I gotta say, you're not having much luck so far.
You two have fun. I'm gonna stay back with Mew and put some cardboard up over our window.
I'm sorry, Nancy! I'll get a new window, I *promise.* I just-- I saw Mew being taken, and I--
Hey. Shh. I would've done *exactly the same.*
The only difference is I wouldn't have let the *catnapper* throw actual garbage at me for *nearly* as long.
Hey! I would've *eventually* returned him--
Her, Howard! Mew's a *lady!*
--I would've returned *her* after someone told me she wasn't Biggs!! I'm a *detective,* lady! I'm not the bad guy here!
So what you're saying is...
...you're not a bad *egg??*
Hey! Has anyone seen a cat named "Biggs"?! Anyone? Come here, Biggs!
The sooner you show up, the sooner I don't have to hang out with this woman anymore!

I'm sorry, Howard, I thought you'd like the duck puns! I'm big into the nut puns myself, so I just assumed. You might even say nut puns are...me in a ***nutshell?***
Ugh I didn't realize this was a crossover with the *PUN*isher.

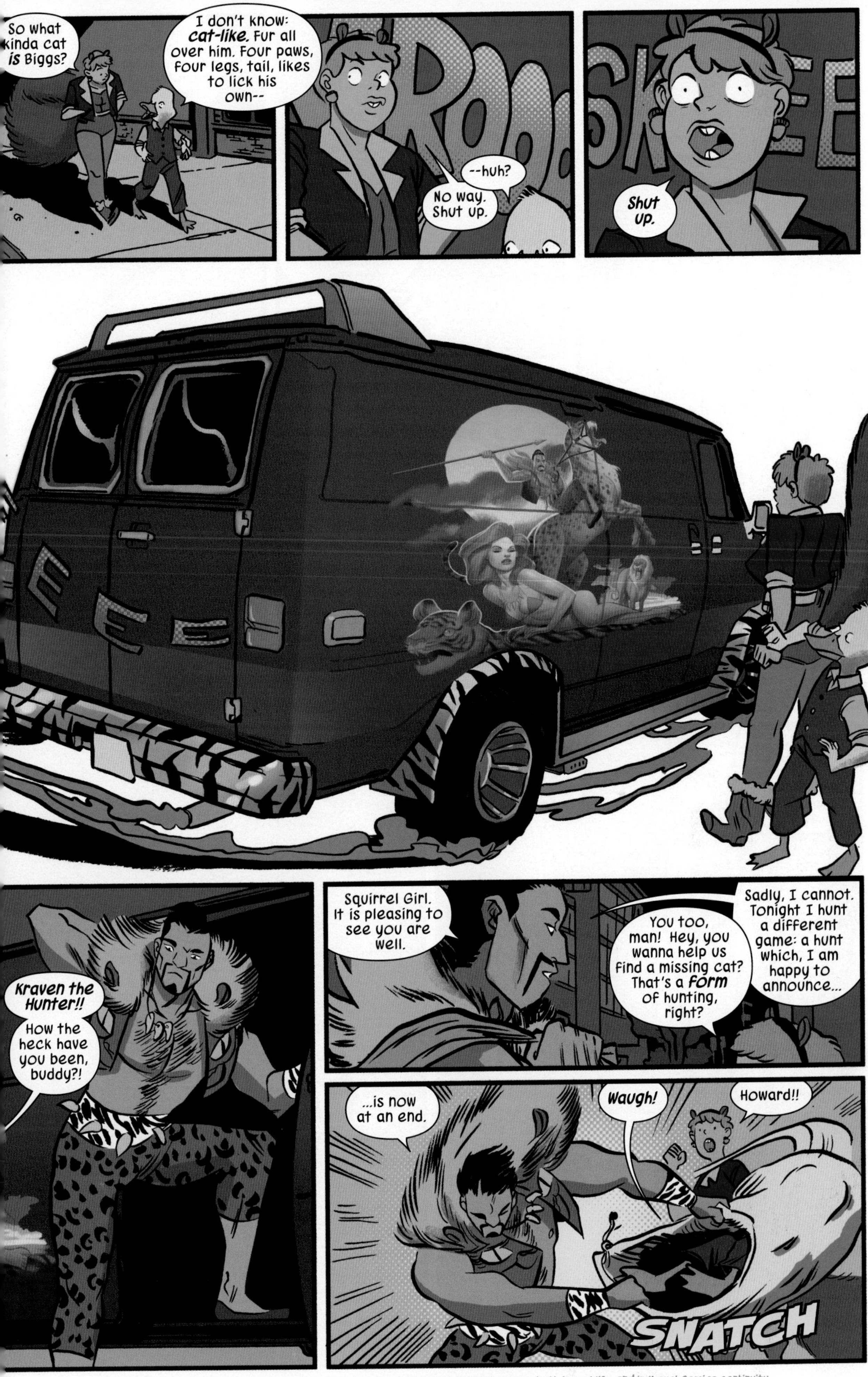
So what kinda cat *is* Biggs?
I don't know: ***cat-like.*** Fur all over him. Four paws, four legs, tail, likes to lick his own--
--huh?
No way. Shut up.
Shut up.
Kraven the Hunter!!
How the heck have you been, buddy?!
Squirrel Girl. It is pleasing to see you are well.
You too, man! Hey, you wanna help us find a missing cat? That's a ***form*** of hunting, right?
Sadly, I cannot. Tonight I hunt a different game: a hunt which, I am happy to announce...
...is now at an end.
Waugh!
Howard!!
SNATCH

I am here to tell you that the Kra-Van is the best thing to happen to Kraven in twenty years, both in real life ***and*** in Marvel Comics continuity.
Really looking forward to the cosplay for this.

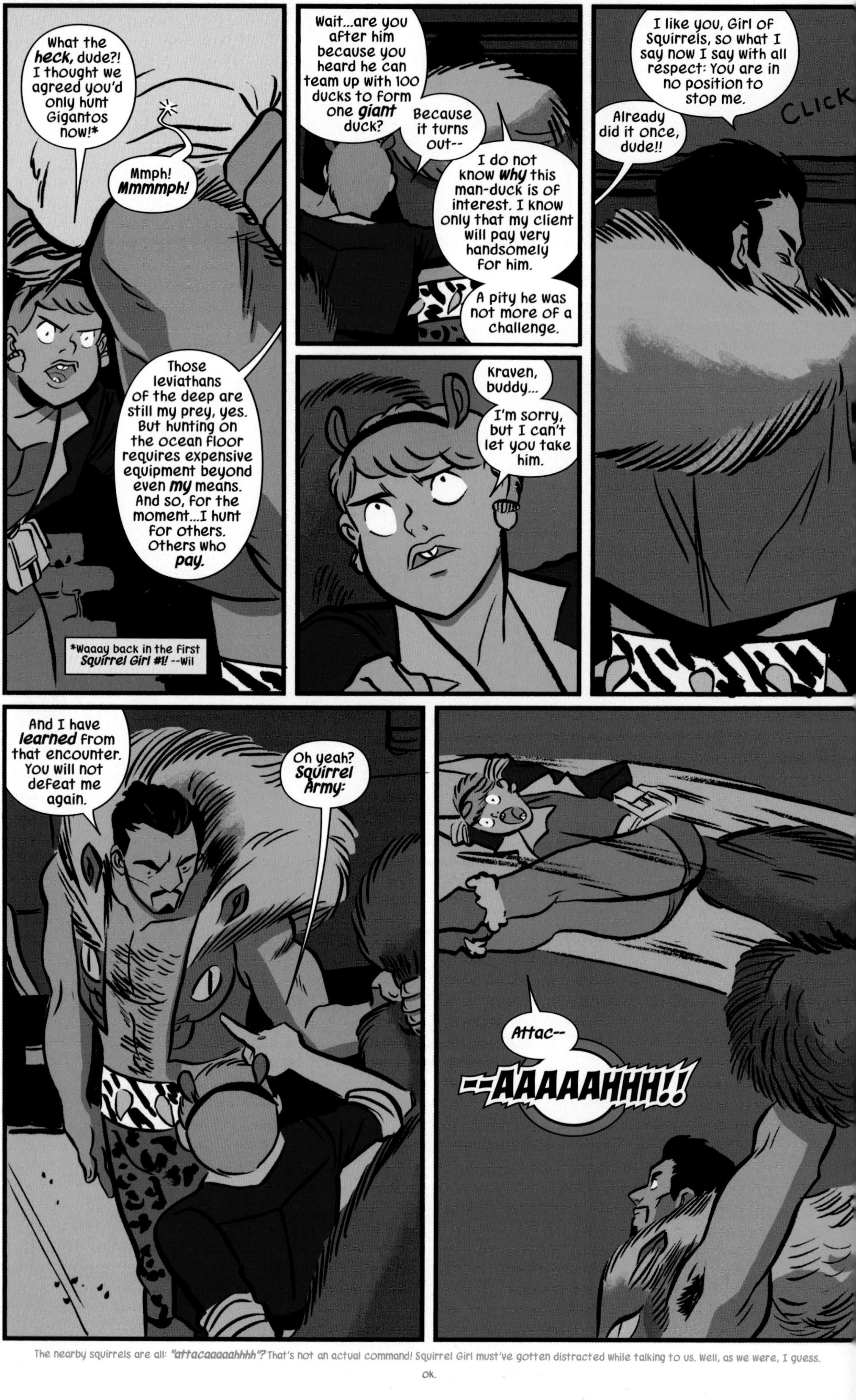
What the heck, dude?! I thought we agreed you'd only hunt Gigantos now!*
Mmph! Mmmmph!
Those leviathans of the deep are still my prey, yes. But hunting on the ocean floor requires expensive equipment beyond even my means. And so, for the moment...I hunt for others. Others who pay.
*Waaay back in the first Squirrel Girl #1! --Wil
Wait...are you after him because you heard he can team up with 100 ducks to form one giant duck?
Because it turns out--
I do not know why this man-duck is of interest. I know only that my client will pay very handsomely for him.
A pity he was not more of a challenge.
Kraven, buddy...
I'm sorry, but I can't let you take him.
I like you, Girl of Squirrels, so what I say now I say with all respect: You are in no position to stop me.
CLICK
Already did it once, dude!!
And I have learned from that encounter. You will not defeat me again.
Oh yeah? Squirrel Army:
Attac--
--AAAAAHHH!!

The nearby squirrels are all: *"attacaaaaahhhh"?* That's not an actual command! Squirrel Girl must've gotten distracted while talking to us. Well, as we were, I guess.

OK.

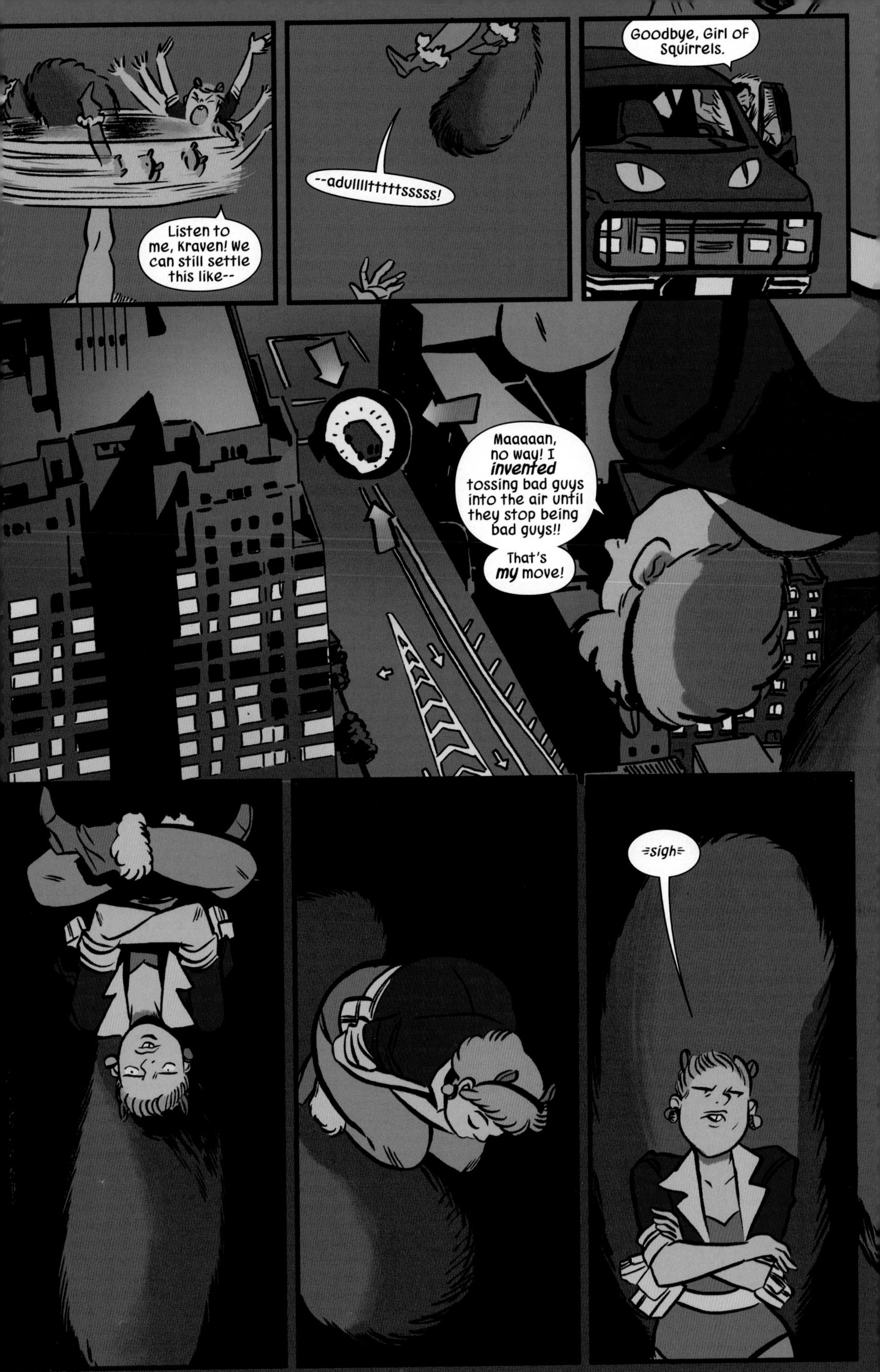
Listen to me, Kraven! We can still settle this like--
--adulllllttttttsssss!
Goodbye, Girl of Squirrels.
Maaaaan, no way! I *invented* tossing bad guys into the air until they stop being bad guys!!
That's *my* move!
=sigh=

Huh! So ***that's*** what that feels like!

I would be so conflicted, 'cause I'm in a battle, but being tossed into the air would be so much fun!

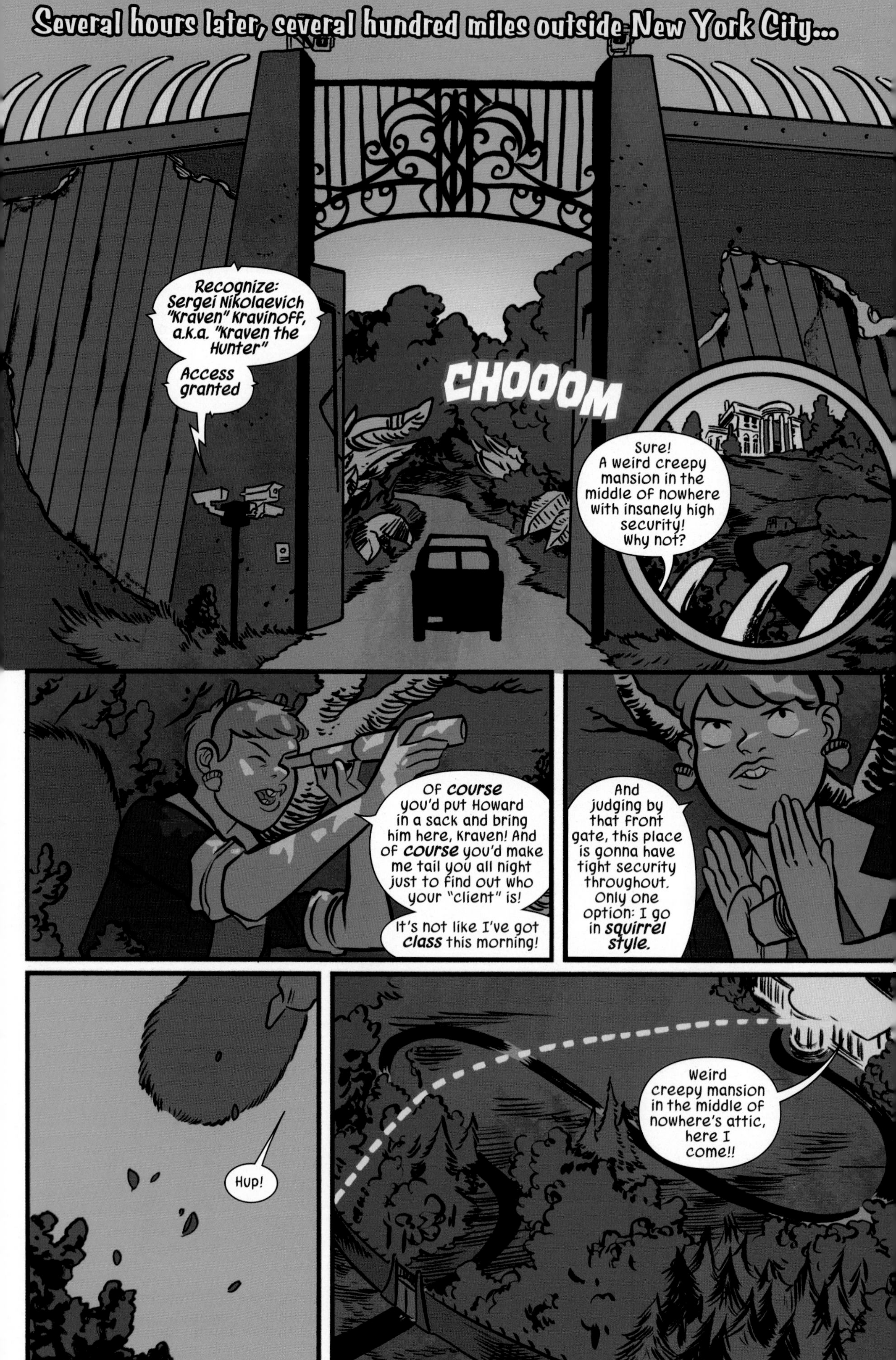
Several hours later, several hundred miles outside New York City...
Recognize: Sergei Nikolaevich "Kraven" Kravinoff, a.k.a. "Kraven the Hunter"
Access granted
CHOOOM
Sure! A weird creepy mansion in the middle of nowhere with insanely high security! Why not?
Of course you'd put Howard in a sack and bring him here, Kraven! And of course you'd make me tail you all night just to find out who your "client" is!
It's not like I've got class this morning!
And judging by that front gate, this place is gonna have tight security throughout. Only one option: I go in squirrel style.
Hup!
Weird creepy mansion in the middle of nowhere's attic, here I come!!

I'm worried about Doreen Green missing class too, but don't worry: she reads ahead, so when she has to miss class like this, she doesn't fall too far behind. Thanks, Doreen! Now we can all enjoy the rest of this comic without worrying.

Hm. I heard she just skims.

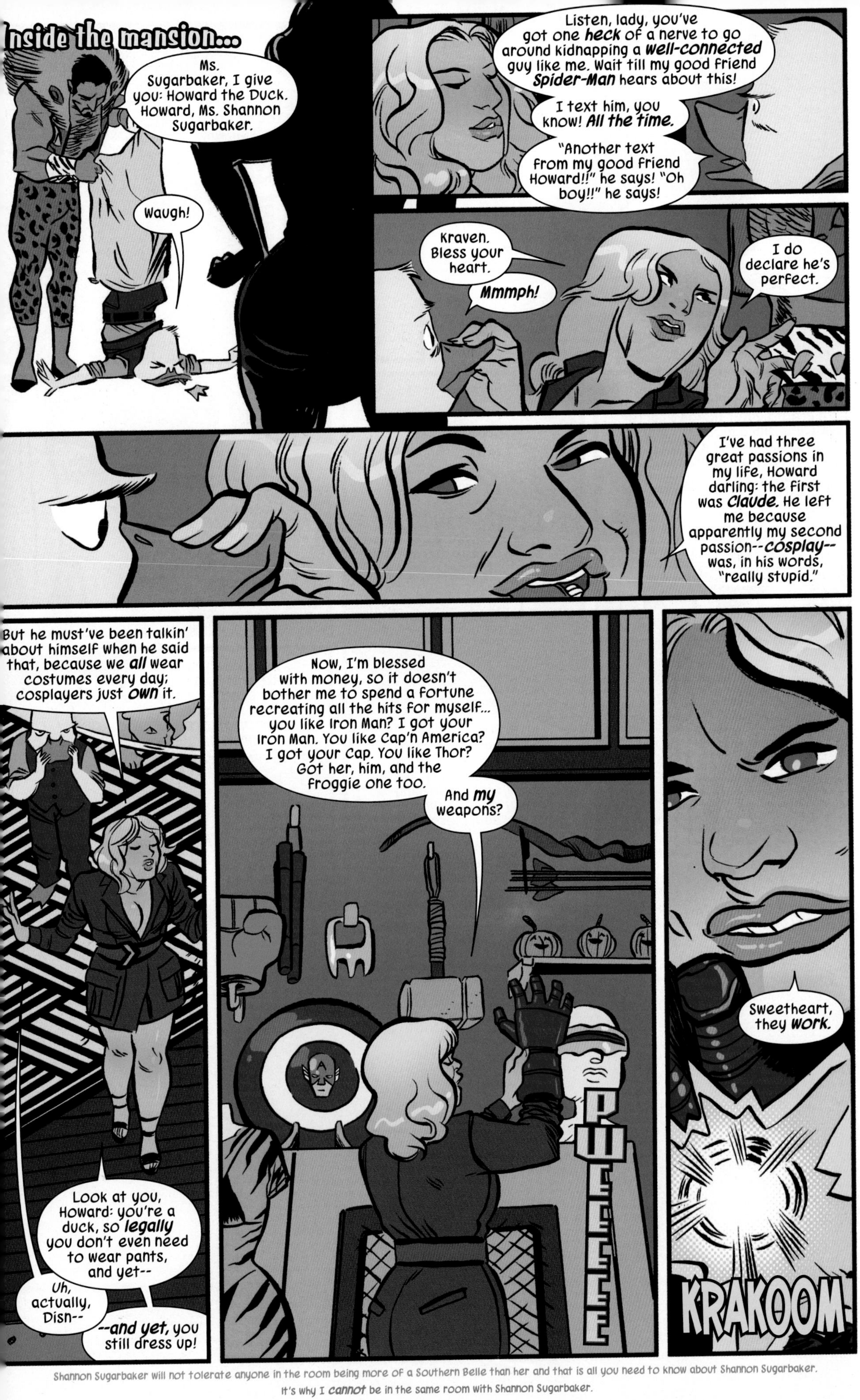
Inside the mansion...
Ms. Sugarbaker, I give you: Howard the Duck. Howard, Ms. Shannon Sugarbaker.
Waugh!
Listen, lady, you've got one heck of a nerve to go around kidnapping a well-connected guy like me. Wait till my good friend Spider-Man hears about this!
I text him, you know! All the time.
"Another text from my good friend Howard!!" he says! "Oh boy!!" he says!
Kraven. Bless your heart.
Mmmph!
I do declare he's perfect.
I've had three great passions in my life, Howard darling: the first was Claude. He left me because apparently my second passion--cosplay--was, in his words, "really stupid."
But he must've been talkin' about himself when he said that, because we all wear costumes every day; cosplayers just own it.
Look at you, Howard: you're a duck, so legally you don't even need to wear pants, and yet--
Uh, actually, Disn--
--and yet, you still dress up!
Now, I'm blessed with money, so it doesn't bother me to spend a fortune recreating all the hits for myself... you like Iron Man? I got your Iron Man. You like Cap'n America? I got your Cap. You like Thor? Got her, him, and the froggie one too.
And my weapons?
PWEEEEE
Sweetheart, they work.
KRAKOOM!

Shannon Sugarbaker will not tolerate anyone in the room being more of a Southern Belle than her and that is all you need to know about Shannon Sugarbaker.

It's why I *cannot* be in the same room with Shannon Sugarbaker.

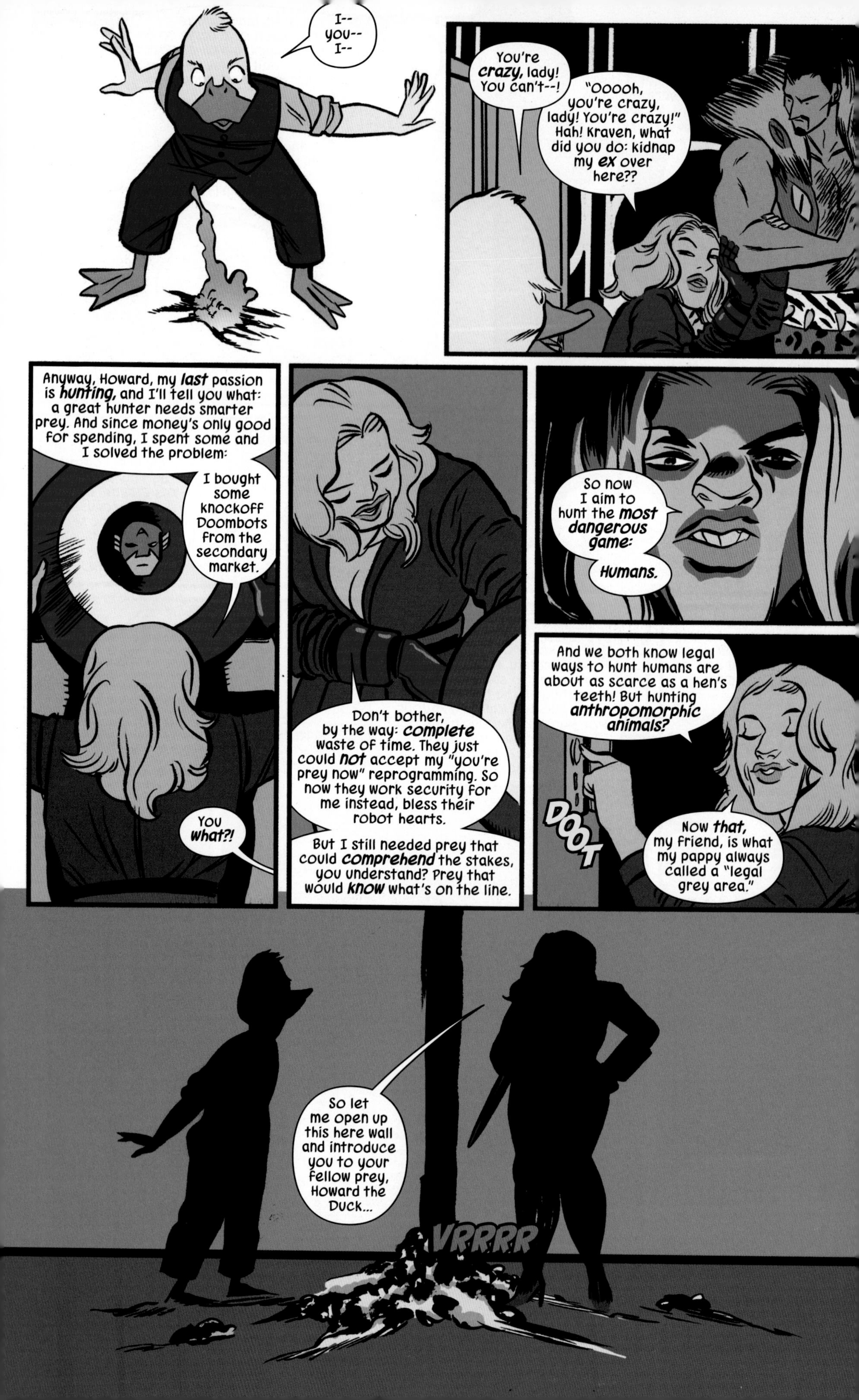
I--
you--
I--
You're crazy, lady! You can't--!
"Ooooh, you're crazy, lady! You're crazy!" Hah! Kraven, what did you do: kidnap my ex over here??
Anyway, Howard, my last passion is hunting, and I'll tell you what: a great hunter needs smarter prey. And since money's only good for spending, I spent some and I solved the problem:
I bought some knockoff Doombots from the secondary market.
You what?!
Don't bother, by the way: complete waste of time. They just could not accept my "you're prey now" reprogramming. So now they work security for me instead, bless their robot hearts.
But I still needed prey that could comprehend the stakes, you understand? Prey that would know what's on the line.
So now I aim to hunt the most dangerous game:
Humans.
And we both know legal ways to hunt humans are about as scarce as a hen's teeth! But hunting anthropomorphic animals?
DOOT
Now that, my friend, is what my pappy always called a "legal grey area."
So let me open up this here wall and introduce you to your fellow prey, Howard the Duck...
VRRRR

Meanwhile, upstairs:

INTRUDER DETECTED*

Oh crap!

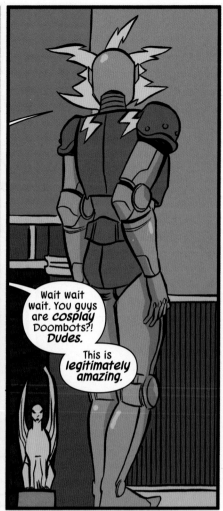

Wait wait wait. You guys are *cosplay* Doombots?! *Dudes.*

This is *legitimately amazing.*

Meanwhile, downstairs:

Rocket Raccoon! This adorable fella went to space, and now he walks on his hind legs and thinks he's people! But he's still vermin.

Hey, Howard, good to see ya. Listen, lady: give me my blasters back and we'll see who's *vermin.*

Adorable.

Beast! Part animal, part human, maybe with some ape and cat in there? I must say, sometimes I can't rightly tell.

Once more, madam, I'm *not* a hybrid. My current appearance is merely the logical end result of a genetic mutation, the particulars of which--

Aww! Who's a wittle beastie-weastie who loves the sound of his own voice??

Biggs, my ex's cat! Kidnapped by yours truly after my ex left, and turned into an unstoppable anthropomorphic cyber *killcat,* so I can hunt him an' kill him.

BIGGS CONFUSED

Now that is just classic Biggs!

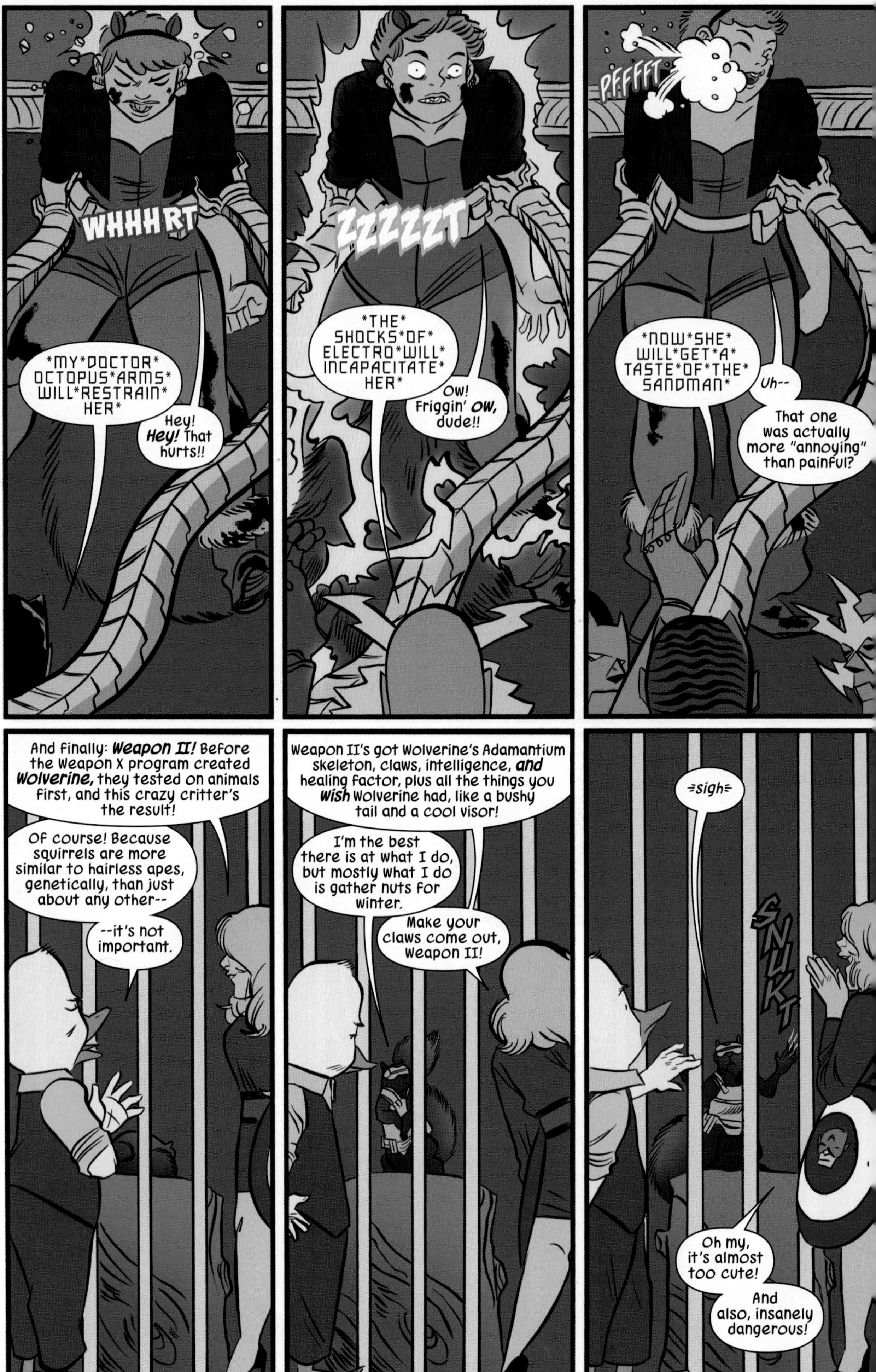
WHHHRT
*MY*DOCTOR*OCTOPUS*ARMS*WILL*RESTRAIN*HER*
Hey! Hey! That hurts!!
ZZZZZT
*THE*SHOCKS*OF*ELECTRO*WILL*INCAPACITATE*HER*
Ow! Friggin' OW, dude!!
PFFFFT
*NOW*SHE*WILL*GET*A*TASTE*OF*THE*SANDMAN*
Uh--
That one was actually more "annoying" than painful?
And finally: Weapon II! Before the Weapon X program created Wolverine, they tested on animals first, and this crazy critter's the result!
Of course! Because squirrels are more similar to hairless apes, genetically, than just about any other--
--it's not important.
Weapon II's got Wolverine's Adamantium skeleton, claws, intelligence, and healing factor, plus all the things you wish Wolverine had, like a bushy tail and a cool visor!
I'm the best there is at what I do, but mostly what I do is gather nuts for winter.
Make your claws come out, Weapon II!
=sigh=
SNUKT
Oh my, it's almost too cute!
And also, insanely dangerous!

*THERE*CAN*BE*NO*ESCAPE*/*MY*SAND*WAS*PROGRAMMED*TO*BE*COARSE*AND*ROUGH*AND*IRRITATING*AND*TO*GET*EVERYWHERE*

SCIENCE CORNER: Interesting sand fact: sand is actually just dirt but different I guess!

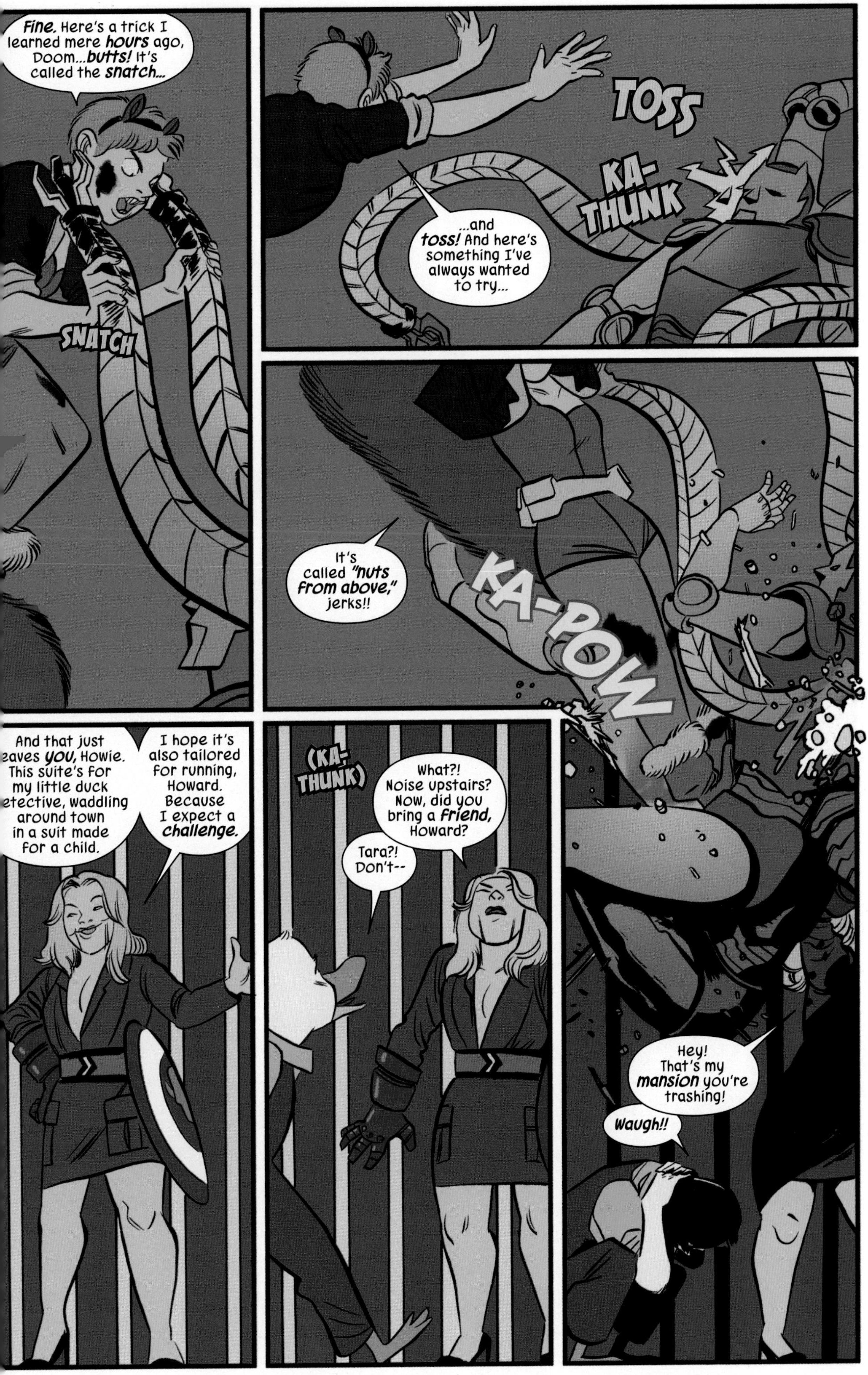

Fine. Here's a trick I learned mere hours ago, Doom...butts! It's called the snatch...
SNATCH
TOSS
KA-THUNK
...and toss! And here's something I've always wanted to try...
It's called "nuts from above," jerks!!
KA-POW
And that just eaves YOU, Howie. This suite's for my little duck etective, waddling around town in a suit made for a child.
I hope it's also tailored for running, Howard. Because I expect a challenge.
(KA-THUNK)
What?! Noise upstairs? Now, did you bring a friend, Howard?
Tara?! Don't--
Hey! That's my mansion you're trashing!
Waugh!!

I didn't ask Chip if it was canon that Howard buys his suits from the children's section, but I feel pretty confident that I am 100% correct

Um, *children* buy their suits from the *Howard* section, *Ryan.*

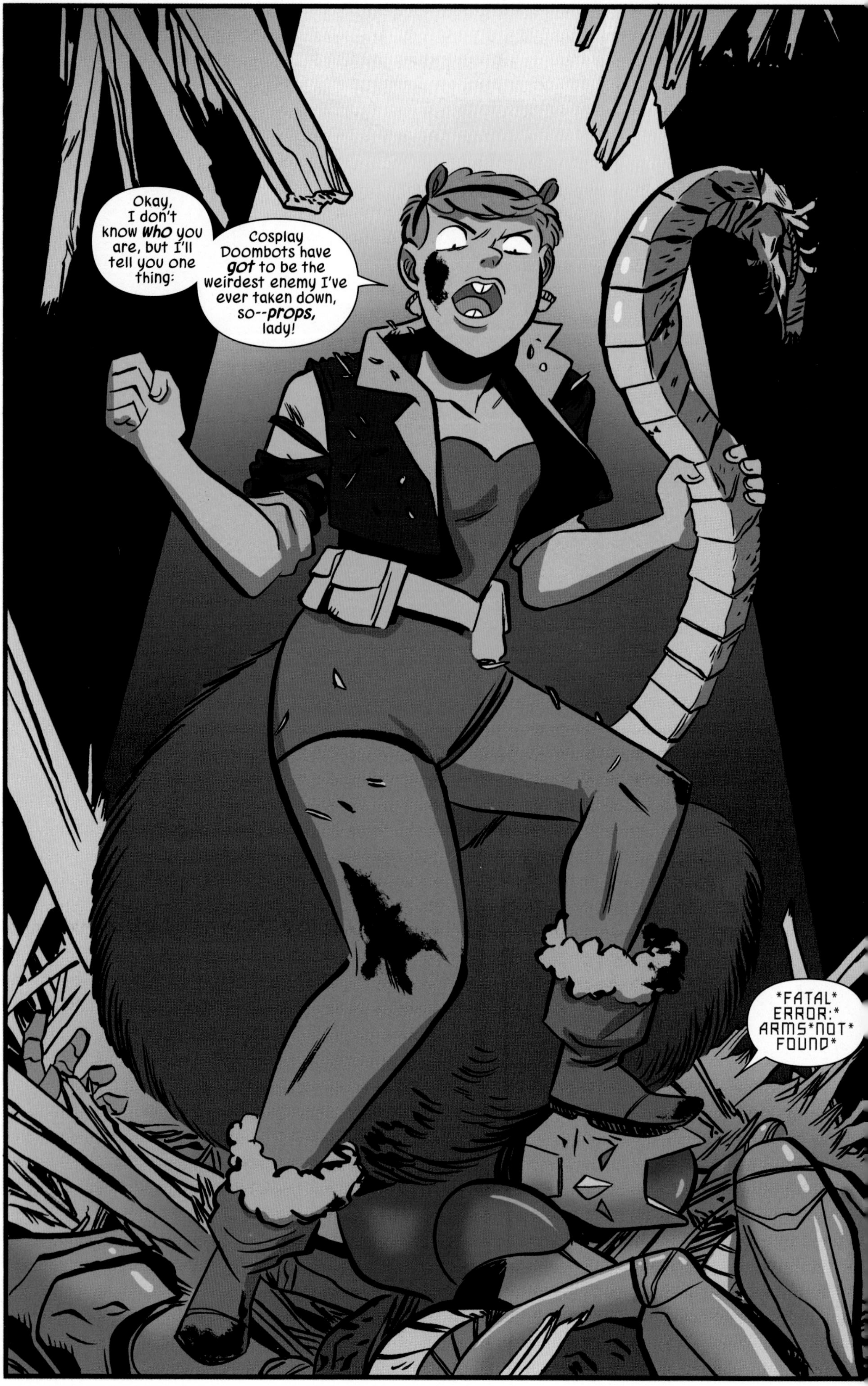
Okay, I don't know **who** you are, but I'll tell you one thing:
Cosplay Doombots have **got** to be the weirdest enemy I've ever taken down, so--**props,** lady!
FATAL ERROR:* ARMS*NOT* FOUND*

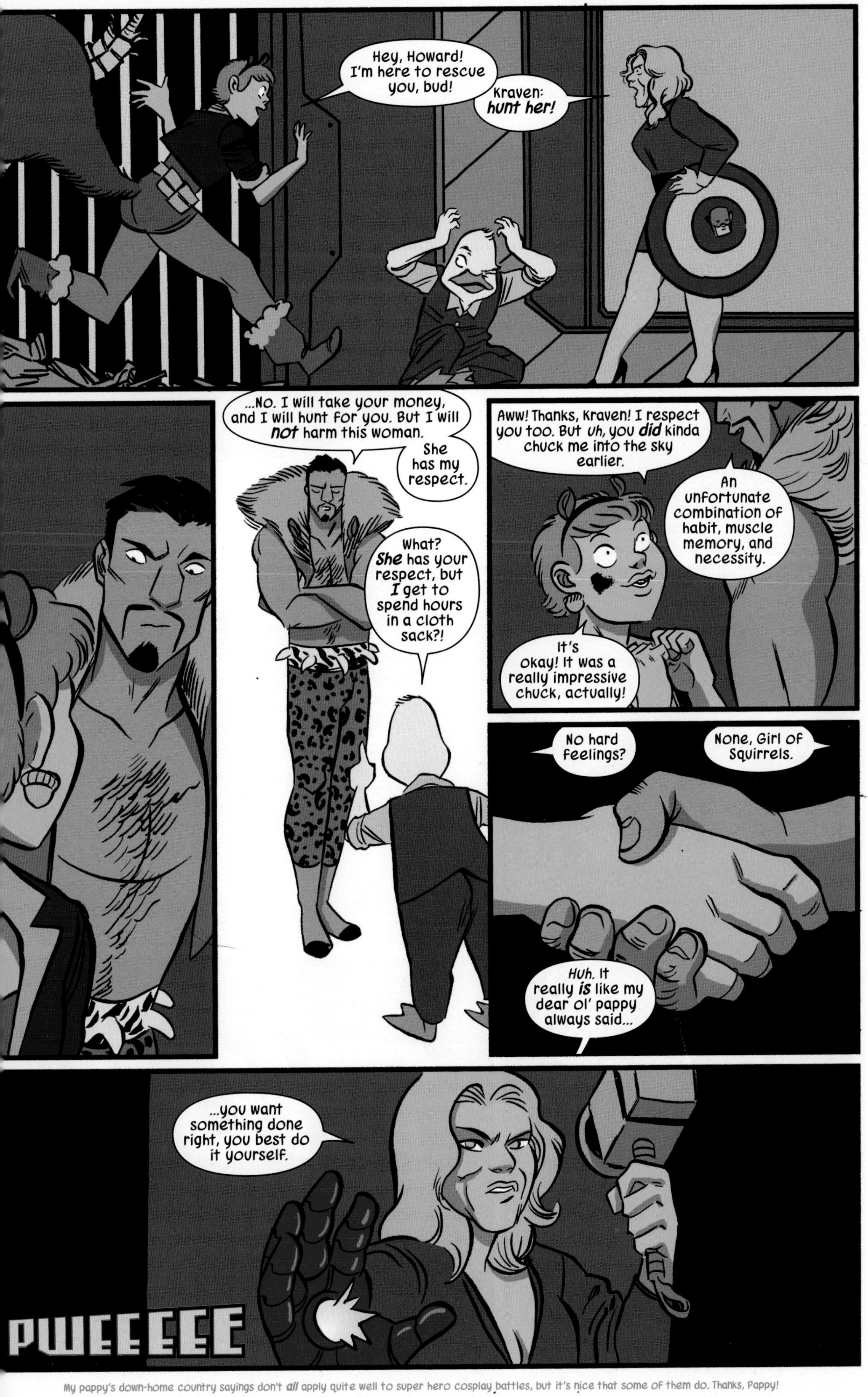
Hey, Howard! I'm here to rescue you, bud!
Kraven: *hunt her!*
...No. I will take your money, and I will hunt for you. But I will *not* harm this woman.
She has my respect.
What? *She* has your respect, but *I* get to spend hours in a cloth sack?!
Aww! Thanks, Kraven! I respect you too. But *uh*, you *did* kinda chuck me into the sky earlier.
An unfortunate combination of habit, muscle memory, and necessity.
It's okay! It was a really impressive chuck, actually!
No hard feelings?
None, Girl of Squirrels.
Huh. It really *is* like my dear ol' pappy always said...
...you want something done right, you best do it yourself.
PWEEEEE

My pappy's down-home country sayings don't ***all*** apply quite well to super hero cosplay battles, but it's nice that some of them do. Thanks, Pappy!
Um, if you want something done right, you hire a person who specializes in the task that needs completing. Your pappy needs to be corrected.

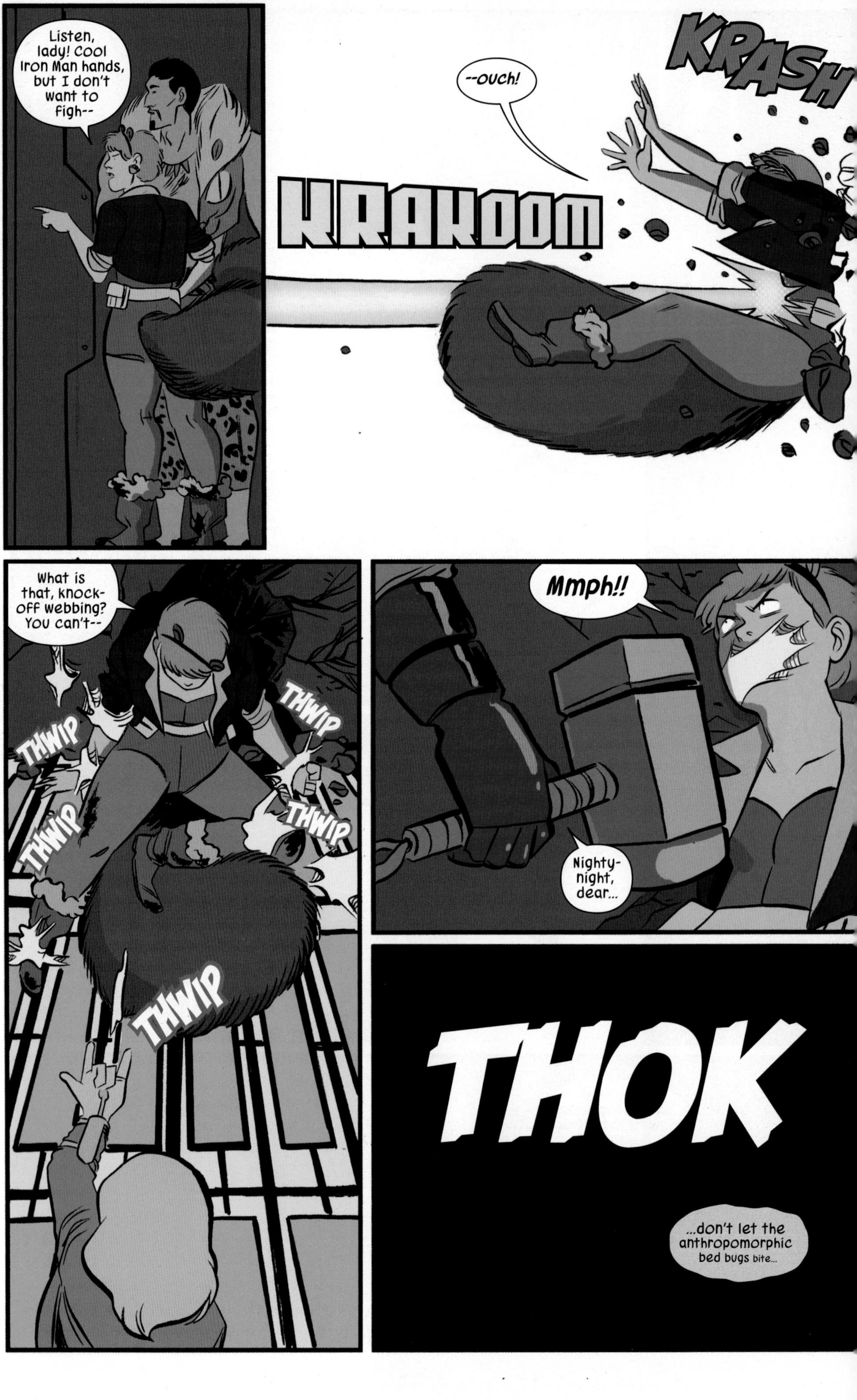
Listen, lady! Cool Iron Man hands, but I don't want to figh--
KRAKOOM
--OUCH!
KRASH
What is that, knock-off webbing? You can't--
THWIP
THWIP
THWIP
THWIP
THWIP
Mmph!!
Nighty-night, dear...
THOK
...don't let the anthropomorphic bed bugs bite...

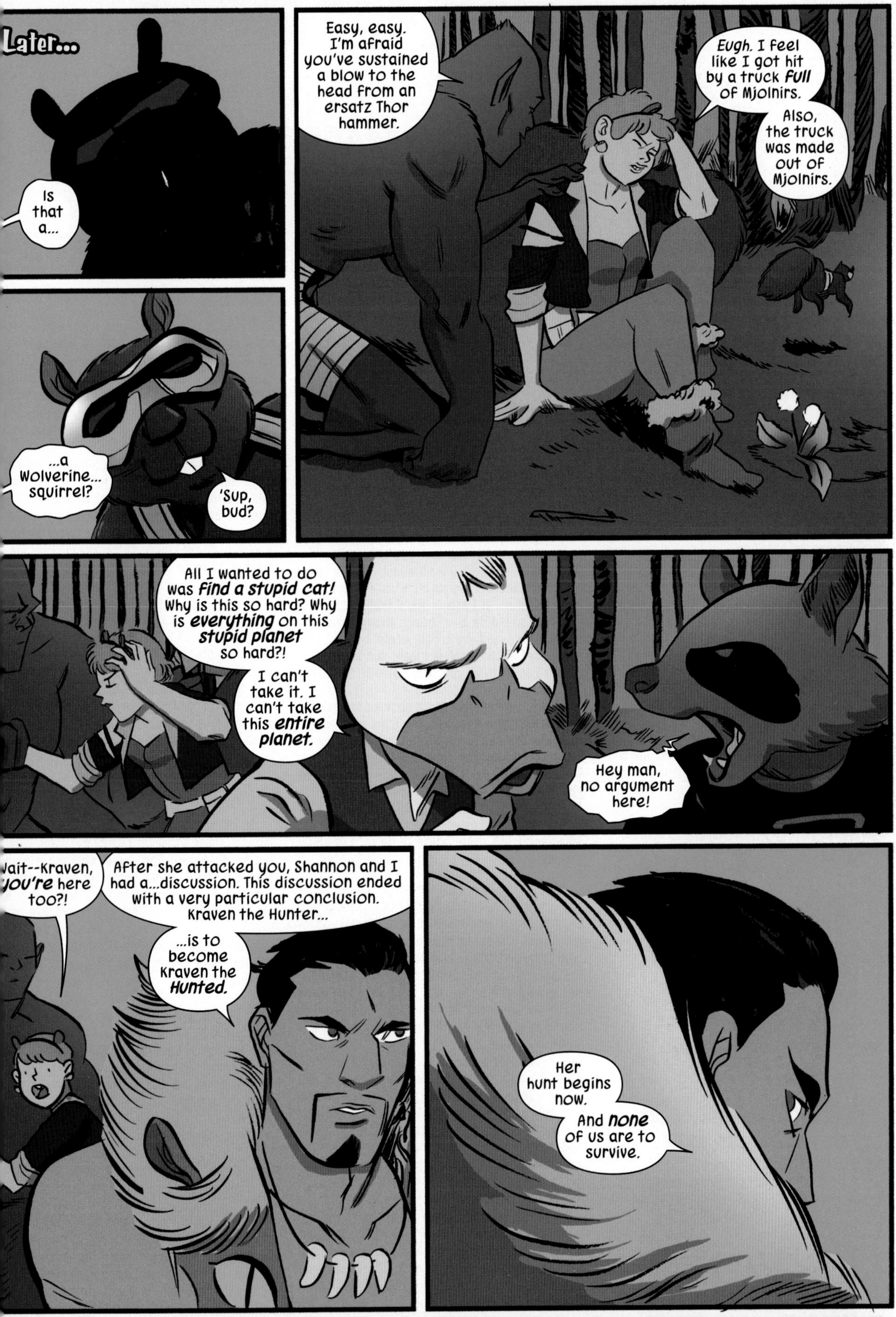
Later...
Is that a...
...a Wolverine... squirrel?
'Sup, bud?
Easy, easy. I'm afraid you've sustained a blow to the head from an ersatz Thor hammer.
Eugh. I feel like I got hit by a truck FULL of Mjolnirs.
Also, the truck was made out of Mjolnirs.
All I wanted to do was find a stupid cat! Why is this so hard? Why is everything on this stupid planet so hard?!
I can't take it. I can't take this entire planet.
Hey man, no argument here!
Wait--Kraven, you're here too?!
After she attacked you, Shannon and I had a...discussion. This discussion ended with a very particular conclusion. Kraven the Hunter...
...is to become Kraven the Hunted.
Her hunt begins now.
And none of us are to survive.

Continued in HOWARD THE DUCK #6, out next month!

But I'll give you a hint: basically what happens in it is (spoiler alert) ADVENTURE??

Also: cosplay. Lots of cosplay.
I'm cosplaying right now! It's as a guy who forgot that he now has to write a whole *Howard the Duck* comic!!

Letters From Nuts

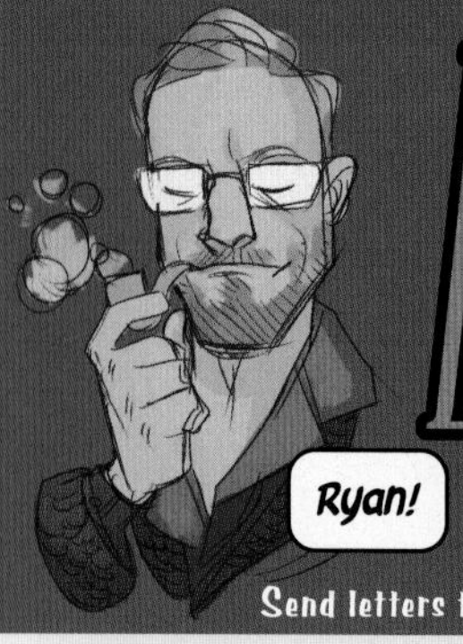
Ryan!

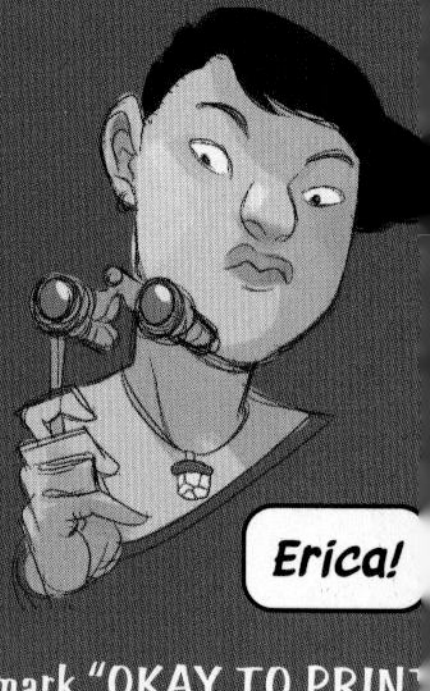
Erica!

Send letters to mheroes@marvel.com or 135 W 50th St, 7th Floor, New York, NY 10020 (Please mark "OKAY TO PRIN

Hey everybody! How'd you like the first part of our crossover with HOWARD THE DUCK? Special thanks to the HOWARD creative team -- Chip Zdarsky & Joe Quinones -- for helping us with this issue. Join us as we go help them tell the second half of this story next month in HOWARD THE DUCK #6! But hey, first let's get to your letters!

Dear Squirrel Girl,

We like you. You're funny! We read your comic every month. Daddy puts the next comic on the calendar so we can count until the day. We have read every single one of your books and comic books. We share them with our friends! We share them with Eva and Bella (our cousins), and now they read them, too! We share them with Tyler, too. He's our Sunday School teacher. He borrows them every Sunday morning, and gives them back in a week. He thinks you are funny, too.

We just read Issue 5, and it was cool. And funny. Our favorite part was when all you girls vexed Doctor Doom. It was just like when your squirrel friends did last time!

We love dressing up! For Halloween we were YOU and COMMANDER KEEN! And we went to Kapow and met Captain America and Luigi, and Tippy-Toe beat up the Red Skull! This happened for real. We have pictures.

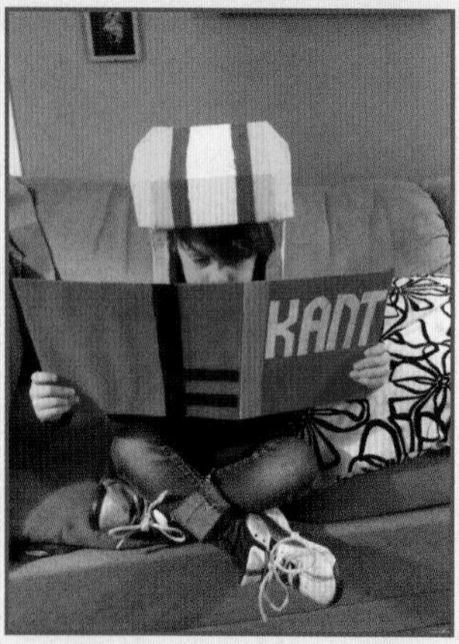

I (Elijah) like to read SQUIRREL GIRL when I pretend to read Kant.

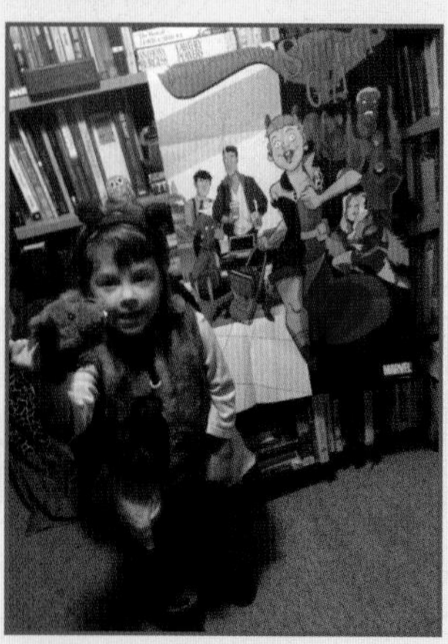

Wally at Kapow says I (Grace) am the biggest Squirrel Girl fan in town, so he gave me the poster to keep!

Love from,
The Unbeatable Twins, Elijah and Grace
(we are five-and-a-half)

RYAN: Aw, that's super great! ESPECIALLY the Commander Keen costume, because I am a Keen fan from way back. Did you know that if you let Keen sit around in Pyramid of the Moons in Keen 4, he'll eventually moon the camera? I played this game LITERALLY 20 YEARS AGO and I still remember that fact.

Anyway, in non-mooning news, I loved your costumes, and the fact that you like our comics AND share them with your friends! This is super great and I bet your friends think you're the coolest for doing that. If I had a friend that loaned me comics, I would be all "Thanks, friend! You ARE the coolest!" and my friend would be all "Yes, obviously I am the coolest friend, due to all these comics I am sharing" and they would be telling the TRUTH.

ERICA: I would also like a moment to geek out over Commander Keen. Do you guys even have a computer that can run those games? Were they re-released? Oh my god, somebody please tell me. I ALSO PLAYED THIS GAME 20 YEARS AGO AND THINK ABOUT IT ALL THE TIME.

You guys got the Squirrel Girl poster!!! That's exciting because I haven't seen that many around. This seems like a fun house to be in. I'm pretty jealous.

Consistently the best book on the racks, I absolutely love what Ryan and Erica are doing with Squirrel Girl. Issue 4 had three brilliant ideas of how to use a time machine to defeat Dr Doom, the third being best of all, and a gorgeous nod to Secret Squirrel with Doreen's sleuthing disguise ensemble. Hey, given that this story was set in the 60s, maybe the creators of Secret Squirrel actually got their idea from seeing Doreen's outfit, which makes for crazy bootstrapping paradox.

We also got an excellent fight with Dr Doom, where in keeping with the book's philosophy that talking with the antagonist can produce better results than fists and power beams, there's a conversation that sparkles with ideas and humour. I mean, when was the last time anyone saw Maslow's Hierarchy in a superhero fight? Plus we learned what Dr Doom thinks of Galactus, and of course Doom's ego is such that he even looks down on Galactus.

It is so refreshing and inspiring to pick up a comic book that uses the medium to the fullest (what other medium could pull off the 'can you spot Doom grinding a rail' gag, or the footnotes?) and also just delights and revels in the idea of having superpowers and the joy that they can bring.

It might have been easy to conceive of a comic book that was an antidote to all the grim, dark, angsty stuff around but to pull off a series that does that whilst showing true love and respect to the tradition of comics and real fondness for the characters is a different matter entirely.

It is a true joy to pick up this comic, thanks for sharing it with us.

Andrew Pack,
Brighton, England

R: Thanks, Andrew! I think it helps th everyone involved in the book really loves comi as a medium, so we're here to have the mo fun we can have. Comics is a terrific way to t stories! Prose is fine I GUESS if there's no arti around, but we all know the REAL medium write like Chaucer and Shakespeare wished they cou have worked in, if only they could've drawn bett

E: This has been way more fun to work on th I ever thought it would be. I think I've mention this before, but nobody on the team really kn one another (Wil and I had exchanged three six emails, Rico and I had said a few words each other), but I think it all really clicked. We wanted the same things and have a similar sen of humor. It's been a great ride.

"Steve Rogers called me 'Son.'" That line had r literally rolling on the floor laughing! I can't tell y what a delight the Squirrel Girl book is. Like a lot long-time readers, I like a lot of fun in my comic so I really appreciate what you do. Oh, and I tota caught the "Secret Squirrel" nod in #4. What a gre and appropriate easter egg! I love the art, Erica, a Ryan, keep making me laugh!

Thank
Brian Langlo

R: I didn't mention it in the answer to the la letter because I thought I could get away with but the jig is up! The Secret Squirrel referen was ALL ERICA. I just wrote her in a trenchco and fedora, and Erica was like "Ryan, this ca be done better." The best part was, there rea WERE hats sold like that in the time period. remember Erica found photo reference. Mode fashion really needs to up its game! I want glasses hat, STAT.

E: I honestly don't even remember how I fou sunglasses hats. I really don't. I purposely look up when Secret Squirrel debuted because I mig not have done the outfit if it weren't from the '60 Then I looked up '60s versions of the things wore. #obsessive

Okay, Marvel people, I know this is a lo shot, but hear me out: We need to bring Netfli Unbreakable Kimmy Schmidt into the Marv universe, and Squirrel Girl can make it happen.

Picture this: Kimmy shows up for her first d of class at Empire State University (Normal Cla for People with Normal Lives 101, natch), only find herself seated next to Doreen Green. Th hit it off immediately as the two most upbeat a enthusiastic accumulations of organic matter in t history of the universe. Kimmy can immediately ta to Tippy-Toe. She takes on the super hero monik of Camel Damsel and joins Squirrel Girl in her que to rid New York City of jerks who suck.

And the theme song...

Un-BEATable!
She's a squirrel, DANGIT.
It's a MIRACLE!

Chaos in the streets. Productivity plummets all-time lows as frenzied excitement for this ɔssover obliterates work attendance and throws stock market into an irreparable downward ral. Civilization as we know it ceases to exist. On ɔond thought, this might not be a great idea. Sorry rought it up.

Zack Miller
Brooklyn, NY

R: Just on the off chance that multinational rporation Marvel/Disney is waiting for MY rmission to make this happen, this is me saying: ke this happen! Marvel, get Netflix on the one! I don't know if they have phones, actually! arvel, send Netflix a DM on Twitter!!

y Ryan, Erica and the rest of the team!

I want to start off by saying how much I'm joying USG -- I've been a fan of Doreen for over years and it's easily my favorite comic so far this ntury! My girlfriend Jo and I eagerly await each w issue every month.

Like you guys, I'm dismayed at the lack of erchandise featuring Squirrel Girl, so I decided take matters into my own hands... I made a stom SG Marvel Legends action figure, complete th custom packaging! She's super-posable, has eal (fake) fur tail (that's also super-posable) and cludes 7 of her squirrels, including Tippy-Toe!

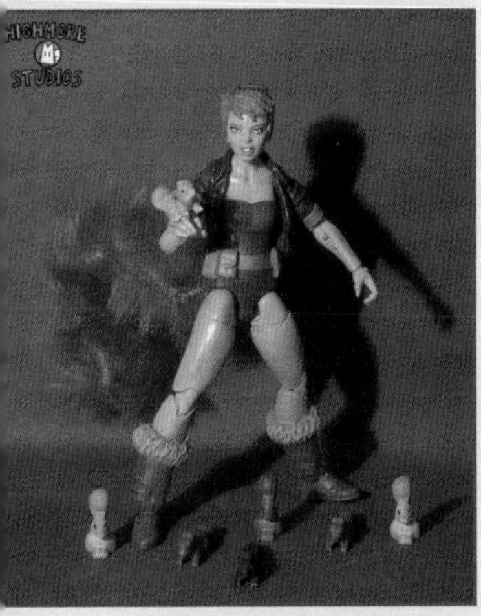
HIGHMORE
STUDIOS

Keep up the squirrelly good work!
Matt Beahan

R: Matt, I LOVE YOUR ACTION FIGURE. It's so eat! We did that action figure variant cover for #3 d my first words to our editor were "YES HELLO N THIS BE A REAL THING PLEASE THANKS IN VANCE." It's my understanding that action ures take much longer to produce than talking uirrel comic books, though, so I don't think we're nna see much OFFICIAL merchandise for a while ut I hold out hope for a figure someday that even proaches how cool this is!!

E: OH MY GOD. I LOVE IT. Did you make the ppy? Did you get it from another set? I love it much.

ar Team Squirrel Girl,

Hi, I'm Tabby, and I truly love The Unbeatable uirrel Girl! I've been collecting pieces for a costume wear to a comic convention, so I could meet Rico nzi, and show it off to him. Unfortunately I got real k, and had to go to the hospital for a while. I ended with a feeding tube, but I wasn't going to let that op me from going to the convention and meeting Rico. The convention was the day after I got home from the hospital, but I let my mother know I would go nuts if she didn't take me.

With my sidekick Tippy-Toe (really my sister Abigail), I made it to the convention and met Rico. He was awesome, and super friendly and signed posters for the both of us. I've included a picture. I'm still fighting to get better, but we are unbeatable just like Squirrel Girl!

Love Tabby!

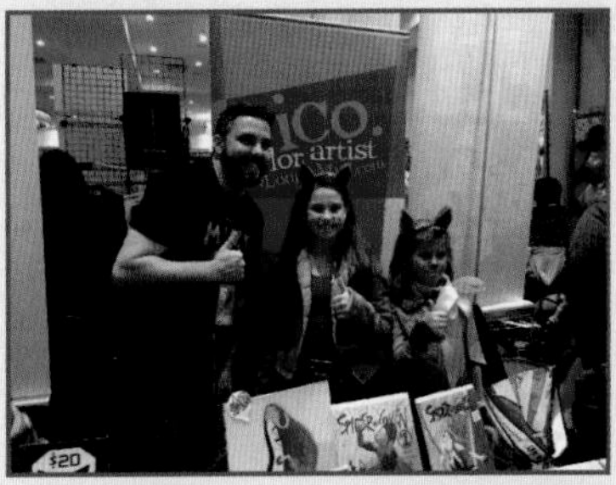
rico.
color artist
$20

R: Aw, Tabby are you the best? IT SEEMS LIKELY. Rico told us about this and he was super excited that you made it out! Both your and Abigail's costumes are terrific, and I'm really glad you were well enough for a day at the comics show, and I hope you feel better soon! I was on a feeding tube once and it was not as fun as it sounded (free food through a tube? SIGN ME UP). I know that you are as unbeatable as your costume is awesome, which is to say: extremely.

E: Agh. You're tougher than I am. The worst I've had is an appendectomy, so they let me eat after a day or two. I'm glad you could make it out after you put all that work in! Great costume!

I have been loving the adventures of Doreen, from vol. 1 and now vol. 2. I particularly enjoy the Computer Science references, and how Doreen and her friends are so excited about their academic studies. Warms this old professor's heart.

But it's a reference in issue 4 that only an "old" professor would get that motivates my letter. When Doreen needs to sneak up and secretly spy on Castle Doom in Central Park, she is dressed as... Secret Squirrel! I LOVED that show when it first aired in 1965 (did I mention the 'old' part?). Now want guest appearances from Morocco Mole, or at least Scott Lang dressed as Atom Ant.

If Doreen or Nancy need any help with their other science courses (hey - you don't just take classes in your major while at college), they should feel free to drop me a line.

I don't have any photos of me dressed like Squirrel Girl, but I do have a drawing (by Gene Ha!) of me as Ryan from the letter column graphic.

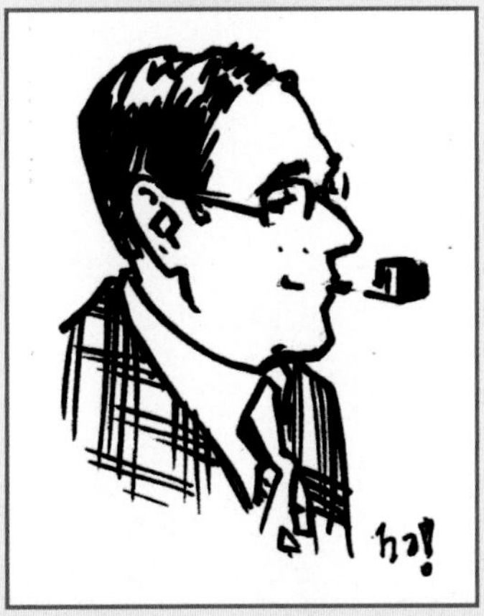
ha!

Off to eat nuts.

Your Friendly Neighborhood Physics Professor,
Jim Kakalios
Taylor Distinguished Professor
School of Physics and Astronomy
The University of Minnesota
Minneapolis, MN 55455

R: Jim, it is amazing to hear from you, because I HAVE READ YOUR BOOK. It's called The Physics of Superheroes and I think of it every time Doreen leaps over NYC and lands like it isn't even a thing. As you can tell, I studied it extremely carefully.

And I love that you have a drawing (by Gene Ha!) of you as ME from our letters page! That is amazing and I would've never expected to live in a world where this is the case. I'm super stoked you like our comics!

E: Morocco Moleman? Huckleberry Havok? Ah, too bad we don't have the rights to those guys.

Next:

You gotta read HOWARD THE DUCK #6, on sale next month, for the rest of this story!

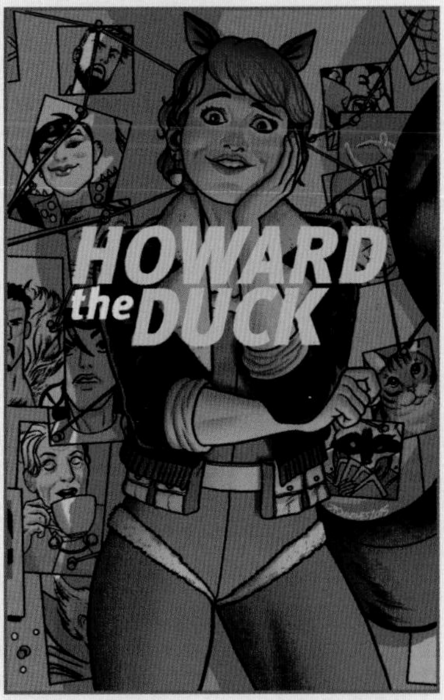
HOWARD the DUCK

And then after that come back here for an insanely awesome new story where YOU call the shots!

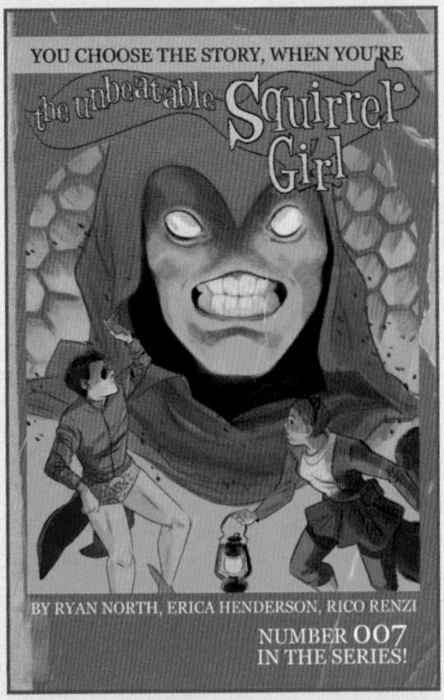
YOU CHOOSE THE STORY, WHEN YOU'RE
the unbeatable Squirrel Girl
BY RYAN NORTH, ERICA HENDERSON, RICO RENZI
NUMBER 007
IN THE SERIES!

ttention, Squirrel Scouts! Make sure to check out our production blog, **unbeatablesquirrelgirl.tumblr.com**, where we post behind-the-scenes stuff on how the book gets made, along with all sorts of cool things *you* make: fanart, cosplay, whatever!

HOWARD THE DUCK #6

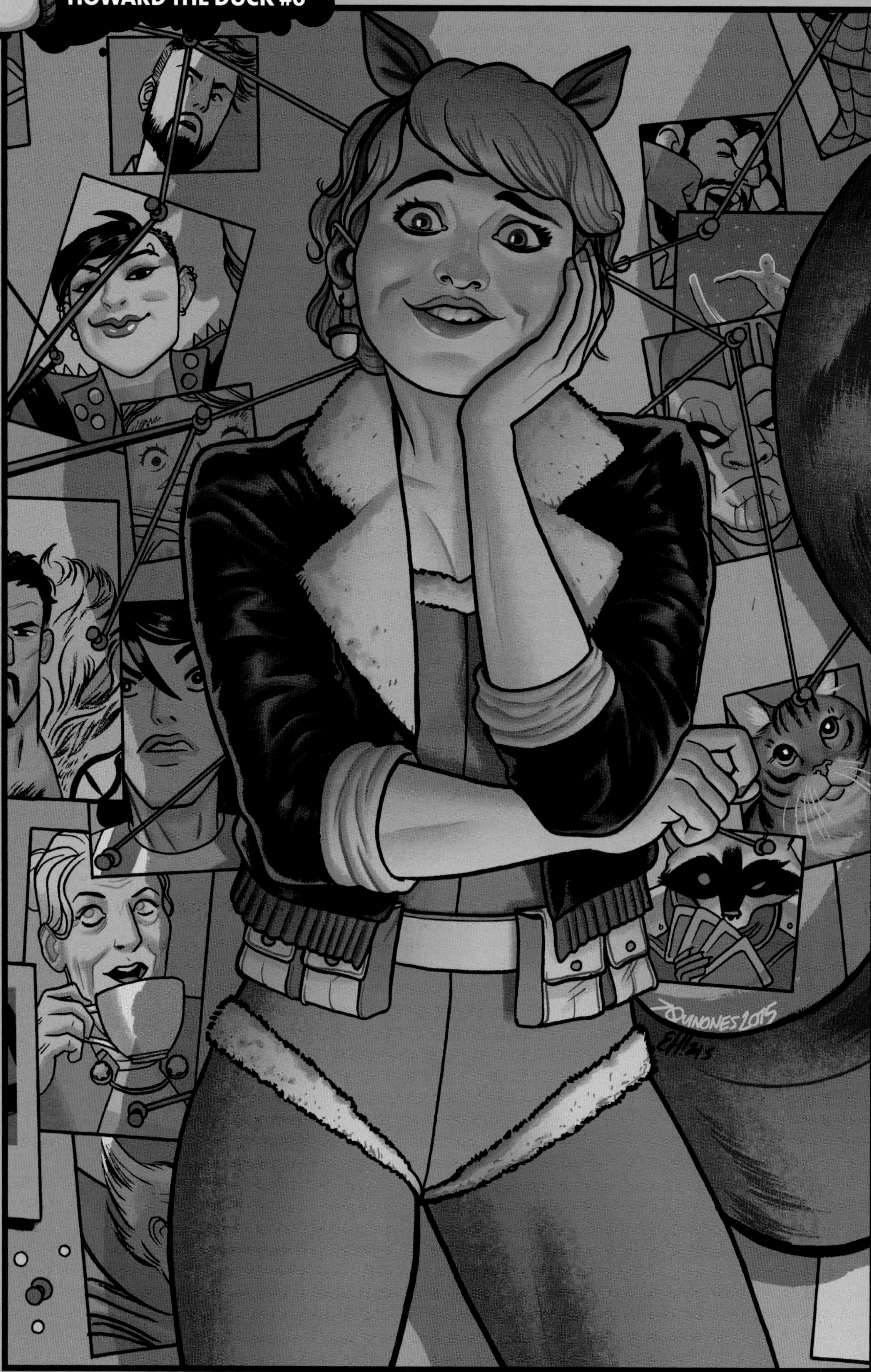

HOWARD the DUCK

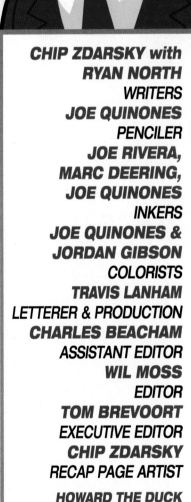

HEY, HOPEFULLY THIS ISN'T NEWS TO YOU, BUT THIS ISSUE RIGHT HERE IS PART TWO OF A TWO-PART STORY THAT BEGAN IN *THE UNBEATABLE SQUIRREL GIRL #6!* HOWARD DOES A PRETTY GOOD JOB ON THE NEXT PAGE OF SUMMARIZING WHAT HAPPENED IN THAT ISSUE, BUT STILL, *U.S.G.* IS REALLY GOOD, YOU SHOULD TRACK THAT ISSUE DOWN. (AND YES YOU *CAN* TRUST THIS TOTALLY UNBIASED RECAPPER!)

ANYWAY, HERE'S SOME ADDITIONAL HOWARD-CENTRIC CONTEXT FOR THIS ISSUE, OKAY?

EVER SINCE THE START OF THIS NEW VOLUME, HOWARD'S HAD WHAT APPEARS TO BE A CYBORG CAT FOR A PET. WHAT IS *UP* WITH THAT CAT? FIND OUT IN THIS VERY ISSUE, WHICH TAKES PLACE BETWEEN THIS VOLUME AND THE LAST ONE. (I KNOW, I KNOW-- COMICS!)

HUH. GUESS THERE WASN'T A WHOLE LOTTA CONTEXT TO SHARE ACTUALLY. YOU'RE FREE TO GO!

CHIP ZDARSKY with **RYAN NORTH**
WRITERS
JOE QUINONES
PENCILER
JOE RIVERA, MARC DEERING, JOE QUINONES
INKERS
JOE QUINONES & JORDAN GIBSON
COLORISTS
TRAVIS LANHAM
LETTERER & PRODUCTION
CHARLES BEACHAM
ASSISTANT EDITOR
WIL MOSS
EDITOR
TOM BREVOORT
EXECUTIVE EDITOR
CHIP ZDARSKY
RECAP PAGE ARTIST

HOWARD THE DUCK CREATED BY **STEVE GERBER** & **VAL MAYERIK**

JOE QUINONES with ERICA HENDERSON
COVER ARTISTS
JOE QUINONES & PAOLO RIVERA; BRADD MOORE & MATTHEW WILSON
VARIANT COVER ARTISTS
AXEL ALONSO EDITOR IN CHIEF JOE QUESADA CHIEF CREATIVE OFFICER
DAN BUCKLEY PUBLISHER ALAN FINE EXECUTIVE PRODUCER

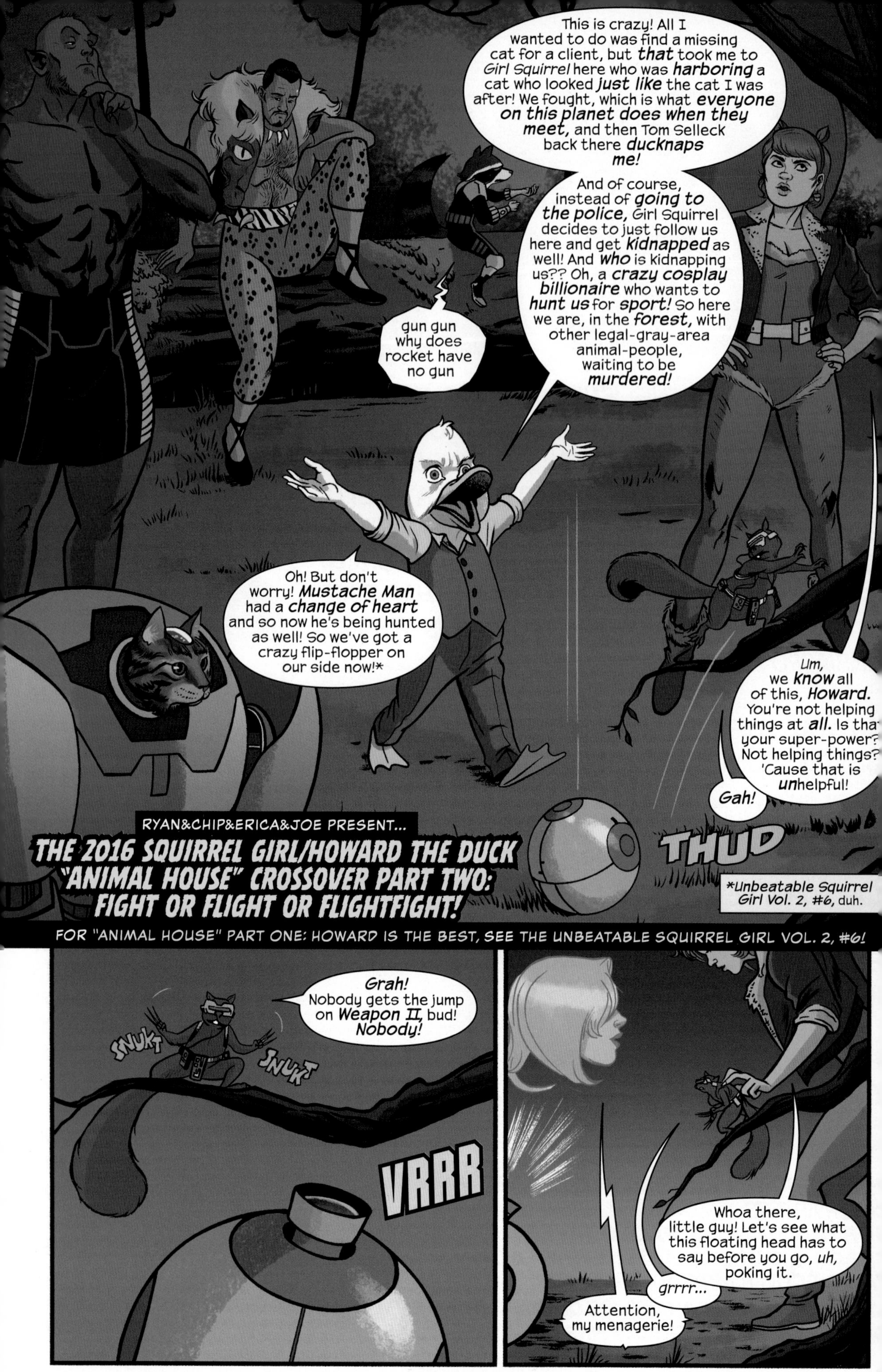
This is crazy! All I wanted to do was find a missing cat for a client, but that took me to Girl Squirrel here who was harboring a cat who looked just like the cat I was after! We fought, which is what everyone on this planet does when they meet, and then Tom Selleck back there ducknaps me!
And of course, instead of going to the police, Girl Squirrel decides to just follow us here and get kidnapped as well! And who is kidnapping us?? Oh, a crazy cosplay billionaire who wants to hunt us for sport! So here we are, in the forest, with other legal-gray-area animal-people, waiting to be murdered!
gun gun why does rocket have no gun
Oh! But don't worry! Mustache Man had a change of heart and so now he's being hunted as well! So we've got a crazy flip-flopper on our side now!*
Um, we know all of this, Howard. You're not helping things at all. Is tha your super-power? Not helping things? 'Cause that is unhelpful!
Gah!
THUD
RYAN&CHIP&ERICA&JOE PRESENT...
THE 2016 SQUIRREL GIRL/HOWARD THE DUCK "ANIMAL HOUSE" CROSSOVER PART TWO: FIGHT OR FLIGHT OR FLIGHTFIGHT!
*Unbeatable Squirrel Girl Vol. 2, #6, duh.
FOR "ANIMAL HOUSE" PART ONE: HOWARD IS THE BEST, SEE THE UNBEATABLE SQUIRREL GIRL VOL. 2, #6!
Grah! Nobody gets the jump on Weapon II, bud! Nobody!
SNUKT
SNUKT
VRRR
Whoa there, little guy! Let's see what this floating head has to say before you go, uh, poking it.
grrrr...
Attention, my menagerie!

So, Ryan does these weird "alt text" things in *Squirrel Girl* to prove that they're not just about "mainstream text," I guess. Cool stuff, guys!
And if you're here from *Squirrel Girl,* you should know normally Chip *doesn't* do this text at the bottom, so if you look at the other issues, you'll just be disappointed!! Okay bye

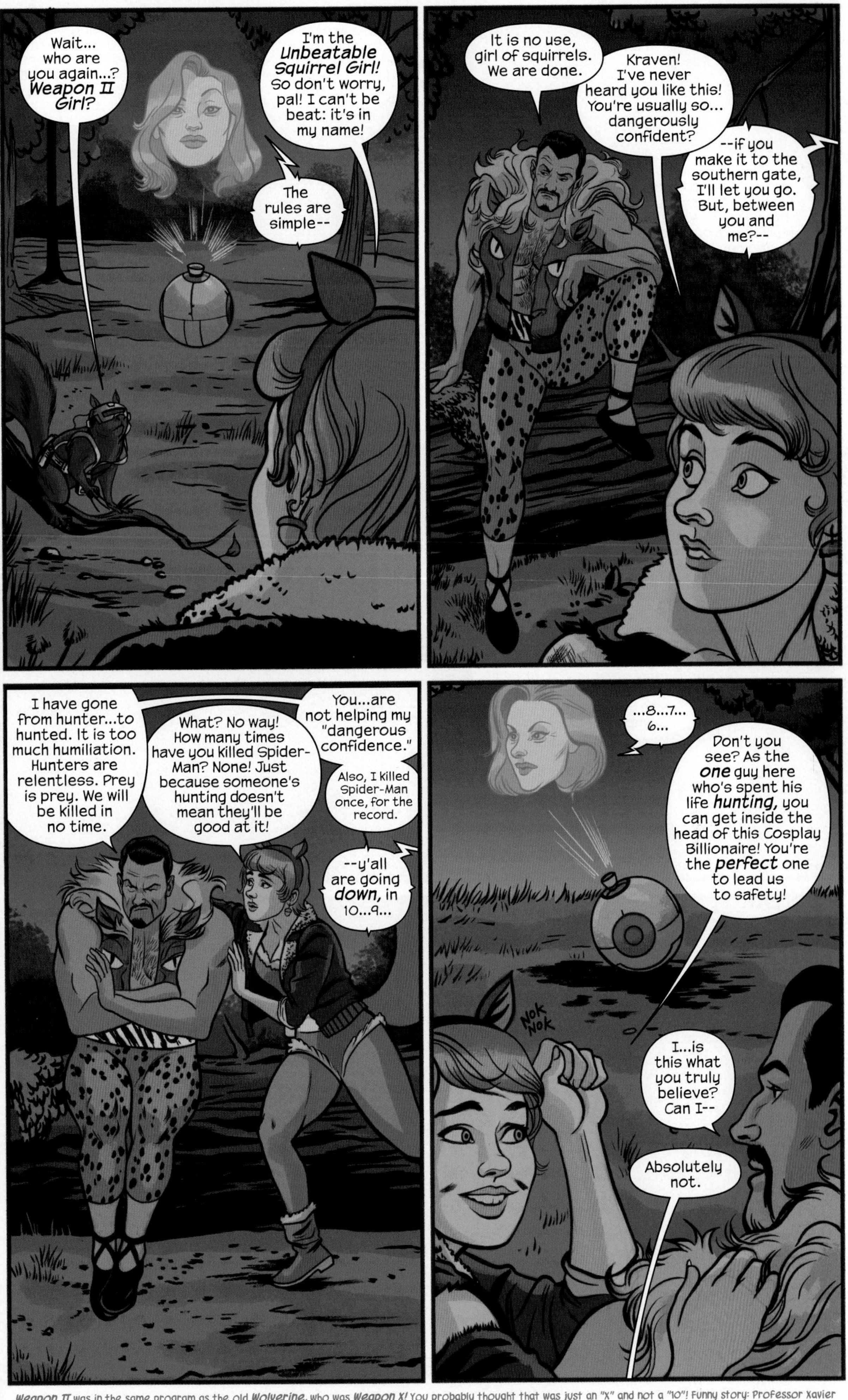
Wait... who are you again...? Weapon II Girl?
I'm the Unbeatable Squirrel Girl! So don't worry, pal! I can't be beat: it's in my name!
The rules are simple--
It is no use, girl of squirrels. We are done.
Kraven! I've never heard you like this! You're usually so... dangerously confident?
--if you make it to the southern gate, I'll let you go. But, between you and me?--
I have gone from hunter...to hunted. It is too much humiliation. Hunters are relentless. Prey is prey. We will be killed in no time.
What? No way! How many times have you killed Spider-Man? None! Just because someone's hunting doesn't mean they'll be good at it!
You...are not helping my "dangerous confidence."
Also, I killed Spider-Man once, for the record.
--y'all are going down, in 10...9...
...8...7... 6...
Don't you see? As the one guy here who's spent his life hunting, you can get inside the head of this Cosplay Billionaire! You're the perfect one to lead us to safety!
NOK NOK
I...is this what you truly believe? Can I--
Absolutely not.

Weapon II was in the same program as the old ***Wolverine,*** who was ***Weapon X!*** You probably thought that was just an "X" and not a "10"! Funny story: Professor Xavier actually named the X-Men ***"Ten-Men,"*** because he wanted ten guys on the team, but nobody got it so he just let people believe it was X-Men.

Now ***that's*** a tenhilarating addition to Marvel canon!

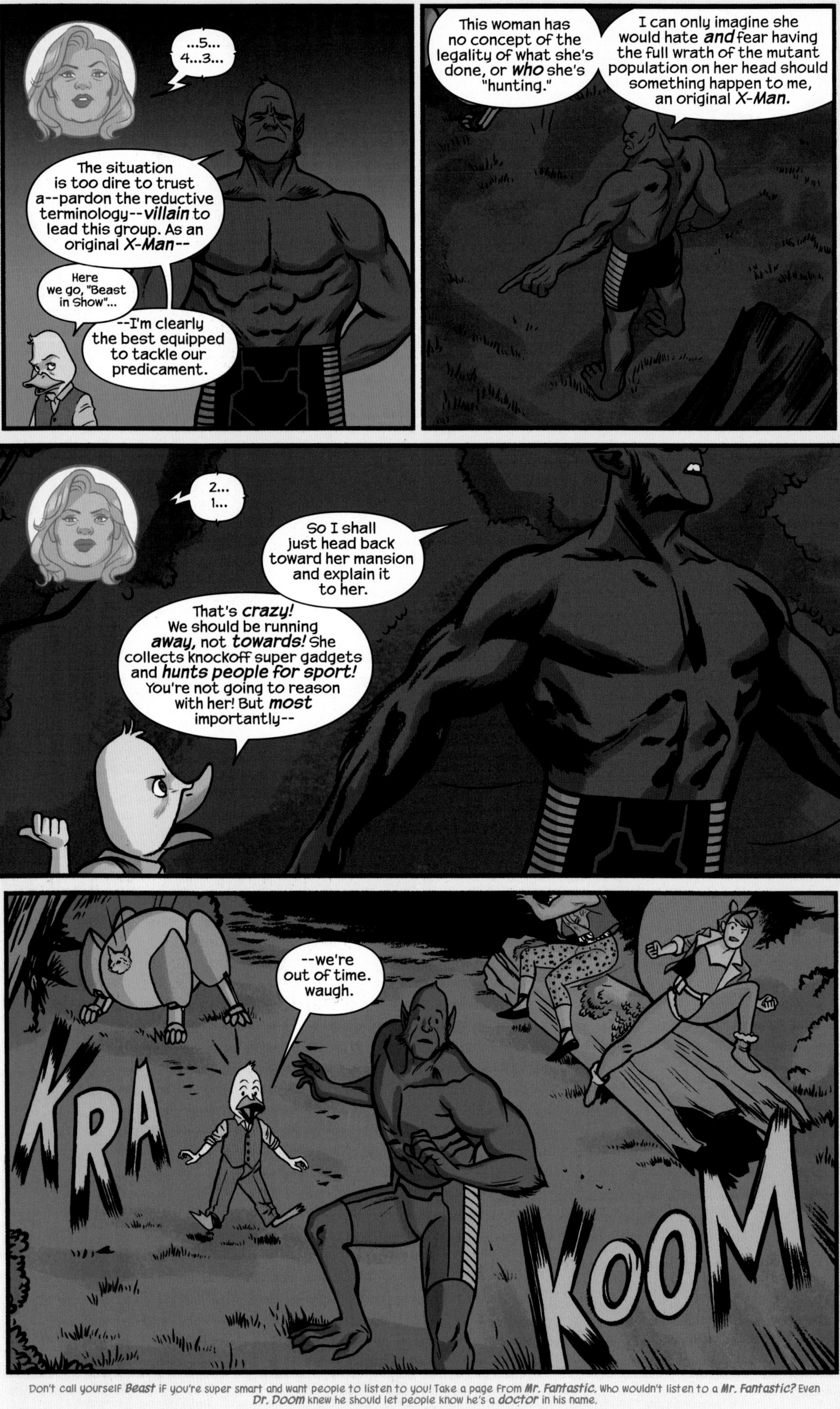
...5...
4...3...
The situation is too dire to trust a--pardon the reductive terminology--villain to lead this group. As an original X-Man--
Here we go, "Beast in Show"...
--I'm clearly the best equipped to tackle our predicament.
This woman has no concept of the legality of what she's done, or who she's "hunting."
I can only imagine she would hate and fear having the full wrath of the mutant population on her head should something happen to me, an original X-Man.
2...
1...
So I shall just head back toward her mansion and explain it to her.
That's crazy! We should be running away, not towards! She collects knockoff super gadgets and hunts people for sport! You're not going to reason with her! But most importantly--
--we're out of time. waugh.
KRA
KOOM

Don't call yourself *Beast* if you're super smart and want people to listen to you! Take a page from ***Mr. Fantastic.*** Who wouldn't listen to a ***Mr. Fantastic?*** Even ***Dr. Doom*** knew he should let people know he's a ***doctor*** in his name.

Thought you could ever only have a character say "...we're out of time" in a time travel story? ***Think again.***

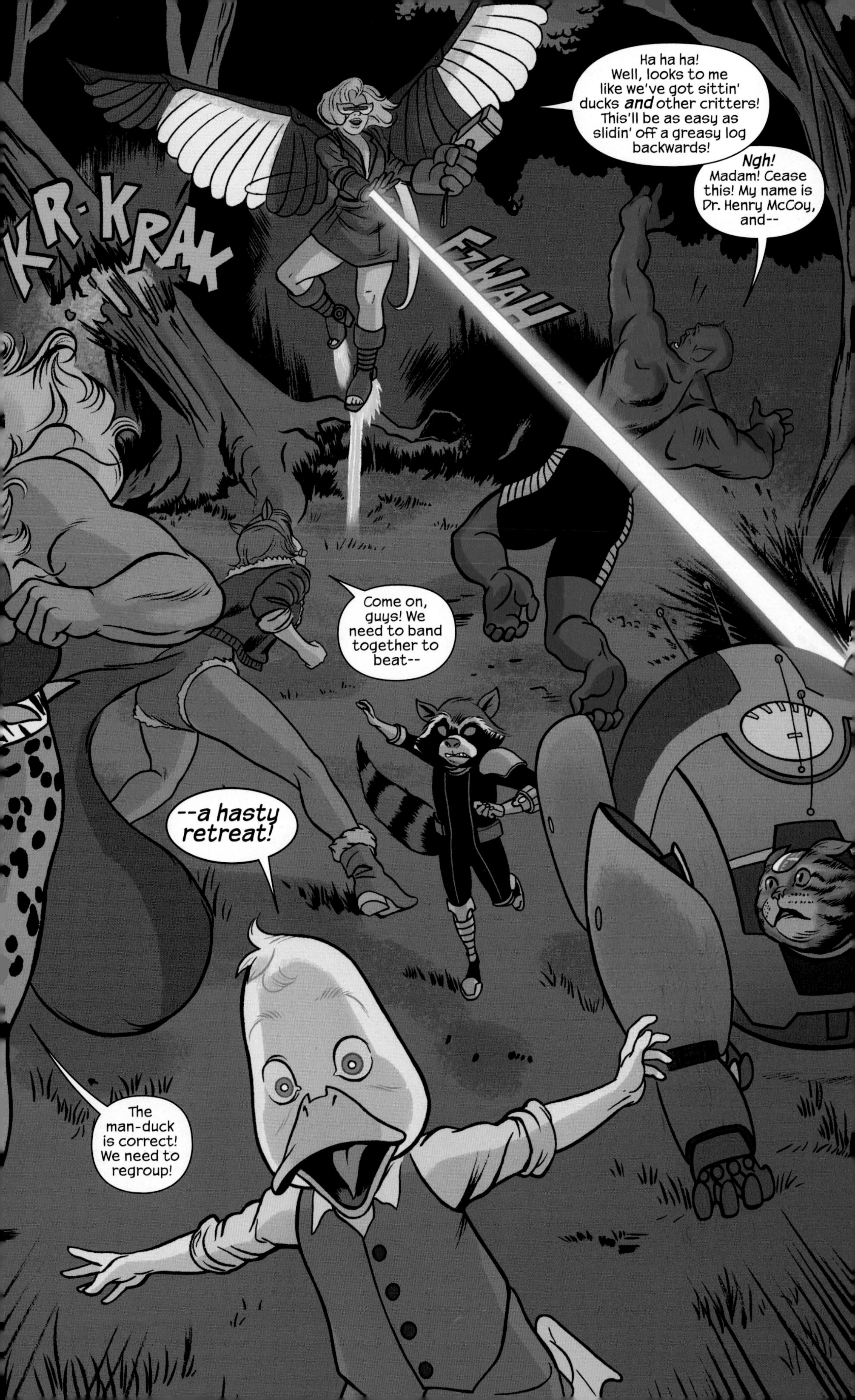
KR-KRAK
Ha ha ha! Well, looks to me like we've got sittin' ducks and other critters! This'll be as easy as slidin' off a greasy log backwards!
FZWAH
Ngh! Madam! Cease this! My name is Dr. Henry McCoy, and--
Come on, guys! We need to band together to beat--
--a hasty retreat!
The man-duck is correct! We need to regroup!

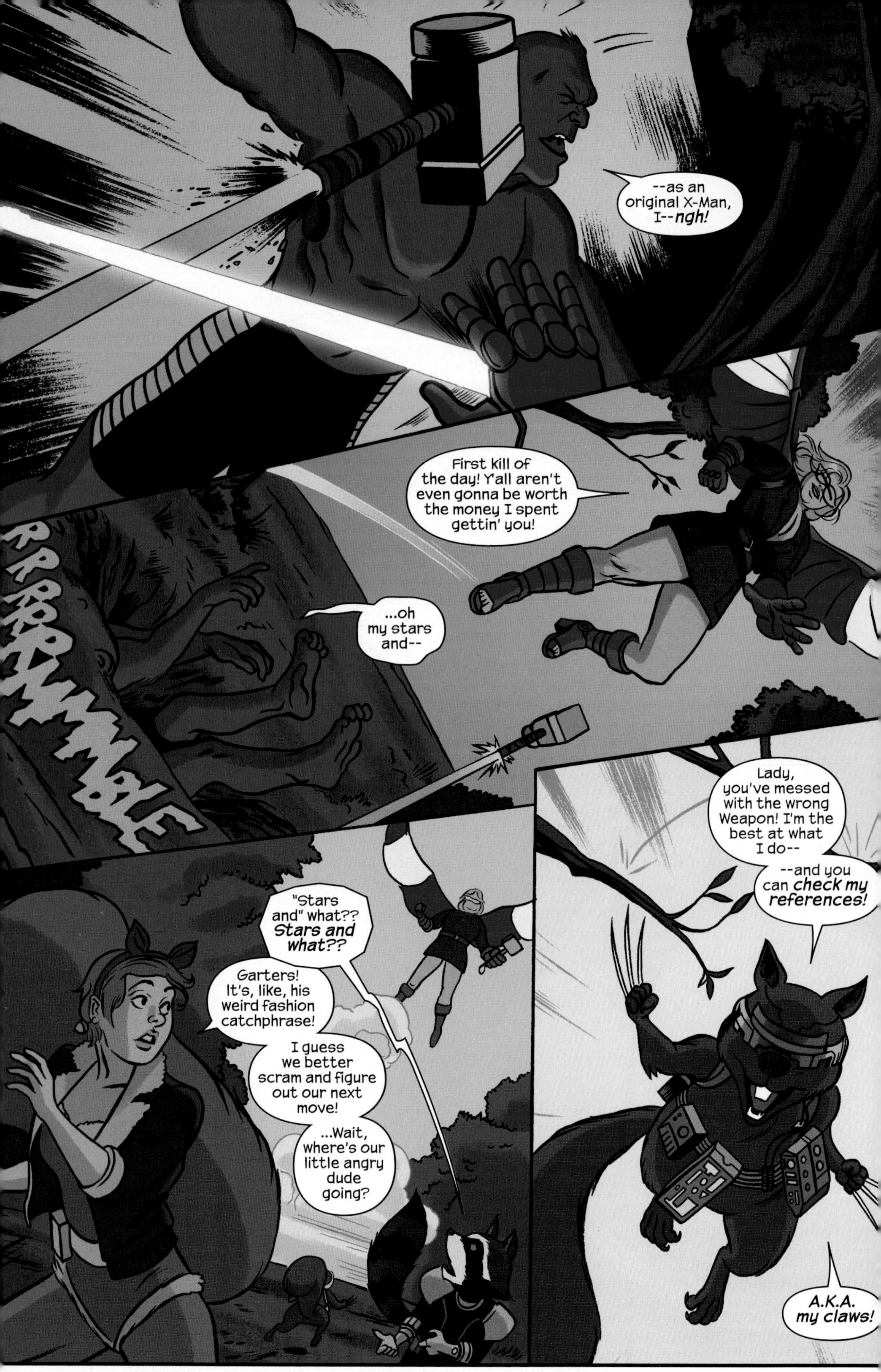
--as an original X-Man, I--*ngh!*
First kill of the day! Y'all aren't even gonna be worth the money I spent gettin' you!
...oh my stars and--
"Stars and" what?? *Stars and what??*
Garters! It's, like, his weird fashion catchphrase!
I guess we better scram and figure out our next move!
...Wait, where's our little angry dude going?
Lady, you've messed with the wrong Weapon! I'm the best at what I do--
--and you can *check my references!*
A.K.A. my claws!

Actually, "garters" in this case refers to the Most Noble Order of the Garter, which is the highest order of chivalry in the U.K. *See, Ryan? I can know things, too.*
I like how your impression of me is "a guy who knows things." I'll take it!

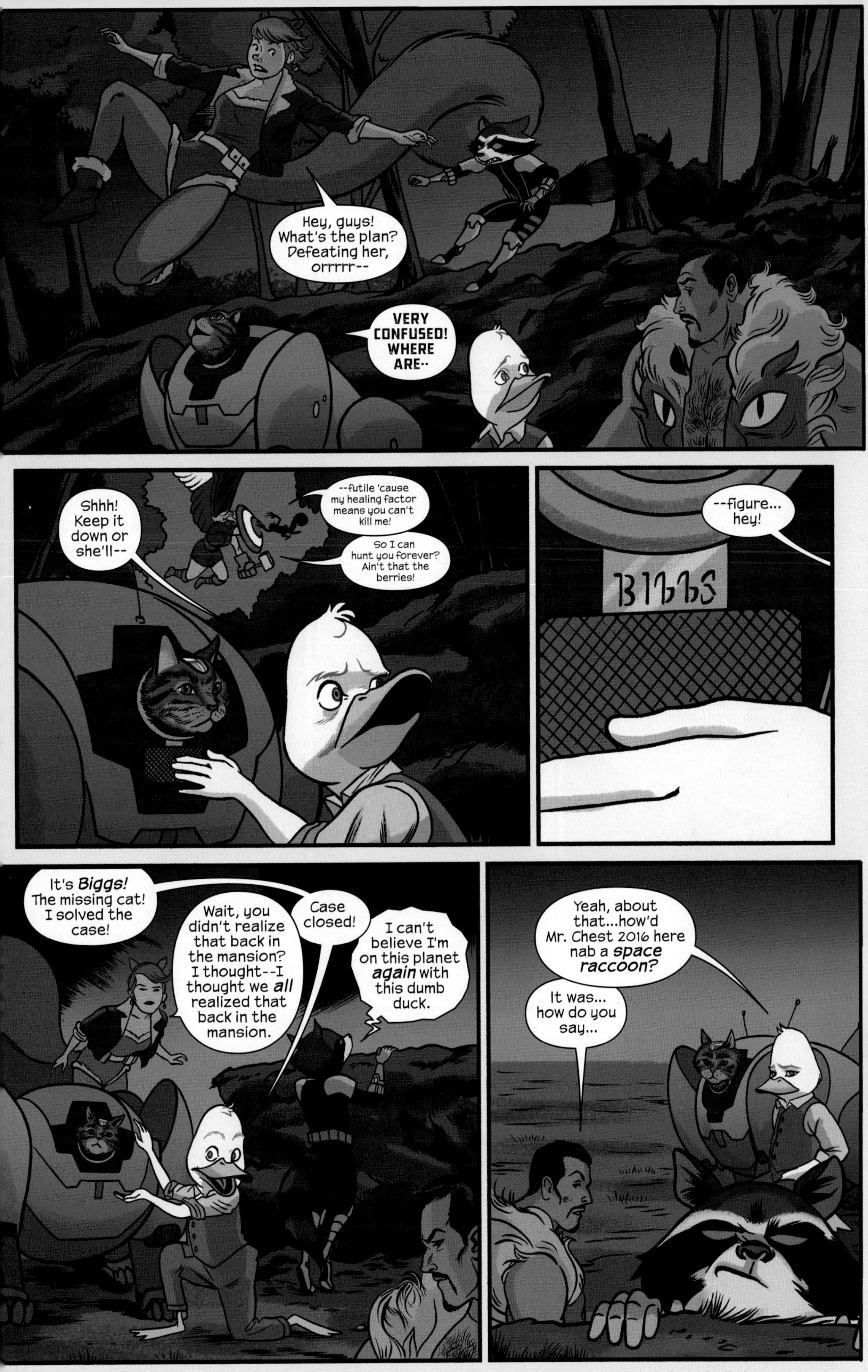
Hey, guys! What's the plan? Defeating her, orrrrr--
VERY CONFUSED! WHERE ARE··
Shhh! Keep it down or she'll--
--futile 'cause my healing factor means you can't kill me!
So I can hunt you forever? Ain't that the berries!
--figure... hey!
It's Biggs! The missing cat! I solved the case!
Case closed!
Wait, you didn't realize that back in the mansion? I thought--I thought we all realized that back in the mansion.
I can't believe I'm on this planet again with this dumb duck.
Yeah, about that...how'd Mr. Chest 2016 here nab a space raccoon?
It was... how do you say...

Ducks actually have excellent vision and can see two, three times farther than humans! But sometimes you can't see the forest for the trees, and Howard is all about complaining about the trees.

As a guy who knows things, I agree.

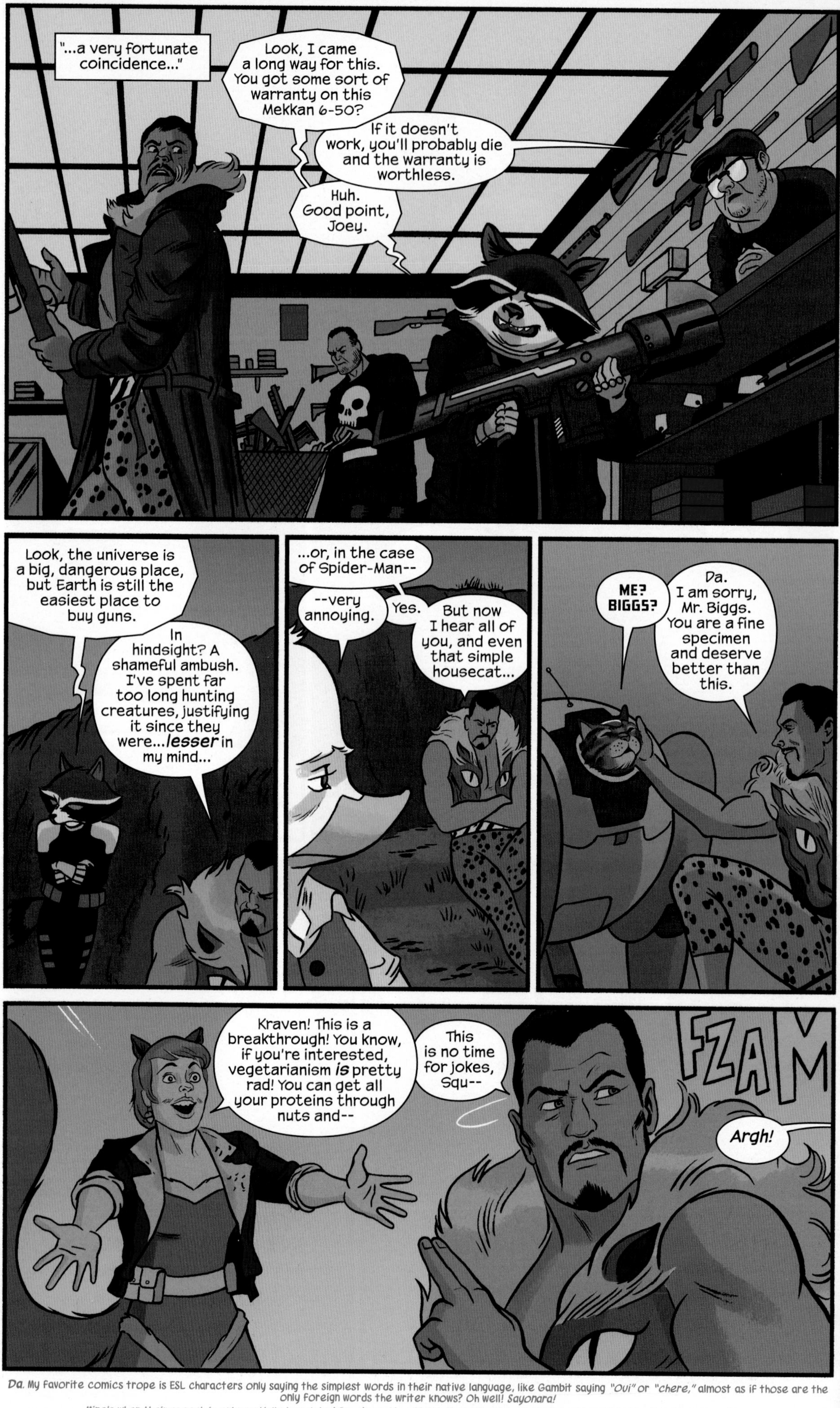
"...a very fortunate coincidence..."
Look, I came a long way for this. You got some sort of warranty on this Mekkan 6-50?
If it doesn't work, you'll probably die and the warranty is worthless.
Huh. Good point, Joey.
Look, the universe is a big, dangerous place, but Earth is still the easiest place to buy guns.
In hindsight? A shameful ambush. I've spent far too long hunting creatures, justifying it since they were...*lesser* in my mind...
...or, in the case of Spider-Man--
--very annoying.
Yes.
But now I hear all of you, and even that simple housecat...
ME? BIGGS?
Da. I am sorry, Mr. Biggs. You are a fine specimen and deserve better than this.
Kraven! This is a breakthrough! You know, if you're interested, vegetarianism *is* pretty rad! You can get all your proteins through nuts and--
This is no time for jokes, Squ--
FZAM
Argh!

Da. My favorite comics trope is ESL characters only saying the simplest words in their native language, like Gambit saying *"Oui"* or *"chere,"* almost as if those are the only foreign words the writer knows? Oh well! *Sayonara!*

Mine's when their speech is only partially translated for dramatic effect. It really gives *un petit quelque chose* to the *mise-en-scène.*

...ngh... my healing factor'll...do its job...like a little...body hospital... and then...

UGH STOP TALKING ABOUT YOUR HEALING FACTOR NOBODY CARES

This ain't over, bud... *urk!*

RRRUMMMMMMBLLLE

Hooookay, so Wolverteeny is down. What now?

Even if we made it to the finish line, there's *no way* she'd just let us go! We'd be back with Avengers and Fantastic Fours and maybe even cops in no time!

Hmm, then our only options are to ambush her here in the woods or head to the mansion. We can then... ugh...call for help...or find something we can use against her.

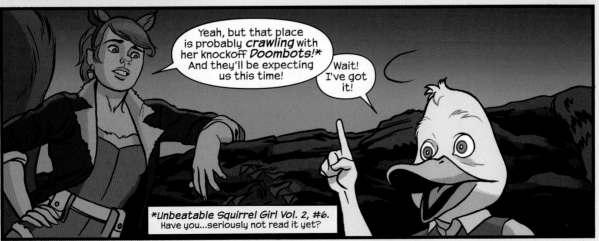

Yeah, but that place is probably *crawling* with her knockoff *Doombots!** And they'll be expecting us this time!

Wait! I've got it!

*Unbeatable Squirrel Girl Vol. 2, #6. Have you...seriously not read it yet?

And who calls their abilities a "Factor"? That's like me saying my "writing Factor" will finish this script in no time, or Ryan saying "My tall Factor will help me get that can on the top shelf." It's weird, man.
Chip, look, do you want the can or not?

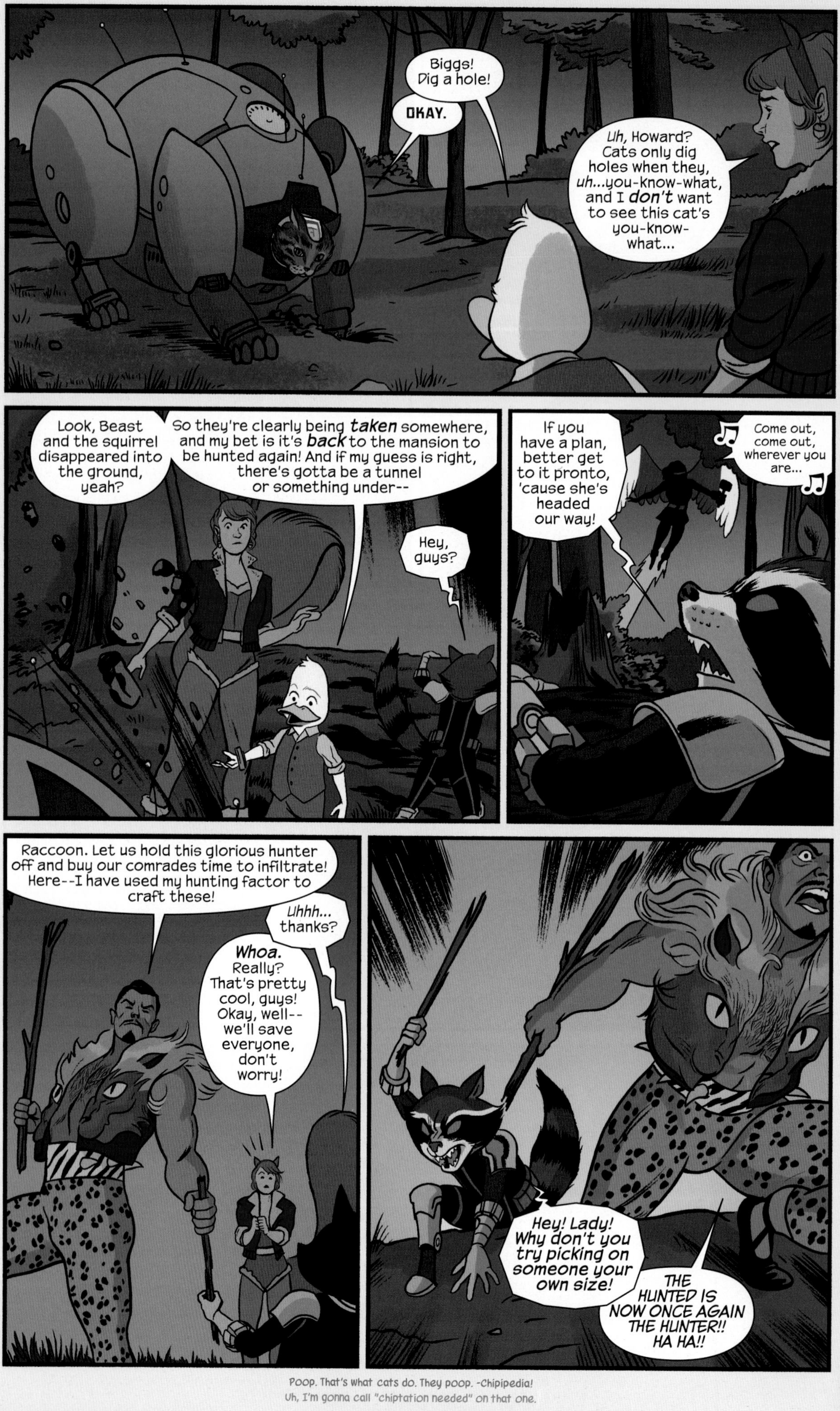
Biggs!
Dig a hole!
OKAY.
Uh, Howard? Cats only dig holes when they, uh...you-know-what, and I don't want to see this cat's you-know-what...
Look, Beast and the squirrel disappeared into the ground, yeah?
So they're clearly being taken somewhere, and my bet is it's back to the mansion to be hunted again! And if my guess is right, there's gotta be a tunnel or something under--
Hey, guys?
If you have a plan, better get to it pronto, 'cause she's headed our way!
♫ Come out, come out, wherever you are... ♫
Raccoon. Let us hold this glorious hunter off and buy our comrades time to infiltrate! Here--I have used my hunting factor to craft these!
Uhhh... thanks?
Whoa. Really? That's pretty cool, guys! Okay, well-- we'll save everyone, don't worry!
Hey! Lady! Why don't you try picking on someone your own size!
THE HUNTED IS NOW ONCE AGAIN THE HUNTER!! HA HA!!

Poop. That's what cats do. They poop. -Chipipedia!
Uh, I'm gonna call "chiptation needed" on that one.

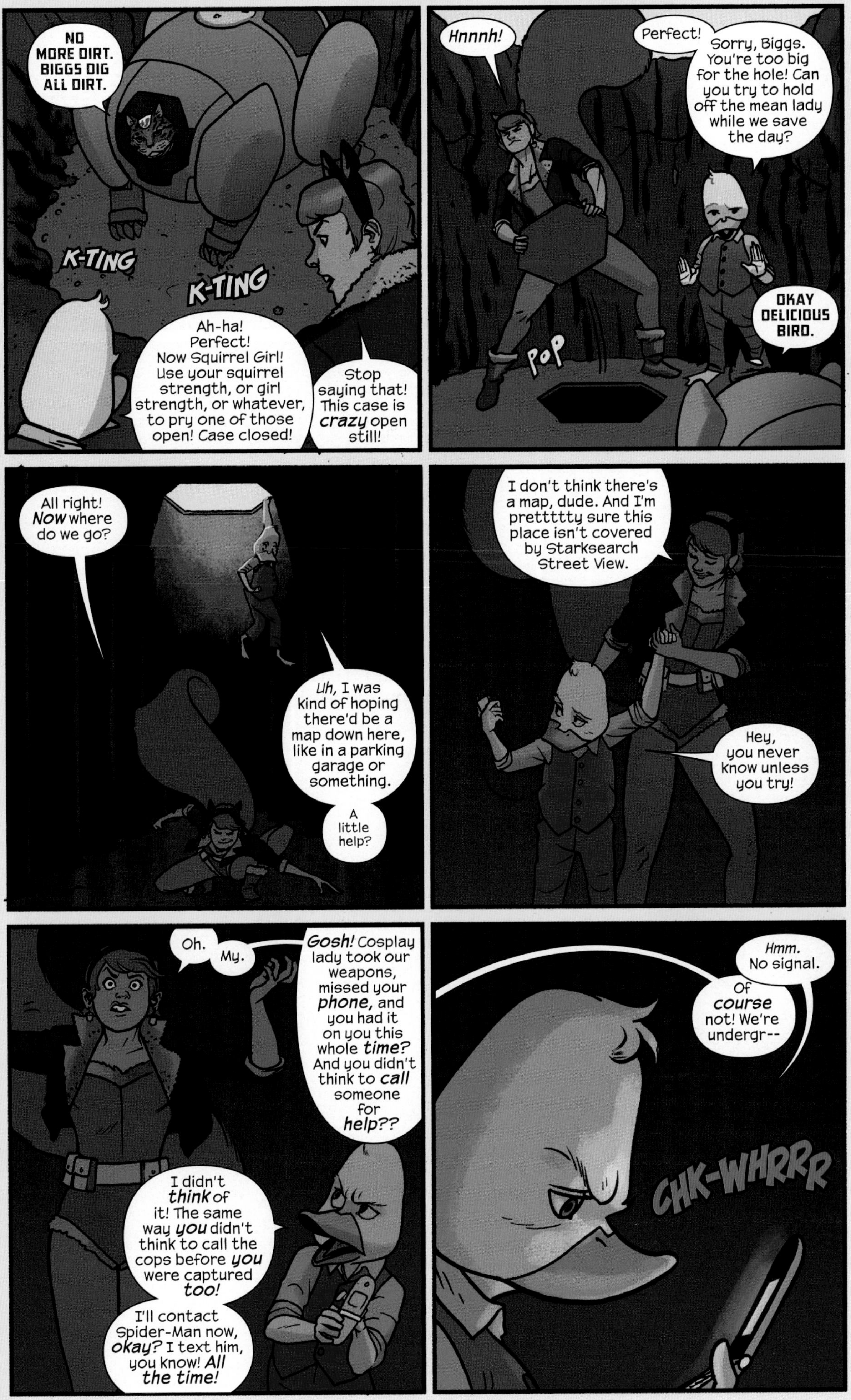
NO MORE DIRT. BIGGS DIG ALL DIRT.
K-TING
K-TING
Ah-ha! Perfect! Now Squirrel Girl! Use your squirrel strength, or girl strength, or whatever, to pry one of those open! Case closed!
Stop saying that! This case is crazy open still!
Hnnnh!
Perfect!
Sorry, Biggs. You're too big for the hole! Can you try to hold off the mean lady while we save the day?
POP
OKAY DELICIOUS BIRD.
All right! NOW where do we go?
Uh, I was kind of hoping there'd be a map down here, like in a parking garage or something.
A little help?
I don't think there's a map, dude. And I'm prettttty sure this place isn't covered by Starksearch Street View.
Hey, you never know unless you try!
Oh.
My.
Gosh! Cosplay lady took our weapons, missed your phone, and you had it on you this whole time? And you didn't think to call someone for help??
I didn't think of it! The same way you didn't think to call the cops before you were captured too!
I'll contact Spider-Man now, okay? I text him, you know! All the time!
Hmm. No signal.
Of course not! We're undergr--
CHK-WHRRR

Always use Safesearch with Starksearch. Just trust me.
Spider-Man set up an autoreply to send "lol no way!!" to every text Howard sends, and he hasn't noticed yet. It's been months.

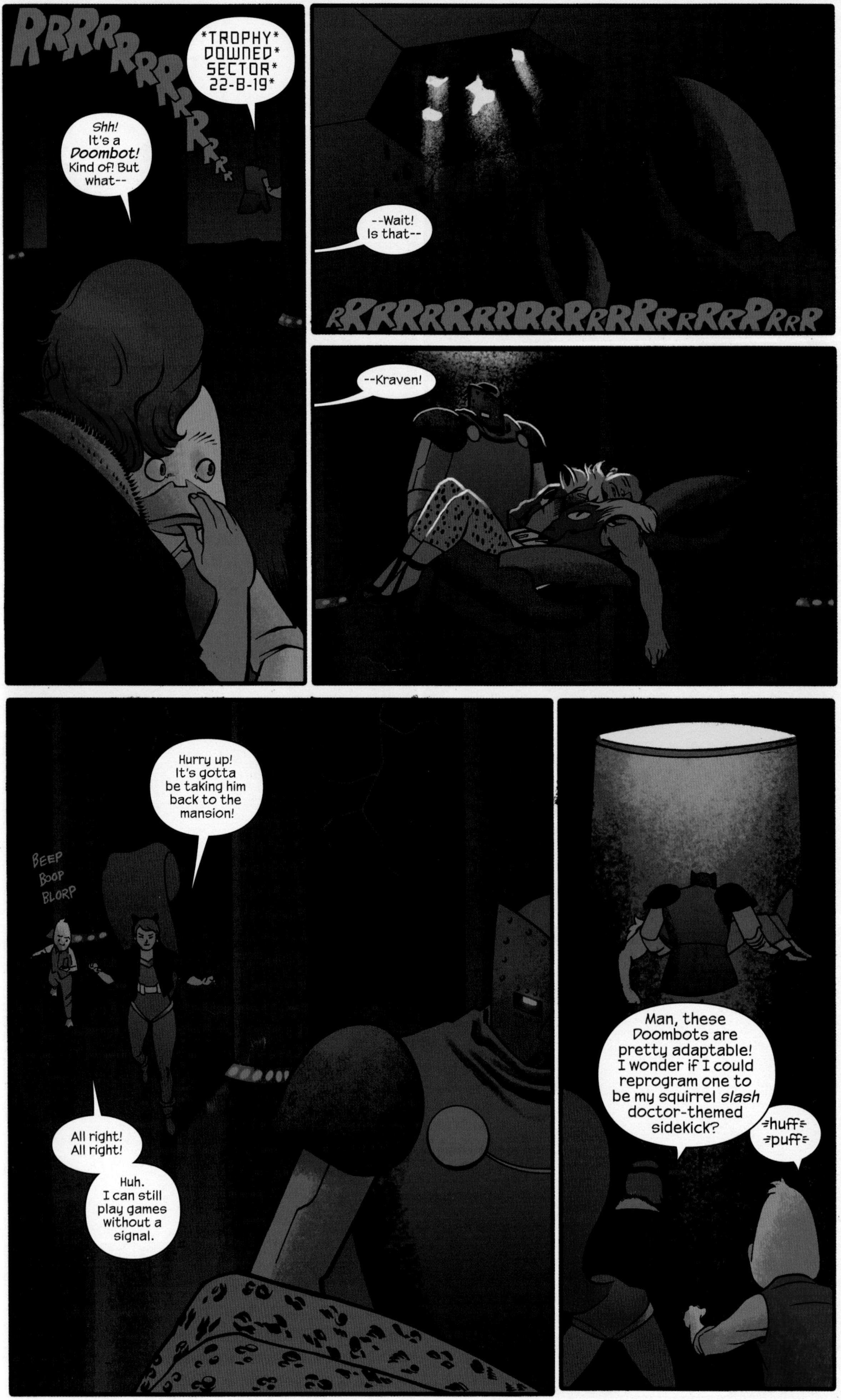
TROPHY DOWNED* SECTOR* 22-B-19*
RRRRRRRRRRRRRRRRRR
Shh! It's a *Doombot!* Kind of! But what--
--Wait! Is that--
RRRRRRRRRRRRRRRRRRRRRRRR
--Kraven!
Hurry up! It's gotta be taking him back to the mansion!
BEEP BOOP BLORP
All right! All right!
Huh. I can still play games without a signal.
Man, these Doombots are pretty adaptable! I wonder if I could reprogram one to be my squirrel *slash* doctor-themed sidekick?
=huff= =puff=

Think about it, Ryan. If you ***don't*** go for it, I'm going to make one Howard's sidekick: ***Dr. Plume.***
Wow. I ***really*** should've read ***Howard the Duck*** before agreeing to this crossover.

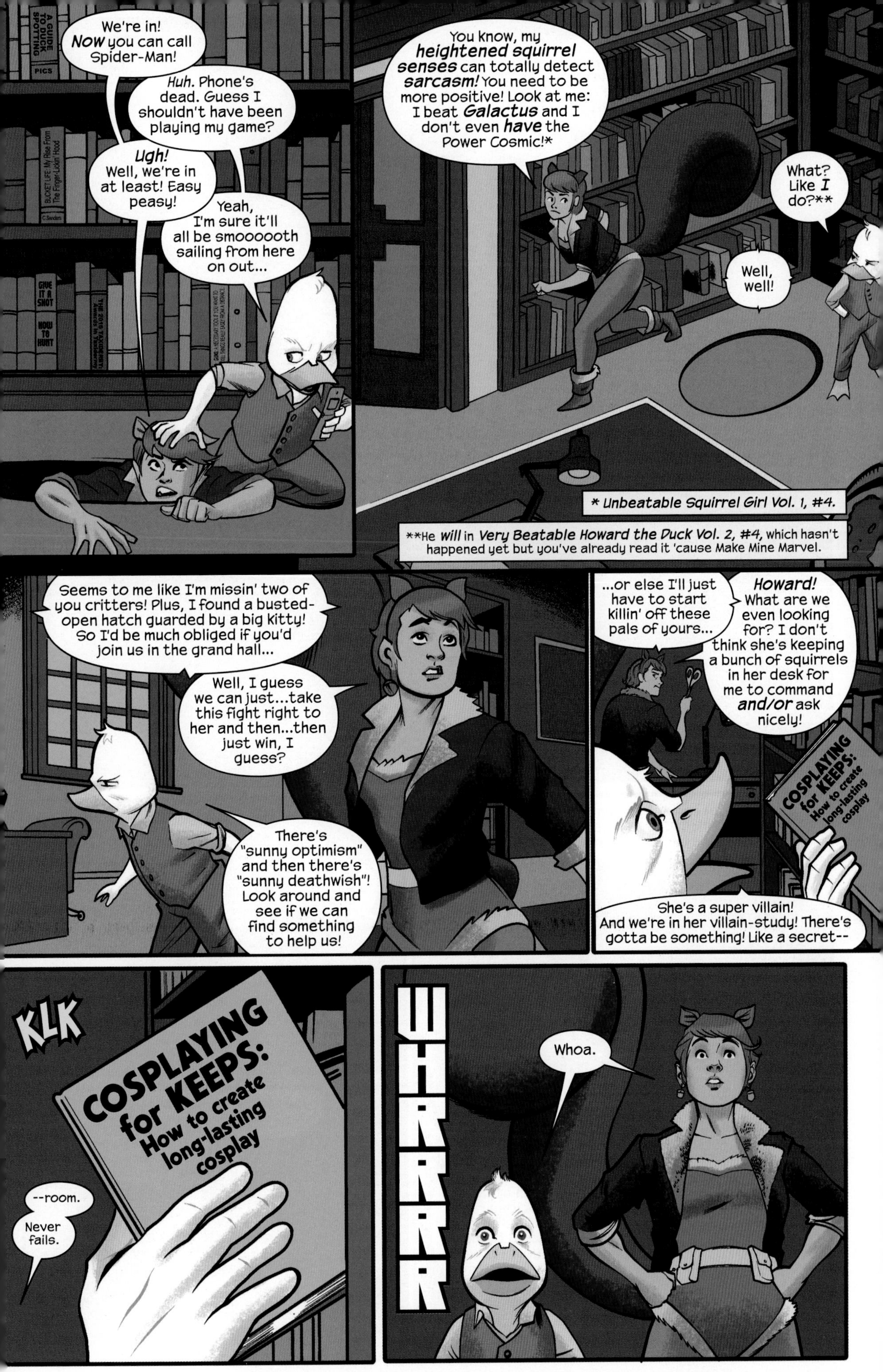
We're in! NOW you can call Spider-Man!
Huh. Phone's dead. Guess I shouldn't have been playing my game?
Ugh! Well, we're in at least! Easy peasy!
Yeah, I'm sure it'll all be smooooth sailing from here on out...
A GUIDE TO DUCK SPOTTING
PICS
GIVE IT A SHOT
HOW TO HUNT
You know, my heightened squirrel senses can totally detect sarcasm! You need to be more positive! Look at me: I beat Galactus and I don't even have the Power Cosmic!*
What? Like I do?**
Well, well!
* Unbeatable Squirrel Girl Vol. 1, #4.
**He will in Very Beatable Howard the Duck Vol. 2, #4, which hasn't happened yet but you've already read it 'cause Make Mine Marvel.
Seems to me like I'm missin' two of you critters! Plus, I found a busted-open hatch guarded by a big kitty! So I'd be much obliged if you'd join us in the grand hall...
Well, I guess we can just...take this fight right to her and then...then just win, I guess?
There's "sunny optimism" and then there's "sunny deathwish"! Look around and see if we can find something to help us!
...or else I'll just have to start killin' off these pals of yours...
Howard! What are we even looking for? I don't think she's keeping a bunch of squirrels in her desk for me to command and/or ask nicely!
COSPLAYING for KEEPS: How to create long-lasting cosplay
She's a super villain! And we're in her villain-study! There's gotta be something! Like a secret--
KLK
COSPLAYING for KEEPS: How to create long-lasting cosplay
--room.
Never fails.
WHRRRR
Whoa.

Other cosplay books: *Be the Hero You Want to See in the World But Without Powers, House of M: Designer Mutant Cosplay, Cos and Effect: Succeed in your Job by Dressing Like Storm.*
Not to mention *Fired With Cos: How You Too Can Get Fired For Dressing like Storm 24/7, We Have a Dress Code Here*

I suppose I'll start with the commie traitor first! You've got ten seconds to get your grade-B butts out here!

10...9...8...

And so ends the life of Sergei Nikolaevich Kravinoff...

PWEE

She really enjoys her countdowns...

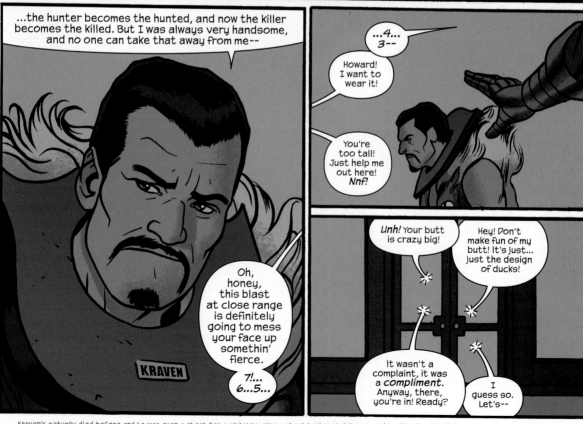

...the hunter becomes the hunted, and now the killer becomes the killed. But I was always very handsome, and no one can take that away from me--

Oh, honey, this blast at close range is definitely going to mess your face up somethin' fierce.

7!...6...5...

KRAVEN

...4...3--

Howard! I want to wear it!

You're too tall! Just help me out here! Nnf!

Unh! Your butt is crazy big!

Hey! Don't make fun of my butt! It's just... just the design of ducks!

It wasn't a complaint, it was a compliment. Anyway, there, you're in! Ready?

I guess so. Let's--

Kraven's actually died before and he was even a ghost for a while! Imagine a ghost hunter skulking around hunting the living? It would be like the opposite of a ghostbuster, and pretty cool. Call me, Hollywood.

Hollywood, my idea is like Chip's, only better because it's also like Die Hard. Call me first.

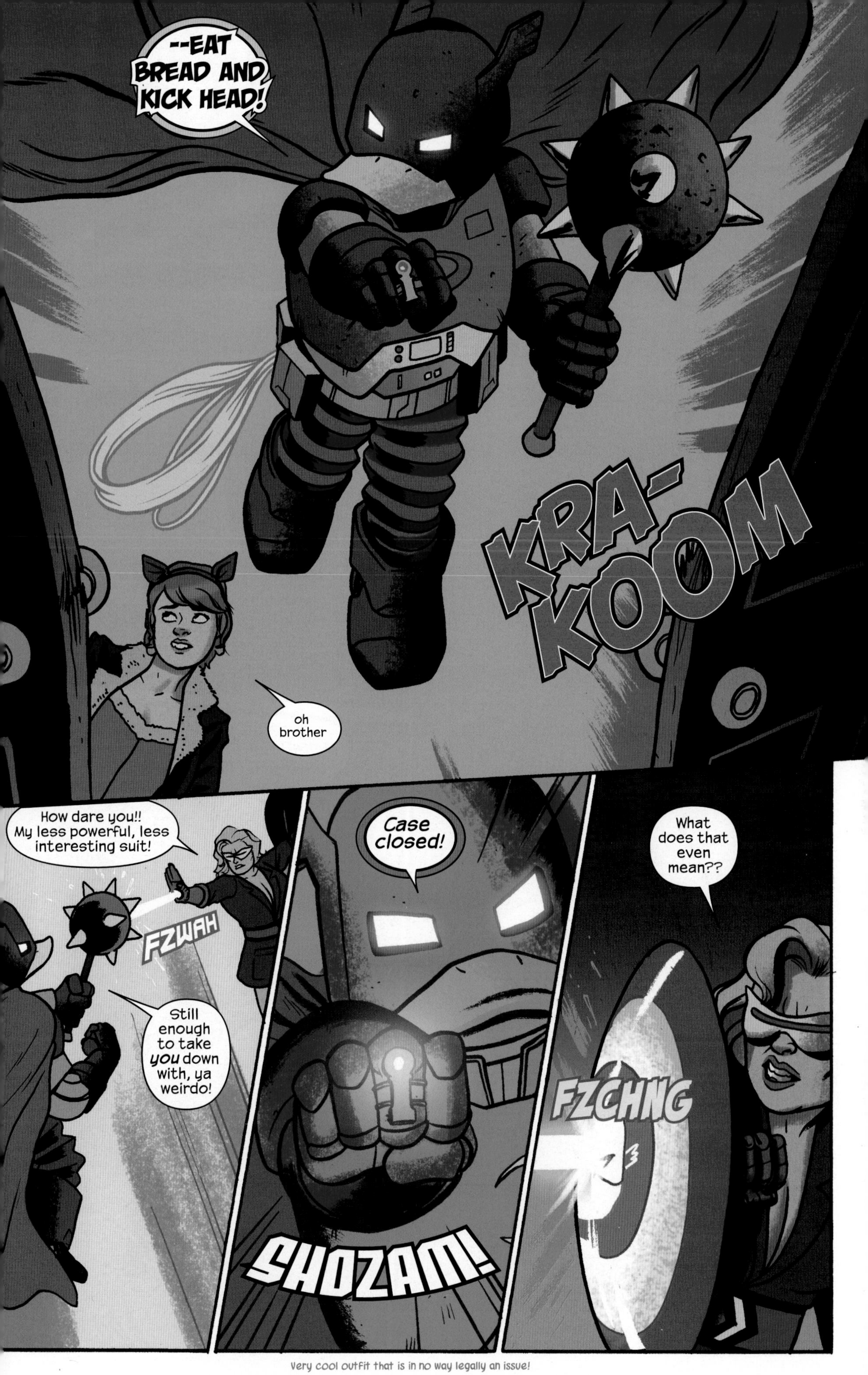
--EAT BREAD AND KICK HEAD!
KRA-KOOM
oh brother
How dare you!! My less powerful, less interesting suit!
FZWAH
Still enough to take *you* down with, ya weirdo!
Case closed!
SHOZAM!
What does that even mean??
FZCHNG

Very cool outfit that is in no way legally an issue!
I take it back, crossing over with ***Howard*** was an excellent idea and I'm 100% on board.

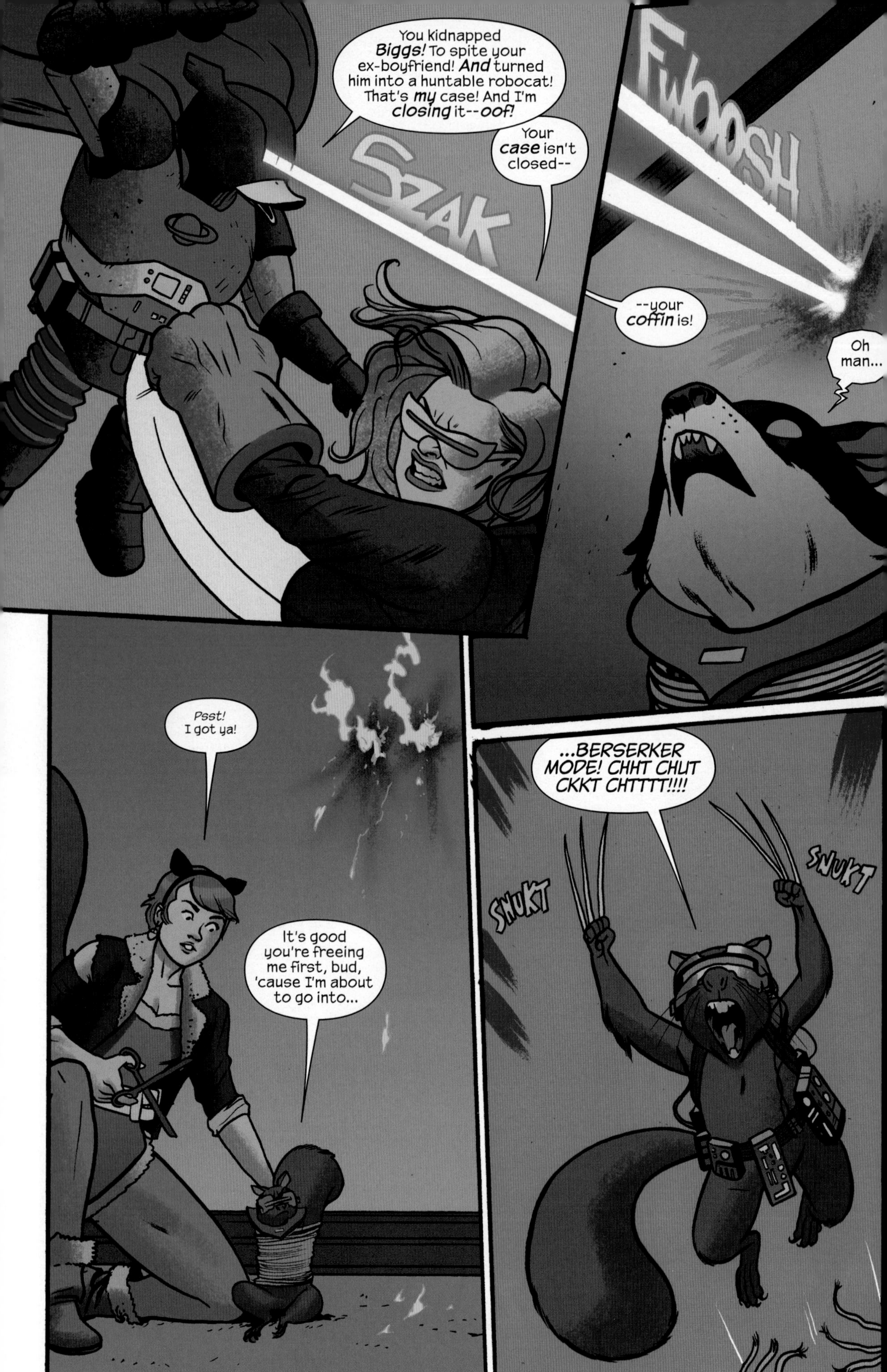
You kidnapped Biggs! To spite your ex-boyfriend! And turned him into a huntable robocat! That's my case! And I'm closing it--oof!
SZAK
Your case isn't closed--
FWOOSH
--your coffin is!
Oh man...
Psst! I got ya!
It's good you're freeing me first, bud, 'cause I'm about to go into...
...BERSERKER MODE! CHHT CHUT CKKT CHTTTT!!!!
SNUKT
SNUKT

Adorable!
Adorable.

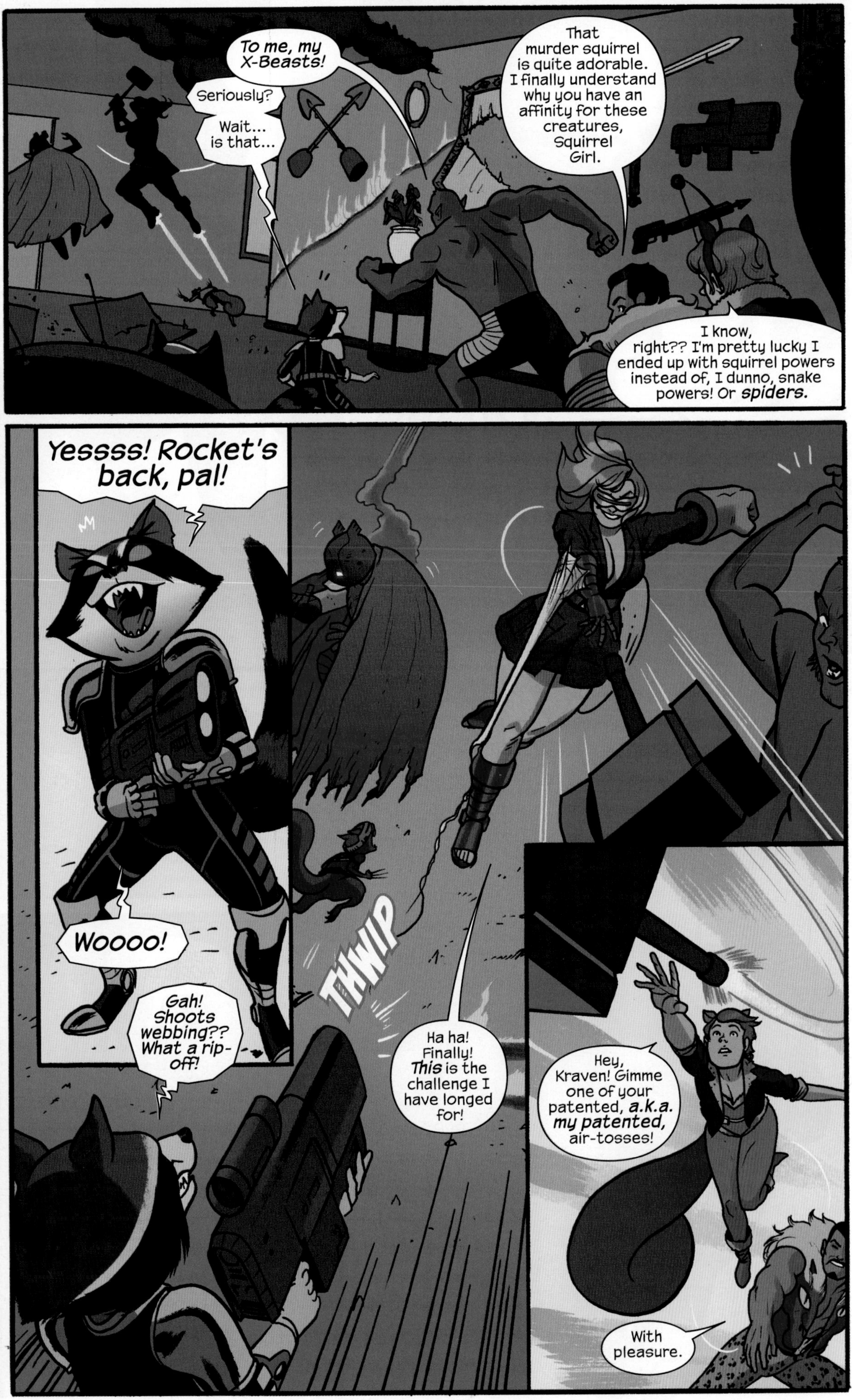
To me, my X-Beasts!
Seriously?
Wait... is that...
That murder squirrel is quite adorable. I finally understand why you have an affinity for these creatures, Squirrel Girl.
I know, right?? I'm pretty lucky I ended up with squirrel powers instead of, I dunno, snake powers! Or spiders.
Yessss! Rocket's back, pal!
Woooo!
Gah! Shoots webbing?? What a rip-off!
THWIP
Ha ha! Finally! This is the challenge I have longed for!
Hey, Kraven! Gimme one of your patented, a.k.a. my patented, air-tosses!
With pleasure.

Snake Girl. There's *another* one for you, *Hollywood!*
I'm more into the idea of a woman who can talk to spiders, and lives in a house full of spiders, and spiders do whatever she says, and she's always covered in spiders. *Nobody would ever mess with her.*

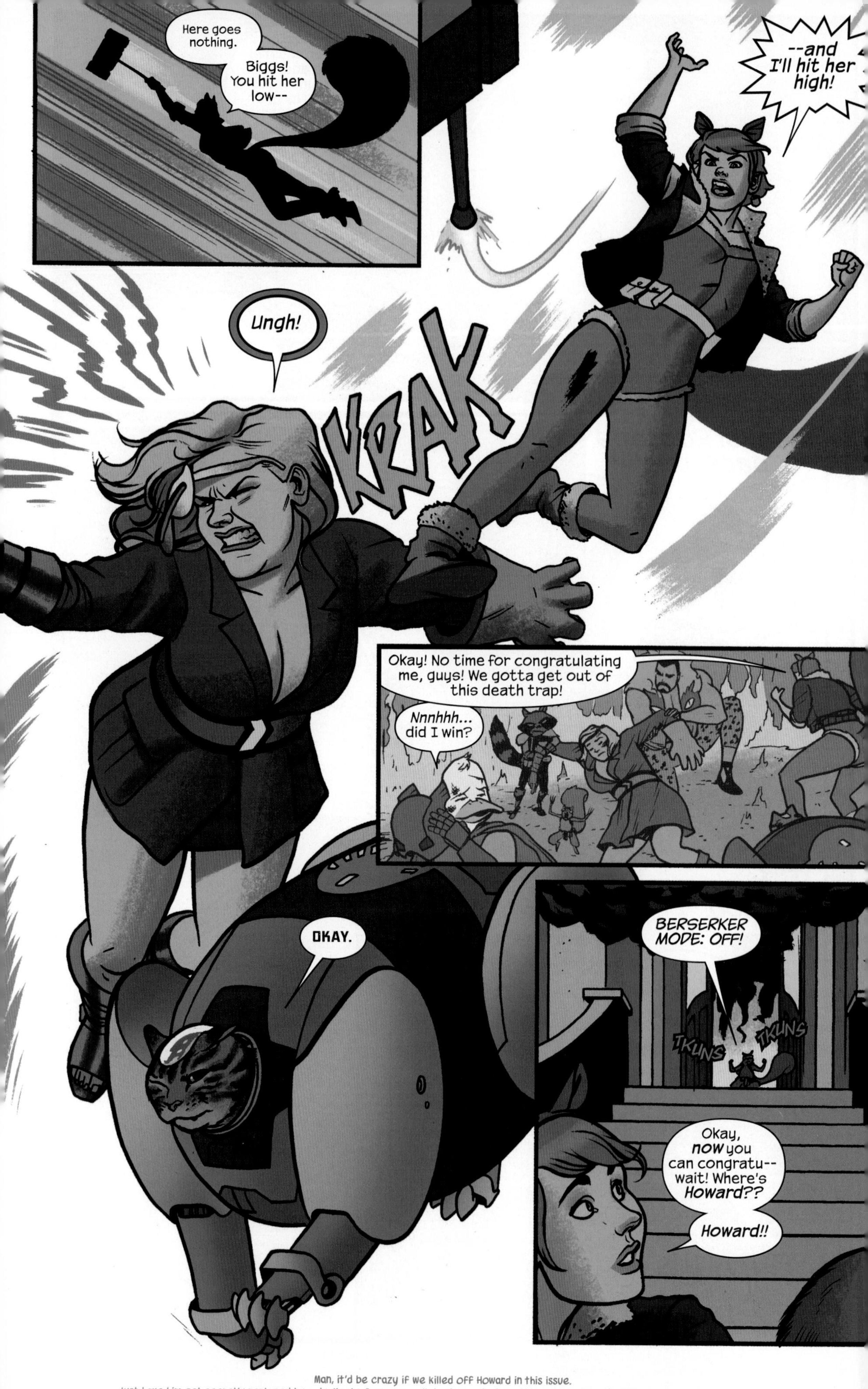

Here goes nothing.
Biggs! You hit her low--
--and I'll hit her high!
Ungh!
KRAK
Okay! No time for congratulating me, guys! We gotta get out of this death trap!
Nnnhhh... did I win?
OKAY.
BERSERKER MODE: OFF!
TKUNS
TKUNS
Okay, *now* you can congratu-- wait! Where's *Howard??*
Howard!!

Man, it'd be crazy if we killed off Howard in this issue.
Just have him get secretly replaced by a duplicate from a parallel universe before this crossover ends. It'll work out great, I promise.

≠cough cough≠ Case...

...closed. Okay, *that* time made sense.

Squirrel Girl. I am... ashamed. This has not been a life well lived.

Aw, Kraven! It's never too late! Look at me! I used to be a terrible person!

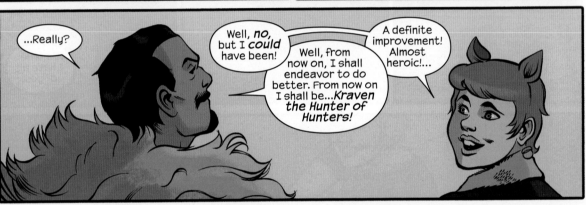

...Really?

Well, *no*, but I *could* have been!

Well, from now on, I shall endeavor to do better. From now on I shall be...*Kraven the Hunter of Hunters!*

A definite improvement! Almost heroic!...

...and look how good you do as a hero!

THE END!

We won't stop until we reform every super villain. Next up? *Doombots.*
This summer...one Doombot discovers the only thing preventing him from taking over the world...is a crazy little thing called "love."

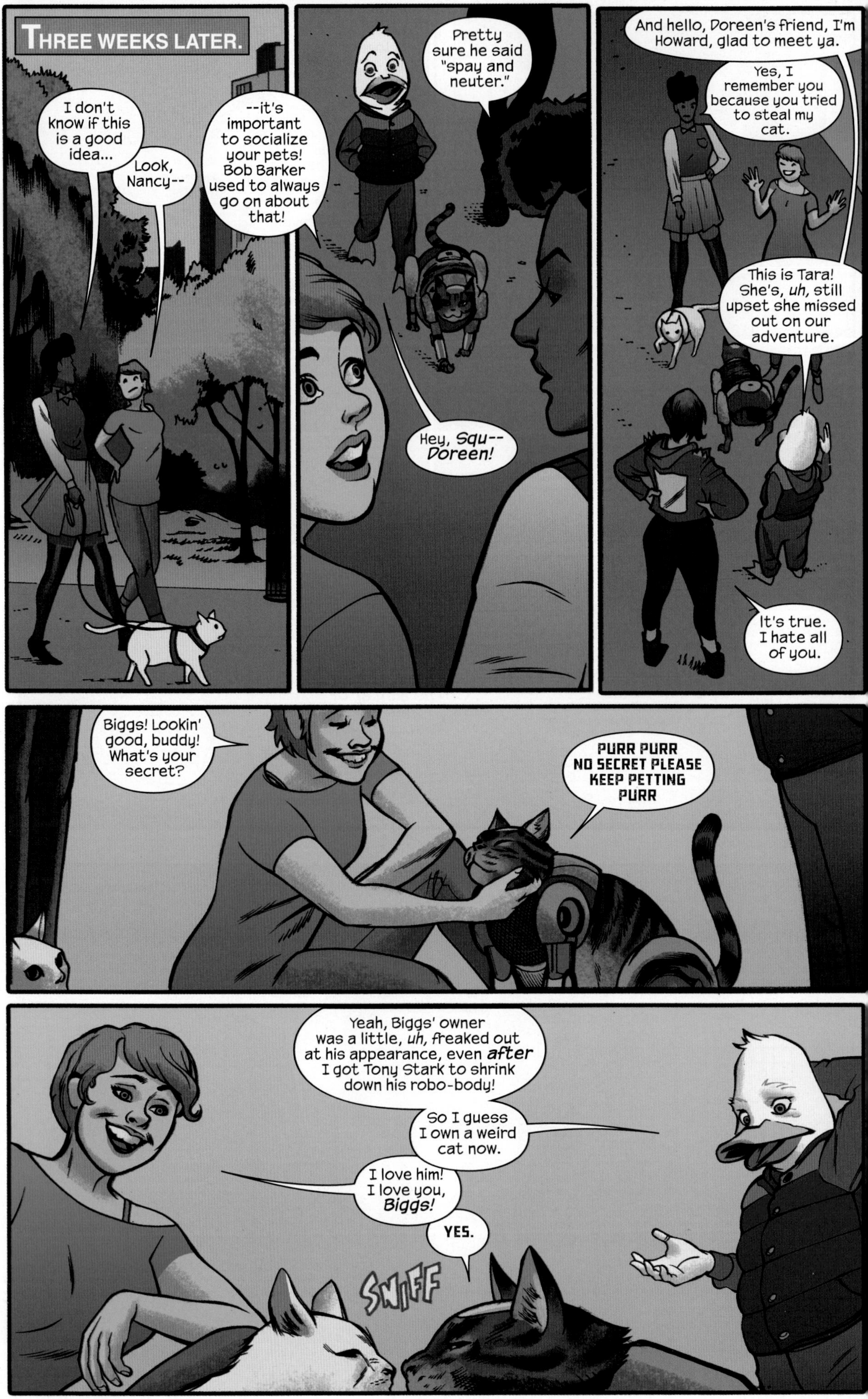
THREE WEEKS LATER.
I don't know if this is a good idea...
Look, Nancy--
--it's important to socialize your pets! Bob Barker used to always go on about that!
Pretty sure he said "spay and neuter."
Hey, Squ-- Doreen!
And hello, Doreen's friend, I'm Howard, glad to meet ya.
Yes, I remember you because you tried to steal my cat.
This is Tara! She's, uh, still upset she missed out on our adventure.
It's true. I hate all of you.
Biggs! Lookin' good, buddy! What's your secret?
PURR PURR NO SECRET PLEASE KEEP PETTING PURR
Yeah, Biggs' owner was a little, uh, freaked out at his appearance, even after I got Tony Stark to shrink down his robo-body!
So I guess I own a weird cat now.
I love him! I love you, Biggs!
YES.
SNIFF

Yes.

That other cat is named "Mew" and she appears in *several Squirrel Girl* issues. That's right. *Our* comic has cats, *too.*

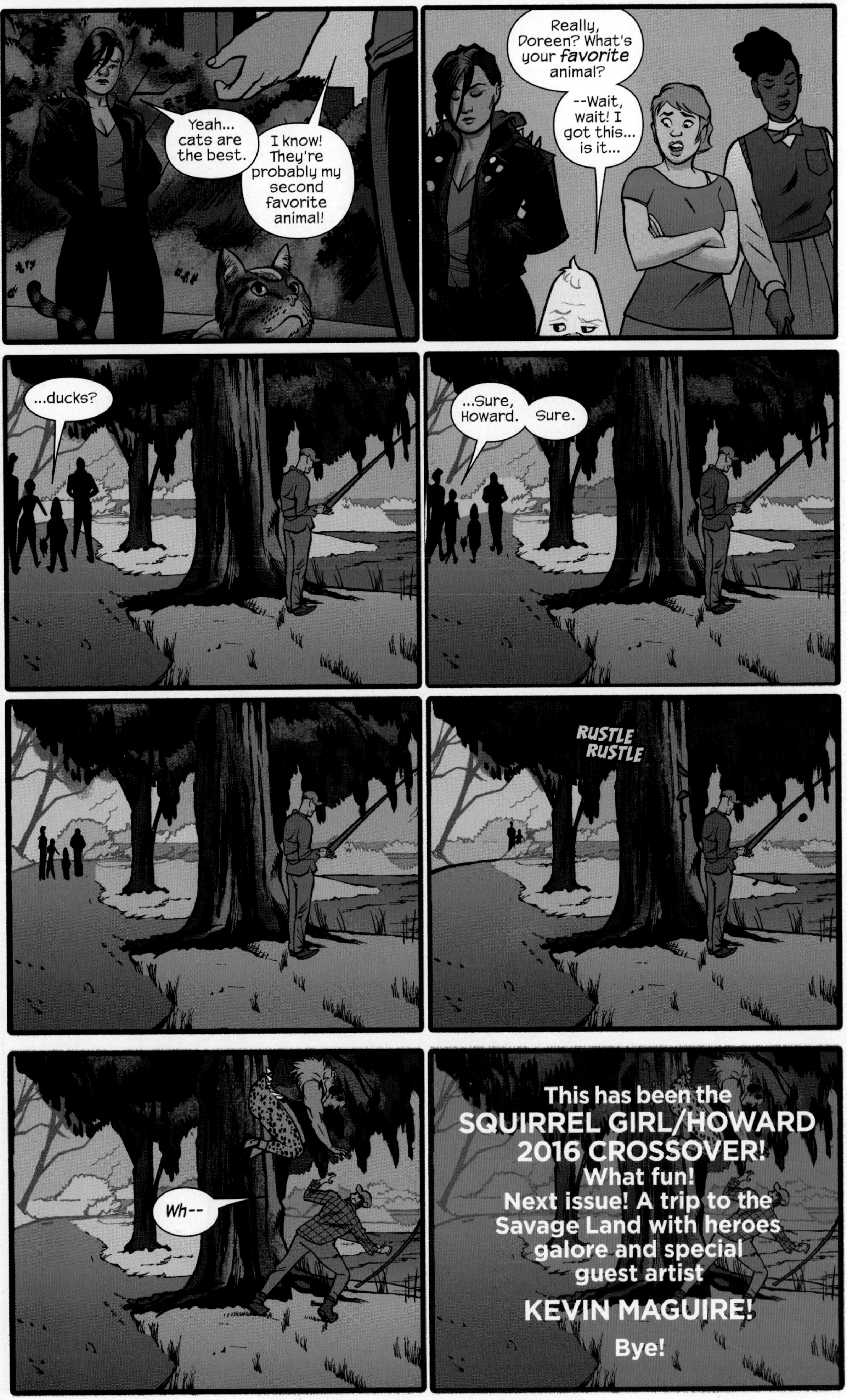
Yeah... cats are the best.
I know! They're probably my second favorite animal!
Really, Doreen? What's your *favorite* animal?
--Wait, wait! I got this... is it...
...ducks?
...Sure, Howard.
Sure.
RUSTLE
RUSTLE
Wh--
This has been the SQUIRREL GIRL/HOWARD 2016 CROSSOVER! What fun!
Next issue! A trip to the Savage Land with heroes galore and special guest artist
KEVIN MAGUIRE!
Bye!

I never wanted this to end. Except I only get paid when it ends.
Chip, it was fun to help you out and write some little words beneath your comic about a talking duck who is mad at things.

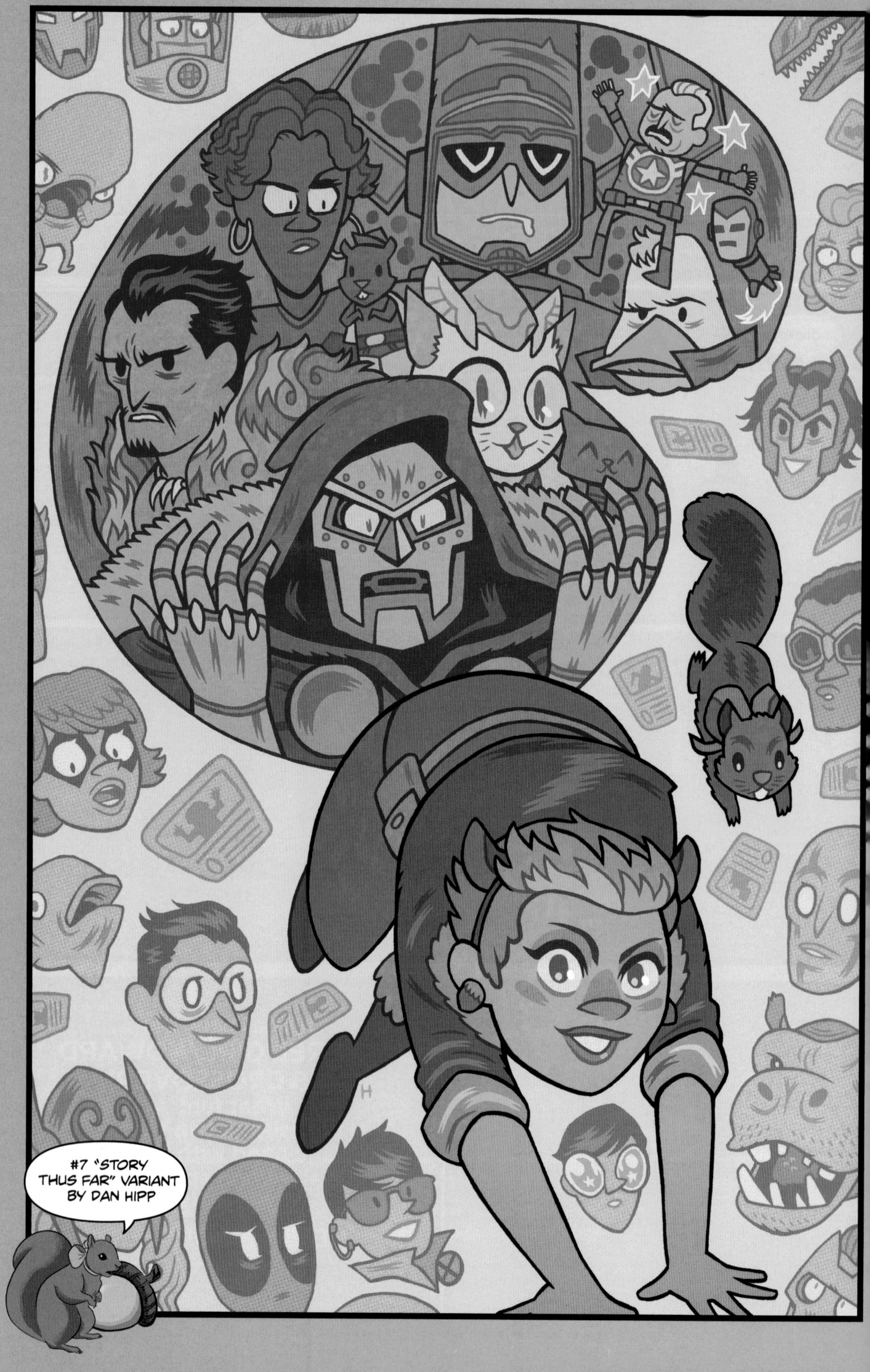
#7 "STORY THUS FAR" VARIANT BY DAN HIPP

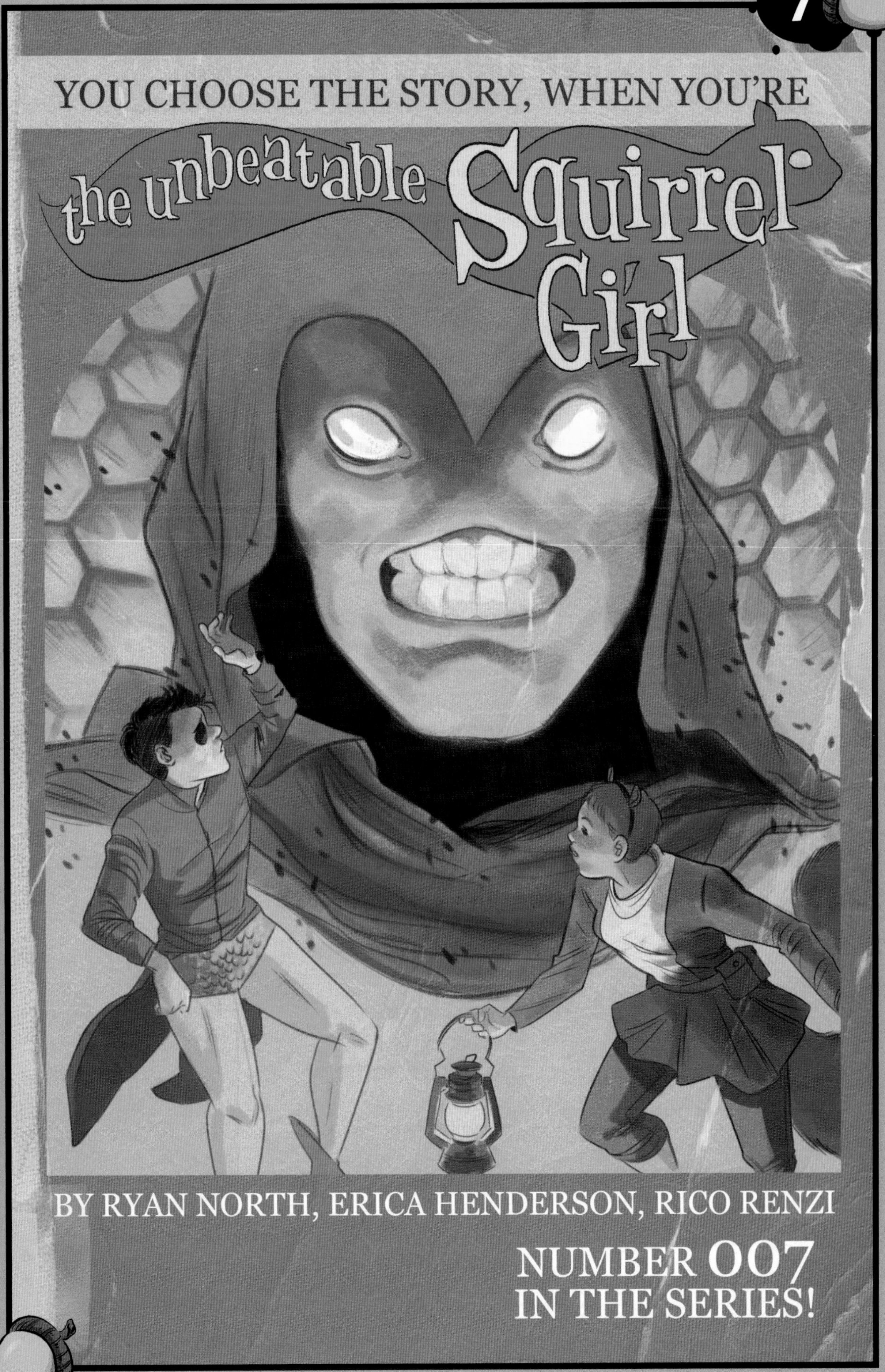
YOU CHOOSE THE STORY, WHEN YOU'RE
the unbeatable Squirrel Girl
BY RYAN NORTH, ERICA HENDERSON, RICO RENZI
NUMBER 007
IN THE SERIES!

Doreen Green isn't just a second-year computer science student: she secretly also has all the powers of both squirrel and girl! She uses her amazing abilities to fight crime **and** be as awesome as possible. You know her as...**The Unbeatable Squirrel Girl!**
Find out what she's been up to, with...

Squirrel Girl *in a nutshell*

search! 🔍

#swarm

#bees

#ironmansplaining

#koiboi

#surfandturfspecial

Squirrel Girl @unbeatablesg
Hey everyone! Great to be back on here after being TRAPPED IN THE PAST WITH DOCTOR DOOM!!

Squirrel Girl @unbeatablesg
p.s. yes, in case you missed it, I was trapped in the past with Doctor Doom

Squirrel Girl @unbeatablesg
Don't worry, me and my friends saved everyone though!! haha nbd

Tony Stark @starkmantony ✓
@unbeatablesg Huh. Seems to me the OTHER super heroes don't run online to talk up whatever Secret Wars THEY were involved in.

Squirrel Girl @unbeatablesg
@starkmantony that's just because they don't have MY level of social media game, Tony! :O

Tony Stark @starkmantony ✓
@unbeatablesg Sure, or because time travel often results in temporal paradoxes where even event participants don't remember what they did!

Squirrel Girl @unbeatablesg
@starkmantony YES TONY, thank you, I do understand how time travel works!!

Squirrel Girl @unbeatablesg
@starkmantony wait, omg, did you just mansplain time travel to me

Squirrel Girl @unbeatablesg
@starkmantony DID IRON MAN JUST IRON MANSPLAIN TIME TRAVEL TO ME

Tony Stark @starkmantony ✓
@unbeatablesg Listen, if I promise not to do that again, can we please not make #ironmansplaining a thing?

Squirrel Girl @unbeatablesg
@starkmantony Haha okay, that's a deal!! ps congratulations on your first hashtag

Tony Stark @starkmantony ✓
@unbeatablesg #ThankYouSquirrelGirlIGuessEvenThe #OlderGenerationKnowsAboutSocialMediaToo

Squirrel Girl @unbeatablesg
@starkmantony oof!! so close, and yet so far

Squirrel Girl @unbeatablesg
Hey, remember when me and Howard the Duck hung out and found a cat and got hunted by a cosplay billionaire?? @imhowatrd

Squirrel Girl @unbeatablesg
haha it sounds crazy to write when I write it out like that but it was actually one of my more sensible adventures

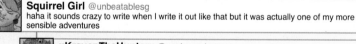

xKravenTheHunterx @unshavenkraven
@unbeatablesg @imhowatrd It was...educational. I must apologize for my role in that escapade, Girl of Squirrels.

Squirrel Girl @unbeatablesg
@unshavenkraven @imhowatrd oh no worries, Kraven!! We all make mistakes but the important thing is we learn from them 💯 💯 💯

Howard The Duck @imhowatrd
@unshavenkraven @unbeatablesg wehat do thre wempoty boxess mwean

Squirrel Girl @unbeatablesg
@imhowatrd they're emoji! Your phone isn't handling them right though. I guess you should get emoji service added to your...BILL??

Howard The Duck @imhowatrd
@unbeatablesg woww

Howard The Duck @imhowatrd
@unbeatablesg siri its howared hiow ddo i delrte my accopunt

Howard The Duck @imhowatrd
@unbeatablesg siri

Howard The Duck @imhowatrd
@unbeatablesg siri helllo

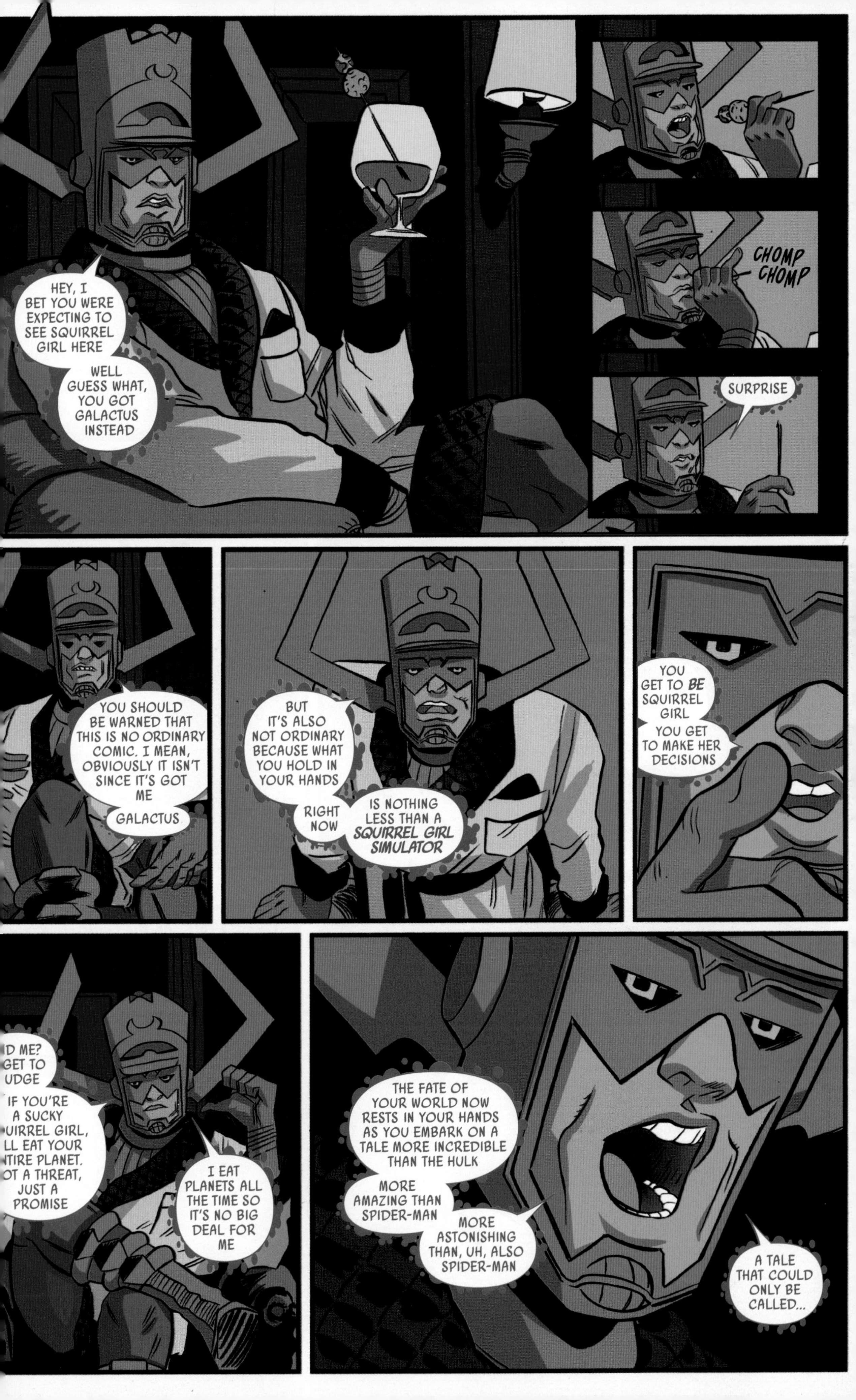
HEY, I BET YOU WERE EXPECTING TO SEE SQUIRREL GIRL HERE
WELL GUESS WHAT, YOU GOT GALACTUS INSTEAD
CHOMP CHOMP
SURPRISE
YOU SHOULD BE WARNED THAT THIS IS NO ORDINARY COMIC. I MEAN, OBVIOUSLY IT ISN'T SINCE IT'S GOT ME
GALACTUS
BUT IT'S ALSO NOT ORDINARY BECAUSE WHAT YOU HOLD IN YOUR HANDS
RIGHT NOW
IS NOTHING LESS THAN A *SQUIRREL GIRL SIMULATOR*
YOU GET TO *BE* SQUIRREL GIRL
YOU GET TO MAKE HER DECISIONS
D ME? GET TO UDGE IF YOU'RE A SUCKY UIRREL GIRL, LL EAT YOUR TIRE PLANET. OT A THREAT, JUST A PROMISE
I EAT PLANETS ALL THE TIME SO IT'S NO BIG DEAL FOR ME
THE FATE OF YOUR WORLD NOW RESTS IN YOUR HANDS AS YOU EMBARK ON A TALE MORE INCREDIBLE THAN THE HULK
MORE AMAZING THAN SPIDER-MAN
MORE ASTONISHING THAN, UH, ALSO SPIDER-MAN
A TALE THAT COULD ONLY BE CALLED...

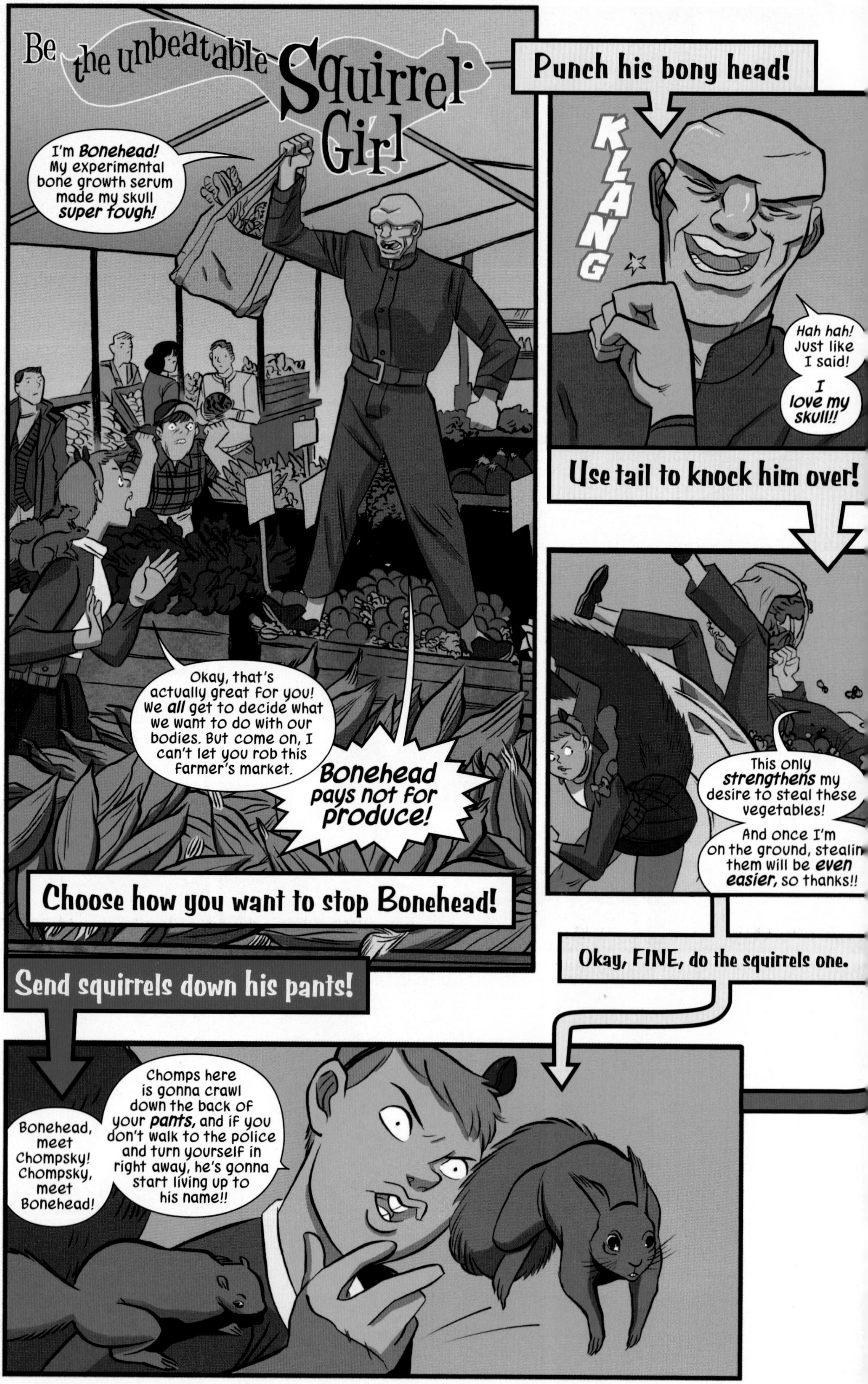

Be the unbeatable Squirrel Girl
I'm Bonehead! My experimental bone growth serum made my skull super tough!
Okay, that's actually great for you! We all get to decide what we want to do with our bodies. But come on, I can't let you rob this farmer's market.
Bonehead pays not for produce!
Choose how you want to stop Bonehead!
Punch his bony head!
KLANG
Hah hah! Just like I said!
I love my skull!!
Use tail to knock him over!
This only strengthens my desire to steal these vegetables!
And once I'm on the ground, stealin them will be even easier, so thanks!!
Okay, FINE, do the squirrels one.
Send squirrels down his pants!
Bonehead, meet Chompsky! Chompsky, meet Bonehead!
Chomps here is gonna crawl down the back of your pants, and if you don't walk to the police and turn yourself in right away, he's gonna start living up to his name!!

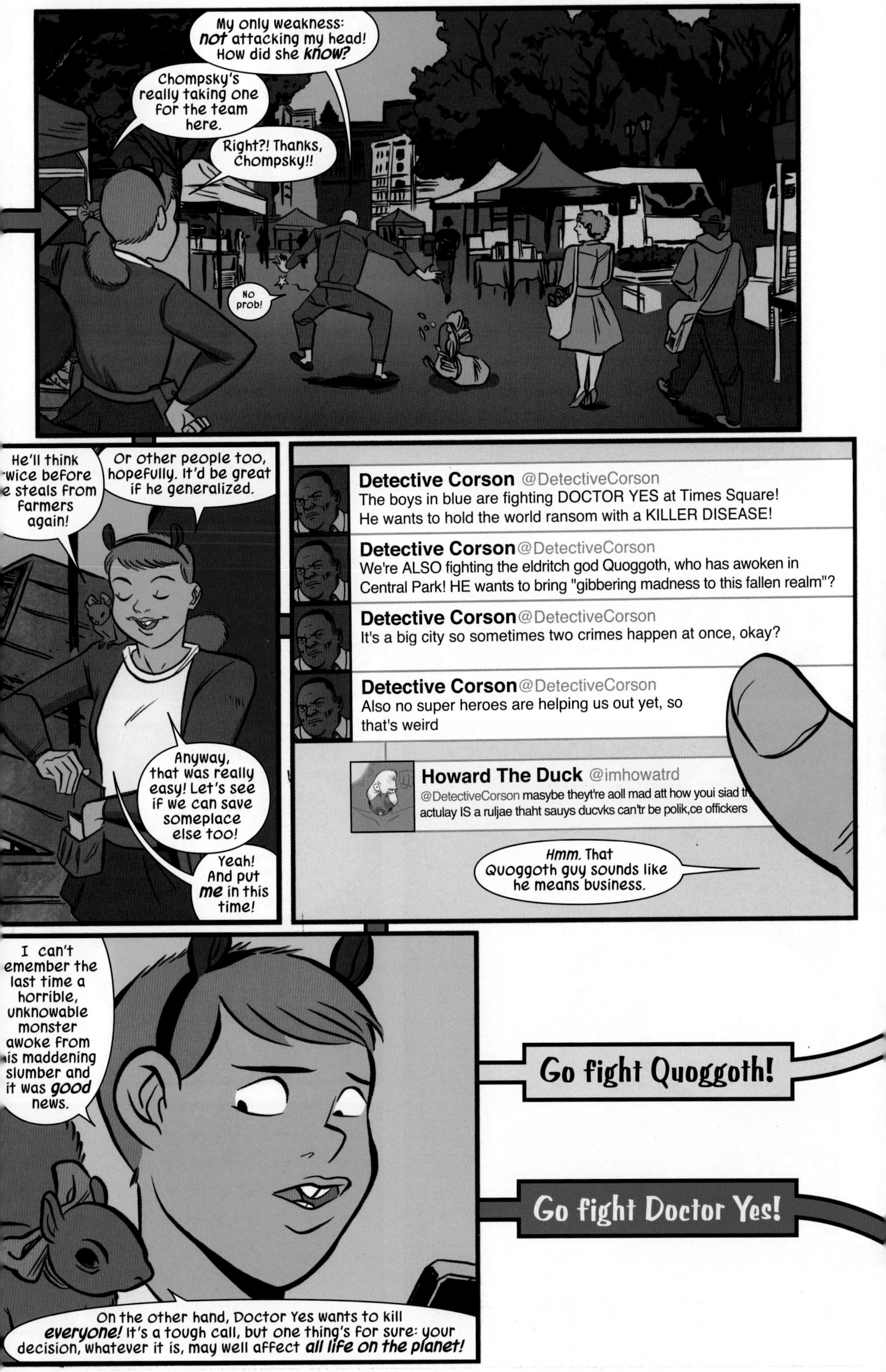
My only weakness: *not* attacking my head! How did she *know?*
Chompsky's really taking one for the team here.
Right?! Thanks, Chompsky!!
No prob!
He'll think wice before e steals from farmers again!
Or other people too, hopefully. It'd be great if he generalized.
Anyway, that was really easy! Let's see if we can save someplace else too!
Yeah! And put *me* in this time!
Detective Corson @DetectiveCorson
The boys in blue are fighting DOCTOR YES at Times Square! He wants to hold the world ransom with a KILLER DISEASE!
Detective Corson @DetectiveCorson
We're ALSO fighting the eldritch god Quoggoth, who has awoken in Central Park! HE wants to bring "gibbering madness to this fallen realm"?
Detective Corson @DetectiveCorson
It's a big city so sometimes two crimes happen at once, okay?
Detective Corson @DetectiveCorson
Also no super heroes are helping us out yet, so that's weird
Howard The Duck @imhowatrd
@DetectiveCorson masybe theyt're aoll mad att how youi siad
actulay IS a ruljae thaht sauys ducvks can'tr be polik,ce offickers
Hmm. That Quoggoth guy sounds like he means business.
I can't emember the last time a horrible, unknowable monster awoke from is maddening slumber and it was *good* news.
Go fight Quoggoth!
Go fight Doctor Yes!
On the other hand, Doctor Yes wants to kill *everyone!* It's a tough call, but one thing's for sure: your decision, whatever it is, may well affect *all life on the planet!*

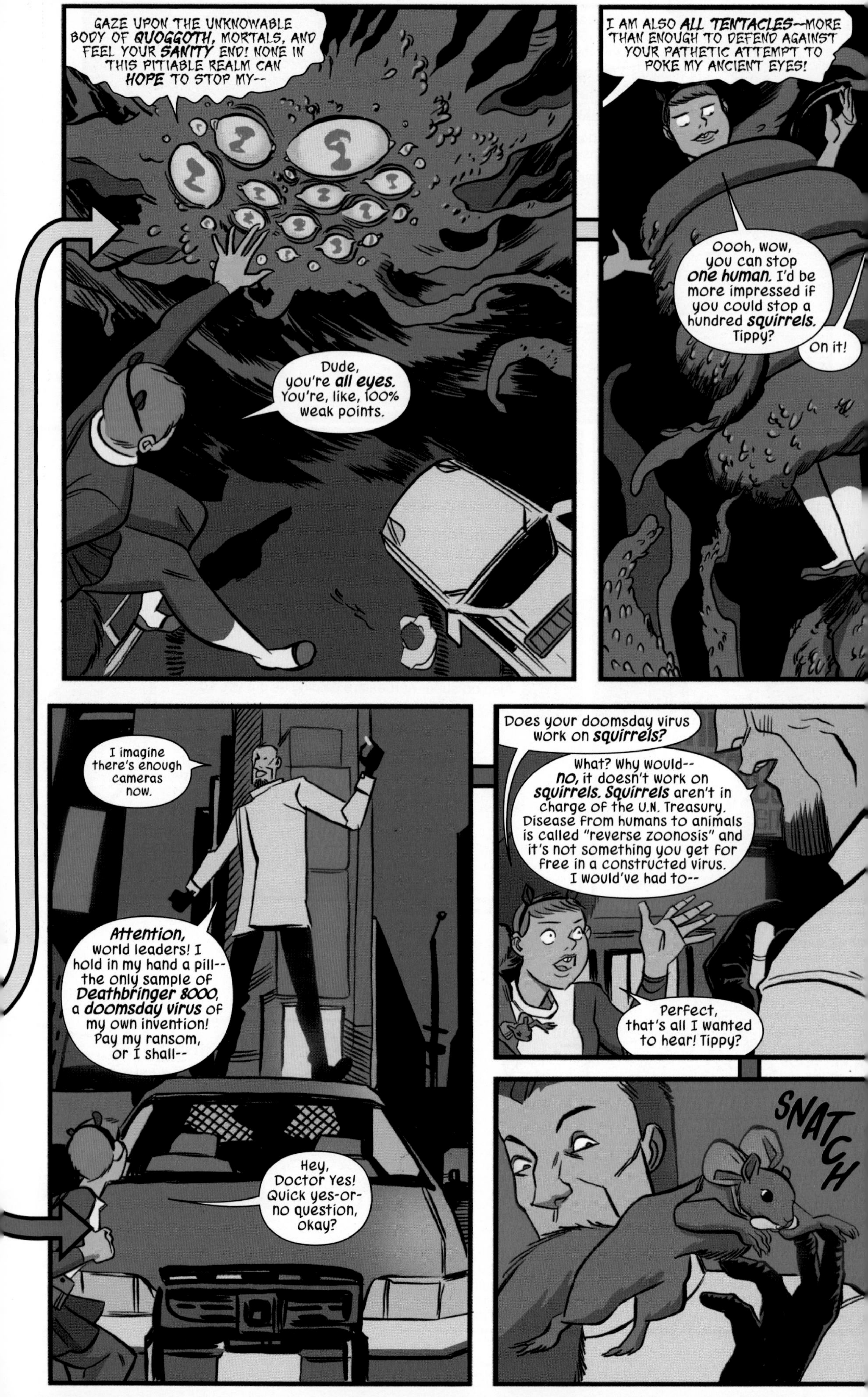
GAZE UPON THE UNKNOWABLE BODY OF QUOGGOTH, MORTALS, AND FEEL YOUR SANITY END! NONE IN THIS PITIABLE REALM CAN HOPE TO STOP MY--
Dude, you're all eyes. You're, like, 100% weak points.
I AM ALSO ALL TENTACLES--MORE THAN ENOUGH TO DEFEND AGAINST YOUR PATHETIC ATTEMPT TO POKE MY ANCIENT EYES!
Oooh, wow, you can stop one human. I'd be more impressed if you could stop a hundred squirrels. Tippy?
On it!
I imagine there's enough cameras now.
Attention, world leaders! I hold in my hand a pill-- the only sample of Deathbringer 8000, a doomsday virus of my own invention! Pay my ransom, or I shall--
Hey, Doctor Yes! Quick yes-or-no question, okay?
Does your doomsday virus work on squirrels?
What? Why would-- no, it doesn't work on squirrels. Squirrels aren't in charge of the U.N. Treasury. Disease from humans to animals is called "reverse zoonosis" and it's not something you get for free in a constructed virus. I would've had to--
Perfect, that's all I wanted to hear! Tippy?
SNATCH

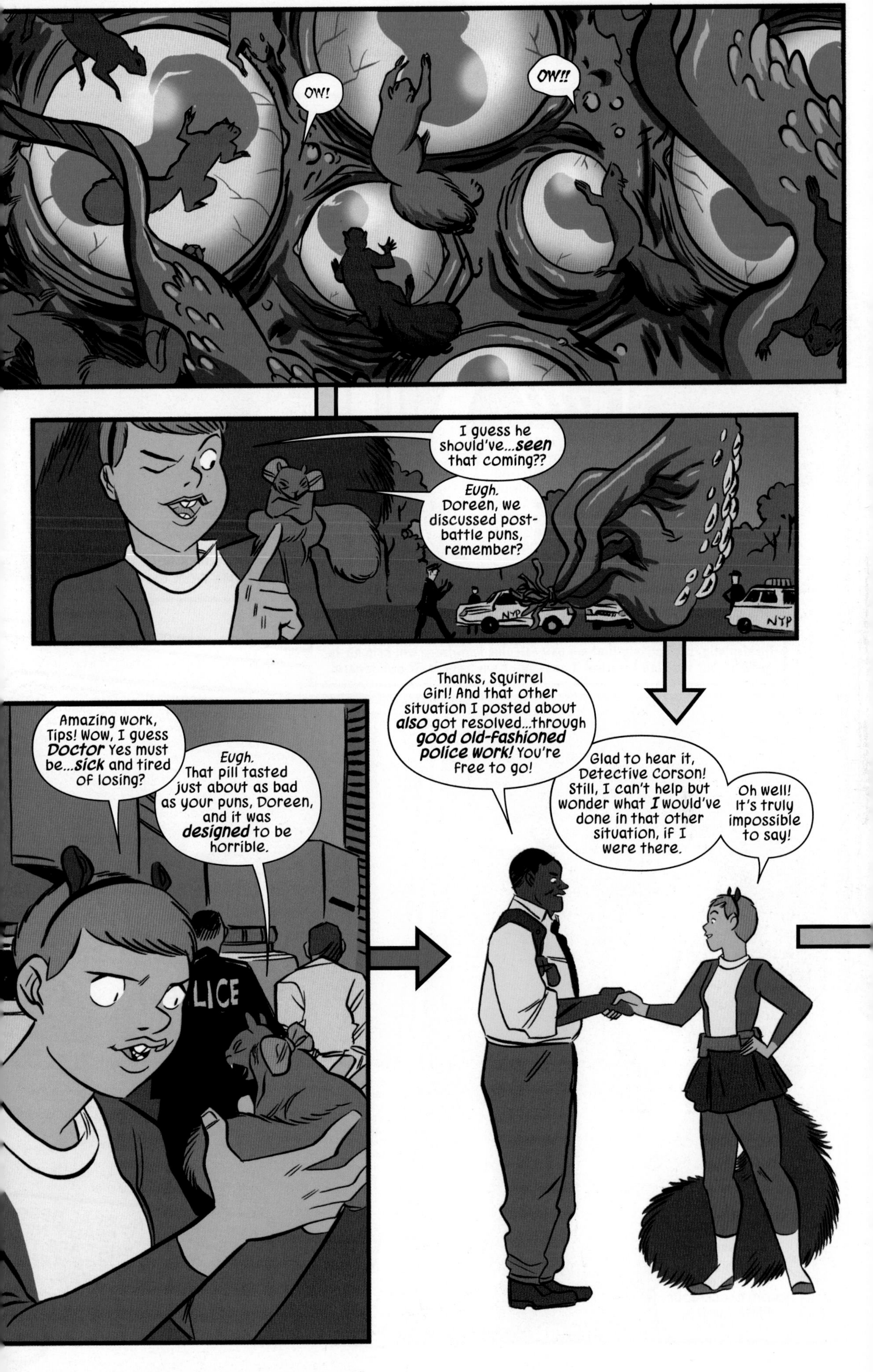
OW!
OW!!
I guess he should've...seen that coming??
Eugh. Doreen, we discussed post-battle puns, remember?
NYP
NYP
Amazing work, Tips! Wow, I guess Doctor Yes must be...sick and tired of losing?
Eugh. That pill tasted just about as bad as your puns, Doreen, and it was designed to be horrible.
LICE
Thanks, Squirrel Girl! And that other situation I posted about also got resolved...through good old-fashioned police work! You're free to go!
Glad to hear it, Detective Corson! Still, I can't help but wonder what I would've done in that other situation, if I were there.
Oh well! It's truly impossible to say!

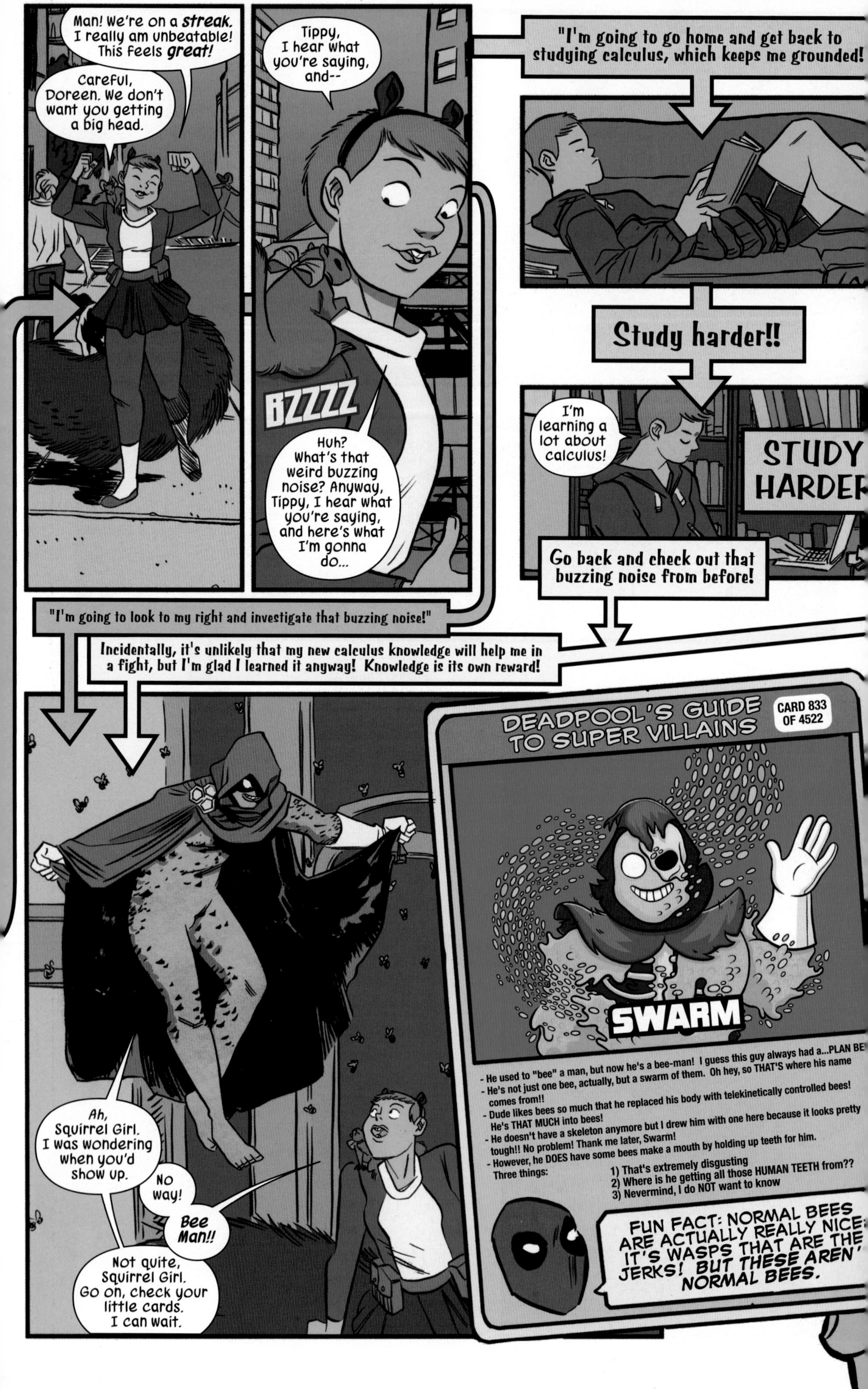

Man! We're on a streak. I really am unbeatable! This feels great!
Careful, Doreen. We don't want you getting a big head.
Tippy, I hear what you're saying, and--
BZZZZ
Huh? What's that weird buzzing noise? Anyway, Tippy, I hear what you're saying, and here's what I'm gonna do...
"I'm going to go home and get back to studying calculus, which keeps me grounded!
Study harder!!
I'm learning a lot about calculus!
STUDY HARDER
Go back and check out that buzzing noise from before!
"I'm going to look to my right and investigate that buzzing noise!"
Incidentally, it's unlikely that my new calculus knowledge will help me in a fight, but I'm glad I learned it anyway! Knowledge is its own reward!
Ah, Squirrel Girl. I was wondering when you'd show up.
No way!
Bee Man!!
Not quite, Squirrel Girl. Go on, check your little cards. I can wait.
DEADPOOL'S GUIDE TO SUPER VILLAINS
CARD 833 OF 4522
SWARM
- He used to "bee" a man, but now he's a bee-man! I guess this guy always had a...PLAN BE
- He's not just one bee, actually, but a swarm of them. Oh hey, so THAT'S where his name
comes from!!
- Dude likes bees so much that he replaced his body with telekinetically controlled bees!
He's THAT MUCH into bees!
- He doesn't have a skeleton anymore but I drew him with one here because it looks pretty
tough!! No problem! Thank me later, Swarm!
- However, he DOES have some bees make a mouth by holding up teeth for him.
Three things:
1) That's extremely disgusting
2) Where is he getting all those HUMAN TEETH from??
3) Nevermind, I do NOT want to know
FUN FACT: NORMAL BEES ARE ACTUALLY REALLY NICE; IT'S WASPS THAT ARE THE JERKS! BUT THESE AREN' NORMAL BEES.

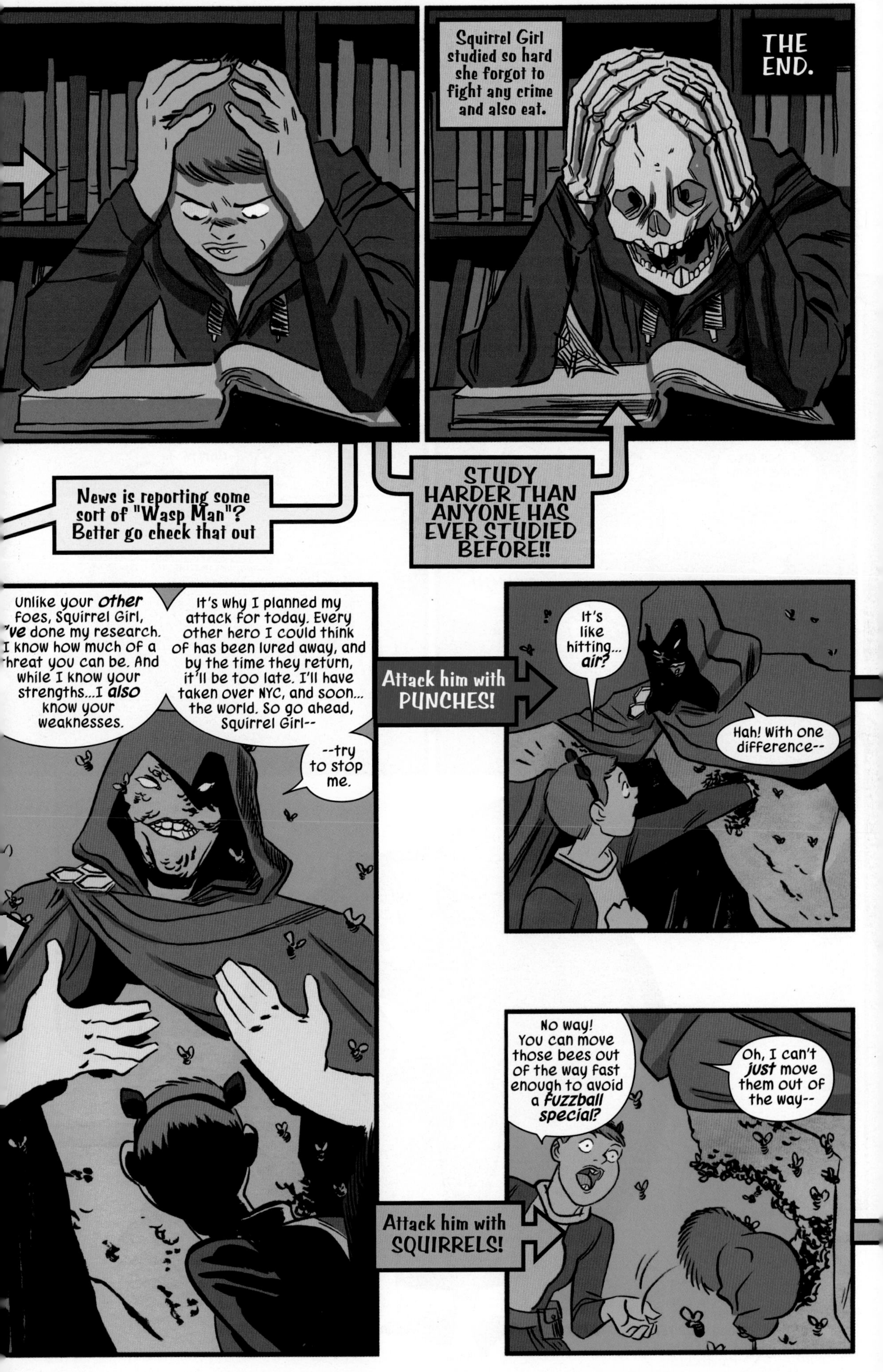

Squirrel Girl studied so hard she forgot to fight any crime and also eat.
THE END.
News is reporting some sort of "Wasp Man"? Better go check that out
STUDY HARDER THAN ANYONE HAS EVER STUDIED BEFORE!!
Unlike your other foes, Squirrel Girl, I've done my research. I know how much of a threat you can be. And while I know your strengths...I also know your weaknesses.
It's why I planned my attack for today. Every other hero I could think of has been lured away, and by the time they return, it'll be too late. I'll have taken over NYC, and soon... the world. So go ahead, Squirrel Girl--
--try to stop me.
Attack him with PUNCHES!
It's like hitting... air?
Hah! With one difference--
Attack him with SQUIRRELS!
No way! You can move those bees out of the way fast enough to avoid a fuzzball special?
Oh, I can't just move them out of the way--

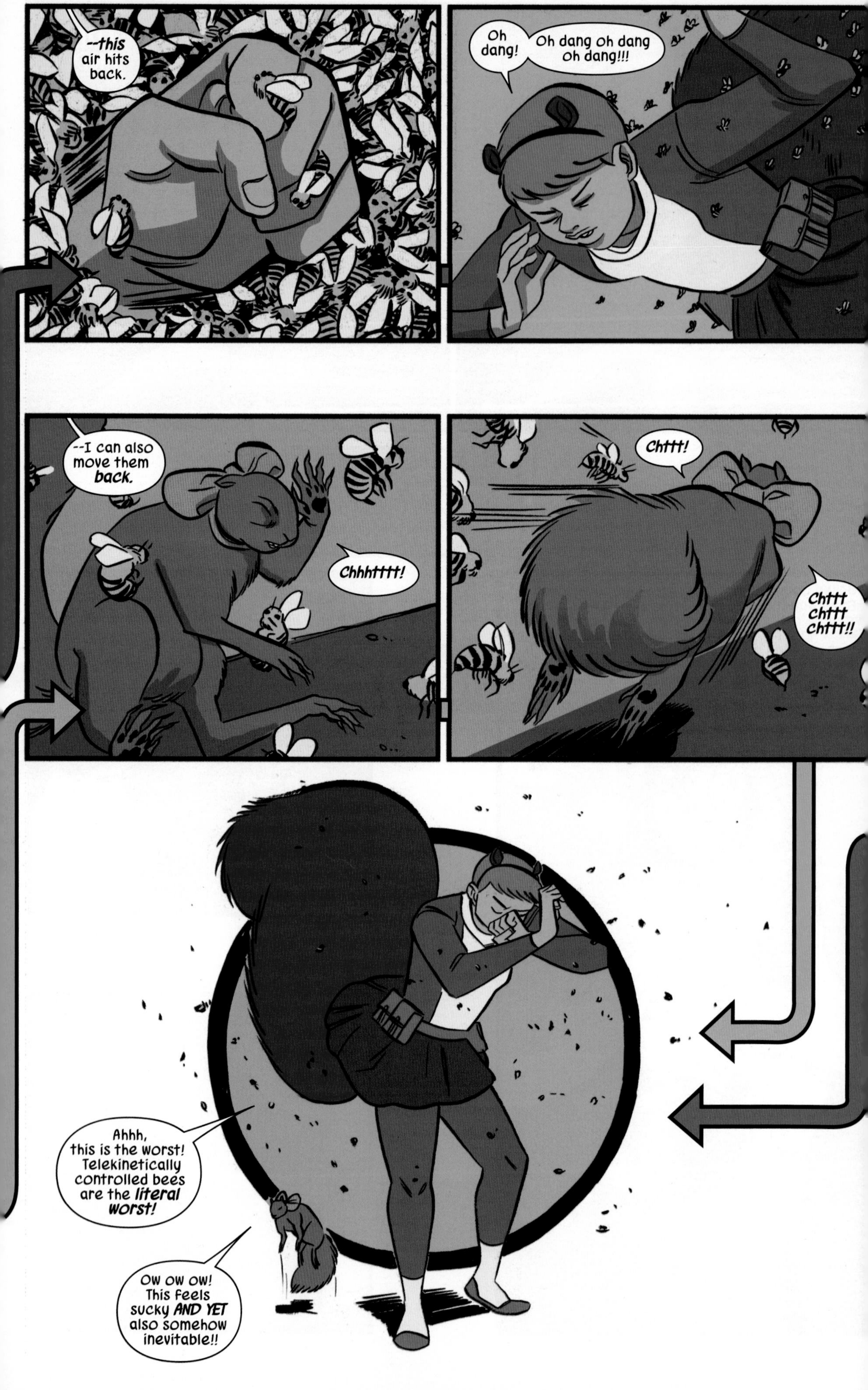
--this air hits back.
Oh dang!
Oh dang oh dang oh dang!!!
--I can also move them back.
Chhhtttt!
Chttt!
Chttt chttt chttt!!
Ahhh, this is the worst! Telekinetically controlled bees are the literal worst!
Ow ow ow! This feels sucky AND YET also somehow inevitable!!

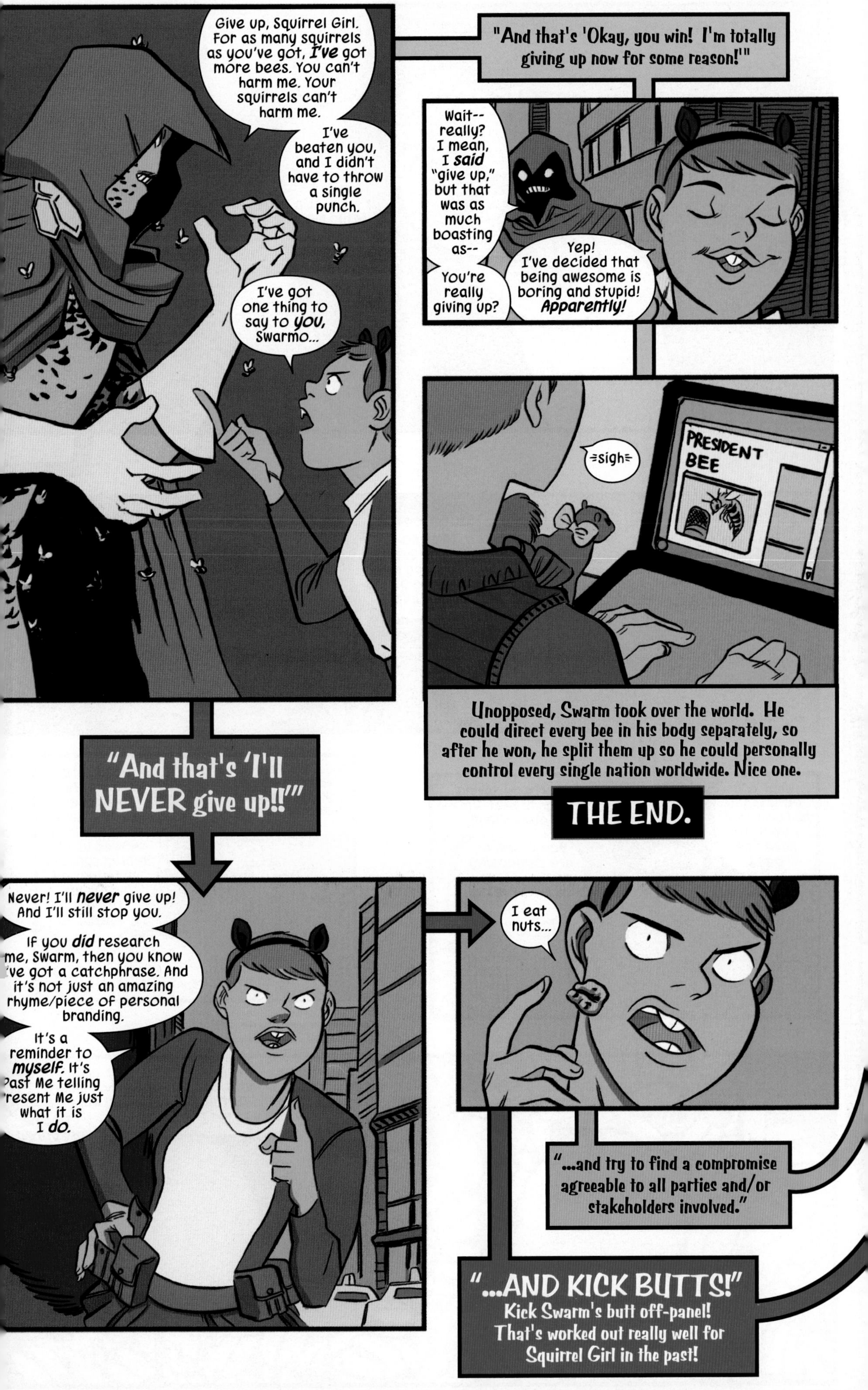
Give up, Squirrel Girl. For as many squirrels as you've got, I've got more bees. You can't harm me. Your squirrels can't harm me.
I've beaten you, and I didn't have to throw a single punch.
I've got one thing to say to you, Swarmo...
"And that's 'Okay, you win! I'm totally giving up now for some reason!'"
Wait-- really? I mean, I said "give up," but that was as much boasting as--
You're really giving up?
Yep! I've decided that being awesome is boring and stupid! Apparently!
PRESIDENT BEE
sigh
Unopposed, Swarm took over the world. He could direct every bee in his body separately, so after he won, he split them up so he could personally control every single nation worldwide. Nice one.
THE END.
"And that's 'I'll NEVER give up!!'"
Never! I'll never give up! And I'll still stop you.
If you did research me, Swarm, then you know I've got a catchphrase. And it's not just an amazing rhyme/piece of personal branding.
It's a reminder to myself. It's Past Me telling Present Me just what it is I do.
I eat nuts...
"...and try to find a compromise agreeable to all parties and/or stakeholders involved."
"...AND KICK BUTTS!"
Kick Swarm's butt off-panel! That's worked out really well for Squirrel Girl in the past!

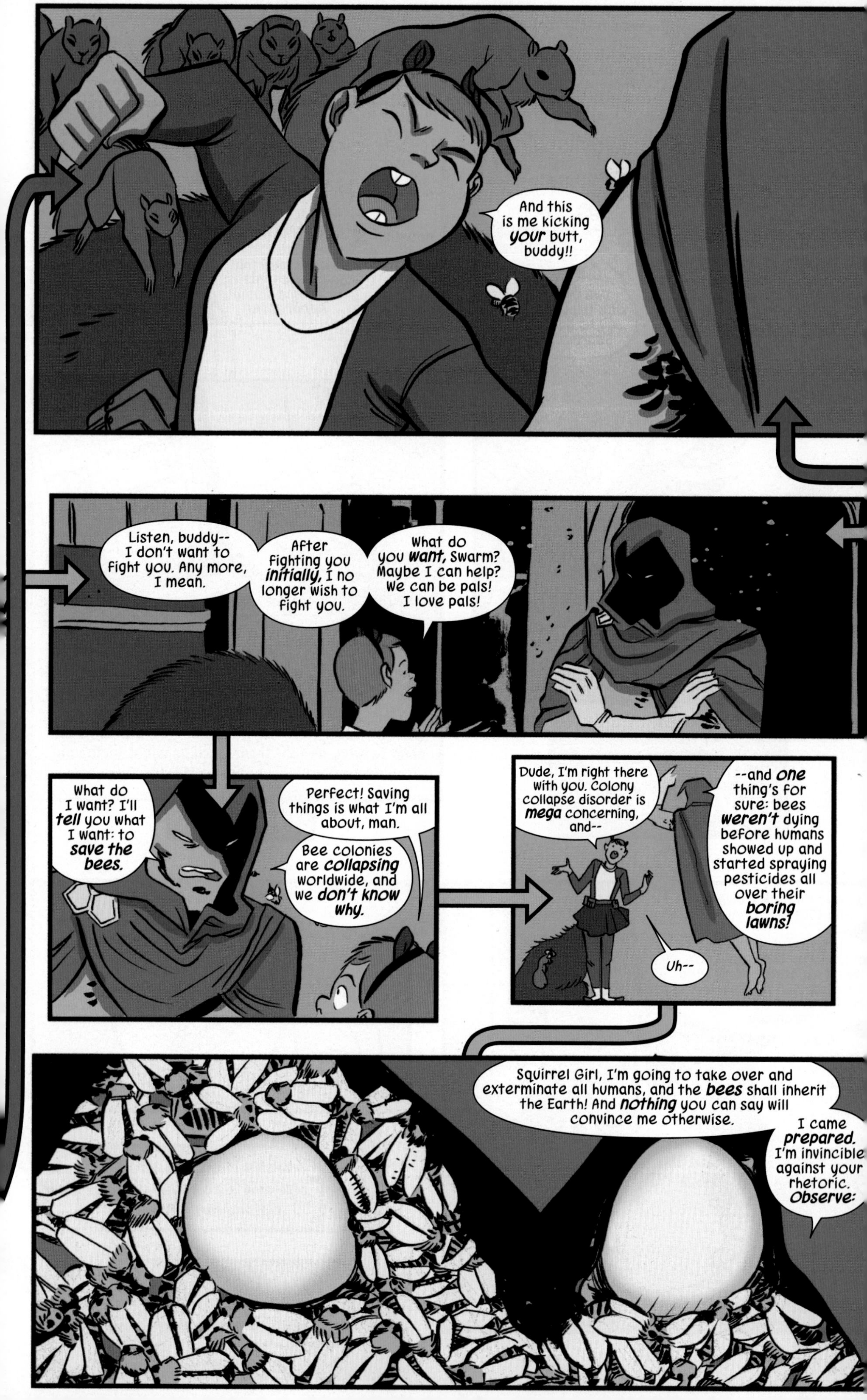
And this is me kicking *your* butt, buddy!!
Listen, buddy-- I don't want to fight you. Any more, I mean.
After fighting you *initially,* I no longer wish to fight you.
What do you *want,* Swarm? Maybe I can help? We can be pals! I love pals!
What do I want? I'll *tell* you what I want: to *save the bees.*
Perfect! Saving things is what I'm all about, man.
Bee colonies are *collapsing* worldwide, and we *don't know why.*
Dude, I'm right there with you. Colony collapse disorder is *mega* concerning, and--
--and *one* thing's for sure: bees *weren't* dying before humans showed up and started spraying pesticides all over their *boring lawns!*
Uh--
Squirrel Girl, I'm going to take over and exterminate all humans, and the *bees* shall inherit the Earth! And *nothing* you can say will convince me otherwise.
I came *prepared.* I'm invincible against your rhetoric. *Observe:*

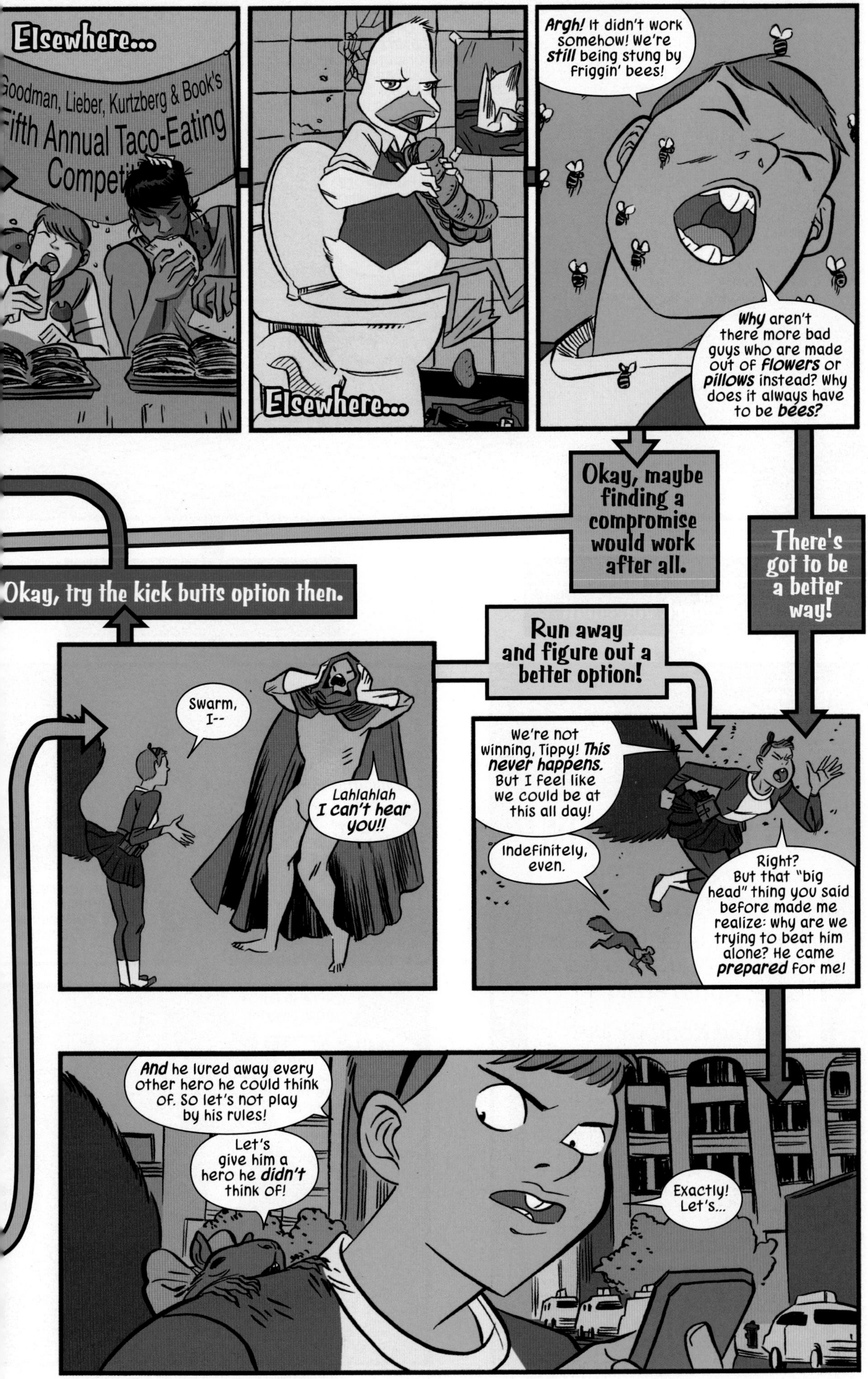
Elsewhere...
Goodman, Lieber, Kurtzberg & Book's Fifth Annual Taco-Eating Competi
Elsewhere...
Argh! It didn't work somehow! We're still being stung by friggin' bees!
Why aren't there more bad guys who are made out of flowers or pillows instead? Why does it always have to be bees?
Okay, maybe finding a compromise would work after all.
There's got to be a better way!
Okay, try the kick butts option then.
Run away and figure out a better option!
Swarm, I--
Lahlahlah I can't hear you!!
We're not winning, Tippy! This never happens. But I feel like we could be at this all day!
Indefinitely, even.
Right? But that "big head" thing you said before made me realize: why are we trying to beat him alone? He came prepared for me!
And he lured away every other hero he could think of. So let's not play by his rules!
Let's give him a hero he didn't think of!
Exactly! Let's...

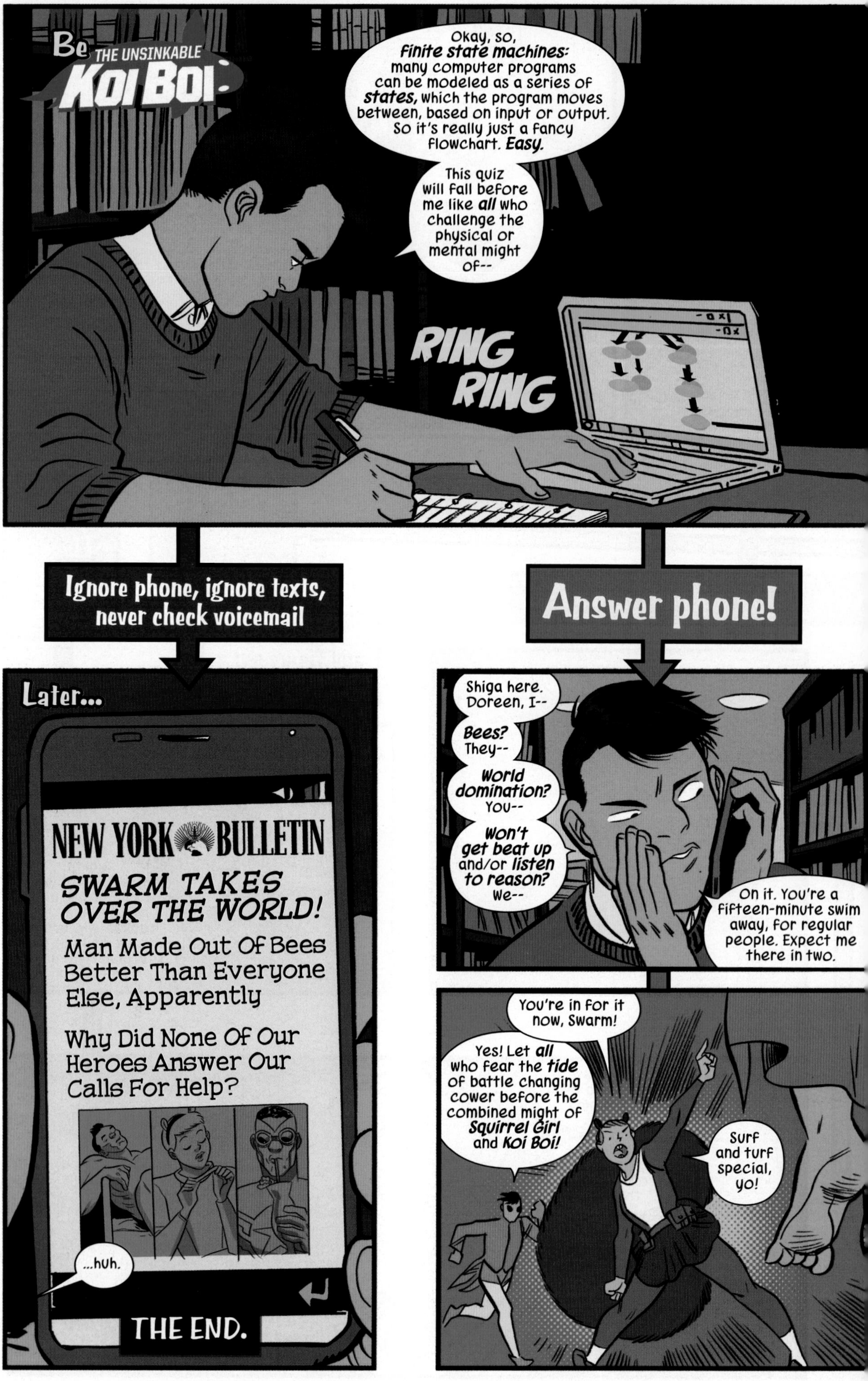
Be THE UNSINKABLE KOI BOI
Okay, so, finite state machines: many computer programs can be modeled as a series of states, which the program moves between, based on input or output. So it's really just a fancy flowchart. Easy.
This quiz will fall before me like all who challenge the physical or mental might of--
RING RING
Ignore phone, ignore texts, never check voicemail
Answer phone!
Later...
NEW YORK BULLETIN
SWARM TAKES OVER THE WORLD!
Man Made Out Of Bees Better Than Everyone Else, Apparently
Why Did None Of Our Heroes Answer Our Calls For Help?
...huh.
THE END.
Shiga here. Doreen, I--
Bees? They--
World domination? You--
Won't get beat up and/or listen to reason? We--
On it. You're a fifteen-minute swim away, for regular people. Expect me there in two.
You're in for it now, Swarm!
Yes! Let all who fear the tide of battle changing cower before the combined might of Squirrel Girl and Koi Boi!
Surf and turf special, yo!

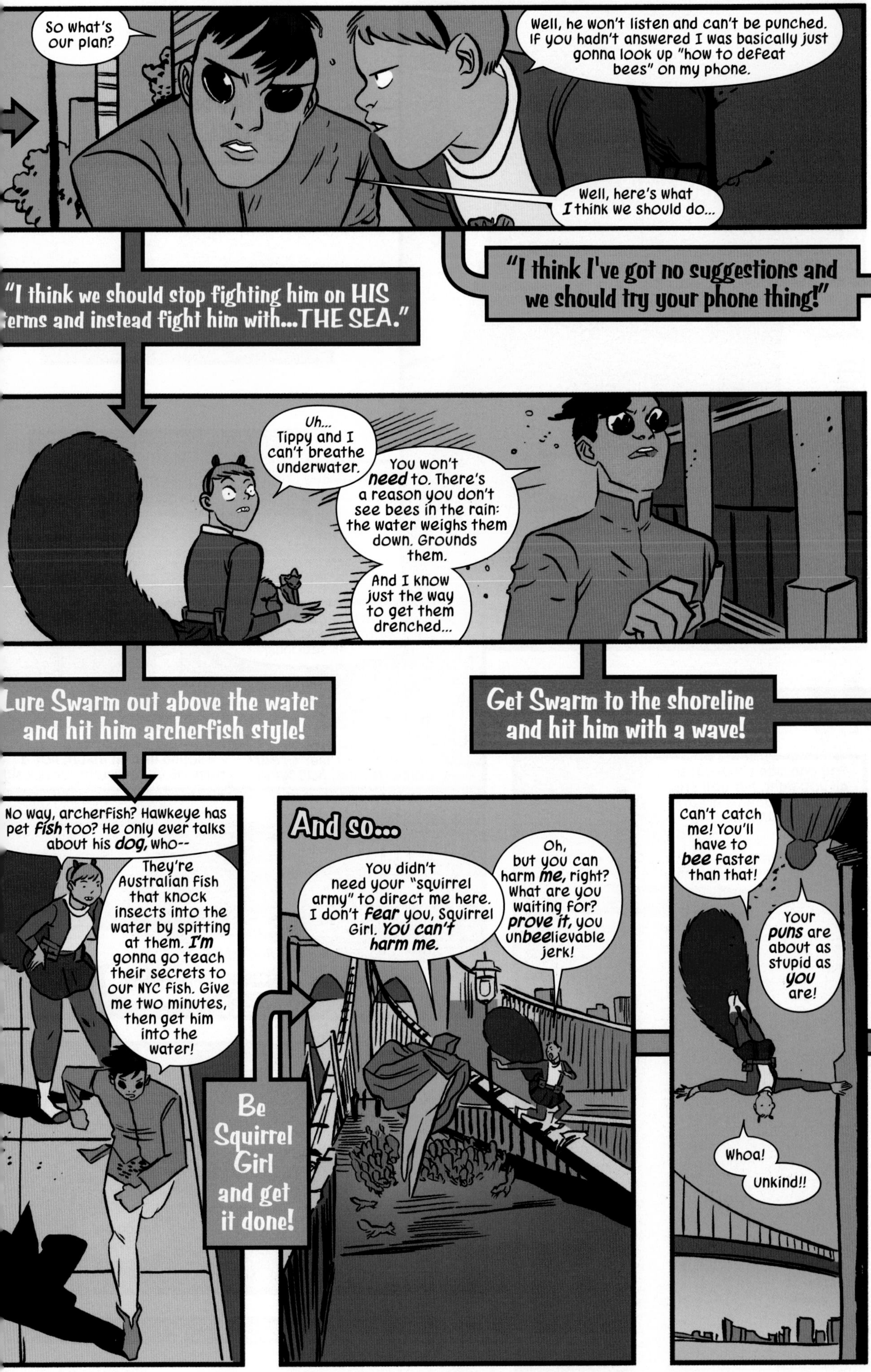

So what's our plan?
Well, he won't listen and can't be punched. If you hadn't answered I was basically just gonna look up "how to defeat bees" on my phone.
Well, here's what I think we should do...
"I think we should stop fighting him on HIS terms and instead fight him with...THE SEA."
"I think I've got no suggestions and we should try your phone thing!"
Uh... Tippy and I can't breathe underwater.
You won't need to. There's a reason you don't see bees in the rain: the water weighs them down. Grounds them.
And I know just the way to get them drenched...
Lure Swarm out above the water and hit him archerfish style!
Get Swarm to the shoreline and hit him with a wave!
No way, archerfish? Hawkeye has pet fish too? He only ever talks about his dog, who--
They're Australian fish that knock insects into the water by spitting at them. I'm gonna go teach their secrets to our NYC fish. Give me two minutes, then get him into the water!
Be Squirrel Girl and get it done!
And so...
You didn't need your "squirrel army" to direct me here. I don't fear you, Squirrel Girl. You can't harm me.
Oh, but you can harm me, right? What are you waiting for? Prove it, you unbeelievable jerk!
Can't catch me! You'll have to bee faster than that!
Your puns are about as stupid as you are!
Whoa!
Unkind!!

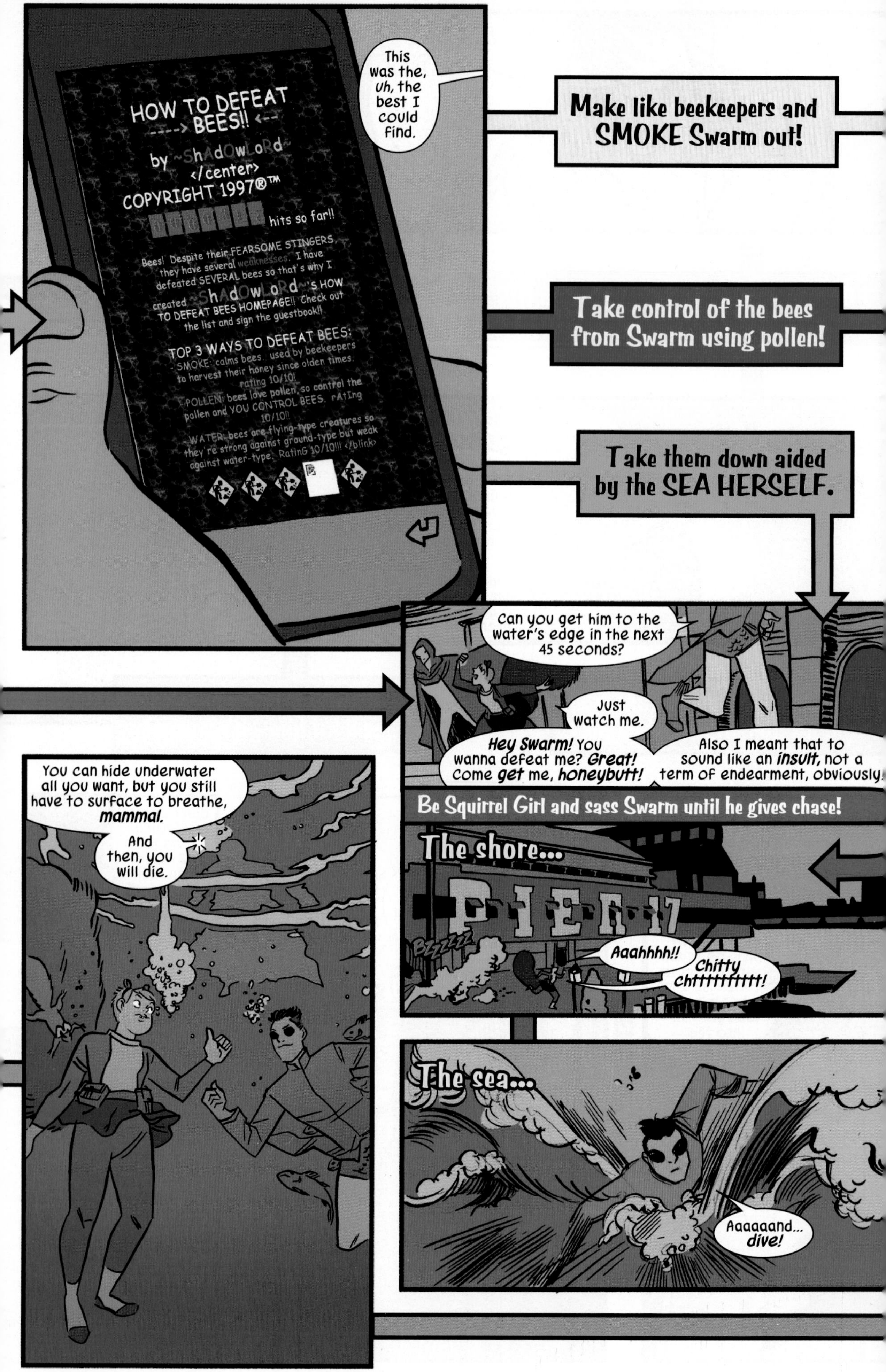
HOW TO DEFEAT BEES!!
----> BEES!! <---
by ~ShAdOwLoRd~
</center>
COPYRIGHT 1997®™
hits so far!!
Bees! Despite their FEARSOME STINGERS, they have several weaknesses. I have defeated SEVERAL bees so that's why I created ~ShAdOwLoRd~'s HOW TO DEFEAT BEES HOMEPAGE!! Check out the list and sign the guestbook!!
TOP 3 WAYS TO DEFEAT BEES:
- SMOKE: calms bees. used by beekeepers to harvest their honey since olden times. rating 10/10!
- POLLEN: bees love pollen, so control the pollen and YOU CONTROL BEES. rAtIng 10/10!!
- WATER: bees are flying-type creatures so they're strong against ground-type but weak against water-type. RatinG 10/10!!! </blink>
This was the, uh, the best I could find.
Make like beekeepers and SMOKE Swarm out!
Take control of the bees from Swarm using pollen!
Take them down aided by the SEA HERSELF.
Can you get him to the water's edge in the next 45 seconds?
Just watch me.
Hey Swarm! You wanna defeat me? Great! Come get me, honeybutt!
Also I meant that to sound like an insult, not a term of endearment, obviously!
Be Squirrel Girl and sass Swarm until he gives chase!
The shore...
PIER 17
Bzzzzz
Aaahhhh!!
Chitty chttttttttt!
The sea...
Aaaaaand... dive!
You can hide underwater all you want, but you still have to surface to breathe, mammal.
And then, you will die.

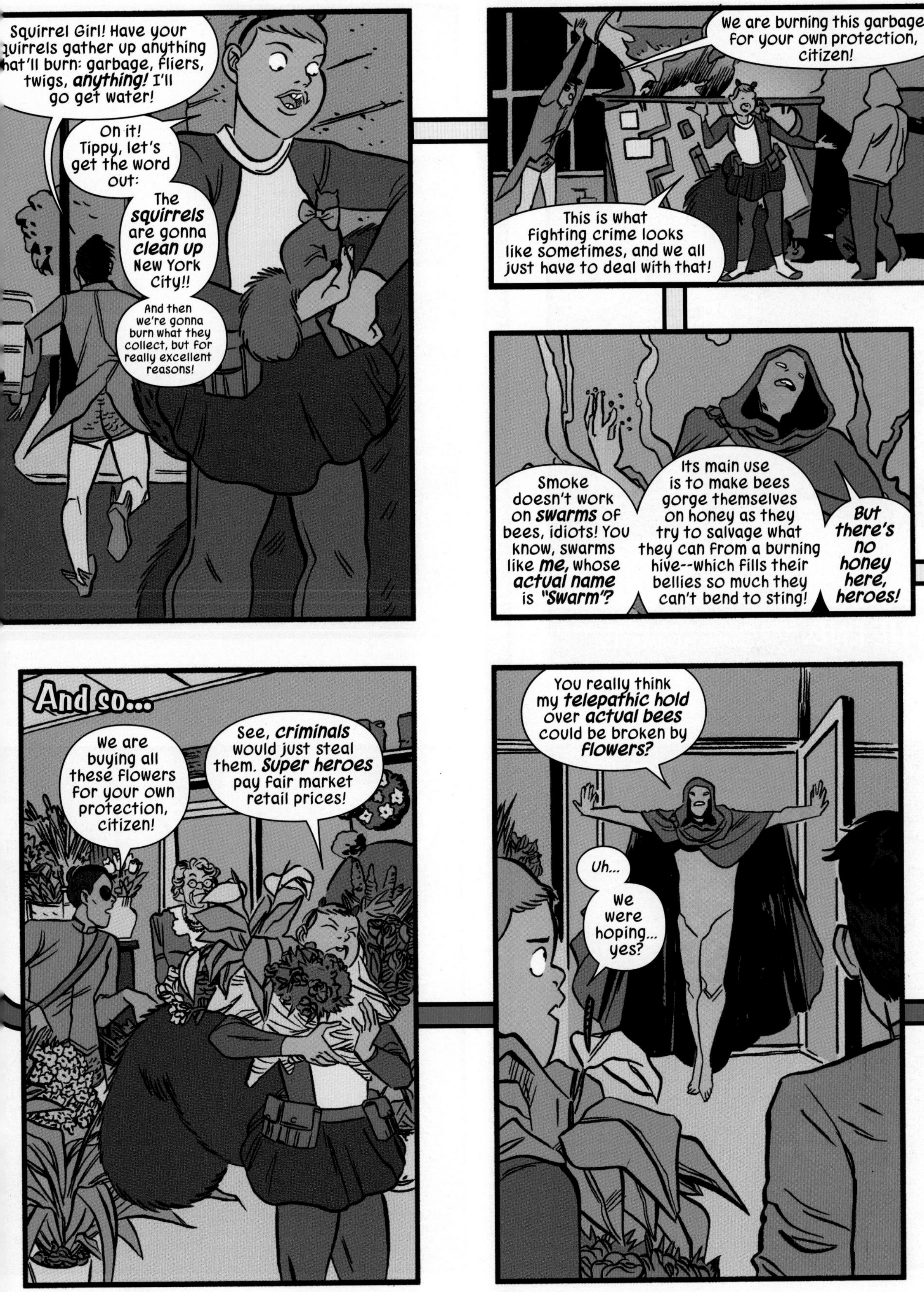
Squirrel Girl! Have your quirrels gather up anything hat'll burn: garbage, fliers, twigs, anything! I'll go get water!
On it! Tippy, let's get the word out:
The squirrels are gonna clean up New York City!!
And then we're gonna burn what they collect, but for really excellent reasons!
We are burning this garbage for your own protection, citizen!
This is what fighting crime looks like sometimes, and we all just have to deal with that!
Smoke doesn't work on swarms of bees, idiots! You know, swarms like me, whose actual name is "Swarm"?
Its main use is to make bees gorge themselves on honey as they try to salvage what they can from a burning hive--which fills their bellies so much they can't bend to sting!
But there's no honey here, heroes!
And so...
We are buying all these flowers for your own protection, citizen!
See, criminals would just steal them. Super heroes pay fair market retail prices!
You really think my telepathic hold over actual bees could be broken by flowers?
Uh...
We were hoping... yes?

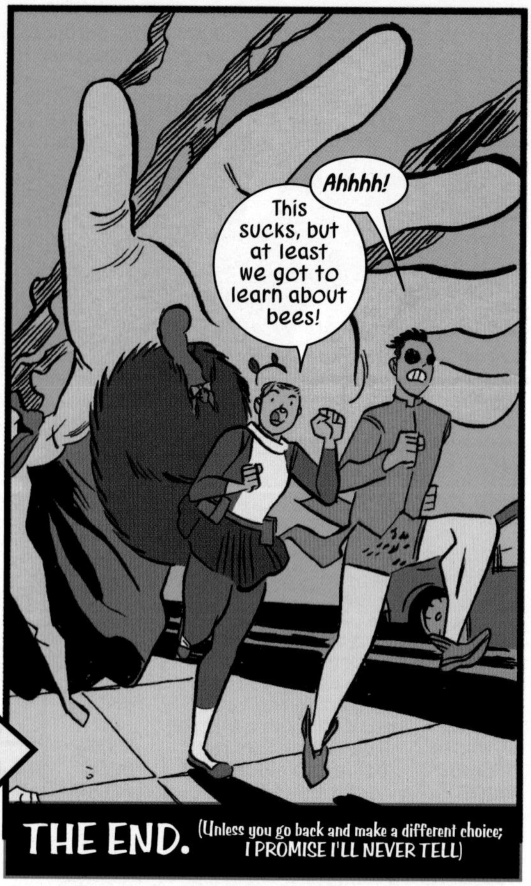
Ahhhh!
This sucks, but at least we got to learn about bees!
THE END. (Unless you go back and make a different choice; I PROMISE I'LL NEVER TELL)

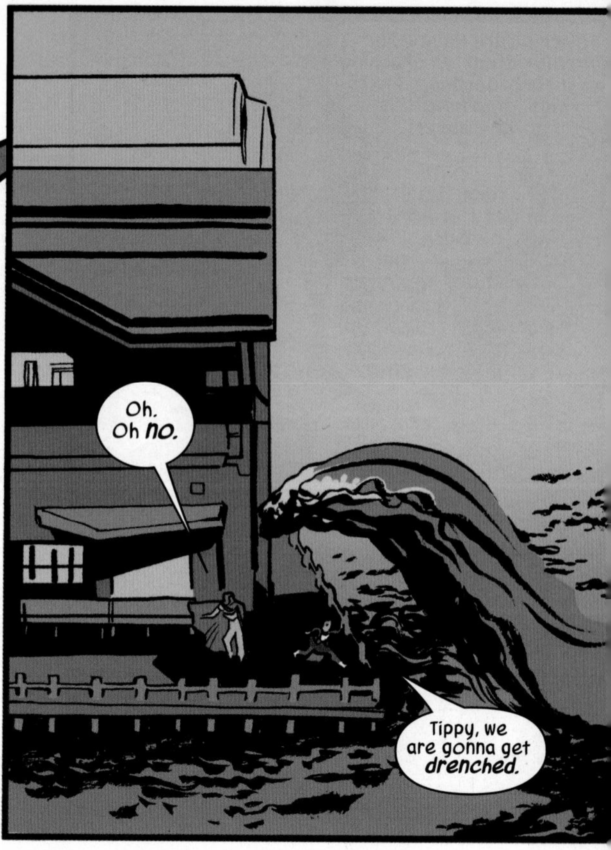
Oh. Oh *no.*
Tippy, we are gonna get *drenched.*

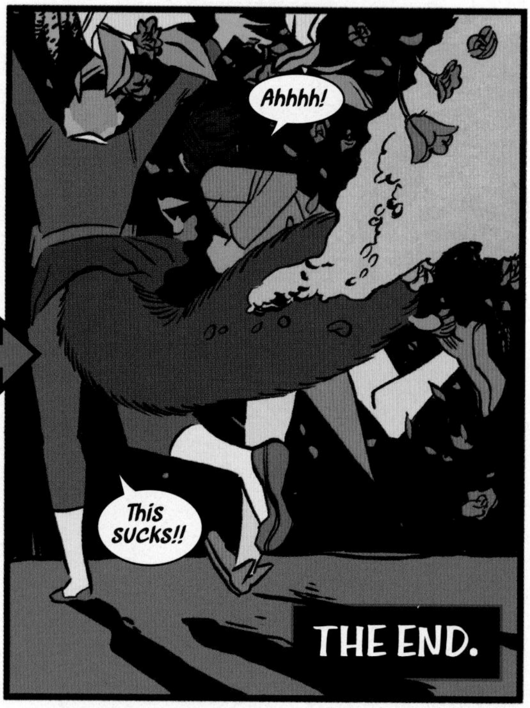
Ahhhh!
This sucks!!
THE END.

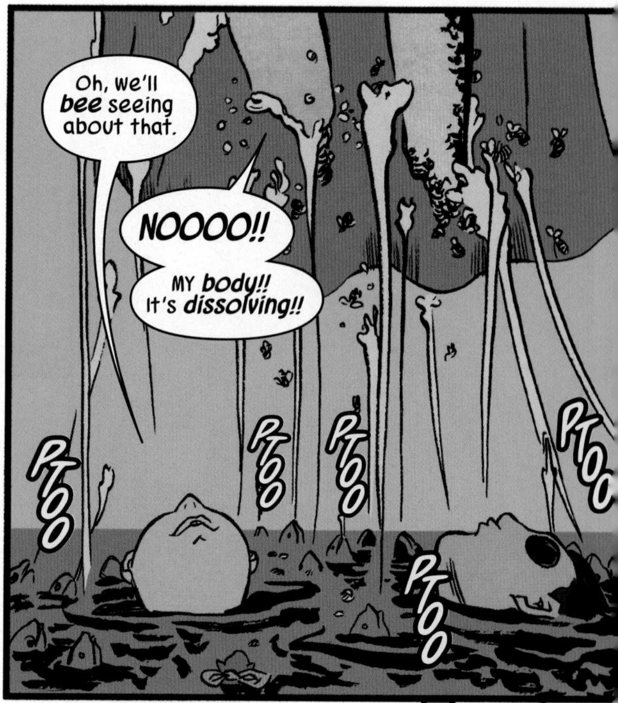
Oh, we'll *bee* seeing about that.
NOOOO!!
MY *body!!* It's *dissolving!!*
PTOO
PTOO
PTOO
PTOO
PTOO

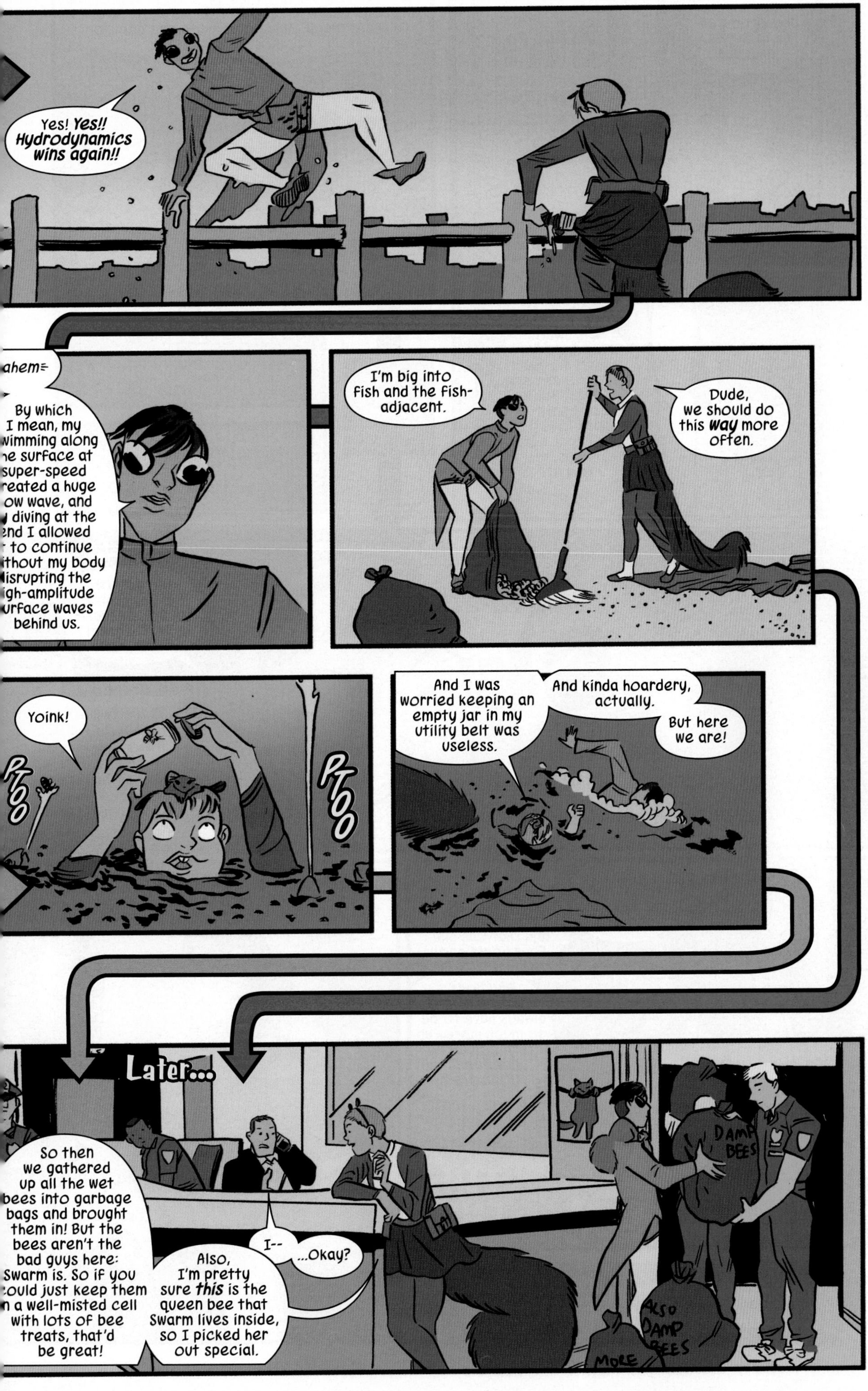
Yes! Yes!! Hydrodynamics wins again!!
ahem=
By which I mean, my wimming along ne surface at super-speed reated a huge ow wave, and diving at the nd I allowed to continue ithout my body isrupting the igh-amplitude urface waves behind us.
I'm big into fish and the fish-adjacent.
Dude, we should do this way more often.
Yoink!
PTOO
PTOO
And I was worried keeping an empty jar in my utility belt was useless.
And kinda hoardery, actually.
But here we are!
Later...
So then we gathered up all the wet bees into garbage bags and brought them in! But the bees aren't the bad guys here: Swarm is. So if you ould just keep them n a well-misted cell with lots of bee treats, that'd be great!
I--
...Okay?
Also, I'm pretty sure this is the queen bee that Swarm lives inside, so I picked her out special.
DAMP BEES
ALSO DAMP BEES
MORE

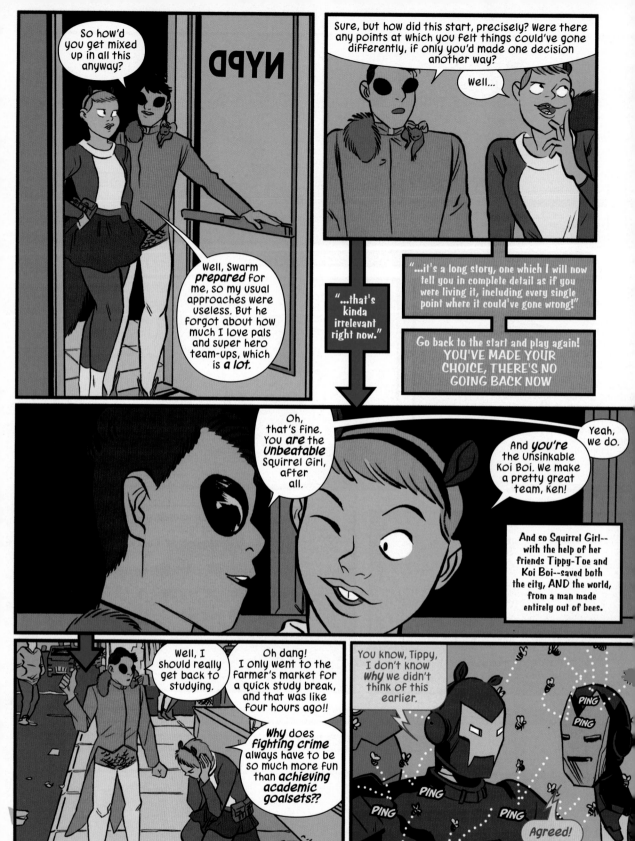

NYPD

So how'd you get mixed up in all this anyway?

Well, Swarm **prepared** for me, so my usual approaches were useless. But he forgot about how much I love pals and super hero team-ups, which is a *lot*.

Sure, but how did this start, precisely? Were there any points at which you felt things could've gone differently, if only you'd made one decision another way?

Well...

"...that's kinda irrelevant right now."

"...it's a long story, one which I will now tell you in complete detail as if you were living it, including every single point where it could've gone wrong!"

Go back to the start and play again! YOU'VE MADE YOUR CHOICE, THERE'S NO GOING BACK NOW

Oh, that's fine. You *are* the *Unbeatable* Squirrel Girl, after all.

And *you're* the Unsinkable Koi Boi. We make a pretty great team, Ken!

Yeah, we do.

And so Squirrel Girl--with the help of her friends Tippy-Toe and Koi Boi--saved both the city, AND the world, from a man made entirely out of bees.

Well, I should really get back to studying.

Oh dang! I only went to the farmer's market for a quick study break, and that was like four hours ago!! Why does fighting crime always have to be so much more fun than achieving academic goalsets??

THE END!

You know, Tippy, I don't know *why* we didn't think of this earlier.

PING PING PING PING PING PING PING PING PING

Agreed!

Special Bonus Secret Ending That Can Only Be Reached By Cheating!

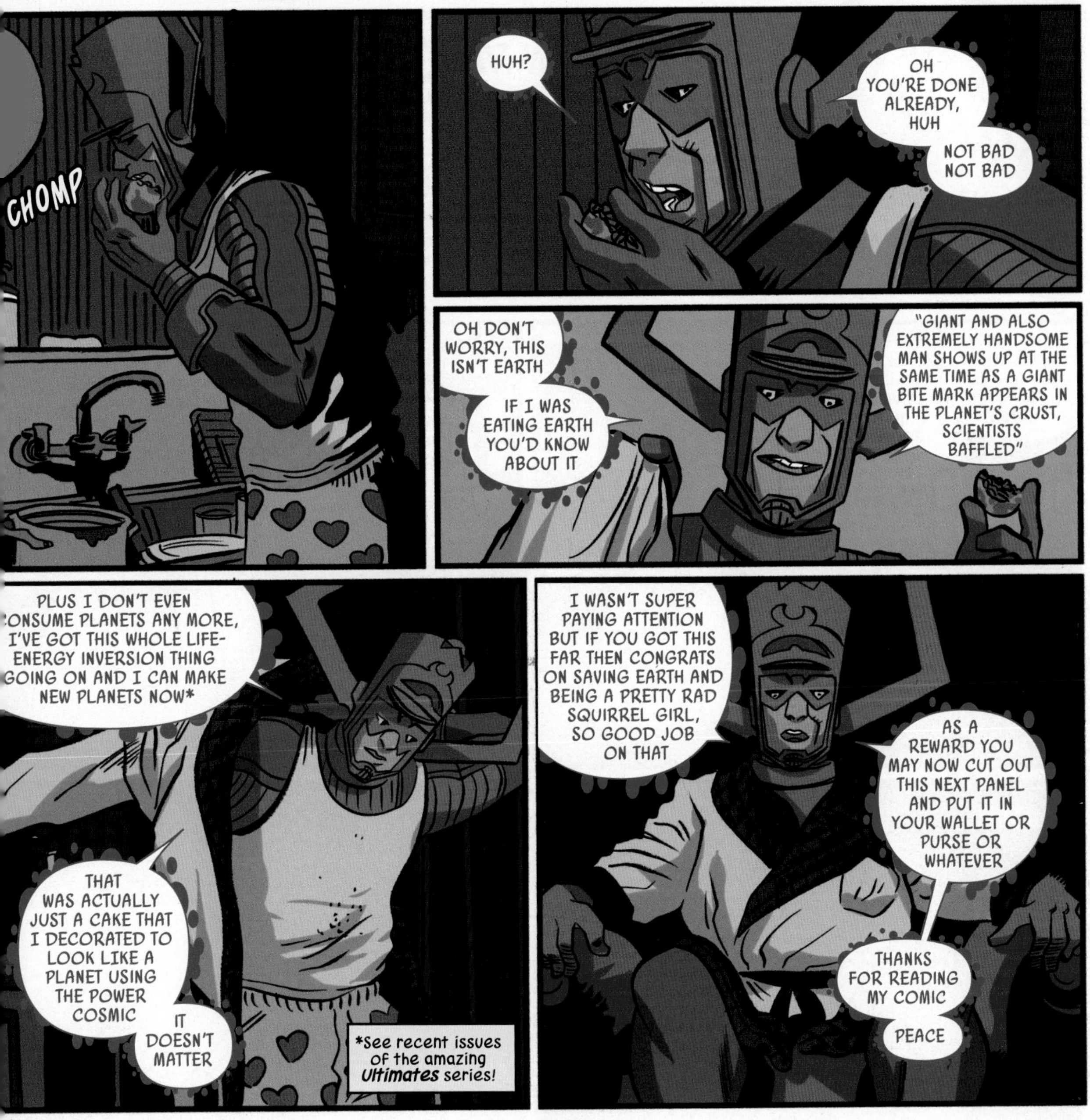
CHOMP
HUH?
OH YOU'RE DONE ALREADY, HUH
NOT BAD NOT BAD
OH DON'T WORRY, THIS ISN'T EARTH
IF I WAS EATING EARTH YOU'D KNOW ABOUT IT
"GIANT AND ALSO EXTREMELY HANDSOME MAN SHOWS UP AT THE SAME TIME AS A GIANT BITE MARK APPEARS IN THE PLANET'S CRUST, SCIENTISTS BAFFLED"
PLUS I DON'T EVEN CONSUME PLANETS ANY MORE, I'VE GOT THIS WHOLE LIFE-ENERGY INVERSION THING GOING ON AND I CAN MAKE NEW PLANETS NOW*
THAT WAS ACTUALLY JUST A CAKE THAT I DECORATED TO LOOK LIKE A PLANET USING THE POWER COSMIC
IT DOESN'T MATTER
*See recent issues of the amazing *Ultimates* series!
I WASN'T SUPER PAYING ATTENTION BUT IF YOU GOT THIS FAR THEN CONGRATS ON SAVING EARTH AND BEING A PRETTY RAD SQUIRREL GIRL, SO GOOD JOB ON THAT
AS A REWARD YOU MAY NOW CUT OUT THIS NEXT PANEL AND PUT IT IN YOUR WALLET OR PURSE OR WHATEVER
THANKS FOR READING MY COMIC
PEACE

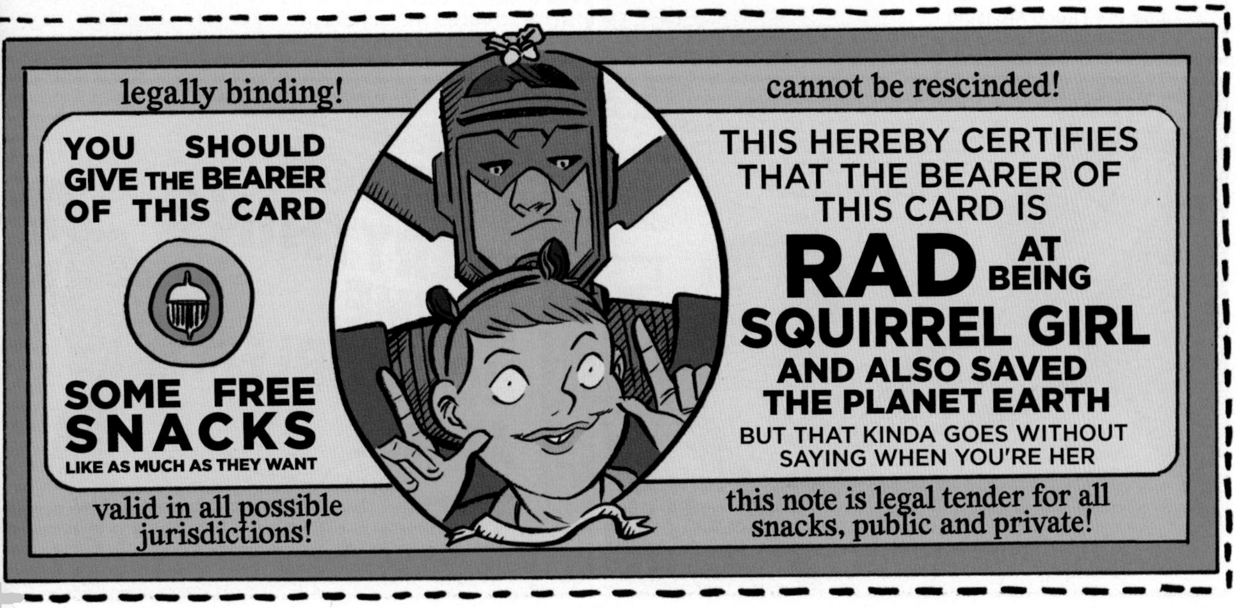
legally binding!
cannot be rescinded!
YOU SHOULD GIVE THE BEARER OF THIS CARD
SOME FREE SNACKS
LIKE AS MUCH AS THEY WANT
THIS HEREBY CERTIFIES THAT THE BEARER OF THIS CARD IS
RAD AT BEING SQUIRREL GIRL
AND ALSO SAVED THE PLANET EARTH
BUT THAT KINDA GOES WITHOUT SAYING WHEN YOU'RE HER
valid in all possible jurisdictions!
this note is legal tender for all snacks, public and private!

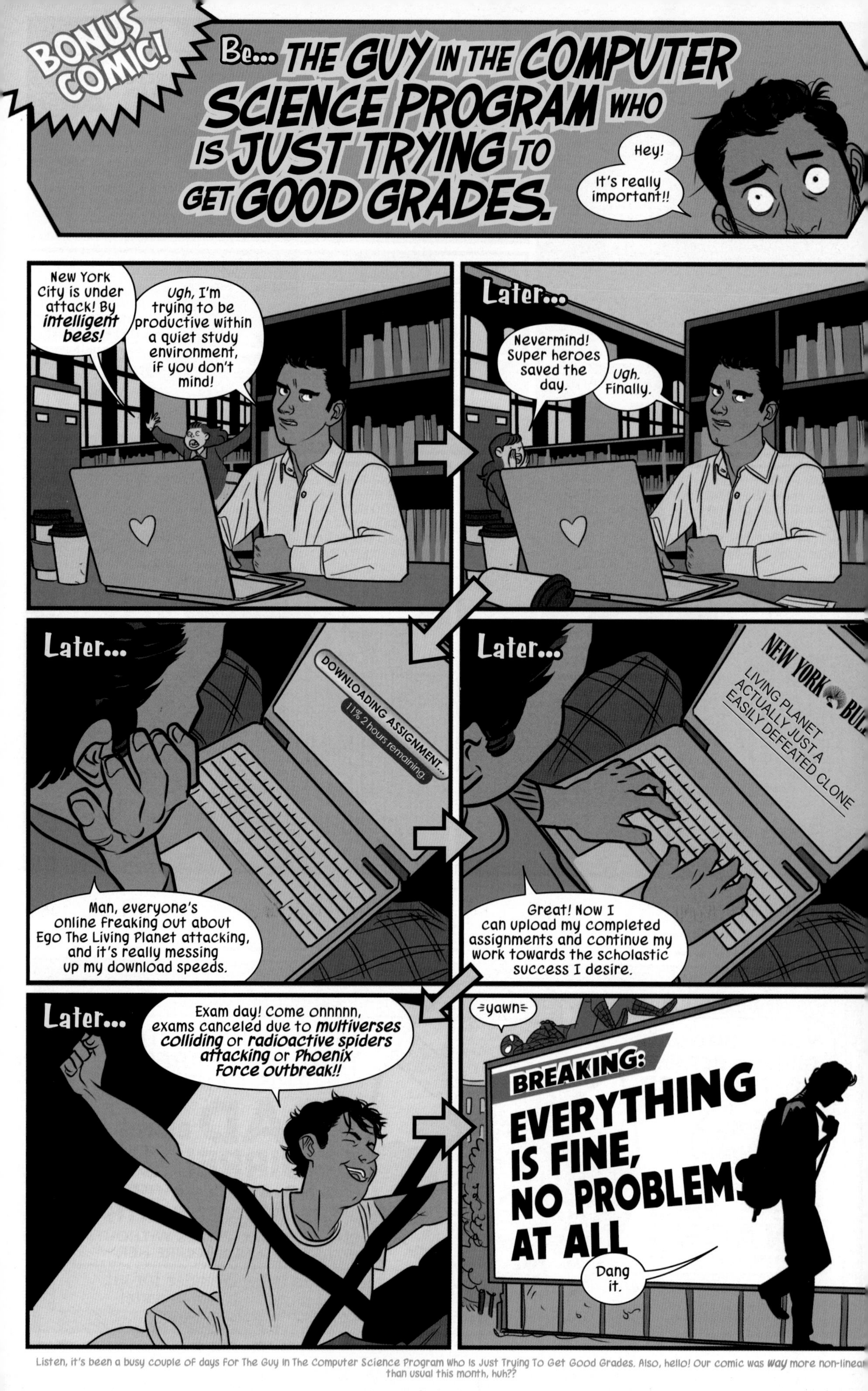
BONUS COMIC!
Be... THE GUY IN THE COMPUTER SCIENCE PROGRAM WHO IS JUST TRYING TO GET GOOD GRADES.
Hey!
It's really important!!
New York City is under attack! By *intelligent bees!*
Ugh, I'm trying to be productive within a quiet study environment, if you don't mind!
Later...
Nevermind! Super heroes saved the day.
Ugh. Finally.
Later...
DOWNLOADING ASSIGNMENT...
11% 2 hours remaining.
Man, everyone's online freaking out about Ego The Living Planet attacking, and it's really messing up my download speeds.
Later...
NEW YORK
LIVING PLANET ACTUALLY JUST A EASILY DEFEATED CLONE
Great! Now I can upload my completed assignments and continue my work towards the scholastic success I desire.
Later...
Exam day! Come onnnnn, exams canceled due to *multiverses colliding* or *radioactive spiders attacking* or *Phoenix Force outbreak!!*
=yawn=
BREAKING:
EVERYTHING IS FINE, NO PROBLEMS AT ALL
Dang it.

Listen, it's been a busy couple of days for The Guy In The Computer Science Program Who Is Just Trying To Get Good Grades. Also, hello! Our comic was *way* more non-linea[r] than usual this month, huh??

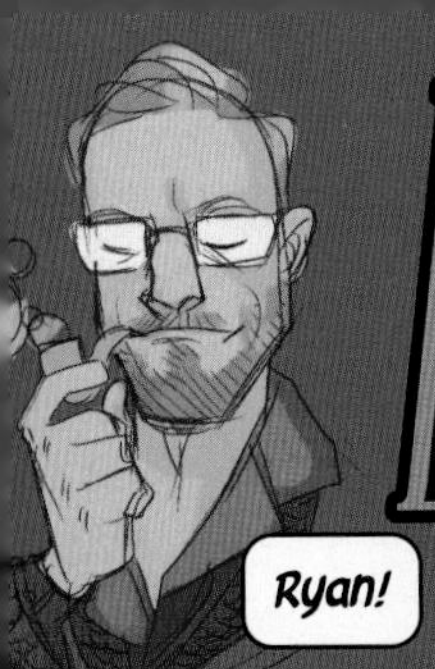
Ryan!

Letters From Nuts

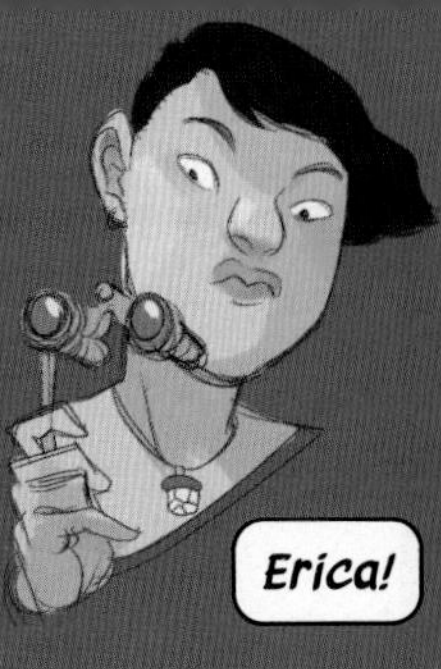
Erica!

Send letters to mheroes@marvel.com or 135 W 50th St, 7th Floor, New York, NY 10020 (Please mark "OKAY TO PRINT")

Dear Erica & Ryan,

I found your comics a couple of months ago and have ıce read every issue. Squirrels are some of my favorite ımals and Squirrel Girl is my new favorite hero. Thank ı for telling this wonderful story.

I work in wildlife rehabilitation and last year fostered veral orphaned baby squirrels, like the girl pictured low. If I am fortunate enough to do so again this year, ıhall tell them tale (tail?) of brave Tippy-Toe and her est to make the work a better place for squirrels and mans. I think it is important for squirrel kids to have meone to look up to and admire. Do you have any vice for a young squirrel just starting out in life?

Thank you.

Jennifer B.
Berkeley, CA

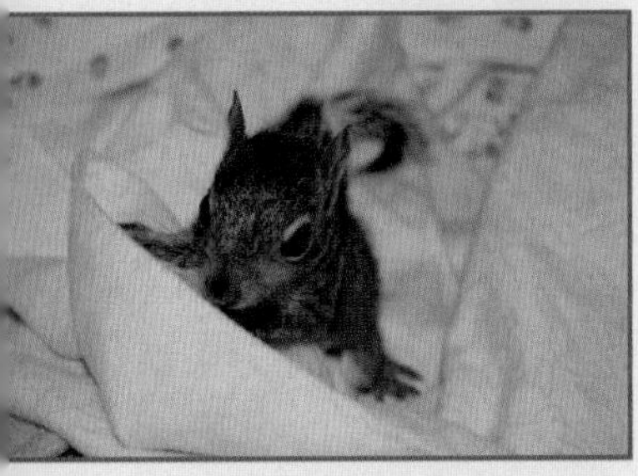

RYAN: I feel like YOU – as an actual real-life ldlife rehabilitator (nice!) – should be giving US vice to give to young squirrels just starting out in e! But from my brief research just now, I think it's portant that they get plenty of fluids, stay warm, d after a few weeks meet other squirrels in a ntrolled environment! Also, be extremely awesome. always helps if you can be extremely awesome, baby uirrels.

ERICA: Please keep sending us photos of wee baby uirrels. We will keep printing them. Send them all.

Well. How annoying. Emmys, Grammys, Oscars, and t one mention of THE UNBEATABLE SQUIRREL GIRL. ıis will not do. So we, The Nabobs who Understand the emendousness of Squirrel Girl (aka "The Academy"), reby announce the First Occasional Ratatoskr Awards, noring the unquestioned brilliance of everyone using a yming animal-themed super-hero name.

Best Leading Actress – Her name's Doreen. It rhymes th "keen." She's inexperienced – a little Green.
Best Leading Actor – Tony Stark, The Irascible Iron an (who now holds the all-time record for fewest tual on-panel appearances by a leading man). Best pporting Actress – Tippy-toe, by a whisker over Nancy ho thinks The Academy is NUTS). Best Supporting tor – Well, Galactus LOOKS male…
Best Screenplay – That classic C++ program 'AN! ("Random Yucks in ASCII Notation"). Best nematography – The Erica! Studio Best Special Effects RICO (nationally guilty of being Suave). Best Sound gineering – Clayton Cowls (ahem: the plural of "cowl" es not have an "e"). Best Subtitles – This time, DO take e Brown ACID. Best Editor – Wil Moss (one does not ake wisecracks about editors). And, finally, Best Sequel – Well, technically, "Only Our Second #1 So Far This Year," but The Academy suggests "Lokat and Katatoskr team up to take down the Cat-Thors," written and drawn by Nancy (who might forgive us now).

Congratulations to all, and in anticipation of the next cancellation and new #1 this year; The Academy (aka Brock J. Hanke).

RYAN: Haha, never have I swept an awards show like this before! But I am very interested in this "Katatoskr" character and look forward to reading about her EXTREMELY canon adventures.

ERICA: AHHHHHHH! I'M GOING TO DISNEYLAND.

Howdy Squirrel Folk,
Long time(ish) reader, first-time writer (sorry, always wanted to say/type that somewhere). First off, looooooooving Squirrel Girl. She's always a hoot and kicks some serious tail. Anyway, I noticed that in the latest issue of Squirrel Girl that Nancy could understand what Tippy was saying. Was that like a hint of things to come for her power-wise, an oversight, or something that I just never noticed? In any case, can't wait to see how things go between Doreen and Howard in the next issue! Now only if you guys could get Doreen and Patsy Walker in an issue (non-cameo-wise). ;)

Mario Barron

RYAN: Hi, Mario! Our first #8 ends with Doreen and Tippy teaching Nancy, Chipmunk Hunk, and Koi Boi the basics of squirrel language, with the idea that it'd come in handy in just such a situation. When Tippy and Nancy were in Asgard and Tippy couldn't talk to Nancy, she found it PRETTY FRUSTRATING, and came up with the idea of brief language lessons as a way of solving that problem! Then, later on several decades in the past, it helped them save the fate of an entire planet, so I guess it was the right call. Good work, Tippy!

As with the first volume of THE UNBEATABLE SQUIRREL GIRL, my four-year-old twin daughters are highly enjoying the second series. It's the only new title coming out besides GUARDIANS OF THE GALAXY that they ask about on a regular basis. Quite awesome, since Doreen is currently my favorite character in comics right now. It's neat to be able to share her adventures with my girls.

I'm also happy to say that I've finally turned a few people outside of my family on to SQUIRREL GIRL. They all agree that it's possibly too humorous for its own good. One of my friends actually thanked me recently for telling him about the book. He stated that it is now his most-liked Marvel comic. That's two of us out there, at least.

Could you just do your readers one favor, Ryan and Erica? A teeny, tiny request. Can we get about sixty more years of you two working on this series before you hand it over to another creative team? That would be super. Thanks!

Darrick Patrick
Dayton, Ohio

P.S. I'm including a photograph of Nola and Logann showing off their second UNBEATABLE collection so far.

P.S.S. That's odd. Are you experiencing a slight feeling of déjà vu too?

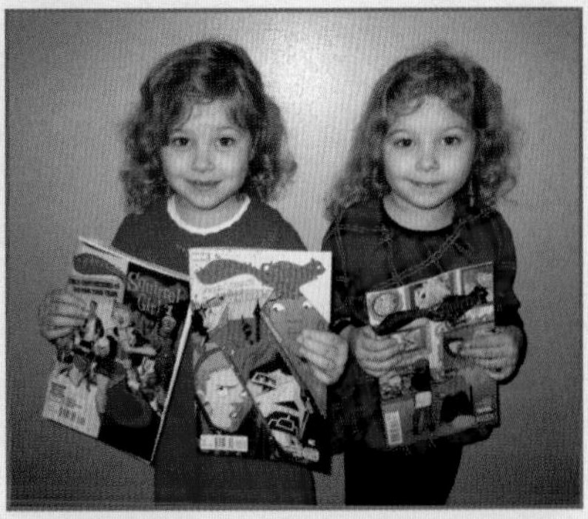

RYAN: Darrick, thank YOU! That's a super-great picture. I love that you're still out there recommending our book not just to your daughters, but also to people who don't live inside your house! That's excellent. Your twins will be happy to know that in our (just announced) UNBEATABLE SQUIRREL GIRL OGN (that's "original graphic novel," presumably to distinguish it from all those plagiarized graphic novels out there) that's coming out in October and that we're working on in parallel with this comic AS WE SPEAK, Squirrel Girl will be facing what's, in effect, her twin – only she and her double have different ideas of the best way to do things. Some of these pages will feature: PUNCHING. As for your request, I think it is entirely feasible and I see no downsides at all. Erica?

ERICA: It should be okay as long as I remember to take a nap every so often.

Thank you, SQUIRREL GIRL team! All of you creative people and miscellaneous mammals, thank you! You put Jubilee in SQUIRREL GIRL #3!!! Yay!!! All I need is X-23/Wolverine to make a cameo and I have my holy trinity of favorite Marvel ladies all in my favorite comic book!

Ryan and Erica, you keep producing a quality, funny, oddball, FANTASTIC book that never fails to entertain. Thank you again for giving us a light in the gloom. Don't stop! (Please!)

Tim Pealing
Plymouth, England

RYAN: Thanks, Tim! My only regret with Jubilee is that I didn't get to have her say that she'd "shed some LIGHT on the situation" – I had a series of old X-Men comics in which she said it twice in as many issues. To the same person, no less! Clearly it was intended to be her catchphrase, but sadly, the scene in which she appeared in our comic was in broad daylight, outdoors, on a sunny day, and therefore extremely well lit. Some other time!

ERICA: I was pretty excited to get Jubilee in there too. The next on my bucket list is Dazzler. ONE DAY! Apparently we just promised to do this book for another sixty years so I'm sure it'll happen.

Ack, out of room! Well, come back next issue for a story about Squirrel Girl's love life! (Or lack thereof!)

ttention, Squirrel Scouts! Make sure to check out our production blog, **unbeatablesquirrelgirl.tumblr.com**, where we post behind-the-scenes stuff on how the book gets made, along with all sorts of cool things *you* make: fanart, cosplay, whatever!

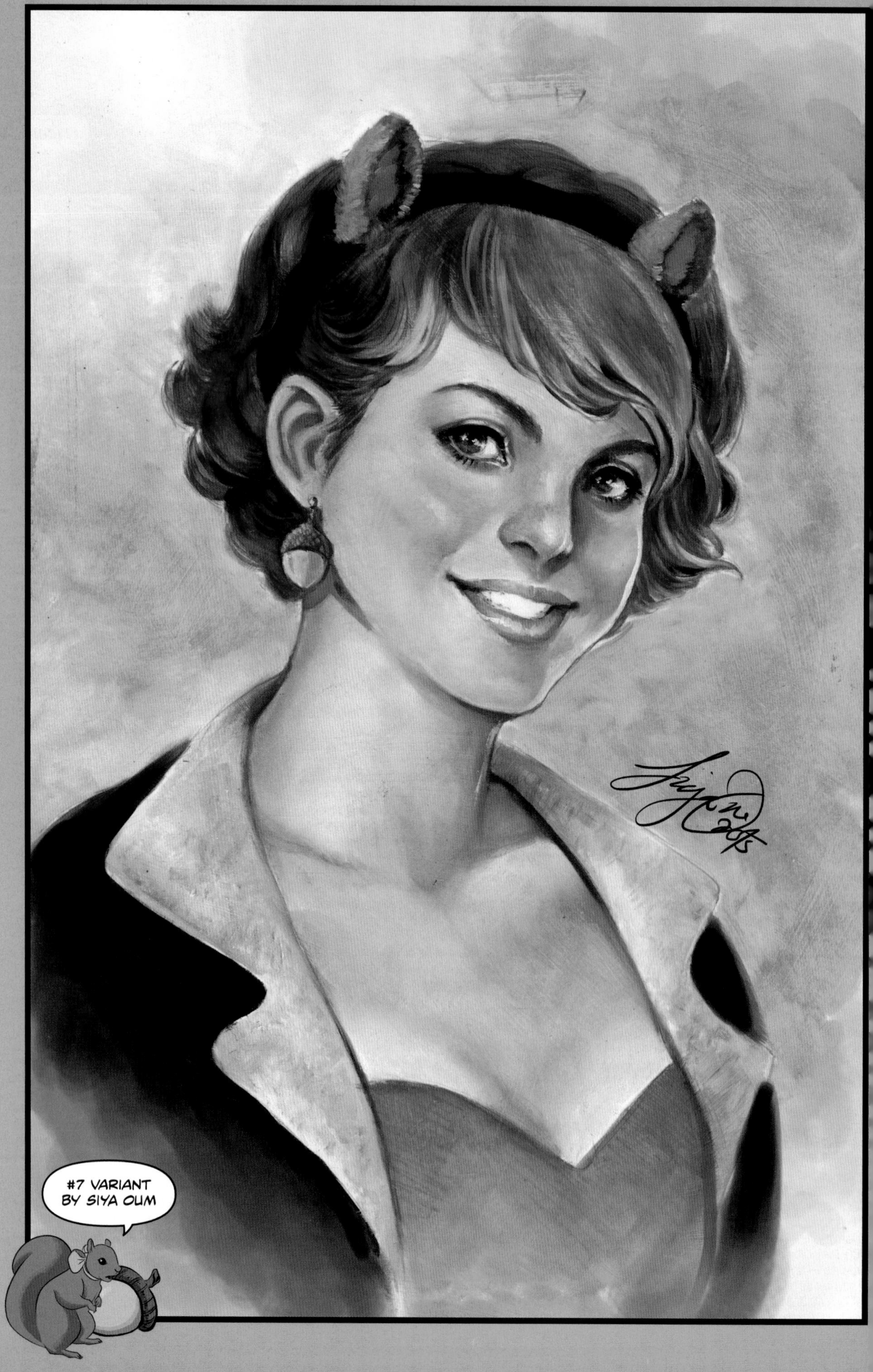
#7 VARIANT
BY SIYA OUM

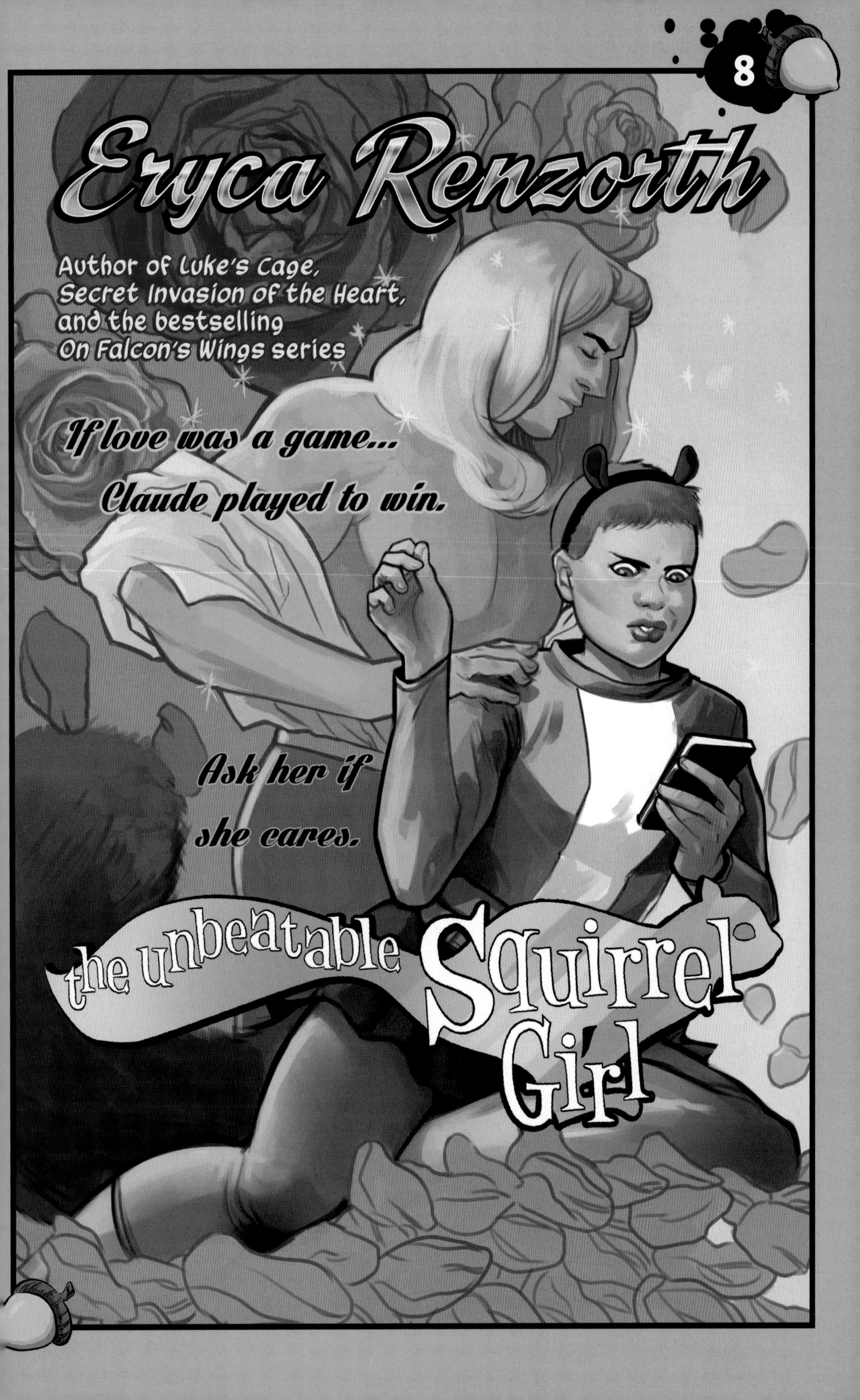
8
Eryca Renzorth
Author of Luke's Cage,
Secret Invasion of the Heart,
and the bestselling
On Falcon's Wings series
If love was a game...
Claude played to win.
Ask her if
she cares.
the unbeatable Squirrel Girl

Doreen Green isn't just a second-year computer science student: she secretly also has all the powers of both squirrel ar girl! She uses her amazing abilities to fight crime **and** be as awesome as possible. You know her as...**The Unbeatable Squirrel Gir**

Find out what she's been up to, with...

Squirrel Girl *in a nutshell*

Squirrel Girl @unbeatablesg
Hey who has two thumbs and took down SWARM in one of SEVERAL different ways?

Squirrel Girl @unbeatablesg
and also a tail

Squirrel Girl @unbeatablesg
Who has two thumbs and a tail and really great computer science skills and a great sense of style and cool friends who she loves and (1/2)

Squirrel Girl @unbeatablesg
(cont) squirrel skills and problem-solving skills and being smart skills AND took down SWARM in one of SEVERAL different ways? (2/2)

Squirrel Girl @unbeatablesg
ME

Squirrel Girl @unbeatablesg
PLEASE RT, IT WAS AMAZING

G. ALACTUS **GALACTUS @xGALACTUSx**
@unbeatablesg ARE YOU SURE YOU DIDN'T FAIL TO TAKE DOWN SWARM, AND THEN HE BECAME PRESIDENT, AND ALL EARTH HAD TO WORSHIP PRESIDENT BEE

Squirrel Girl @unbeatablesg
@xGALACTUSx YES GALACTUS, I'm sure!! If that were true things would be different and PROBABLY way worse? So let's all stop talking about it

Squirrel Girl @unbeatablesg
@xGALACTUSx Also great to see you here! You never post on this dang site!!

G. ALACTUS **GALACTUS @xGALACTUSx**
@unbeatablesg IT'S TRUE I GOT LOCKED OUT OF MY ACCOUNT

G. ALACTUS **GALACTUS @xGALACTUSx**
@unbeatablesg THEY HAD A SECURITY QUESTION THAT I HAD TO ANSWER TO UNLOCK IT AND GUESS WHAT I SET THE QUESTION AS

G. ALACTUS **GALACTUS @xGALACTUSx**
@unbeatablesg GO ON, GUESS

Squirrel Girl @unbeatablesg
@xGALACTUSx um... "Universe's maiden name"? "Name of first Universe"? "Favorite power cosmic"?

G. ALACTUS **GALACTUS @xGALACTUSx**
@unbeatablesg APPARENTLY WHEN I FIRST SIGNED UP I'D SET IT TO "HI GALACTUS, IT'S YOU FROM THE PAST!! NO QUESTIONS HERE, YOU RULE BUDDY!!"

G. ALACTUS **GALACTUS @xGALACTUSx**
@unbeatablesg IT'S LIKE, THANKS PAST ME, JUST SOME REAL TERRIFIC WORK THERE

G. ALACTUS **GALACTUS @xGALACTUSx**
@unbeatablesg ANYWAY I USED THE POWER COSMIC TO REWIND TIME AND CHANGE THINGS SO I NEVER CHOSE THAT SECURITY QUESTION

G. ALACTUS **GALACTUS @xGALACTUSx**
@unbeatablesg AS A SIDE EFFECT IT CAUSED TWO SOLAR SYSTEMS TO NEVER HAVE BEEN FORMED BUT THEY WERE DUDS ANYWAY, JUST REAL DUD SOLAR SYSTEMS

Squirrel Girl @unbeatablesg
@xGALACTUSx ...

G. ALACTUS **GALACTUS @xGALACTUSx**
@unbeatablesg ALSO

G. ALACTUS **GALACTUS @xGALACTUSx**
@unbeatablesg I HAVE ALREADY FORGOTTEN MY NEW PASSWORD

G. ALACTUS **GALACTUS @xGALACTUSx**
@unbeatablesg SO THAT'S A THING

search!

#treelobsters

#thenotsogoodshipMakambo

#archiepelago

#molemoneymoleproblems

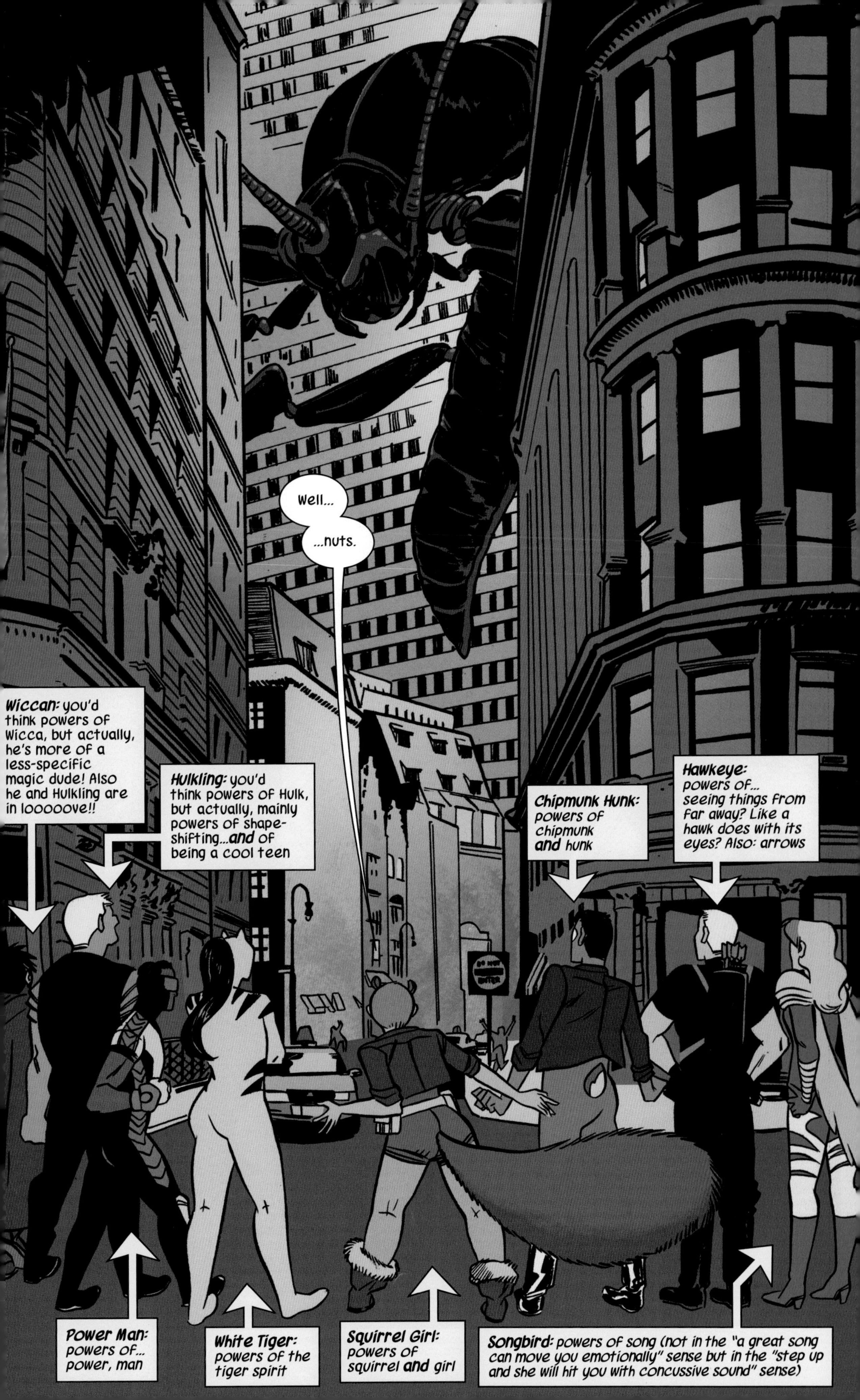

Well...
...nuts.
Wiccan: you'd think powers of Wicca, but actually, he's more of a less-specific magic dude! Also he and Hulkling are in looooove!!
Hulkling: you'd think powers of Hulk, but actually, mainly powers of shape-shifting...and of being a cool teen
Chipmunk Hunk: powers of chipmunk and hunk
Hawkeye: powers of... seeing things from far away? Like a hawk does with its eyes? Also: arrows
Power Man: powers of... power, man
White Tiger: powers of the tiger spirit
Squirrel Girl: powers of squirrel and girl
Songbird: powers of song (not in the "a great song can move you emotionally" sense but in the "step up and she will hit you with concussive sound" sense)

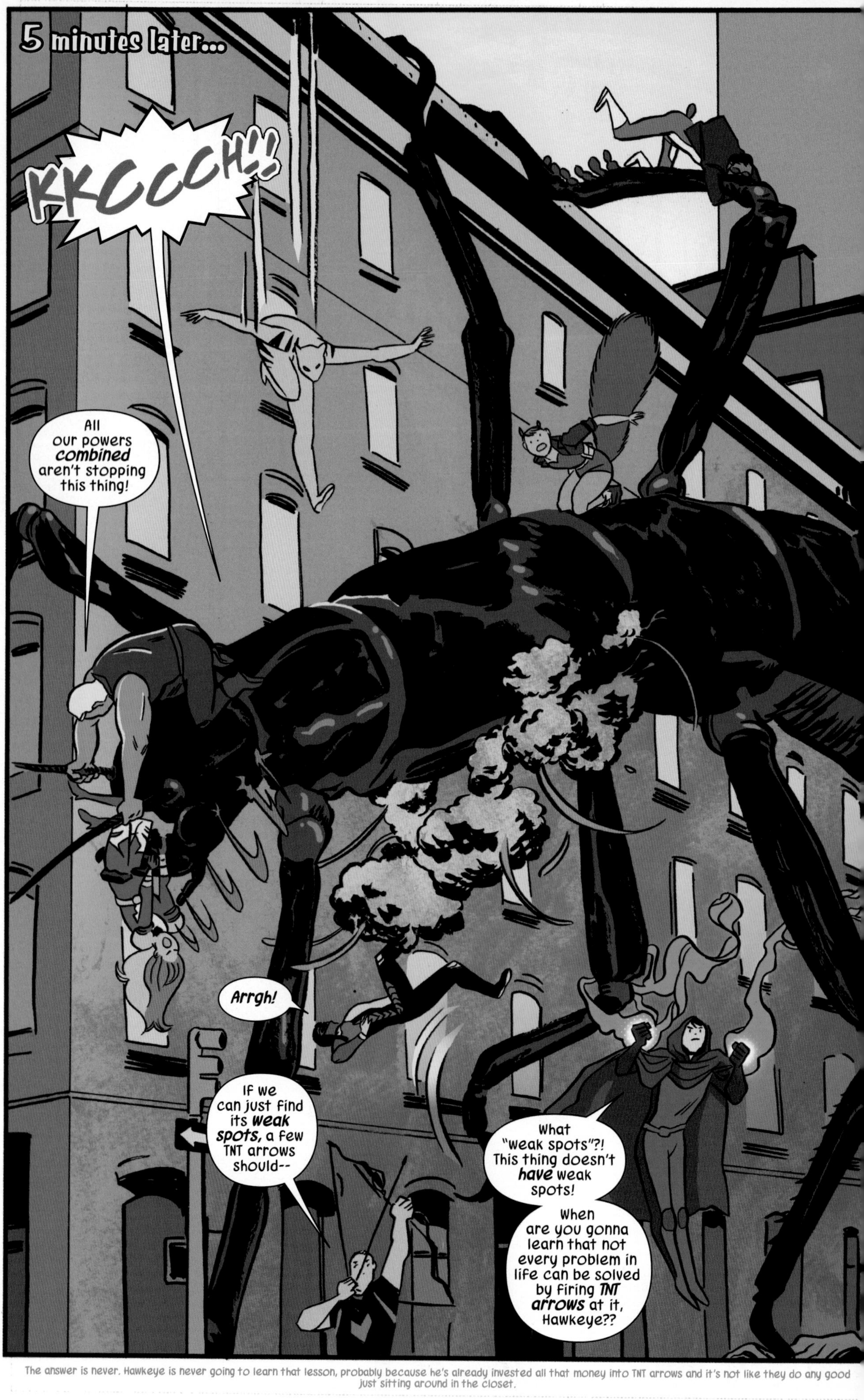
5 minutes later...
KKCOCCH!!
All our powers combined aren't stopping this thing!
Arrgh!
If we can just find its weak spots, a few TNT arrows should--
What "weak spots"?! This thing doesn't have weak spots!
When are you gonna learn that not every problem in life can be solved by firing TNT arrows at it, Hawkeye??

The answer is never. Hawkeye is never going to learn that lesson, probably because he's already invested all that money into TNT arrows and it's not like they do any good just sitting around in the closet.

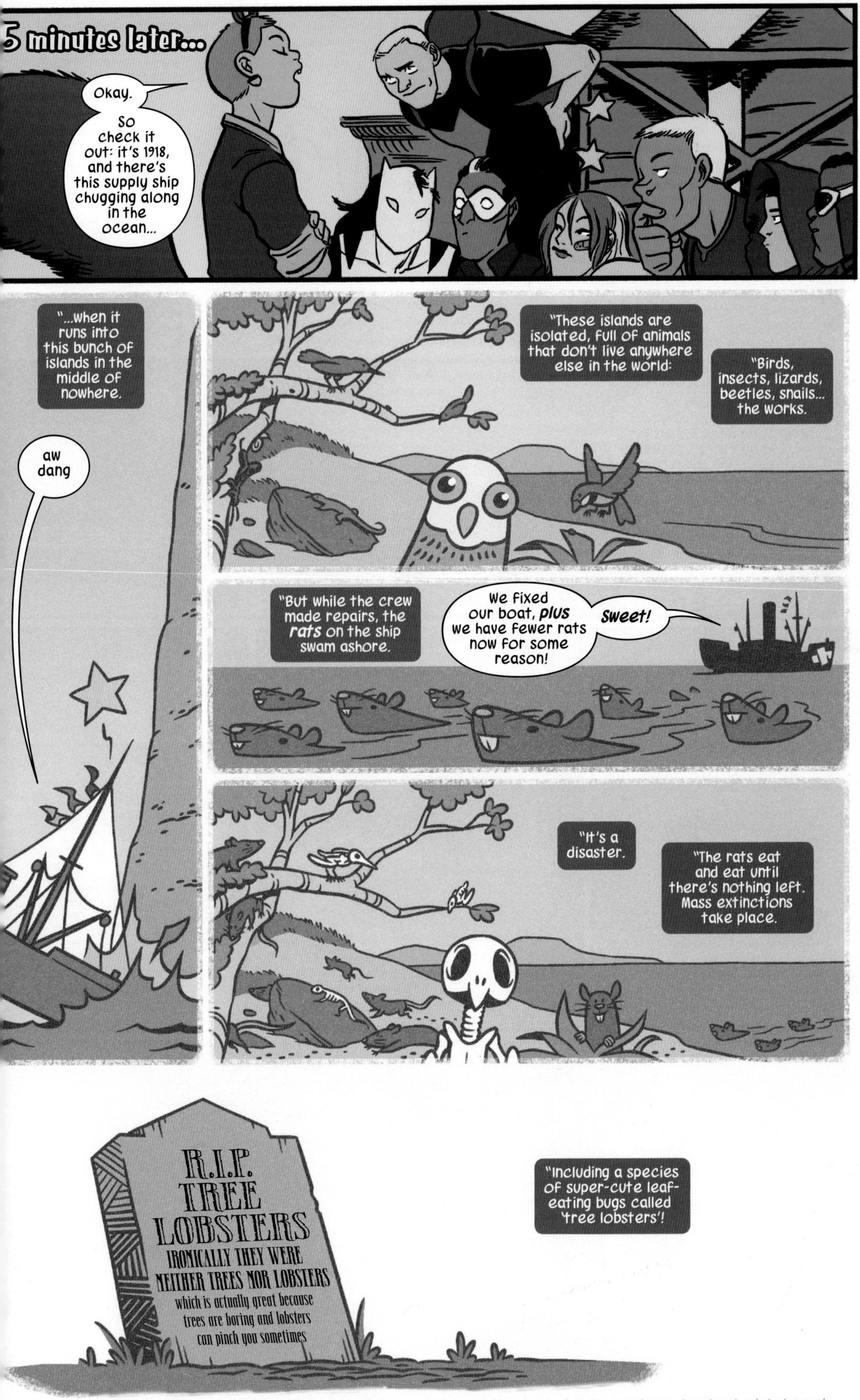
5 minutes later...
Okay.
So check it out: it's 1918, and there's this supply ship chugging along in the ocean...
"...when it runs into this bunch of islands in the middle of nowhere.
aw dang
"These islands are isolated, full of animals that don't live anywhere else in the world:
"Birds, insects, lizards, beetles, snails... the works.
"But while the crew made repairs, the rats on the ship swam ashore.
We fixed our boat, plus we have fewer rats now for some reason!
Sweet!
"It's a disaster.
"The rats eat and eat until there's nothing left. Mass extinctions take place.
R.I.P. TREE LOBSTERS
IRONICALLY THEY WERE NEITHER TREES NOR LOBSTERS
which is actually great because trees are boring and lobsters can pinch you sometimes
"Including a species of super-cute leaf-eating bugs called 'tree lobsters'!

"A bunch of islands" is called an "archipelago." If Squirrel Girl ever fights a guy who can split into a bunch of smaller guys whenever he gets wet and who is named "Archie Pelago," then you will know precisely where I got my inspiration.

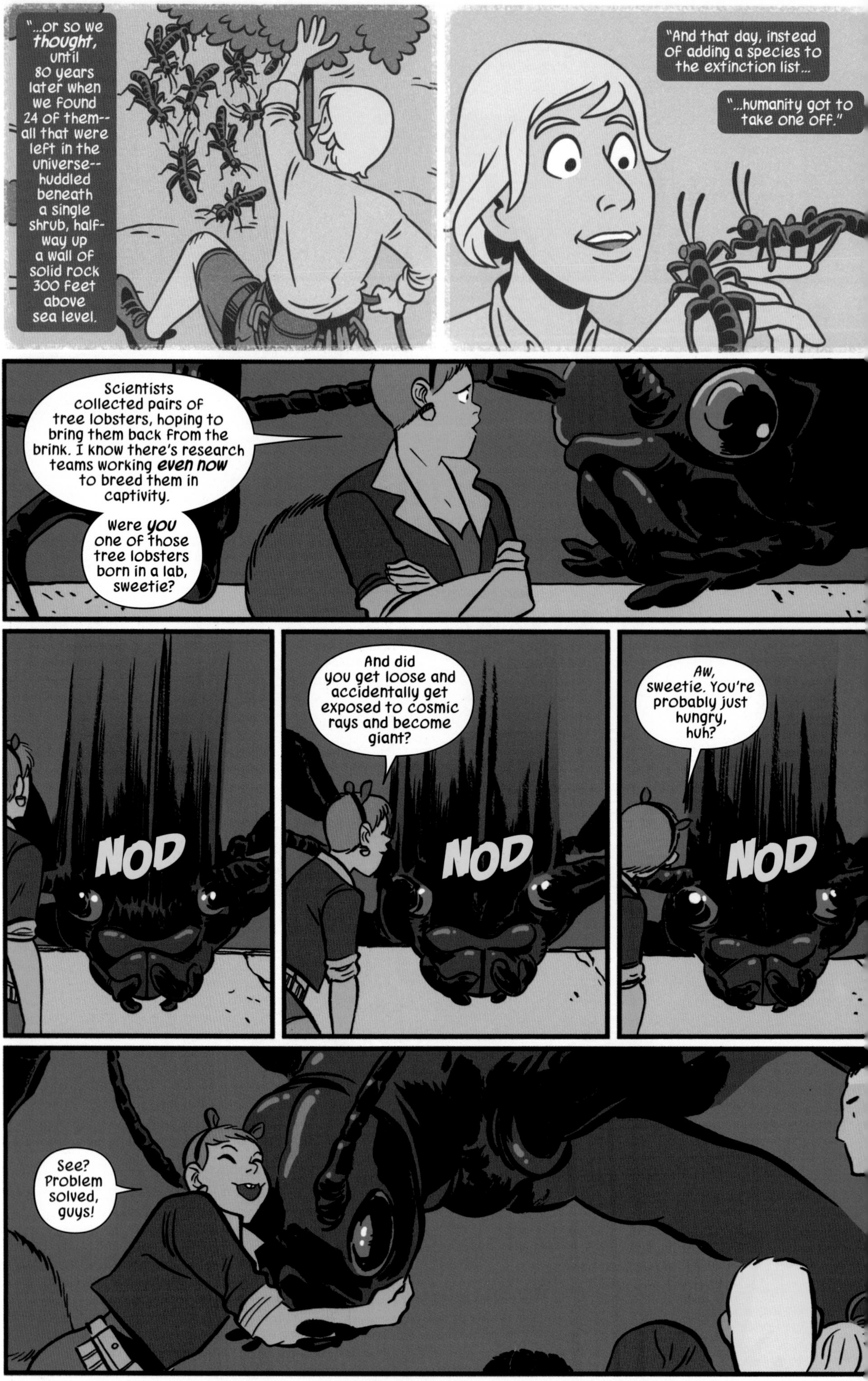
"...or so we thought, until 80 years later when we found 24 of them--all that were left in the universe--huddled beneath a single shrub, half-way up a wall of solid rock 300 feet above sea level.
"And that day, instead of adding a species to the extinction list...
"...humanity got to take one off."
Scientists collected pairs of tree lobsters, hoping to bring them back from the brink. I know there's research teams working even now to breed them in captivity.
Were you one of those tree lobsters born in a lab, sweetie?
NOD
And did you get loose and accidentally get exposed to cosmic rays and become giant?
NOD
Aw, sweetie. You're probably just hungry, huh?
NOD
See? Problem solved, guys!

Tree lobsters are *the cutest.* They pair off in couples and follow each other around, and when they sleep they cuddle up together so that one insect's legs protectively cover the other. *They're insects that spoon each other, it's the cutest--I love you, tree lobsters!*

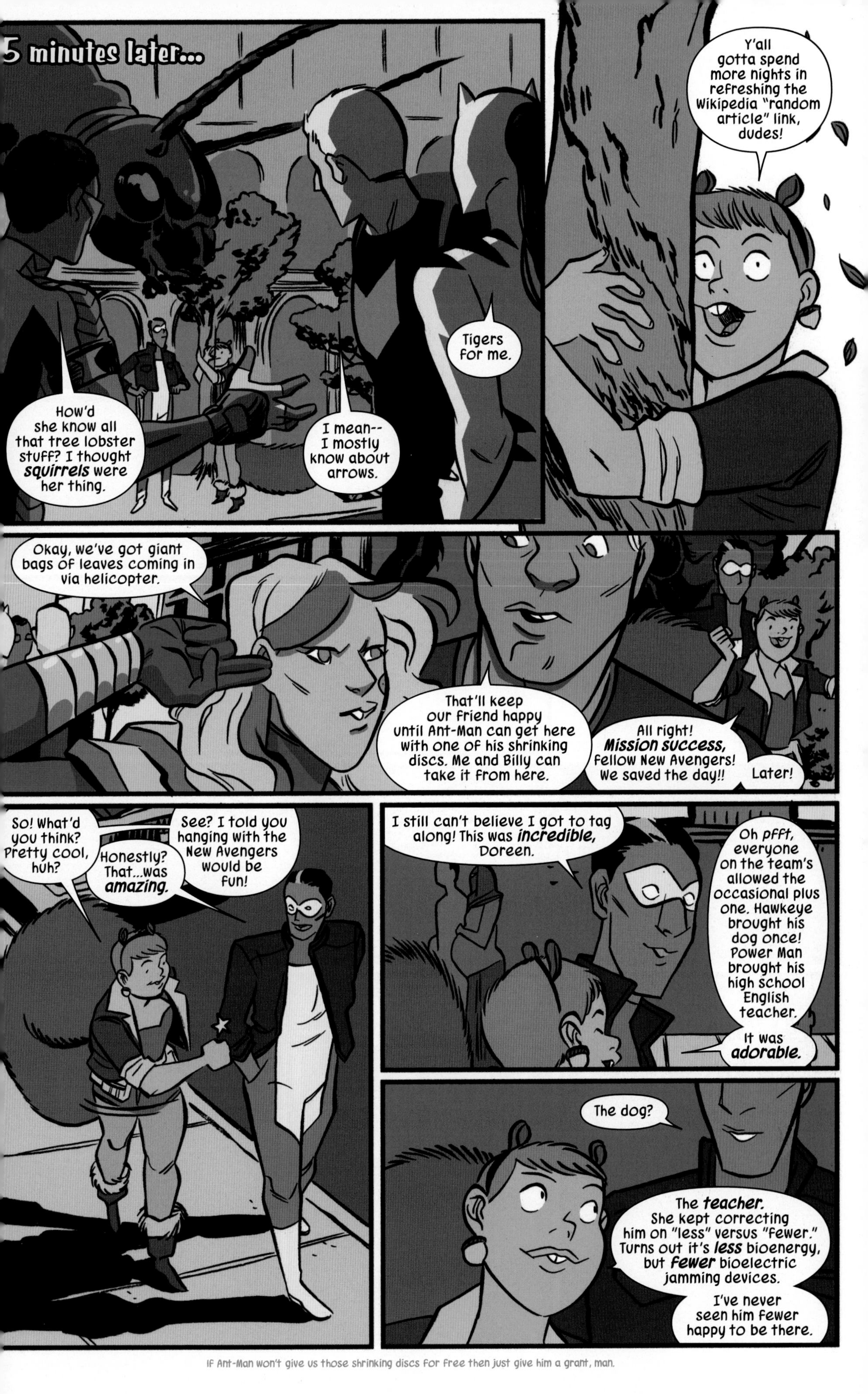
5 minutes later...
Y'all gotta spend more nights in refreshing the Wikipedia "random article" link, dudes!
How'd she know all that tree lobster stuff? I thought squirrels were her thing.
I mean-- I mostly know about arrows.
Tigers for me.
Okay, we've got giant bags of leaves coming in via helicopter.
That'll keep our friend happy until Ant-Man can get here with one of his shrinking discs. Me and Billy can take it from here.
All right! Mission success, fellow New Avengers! We saved the day!!
Later!
So! What'd you think? Pretty cool, huh?
Honestly? That...was amazing.
See? I told you hanging with the New Avengers would be fun!
I still can't believe I got to tag along! This was incredible, Doreen.
Oh pfft, everyone on the team's allowed the occasional plus one. Hawkeye brought his dog once! Power Man brought his high school English teacher.
It was adorable.
The dog?
The teacher. She kept correcting him on "less" versus "fewer." Turns out it's less bioenergy, but fewer bioelectric jamming devices.
I've never seen him fewer happy to be there.

If Ant-Man won't give us those shrinking discs for free then just give him a grant, man.

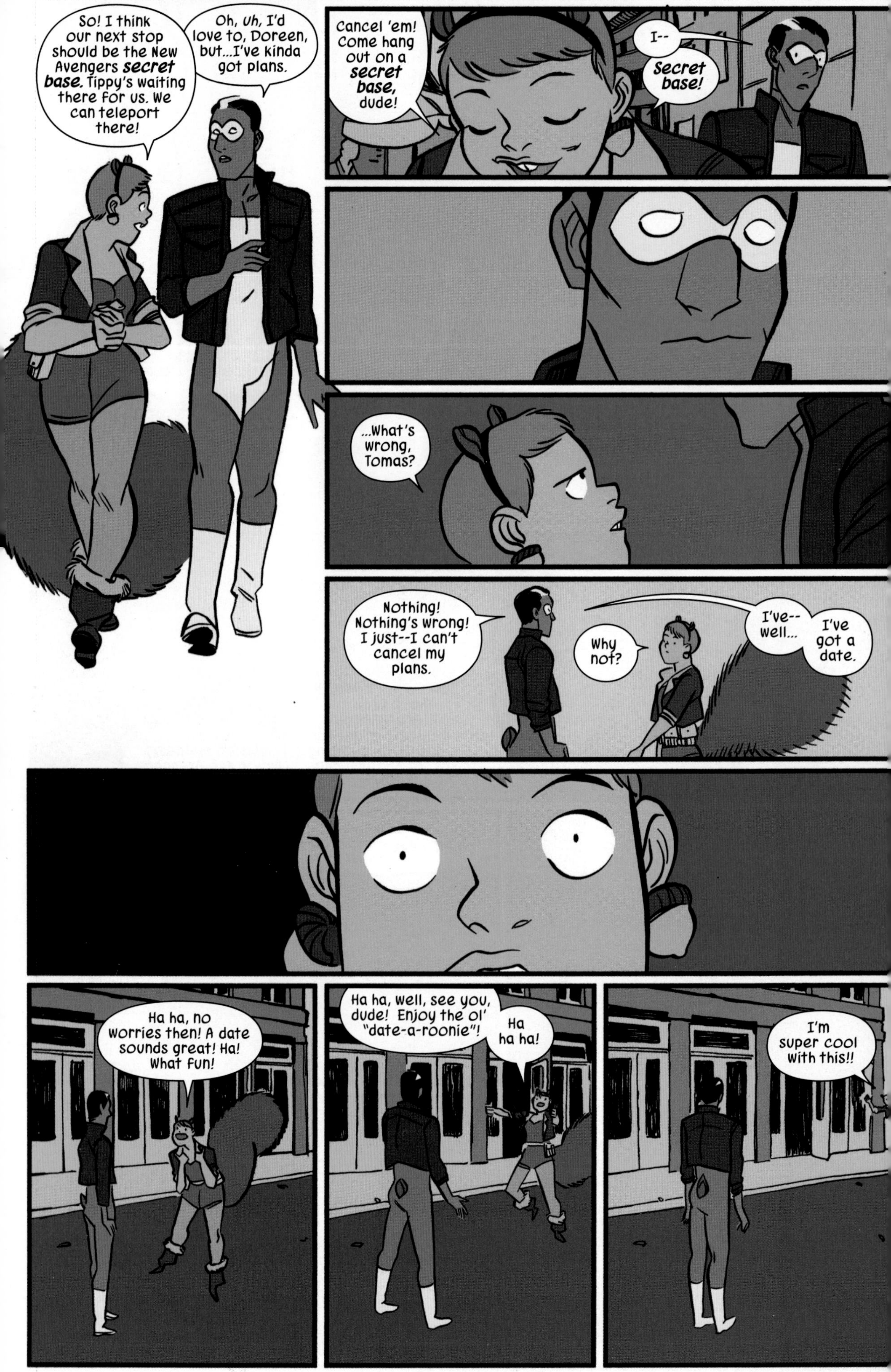
So! I think our next stop should be the New Avengers **secret base.** Tippy's waiting there for us. We can teleport there!
Oh, uh, I'd love to, Doreen, but...I've kinda got plans.
Cancel 'em! Come hang out on a **secret base,** dude!
I--
Secret base!
...What's wrong, Tomas?
Nothing! Nothing's wrong! I just--I can't cancel my plans.
Why not?
I've-- well...
I've got a date.
Ha ha, no worries then! A date sounds great! Ha! What fun!
Ha ha, well, see you, dude! Enjoy the ol' "date-a-roonie"!
Ha ha ha!
I'm super cool with this!!

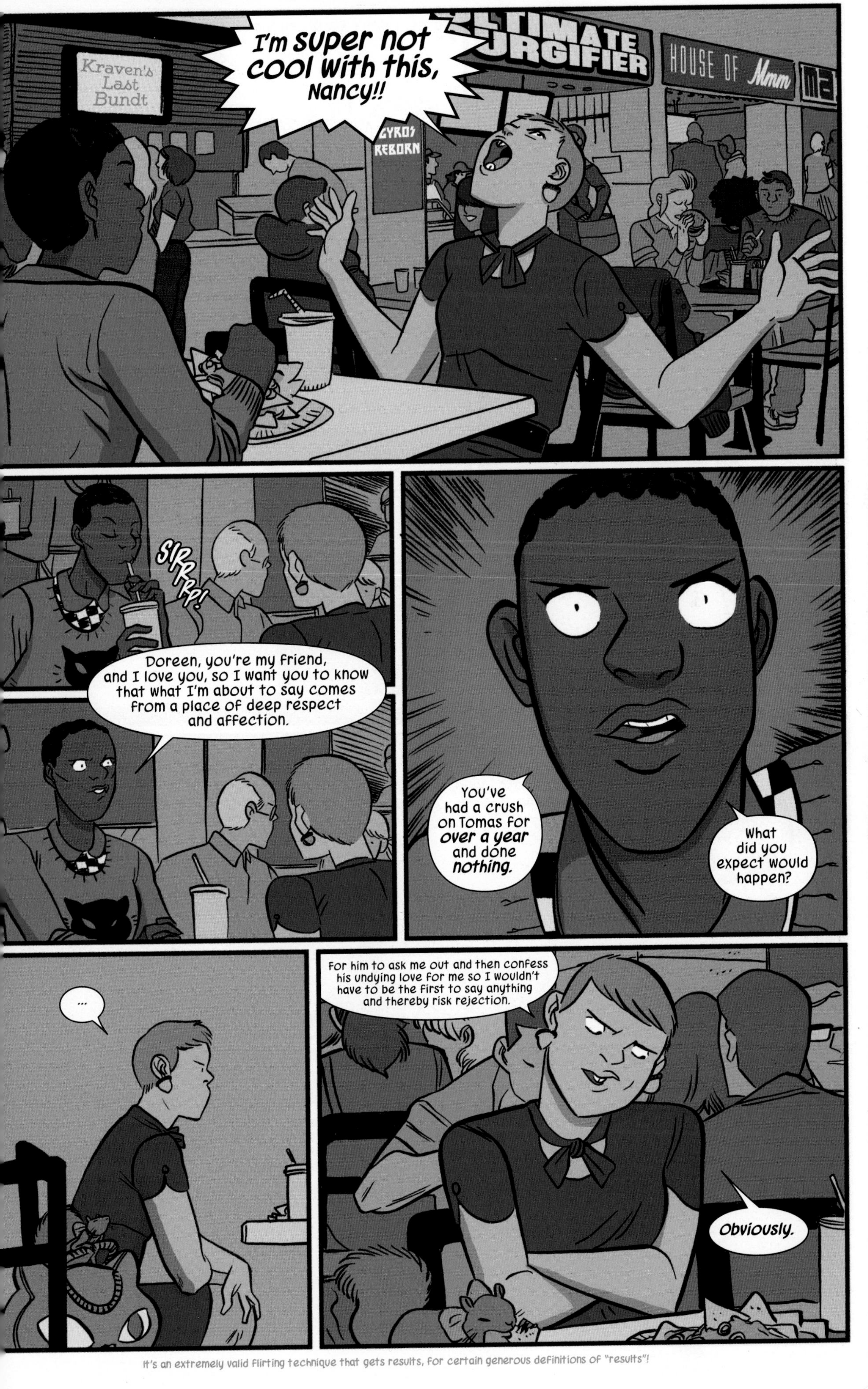
Kraven's Last Bundt
I'm super not cool with this, Nancy!!
GYROS REBORN
HOUSE OF Mmm
SIRRRP!
Doreen, you're my friend, and I love you, so I want you to know that what I'm about to say comes from a place of deep respect and affection.
You've had a crush on Tomas for over a year and done nothing.
What did you expect would happen?
...
For him to ask me out and then confess his undying love for me so I wouldn't have to be the first to say anything and thereby risk rejection.
Obviously.

It's an extremely valid flirting technique that gets results, for certain generous definitions of "results"!

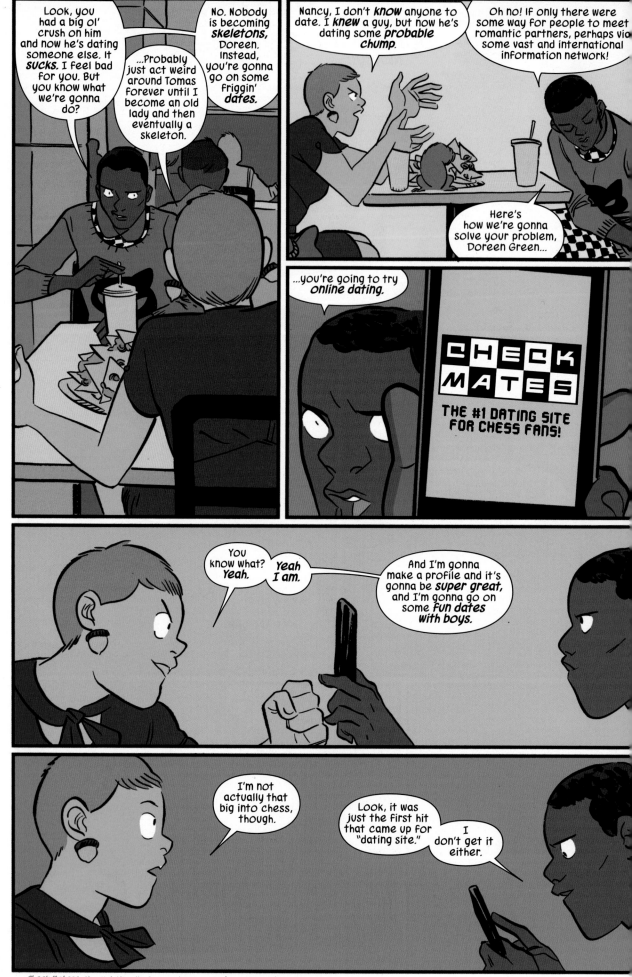

Look, you had a big ol' crush on him and now he's dating someone else. It **SUCKS.** I feel bad for you. But you know what we're gonna do?

...Probably just act weird around Tomas forever until I become an old lady and then eventually a skeleton.

No. Nobody is becoming **skeletons,** Doreen. Instead, you're gonna go on some **friggin' dates.**

Nancy, I don't **KNOW** anyone to date. I **KNEW** a guy, but now he's dating some **probable chump.**

Oh no! If only there were some way for people to meet romantic partners, perhaps via some vast and international information network!

Here's how we're gonna solve your problem, Doreen Green...

...you're going to try **online dating.**

CHECK MATES

THE #1 DATING SITE FOR CHESS FANS!

You know what? Yeah.

Yeah I am.

And I'm gonna make a profile and it's gonna be **super great,** and I'm gonna go on some **fun dates** with boys.

I'm not actually that big into chess, though.

Look, it was just the first hit that came up for "dating site."

I don't get it either.

Check Mates is the #1 dating site for grandmasters...*and grandsmoochers.* And to answer your question, no, I don't know if it exists outside the Marvel Universe, and yes, I really really really hope it does too. Also, yes, it showed up in our first issue #2! Geez! Doreen could've been smooching for *literally months.*

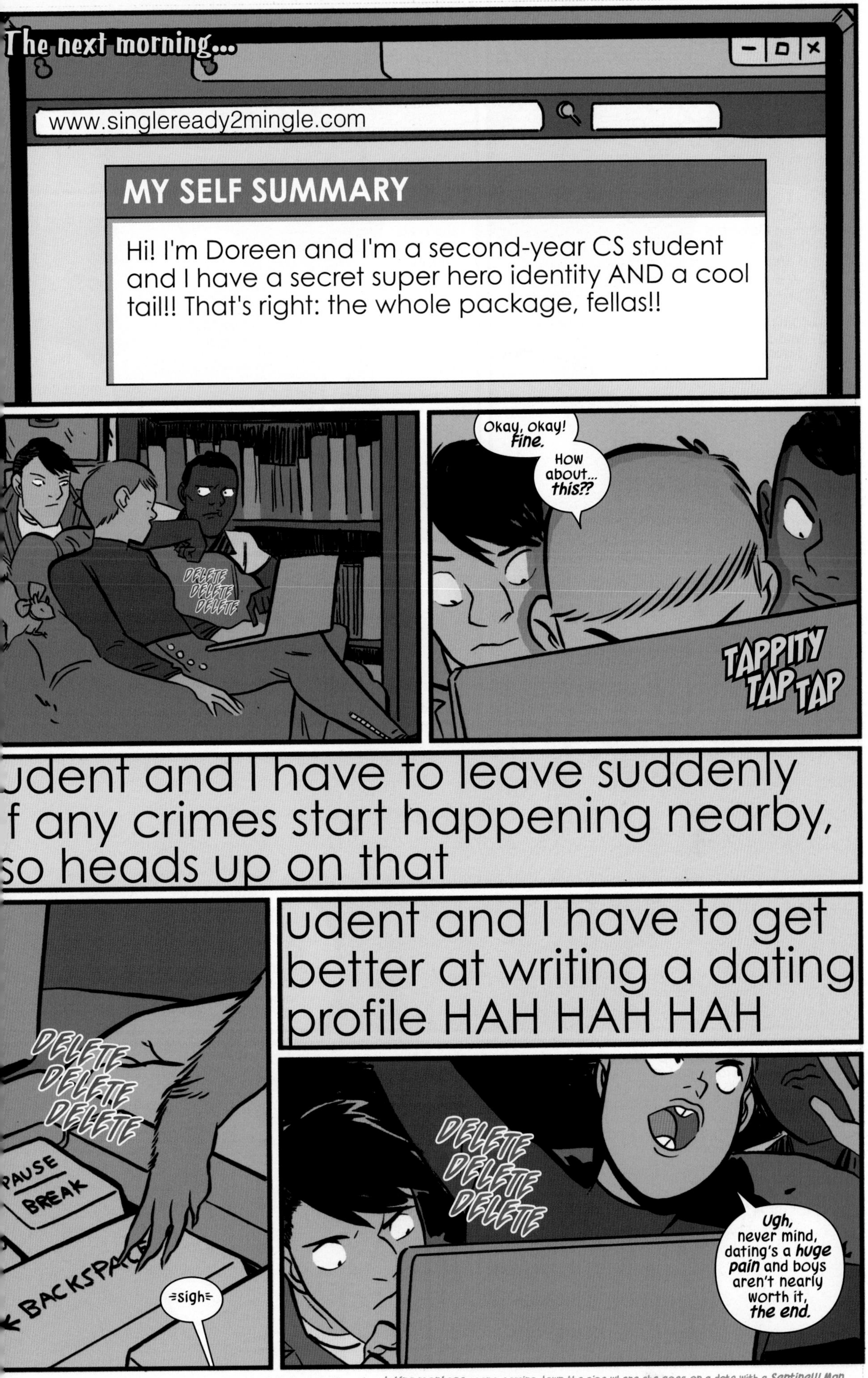
The next morning...
www.singleready2mingle.com
MY SELF SUMMARY
Hi! I'm Doreen and I'm a second-year CS student and I have a secret super hero identity AND a cool tail!! That's right: the whole package, fellas!!
DELETE DELETE DELETE
Okay, okay! Fine.
How about... this??
TAPPITY TAP TAP
udent and I have to leave suddenly f any crimes start happening nearby, so heads up on that
udent and I have to get better at writing a dating profile HAH HAH HAH
DELETE DELETE DELETE
PAUSE BREAK
BACKSPACE
=sigh=
DELETE DELETE DELETE
Ugh, never mind, dating's a huge pain and boys aren't nearly worth it, the end.

Doreen's kidding: there's still way more story! In fact, we've actually got a *dating montage* scene coming down the pipe where she goes on a date with a *Sentinel!! Man.* We probably should've shouted about that on the cover instead of burying it here in tiny text hidden halfway through the book, huh? Oh well, live and learn!

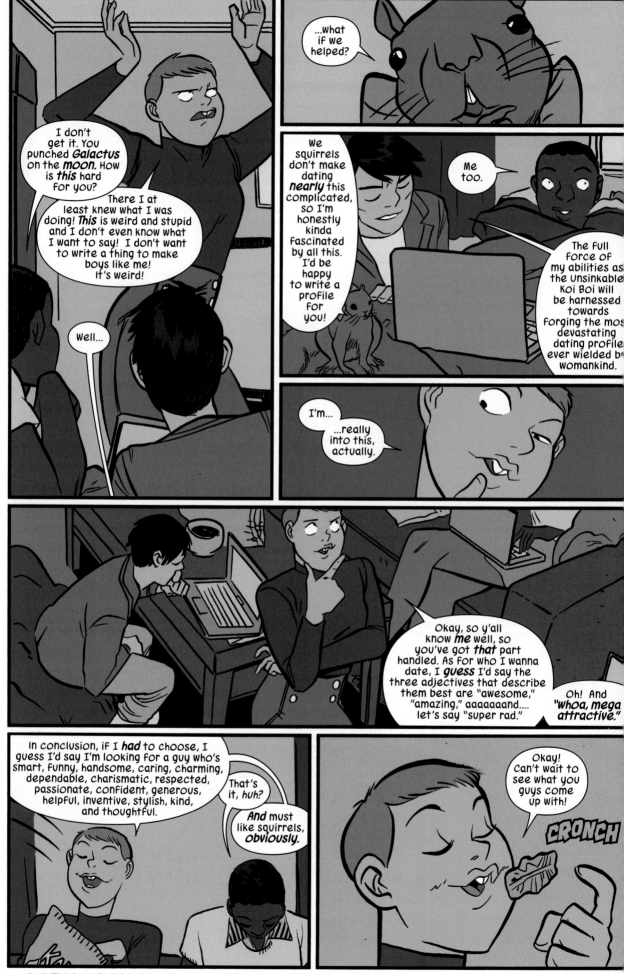

...what if we helped?

I don't get it. You punched *Galactus* on the *moon*. How is *this* hard for you?

There I at least knew what I was doing! *This* is weird and stupid and I don't even know what I want to say! I don't want to write a thing to make boys like me! It's weird!

Well...

We squirrels don't make dating *nearly* this complicated, so I'm honestly kinda fascinated by all this. I'd be happy to write a profile for you!

Me too.

The full force of my abilities as the Unsinkable Koi Boi will be harnessed towards forging the most devastating dating profile ever wielded by womankind.

I'm... ...really into this, actually.

Okay, so y'all know *me* well, so you've got *that* part handled. As for who I wanna date, I *guess* I'd say the three adjectives that describe them best are "awesome," "amazing," aaaaaaand.... let's say "super rad."

Oh! And *"whoa, mega attractive."*

In conclusion, if I *had* to choose, I guess I'd say I'm looking for a guy who's smart, funny, handsome, caring, charming, dependable, charismatic, respected, passionate, confident, generous, helpful, inventive, stylish, kind, and thoughtful.

That's it, *huh?*

And must like squirrels, *obviously.*

Okay! Can't wait to see what you guys come up with!

CRONCH

Look, it's not complicated. All I'm looking for are boys who like squirrels who like girls who like squirrels who like boys who like girls who like squirrels who like boys.

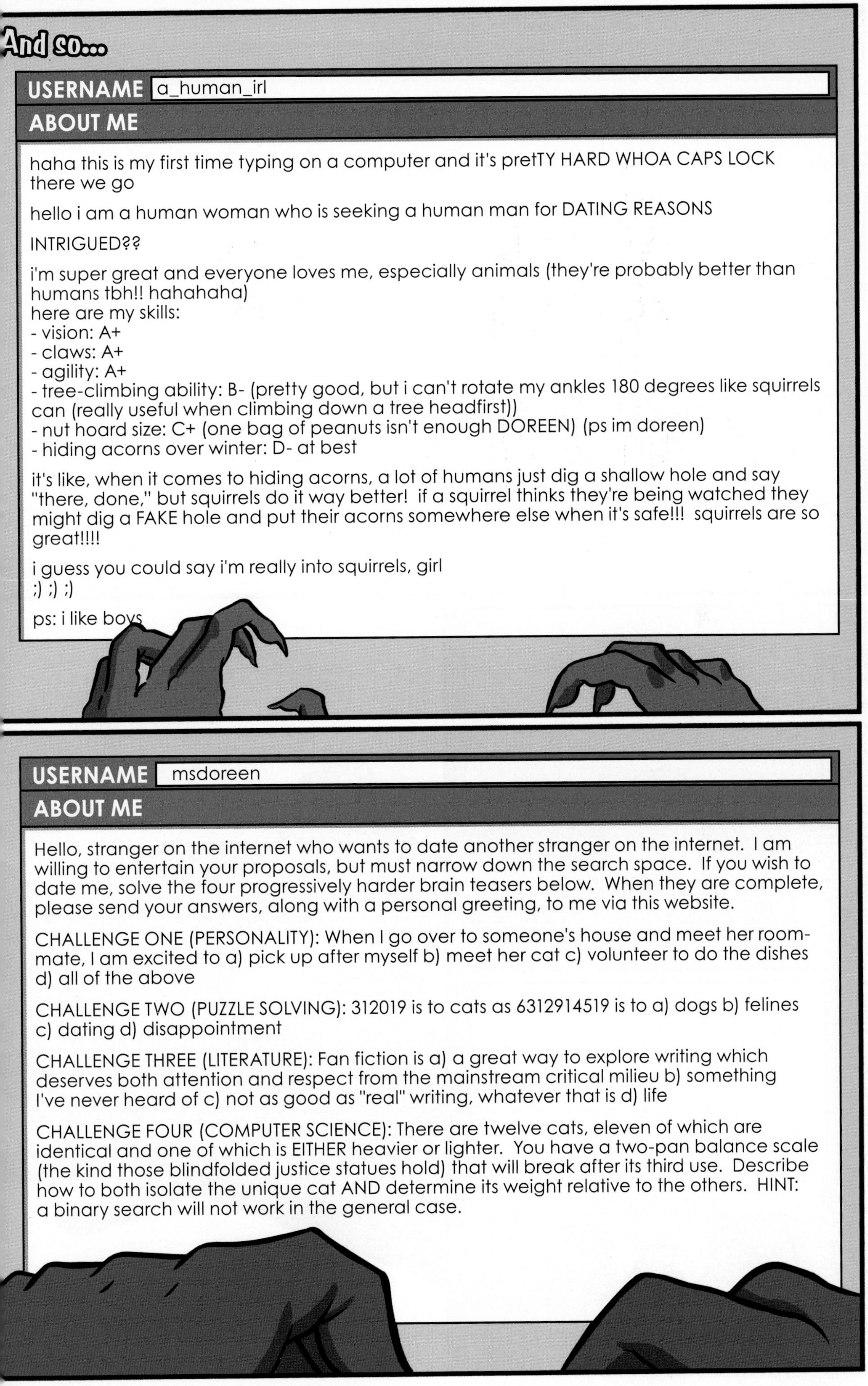
And so...
USERNAME a_human_irl
ABOUT ME
haha this is my first time typing on a computer and it's pretTY HARD WHOA CAPS LOCK there we go
hello i am a human woman who is seeking a human man for DATING REASONS
INTRIGUED??
i'm super great and everyone loves me, especially animals (they're probably better than humans tbh!! hahahaha)
here are my skills:
- vision: A+
- claws: A+
- agility: A+
- tree-climbing ability: B- (pretty good, but i can't rotate my ankles 180 degrees like squirrels can (really useful when climbing down a tree headfirst))
- nut hoard size: C+ (one bag of peanuts isn't enough DOREEN) (ps im doreen)
- hiding acorns over winter: D- at best
it's like, when it comes to hiding acorns, a lot of humans just dig a shallow hole and say "there, done," but squirrels do it way better! if a squirrel thinks they're being watched they might dig a FAKE hole and put their acorns somewhere else when it's safe!!! squirrels are so great!!!!
i guess you could say i'm really into squirrels, girl
;) ;) ;)
ps: i like boys
USERNAME msdoreen
ABOUT ME
Hello, stranger on the internet who wants to date another stranger on the internet. I am willing to entertain your proposals, but must narrow down the search space. If you wish to date me, solve the four progressively harder brain teasers below. When they are complete, please send your answers, along with a personal greeting, to me via this website.
CHALLENGE ONE (PERSONALITY): When I go over to someone's house and meet her roommate, I am excited to a) pick up after myself b) meet her cat c) volunteer to do the dishes d) all of the above
CHALLENGE TWO (PUZZLE SOLVING): 312019 is to cats as 6312914519 is to a) dogs b) felines c) dating d) disappointment
CHALLENGE THREE (LITERATURE): Fan fiction is a) a great way to explore writing which deserves both attention and respect from the mainstream critical milieu b) something I've never heard of c) not as good as "real" writing, whatever that is d) life
CHALLENGE FOUR (COMPUTER SCIENCE): There are twelve cats, eleven of which are identical and one of which is EITHER heavier or lighter. You have a two-pan balance scale (the kind those blindfolded justice statues hold) that will break after its third use. Describe how to both isolate the unique cat AND determine its weight relative to the others. HINT: a binary search will not work in the general case.

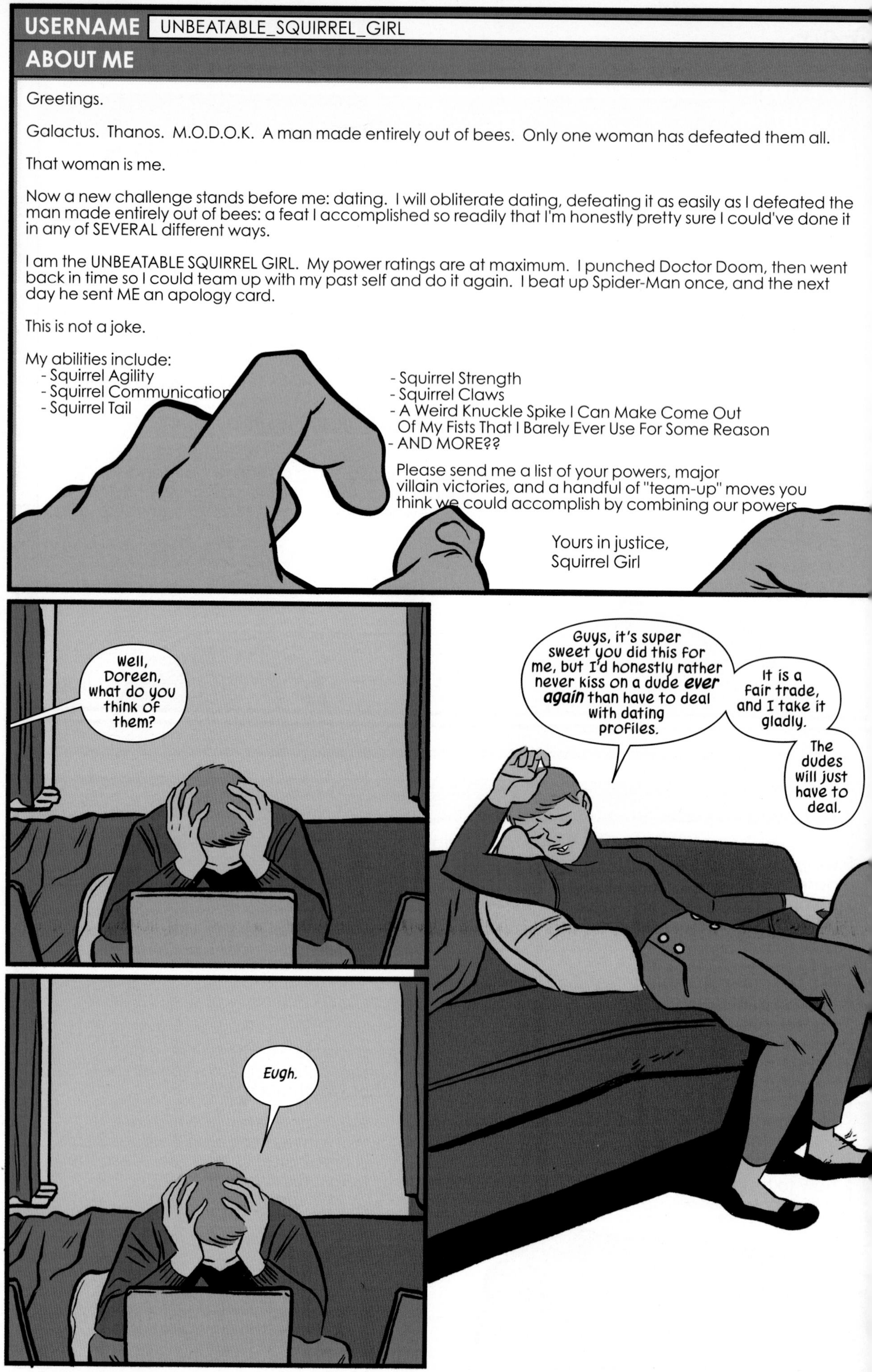
USERNAME UNBEATABLE_SQUIRREL_GIRL
ABOUT ME
Greetings.
Galactus. Thanos. M.O.D.O.K. A man made entirely out of bees. Only one woman has defeated them all.
That woman is me.
Now a new challenge stands before me: dating. I will obliterate dating, defeating it as easily as I defeated the man made entirely out of bees: a feat I accomplished so readily that I'm honestly pretty sure I could've done it in any of SEVERAL different ways.
I am the UNBEATABLE SQUIRREL GIRL. My power ratings are at maximum. I punched Doctor Doom, then went back in time so I could team up with my past self and do it again. I beat up Spider-Man once, and the next day he sent ME an apology card.
This is not a joke.
My abilities include:
- Squirrel Agility
- Squirrel Communication
- Squirrel Tail
- Squirrel Strength
- Squirrel Claws
- A Weird Knuckle Spike I Can Make Come Out Of My Fists That I Barely Ever Use For Some Reason
- AND MORE??
Please send me a list of your powers, major villain victories, and a handful of "team-up" moves you think we could accomplish by combining our powers.
Yours in justice,
Squirrel Girl
Well, Doreen, what do you think of them?
Eugh.
Guys, it's super sweet you did this for me, but I'd honestly rather never kiss on a dude *ever again* than have to deal with dating profiles.
It is a fair trade, and I take it gladly.
The dudes will just have to deal.

Somewhere, in the middle of the night, the dudes are suddenly sitting up in bed, drenched in sweat. *"Oh no I can't deal with this,"* the dudes are whispering.

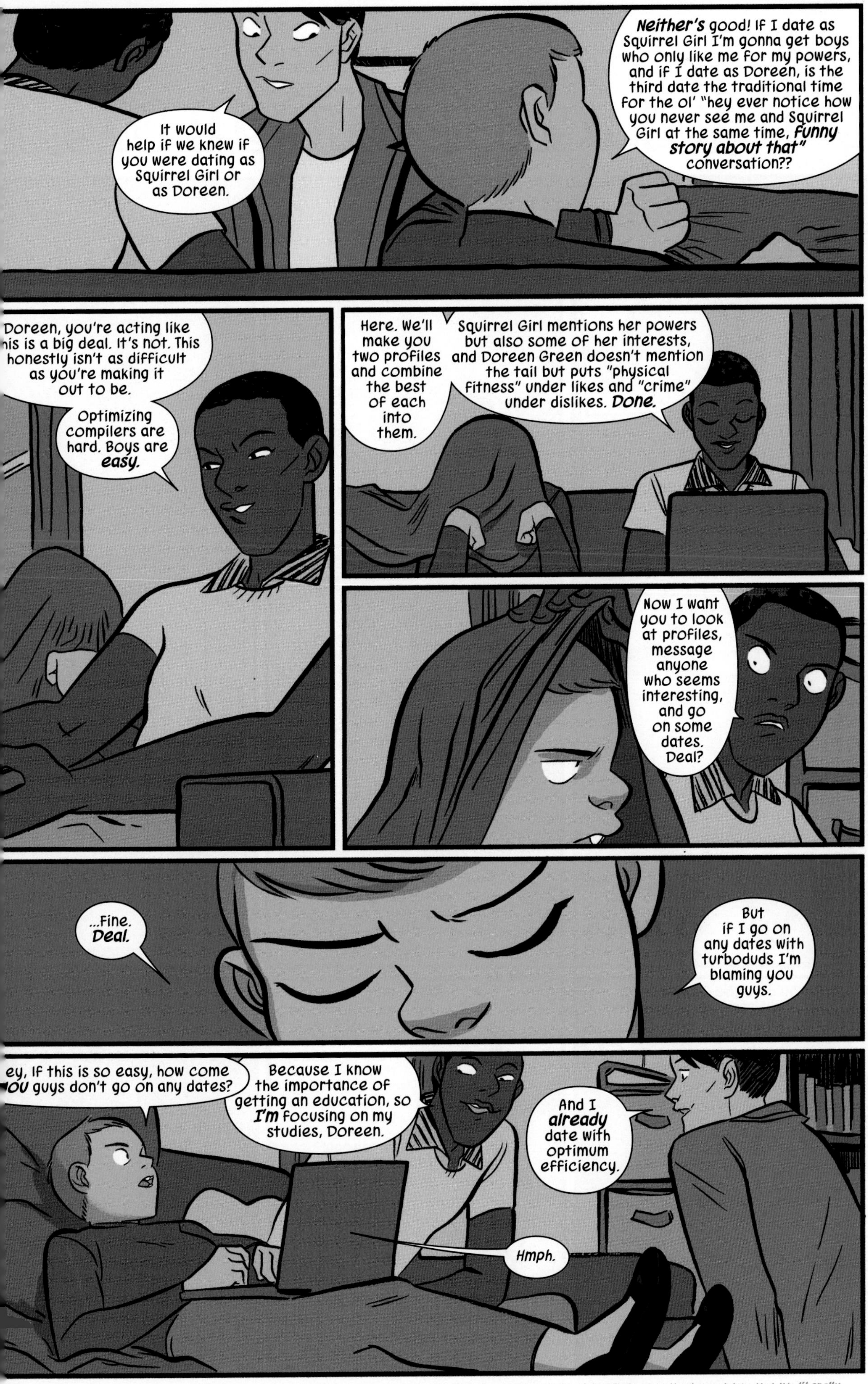
It would help if we knew if you were dating as Squirrel Girl or as Doreen.
Neither's good! If I date as Squirrel Girl I'm gonna get boys who only like me for my powers, and if I date as Doreen, is the third date the traditional time for the ol' "hey ever notice how you never see me and Squirrel Girl at the same time, funny story about that" conversation??
Doreen, you're acting like nis is a big deal. It's not. This honestly isn't as difficult as you're making it out to be.
Optimizing compilers are hard. Boys are easy.
Here. We'll make you two profiles and combine the best of each into them.
Squirrel Girl mentions her powers but also some of her interests, and Doreen Green doesn't mention the tail but puts "physical fitness" under likes and "crime" under dislikes. Done.
Now I want you to look at profiles, message anyone who seems interesting, and go on some dates. Deal?
...Fine. Deal.
But if I go on any dates with turboduds I'm blaming you guys.
ey, if this is so easy, how come OU guys don't go on any dates?
Because I know the importance of getting an education, so I'm focusing on my studies, Doreen.
And I already date with optimum efficiency.
Hmph.

To be fair to boys, optimizing compilers *are* super hard. Some of the problems involved have been proven undecidable! That means they're so tricky that it's *literally impossible* to come up with a single algorithm that will always produce a correct yes or no answer. That's a hard problem, yo! Also, an extremely fascinating one!

And then Doreen went

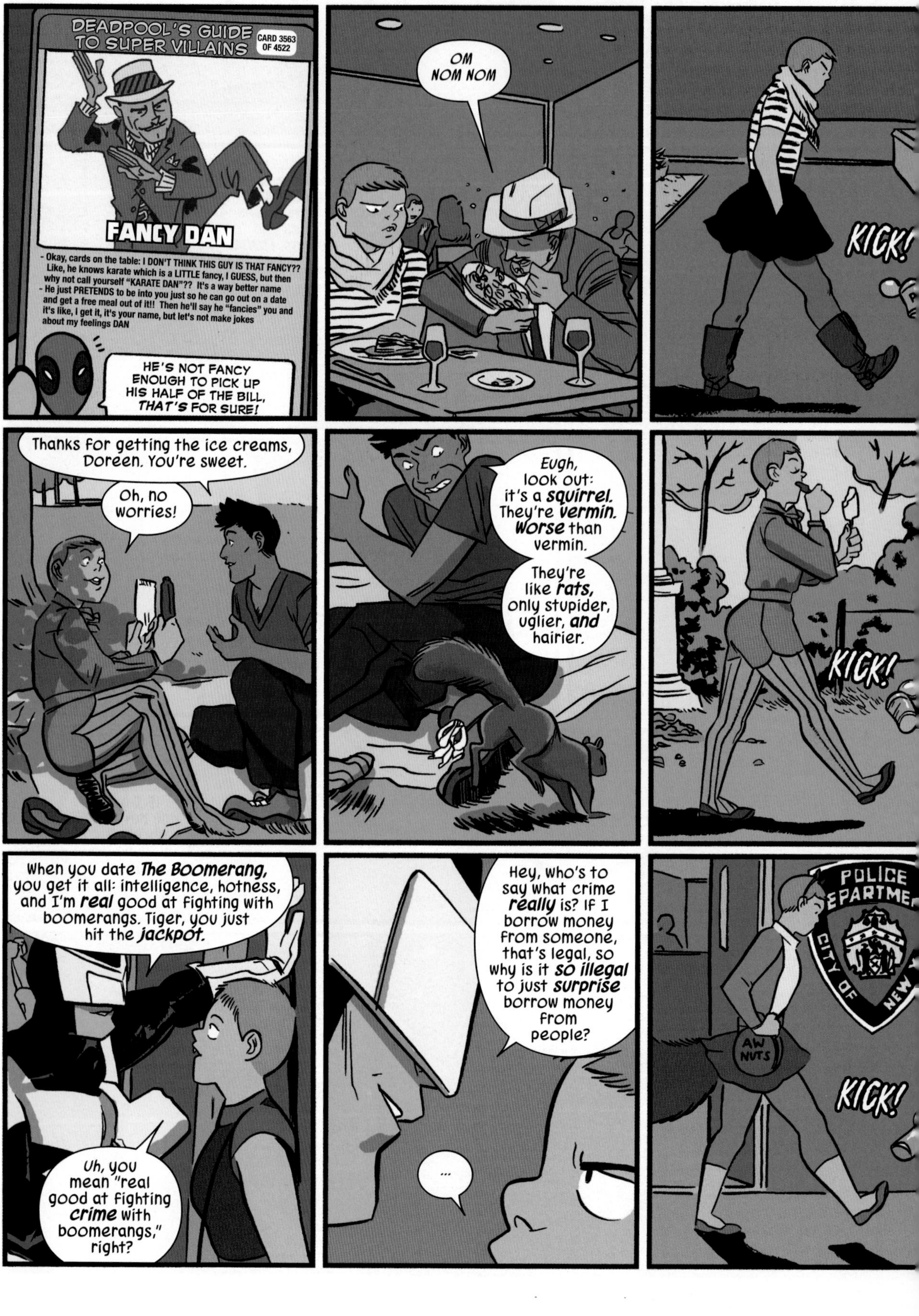

DEADPOOL'S GUIDE TO SUPER VILLAINS
CARD 3563 OF 4522
FANCY DAN
- Okay, cards on the table: I DON'T THINK THIS GUY IS THAT FANCY?? Like, he knows karate which is a LITTLE fancy, I GUESS, but then why not call yourself "KARATE DAN"?? It's a way better name
- He just PRETENDS to be into you just so he can go out on a date and get a free meal out of it!! Then he'll say he "fancies" you and it's like, I get it, it's your name, but let's not make jokes about my feelings DAN
HE'S NOT FANCY ENOUGH TO PICK UP HIS HALF OF THE BILL, THAT'S FOR SURE!
OM NOM NOM
KICK!
Thanks for getting the ice creams, Doreen. You're sweet.
Oh, no worries!
Eugh, look out: it's a squirrel. They're vermin. Worse than vermin.
They're like rats, only stupider, uglier, and hairier.
KICK!
When you date The Boomerang, you get it all: intelligence, hotness, and I'm real good at fighting with boomerangs. Tiger, you just hit the jackpot.
Uh, you mean "real good at fighting crime with boomerangs," right?
Hey, who's to say what crime really is? If I borrow money from someone, that's legal, so why is it so illegal to just surprise borrow money from people?
...
POLICE DEPARTME
CITY OF NEW
AW NUTS
KICK!

on a bunch of dates.

Whoa whoa whoa! **My soup came hot enough--** what are you doing?!

Doin' what Human Torches do best: *Bringing the heat, baby! Flame on!!*

Oh. Smoke detector.

...Riiiiiight.

KICK!

I've always believed what Mandela said: that real courage isn't the *absence* of fear, but rather our triumph *over* it.

Right?!

Heh. Truth is, there *is* one thing I'm afraid of, though: *squirrels. Total* phobia, I know, but I'm fine as long as I avoid them entirely! *Forever.*

Oof. So close, Steve.

KICK!

I'm sorry, Sentinel #X-42903-22, but I can't date anyone who hates and fears mutants.

BUT THAT IS WHAT I WAS PROGRAMMED TO DO. IT IS MY PURPOSE.

KA-BOOM!

WHY WAS I ALSO PROGRAMMED...TO FEEL HEARTBREAK??

Called it.

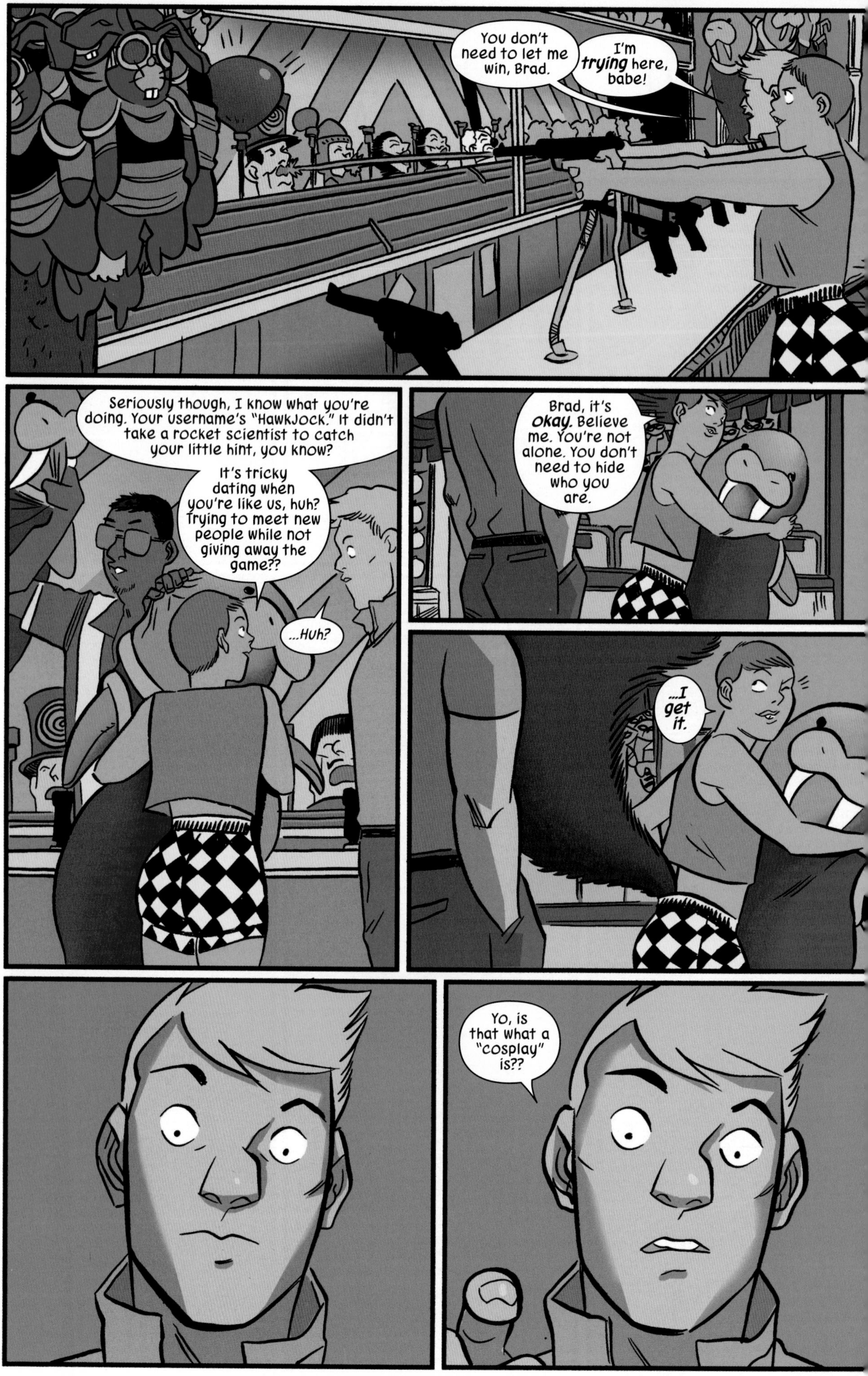
You don't need to let me win, Brad.
I'm trying here, babe!
Seriously though, I know what you're doing. Your username's "HawkJock." It didn't take a rocket scientist to catch your little hint, you know?
It's tricky dating when you're like us, huh? Trying to meet new people while not giving away the game??
...Huh?
Brad, it's okay. Believe me. You're not alone. You don't need to hide who you are.
...I get it.
Yo, is that what a "cosplay" is??

Is that a cosplay? Hey, how many cosplays did it take to make that?? Wow, it sure looks like it cost a lot of cosplays.

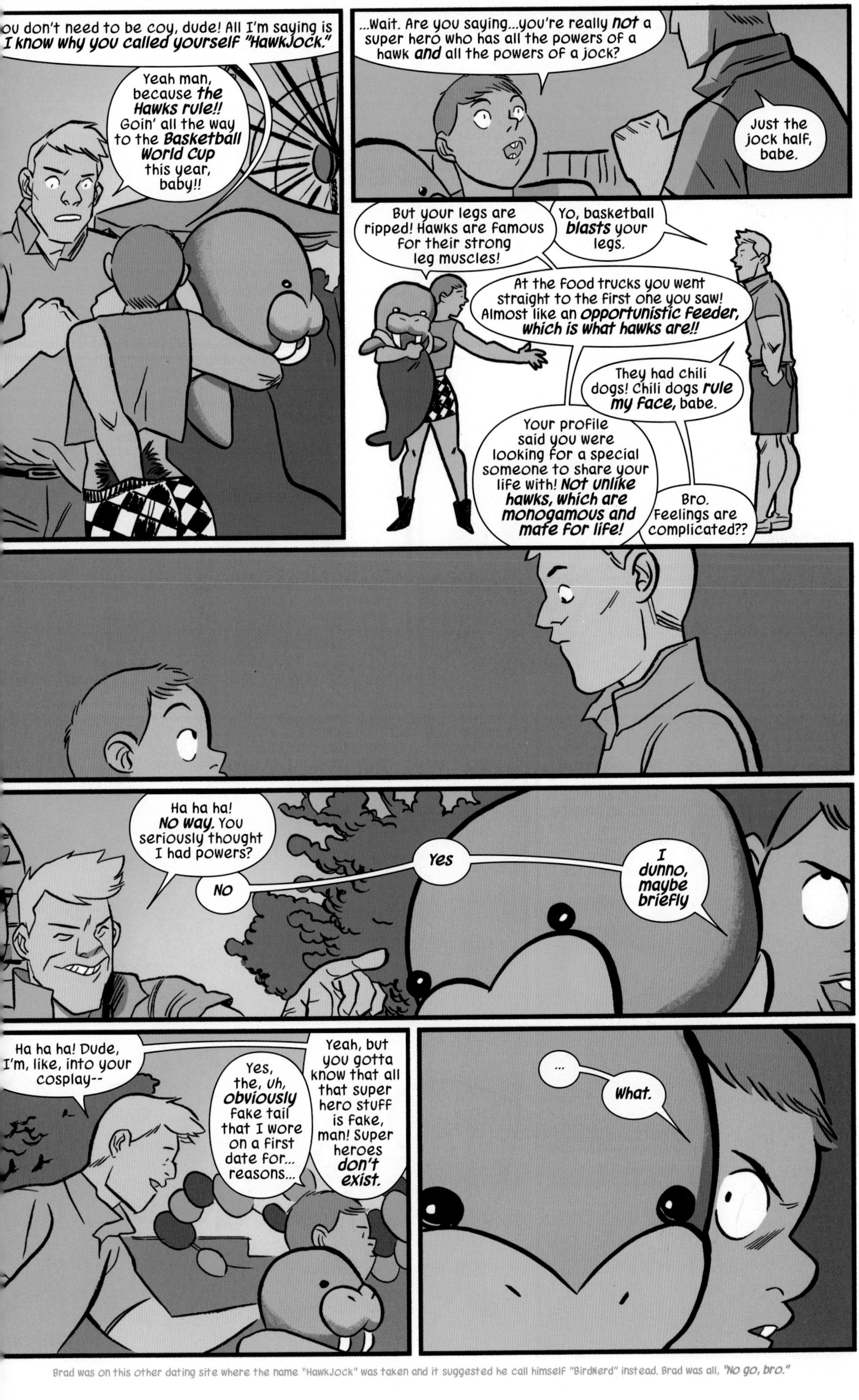
ou don't need to be coy, dude! All I'm saying is I know why you called yourself "HawkJock."
Yeah man, because the Hawks rule!! Goin' all the way to the Basketball World Cup this year, baby!!
...Wait. Are you saying...you're really not a super hero who has all the powers of a hawk and all the powers of a jock?
Just the jock half, babe.
But your legs are ripped! Hawks are famous for their strong leg muscles!
Yo, basketball blasts your legs.
At the food trucks you went straight to the first one you saw! Almost like an opportunistic feeder, which is what hawks are!!
They had chili dogs! Chili dogs rule my face, babe.
Your profile said you were looking for a special someone to share your life with! Not unlike hawks, which are monogamous and mate for life!
Bro. Feelings are complicated??
Ha ha ha! No way. You seriously thought I had powers?
NO
Yes
I dunno, maybe briefly
Ha ha ha! Dude, I'm, like, into your cosplay--
Yes, the, uh, obviously fake tail that I wore on a first date for... reasons...
Yeah, but you gotta know that all that super hero stuff is fake, man! Super heroes don't exist.
...
What.

Brad was on this other dating site where the name "HawkJock" was taken and it suggested he call himself "BirdNerd" instead. Brad was all, *"No go, bro."*

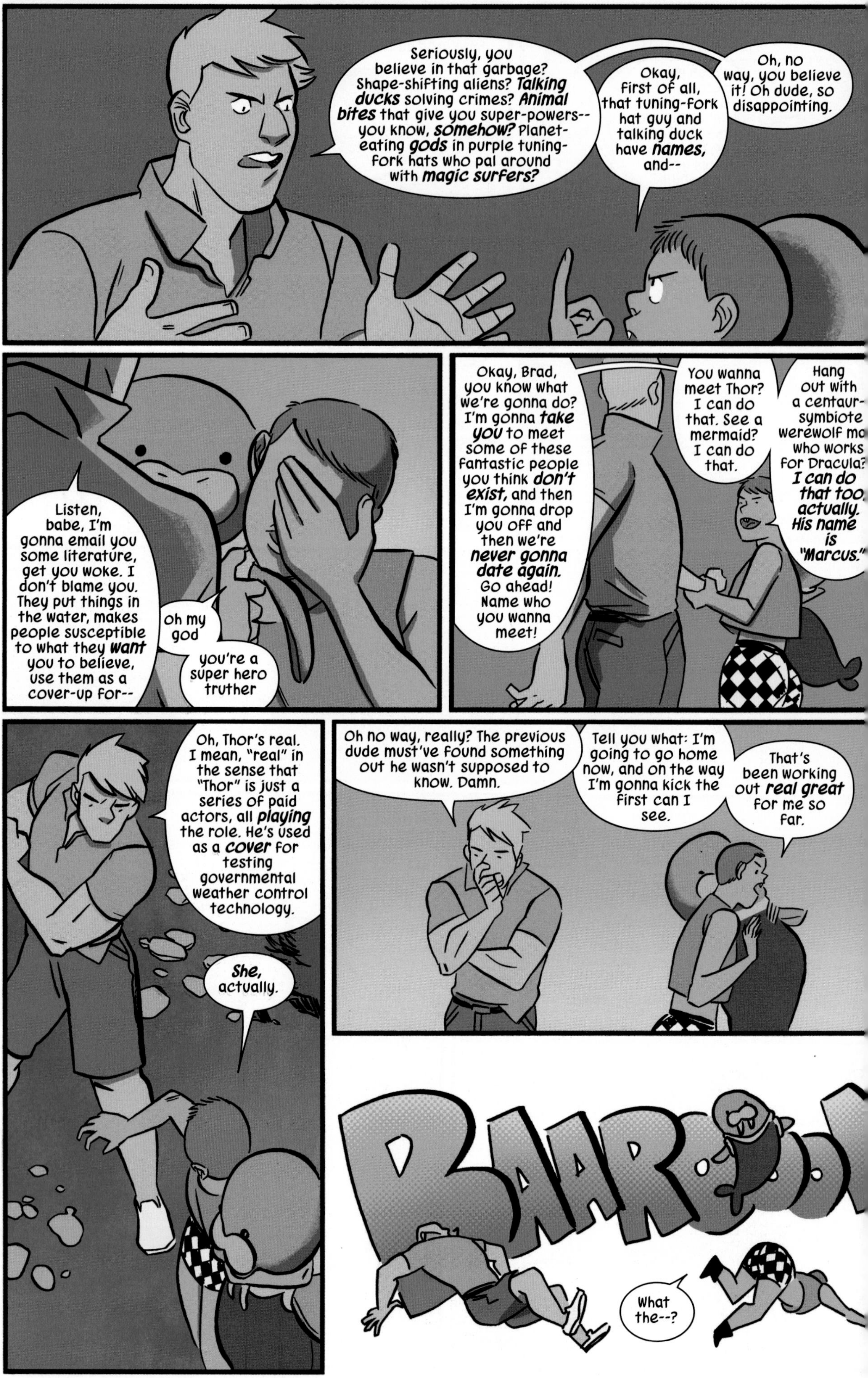
Seriously, you believe in that garbage? Shape-shifting aliens? Talking ducks solving crimes? Animal bites that give you super-powers--you know, somehow? Planet-eating gods in purple tuning-fork hats who pal around with magic surfers?
Okay, first of all, that tuning-fork hat guy and talking duck have names, and--
Oh, no way, you believe it! Oh dude, so disappointing.
Listen, babe, I'm gonna email you some literature, get you woke. I don't blame you. They put things in the water, makes people susceptible to what they want you to believe, use them as a cover-up for--
Oh my god
you're a super hero truther
Okay, Brad, you know what we're gonna do? I'm gonna take you to meet some of these fantastic people you think don't exist, and then I'm gonna drop you off and then we're never gonna date again. Go ahead! Name who you wanna meet!
You wanna meet Thor? I can do that. See a mermaid? I can do that.
Hang out with a centaur-symbiote werewolf man who works for Dracula? I can do that too, actually. His name is "Marcus."
Oh, Thor's real. I mean, "real" in the sense that "Thor" is just a series of paid actors, all playing the role. He's used as a cover for testing governmental weather control technology.
She, actually.
Oh no way, really? The previous dude must've found something out he wasn't supposed to know. Damn.
Tell you what: I'm going to go home now, and on the way I'm gonna kick the first can I see.
That's been working out real great for me so far.
What the--?

Marcus is a real guy, but sadly he's a bad guy - in the Marvel Universe, anyway! In the real world guys named Marcus are a thing too, and they're pretty chill, but sadly none of them have centaur-symbiote-werewolf powers. *Yet.*

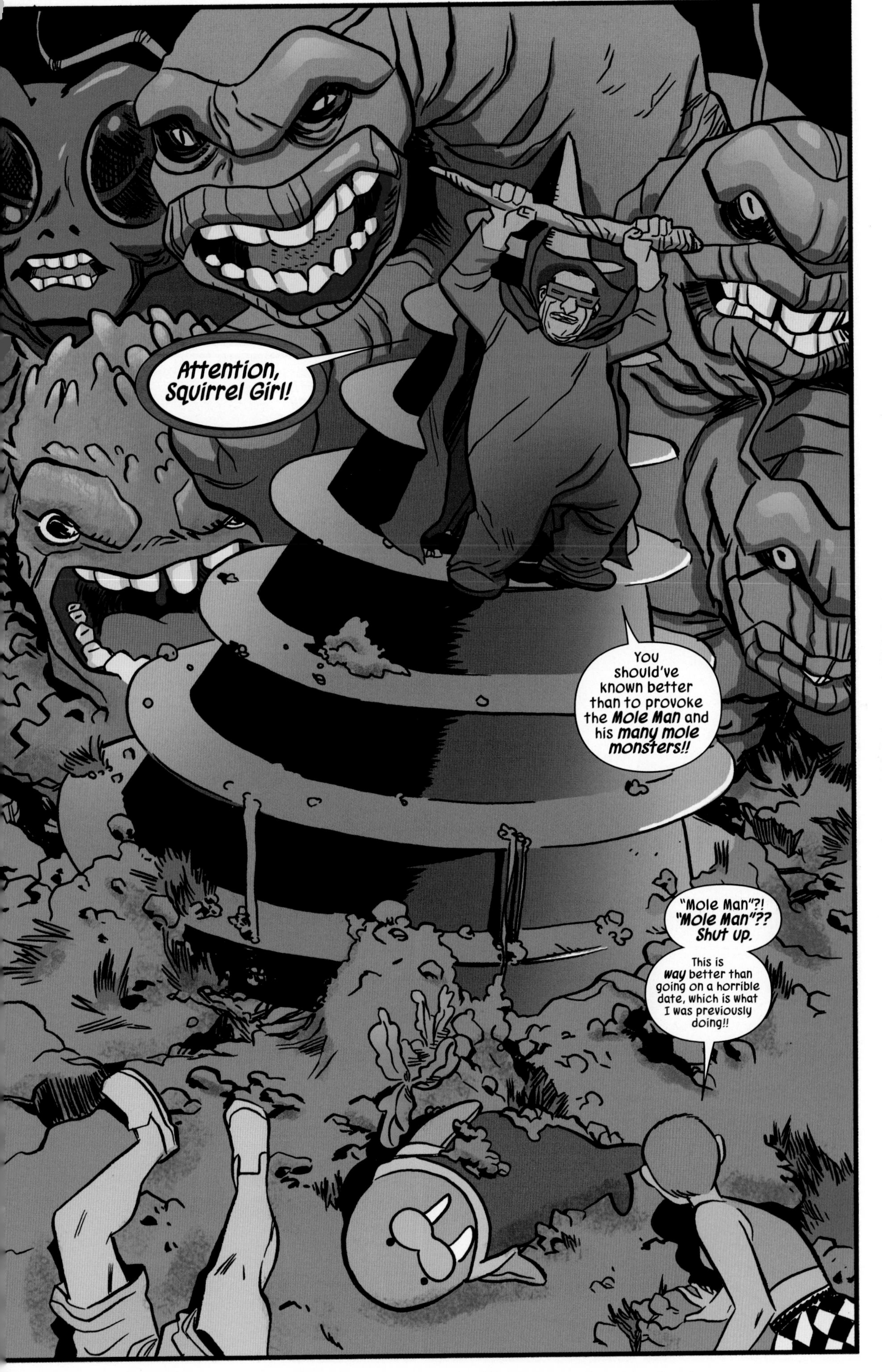
Attention, Squirrel Girl!
You should've known better than to provoke the Mole Man and his many mole monsters!!
"Mole Man"?! "Mole Man"?? Shut up.
This is way better than going on a horrible date, which is what I was previously doing!!

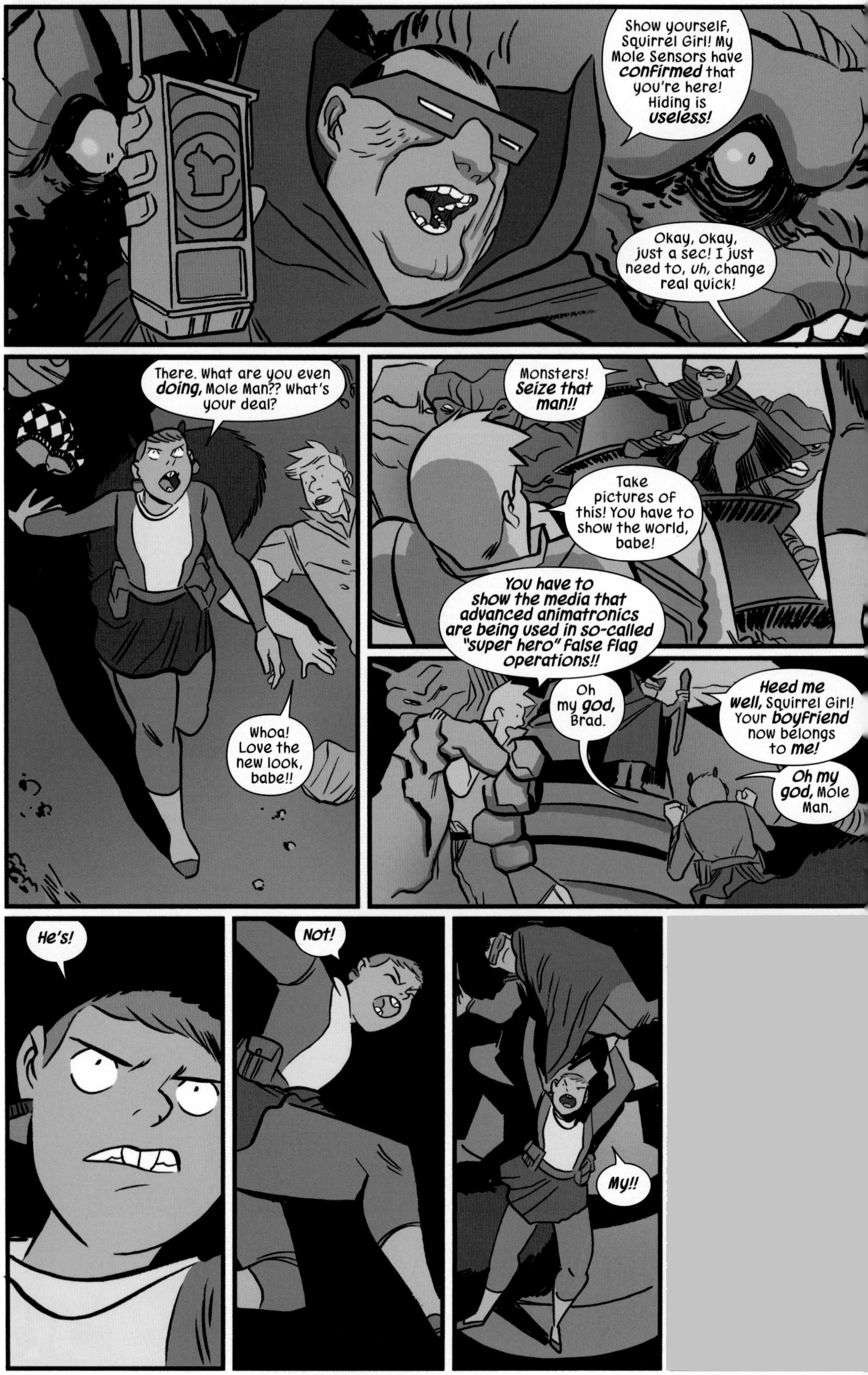
Show yourself, Squirrel Girl! My Mole Sensors have confirmed that you're here! Hiding is useless!
Okay, okay, just a sec! I just need to, uh, change real quick!
There. What are you even doing, Mole Man?? What's your deal?
Whoa! Love the new look, babe!!
Monsters! Seize that man!!
Take pictures of this! You have to show the world, babe!
You have to show the media that advanced animatronics are being used in so-called "super hero" false flag operations!!
Oh my god, Brad.
Heed me well, Squirrel Girl! Your boyfriend now belongs to me!
Oh my god, Mole Man.
He's!
Not!
My!!

I guess this fair really *is* foul, now that Mole Man's here, huh? And *yes*, that *was* a Shakespeare reference. We keep it *classy* here. Welcome to the tiny text beneath your Squirrel Girl comic, or as we call it: The Lounge.

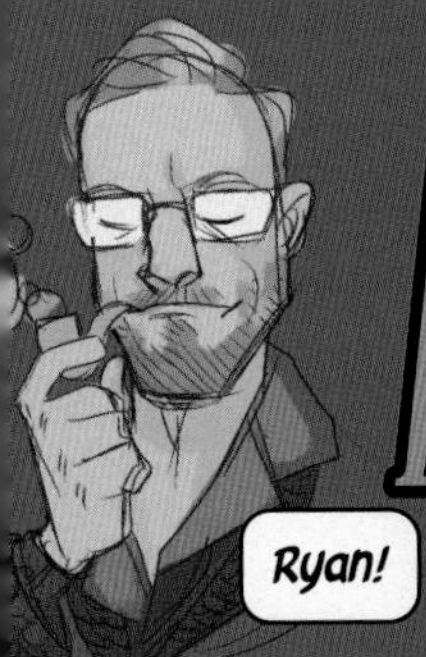
Ryan!

Letters From Nuts

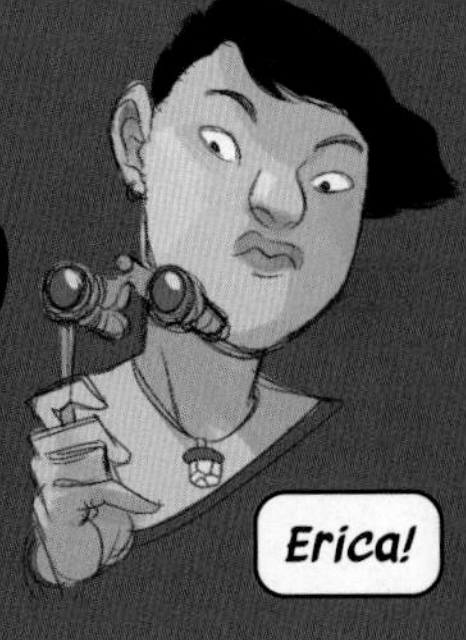
Erica!

Send letters to mheroes@marvel.com or 135 W 50th St, 7th Floor, New York, NY 10020 (Please mark "OKAY TO PRINT")

Howdy, Nut-heads.

Unbeatable Assistant Editor Charles Beacham here! :at a crazy issue, am I right? Poor Doreen. There's thing I miss less about college than the awkwardness dating...Now that I'm married I only have to feel bad out making ONE woman feel uncomfortable with my pid jokes.... Anyway, you're not here to listen to me. I want to hear from Ryan and Erica.

Dear Awesome Makers of Squirrel Girl,

I just want to say that I'm so in love with SQUIRREL RL!! The writing is hilarious, the artwork is amazing, and I e that she's badass, has a cool squirrel pal named Tippy-e and has a relatable personality and body type! Ahhh, just much love!! Hope you guys keep making this comic, it's the top of my reading list every month!

Love (and nuts!) from,
Brittany P.
Philadelphia, PA

P.S. I know that's a lot of exclamation points but you ys so deserve it!

RYAN: Haha, I'm not able to call anyone ELSE out overuse of exclamation marks! You are A-OK for em in my books, Brittany. Also you're A-OK in general,)! I don't know you THAT well, but I do know you have cellent taste in comics, so thanks!

ERICA: I'M GLAD YOU LIKE IT!!!!!!!!!!!!!!!

Hey y'all!

This past weekend I met Erica as the one and only reen Green! I love this comic so much, it's what actually t me into reading comics. Now I can't stop!

Thanks for being amazing!
Madeline Davis

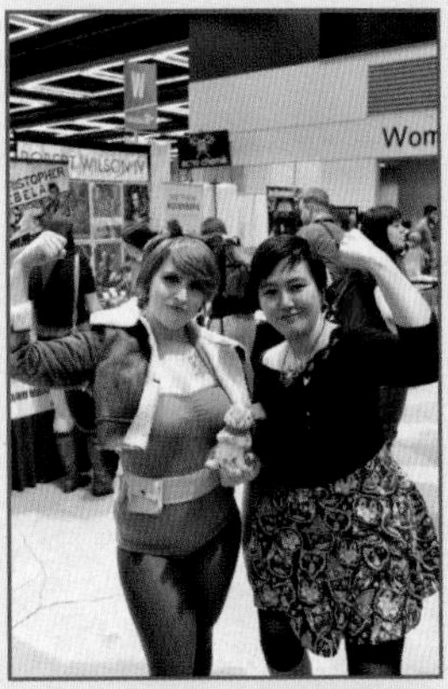

RYAN: Madeline, I am so jealous because GUESS HAT: I haven't been to a convention since we started aking this comic! I have never met a Squirrel Girl in al life. It's my goal to change that this year. This is an nazing picture. Also, I'm glad we could be your gateway to the not-inexpensive habit of comic books! Hooray!! S. Keep reading comics, they're amazing, I'm sorry we n't give them away for free but paper costs money.)

ERICA: Ryan, I highly recommend meeting more uirrel Girls. It is pretty boss. And your costume was IAZING, MADELINE! It was awesome meeting you in al life.

Dear Erica and Ryan,

I just finished issue #5, and as an 8th grade science teacher I was beyond excited for Squirrel Girl to bring up STEM when fighting Doom at the museum. I'm seriously going to incorporate acorns as part of my students' catapult project to honor her being a nerdy hero for us all. Would Tippy-Toe and Squirrel Girl be able to judge who makes the best design? I can share as needed because I realize making a real-life appearance to a classroom when you need to be fighting crime may be difficult.

P.S. I absolutely must see a picture of Tippy-Toe with her acorn dumbbell doing squats like a boss.

Lillian

RYAN: I like how you just slide "catapult project" into your letter like it isn't a big deal. Your students are doing a CATAPULT PROJECT. That's amazing! Building a trebuchet has been on my to-do list for YEARS. All this to say, if you send in pictures of your students' work, Doreen and Tippy will absolutely judge them!! THIS I CLAIM. Please send in pictures along with their maximum distance and airborne time (best of three trials) for sending an acorn into the sky. Please!!

ERICA: Man. I never got to make catapults in school. Where is this school? Why is it so much cooler than mine?

Ryan and Erica,

When I sent a note and said how much I liked the new costume, I totally didn't expect to get an origin story for said costume. Or, frankly, the Kra-Van which is not merely the best thing to happen to Kraven in Marvel continuity, but quite possibly the best thing to happen in Marvel continuity, period. Can we please get a Hot Wheels Kra-Van with a little lens in the back window that shows Erica's van mural in detail (for small values of detail)? Please!

USG remains the comic of record for 2016. My sincere admiration!

Regards,
Gary

RYAN: Right? I'd like to say the Kra-Van was the entire REASON for the crossover, but we didn't come up with it until later. I don't know who at Marvel is in charge of licensing (is it me? I, uh, haven't been doing my job at all, then), but WHOEVER IT IS: please make Kra-Van stuff. Also: Squirrel Girl stuff. Thank you, Gary!

ERICA: Also, after we've tracked down the marketing guy, can we look into getting custom painted denim jackets with the van art on the back? Also, to give credit, I drew the design but Joe Quinones is the one that painted it.

Dear Ryan & Erica,

This is Amanda and Scott (the squirrel and dinosaur researchers from original issues #5 and #8). We have been greatly enjoying Doreen's time-traveling adventures, although she hasn't traveled far enough back in time for one of our tastes. Anyway, we wanted to say hello and follow up on your request for an invitation to a friggin' cool party. On July 25th, you're invited to our wedding! Actually, everyone is invited (but we'll save you a special seat). We aren't much for tradition and are partnering with Nerd Nite Edmonton to turn our marital ceremony into an evening of scintillating science. Scott's paleontological senseis Dr. Robert Bakker and Prof. Philip Currie will give a talk on raptor courtship and tyrannosaur family values, and we will tell the story of our nerdy romance and adventures together. That means dinosaurs, love, interesting facts, and lots of squirrels!

Stay nuts and keep kicking buts!
Amanda Kelley and W. Scott Persons, IV

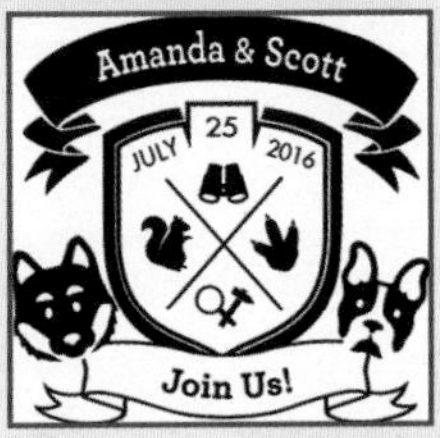
Amanda & Scott
JULY
25
2016
Join Us!

RYAN: Amanda and Scott, you just invited a WORLD of squirrel and/or dinosaur enthusiasts to your wedding. I hope you are prepared! And actually, this sounds amazing: a wedding that's also a SCIENCE LECTURE? About dinosaurs and squirrels? I would crash WAY more weddings if this were the case. In any case, thank you for this invitation, and while I can't RSVP just yet – I don't know if I'll be in Edmonton then – if I am, expect a very tall man to show up, attend your lectures, and eat all your food! And also to wish you all the best.

ERICA: Oh my God. Ryan, what do we have to do to find ourselves in Edmonton with a set of dress clothes that weekend? Maybe you'll see a tall man with his friend who is literally and exactly a foot shorter than him.

Hey, Ryan and Erica!

I was mad into SQUIRREL GIRL, a couple months back, until your first volume ended and I got kind sidetracked... But I just recently got back into it more than before AND I LOVE IT. The plan is to cosplay Squirrel-Earl in the near-future! :) Is there a chance Un-B S-G could go tri-monthly? Love you, folks!

EriK Town

RYAN: Haha! Thanks, Erik! Please send me all Squirrel Earl pics. I'll leave it to Erica to decide if we can put out an issue three times a month, since the art is the hard part of comics, but I feel reasonably sure there are absolutely no reasons why we couldn't go at LEAST quad-monthly, minimum. Right, Erica?

ERICA: Of course. Four monthly publications that are each 5 pages.

Well, that's all she wrote. Come back next month to see how Doreen deals with her new subterranean stalker!

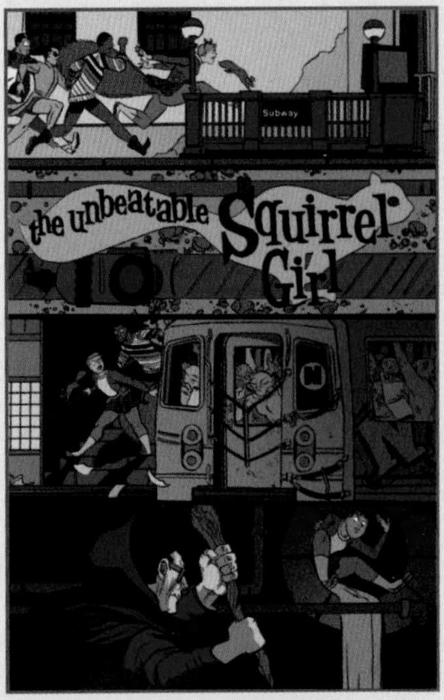
Subway
the unbeatable Squirrel Girl

ANSWER KEY TO NANCY'S CHALLENGES: 1) d, 2) b, 3) d, 4) A truly marvelous proof exists, but this margin is too narrow to contain it.

Attention, Squirrel Scouts! Make sure to check out our production blog, **unbeatablesquirrelgirl.tumblr.com**, where we post behind-the-scenes stuff on how the book gets made, along with all sorts of cool things *you* make: fanart, cosplay, whatever!

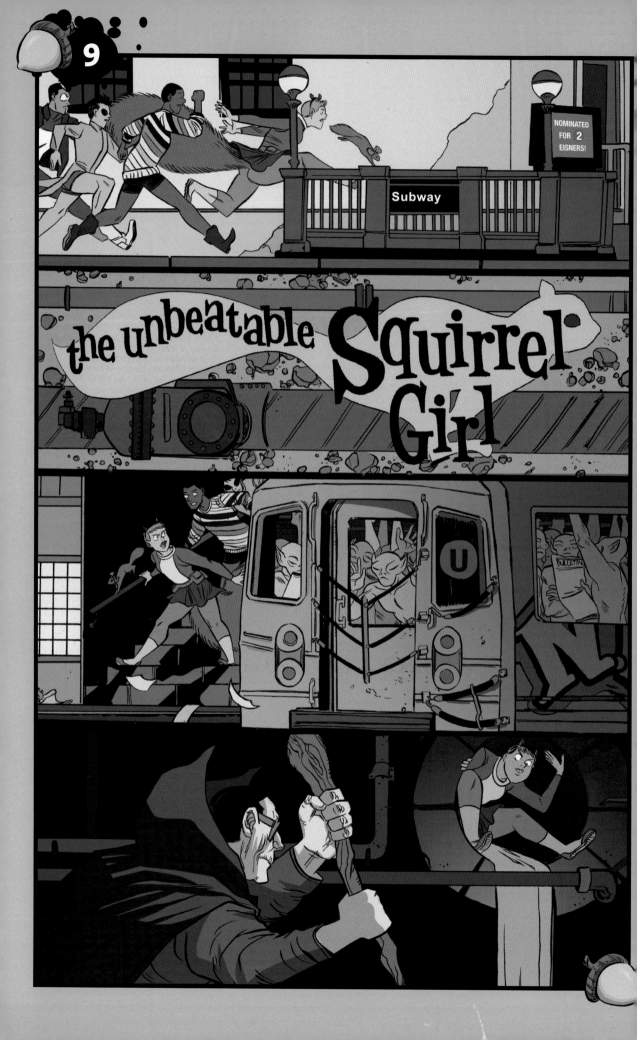

9

NOMINATED FOR 2 EISNERS!

Subway

the unbeatable Squirrel Girl

oreen Green isn't just a second-year computer science student: she secretly also has all the powers of both squirrel and
irl! She uses her amazing abilities to fight crime **and** be as awesome as possible. You know her as...*The Unbeatable Squirrel Girl!*
Find out what she's been up to, with...

Squirrel Girl *in a nutshell*

search! 🔍

#lookatthesizeofthatrock

#bigbenmorelikelittlebennow

#weisenheimer

#saucyhoyden

Squirrel Girl @unbeatablesg
Which bold, confident, attractive woman is going on an internet date tonight? THIS LADY
RIGHT HERE, PEACE OUT Y'ALL!!

Squirrel Girl @unbeatablesg
UPDATE, SEVERAL HOURS LATER: haha nevermind DATING IS THE WORST, THE END

xKravenTheHunterx @unshavenkraven
@unbeatablesg What is wrong, Girl of Squirrels?

Squirrel Girl @unbeatablesg
@unshavenkraven hahah where do i even begin?

Squirrel Girl @unbeatablesg
@unshavenkraven let's just say that my best date so far has been with a giant
Sentinel robot, and even THAT was awful

xKravenTheHunterx @unshavenkraven
@unbeatablesg I was not aware that Sentinels were programmed for dating.

Squirrel Girl @unbeatablesg
@unshavenkraven Kraven

Squirrel Girl @unbeatablesg
@unshavenkraven THEY'RE NOT

Squirrel Girl @unbeatablesg
@unshavenkraven IT'S THE WORST

Tony Stark @starkmantony ✓
@unbeatablesg Hey someone named "Brad" has sent me 7 separate emails claiming
you admitted that super heroes are a government conspiracy??

Tony Stark @starkmantony ✓
@unbeatablesg And that I'm part of it, and that, I quote, "THE FACTS WILL SPEAK
FOR THEMSELVES WHEN WILL YOUR LIES END DEMAND TRUTH NOW"?

Squirrel Girl @unbeatablesg
@starkmantony OH GOD, NEVER DATE BRAD, TONY

Squirrel Girl @unbeatablesg
@starkmantony NEVER DO IT

Tony Stark @starkmantony ✓
@starkmantony I...wasn't planning to

Squirrel Girl @unbeatablesg
@starkmantony HE'LL MAKE UP STORIES ABOUT YOU, PLUS HE DOESN'T HAVE THE
POWERS OF HAWK AND JOCK EVEN THO HE'S "HAWKJOCK" ON THE DATING SITE

Squirrel Girl @unbeatablesg
@starkmantony AND THEN MOLE MAN WILL SHOW UP FOR SOME REASON

Squirrel Girl @unbeatablesg
@starkmantony WHICH REMINDS ME, I SHOULD PROBABLY GET BACK TO THAT

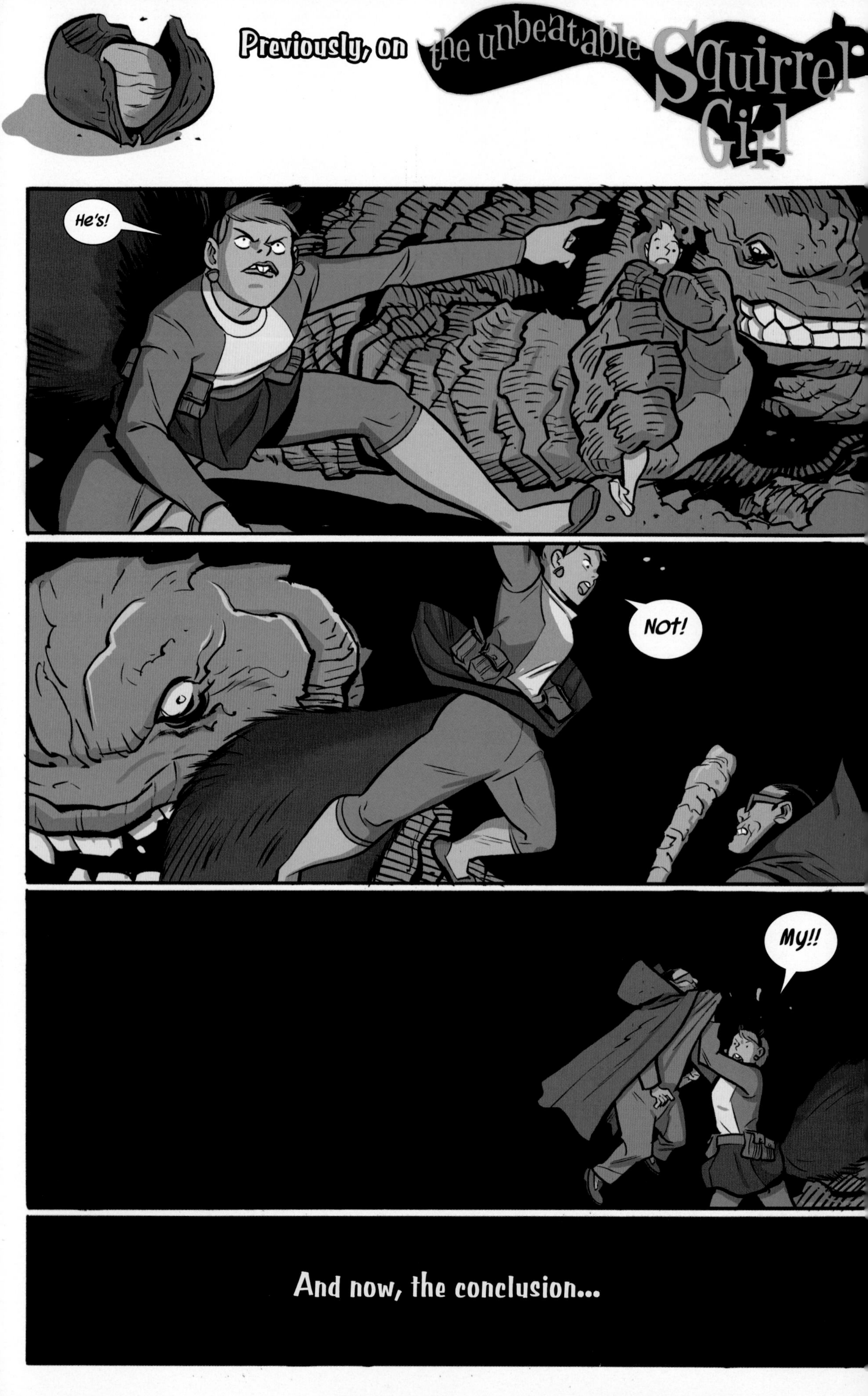
Previously, on the unbeatable Squirrel Girl
He's!
Not!
My!!
And now, the conclusion...

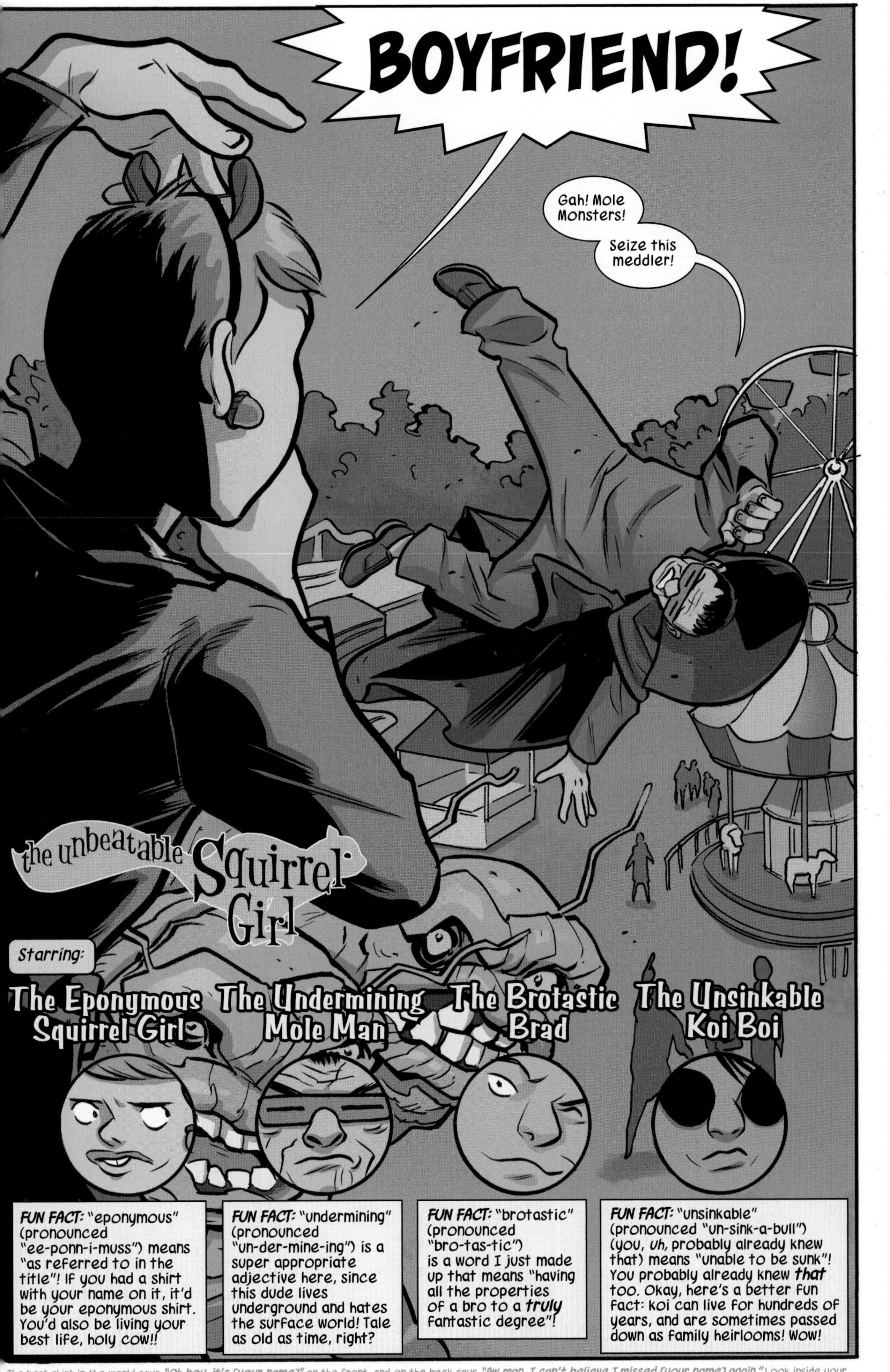
BOYFRIEND!
Gah! Mole Monsters!
Seize this meddler!
the unbeatable Squirrel Girl
Starring:
The Eponymous Squirrel Girl
The Undermining Mole Man
The Brotastic Brad
The Unsinkable Koi Boi
FUN FACT: "eponymous" (pronounced "ee-ponn-i-muss") means "as referred to in the title"! If you had a shirt with your name on it, it'd be your eponymous shirt. You'd also be living your best life, holy cow!!
FUN FACT: "undermining" (pronounced "un-der-mine-ing") is a super appropriate adjective here, since this dude lives underground and hates the surface world! Tale as old as time, right?
FUN FACT: "brotastic" (pronounced "bro-tas-tic") is a word I just made up that means "having all the properties of a bro to a *truly* fantastic degree"!
FUN FACT: "unsinkable" (pronounced "un-sink-a-bull") (you, *uh*, probably already knew that) means "unable to be sunk"! You probably already knew *that* too. Okay, here's a better fun fact: koi can live for hundreds of years, and are sometimes passed down as family heirlooms! WOW!

The best shirt in the world says *"Oh boy, it's [your name]"* on the front, and on the back says *"Aw man, I can't believe I missed [your name] again."* Look inside your heart; you know it's true!!

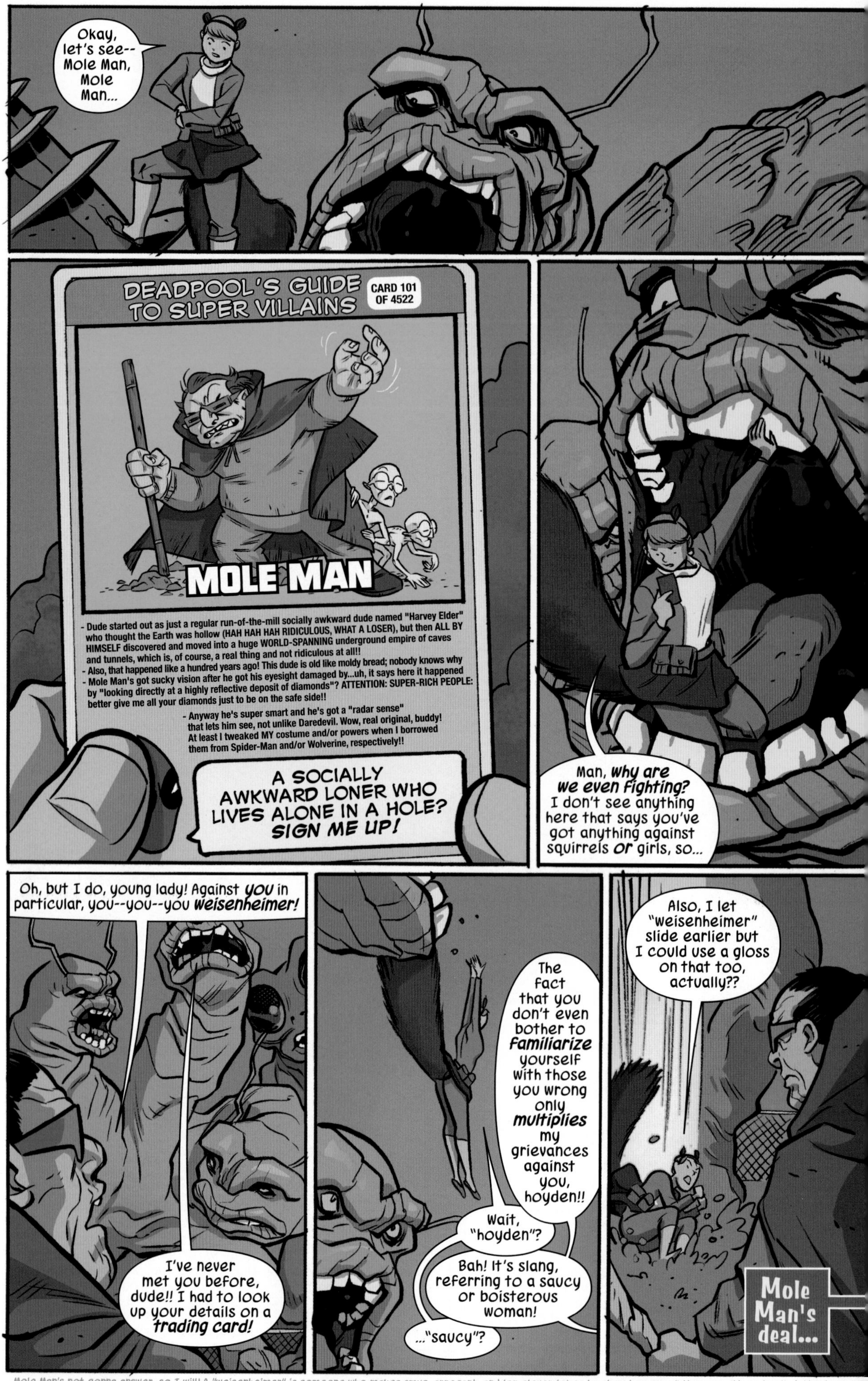

Okay, let's see-- Mole Man, Mole Man...
DEADPOOL'S GUIDE TO SUPER VILLAINS
CARD 101 OF 4522
MOLE MAN
- Dude started out as just a regular run-of-the-mill socially awkward dude named "Harvey Elder" who thought the Earth was hollow (HAH HAH HAH RIDICULOUS, WHAT A LOSER), but then ALL BY HIMSELF discovered and moved into a huge WORLD-SPANNING underground empire of caves and tunnels, which is, of course, a real thing and not ridiculous at all!!
- Also, that happened like a hundred years ago! This dude is old like moldy bread; nobody knows why
- Mole Man's got sucky vision after he got his eyesight damaged by...uh, it says here it happened by "looking directly at a highly reflective deposit of diamonds"? ATTENTION: SUPER-RICH PEOPLE: better give me all your diamonds just to be on the safe side!!
- Anyway he's super smart and he's got a "radar sense" that lets him see, not unlike Daredevil. Wow, real original, buddy! At least I tweaked MY costume and/or powers when I borrowed them from Spider-Man and/or Wolverine, respectively!!
A SOCIALLY AWKWARD LONER WHO LIVES ALONE IN A HOLE? SIGN ME UP!
Man, why are we even fighting? I don't see anything here that says you've got anything against squirrels or girls, so...
Oh, but I do, young lady! Against you in particular, you--you--you weisenheimer!
I've never met you before, dude!! I had to look up your details on a trading card!
The fact that you don't even bother to familiarize yourself with those you wrong only multiplies my grievances against you, hoyden!!
Wait, "hoyden"?
Bah! It's slang, referring to a saucy or boisterous woman!
..."saucy"?
Also, I let "weisenheimer" slide earlier but I could use a gloss on that too, actually??
Mole Man's deal...

Mole Man's not gonna answer, so I will! A "weisenheimer" is someone who makes smug, arrogant, and/or clever jokes to show how smart they are. It's an insult dating back to the early 1900s...***not unlike Mole Man himself??*** Zing! Look at me, I'm a regular saucy weisenheimer down here!

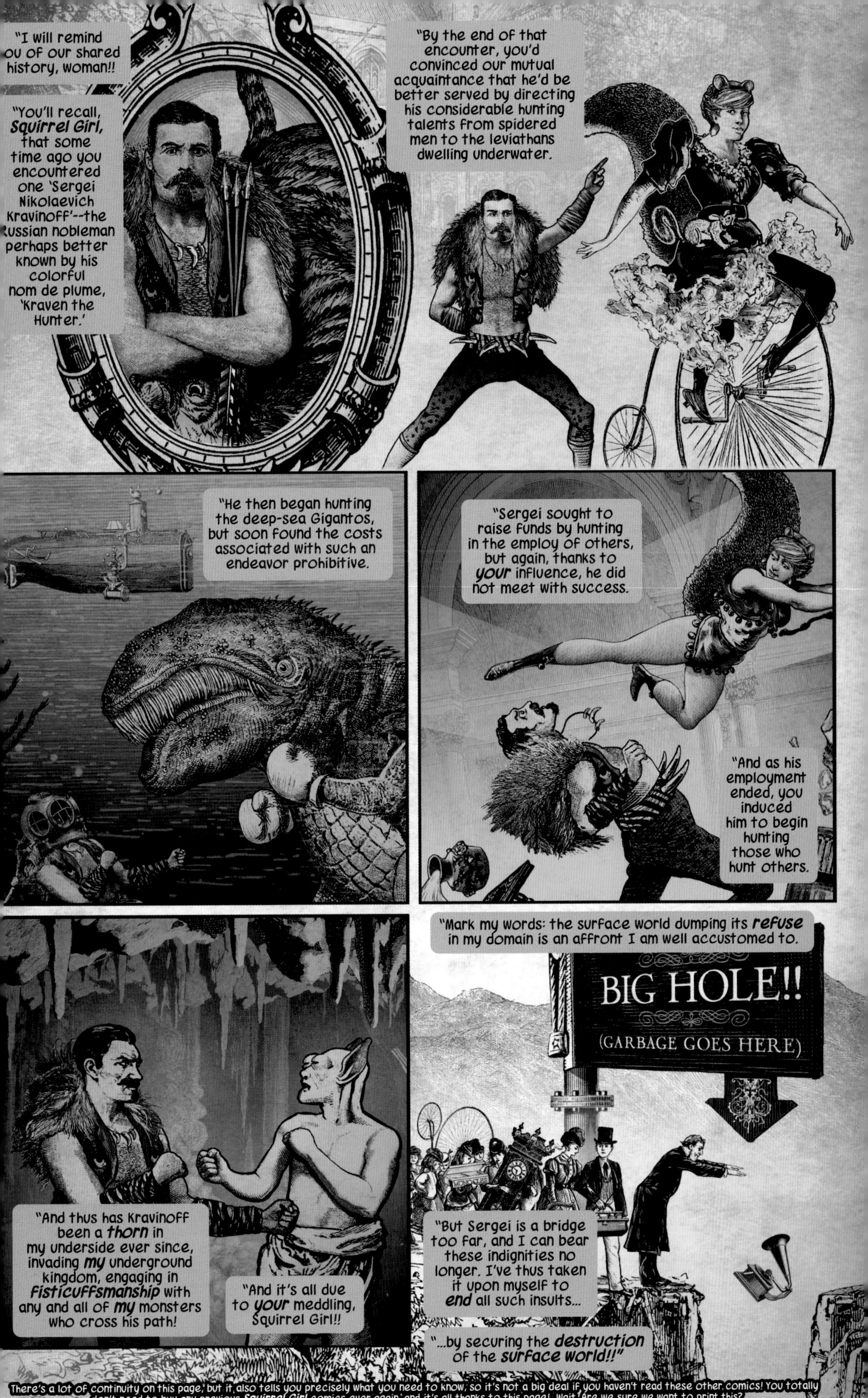
"I will remind ou of our shared history, woman!!
"You'll recall, *Squirrel Girl,* that some time ago you encountered one 'Sergei Nikolaevich Kravinoff'--the ussian nobleman perhaps better known by his colorful nom de plume, 'Kraven the Hunter.'
"By the end of that encounter, you'd convinced our mutual acquaintance that he'd be better served by directing his considerable hunting talents from spidered men to the leviathans dwelling underwater.
"He then began hunting the deep-sea Gigantos, but soon found the costs associated with such an endeavor prohibitive.
"Sergei sought to raise funds by hunting in the employ of others, but again, thanks to *your* influence, he did not meet with success.
"And as his employment ended, you induced him to begin hunting those who hunt others.
"And thus has Kravinoff been a *thorn* in my underside ever since, invading *my* underground kingdom, engaging in *fisticuffsmanship* with any and all of *my* monsters who cross his path!
"And it's all due to *your* meddling, Squirrel Girl!!
"Mark my words: the surface world dumping its *refuse* in my domain is an affront I am well accustomed to.
BIG HOLE!!
(GARBAGE GOES HERE)
"But Sergei is a bridge too far, and I can bear these indignities no longer. I've thus taken it upon myself to *end* all such insults...
"...by securing the *destruction* of the *surface world!!"*

There's a lot of continuity on this page, but it also tells you precisely what you need to know, so it's not a big deal if you haven't read these other comics! You totally don't need to buy any previous *Squirrel Girl* comics ever again, and it's all thanks to this page!...Wait. Are we sure we want to print this?

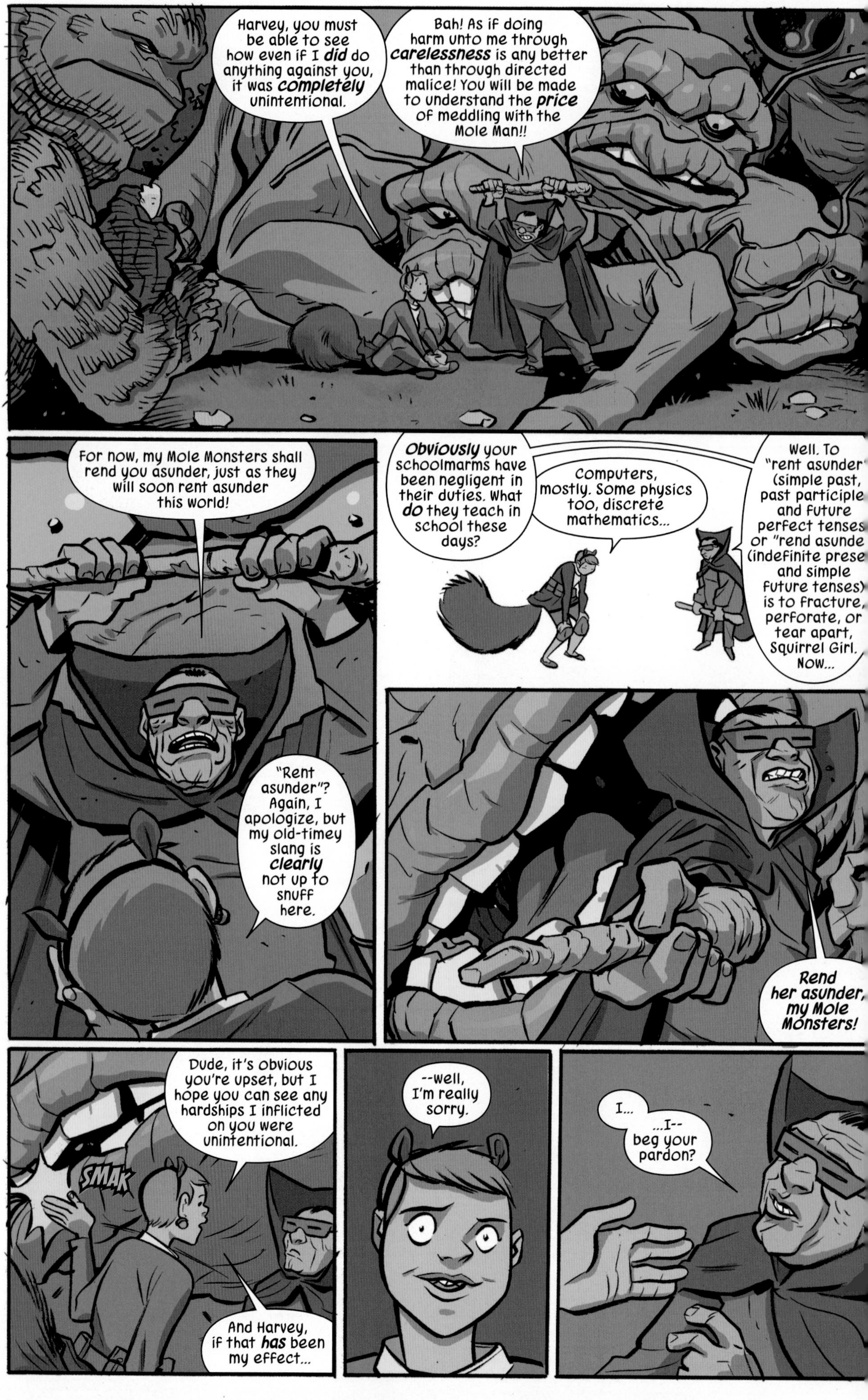
Harvey, you must be able to see how even if I did do anything against you, it was completely unintentional.
Bah! As if doing harm unto me through carelessness is any better than through directed malice! You will be made to understand the price of meddling with the Mole Man!!
For now, my Mole Monsters shall rend you asunder, just as they will soon rent asunder this world!
"Rent asunder"? Again, I apologize, but my old-timey slang is clearly not up to snuff here.
Obviously your schoolmarms have been negligent in their duties. What do they teach in school these days?
Computers, mostly. Some physics too, discrete mathematics...
Well. To "rent asunder" (simple past, past participle and future perfect tenses or "rend asunde (indefinite prese and simple future tenses) is to fracture, perforate, or tear apart, Squirrel Girl. Now...
Rend her asunder, my Mole Monsters!
Dude, it's obvious you're upset, but I hope you can see any hardships I inflicted on you were unintentional.
SMAK
And Harvey, if that has been my effect...
--well, I'm really sorry.
I...
...I-- beg your pardon?

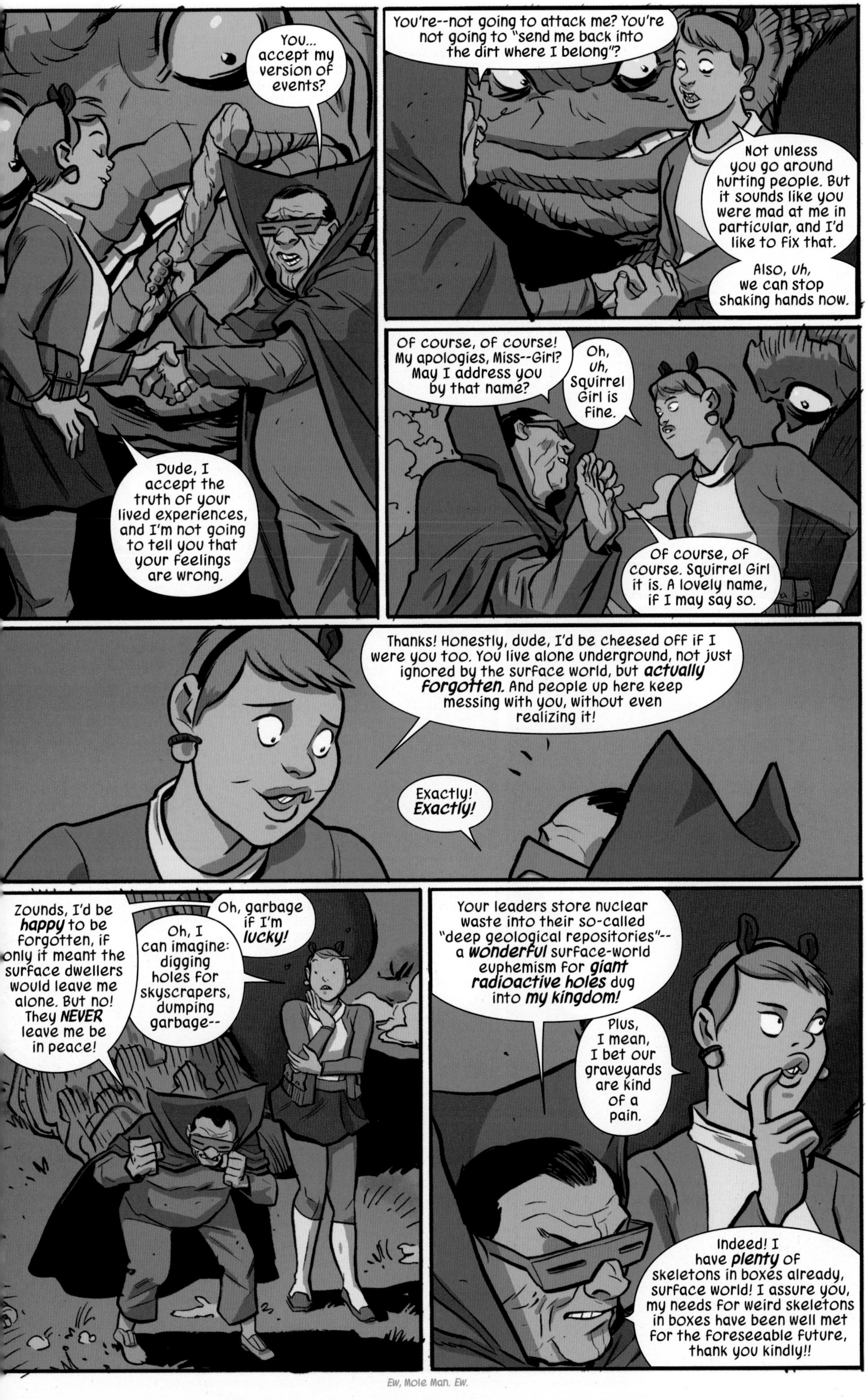
You... accept my version of events?
Dude, I accept the truth of your lived experiences, and I'm not going to tell you that your feelings are wrong.
You're--not going to attack me? You're not going to "send me back into the dirt where I belong"?
Not unless you go around hurting people. But it sounds like you were mad at me in particular, and I'd like to fix that.
Also, uh, we can stop shaking hands now.
Of course, of course! My apologies, Miss--Girl? May I address you by that name?
Oh, uh, Squirrel Girl is fine.
Of course, of course. Squirrel Girl it is. A lovely name, if I may say so.
Thanks! Honestly, dude, I'd be cheesed off if I were you too. You live alone underground, not just ignored by the surface world, but **actually forgotten.** And people up here keep messing with you, without even realizing it!
Exactly! ***Exactly!***
Zounds, I'd be ***happy*** to be forgotten, if only it meant the surface dwellers would leave me alone. But no! They ***NEVER*** leave me be in peace!
Oh, I can imagine: digging holes for skyscrapers, dumping garbage--
Oh, garbage if I'm ***lucky!***
Your leaders store nuclear waste into their so-called "deep geological repositories"-- a ***wonderful*** surface-world euphemism for ***giant radioactive holes*** dug into ***my kingdom!***
Plus, I mean, I bet our graveyards are kind of a pain.
Indeed! I have ***plenty*** of skeletons in boxes already, surface world! I assure you, my needs for weird skeletons in boxes have been well met for the foreseeable future, thank you kindly!!

Ew, Mole Man. Ew.

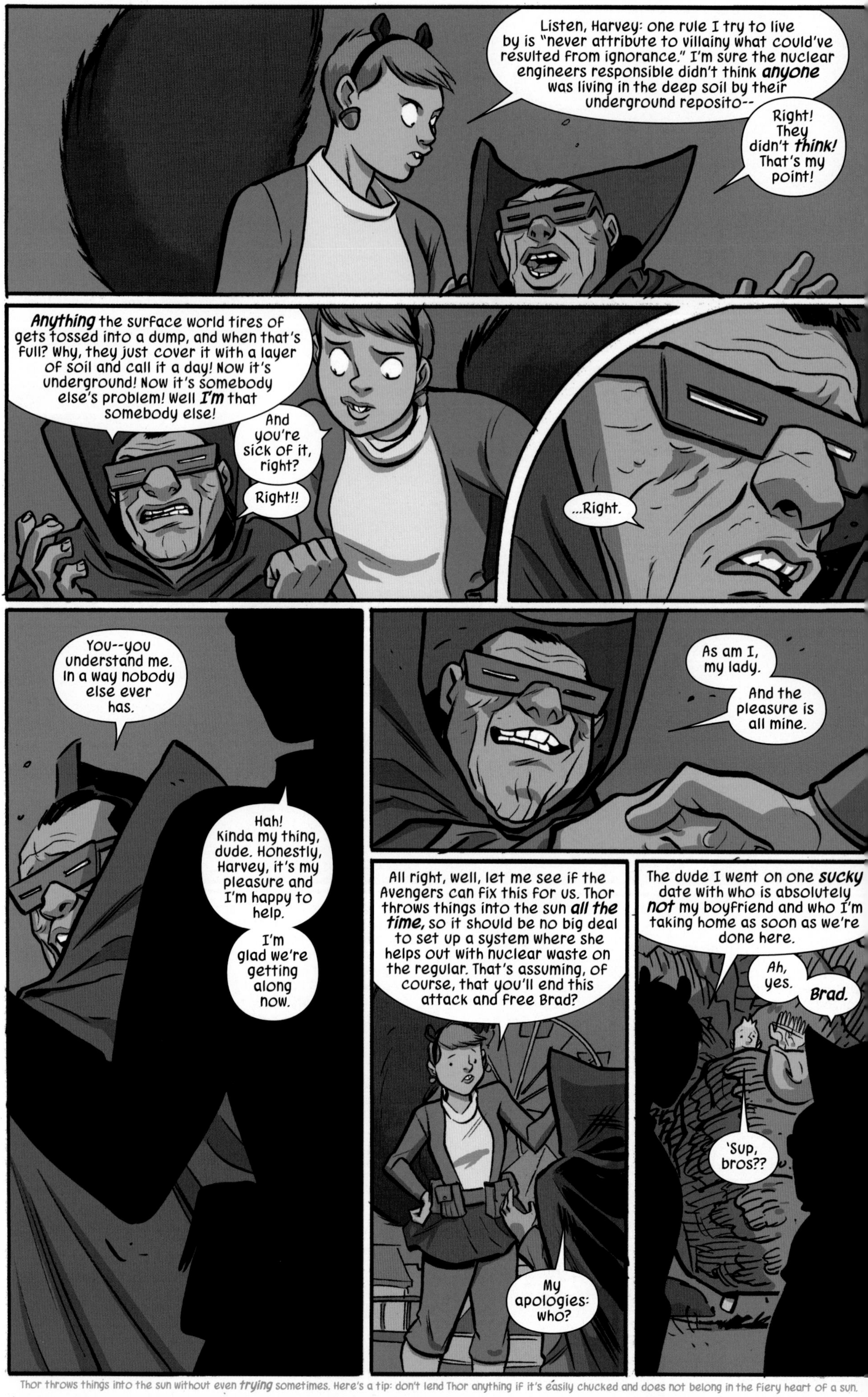
Listen, Harvey: one rule I try to live by is "never attribute to villainy what could've resulted from ignorance." I'm sure the nuclear engineers responsible didn't think *anyone* was living in the deep soil by their underground reposito--
Right! They didn't *think!* That's my point!
Anything the surface world tires of gets tossed into a dump, and when that's full? Why, they just cover it with a layer of soil and call it a day! Now it's underground! Now it's somebody else's problem! Well *I'm* that somebody else!
And you're sick of it, right?
Right!!
...Right.
You--you understand me. In a way nobody else ever has.
Hah! Kinda my thing, dude. Honestly, Harvey, it's my pleasure and I'm happy to help.
I'm glad we're getting along now.
As am I, my lady.
And the pleasure is all mine.
All right, well, let me see if the Avengers can fix this for us. Thor throws things into the sun *all the time,* so it should be no big deal to set up a system where she helps out with nuclear waste on the regular. That's assuming, of course, that you'll end this attack and free Brad?
My apologies: who?
The dude I went on one *sucky* date with who is absolutely *not* my boyfriend and who I'm taking home as soon as we're done here.
Ah, yes.
Brad.
'Sup, bros??

Thor throws things into the sun without even *trying* sometimes. Here's a tip: don't lend Thor anything if it's easily chucked and does not belong in the fiery heart of a sun.

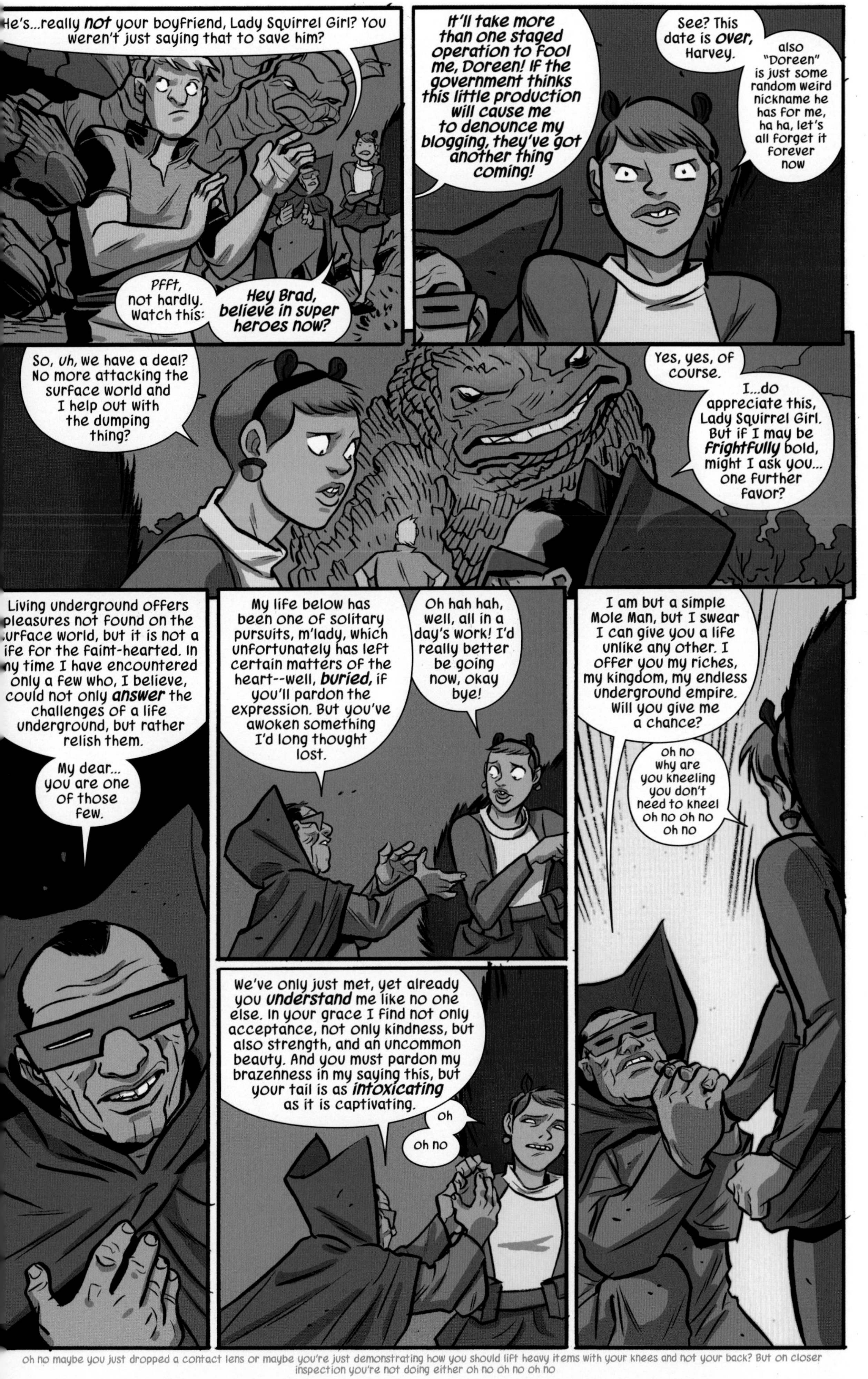
He's...really not your boyfriend, Lady Squirrel Girl? You weren't just saying that to save him?
Pfft, not hardly. Watch this:
Hey Brad, believe in super heroes now?
It'll take more than one staged operation to fool me, Doreen! If the government thinks this little production will cause me to denounce my blogging, they've got another thing coming!
See? This date is over, Harvey.
also "Doreen" is just some random weird nickname he has for me, ha ha, let's all forget it forever now
So, uh, we have a deal? No more attacking the surface world and I help out with the dumping thing?
Yes, yes, of course.
I...do appreciate this, Lady Squirrel Girl. But if I may be frightfully bold, might I ask you... one further favor?
Living underground offers pleasures not found on the surface world, but it is not a life for the faint-hearted. In my time I have encountered only a few who, I believe, could not only answer the challenges of a life underground, but rather relish them.
My dear... you are one of those few.
My life below has been one of solitary pursuits, m'lady, which unfortunately has left certain matters of the heart--well, buried, if you'll pardon the expression. But you've awoken something I'd long thought lost.
Oh hah hah, well, all in a day's work! I'd really better be going now, okay bye!
We've only just met, yet already you understand me like no one else. In your grace I find not only acceptance, not only kindness, but also strength, and an uncommon beauty. And you must pardon my brazenness in my saying this, but your tail is as intoxicating as it is captivating.
oh
oh no
I am but a simple Mole Man, but I swear I can give you a life unlike any other. I offer you my riches, my kingdom, my endless underground empire. Will you give me a chance?
oh no why are you kneeling you don't need to kneel oh no oh no oh no

oh no maybe you just dropped a contact lens or maybe you're just demonstrating how you should lift heavy items with your knees and not your back? But on closer inspection you're not doing either oh no oh no oh no

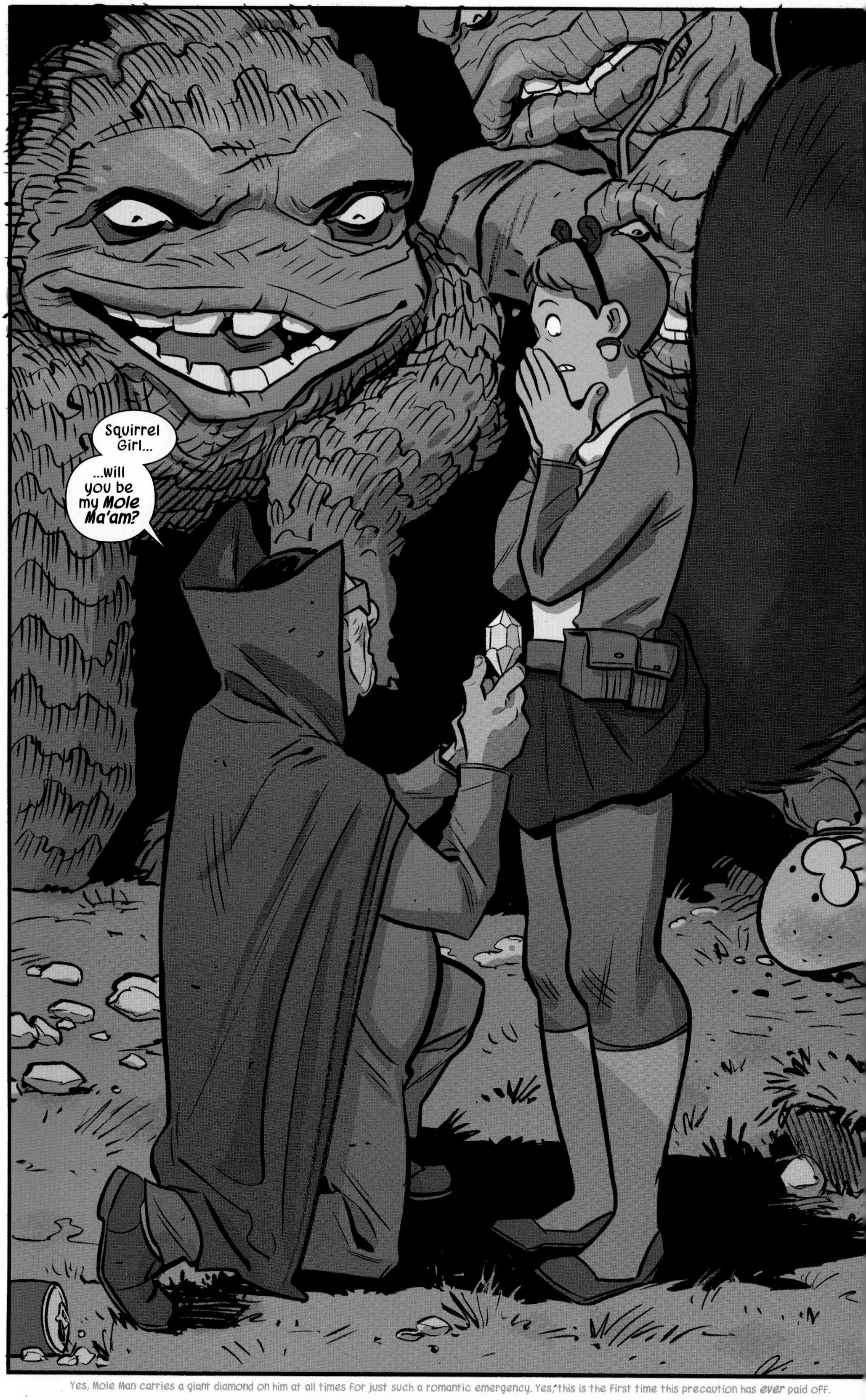
Squirrel Girl...
...will you be my *Mole Ma'am?*

Yes, Mole Man carries a giant diamond on him at all times for just such a romantic emergency. Yes, this is the first time this precaution has *ever* paid off.

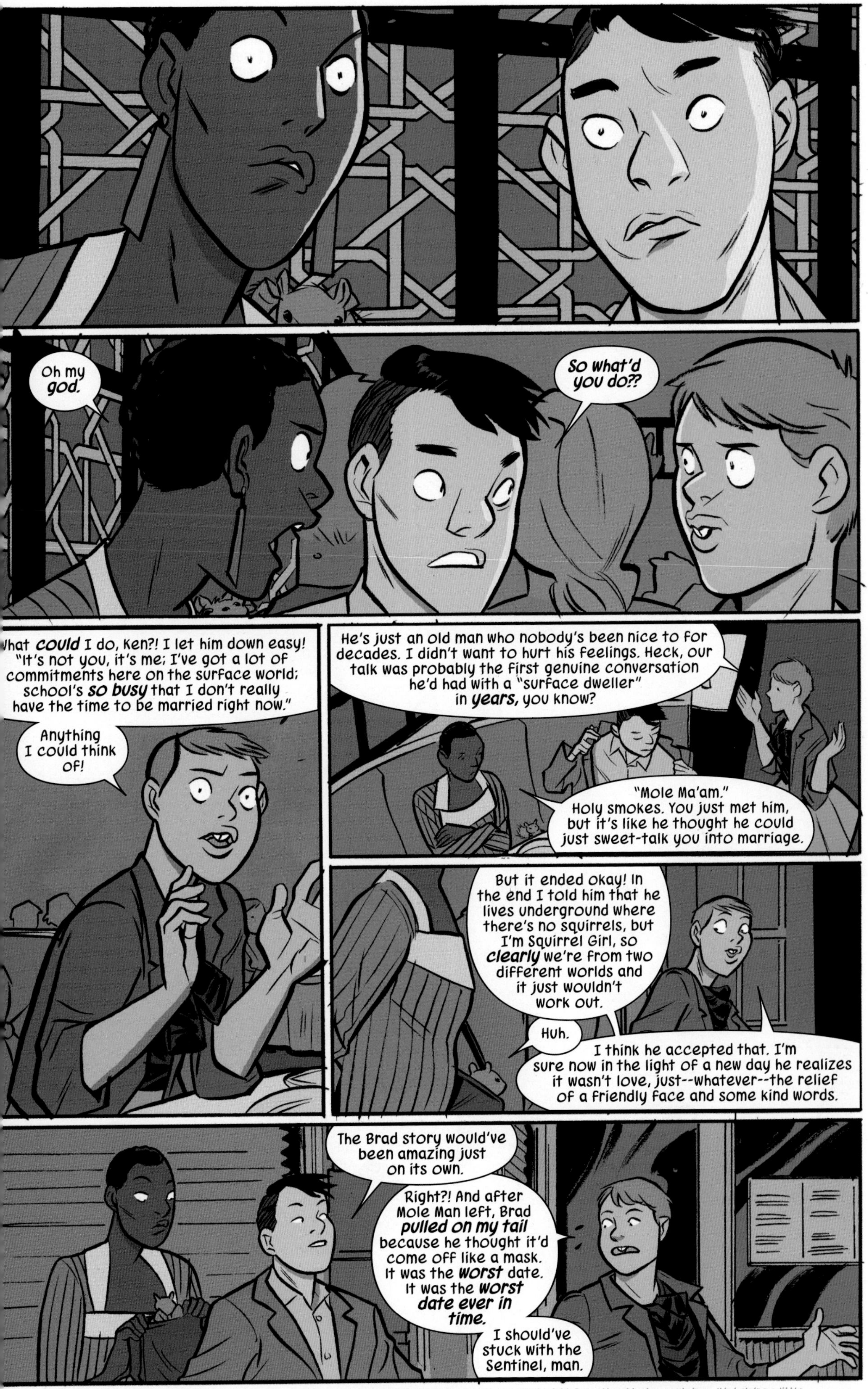
Oh my god.
So what'd you do??
What could I do, Ken?! I let him down easy! "It's not you, it's me; I've got a lot of commitments here on the surface world; school's so busy that I don't really have the time to be married right now."
Anything I could think of!
He's just an old man who nobody's been nice to for decades. I didn't want to hurt his feelings. Heck, our talk was probably the first genuine conversation he'd had with a "surface dweller" in years, you know?
"Mole Ma'am." Holy smokes. You just met him, but it's like he thought he could just sweet-talk you into marriage.
But it ended okay! In the end I told him that he lives underground where there's no squirrels, but I'm Squirrel Girl, so clearly we're from two different worlds and it just wouldn't work out.
Huh.
I think he accepted that. I'm sure now in the light of a new day he realizes it wasn't love, just--whatever--the relief of a friendly face and some kind words.
The Brad story would've been amazing just on its own.
Right?! And after Mole Man left, Brad pulled on my tail because he thought it'd come off like a mask. It was the worst date. It was the worst date ever in time.
I should've stuck with the Sentinel, man.

Somewhere out there, a Sentinel is trying to make himself feel better by gorging on ice cream straight from the shipping container. It's helping a little.

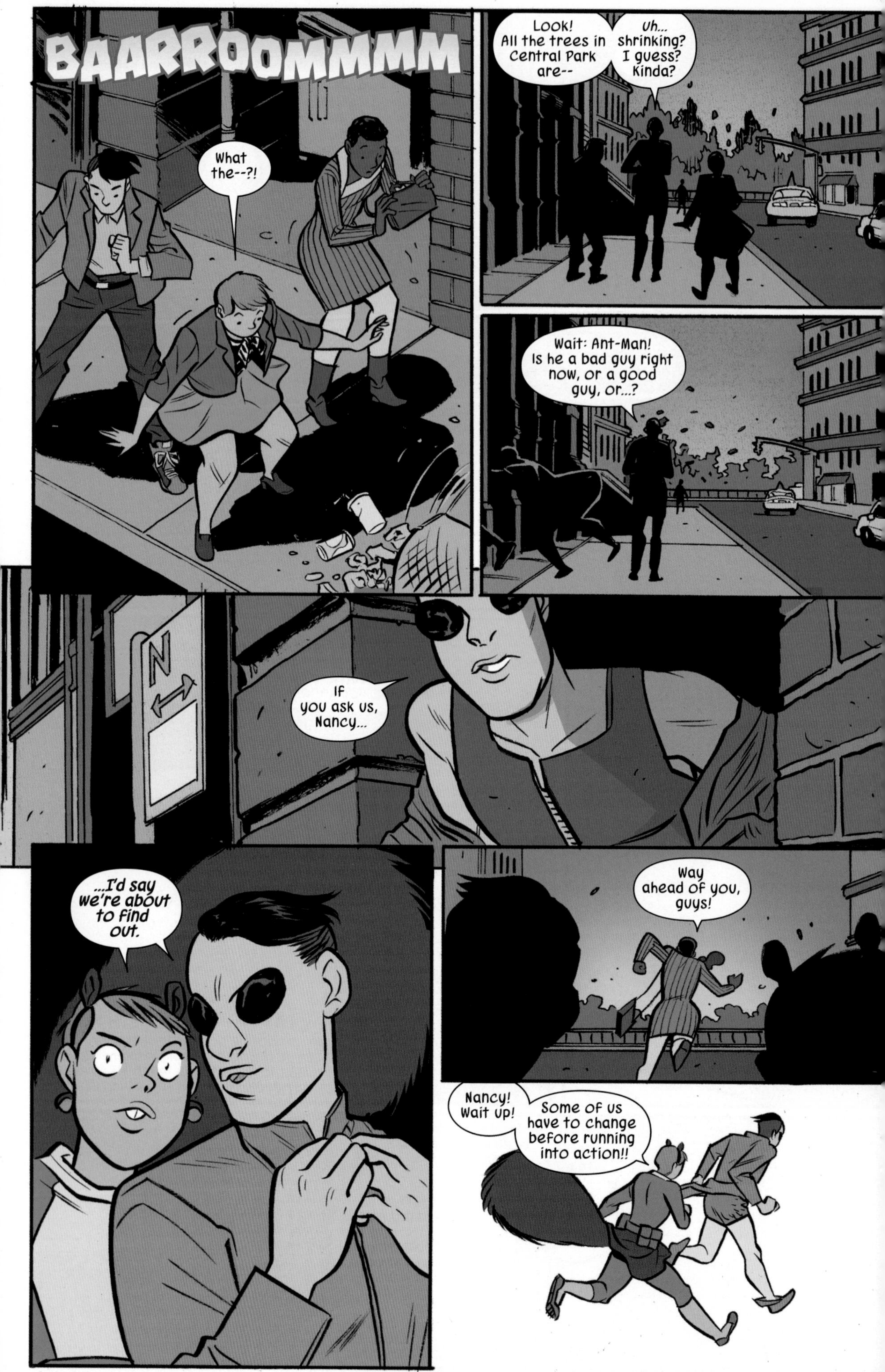
BAARROOMMMMM
What the--?!
Look! All the trees in Central Park are--
Uh... shrinking? I guess? Kinda?
Wait: Ant-Man! Is he a bad guy right now, or a good guy, or...?
If you ask us, Nancy...
...I'd say we're about to find out.
Way ahead of you, guys!
Nancy! Wait up!
Some of us have to change before running into action!!

Squirrel Girl was wearing her costume underneath her clothes, which I guess means...dressing in layers really *does* keep you prepared for whatever the day throws at you?! My parents were *right??*

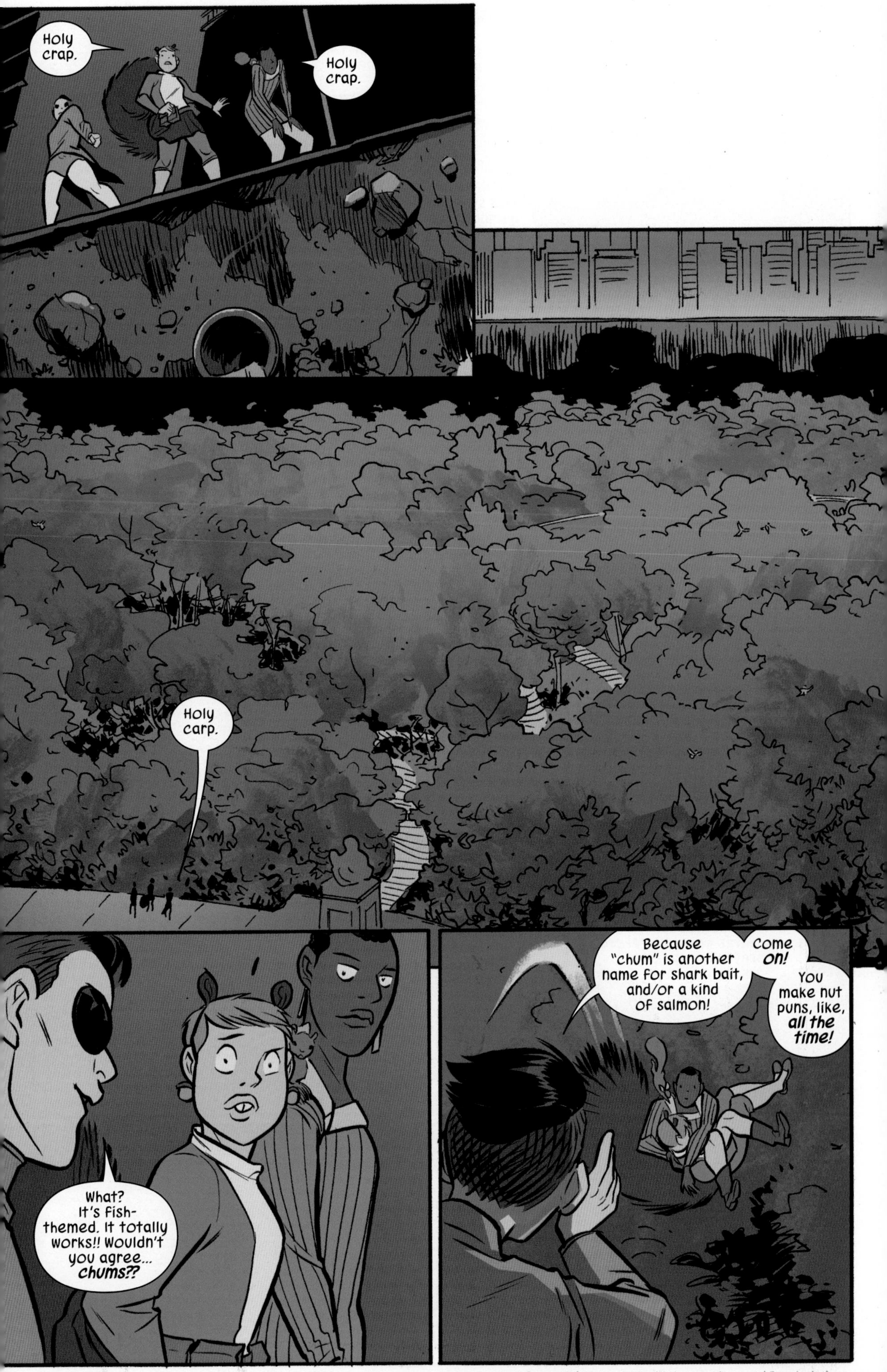
Holy crap.
Holy crap.
Holy carp.
What? It's fish-themed. It totally works!! Wouldn't you agree... chums??
Because "chum" is another name for shark bait, and/or a kind of salmon!
Come on!
You make nut puns, like, all the time!

How are we seventeen issues into this book and this is the *first* time Koi Boi called someone "chum"? *Someone's* been slacking (that person is me, and I apologize).

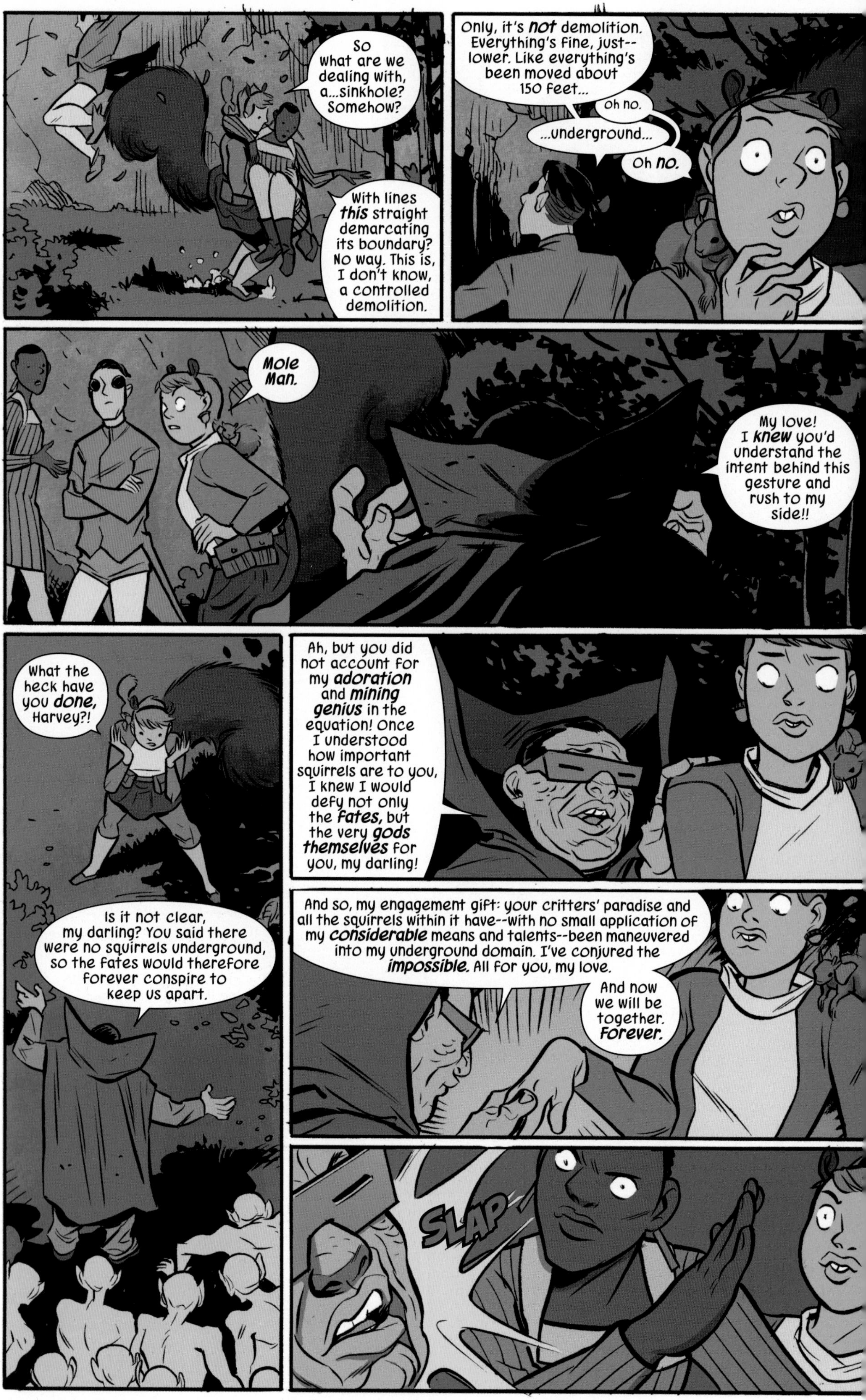

So what are we dealing with, a...sinkhole? Somehow?
With lines this straight demarcating its boundary? No way. This is, I don't know, a controlled demolition.
Only, it's not demolition. Everything's fine, just--lower. Like everything's been moved about 150 feet...
Oh no.
...underground...
Oh no.
Mole Man.
My love! I knew you'd understand the intent behind this gesture and rush to my side!!
What the heck have you done, Harvey?!
Ah, but you did not account for my adoration and mining genius in the equation! Once I understood how important squirrels are to you, I knew I would defy not only the fates, but the very gods themselves for you, my darling!
Is it not clear, my darling? You said there were no squirrels underground, so the fates would therefore forever conspire to keep us apart.
And so, my engagement gift: your critters' paradise and all the squirrels within it have--with no small application of my considerable means and talents--been maneuvered into my underground domain. I've conjured the impossible. All for you, my love.
And now we will be together. Forever.
SLAP

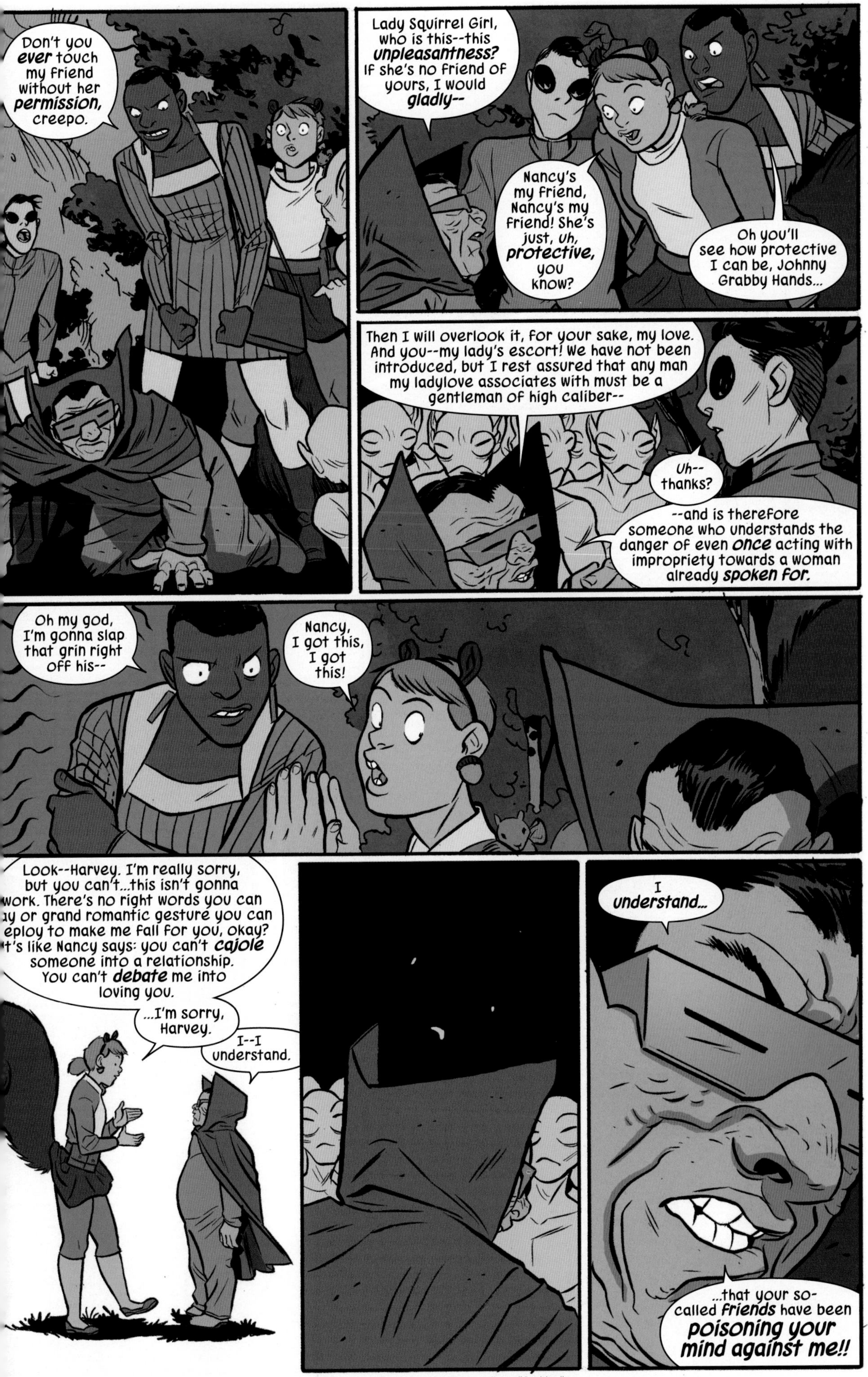
Don't you ever touch my friend without her permission, creepo.
Lady Squirrel Girl, who is this--this unpleasantness? If she's no friend of yours, I would gladly--
Nancy's my friend, Nancy's my friend! She's just, uh, protective, you know?
Oh you'll see how protective I can be, Johnny Grabby Hands...
Then I will overlook it, for your sake, my love. And you--my lady's escort! We have not been introduced, but I rest assured that any man my ladylove associates with must be a gentleman of high caliber--
Uh--thanks?
--and is therefore someone who understands the danger of even once acting with impropriety towards a woman already spoken for.
Oh my god, I'm gonna slap that grin right off his--
Nancy, I got this, I got this!
Look--Harvey. I'm really sorry, but you can't...this isn't gonna work. There's no right words you can ay or grand romantic gesture you can eploy to make me fall for you, okay? t's like Nancy says: you can't cajole someone into a relationship. You can't debate me into loving you.
...I'm sorry, Harvey.
I--I understand.
I understand...
...that your so-called friends have been poisoning your mind against me!!

Please, "Mr. Hands" was my Father. Call me "Grabby."

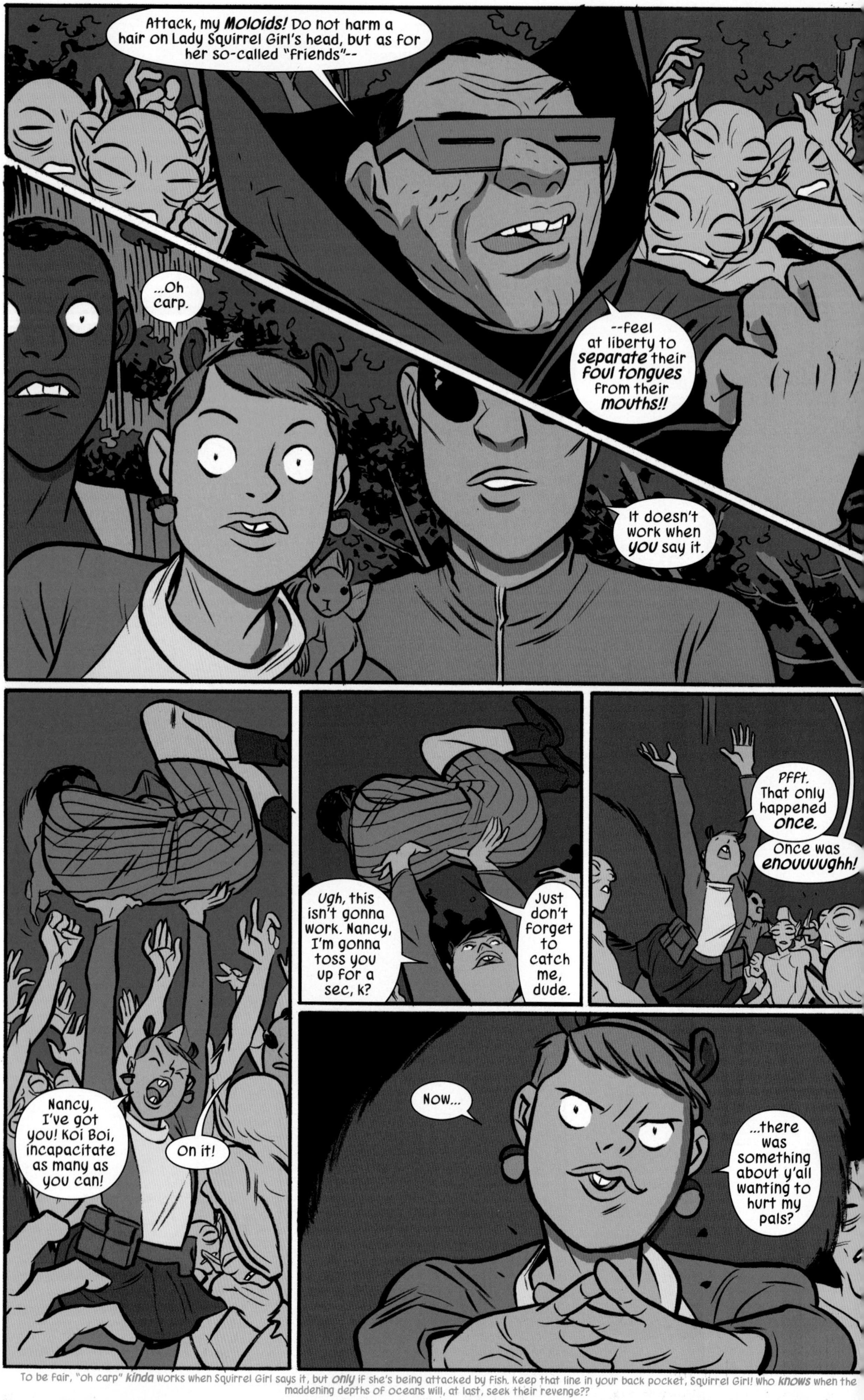
Attack, my *Moloids!* Do not harm a hair on Lady Squirrel Girl's head, but as for her so-called "friends"--
--feel at liberty to *separate* their *foul tongues* from their *mouths!!*
...Oh carp.
It doesn't work when *you* say it.
Ugh, this isn't gonna work. Nancy, I'm gonna toss you up for a sec, k?
Just don't forget to catch me, dude.
Pfft. That only happened *once.*
Once was *enouuuughh!*
Nancy, I've got you! Koi Boi, incapacitate as many as you can!
On it!
Now...
...there was something about y'all wanting to hurt my pals?

To be fair, "oh carp" *kinda* works when Squirrel Girl says it, but *only* if she's being attacked by fish. Keep that line in your back pocket, Squirrel Girl! Who *knows* when the maddening depths of oceans will, at last, seek their revenge??

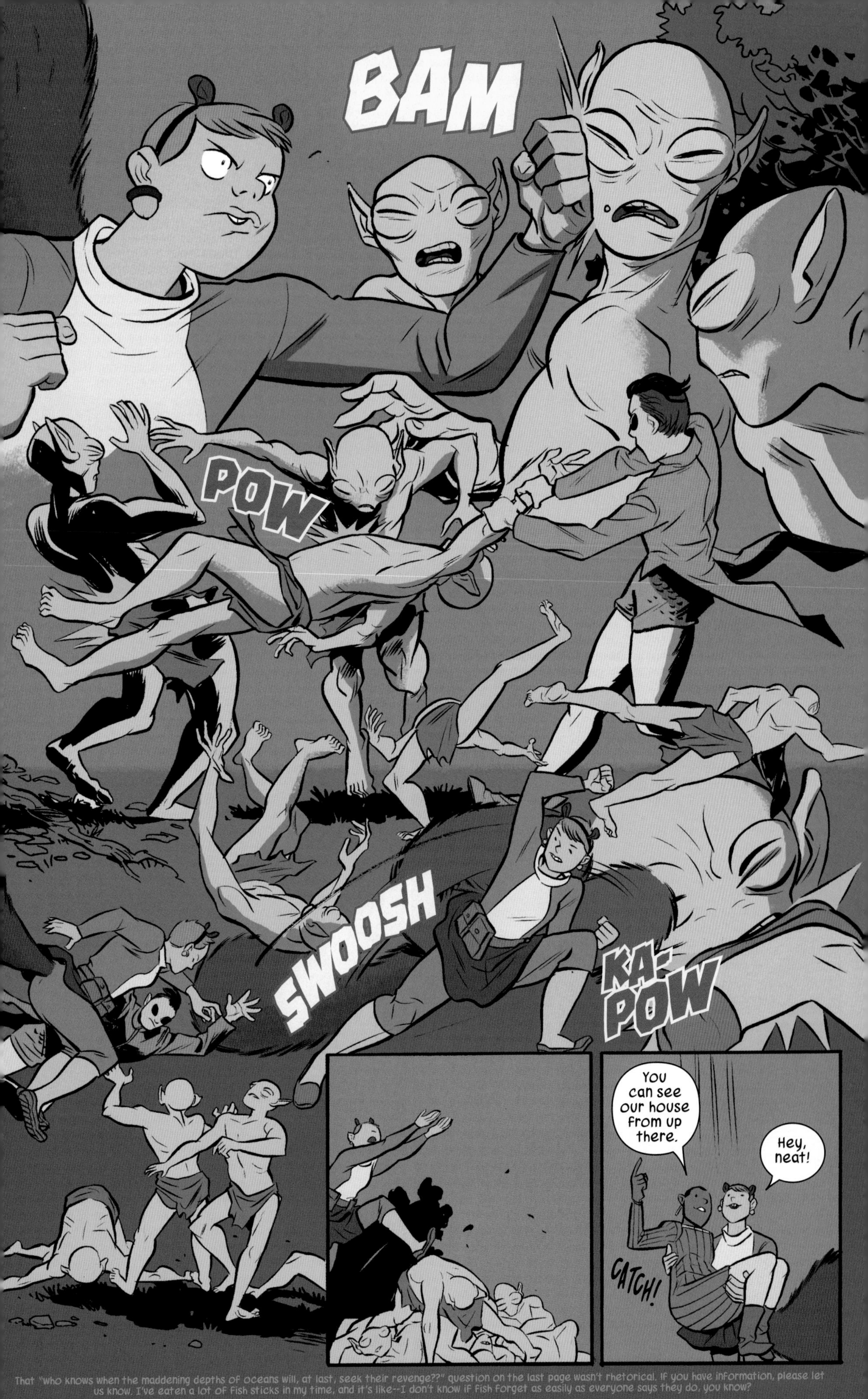
BAM
POW
SWOOSH
KA-POW
You can see our house from up there.
Hey, neat!
CATCH!

That "who knows when the maddening depths of oceans will, at last, seek their revenge??" question on the last page wasn't rhetorical. If you have information, please let us know. I've eaten a lot of fish sticks in my time, and it's like--I don't know if fish forget as easily as everyone says they do, you know?

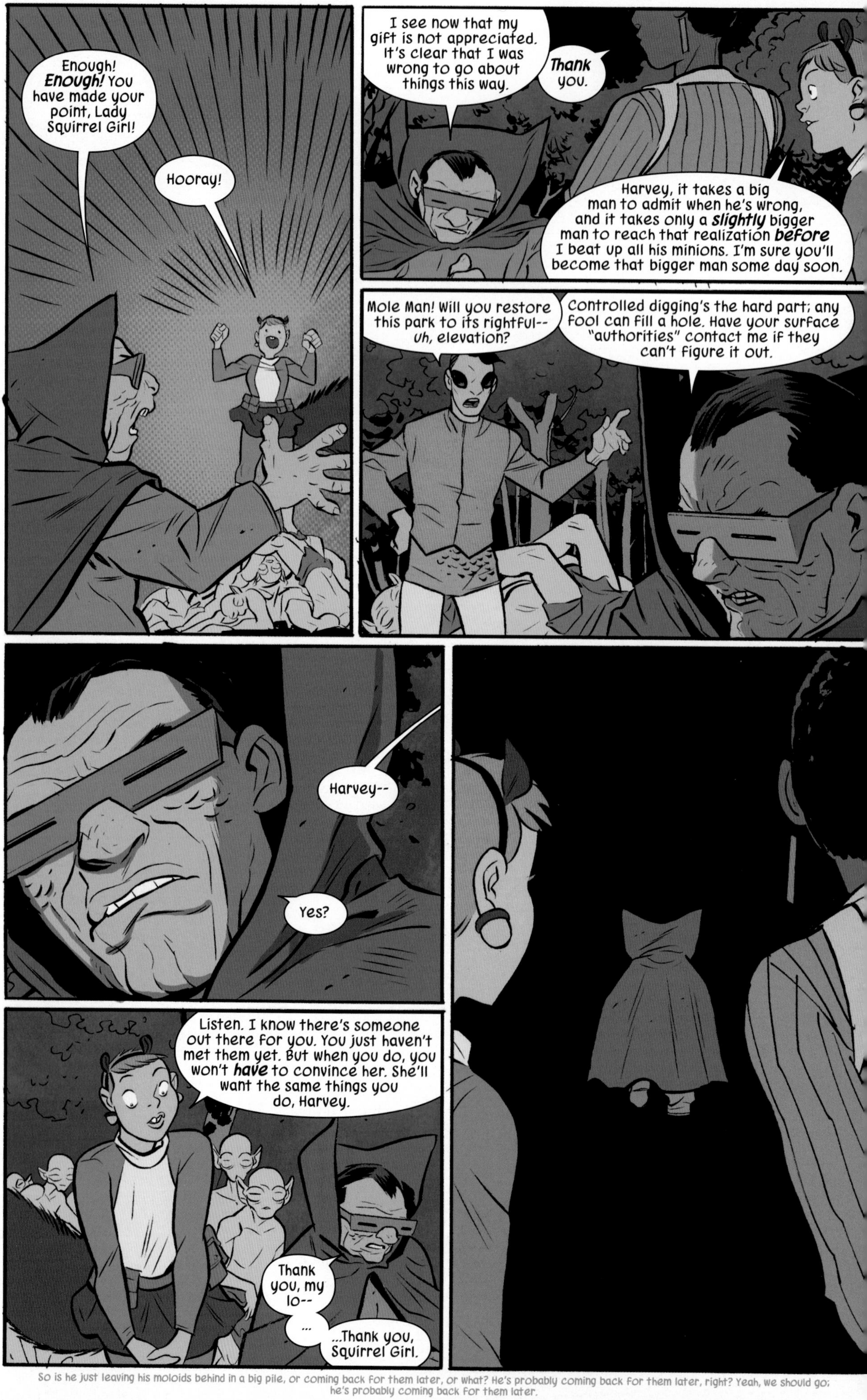
Enough! **Enough!** You have made your point, Lady Squirrel Girl!
Hooray!
I see now that my gift is not appreciated. It's clear that I was wrong to go about things this way.
Thank you.
Harvey, it takes a big man to admit when he's wrong, and it takes only a **slightly** bigger man to reach that realization **before** I beat up all his minions. I'm sure you'll become that bigger man some day soon.
Mole Man! Will you restore this park to its rightful-- uh, elevation?
Controlled digging's the hard part; any fool can fill a hole. Have your surface "authorities" contact me if they can't figure it out.
Harvey--
Yes?
Listen. I know there's someone out there for you. You just haven't met them yet. But when you do, you won't **have** to convince her. She'll want the same things you do, Harvey.
Thank you, my lo--
...
...Thank you, Squirrel Girl.

So is he just leaving his moloids behind in a big pile, or coming back for them later, or what? He's probably coming back for them later, right? Yeah, we should go; he's probably coming back for them later.

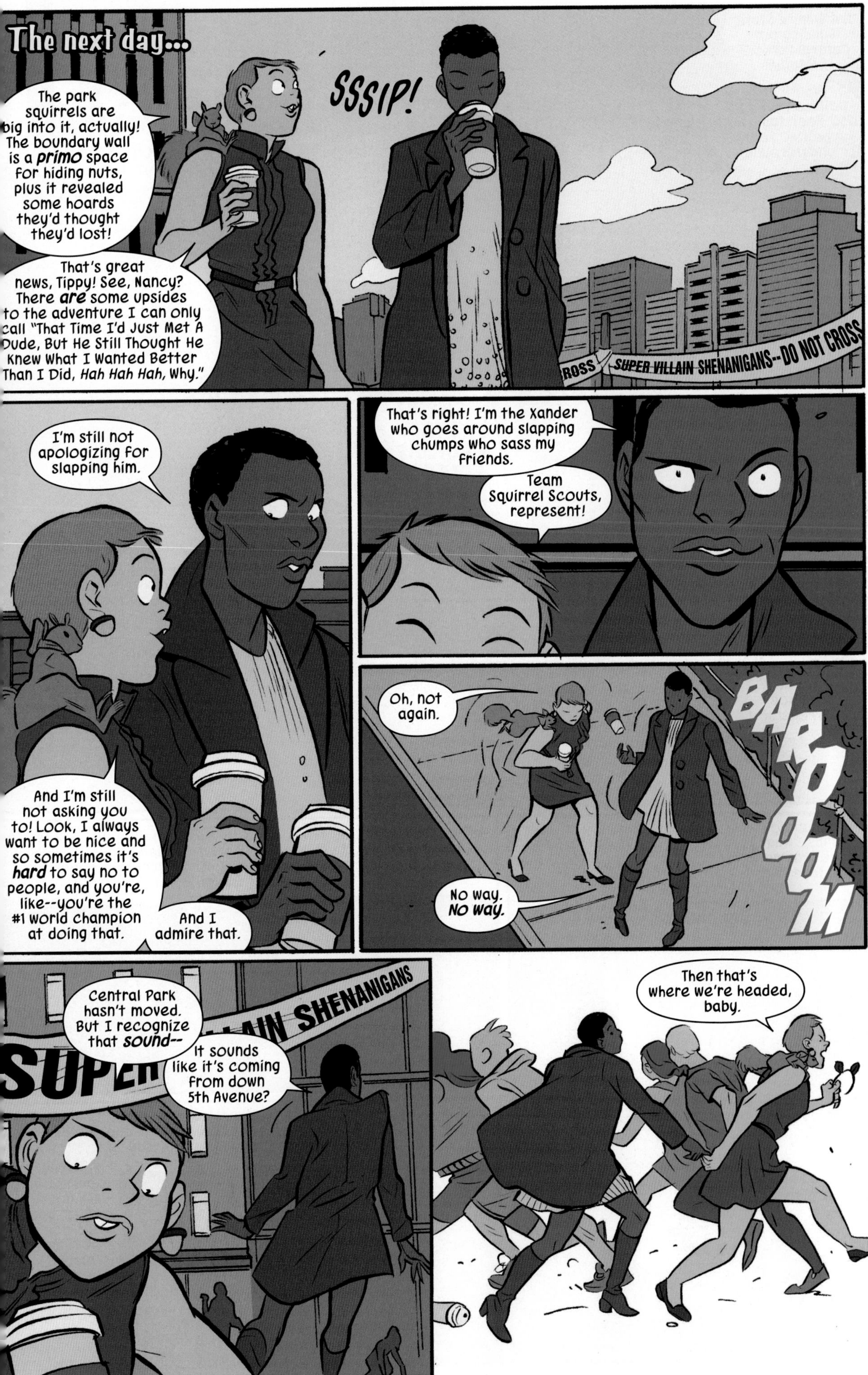
The next day...
The park squirrels are big into it, actually! The boundary wall is a *primo* space for hiding nuts, plus it revealed some hoards they'd thought they'd lost!
SSSIP!
That's great news, Tippy! See, Nancy? There *are* some upsides to the adventure I can only call "That Time I'd Just Met A Dude, But He Still Thought He Knew What I Wanted Better Than I Did, *Hah Hah Hah, Why.*"
ROSS
SUPER VILLAIN SHENANIGANS--DO NOT CROSS
I'm still not apologizing for slapping him.
And I'm still not asking you to! Look, I always want to be nice and so sometimes it's *hard* to say no to people, and you're, like--you're the #1 world champion at doing that.
And I admire that.
That's right! I'm the Xander who goes around slapping chumps who sass my friends.
Team Squirrel Scouts, represent!
Oh, not again.
BAROOOOM
No way. *No way.*
SUPER VILLAIN SHENANIGANS
Central Park hasn't moved. But I recognize that *sound--*
It sounds like it's coming from down 5th Avenue?
Then that's where we're headed, baby.

If you don't know New York roadways and thought "Well, certainly I can read my talking squirrel comic and not be made to feel bad about that particular gap in my knowledge," no worries! 5th Avenue is just, like, a road that runs along Central Park. They named a chocolate bar after it.

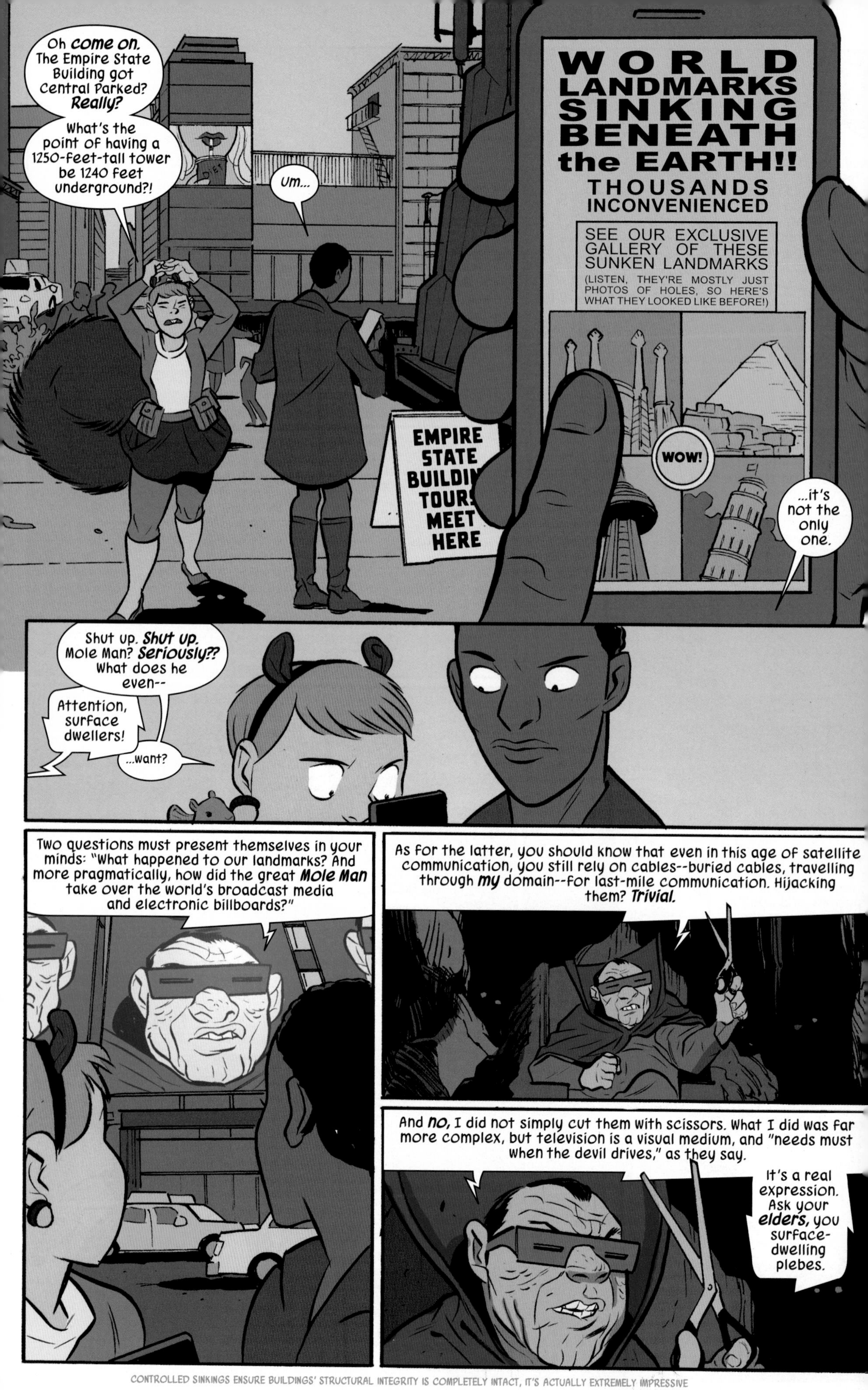
Oh come on. The Empire State Building got Central Parked? Really?
What's the point of having a 1250-feet-tall tower be 1240 feet underground?!
Um...
WORLD LANDMARKS SINKING BENEATH the EARTH!!
THOUSANDS INCONVENIENCED
SEE OUR EXCLUSIVE GALLERY OF THESE SUNKEN LANDMARKS
(LISTEN, THEY'RE MOSTLY JUST PHOTOS OF HOLES, SO HERE'S WHAT THEY LOOKED LIKE BEFORE!)
WOW!
EMPIRE STATE BUILDIN TOUR MEET HERE
...it's not the only one.
Shut up. Shut up. Mole Man? Seriously?? What does he even--
Attention, surface dwellers!
...want?
Two questions must present themselves in your minds: "What happened to our landmarks? And more pragmatically, how did the great Mole Man take over the world's broadcast media and electronic billboards?"
As for the latter, you should know that even in this age of satellite communication, you still rely on cables--buried cables, travelling through my domain--for last-mile communication. Hijacking them? Trivial.
And no, I did not simply cut them with scissors. What I did was far more complex, but television is a visual medium, and "needs must when the devil drives," as they say.
It's a real expression. Ask your elders, you surface-dwelling plebes.

CONTROLLED SINKINGS ENSURE BUILDINGS' STRUCTURAL INTEGRITY IS COMPLETELY INTACT, IT'S ACTUALLY EXTREMELY IMPRESSIVE

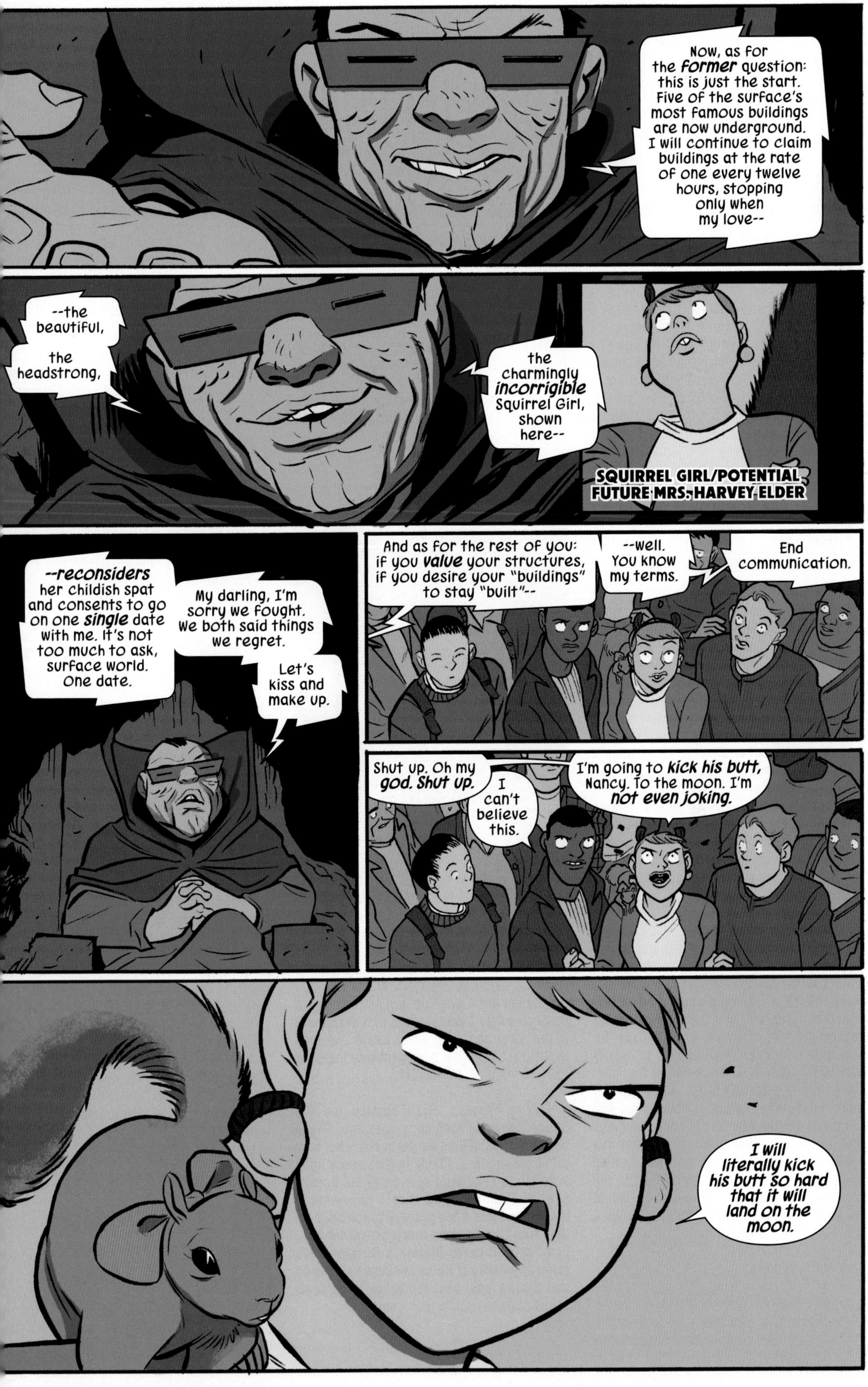
Now, as for the former question: this is just the start. Five of the surface's most famous buildings are now underground. I will continue to claim buildings at the rate of one every twelve hours, stopping only when my love--
--the beautiful,
the headstrong,
the charmingly incorrigible Squirrel Girl, shown here--
SQUIRREL GIRL/POTENTIAL FUTURE MRS. HARVEY ELDER
--reconsiders her childish spat and consents to go on one single date with me. It's not too much to ask, surface world. One date.
My darling, I'm sorry we fought. We both said things we regret.
Let's kiss and make up.
And as for the rest of you: if you value your structures, if you desire your "buildings" to stay "built"--
--well. You know my terms.
End communication.
Shut up. Oh my god. Shut up.
I can't believe this.
I'm going to kick his butt, Nancy. To the moon. I'm not even joking.
I will literally kick his butt so hard that it will land on the moon.

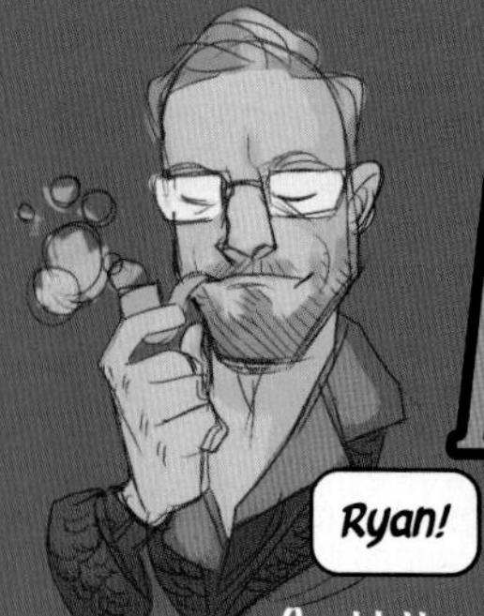
Ryan!

Letters From Nuts

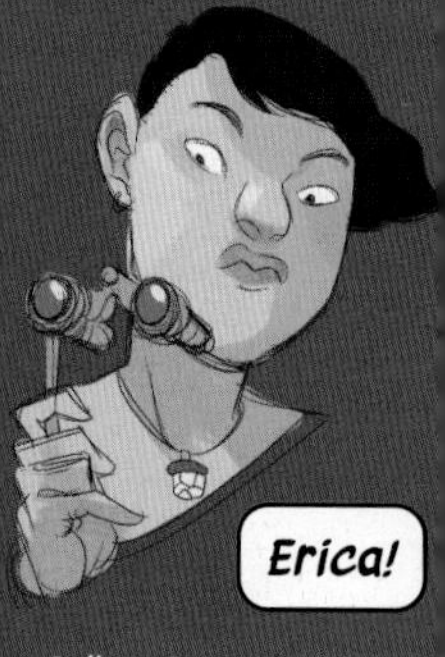
Erica!

Send letters to mheroes@marvel.com or 135 W 50th St, 7th Floor, New York, NY 10020 (Please mark "OKAY TO PRINT

Helloooo, Ryan and Erica!

My wife and I have been reading Squirrel Girl since the first new #1 (and have been reading Ryan's material for rather longer), but issue #8 is the first time I felt it necessary to write in, as I noticed a few things. 1.) Nancy's puzzle solving challenge is potentially incorrect. Unless she lapsed into l33t for a single keystroke, the second number string's second digit should be 5. 2.) Considering no one on the internet is what they seem in the first place, online dating for people who need to maintain a secret identity WOULD be even more difficult than usual. 3.) The dress Doreen wore on her date with Human Torch is SUPER CUTE. Most of her outfits are cute, but this stood out to me for some reason. Keep up the top-notch work, folks!

Ray Davis

RYAN: Ray, you are correct! Nancy has an off-by-one style error in one puzzle, which I initially felt bad about (because it was ME who made the mistake), but then it was pointed out to me that challenging someone with a computer science puzzle and then making a mistake in the implementation is PEAK second-year computer science student, and I felt a lot better about it. So I made it Nancy's mistake, which leaves me still amazingly mistake-free! And yeah, Erica's outfits are amazing. I'm not sure if we said this before, but in the first draft of the Doctor Doom time travel story they originally went back to the '50s, and we changed it to the '60s on Erica's suggestion: there's way better fashions there.

ERICA: That dress is one that I bought thinking it would fit my body type and wound up being one of the worst. I think that was a tribute to the dress I thought I was buying. Ryan, I think it was more about the fact that everyone does the '50s because for some reason it's the "bygone era" decade for Americans so EVERYONE does it to signify THE PAST but I'm done looking at the '50s. There are OTHER DECADES, PEOPLE. And yeah, mod design is pretty cool. It's too bad we didn't see the interiors of many buildings that weren't 1. abandoned space that can be used for meetings 2. abandoned castles in Central Park or 3. a museum built in the previous century because everyone would be sitting in a round chair with op art behind them. AS THEY SHOULD BE.

Dear Nutty Buddies,

Wow, USG #8 was such a great issue! I don't who this new talent Eryca Renzorth is, but she's got all the storytelling skill of Erica Henderson, Rico Renzi and Ryan North combined. Oh, and I SO want my own Wal Rus stuffy now, too! Speaking of stuffies, when I met Ryan at the Toronto Comic Arts Festival a few weeks ago, I told him about the Tippy-Toe stuffy I'd tricked out with her very own Stark-Tech flight suit, based on the design from USG #3 (Vol. 1). Ryan was so excited hearing about it, he asked me to send a him a pic, which I have, but I wanted to share it with everyone! So without much further ado, here's "Space-Tippy" ready for another intergalactic adventure!

Darryl Etheridge
St. Catharines, ON.

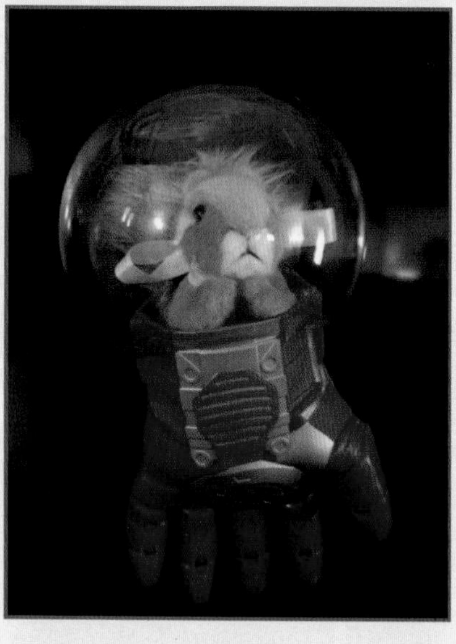

RYAN: THIS IS AMAZING; I can't believe how great the readers we have are. Holy smokes. What Darryl doesn't mention is when he came by and said hi, he casually mentioned this Tippy-Toe Iron Astronaut he'd made and then I kept making him describe it to me, over and over, while I said "no way, SERIOUSLY??". We were probably there for like, 15 minutes, MINIMUM.

ERICA: Yesssss. Ryan showed me the Space Tippy on Facebook a week ago. She is so beautiful. I'm glad we get to share her with all of our readers. I think in that scene Ryan asked for a Fin Fang Foom plush but Doreen already HAS ONE and then I remembered that Marvel has a ton of crazy space animals that aren't really seen much except for one. Fun Fact: All those Blackjack O'Hares were originally Bucky O'Hares because I was tired and they're both cool (as in warm vs cool) colored space rabbits with guns.

Friends,

Some of us just can't get enough Hawkeye We also have a fondness for the Wiccan Hulkling team, and never get enough of them More! More!

Tree lobsters, heartbroken Sentinenls, Mol Man... I like the way we never know wha we're going to get in a Squirrel Girl comic Even more, I like the way there's just s much reading material in this comic. So man words, most of them funny and clever. It' verbally substantial Confession: I laughed ou loud at the less/fewer joke, being an incurabl grammar nerd.

Dorren should hold off on the online dating Who knows who she'll meet in the norma course of things? I think Galactus has a crus on her, but I wouldn't look at him for long-tern prospects.

namaste
Elizabeth Holde
Ottawa, Canad

RYAN: I'm glad you enjoy it, Elizabeth I saw some people saying "wait, that tre lobster thing was REAL??" so let me jus say: yes, the tree lobster science in ou comic is all 100% real (except for the pa where cosmic rays make you giant; jury i still out on that bit). They're called "Lazaru species": a species thought extinct, that the "comes back" when we found out we were wrong. Second chances!

ERICA: MORE FUN FACTS: I knew that could get under Ryan's skin by asking hin how our tree lobster got around the squar cube law and it worked! An insect the size of a whale would collapse under its own weight! They also breathe differently (n lungs!) which restricts their size. 400 millio years ago we had giant bugs but also a LO more oxygen in the air.

I did the online dating thing and it seem to have worked out. Although the difference is my job involves me sitting at home al day and occasionally talking to the people work with, PLUS Ryan, Wil and Rico are al already married! (sorry ladies)

Dear Squirrel Girl,

My name is Kaylee and I'm 7 1/2 years old

I have read all of your comics, I really like them. I like squirrel girl because she has tippy toe and squirrels are cute. I like Nancy Whitehead because I just like her. I like Erica's drawings and I like Ryan's writing. For fan expo 2015 I was squirrel girl and in my hand he didn't make the squirrel she bought it from e store but she made the whole costume! I'm onna read squirrel girl every single day.

eep on drawing and writing more squirrel rls,

Kaylee Boyer

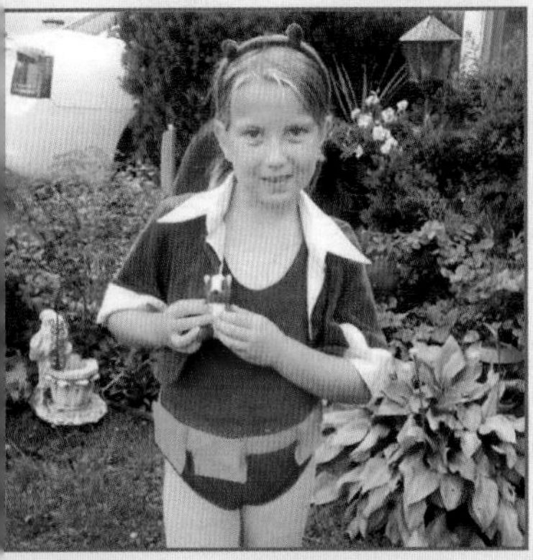

YAN: Kaylee, your outfit is SO GREAT, and our Nana did a great job helping you! Give er a high five for me. We'll keep writing ore squirrel girls, promise!! I wish I was at an Expo, I could've met you!

ERICA: YOUR COSTUME IS SO GOOD. I can ee a hint of that tail in the back. Good job, ou guys, that's the hardest part! I also like ancy.

ear Ryan and Erica,

Just wanted you to know that we (librarians) ot your secret? subliminal? message re: the opropriate shelving location for Unbeatable quirrel Girl. After careful consideration, we greed that it is TOTALLY appropriate and not in ny way misleading to place them in the *Wow! cience Facts!* area of the library.

We took care of it here, and you will robably soon find this to be the case in your wn public library. That is, if it is as awesome s we are... which is likely, since public libraries otally rule.

Keep up the great work!!

Sincerely,
Renee (Special Collections Librarian) &
Brooke (Teen Librarian)

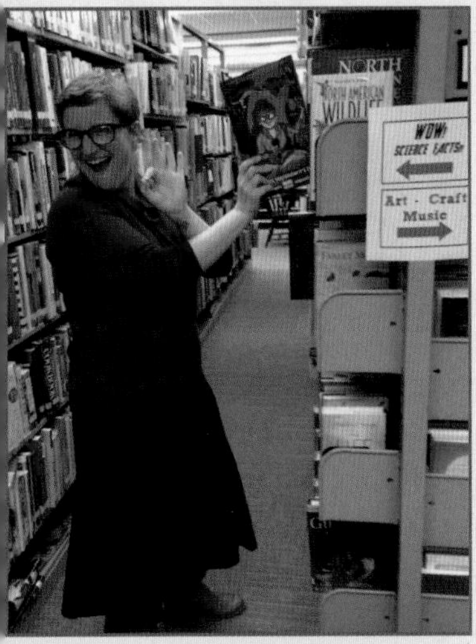
WOW!
SCIENCE FACTS!
Art - Craft
Music

RYAN: THIS IS ALSO AMAZING, and hat picture is all I dreamed of and more. Libraries, everyone! They're ALREADY awesome, and that's before you realize that they're full of librarians, which only increases their awesomness by a factor of 1000!!

ERICA: Bummer! I wish my libraries from when I was a kid had "WOW Science Facts" sections. I owned a lot of Zoobooks as a kid. Remember Zoobooks? What a time to be alive.

Dearest Unbeatable Squirrel Group,

Aaaah! How did I not know about this? I just discovered your wonderful comic last week in a roundabout series of tracing back crossovers, and have since read everything. I feel like a squirrel who just found a cheerful old couple in the park who can be counted on for food every day. Great story, great art, and occasional educational bits. Each issue, I think, "Wow, that was the best. How can you beat that?" But every time you found a way. Small example, this time, I got an amazing story that also made Squirrel Girl more relatable; I, too, make heavy use of Wikipedia's random article button.

I was going to wait until I finished making a Squirrel Earl cosplay (sorry Chipmunk Hunk, but I do not pull off the tiny tail) and could send pics, but I couldn't wait. Also, I need an answer to guide my design. I'm assuming his secret identity isn't named Earl, since that'd be too obvious, so I have to wonder, is it a title? Is he a member of nobility or aristocracy or whatever? Do I get to add a monocle to a non-steampunk cosplay? Also, should Steampunk Squirrel Earl be on my list of future plans? The answer to the last one is yes, so you can skip that one.

Thanks for the great comics,
Simon Nading

PS. I totally nailed Nancy's dating profile quiz. Question 4? I have held enough cats to judge their weight without your sad scale, so I'd just use it once to prove I was right.

PPS. Sentinel X-42903-22 needs a spin-off, along with just about every other character we've met.

RYAN: I always assumed Squirrel Earl was just a guy named Earl who had squirrel powers, but you're right: THAT IS NOT SO GREAT FOR A SECRET IDENTITY. So let's jettison that subpar backstory and say YES, he is definitely a member of the aristocracy, and a monocle would NOT be out of place (in this cosplay, or just in your day-to-day life). I feel like using your super determining-the-relative-mass-of-cats superpower is cheating on Nancy's quiz, though! NO SUPERPOWERS ALLOWED.

ERICA: You know that Squirrel Earl is one of those dudes that went on one of the lineage websites and then bragged to everyone about how he's DEFINITELY ROYALTY.

Dear Team Squirrel,

Just wanted to share these super cute, nut eating, butt kicking pictures of my daughter, Willow. She adores Squirrel Girl so I whipped up (meaning worked long into the night, stabbing myself repeatedly with a needle) this for her to celebrate Free Comic Book Day at our local comic shop. She had a great time being our favourite rodent-based superhero for the day and was delighted every time someone commented on what an awesome SG she made and how fabulous her tail was! Her day was complete when Ryan, Rico and Squirrel Girl herself retweeted her image. Thank you for the superb read and making my kid feel unbeatable.

Much love,

Liz Gallagher
Cambridge, UK.

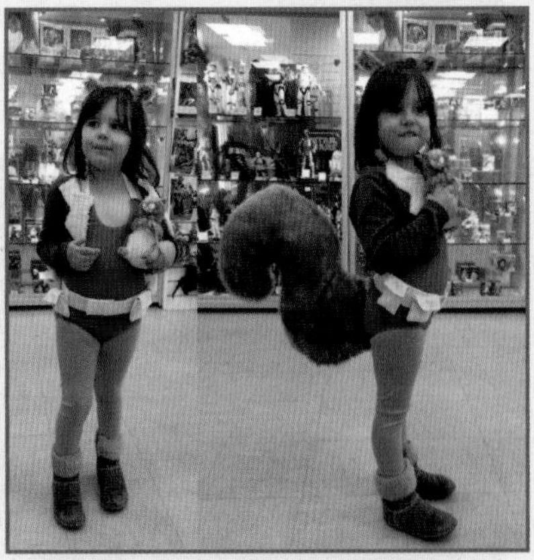

RYAN: Liz, Willow IS unbeatable (as is that costume: great work, my condolences for your multiple stab wounds) and honestly, one of the greatest parts of this job is when stuff like this happens. I love it. LOVE IT. Thank you for supporting Free Comic Book Day too! The more people reading comics, the better, and FCBD is a great way for people who might not normally consider the medium to give it a try. But you know that! You're literally reading this in a comic book right now!!

ERICA: Oh my god. How did I miss these photos on twitter? That is amazing for one night, but I've also CLEARLY had way less practice than you have.

P.S. I have that same squirrel toy in grey.

Next:

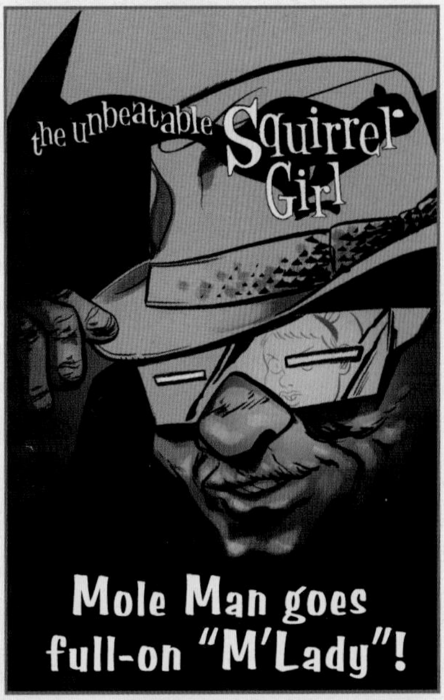
the unbeatable Squirrel Girl
Mole Man goes full-on "M'Lady"!

Attention, Squirrel Scouts! Make sure to check out our production blog, **unbeatablesquirrelgirl.tumblr.com**, where we post behind-the-scenes stuff on how the book gets made, along with all sorts of cool things *you* make: fanart, cosplay, whatever!

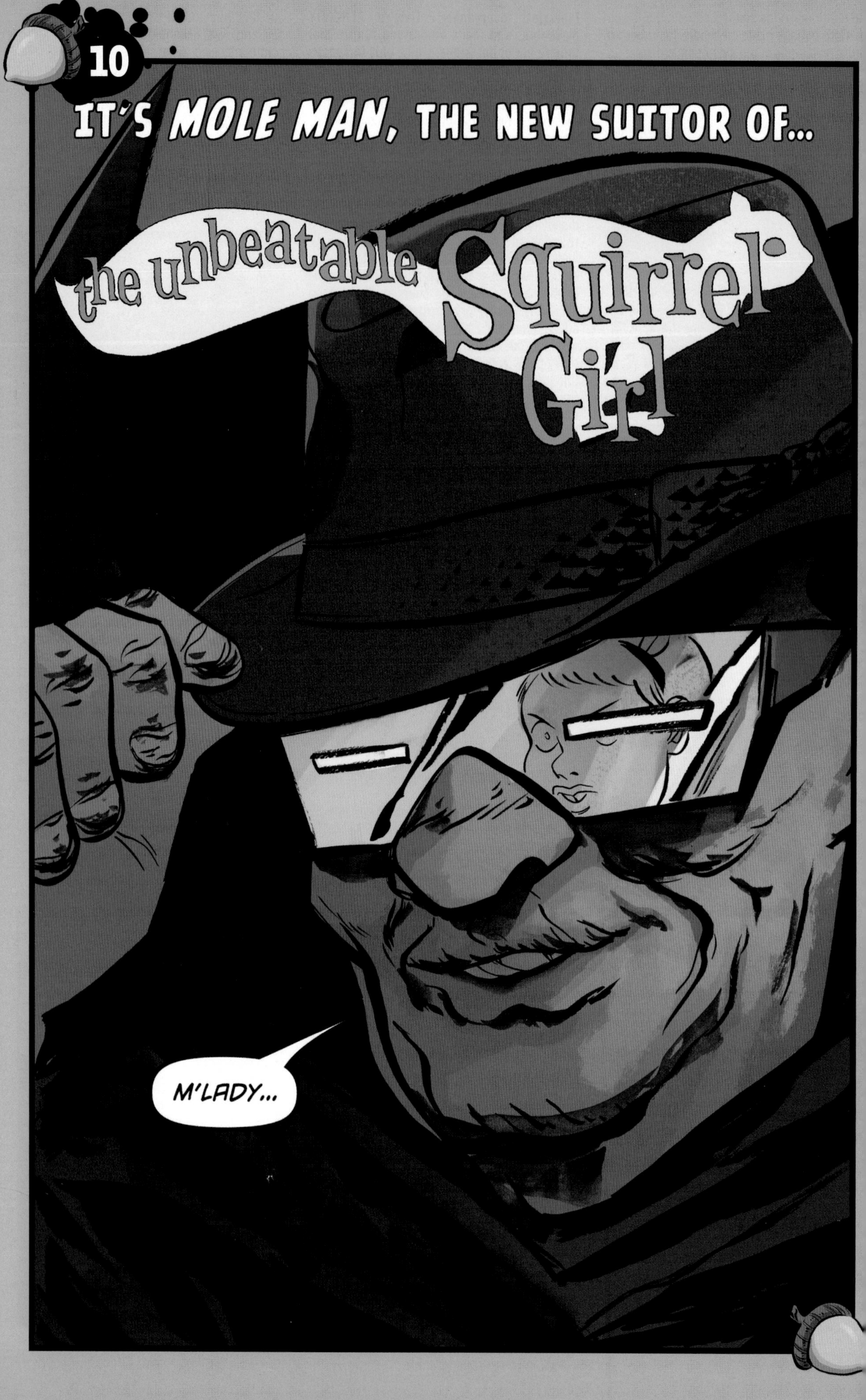
10
IT'S MOLE MAN, THE NEW SUITOR OF...
the unbeatable Squirrel Girl
M'LADY...

oreen Green isn't just a second-year computer science student: she secretly also has all the powers of both squirrel and
l! She uses her amazing abilities to fight crime and be as awesome as possible. You know her as...**The Unbeatable Squirrel Girl!**
Find out what she's been up to, with...

Squirrel Girl in a nutshell

search!

#moleman
#molemaam
#evenmolemoneyevenmoleproblems
#holycarp
#voteloki

Squirrel Girl @unbeatablesg
RT if you got like 9999999 new followers b/c Mole Man went on tv, NAMED YOU, and said he'd only stop stealing buildings if you dated him!!

Squirrel Girl @unbeatablesg
No RTs huh? Haha weird how I'M THE ONLY ONE THIS IS HAPPENING TO FOR SOME FRIGGIN' REASON

Squirrel Girl @unbeatablesg
hahaha what even is reality

Howard The Duck @imhowatrd
@unbeatablesg humnas makr datign pretty weikrd, huh??

Squirrel Girl @unbeatablesg
@imhowatrd oh Howard, you have no idea. NO IDEA

Squirrel Girl @unbeatablesg
@imhowatrd I went on a date with a giant purple robot and that was like the most normal part of the past few days!!

Squirrel Girl @unbeatablesg
@imhowatrd I hope he's doing well

SENTINEL X-42903-22 @X4290322
@unbeatablesg HEY

SENTINEL X-42903-22 @X4290322
@unbeatablesg ERROR 552255: DON'T SUBTWEET ME

Egg @imduderadtude
@unbeatablesg just date him alreayd

Squirrel Girl @unbeatablesg
@imduderadtude YOU DATE HIM

Egg @imduderadtude
@unbeatablesg im 12

Squirrel Girl @unbeatablesg
@imduderadtude 100 YEARS OF COMPUTATIONAL MACHINERY DEVELOPMENT SO A 12-YEAR-OLD BOY I DON'T KNOW CAN GIVE ME UNSOLICITED DATING ADVICE

Egg @imduderadtude
@unbeatablesg lol

Egg @imduderadtude
@unbeatablesg i also make memes

Squirrel Girl @unbeatablesg
@imduderadtude ...Any good ones?

Tony Stark @starkmantony
@unbeatablesg @imduderadtude No they're super bad!! Don't waste your time

Squirrel Girl @unbeatablesg
@starkmantony Tony Stark!! YOU consume THE FRESHEST OF MEMES??

Tony Stark @starkmantony
@unbeatablesg @imduderadtude Haha not with this kid I don't!

Egg @imduderadtude
@starkmantony UM WOW WHAT DOES IT SYA IN MY BIO,, MR STARK?? WHAT DOES IT SAY

Egg @imduderadtude
@starkmantony IT SAYS "DONT @ ME IF U DON'T LIKE MY MEMES!!!"!!! THAT'S WHAT IT SAYS

Egg @imduderadtude
@starkmantony BLOCKED

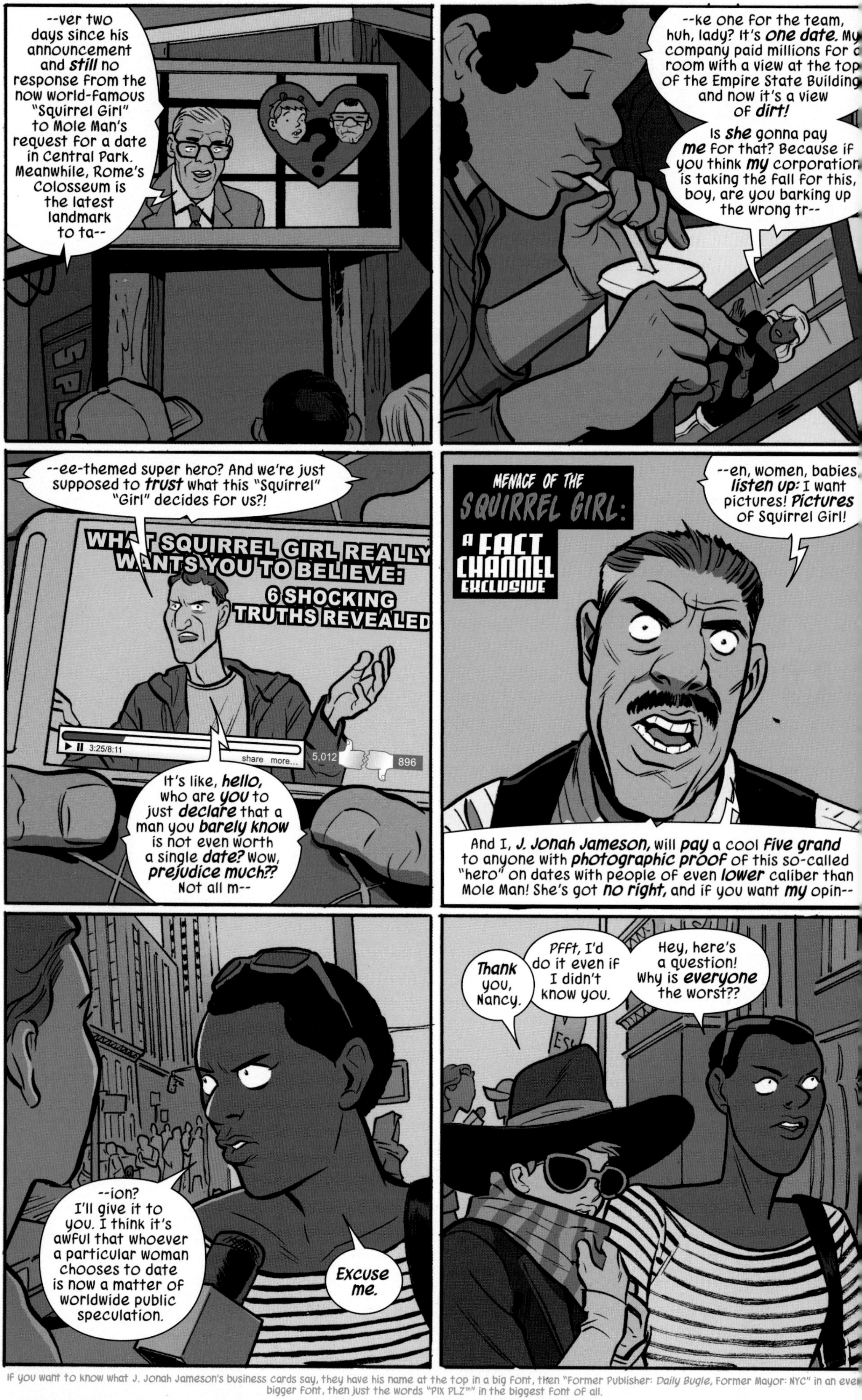

--ver two days since his announcement and still no response from the now world-famous "Squirrel Girl" to Mole Man's request for a date in Central Park. Meanwhile, Rome's Colosseum is the latest landmark to ta--
--ke one for the team, huh, lady? It's one date. My company paid millions for a room with a view at the top of the Empire State Building and now it's a view of dirt!
Is she gonna pay me for that? Because if you think my corporation is taking the fall for this, boy, are you barking up the wrong tr--
--ee-themed super hero? And we're just supposed to trust what this "Squirrel" "Girl" decides for us?!
WHAT SQUIRREL GIRL REALLY WANTS YOU TO BELIEVE: 6 SHOCKING TRUTHS REVEALED
3:25/8:11
share more...
5,012
896
It's like, hello, who are you to just declare that a man you barely know is not even worth a single date? Wow, prejudice much?? Not all m--
MENACE OF THE SQUIRREL GIRL: A FACT CHANNEL EXCLUSIVE
--en, women, babies, listen up: I want pictures! Pictures of Squirrel Girl!
And I, J. Jonah Jameson, will pay a cool five grand to anyone with photographic proof of this so-called "hero" on dates with people of even lower caliber than Mole Man! She's got no right, and if you want my opin--
--ion? I'll give it to you. I think it's awful that whoever a particular woman chooses to date is now a matter of worldwide public speculation.
Excuse me.
Thank you, Nancy.
Pfft, I'd do it even if I didn't know you.
Hey, here's a question! Why is everyone the worst??

If you want to know what J. Jonah Jameson's business cards say, they have his name at the top in a big font, then "Former Publisher: *Daily Bugle*, Former Mayor: NYC" in an even bigger font, then just the words "PIX PLZ™" in the biggest font of all.

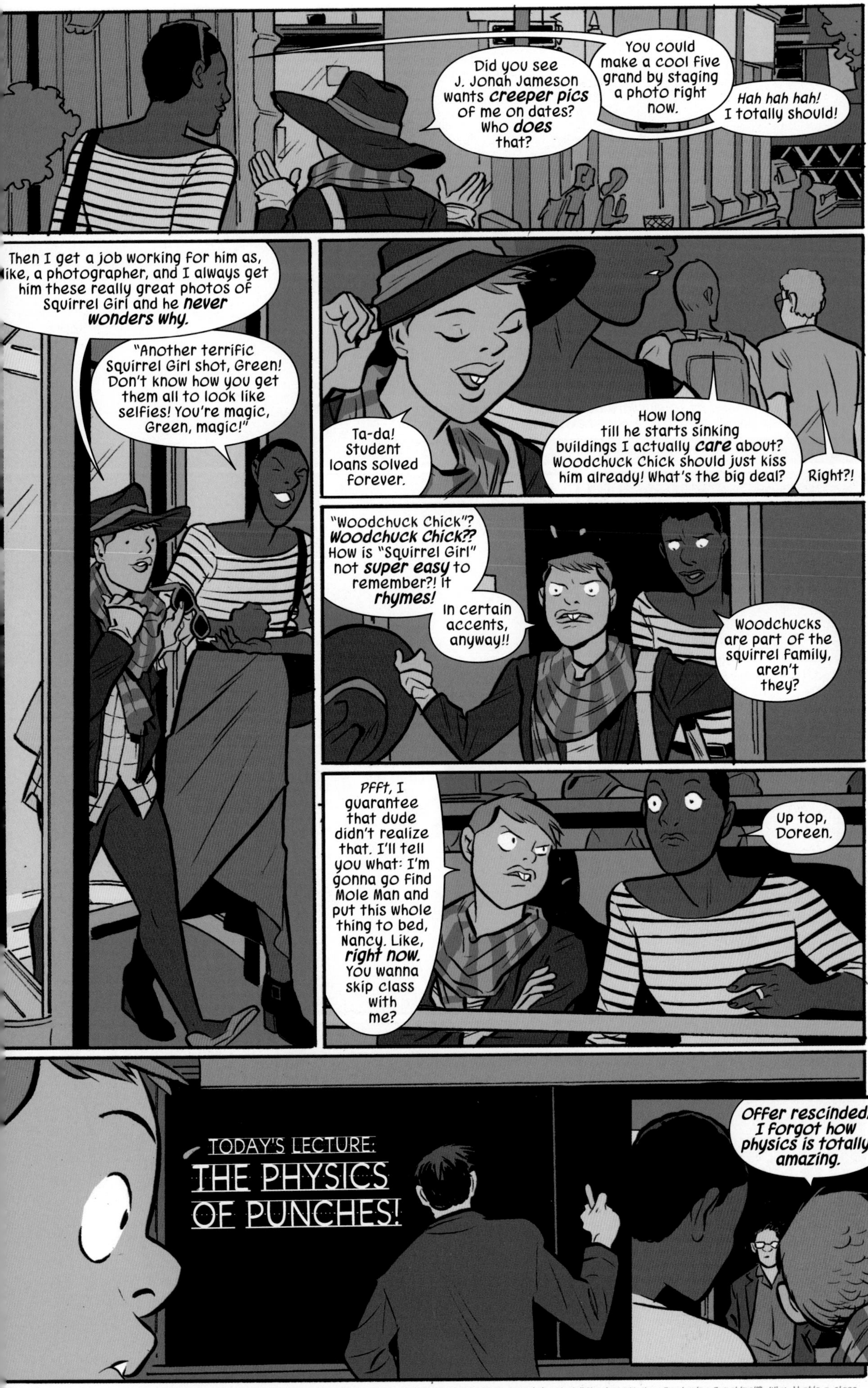
Did you see J. Jonah Jameson wants creeper pics of me on dates? Who does that?
You could make a cool five grand by staging a photo right now.
Hah hah hah! I totally should!
Then I get a job working for him as, like, a photographer, and I always get him these really great photos of Squirrel Girl and he never wonders why.
"Another terrific Squirrel Girl shot, Green! Don't know how you get them all to look like selfies! You're magic, Green, magic!"
Ta-da! Student loans solved forever.
How long till he starts sinking buildings I actually care about? Woodchuck Chick should just kiss him already! What's the big deal?
Right?!
"Woodchuck Chick"? Woodchuck Chick?? How is "Squirrel Girl" not super easy to remember?! It rhymes!
In certain accents, anyway!!
Woodchucks are part of the squirrel family, aren't they?
Pfft, I guarantee that dude didn't realize that. I'll tell you what: I'm gonna go find Mole Man and put this whole thing to bed, Nancy. Like, right now. You wanna skip class with me?
Up top, Doreen.
TODAY'S LECTURE:
THE PHYSICS OF PUNCHES!
Offer rescinded; I forgot how physics is totally amazing.

Teaching tip: Add punching to any lecture title to make it way more interesting! "Physics 101" might sound dry, but "Physics 101, Now Featuring Punching"? Why, that's a class I wish I were taking *right now!*

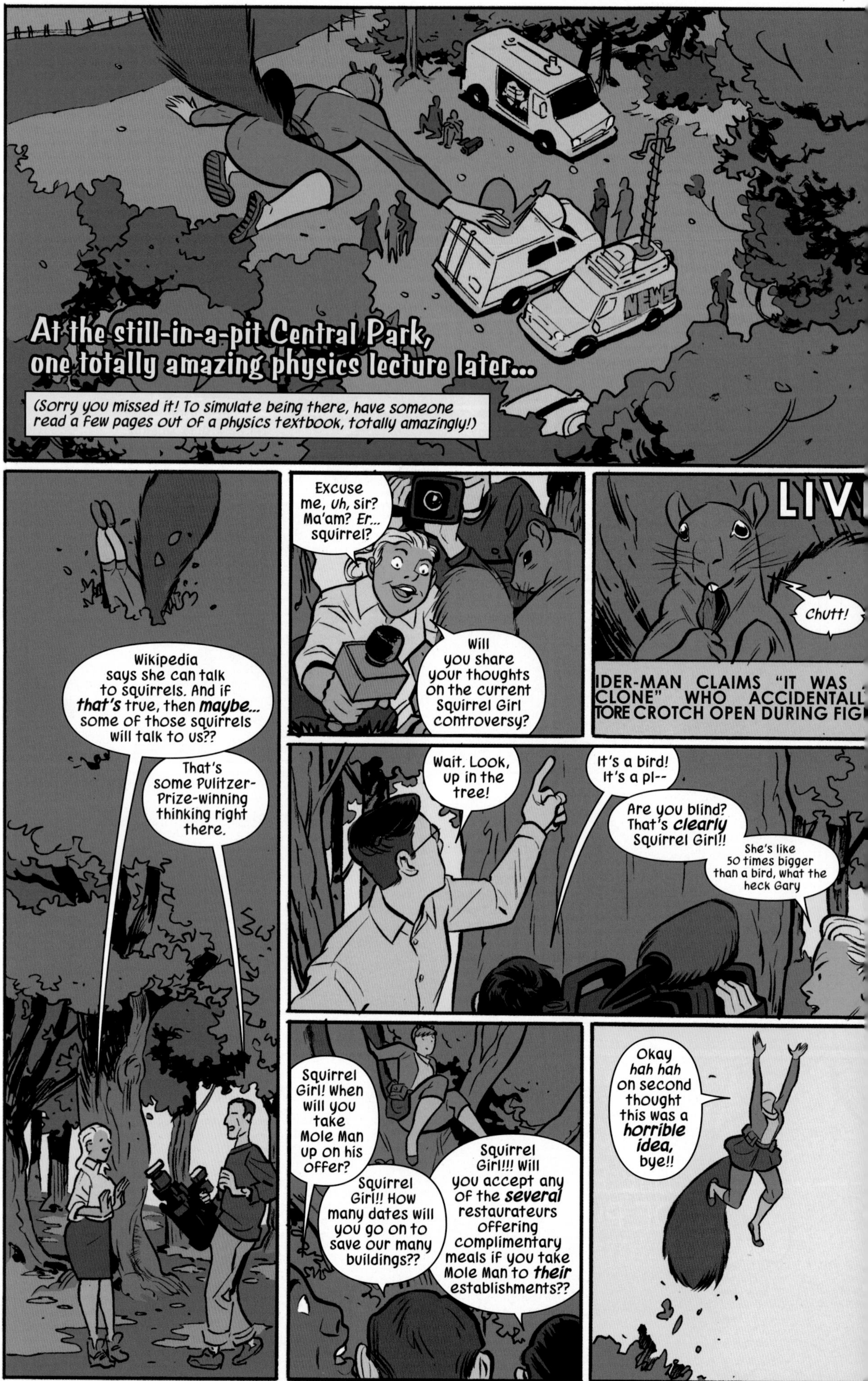
At the still-in-a-pit Central Park, one totally amazing physics lecture later...
(Sorry you missed it! To simulate being there, have someone read a few pages out of a physics textbook, totally amazingly!)
NEWS
Wikipedia says she can talk to squirrels. And if that's true, then maybe... some of those squirrels will talk to us??
That's some Pulitzer-Prize-winning thinking right there.
Excuse me, uh, sir? Ma'am? Er... squirrel?
Will you share your thoughts on the current Squirrel Girl controversy?
LIV
Chutt!
IDER-MAN CLAIMS "IT WAS
CLONE" WHO ACCIDENTALL
TORE CROTCH OPEN DURING FIG
Wait. Look, up in the tree!
It's a bird! It's a pl--
Are you blind? That's clearly Squirrel Girl!!
She's like 50 times bigger than a bird, what the heck Gary
Squirrel Girl! When will you take Mole Man up on his offer?
Squirrel Girl!! How many dates will you go on to save our many buildings??
Squirrel Girl!!! Will you accept any of the several restaurateurs offering complimentary meals if you take Mole Man to their establishments??
Okay hah hah on second thought this was a horrible idea, bye!!

Spider-Man Claims "It Was A Clone" Who Was Caught On Video Landing In A Dumpster Full Of Dirty Diapers, But Only Because He Ran Out Of Web-Fluid Mid-Swing, Which Really Could Happen To Anyone, So Let's Not Be So Quick To Judge Okay

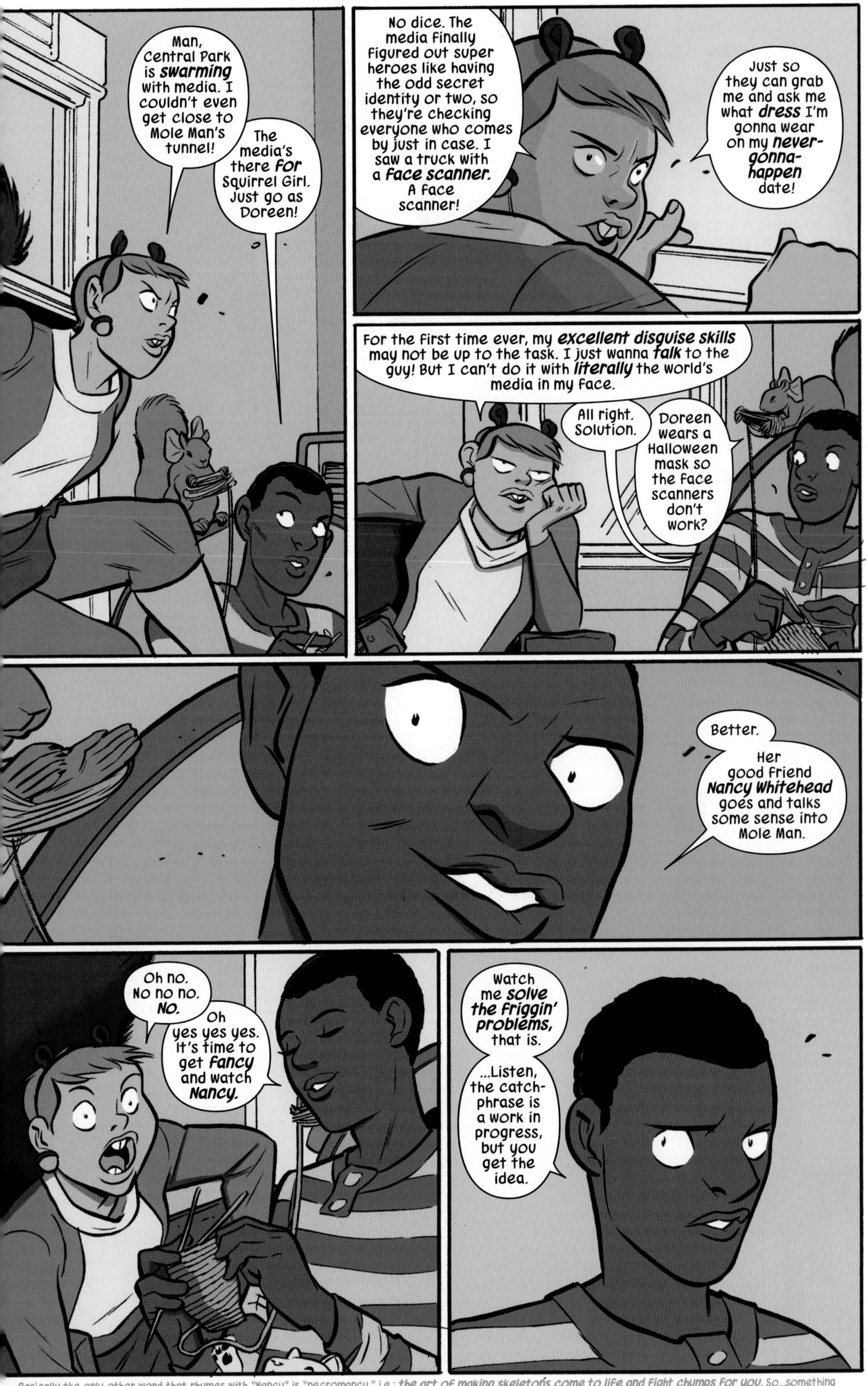
Man, Central Park is swarming with media. I couldn't even get close to Mole Man's tunnel!
The media's there for Squirrel Girl. Just go as Doreen!
No dice. The media finally figured out super heroes like having the odd secret identity or two, so they're checking everyone who comes by just in case. I saw a truck with a face scanner. A face scanner!
Just so they can grab me and ask me what dress I'm gonna wear on my never-gonna-happen date!
For the first time ever, my excellent disguise skills may not be up to the task. I just wanna talk to the guy! But I can't do it with literally the world's media in my face.
All right. Solution.
Doreen wears a Halloween mask so the face scanners don't work?
Better.
Her good friend Nancy Whitehead goes and talks some sense into Mole Man.
Oh no. No no no. NO.
Oh yes yes yes. It's time to get fancy and watch Nancy.
Watch me solve the friggin' problems, that is.
...Listen, the catch-phrase is a work in progress, but you get the idea.

Basically the only other word that rhymes with "Nancy" is "necromancy," i.e.: *the art of making skeletons come to life and fight chumps for you.* So...something to look forward to, I guess??

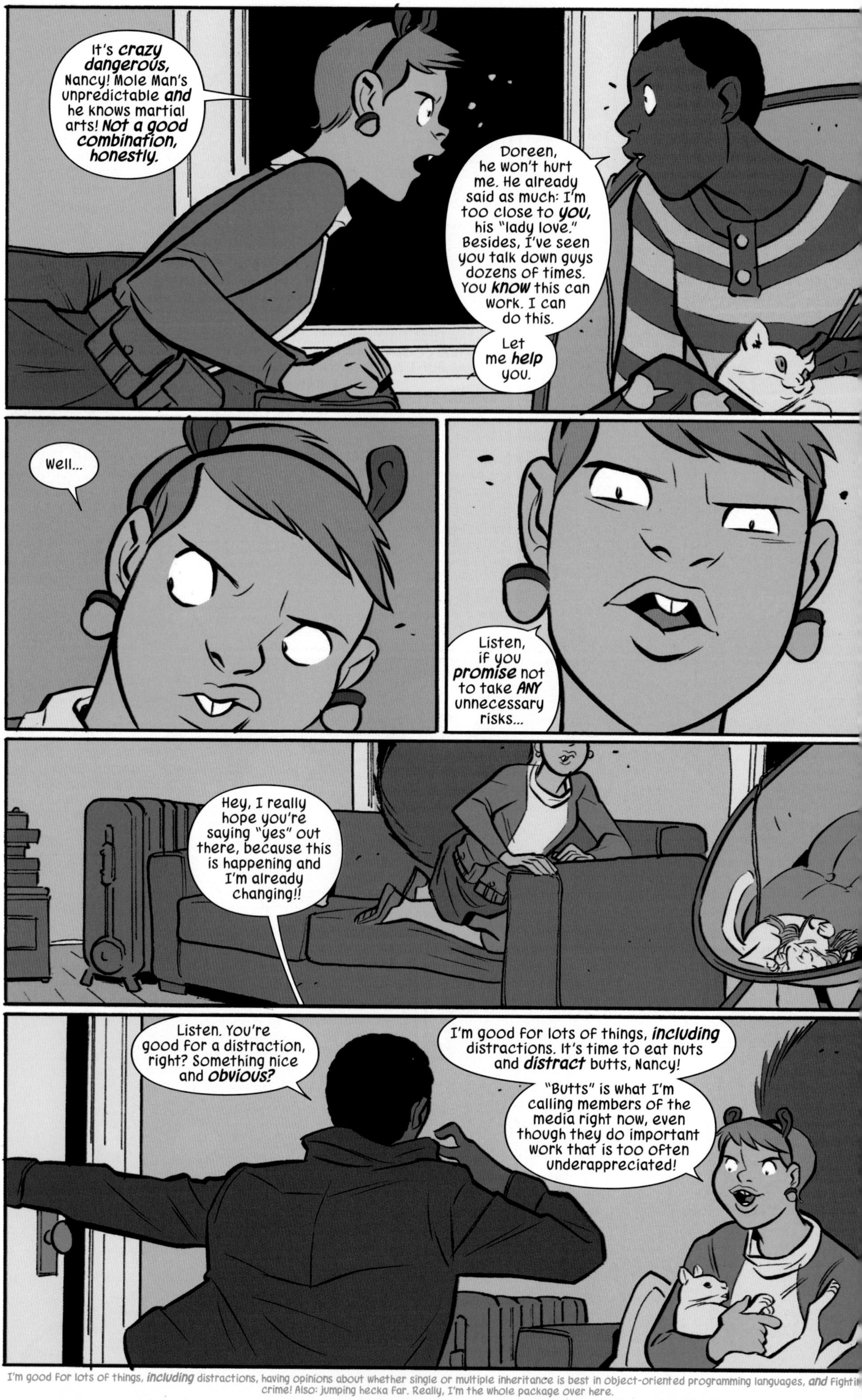
It's *crazy dangerous,* Nancy! Mole Man's unpredictable *and* he knows martial arts! *Not a good combination, honestly.*
Doreen, he won't hurt me. He already said as much: I'm too close to *you,* his "lady love." Besides, I've seen you talk down guys dozens of times. You *know* this can work. I can do this.
Let me *help* you.
Well...
Listen, if you *promise* not to take *ANY* unnecessary risks...
Hey, I really hope you're saying "yes" out there, because this is happening and I'm already changing!!
Listen. You're good for a distraction, right? Something nice and *obvious?*
I'm good for lots of things, *including* distractions. It's time to eat nuts and *distract* butts, Nancy!
"Butts" is what I'm calling members of the media right now, even though they do important work that is too often underappreciated!

I'm good for lots of things, *including* distractions, having opinions about whether single or multiple inheritance is best in object-oriented programming languages, *and* fighti
crime! Also: jumping hecka far. Really, I'm the whole package over here.

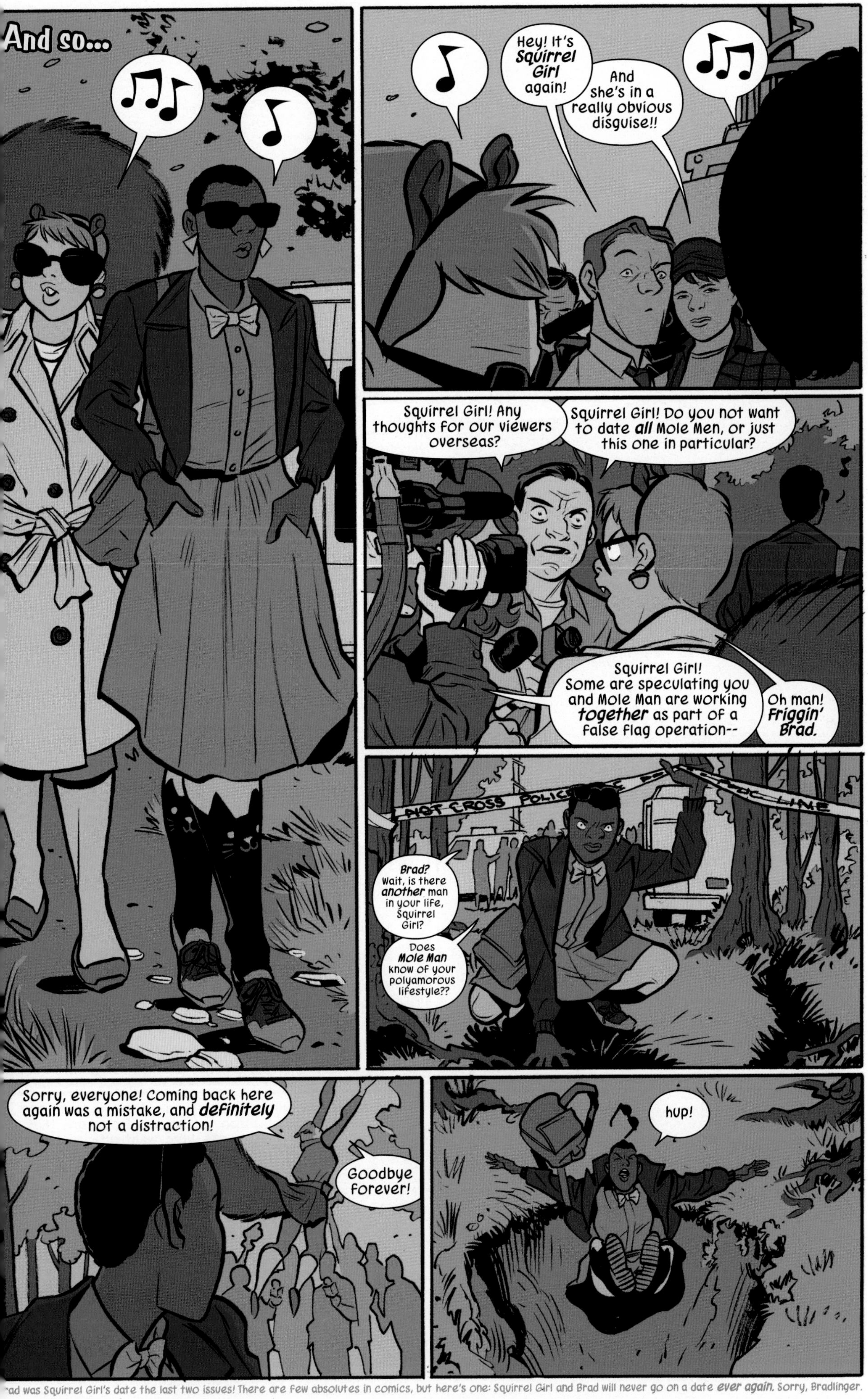
And so...
Hey! It's Squirrel Girl again!
And she's in a really obvious disguise!!
Squirrel Girl! Any thoughts for our viewers overseas?
Squirrel Girl! Do you not want to date all Mole Men, or just this one in particular?
Squirrel Girl! Some are speculating you and Mole Man are working together as part of a false flag operation--
Oh man! Friggin' Brad.
Brad? Wait, is there another man in your life, Squirrel Girl?
Does Mole Man know of your polyamorous lifestyle??
Sorry, everyone! Coming back here again was a mistake, and definitely not a distraction!
Goodbye forever!
hup!

'rad was Squirrel Girl's date the last two issues! There are few absolutes in comics, but here's one: Squirrel Girl and Brad will never go on a date *ever again*. Sorry, Bradlinger.

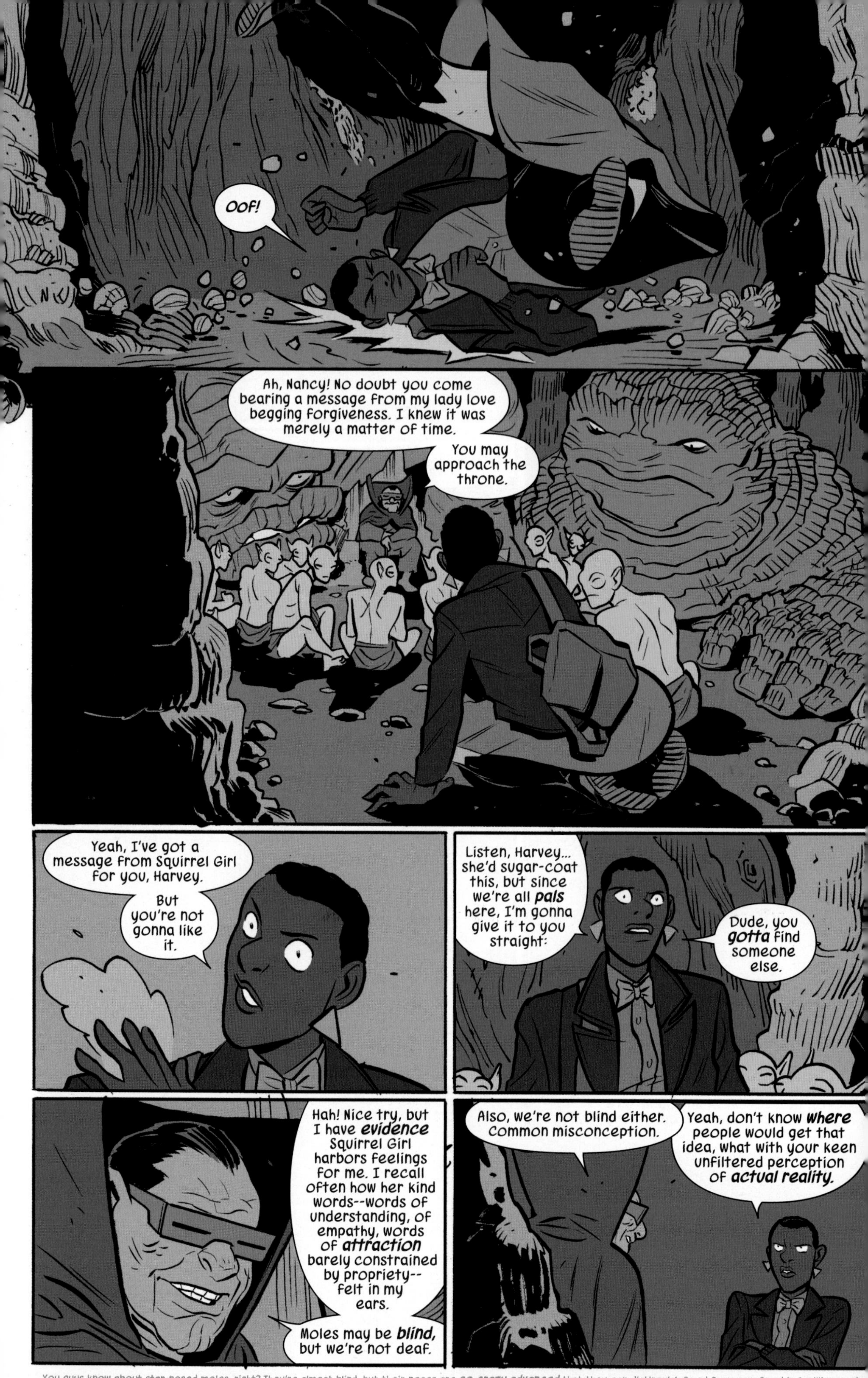

Oof!
Ah, Nancy! No doubt you come bearing a message from my lady love begging forgiveness. I knew it was merely a matter of time.
You may approach the throne.
Yeah, I've got a message from Squirrel Girl for you, Harvey.
But you're not gonna like it.
Listen, Harvey... she'd sugar-coat this, but since we're all pals here, I'm gonna give it to you straight:
Dude, you gotta find someone else.
Hah! Nice try, but I have evidence Squirrel Girl harbors feelings for me. I recall often how her kind words--words of understanding, of empathy, words of attraction barely constrained by propriety--felt in my ears.
Moles may be blind, but we're not deaf.
Also, we're not blind either. Common misconception.
Yeah, don't know where people would get that idea, what with your keen unfiltered perception of actual reality.

You guys know about star-nosed moles, right? They're almost blind, but their noses are *so crazy advanced* that they can distinguish food from non-food in 8 milliseconds. In contrast, it takes your brain at least 100 milliseconds just to figure out what it's looking at. Moles, man!

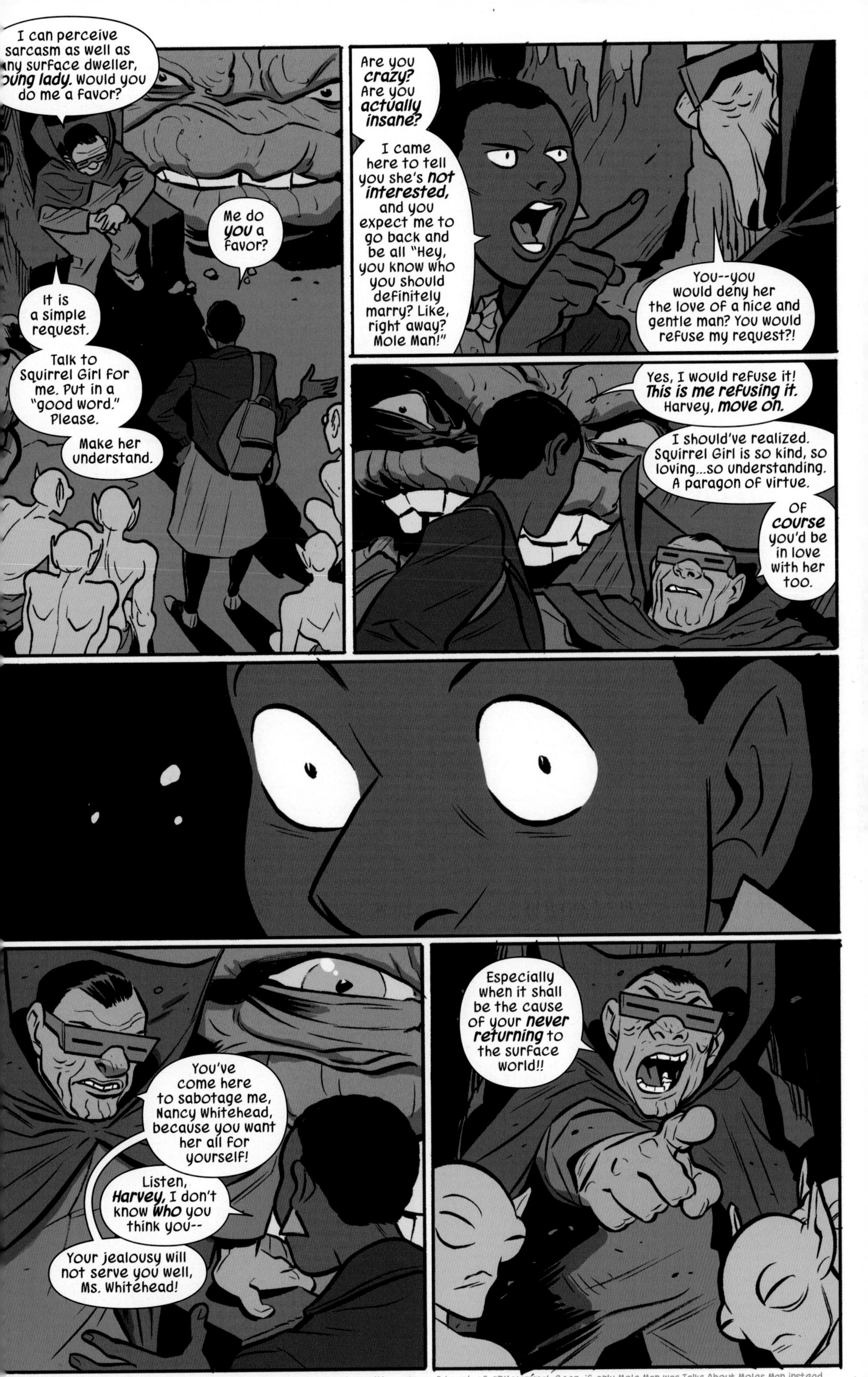
I can perceive sarcasm as well as ny surface dweller, oung lady. Would you do me a favor?
Me do YOU a favor?
It is a simple request.
Talk to Squirrel Girl for me. Put in a "good word." Please.
Make her understand.
Are you crazy? Are you actually insane?
I came here to tell you she's not interested, and you expect me to go back and be all "Hey, you know who you should definitely marry? Like, right away? Mole Man!"
You--you would deny her the love of a nice and gentle man? You would refuse my request?!
Yes, I would refuse it! This is me refusing it. Harvey, move on.
I should've realized. Squirrel Girl is so kind, so loving...so understanding. A paragon of virtue.
Of course you'd be in love with her too.
You've come here to sabotage me, Nancy Whitehead, because you want her all for yourself!
Listen, Harvey, I don't know who you think you--
Your jealousy will not serve you well, Ms. Whitehead!
Especially when it shall be the cause of your never returning to the surface world!!

I'm still big into star-nosed moles. They've got what's likely the most sensitive sense of touch of *any* mammal. Geez, if only Mole Man was Talks About Moles Man instead, we could've all learned cool mole facts *and* nobody's buildings would've gotten sunk!

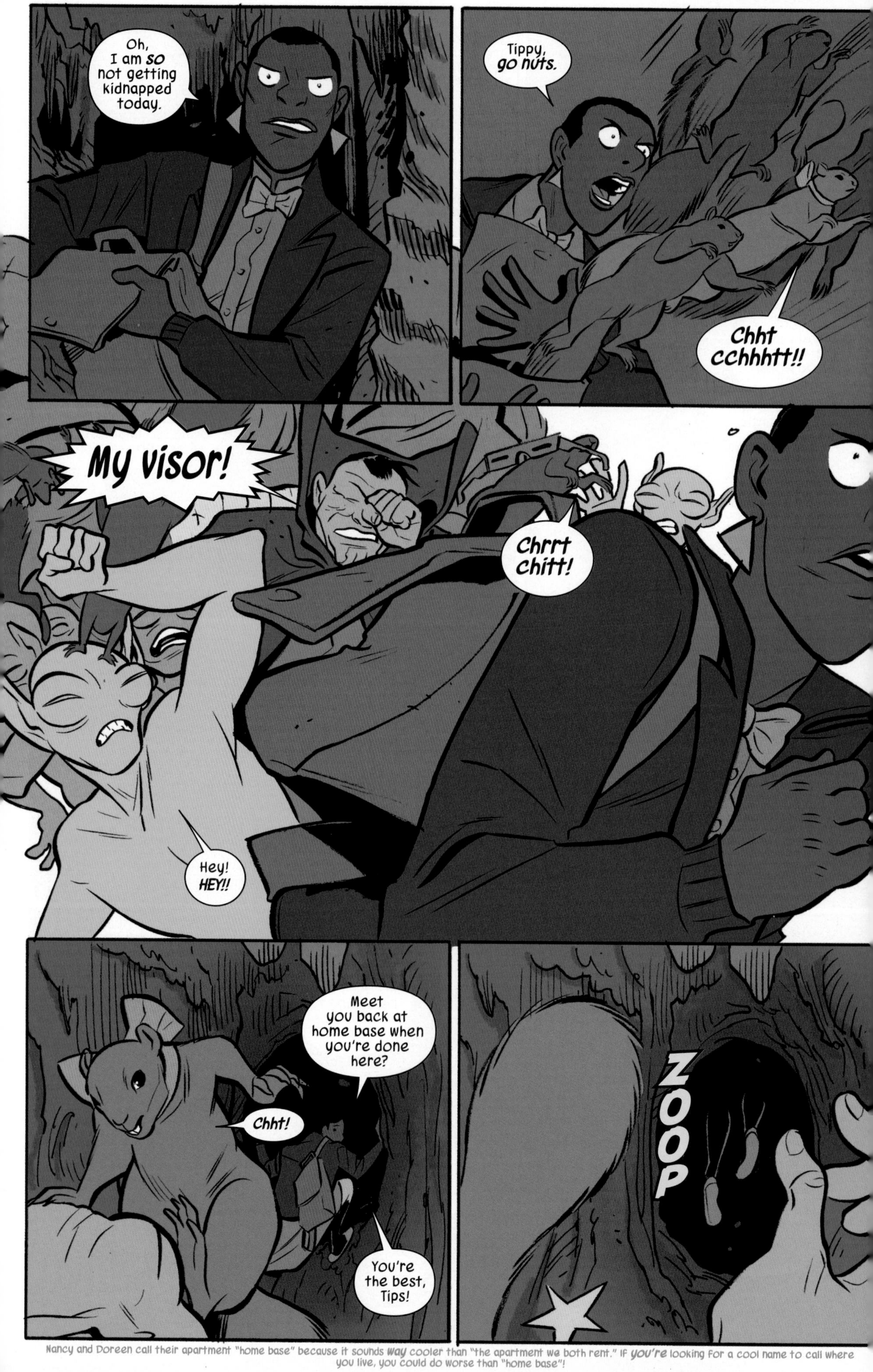
Oh, I am *so* not getting kidnapped today.
Tippy, *go nuts.*
Chht cchhhtt!!
My visor!
Chrrt chitt!
Hey! *HEY!!*
Meet you back at home base when you're done here?
Chht!
You're the best, Tips!
ZOOP

Nancy and Doreen call their apartment "home base" because it sounds *way* cooler than "the apartment we both rent." If *you're* looking for a cool name to call where you live, you could do worse than "home base"!

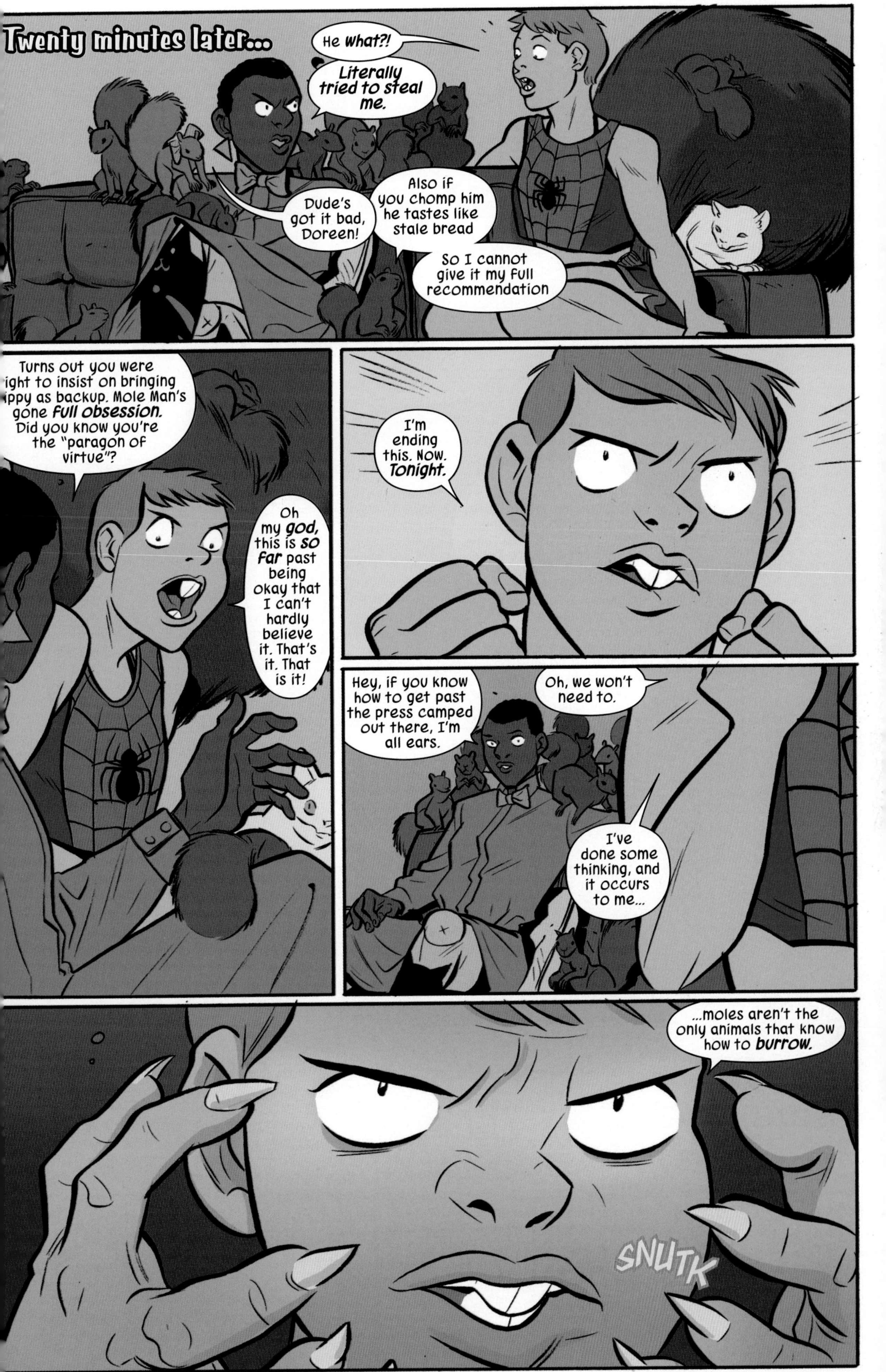
Twenty minutes later...
He what?!
Literally tried to steal me.
Dude's got it bad, Doreen!
Also if you chomp him he tastes like stale bread
So I cannot give it my full recommendation
Turns out you were
ight to insist on bringing
ippy as backup. Mole Man's gone full obsession. Did you know you're the "paragon of virtue"?
Oh my god, this is so far past being okay that I can't hardly believe it. That's it. That is it!
I'm ending this. Now. Tonight.
Hey, if you know how to get past the press camped out there, I'm all ears.
Oh, we won't need to.
I've done some thinking, and it occurs to me...
...moles aren't the only animals that know how to burrow.
SNUTK

Squirrel Girl's been practicing a lot to make her nails make that sound. Hard work pays off! The only sound my nails can make is this incredibly awful *"screeetch"* noise, and then only if I run them down a blackboard.

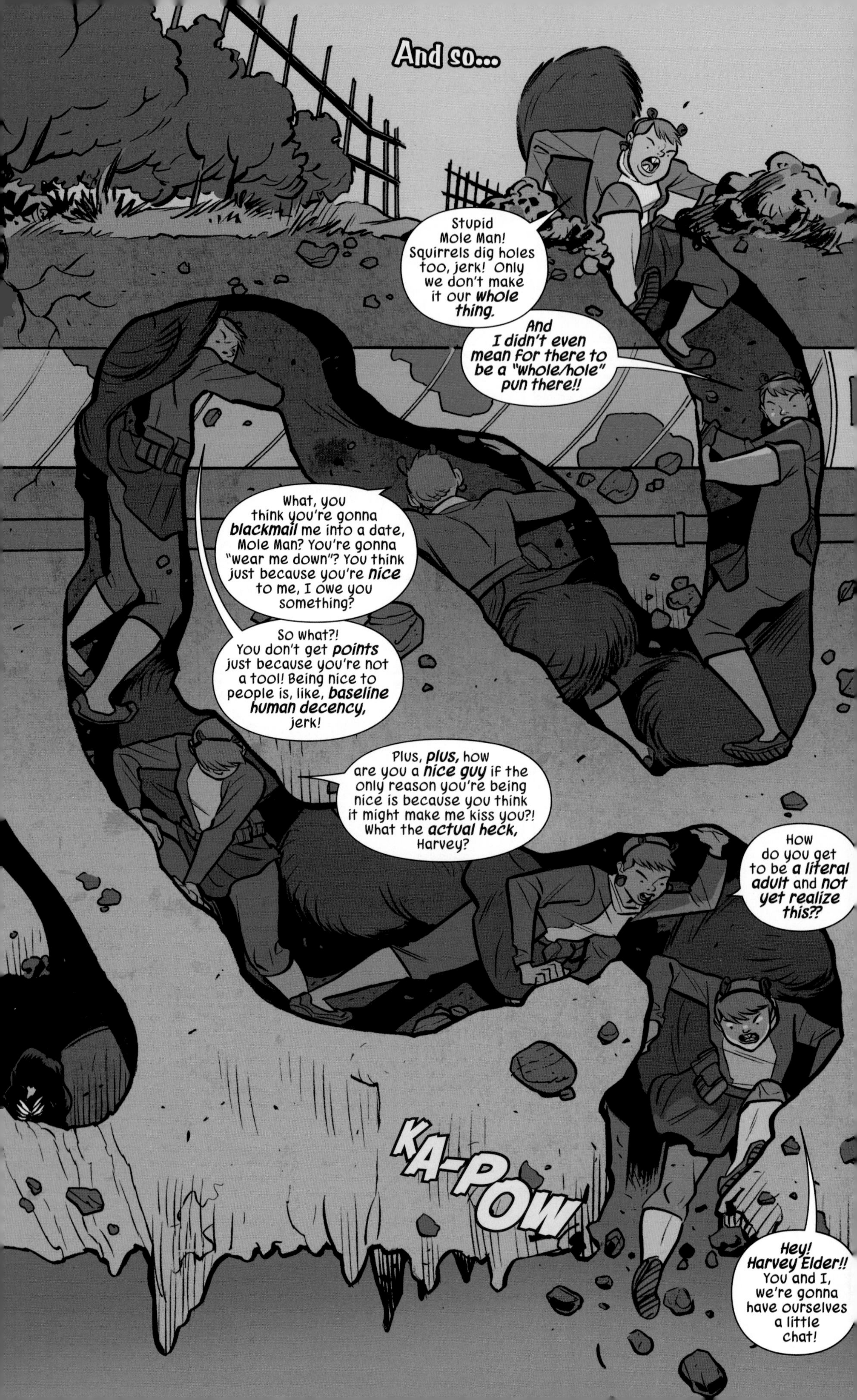
And so...
Stupid Mole Man! Squirrels dig holes too, jerk! Only we don't make it our whole thing.
And I didn't even mean for there to be a "whole/hole" pun there!!
What, you think you're gonna blackmail me into a date, Mole Man? You're gonna "wear me down"? You think just because you're nice to me, I owe you something?
So what?! You don't get points just because you're not a tool! Being nice to people is, like, baseline human decency, jerk!
Plus, plus, how are you a nice guy if the only reason you're being nice is because you think it might make me kiss you?! What the actual heck, Harvey?
How do you get to be a literal adult and not yet realize this??
KA-POW
Hey! Harvey Elder!! You and I, we're gonna have ourselves a little chat!

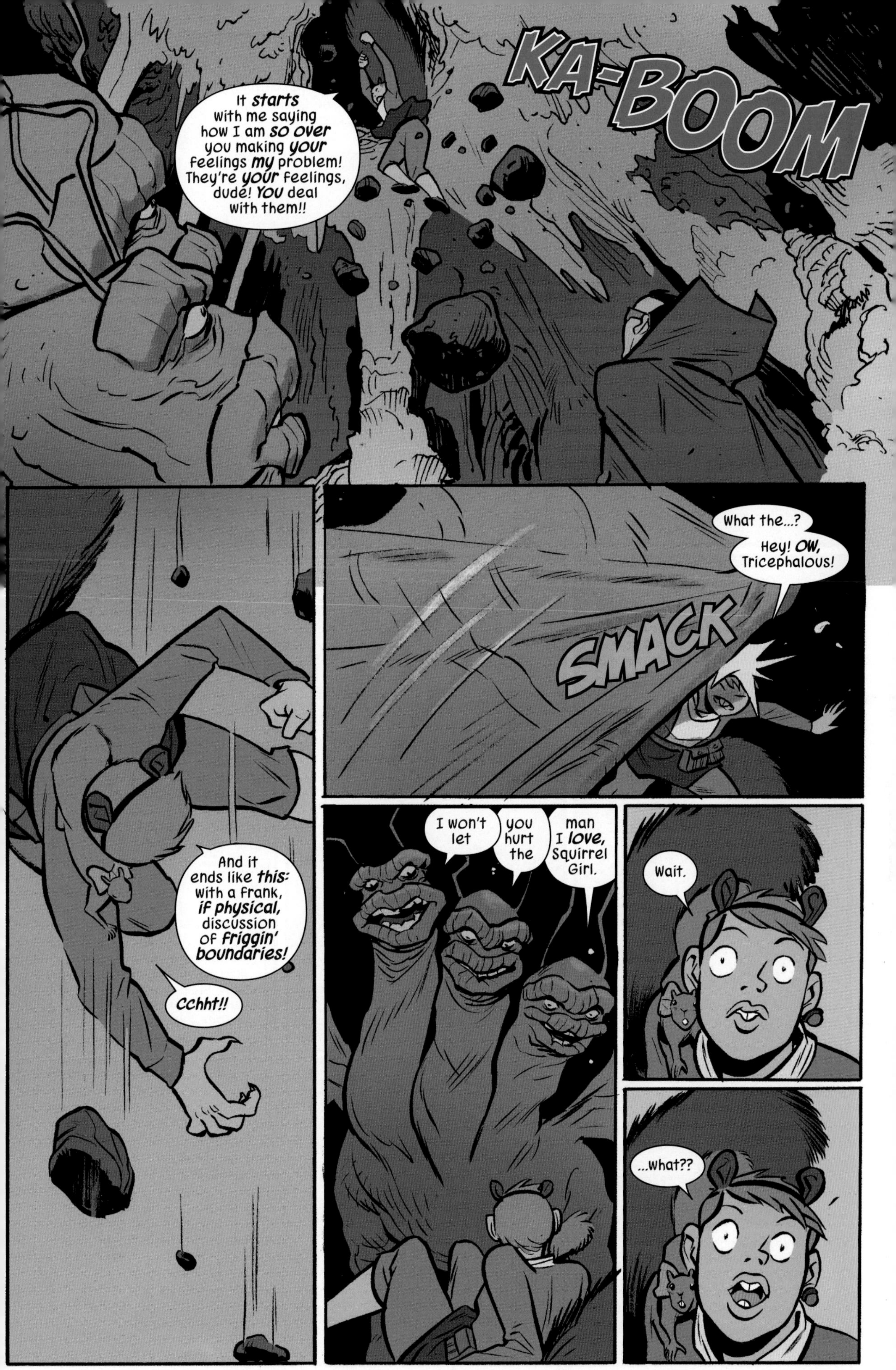
KA-BOOM
It starts with me saying how I am so over you making your feelings my problem! They're your feelings, dude! You deal with them!!
And it ends like this: with a frank, if physical, discussion of friggin' boundaries!
Cchht!!
What the...?
Hey! OW, Tricephalous!
SMACK
I won't let
you hurt the
man I love, Squirrel Girl.
Wait.
...what??

We're gonna have a *chat,* Harvey! And in the *middle* of our chat, we're gonna have some snacks! And they're gonna be real tasty chocolate-covered almonds! And I'm *barely* gonna share with you, because you've made me *that angry!!*

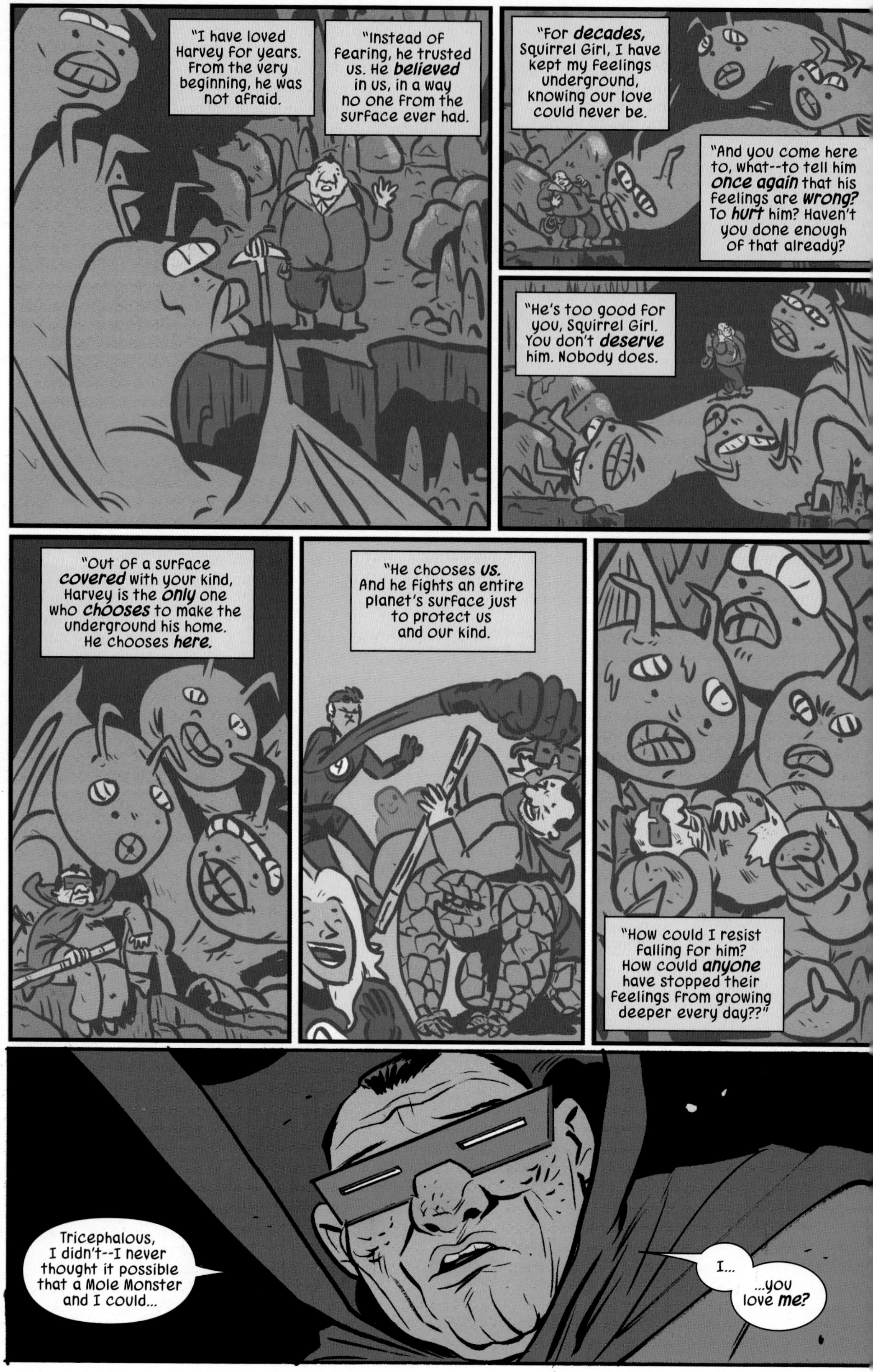
"I have loved Harvey for years. From the very beginning, he was not afraid.
"Instead of fearing, he trusted us. He believed in us, in a way no one from the surface ever had.
"For decades, Squirrel Girl, I have kept my feelings underground, knowing our love could never be.
"And you come here to, what--to tell him once again that his feelings are wrong? To hurt him? Haven't you done enough of that already?
"He's too good for you, Squirrel Girl. You don't deserve him. Nobody does.
"Out of a surface covered with your kind, Harvey is the only one who chooses to make the underground his home. He chooses here.
"He chooses us. And he fights an entire planet's surface just to protect us and our kind.
"How could I resist falling for him? How could anyone have stopped their feelings from growing deeper every day??"
Tricephalous, I didn't--I never thought it possible that a Mole Monster and I could...
I...
...you love me?

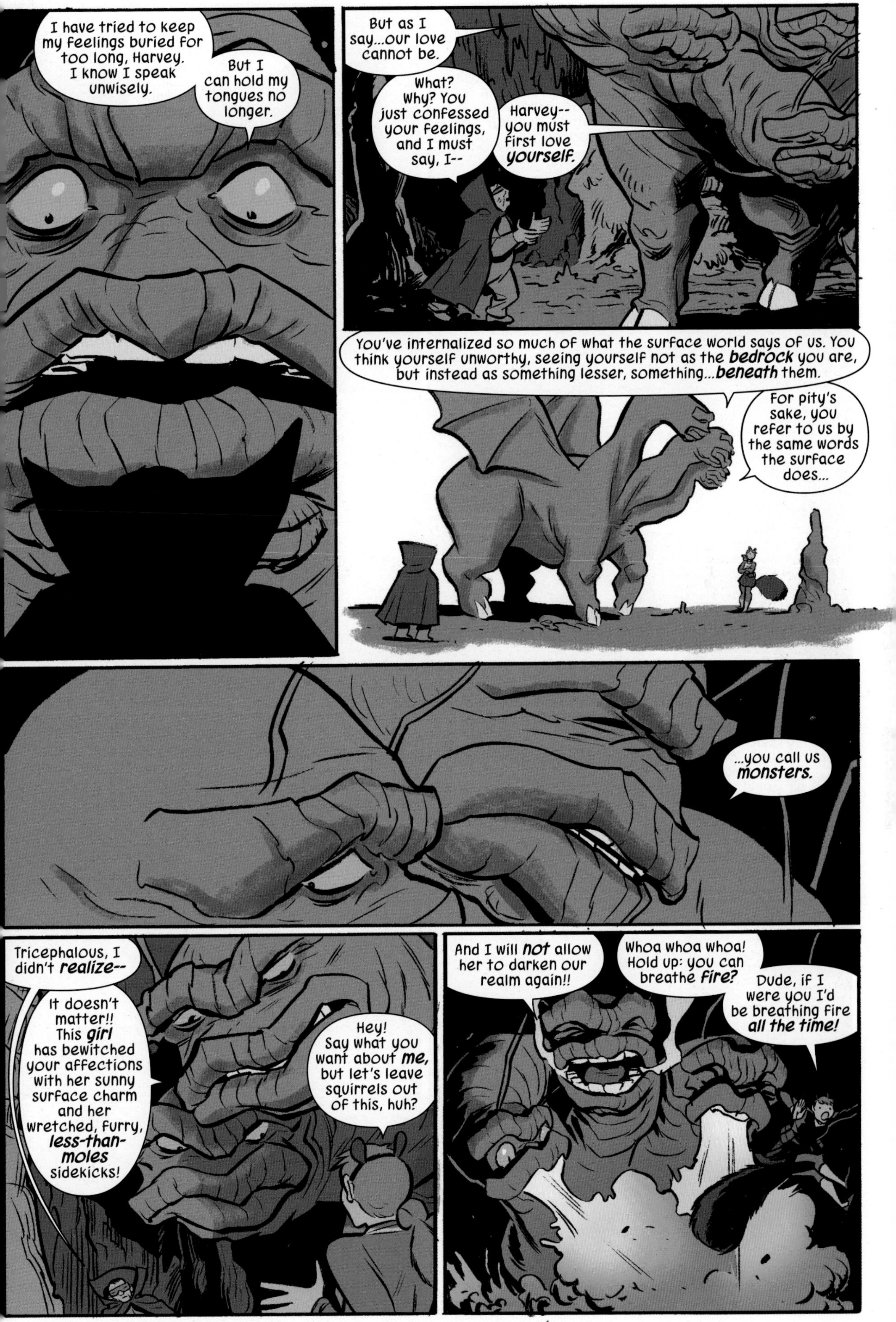
I have tried to keep my feelings buried for too long, Harvey. I know I speak unwisely.
But I can hold my tongues no longer.
But as I say...our love cannot be.
What? Why? You just confessed your feelings, and I must say, I--
Harvey-- you must first love yourself.
You've internalized so much of what the surface world says of us. You think yourself unworthy, seeing yourself not as the bedrock you are, but instead as something lesser, something...beneath them.
For pity's sake, you refer to us by the same words the surface does...
...you call us monsters.
Tricephalous, I didn't realize--
It doesn't matter!! This girl has bewitched your affections with her sunny surface charm and her wretched, furry, less-than-moles sidekicks!
Hey! Say what you want about me, but let's leave squirrels out of this, huh?
And I will not allow her to darken our realm again!!
Whoa whoa whoa! Hold up: you can breathe fire?
Dude, if I were you I'd be breathing fire all the time!

If I were you I'd be flying *everywhere*, breathing fire *nonstop*, and shouting "Bet you didn't know squirrels could do *this*, huh??"

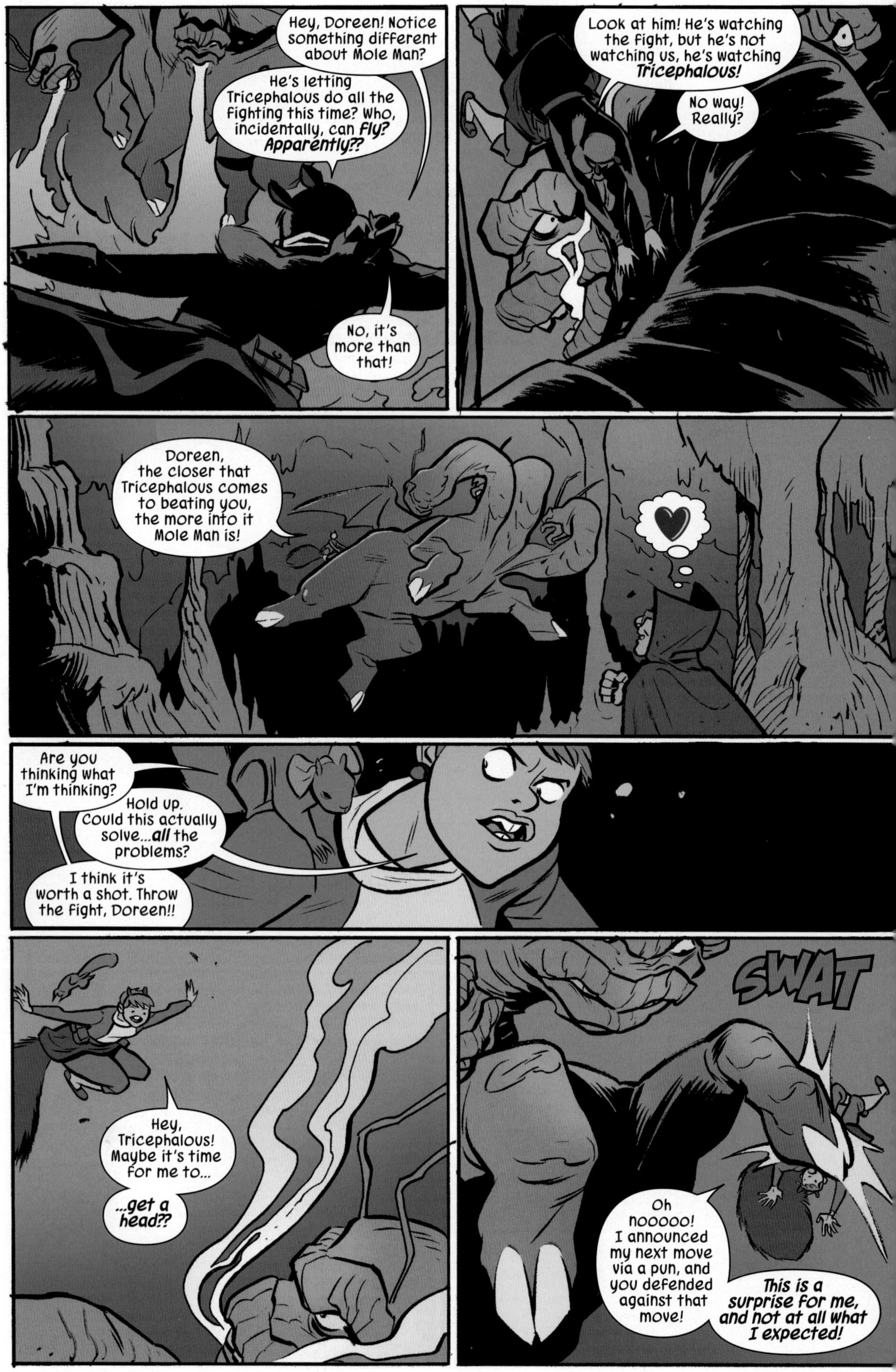
Hey, Doreen! Notice something different about Mole Man?
He's letting Tricephalous do all the fighting this time? Who, incidentally, can fly? Apparently??
No, it's more than that!
Look at him! He's watching the fight, but he's not watching us, he's watching Tricephalous!
No way! Really?
Doreen, the closer that Tricephalous comes to beating you, the more into it Mole Man is!
Are you thinking what I'm thinking?
Hold up. Could this actually solve...all the problems?
I think it's worth a shot. Throw the fight, Doreen!!
Hey, Tricephalous! Maybe it's time for me to...
...get a head??
SWAT
Oh nooooo! I announced my next move via a pun, and you defended against that move!
This is a surprise for me, and not at all what I expected!

To be fair, if you were suddenly knocked out of the air by a fire-breathing three-headed dinosaur-looking thing, you might say "This is a surprise for me, and not at all what I expected" too. And you'd mean it!

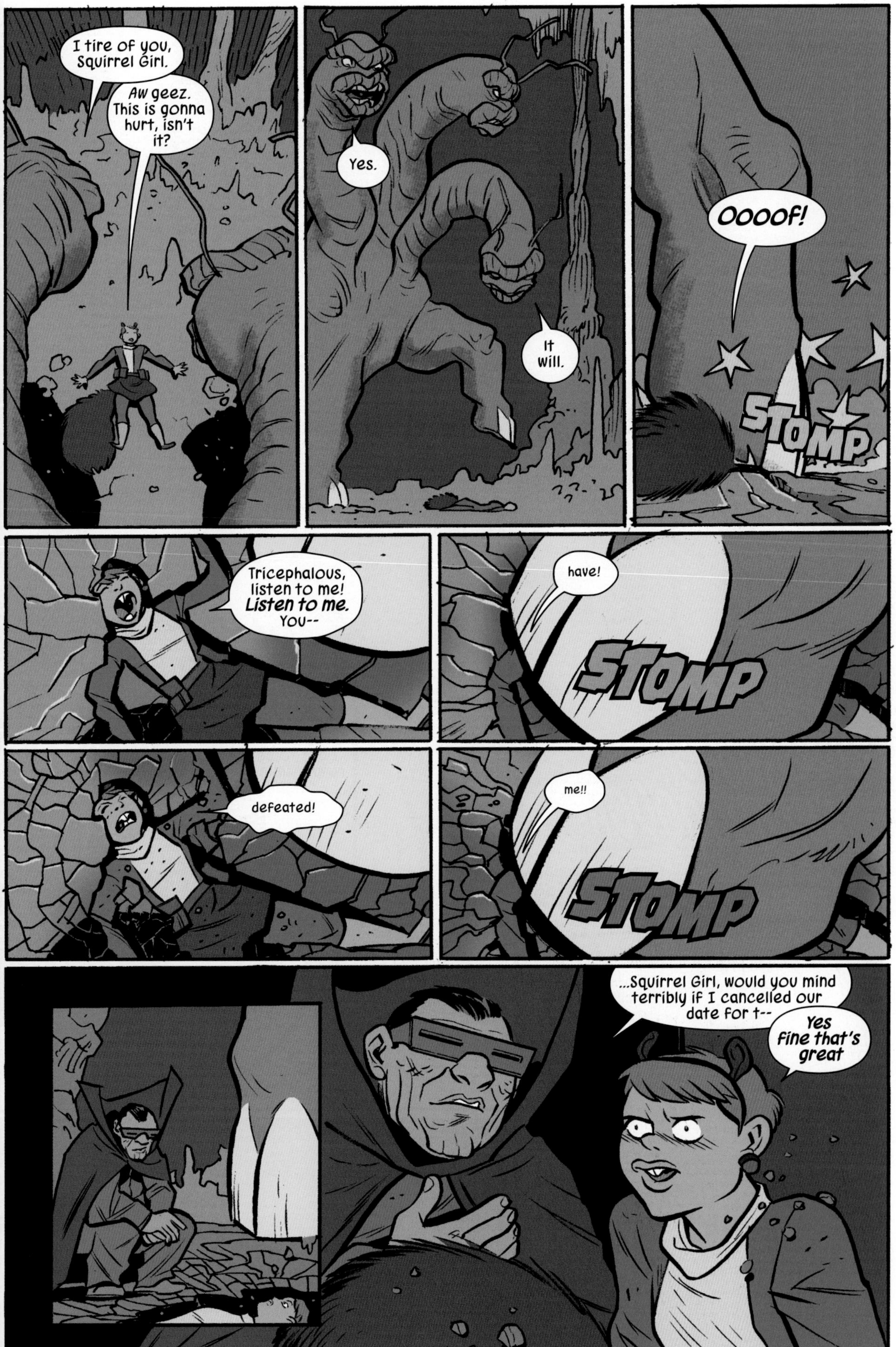
I tire of you, Squirrel Girl.
Aw geez. This is gonna hurt, isn't it?
Yes.
It will.
OOOOF!
STOMP
Tricephalous, listen to me! Listen to me. You--
have!
STOMP
defeated!
me!!
STOMP
...Squirrel Girl, would you mind terribly if I cancelled our date for t--
Yes fine that's great

Tricephalous, more like Tricea*ilus*, am I right? Because we were ailed by it three times? Nevermind, it was--it was a stretch to begin with.

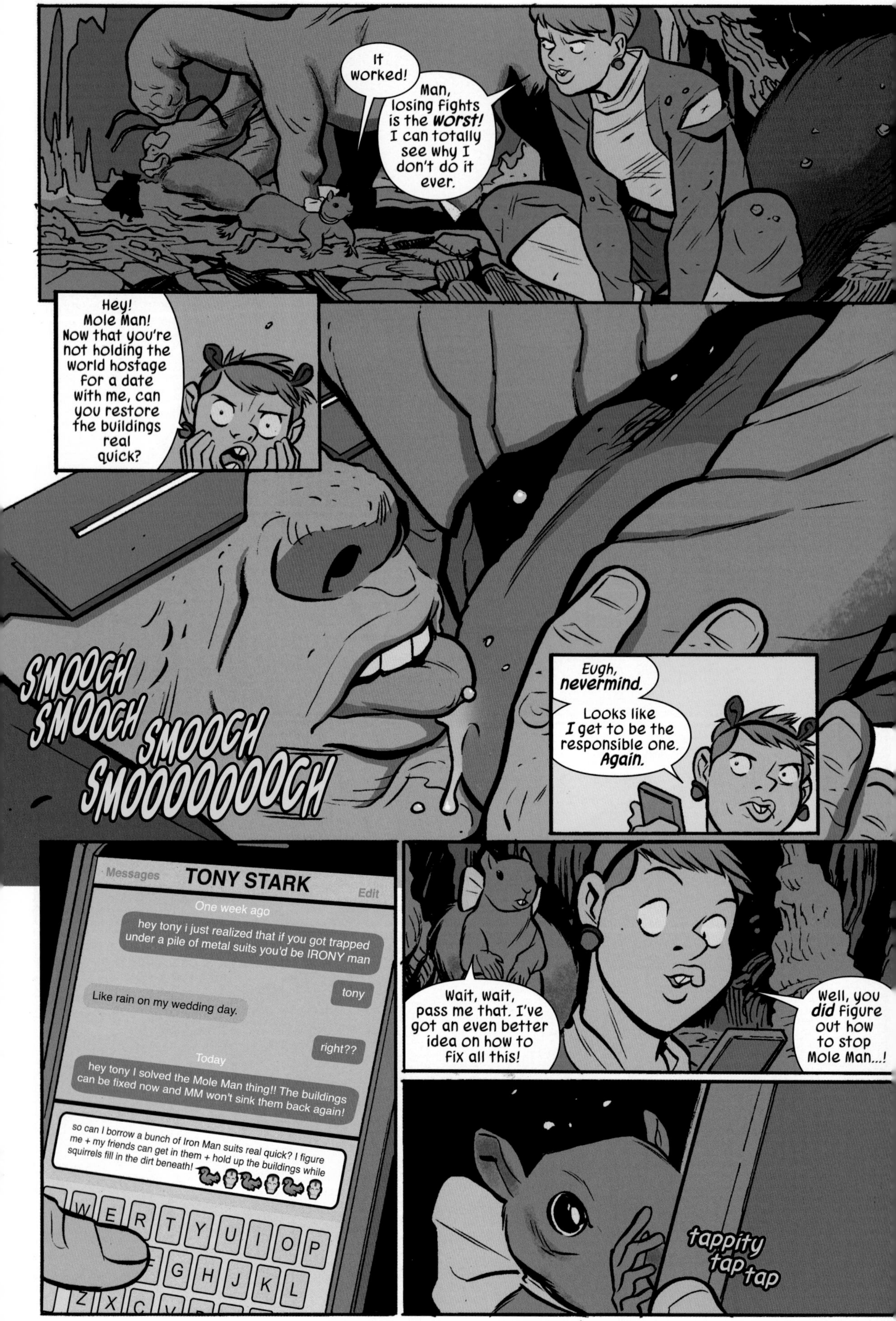

It worked!
Man, losing fights is the **worst!** I can totally see why I don't do it ever.
Hey! Mole Man! Now that you're not holding the world hostage for a date with me, can you restore the buildings real quick?
SMOOCH SMOOCH SMOOCH SMOOOOOOOOCH
Eugh, **nevermind.**
Looks like *I* get to be the responsible one. **Again.**
Well, you **did** figure out how to stop Mole Man...!
Wait, wait, pass me that. I've got an even better idea on how to fix all this!
Messages
TONY STARK
Edit
One week ago
hey tony i just realized that if you got trapped under a pile of metal suits you'd be IRONY man
tony
Like rain on my wedding day.
right??
Today
hey tony I solved the Mole Man thing!! The buildings can be fixed now and MM won't sink them back again!
so can I borrow a bunch of Iron Man suits real quick? I figure me + my friends can get in them + hold up the buildings while squirrels fill in the dirt beneath!
tappity tap tap

If Tony was named Ron instead, he could be "I, Ron" Man. Missed opportunities, Tony! Get on this, Tony!

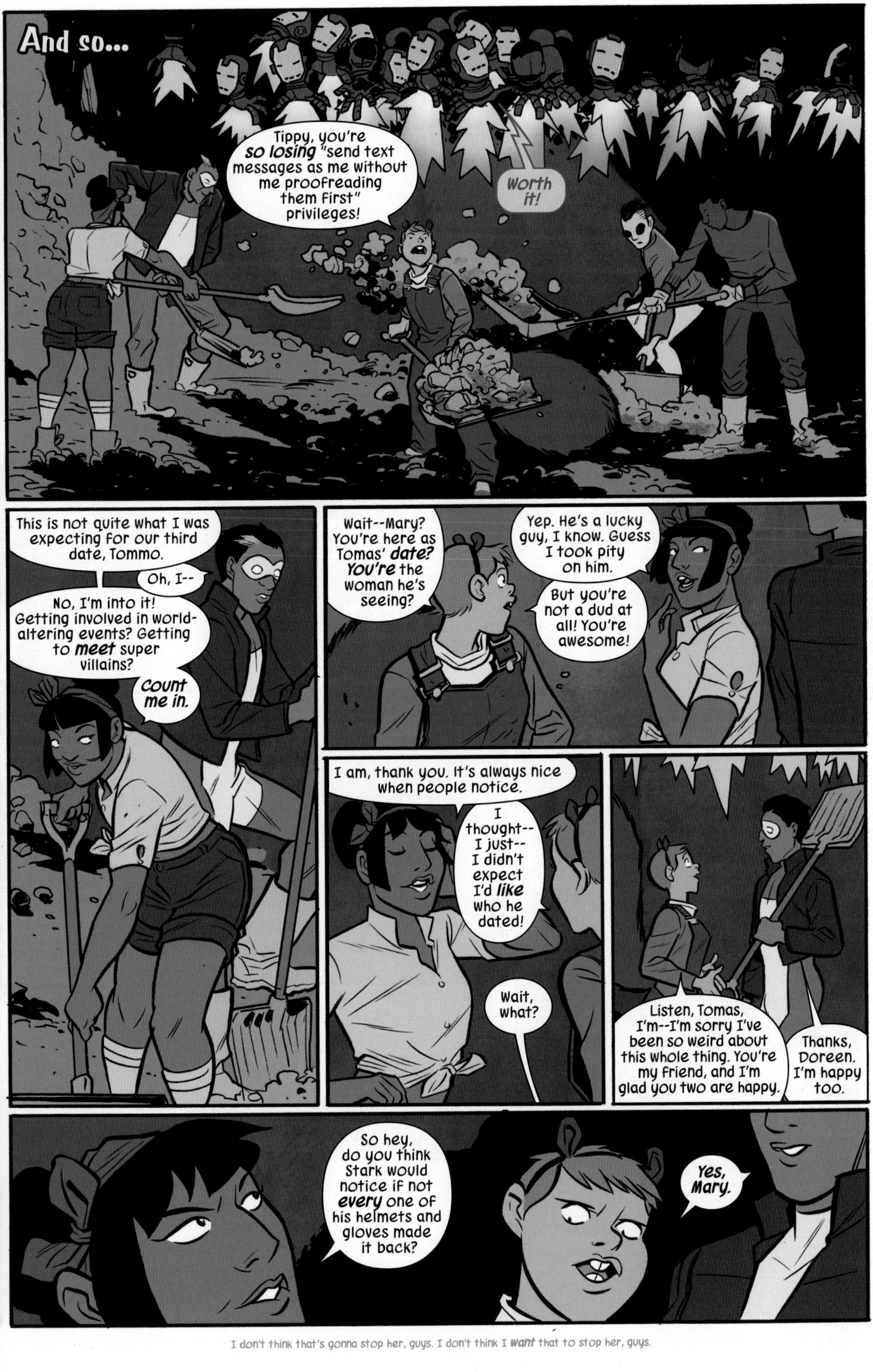
And so...
Tippy, you're so losing "send text messages as me without me proofreading them first" privileges!
Worth it!
This is not quite what I was expecting for our third date, Tommo.
Oh, I--
No, I'm into it! Getting involved in world-altering events? Getting to meet super villains?
Count me in.
Wait--Mary? You're here as Tomas' date? You're the woman he's seeing?
Yep. He's a lucky guy, I know. Guess I took pity on him.
But you're not a dud at all! You're awesome!
I am, thank you. It's always nice when people notice.
I thought-- I just-- I didn't expect I'd like who he dated!
Wait, what?
Listen, Tomas, I'm--I'm sorry I've been so weird about this whole thing. You're my friend, and I'm glad you two are happy.
Thanks, Doreen. I'm happy too.
So hey, do you think Stark would notice if not every one of his helmets and gloves made it back?
Yes, Mary.
I don't think that's gonna stop her, guys. I don't think I *want* that to stop her, guys.

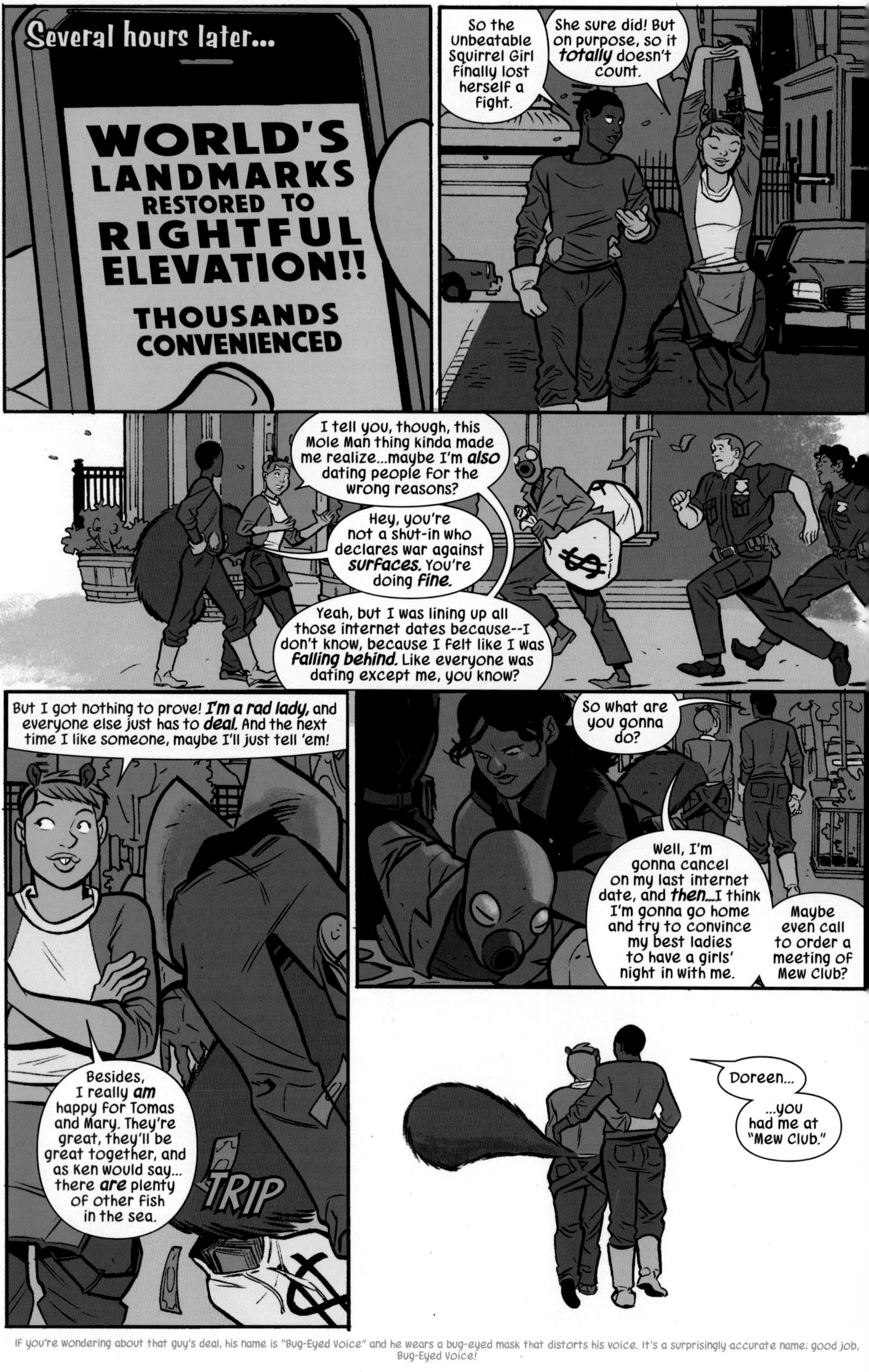
Several hours later...
WORLD'S LANDMARKS RESTORED TO RIGHTFUL ELEVATION!!
THOUSANDS CONVENIENCED
So the Unbeatable Squirrel Girl finally lost herself a fight.
She sure did! But on purpose, so it totally doesn't count.
I tell you, though, this Mole Man thing kinda made me realize...maybe I'm also dating people for the wrong reasons?
Hey, you're not a shut-in who declares war against surfaces. You're doing fine.
Yeah, but I was lining up all those internet dates because--I don't know, because I felt like I was falling behind. Like everyone was dating except me, you know?
But I got nothing to prove! I'm a rad lady, and everyone else just has to deal. And the next time I like someone, maybe I'll just tell 'em!
Besides, I really am happy for Tomas and Mary. They're great, they'll be great together, and as Ken would say... there are plenty of other fish in the sea.
TRIP
So what are you gonna do?
Well, I'm gonna cancel on my last internet date, and then...I think I'm gonna go home and try to convince my best ladies to have a girls' night in with me.
Maybe even call to order a meeting of Mew Club?
Doreen...
...you had me at "Mew Club."

If you're wondering about that guy's deal, his name is "Bug-Eyed Voice" and he wears a bug-eyed mask that distorts his voice. It's a surprisingly accurate name; good job, Bug-Eyed Voice!

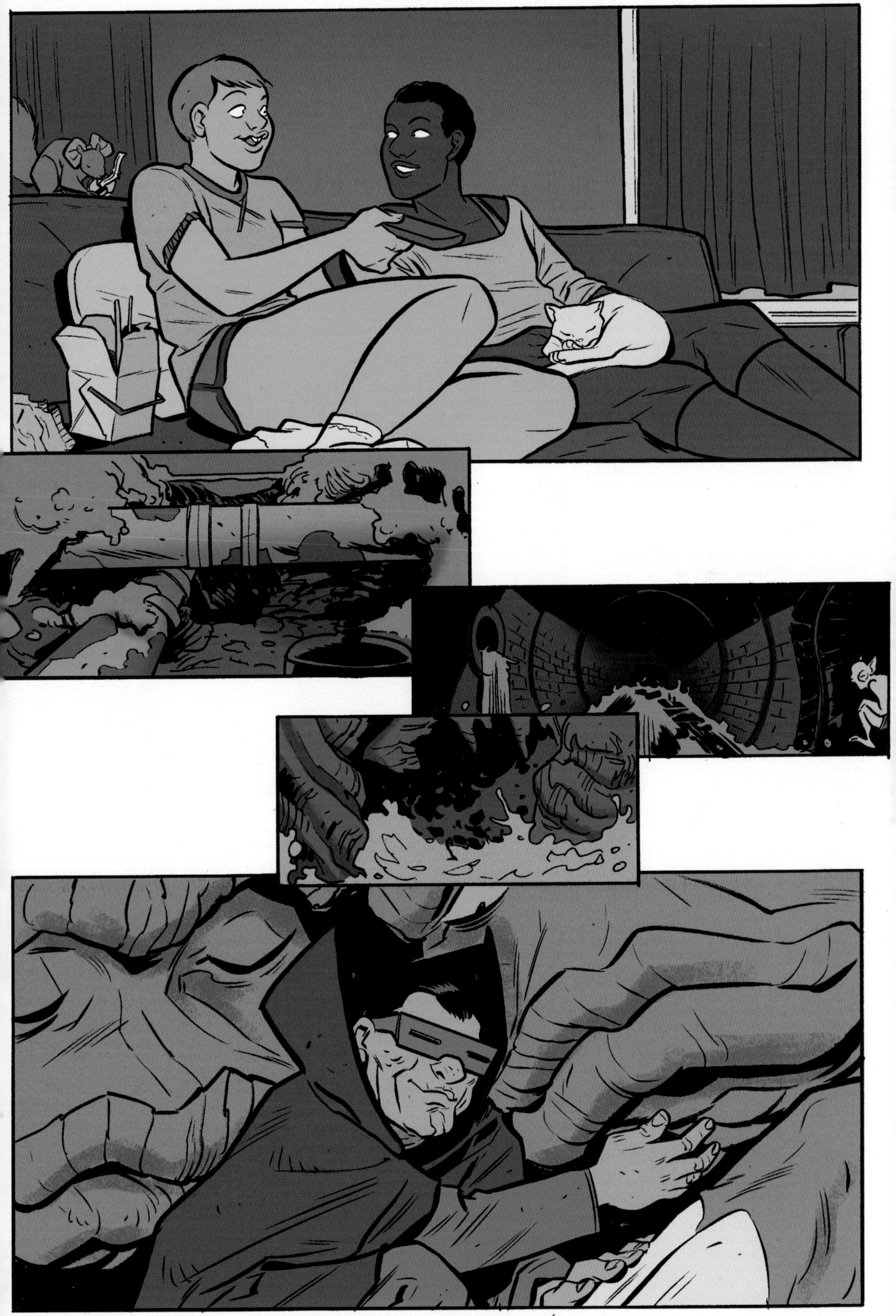

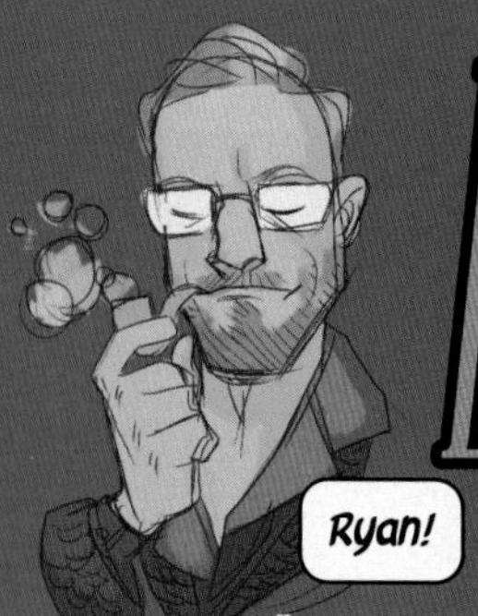
Ryan!

Letters From Nuts

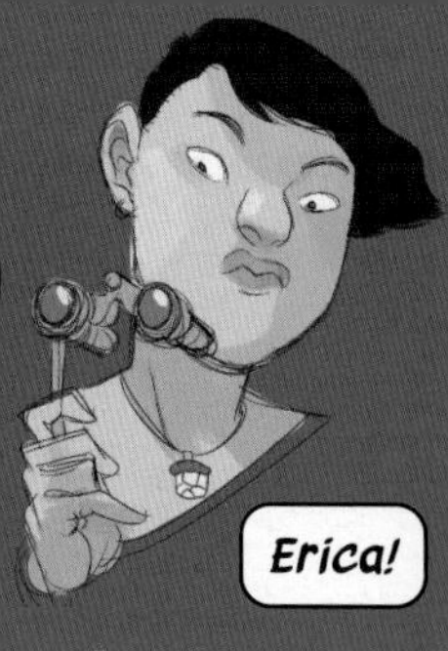
Erica!

Send letters to mheroes@marvel.com or 135 W 50th St, 7th Floor, New York, NY 10020 (Please mark "OKAY TO PRINT"

Dear Erica and Ryan,

I am 10 years old and I have been following Squirrel Girl for 2 years. I think she is the best superhero ever. Tippy-toe is my favorite character. I also love the little notes at the bottom. They make the comics much better!

I had my hair cut like Squirrel Girls's and I made a headband like her's.

Why isn't there a Squirrel Girl movie yet? She is way better than Superman and he has 9 movies. Please beg the Marvel people to make her a movie.

Also, there should be an issue about a mean villain who doesn't want squirrels her yard

Yours in Squirrels,
Noemi

RYAN: Noemi, thank you! What makes your letter extra special to me is you're 10 and have been reading for 2 years: that's 20% of your ENTIRE LIFE spent reading our comics! And it's even more, really, since those first few years you were a baby who didn't even know HOW to read yet. In contrast, I've only been writing them for 5.7% of my life (I'm 35) so it's a really great compliment that you'd spend so much of your life with our crazy comic so far! Thank you.

ERICA: Let's continue down this math path. Superman debuted in 1938, and the first Superman movie wasn't until 1978 (although he was on TV and serials before that- but Doreen's been on TV). So it wasn't until he was 40 years old that he got his own movie! So if Squirrel Girl is in a movie in the next 15 years she'll still beat Superman.

Dear Erica and Ryan:

I just finished your second issue #8 of TUSG, and am happy to report that it's every bit as good as the other issue #8 you made last year. That part where Doreen goes on a date with a sentinel is the kind of thing I buy this excellent comic book for.

However! I noticed an error in the brain-teaser that Nancy wrote for Doreen's dating site profile. For the number to represent the word "felines," it should have been 6512914519, but Nancy typed the number 6312914519. Obviously, this was an intentional error, which Nancy put in to check who was smart enough to notice. Well played, Nancy, well played.

Make Mine Marvel!
Michael Katsuro
Ricksand, Sweden

RYAN: The best part of writing fictional characters is you can make THEM take the fall for your mistakes. So this was ABSOLUTELY Nancy putting that in as a test, and we can all agree that I, the author, definitely did not make a simple off-by-one error of the type which has plagued me for my entire programming career!!

ERICA: I'm pretty excited that we've been able (by the time this comes out, actually 9 just came out on the day I'm typing this) to start just saying the number of the issue instead of "issue 3, no, the second issue 3".

Dear Ryan, Erica, and the whole Unbeatable Squirrel Girl crew,

I'm a child psychologist and have worked with many kids who have trouble reading or simply do not like to read. In that comics both helped me learn to read and learn to love to read, I've used them in my work with these youngsters and it's proven a very successful strategy. I wanted to reach out and thank you all because The Unbeatable Squirrel Girl has far and away been the comic that has most excited these kids and helped to imbue a love for reading. The art, the stories, the humor, and action has been the perfect mix. On top of that, I have enjoyed the issues just as much (if not more) than my patients.

Some quick questions from me and a few of the children and adolescents I work for:

1. Can Squirrel Girl communicate with other members of the sciuridae genius (like marmots and woodchucks)?
2. Is Squirrel Girl's 'unbeatable-ness' one of her super powers or just a product of her attitude?
3. Would Doreen ever date Dr. Doom's son, Werner? Because that would be fun.
4. What is Squirrel Girl's favorite TV show?

Thanks again for all of the wonderful stories. When I'm not doing my doctor thing, I sometimes make fan art. Included is a portrait of Nancy and Mew (my personal favorites among the extended cast). Hope you like it.

Your fan,
Dr. Nathaniel Goldblatt, Psy D

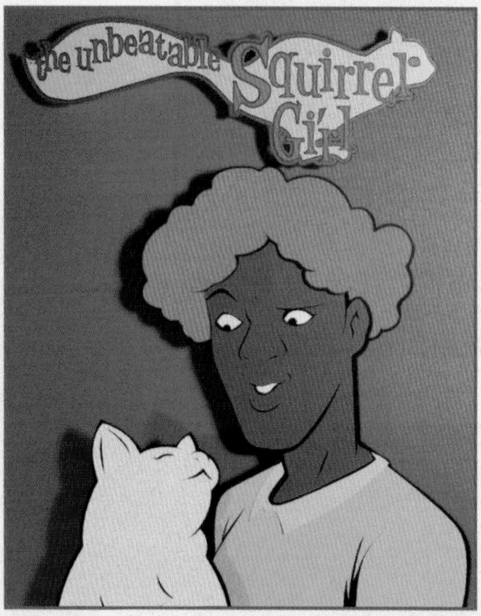
the unbeatable Squirrel Girl

ERICA: I love that this book is useful in your work! Before I started on this book I worked with a local group to put together a picture book for them to use in group therapy sessions for raising mentally ill children so this is something I have some interest in. OKAY.

1. This is literally one of the first questions I asked Ryan. I think we decided that yes, all members of the genus sciuridae speak the same language but it's like different accents.

2. It's all in the attitude.

3. What are his views on vegetarianism?

4. Brooklyn 9-9. It's about friendship and solving crimes!

RYAN: I DIDN'T KNOW DOCTOR DOOM HAD A SON UNTIL RIGHT NOW. This changes everything!! P.S.: I am a Marvel writer.

Ryan and Erica:

Have been super enjoying your book and everything about it... up until this last issue. About dating profiles.

Too real, guys. Just... too real.

Hugs,
Jon

P.S. I think Sentinel #X-42903-22 may be my spirit animal now.

ERICA: I have written my fair share. I know how hard it is. SOLIDARITY.

RYAN: I met and married my wife before online dating was a thing, so I NEVER GOT TO MAKE A DATING PROFILE. I feel like I missed out on all the fun! Then I talk to friends who HAVE done online dating, and when I say that, they look at me like I'm completely crazy. Oh well??

Hi Ryan and Erica!!

First off thanks for making one of the best comics they are seriously that highlight of my day when they come out!!! C:\Users\cbeacham\Desktop\image1.JPG

After reading issue #8 I'm laughing so hard at all the bad dates. Poor sentinel #x-42903-22 he can't help it i he is bad.

Also here is my squirrel girl cosplay and yes it did cost a lot of cosplay .

alyson fand

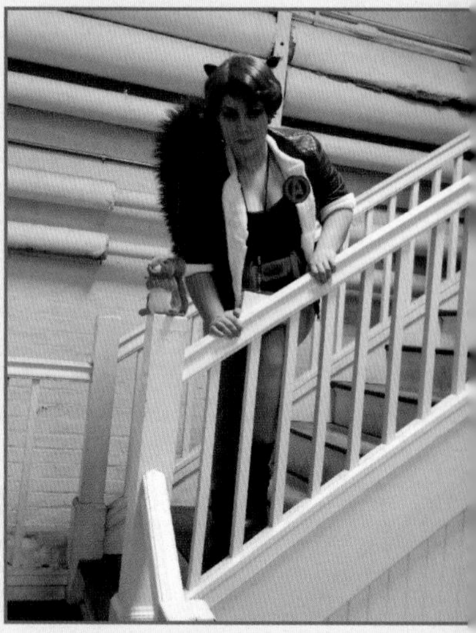

RYAN: Alyson, thank you, and that is a TERRIFIC cosplay. All the cosplay you spent on that cosplay clearly shows up as very good cosplay!! Also, I was really happy to see everyone being so into Sentinel #X-42903-22! Marvel, if you want to make a comic called "LOOKING FOR LOVE IN THE MARVEL UNIVERSE WITH THIS ONE GIANT, BUILDING-SIZED PURPLE ROBOT", know this: Erica and I stand ready.

Dear Erica and Ryan,

I had heard on the internet that Squirrel Girl was an amazing comic and the indeterminate voices of the internet were correct! USG is witty, creative and truly unbeatable. But issue #8 was truly wonderful. I so related to Doreen's boy struggles (especially the "HAHAHA, I AM TOTALLY COOL WITH YOU DATING SOMEONE NOT ME") and laughed and cringed along with her in the making of an online dating profile. Thanks for making a comic that I can really relate to!

Much love
Stacy

RYAN: Thanks, Stacy! As a guy who was afraid to share my feelings with people I wanted to kiss for a long time, I can, uh, kinda really relate too. Also thank you, internet! Not only are you a vast global repository of knowledge, but you can tell people about our comics. So that's TWO things I like about you!

ERICA: This story was one that we talked about when my boyfriend and I hung out at Ryan's place in Toronto for a Christmas party (and to see Force Awakens). I think we were really ready for something that focused on personal life more.

That's all for this issue. See y'all next month!

Attention, Squirrel Scouts! Make sure to check out our production blog, **unbeatablesquirrelgirl.tumblr.com**, where we post behind-the-scenes stuff on how the book gets made, along with all sorts of cool things *you* make: fanart, cosplay, whatever!

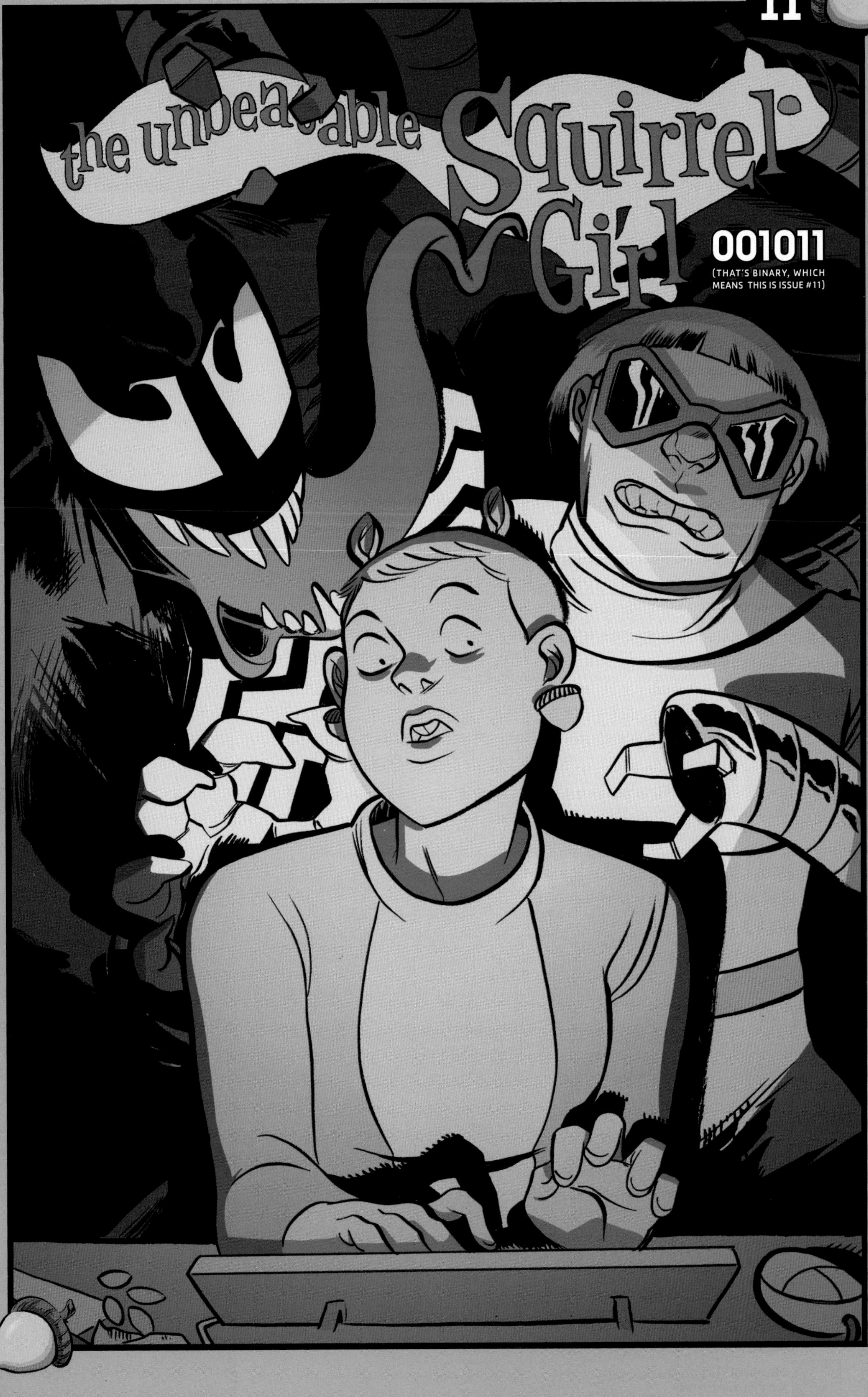
the unbeatable Squirrel Girl
001011
(THAT'S BINARY, WHICH MEANS THIS IS ISSUE #11)

Doreen Green isn't just a second-year computer science student: she secretly also has all the powers of both squirrel and girl! She uses her amazing abilities to fight crime **and** be as awesome as possible. You know her as...**The Unbeatable Squirrel Girl.** Find out what she's been up to, with...

Squirrel Girl in a nutshell

Squirrel Girl @unbeatablesg
Hey everyone guess who saved the world from oh I don't know MOLE MAN? THIS girl, right here. And I had a little help too!

Tippy-Toe @yoitstippytoe
@unbeatablesg CHHTT! CHTT CHTTT CHTTY CHUK

Squirrel Girl @unbeatablesg
@yoitstippytoe tippy YOU WERE THE PERSON I WAS IMPLYING WHEN I SAID I HAD A LITTLE HELP

Tippy-Toe @yoitstippytoe
@unbeatablesg chitty chukk chtt

Squirrel Girl @unbeatablesg
@yoitstippytoe oh my gosh FINE

Squirrel Girl @unbeatablesg
Hey everyone guess who saved the world from MOLE MAN? Me and @yoitstippytoe who posts acorn pics and always welcomes new followers #ff

Nancy Whitehead @sewwiththeflo
@unbeatablesg ...Hello

Squirrel Girl @unbeatablesg
@sewwiththeflo oh my gosh Nancy

Squirrel Girl @unbeatablesg
Hey everyone, who saved the world from MOLE MAN? Me and @yoitstippytoe and @sewwiththeflo who I guess was a random citizen who helped out!

Spider-Man @aspidercan
@unbeatablesg um I helped too #spidermanhelpedtoo

Squirrel Girl @unbeatablesg
@aspidercan what? No you didn't!! Koi Boi and Chipmunk Hunk helped but I didn't see you there at all!

Spider-Man @aspidercan
@unbeatablesg No I was there but always just out of sight! I was thwipping monsters, which were themselves also just out of sight

Spider-Man @aspidercan
@unbeatablesg I guess you didn't notice because my web-shooters make a "thwip" sound but it's pretty quiet

Spider-Man @aspidercan
@unbeatablesg which really just speaks to my high level of thwipping skill

Squirrel Girl @unbeatablesg
@aspidercan WHATEVER SPIDER-MAN, FINE

Squirrel Girl @unbeatablesg
Hey everyone guess who saved the world from MOLE MAN? Me and all my varied friends!! They're all great and I endorse them wholeheartedly.

Nancy Whitehead @sewwiththeflo
@unbeatablesg <3

Spider-Man @aspidercan
@unbeatablesg <3

Tippy-Toe @yoitstippytoe
@unbeatablesg <CHUK

Tony Stark @starkmantony
@unbeatablesg Thanks! My patented Iron Man suits did help out a lot in that adventure, and it's nice to see them get the credit!!

Tony Stark @starkmantony
@unbeatablesg Hey, you mind if we use your endorsement in a commercial?

Squirrel Girl @unbeatablesg
omg i'm going to bed

search!

#doc-ock
#doctorocktor
#frightmares
#throwingupsigns
#counttoten

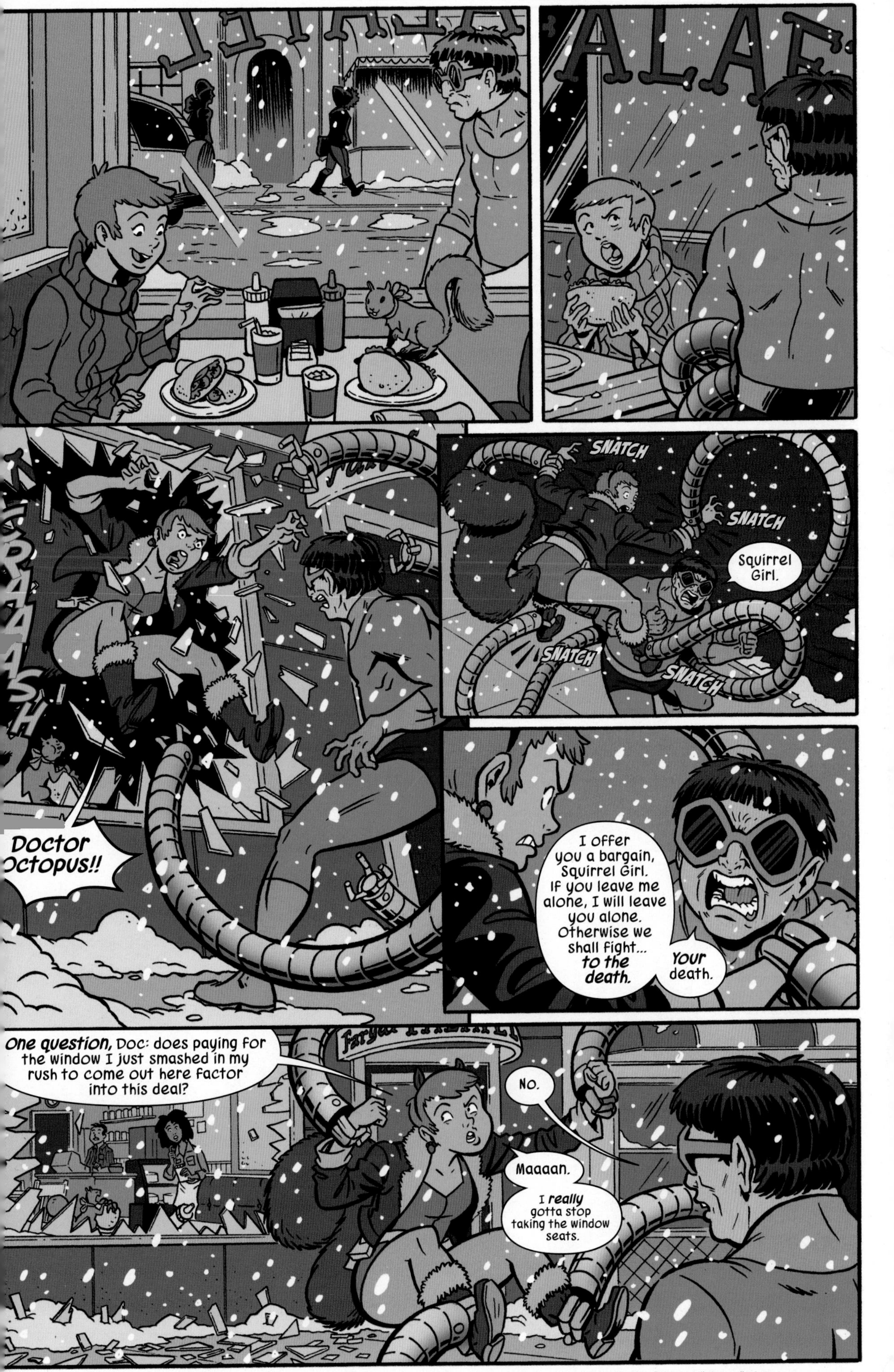
SNATCH
SNATCH
Squirrel Girl.
SNATCH
SNATCH
KRAAASH
Doctor Octopus!!
I offer you a bargain, Squirrel Girl. If you leave me alone, I will leave you alone. Otherwise we shall fight... to the death.
Your death.
One question, Doc: does paying for the window I just smashed in my rush to come out here factor into this deal?
No.
Maaaan.
I really gotta stop taking the window seats.

Hello, I am a regular human who would like to eat falafel. Do you have a "patrons must pay for broken glass" policy? No, not "glasses": glass. Ah, I see. Well, just--just seat me at whatever table is farthest from all the windows.

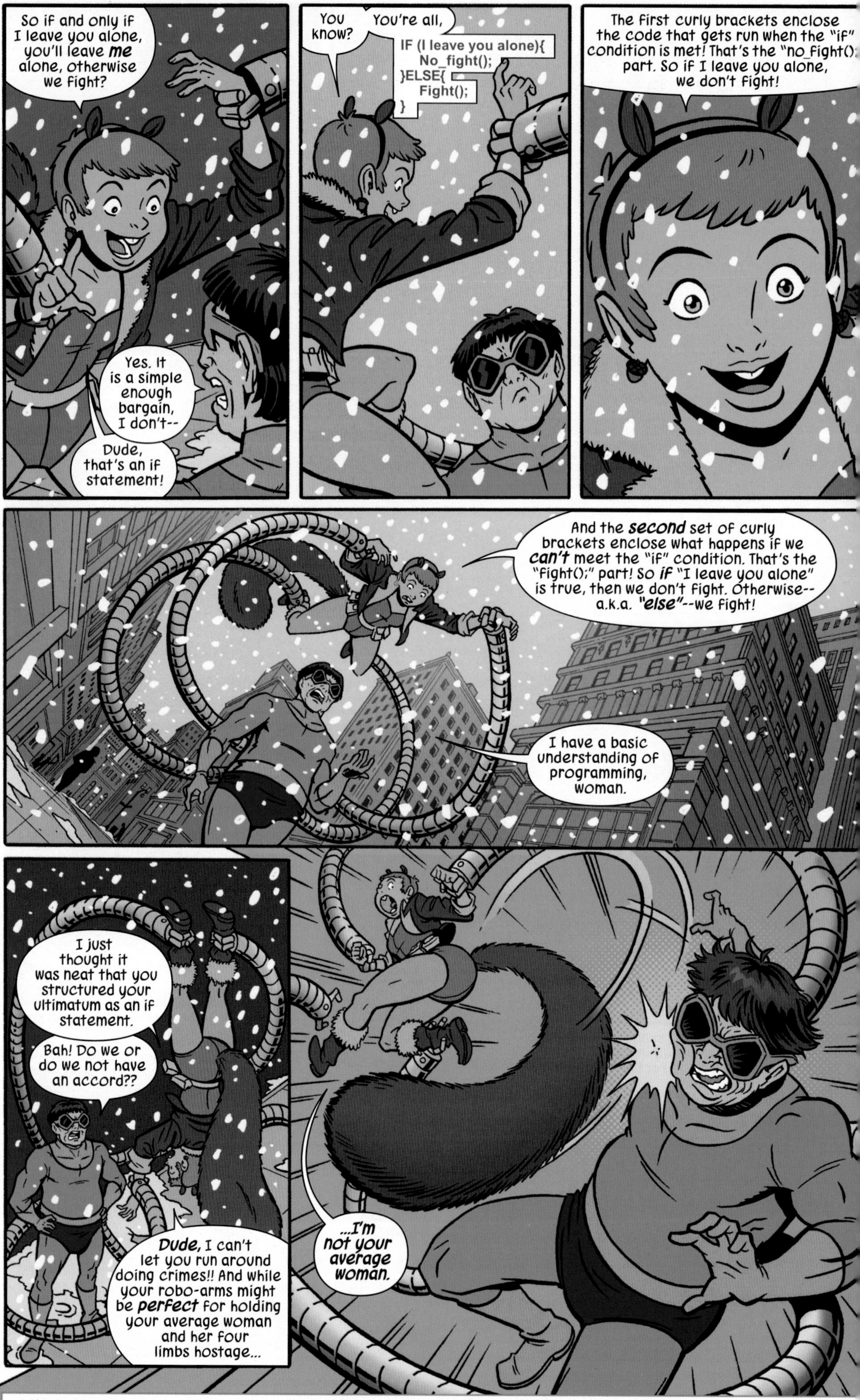
So if and only if I leave you alone, you'll leave *me* alone, otherwise we fight?
Yes. It is a simple enough bargain, I don't--
Dude, that's an if statement!
You know?
You're all,
IF (I leave you alone){
No_fight();
}ELSE{
Fight();
}
The first curly brackets enclose the code that gets run when the "if" condition is met! That's the "no_fight();" part. So if I leave you alone, we don't fight!
And the *second* set of curly brackets enclose what happens if we *can't* meet the "if" condition. That's the "fight();" part! So *if* "I leave you alone" is true, then we don't fight. Otherwise--a.k.a. *"else"*--we fight!
I have a basic understanding of programming, woman.
I just thought it was neat that you structured your ultimatum as an if statement.
Bah! Do we or do we not have an accord??
Dude, I can't let you run around doing crimes!! And while your robo-arms might be *perfect* for holding your average woman and her four limbs hostage...
...I'm not your average woman.

Spider-Man is watching this and suddenly realizing all the times having a tail would've helped him. The answer: approximately one zillion. But then they'd all be much shorter comics, so I guess the real winner is *you*, the reader!!!

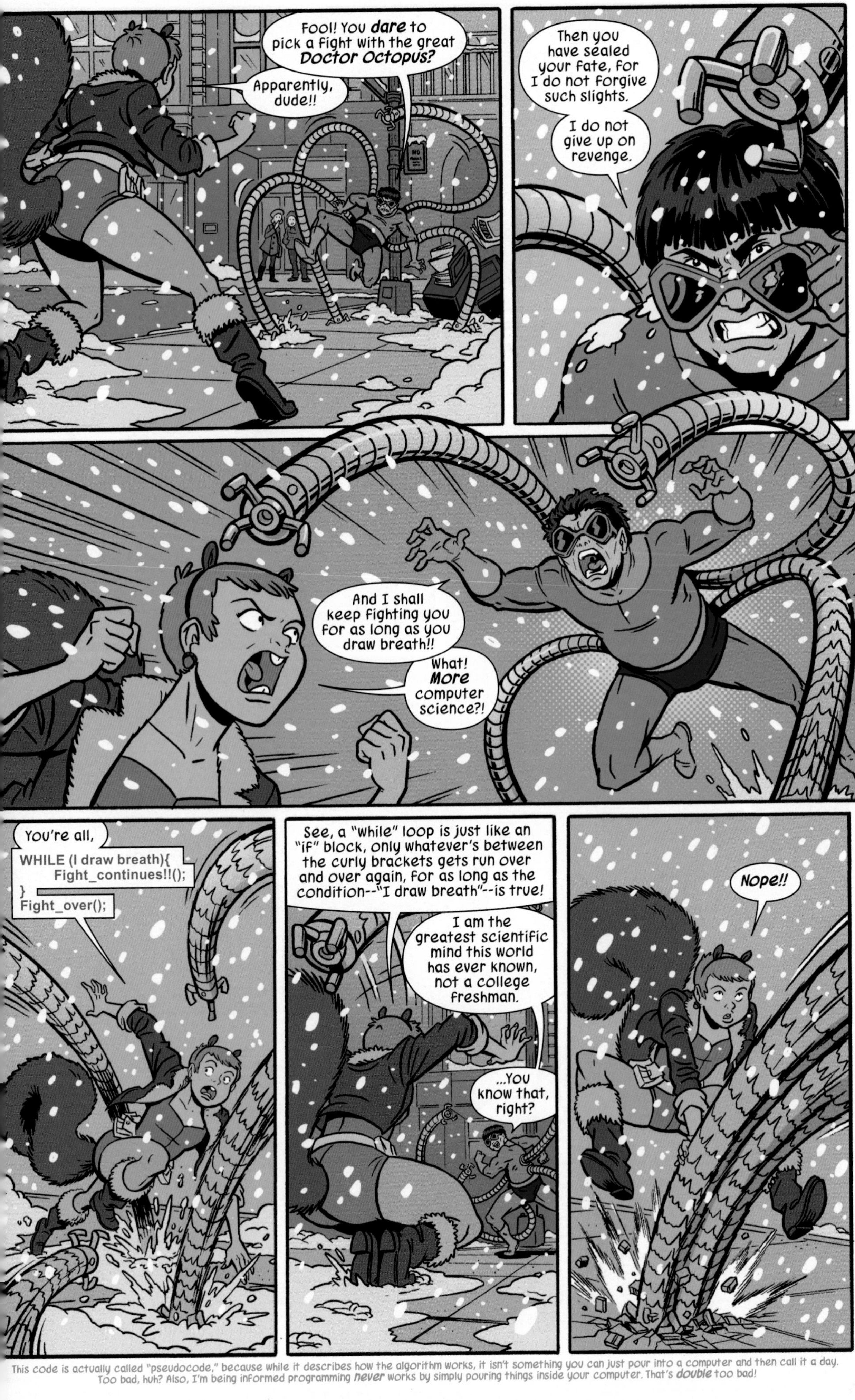
Fool! You dare to pick a fight with the great Doctor Octopus?
Apparently, dude!!
Then you have sealed your fate, for I do not forgive such slights.
I do not give up on revenge.
And I shall keep fighting you for as long as you draw breath!!
What! More computer science?!
You're all,
WHILE (I draw breath){
Fight_continues!!();
}
Fight_over();
See, a "while" loop is just like an "if" block, only whatever's between the curly brackets gets run over and over again, for as long as the condition--"I draw breath"--is true!
I am the greatest scientific mind this world has ever known, not a college freshman.
...You know that, right?
Nope!!

This code is actually called "pseudocode," because while it describes how the algorithm works, it isn't something you can just pour into a computer and then call it a day. Too bad, huh? Also, I'm being informed programming *never* works by simply pouring things inside your computer. That's *double* too bad!

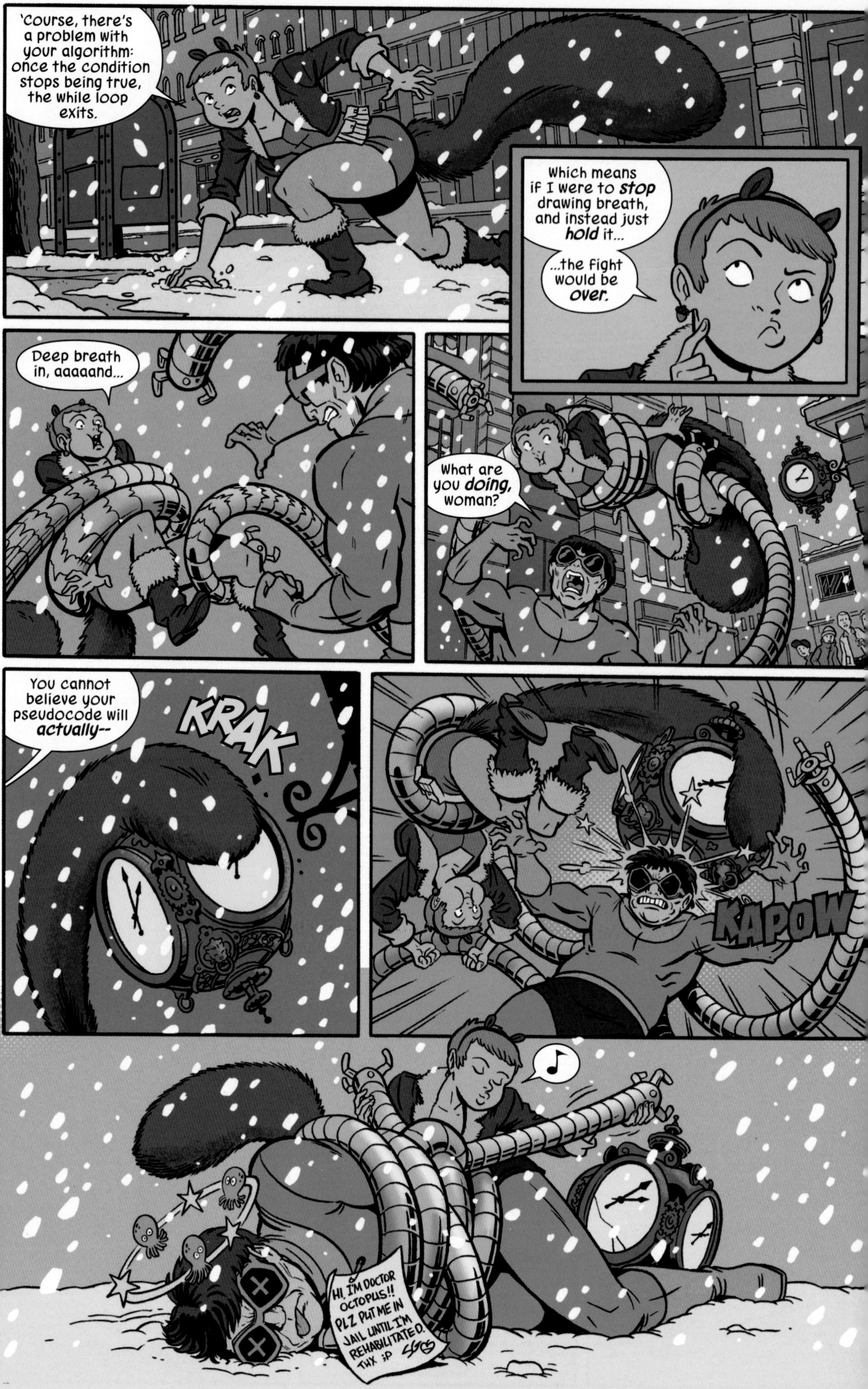
'Course, there's a problem with your algorithm: once the condition stops being true, the while loop exits.
Which means if I were to *stop* drawing breath, and instead just *hold* it...
...the fight would be *over.*
Deep breath in, aaaaand...
What are you *doing,* woman?
You cannot believe your pseudocode will *actually*--
KRAK
KAPOW
♪
HI, I'M DOCTOR OCTOPUS!! PLZ PUT ME IN JAIL UNTIL I'M REHABILITATED. THX :P

The cops are like, hey fellow officers, look at this helpful note! It tells us exactly what we should do, including the term of his rehabilitative sentence! Done!

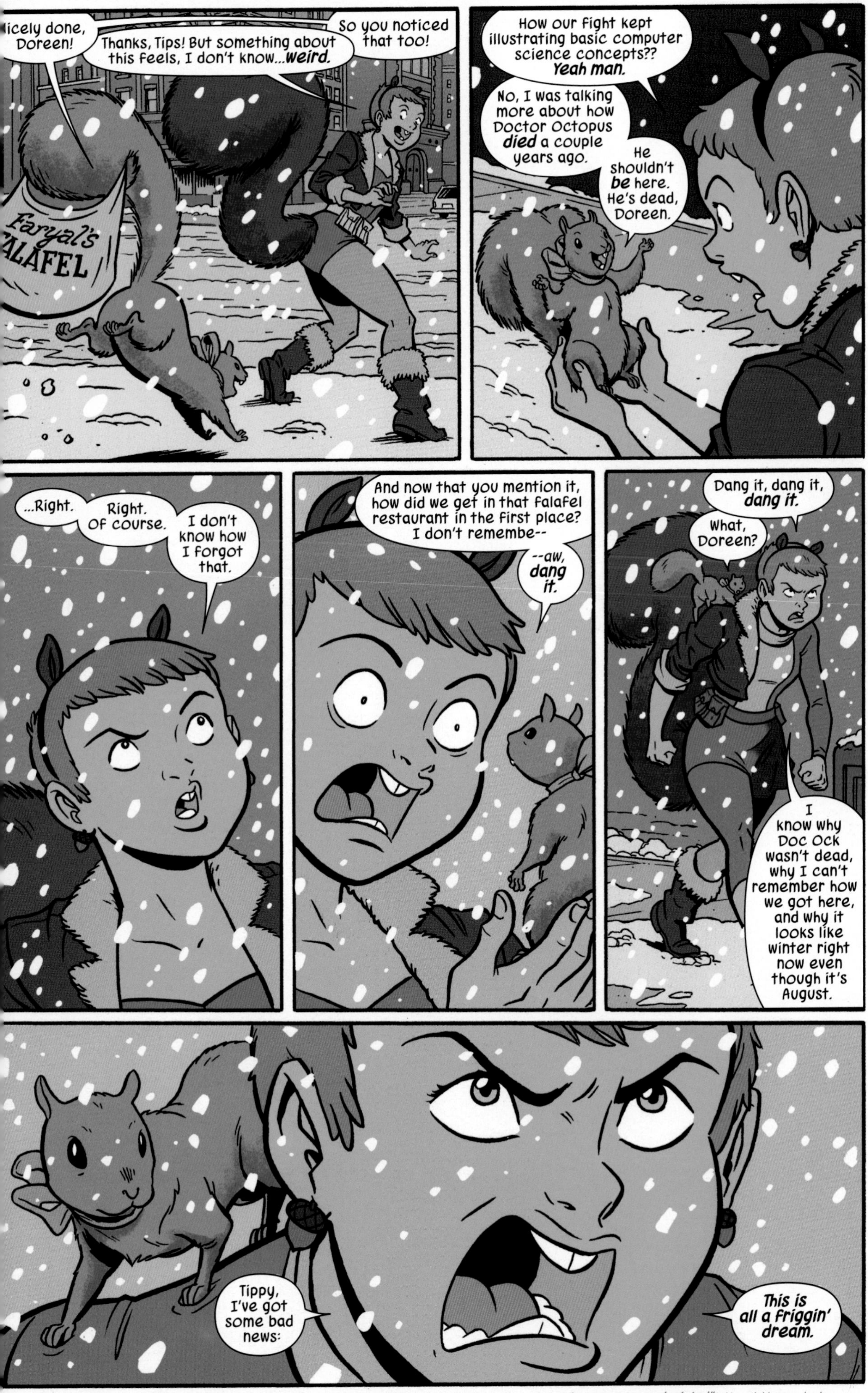

Nicely done, Doreen!
Thanks, Tips! But something about this feels, I don't know...weird.
So you noticed that too!
Faryal's FALAFEL
How our fight kept illustrating basic computer science concepts?? Yeah man.
No, I was talking more about how Doctor Octopus died a couple years ago.
He shouldn't be here. He's dead, Doreen.
...Right.
Right. Of course.
I don't know how I forgot that.
And now that you mention it, how did we get in that falafel restaurant in the first place? I don't remembe--
--aw, dang it.
Dang it, dang it, dang it.
What, Doreen?
I know why Doc Ock wasn't dead, why I can't remember how we got here, and why it looks like winter right now even though it's August.
Tippy, I've got some bad news:
This is all a friggin' dream.

There is a *Squirrel Girl* reader who is halfway through their ***"Excuse me, Doctor Octopus cannot appear in Squirrel Girl as depicted"*** letter right now who is ***really*** wishing they finished reading their comic before bustin' out the ol' email client. Hi there, *Squirrel Girl* reader! Thanks for reading our comic, even though you must be pretty annoyed with us right now! Just save that letter as a draft until we make some other Doc Ock mistake, okay??

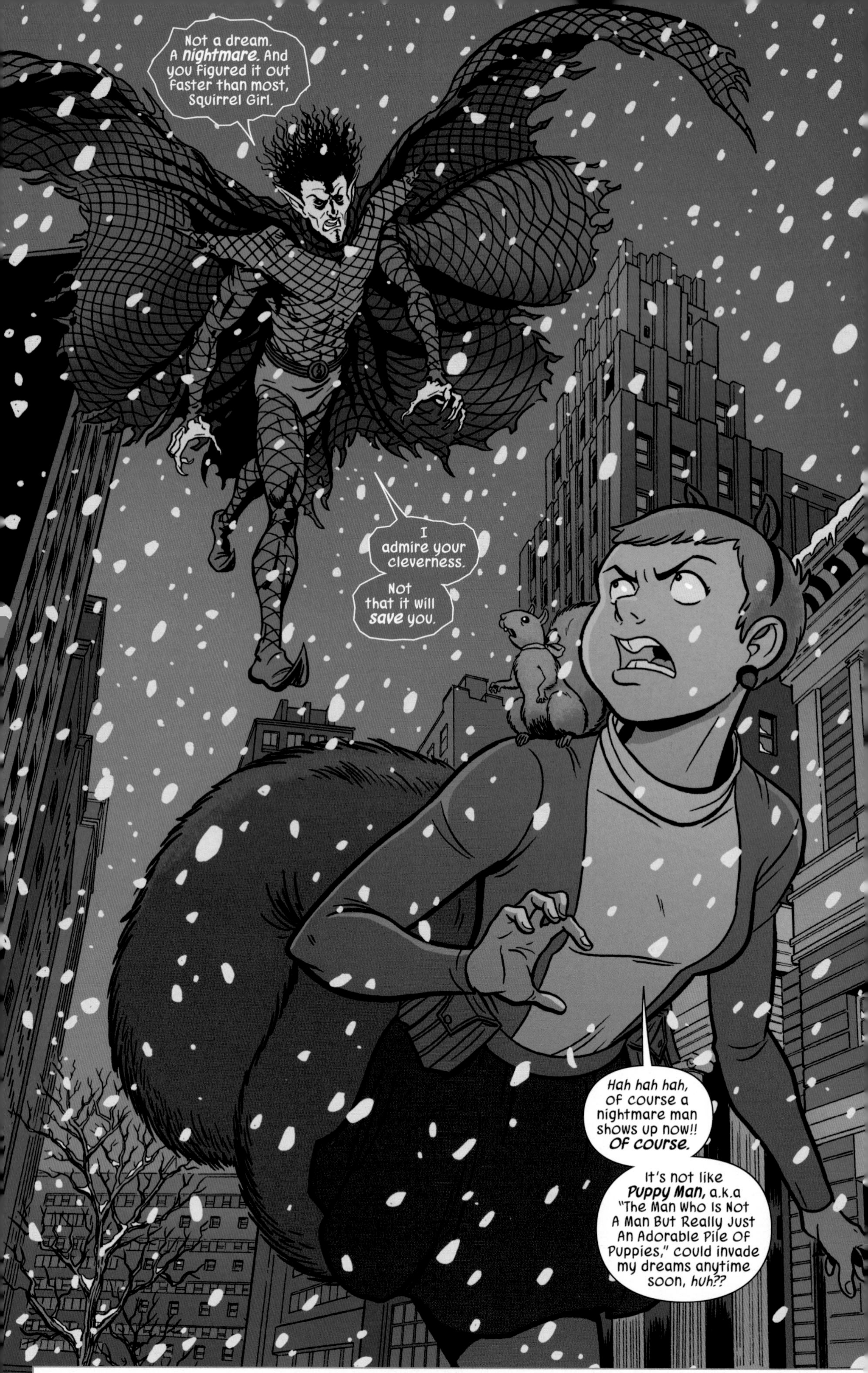
Not a dream. A *nightmare.* And you figured it out faster than most, Squirrel Girl.
I admire your cleverness.
Not that it will *save* you.
Hah hah hah, of course a nightmare man shows up now!! ***OF COURSE.***
It's not like ***Puppy Man,*** a.k.a "The Man Who Is Not A Man But Really Just An Adorable Pile Of Puppies," could invade my dreams anytime soon, *huh??*

You might think Puppy Man has no powers because he is literally just an adorable pile of puppies, but I call that the power of making everyone who sees him involuntarily say *"oh my goodness, so cute."*

Panel 1: "Nightmare" is right, Squirrel Girl. For that is my name. *And* my game.

Oh my gosh, Tips, his lines are stale like day-old bread.

I can hear you in your own dream, Squirrel Girl.

Panel 2: Yeah?! Well how about you tell me what your deal is so I can get back to imagining fake things that never even happened for six hours each night, a.k.a. "dreaming"?!

Oh, I will, Squirrel Girl. I'm here to take your *sanity* from you.

Panel 3: Every time you sleep, your subconscious comes here. To your own bespoke nightmare.

And it is here, in the dream world, where I shall destroy your sanity. It is here where I shall *beat* you.

Wait, I'm not *me*? I'm actually just my own subconscious?

Correct.

Panel 4: *Huh.* Well, seeing as I'm actually doing pretty well so far, I'm not *super* concerned about your whole "nightmare" thing! *This* subconscious just took down *Doc Ock* no problem.

Ah, but the nightmare is just beginning. And you will fall.

And when you fall, so too falls her sanity.

Panel 5: Well bring it on, dude! I'll kick your butt *subconsciously!*

Oh no, I prefer *not* to get my hands dirty. But I know someone who has no such qualms. In my place, I now summon the most feared super villain of all...

COUNT NEFARIA!!

Panel 6: *POOF!*

...Who?

r. and Mrs. Nefaria probably *acted* surprised when their baby boy became a super villain, but Mr. and Mrs. Nefaria probably should've considered the risks when deciding to go through life literally named *Mr. and Mrs. Nefaria.*

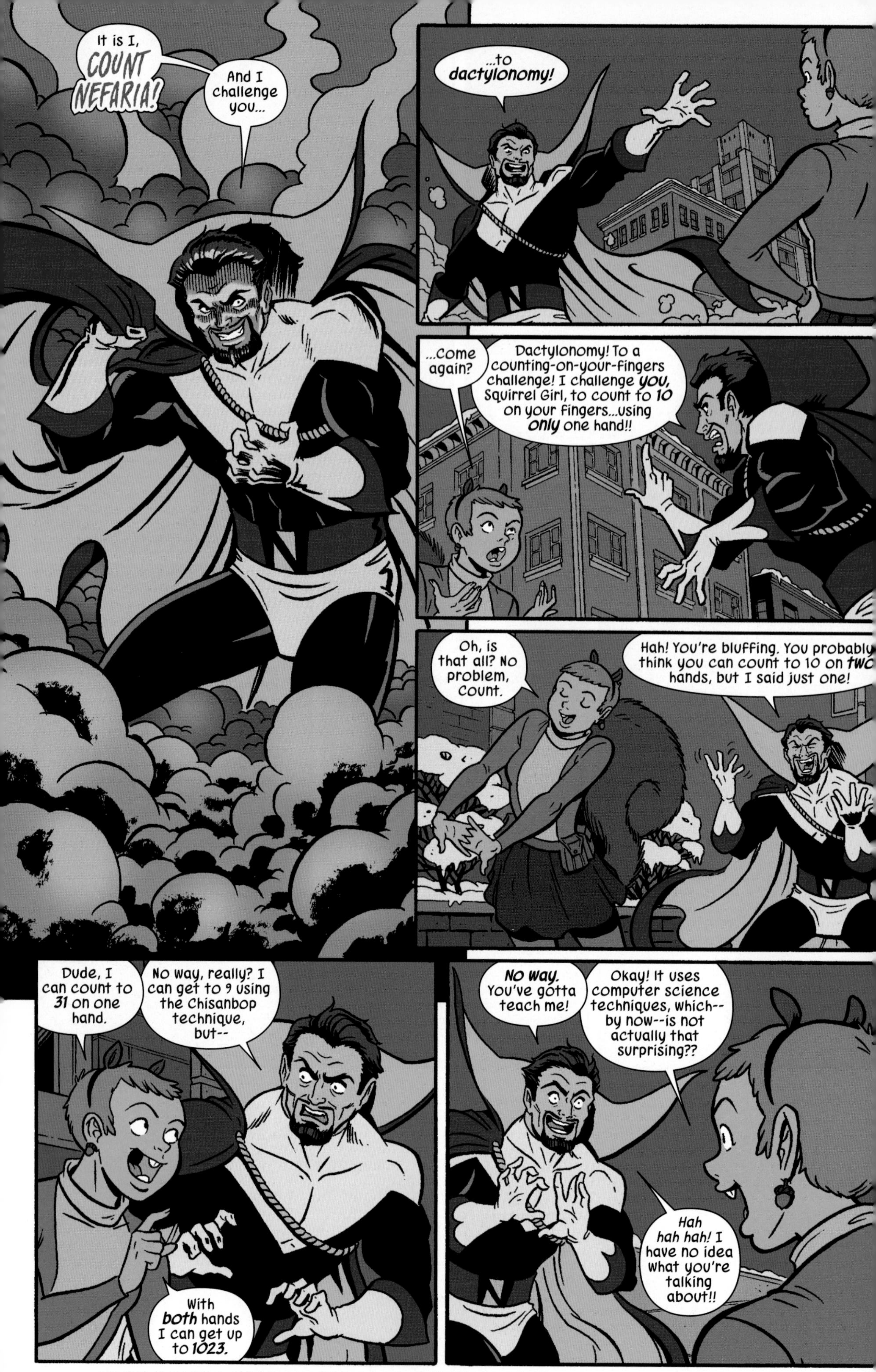
It is I, COUNT NEFARIA!
And I challenge you...
...to dactylonomy!
...Come again?
Dactylonomy! To a counting-on-your-fingers challenge! I challenge YOU, Squirrel Girl, to count to 10 on your fingers...using ONLY one hand!!
Oh, is that all? No problem, Count.
Hah! You're bluffing. You probably think you can count to 10 on two hands, but I said just one!
Dude, I can count to 31 on one hand.
No way, really? I can get to 9 using the Chisanbop technique, but--
With both hands I can get up to 1023.
NO WAY. You've gotta teach me!
Okay! It uses computer science techniques, which--by now--is not actually that surprising??
Hah hah hah! I have no idea what you're talking about!!

How often do you think Count Nefaria gets called Count Nefarious by his barista? Probably 100% of the time, huh. Yeah. Probably 100% of the time.

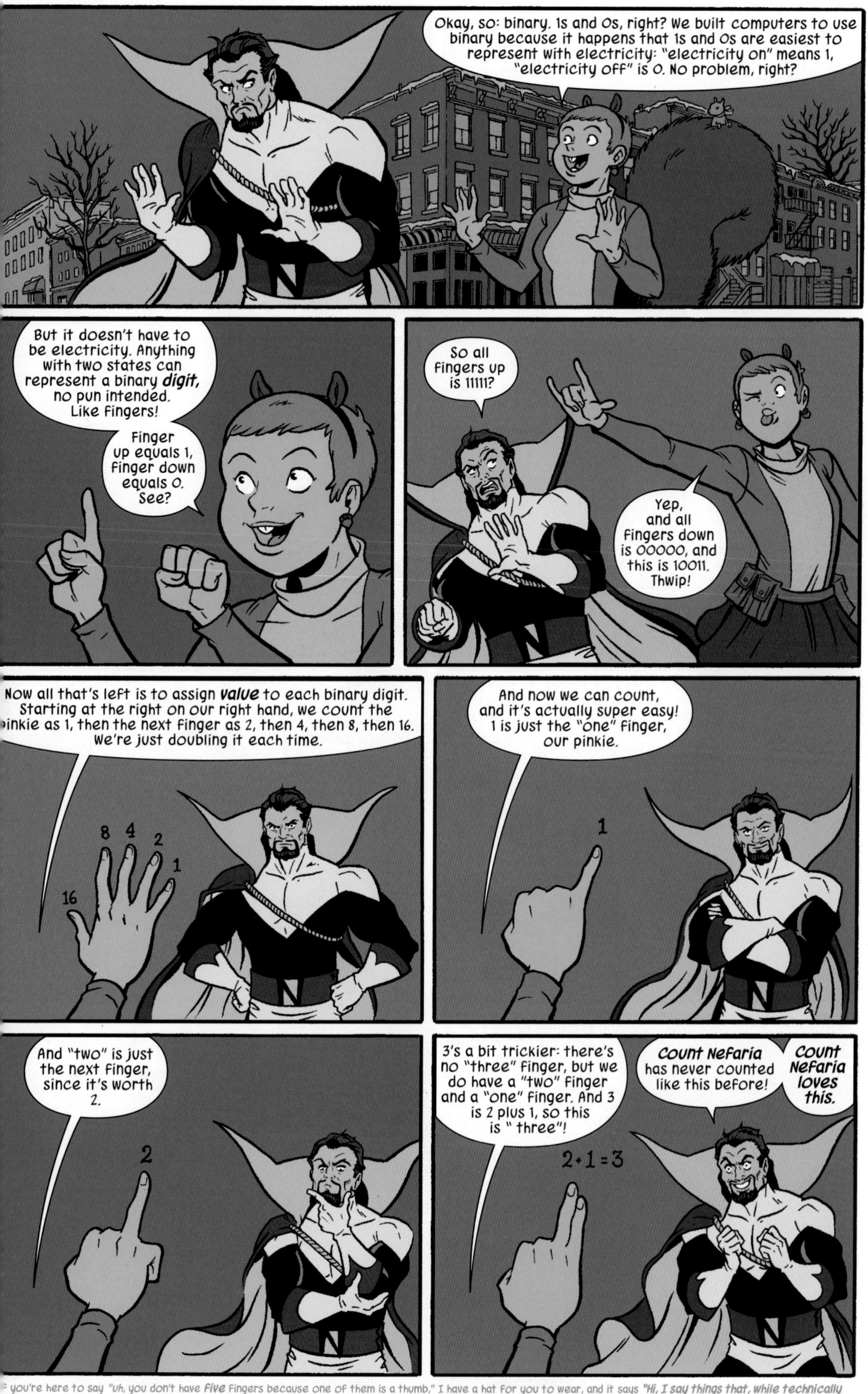
Okay, so: binary. 1s and 0s, right? We built computers to use binary because it happens that 1s and 0s are easiest to represent with electricity: "electricity on" means 1, "electricity off" is 0. No problem, right?
But it doesn't have to be electricity. Anything with two states can represent a binary *digit*, no pun intended. Like fingers!
Finger up equals 1, finger down equals 0. See?
So all fingers up is 11111?
Yep, and all fingers down is 00000, and this is 10011. Thwip!
Now all that's left is to assign *value* to each binary digit. Starting at the right on our right hand, we count the pinkie as 1, then the next finger as 2, then 4, then 8, then 16. We're just doubling it each time.
8
4
2
1
16
And now we can count, and it's actually super easy! 1 is just the "one" finger, our pinkie.
1
And "two" is just the next finger, since it's worth 2.
2
3's a bit trickier: there's no "three" finger, but we do have a "two" finger and a "one" finger. And 3 is 2 plus 1, so this is "three"!
2+1=3
Count Nefaria has never counted like this before!
Count Nefaria loves this.

If you're here to say "Uh, you don't have *five* fingers because one of them is a thumb," I have a hat for you to wear, and it says ***"Hi, I say things that, while technically correct, still get in the way of the clear communication of ideas."*** It's cute! It'll warn the rest of us!!

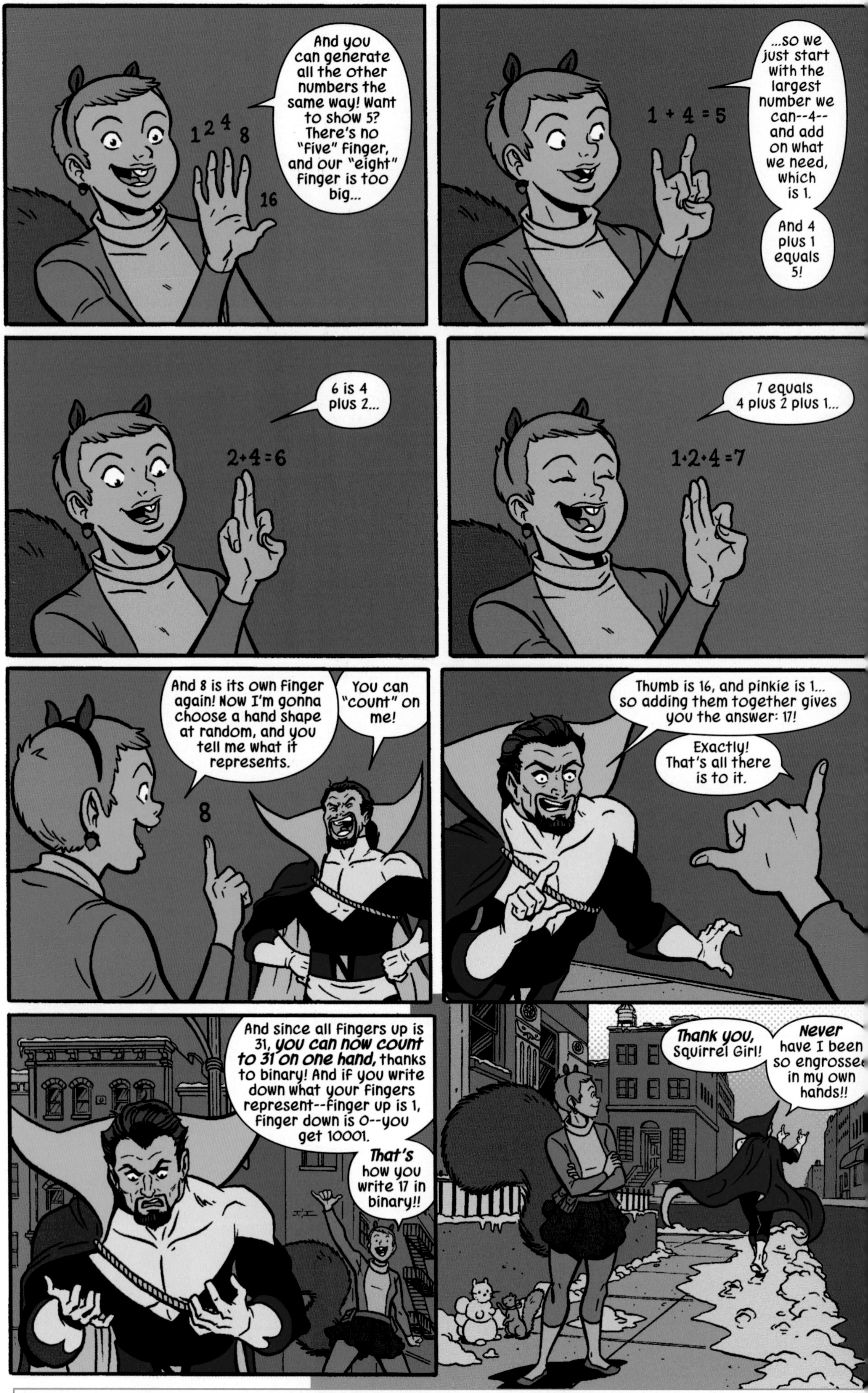
1 2 4 8
16
And you can generate all the other numbers the same way! Want to show 5? There's no "five" finger, and our "eight" finger is too big...
1 + 4 = 5
...so we just start with the largest number we can--4--and add on what we need, which is 1.
And 4 plus 1 equals 5!
2+4=6
6 is 4 plus 2...
1+2+4=7
7 equals 4 plus 2 plus 1...
8
And 8 is its own finger again! Now I'm gonna choose a hand shape at random, and you tell me what it represents.
You can "count" on me!
Thumb is 16, and pinkie is 1... so adding them together gives you the answer: 17!
Exactly! That's all there is to it.
And since all fingers up is 31, *you can now count to 31 on one hand,* thanks to binary! And if you write down what your fingers represent--finger up is 1, finger down is 0--you get 10001.
That's how you write 17 in binary!!
Thank you, Squirrel Girl!
Never have I been so engrosse in my own hands!!

It's okay if you're trying these out on your own hands right now. I did it when I wrote this page, and I guarantee Jacob made the gestures when he drew them. I believe t
basically makes counting on your fingers in binary is the official *Squirrel Girl secret handshake??*

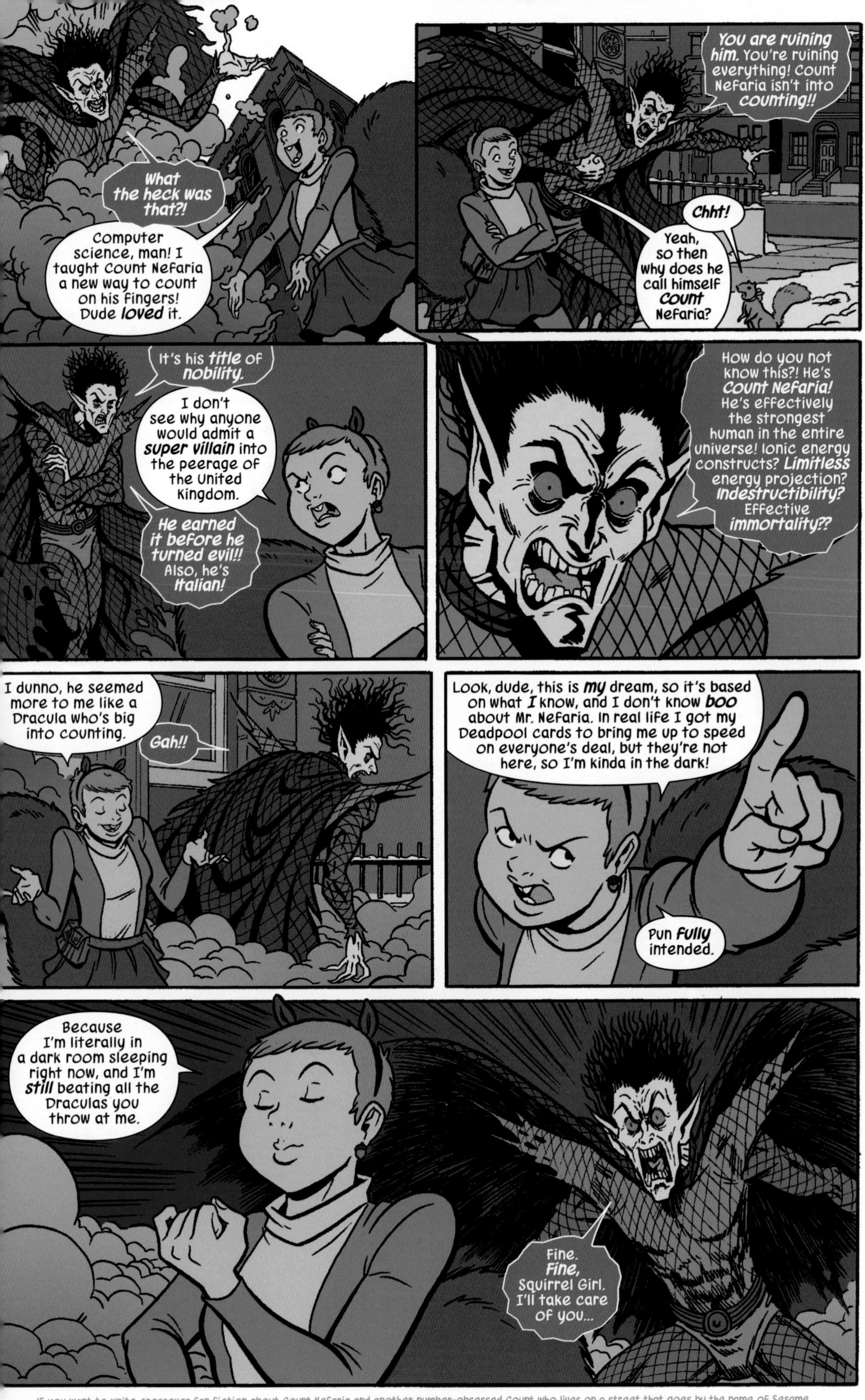

What the heck was that?!
Computer science, man! I taught Count Nefaria a new way to count on his fingers! Dude *loved* it.
You are ruining him. You're ruining everything! Count Nefaria isn't into *counting!!*
Chht!
Yeah, so then why does he call himself *Count* Nefaria?
It's his *title* of *nobility.*
I don't see why anyone would admit a *super villain* into the peerage of the United Kingdom.
He earned it before he turned evil!! Also, he's *Italian!*
How do you not know this?! He's *Count Nefaria!* He's effectively the strongest human in the entire universe! Ionic energy constructs? *Limitless* energy projection? *Indestructibility?* Effective *immortality??*
I dunno, he seemed more to me like a Dracula who's big into counting.
Gah!!
Look, dude, this is *my* dream, so it's based on what *I* know, and I don't know *boo* about Mr. Nefaria. In real life I got my Deadpool cards to bring me up to speed on everyone's deal, but they're not here, so I'm kinda in the dark!
Pun *fully* intended.
Because I'm literally in a dark room sleeping right now, and I'm *still* beating all the Draculas you throw at me.
Fine. *Fine,* Squirrel Girl. I'll take care of you...

If you want to write crossover fan fiction about Count Nefaria and another number-obsessed Count who lives on a street that goes by the name of Sesame, let me just say that I am *way* ahead of you.

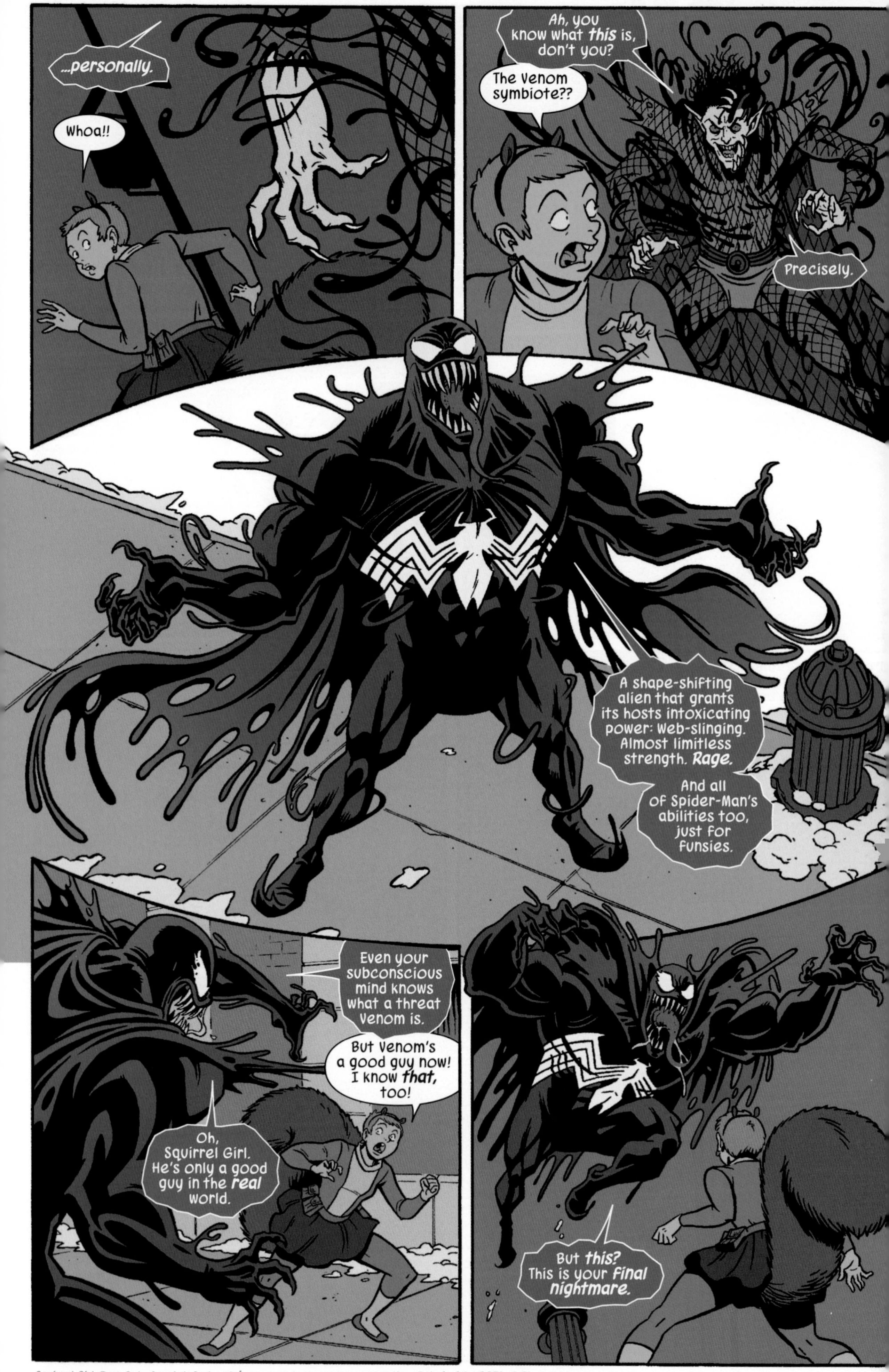
...personally.
Whoa!!
Ah, you know what this is, don't you?
The Venom symbiote??
Precisely.
A shape-shifting alien that grants its hosts intoxicating power: Web-slinging. Almost limitless strength. Rage.
And all of Spider-Man's abilities too, just for funsies.
Even your subconscious mind knows what a threat Venom is.
But Venom's a good guy now! I know that, too!
Oh, Squirrel Girl. He's only a good guy in the real world.
But this? This is your final nightmare.

Squirrel Girl, Doc Ock, Count Nefaria, *and* Venom all in the *same* comic? *Yes. Only in SQUIRREL GIRL.* I don't know what the deal is with all those *other* comics who just give you a talking duck instead and hope it'll be enough. Hi Chip!!

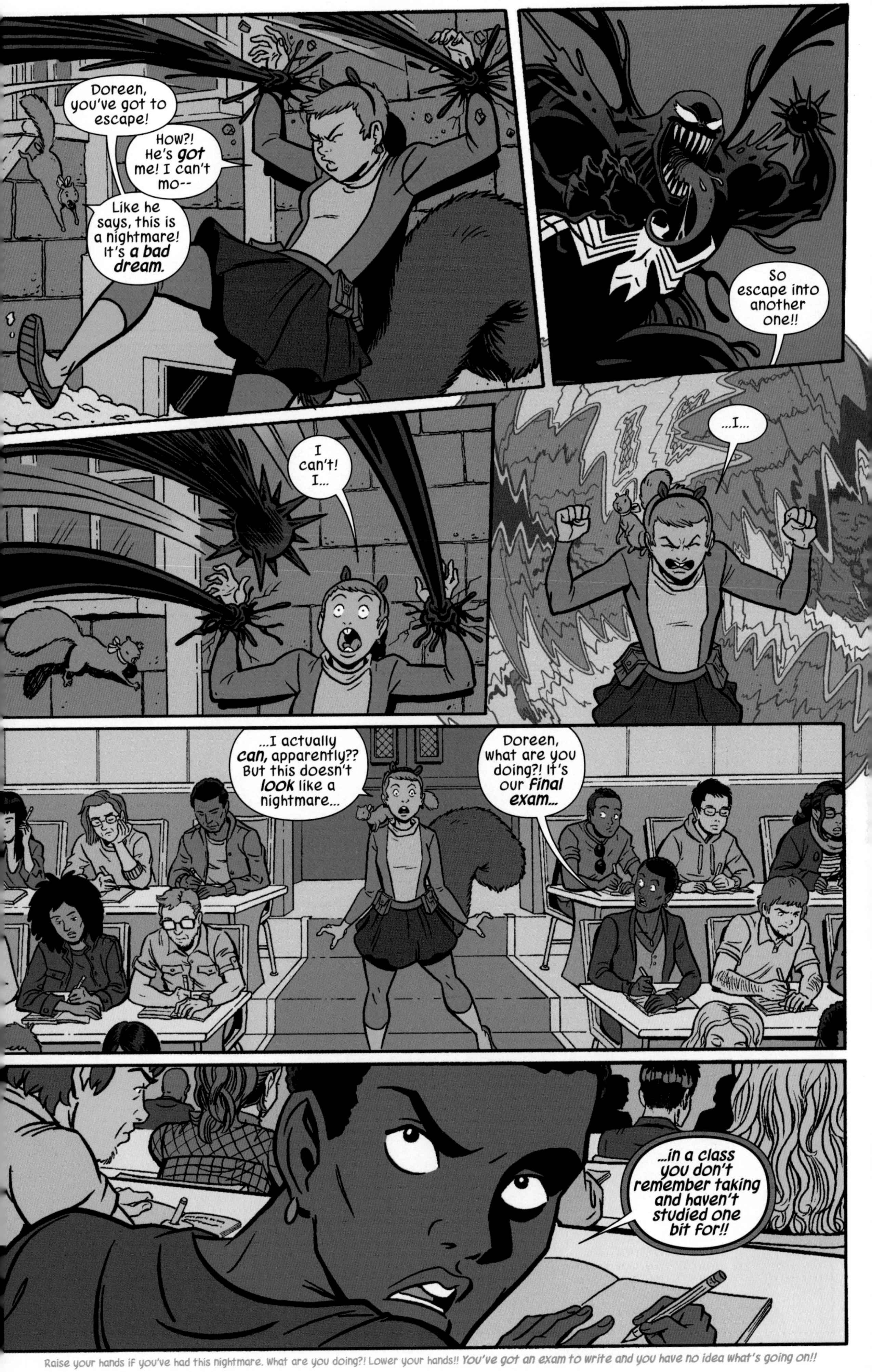
Doreen, you've got to escape!
HOW?! He's got me! I can't mo--
Like he says, this is a nightmare! It's a bad dream.
So escape into another one!!
I can't! I...
...I...
...I actually can, apparently?? But this doesn't look like a nightmare...
Doreen, what are you doing?! It's our final exam...
...in a class you don't remember taking and haven't studied one bit for!!

Raise your hands if you've had this nightmare. What are you doing?! Lower your hands!! *You've got an exam to write and you have no idea what's going on!!*

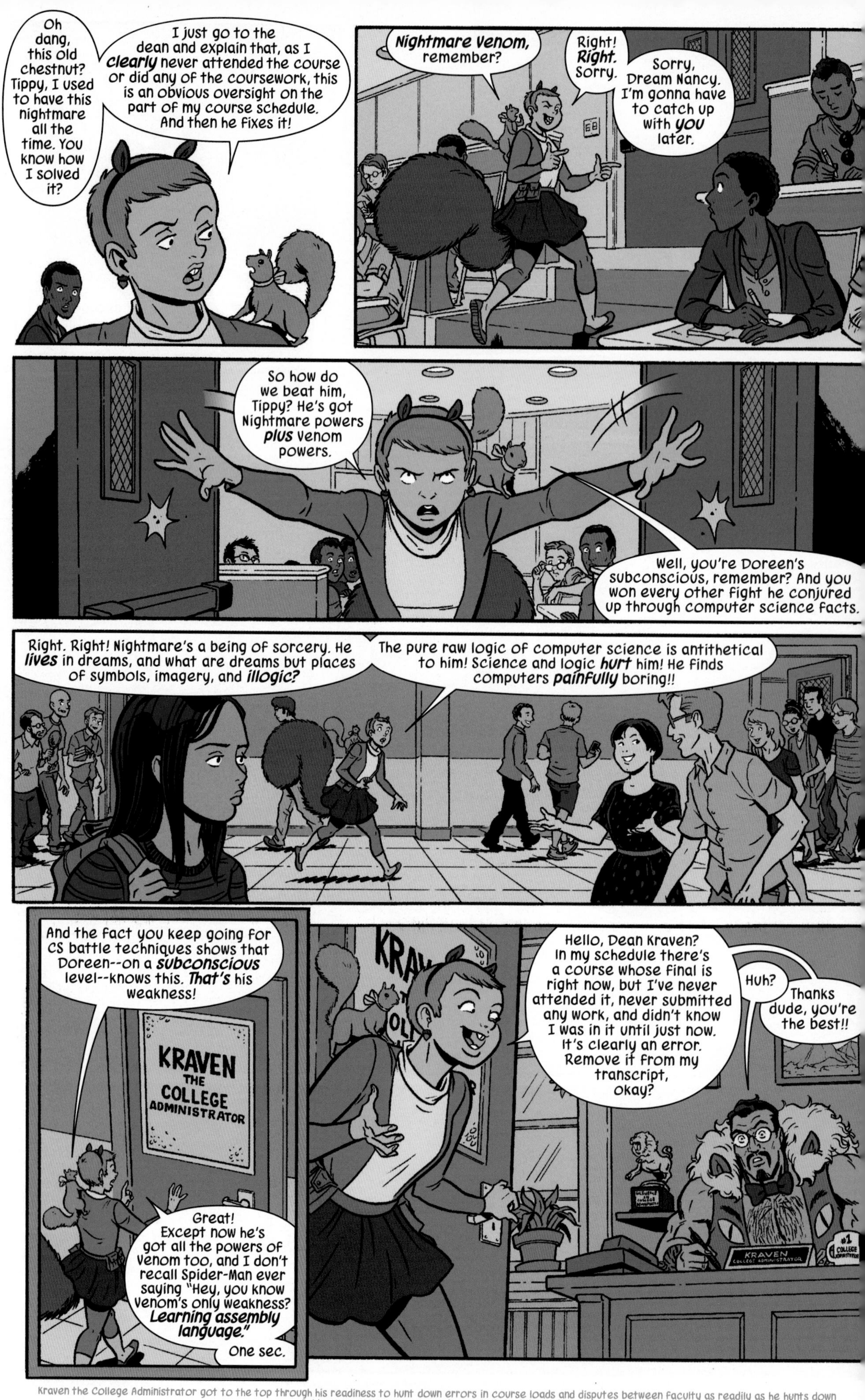
Oh dang, this old chestnut? Tippy, I used to have this nightmare all the time. You know how I solved it?
I just go to the dean and explain that, as I clearly never attended the course or did any of the coursework, this is an obvious oversight on the part of my course schedule. And then he fixes it!
Nightmare Venom, remember?
Right! Right. Sorry.
Sorry, Dream Nancy. I'm gonna have to catch up with you later.
So how do we beat him, Tippy? He's got Nightmare powers plus Venom powers.
Well, you're Doreen's subconscious, remember? And you won every other fight he conjured up through computer science facts.
Right. Right! Nightmare's a being of sorcery. He lives in dreams, and what are dreams but places of symbols, imagery, and illogic?
The pure raw logic of computer science is antithetical to him! Science and logic hurt him! He finds computers painfully boring!!
And the fact you keep going for CS battle techniques shows that Doreen--on a subconscious level--knows this. That's his weakness!
KRAVEN THE COLLEGE ADMINISTRATOR
Great! Except now he's got all the powers of Venom too, and I don't recall Spider-Man ever saying "Hey, you know Venom's only weakness? Learning assembly language."
One sec.
Hello, Dean Kraven? In my schedule there's a course whose final is right now, but I've never attended it, never submitted any work, and didn't know I was in it until just now. It's clearly an error. Remove it from my transcript, okay?
Huh?
Thanks dude, you're the best!!
KRAVEN COLLEGE ADMINISTRATOR
#1 COLLEGE ADMINISTRATOR
Kraven the College Administrator got to the top through his readiness to hunt down errors in course loads and disputes between faculty as readily as he hunts down Spider-Man, which is to say: *extremely friggin' readily.*

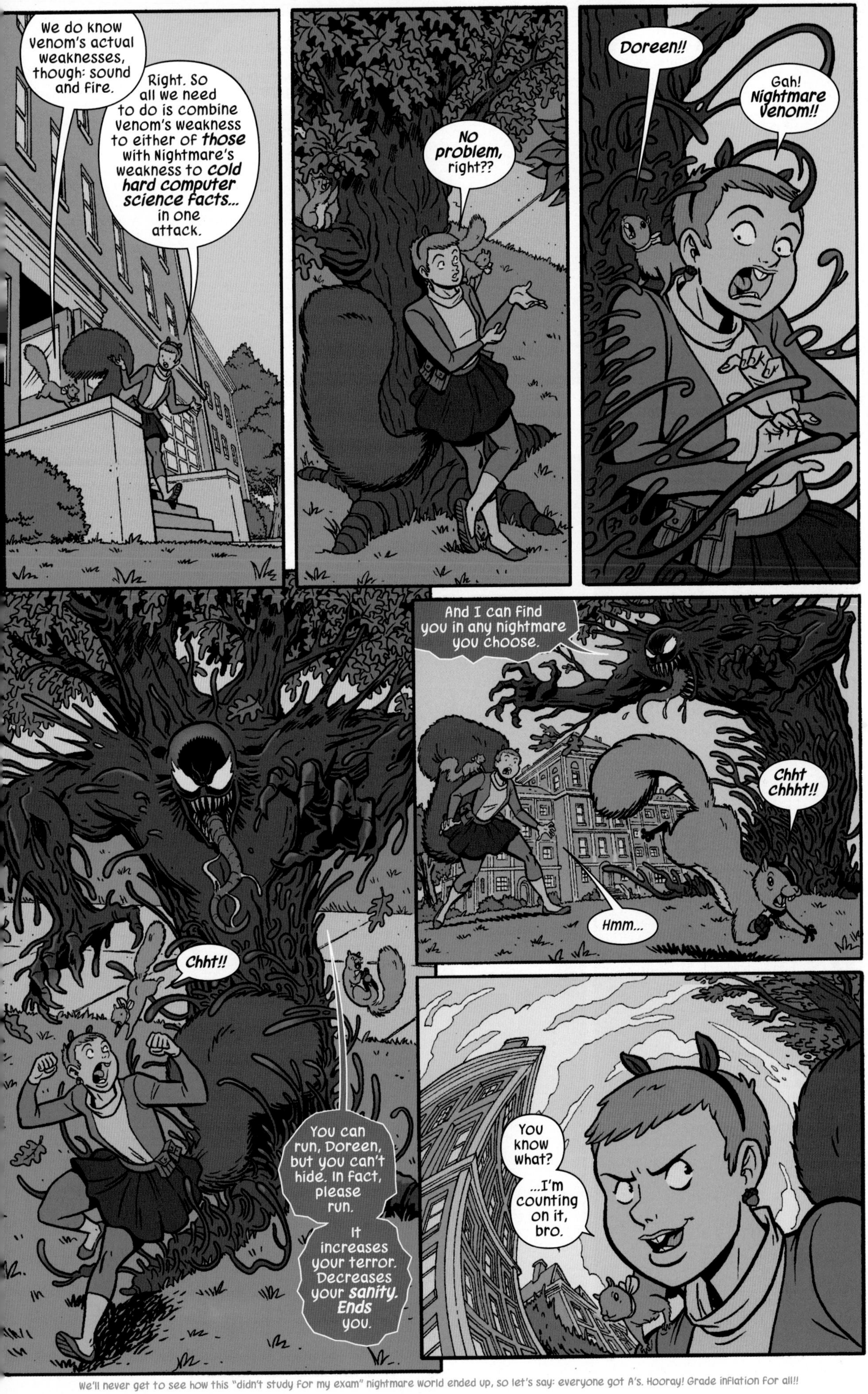
We do know Venom's actual weaknesses, though: sound and fire.
Right. So all we need to do is combine Venom's weakness to either of those with Nightmare's weakness to cold hard computer science facts... in one attack.
No problem, right??
Doreen!!
Gah! Nightmare Venom!!
Chht!!
You can run, Doreen, but you can't hide. In fact, please run.
It increases your terror. Decreases your sanity. Ends you.
And I can find you in any nightmare you choose.
Chht Chhht!!
Hmm...
You know what?
...I'm counting on it, bro.

We'll never get to see how this "didn't study for my exam" nightmare world ended up, so let's say: everyone got A's. Hooray! Grade inflation for all!!

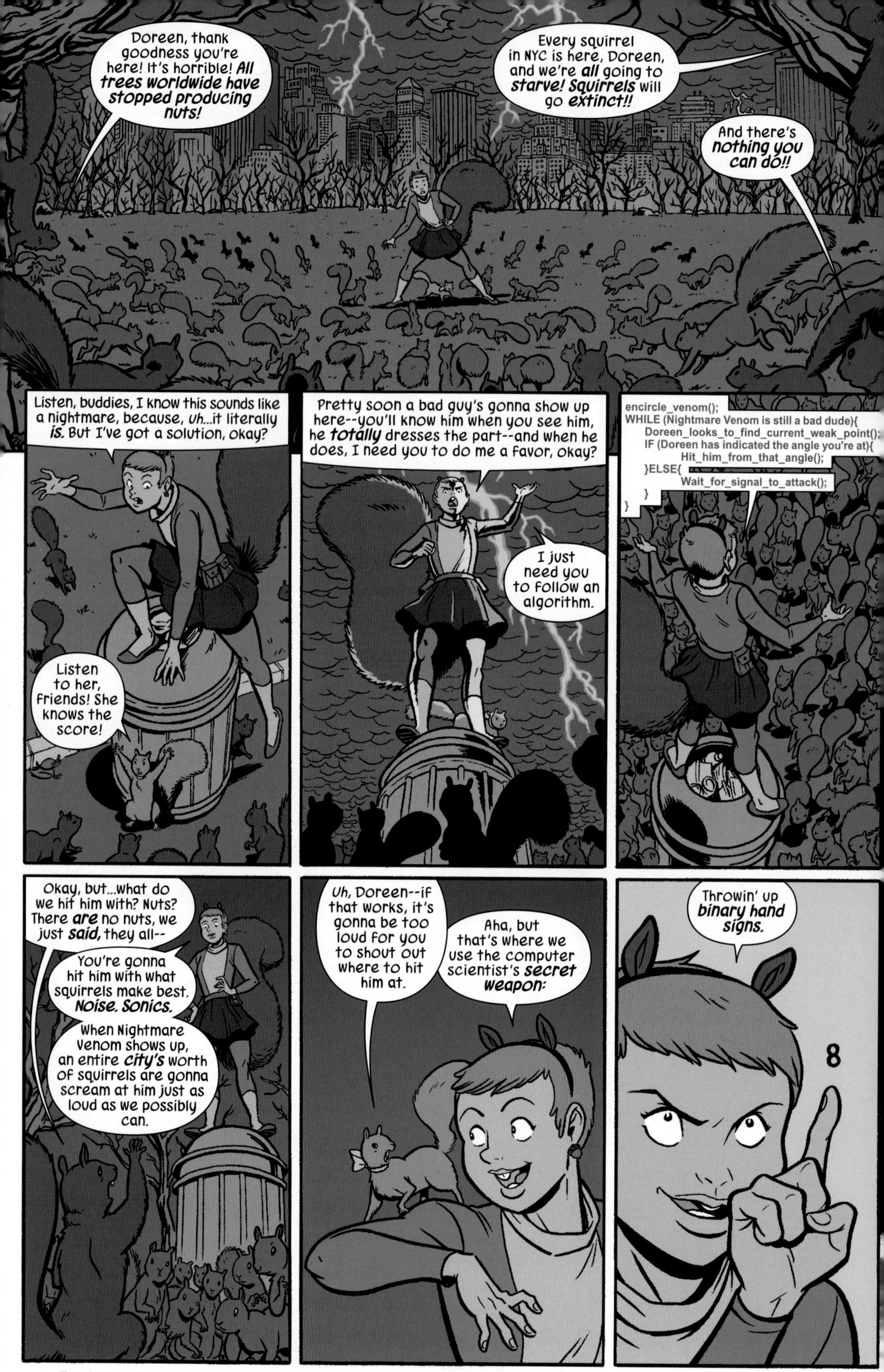

Doreen, thank goodness you're here! It's horrible! All trees worldwide have stopped producing nuts!
Every squirrel in NYC is here, Doreen, and we're all going to starve! Squirrels will go extinct!!
And there's nothing you can do!!
Listen, buddies, I know this sounds like a nightmare, because, uh...it literally is. But I've got a solution, okay?
Listen to her, friends! She knows the score!
Pretty soon a bad guy's gonna show up here--you'll know him when you see him, he totally dresses the part--and when he does, I need you to do me a favor, okay?
I just need you to follow an algorithm.
encircle_venom();
WHILE (Nightmare Venom is still a bad dude){
Doreen_looks_to_find_current_weak_point();
IF (Doreen has indicated the angle you're at){
Hit_him_from_that_angle();
}ELSE{
Wait_for_signal_to_attack();
}
}
Okay, but...what do we hit him with? Nuts? There are no nuts, we just said, they all--
You're gonna hit him with what squirrels make best. Noise. Sonics.
When Nightmare Venom shows up, an entire city's worth of squirrels are gonna scream at him just as loud as we possibly can.
Uh, Doreen--if that works, it's gonna be too loud for you to shout out where to hit him at.
Aha, but that's where we use the computer scientist's secret weapon:
Throwin' up binary hand signs.
8

I'm not gonna say you can recognize a computer scientist by the way they're constantly throwing up binary hand signs. I'm just saying, in a just world, you *could.*

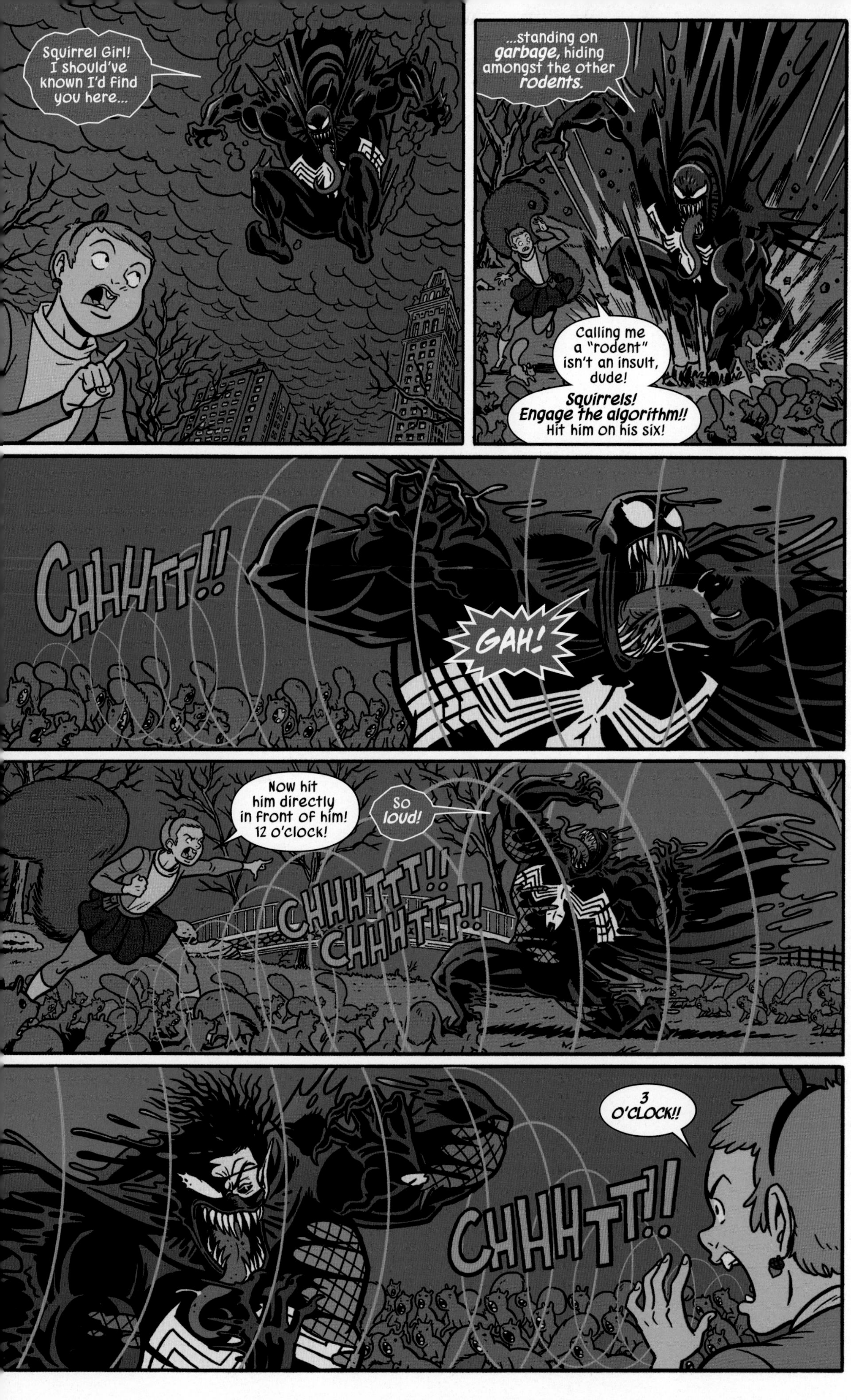
Squirrel Girl! I should've known I'd find you here...
...standing on garbage, hiding amongst the other rodents.
Calling me a "rodent" isn't an insult, dude!
Squirrels! Engage the algorithm!! Hit him on his six!
CHHHTT!!
GAH!
Now hit him directly in front of him! 12 o'clock!
So loud!
CHHHTTT!!
CHHHTTT!!
3 O'CLOCK!!
CHHHTT!!

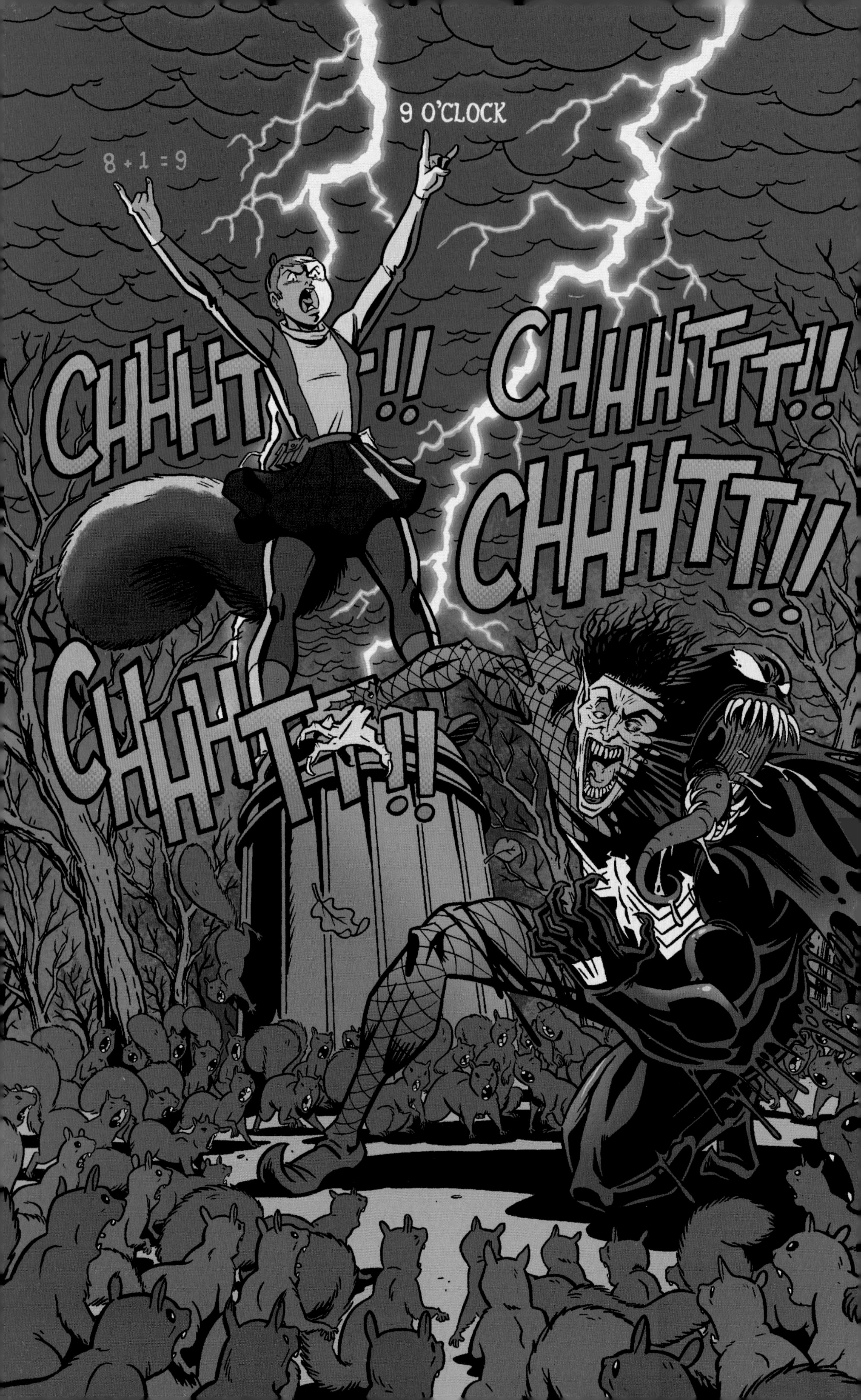

8 + 1 = 9
9 O'CLOCK
CHHHTT!!
CHHHTTT!!
CHHHTTT!!
CHHHTT!!

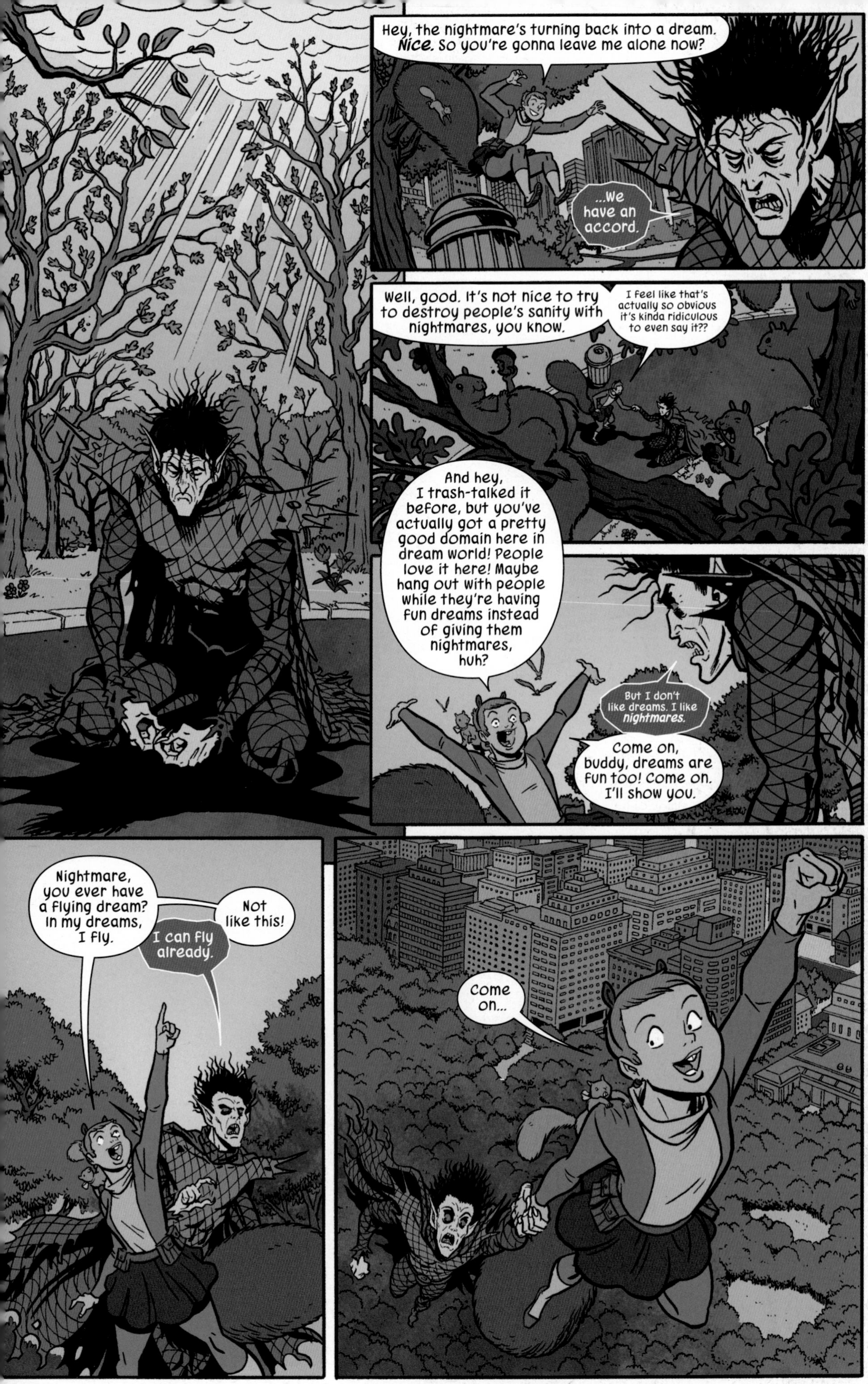
Hey, the nightmare's turning back into a dream. *Nice.* So you're gonna leave me alone now?
...We have an accord.
Well, good. It's not nice to try to destroy people's sanity with nightmares, you know.
I feel like that's actually so obvious it's kinda ridiculous to even say it??
And hey, I trash-talked it before, but you've actually got a pretty good domain here in dream world! People love it here! Maybe hang out with people while they're having fun dreams instead of giving them nightmares, huh?
But I don't like dreams. I like *nightmares.*
Come on, buddy, dreams are fun too! Come on. I'll show you.
Nightmare, you ever have a flying dream? In my dreams, I fly.
I can fly already.
Not like this!
Come on...

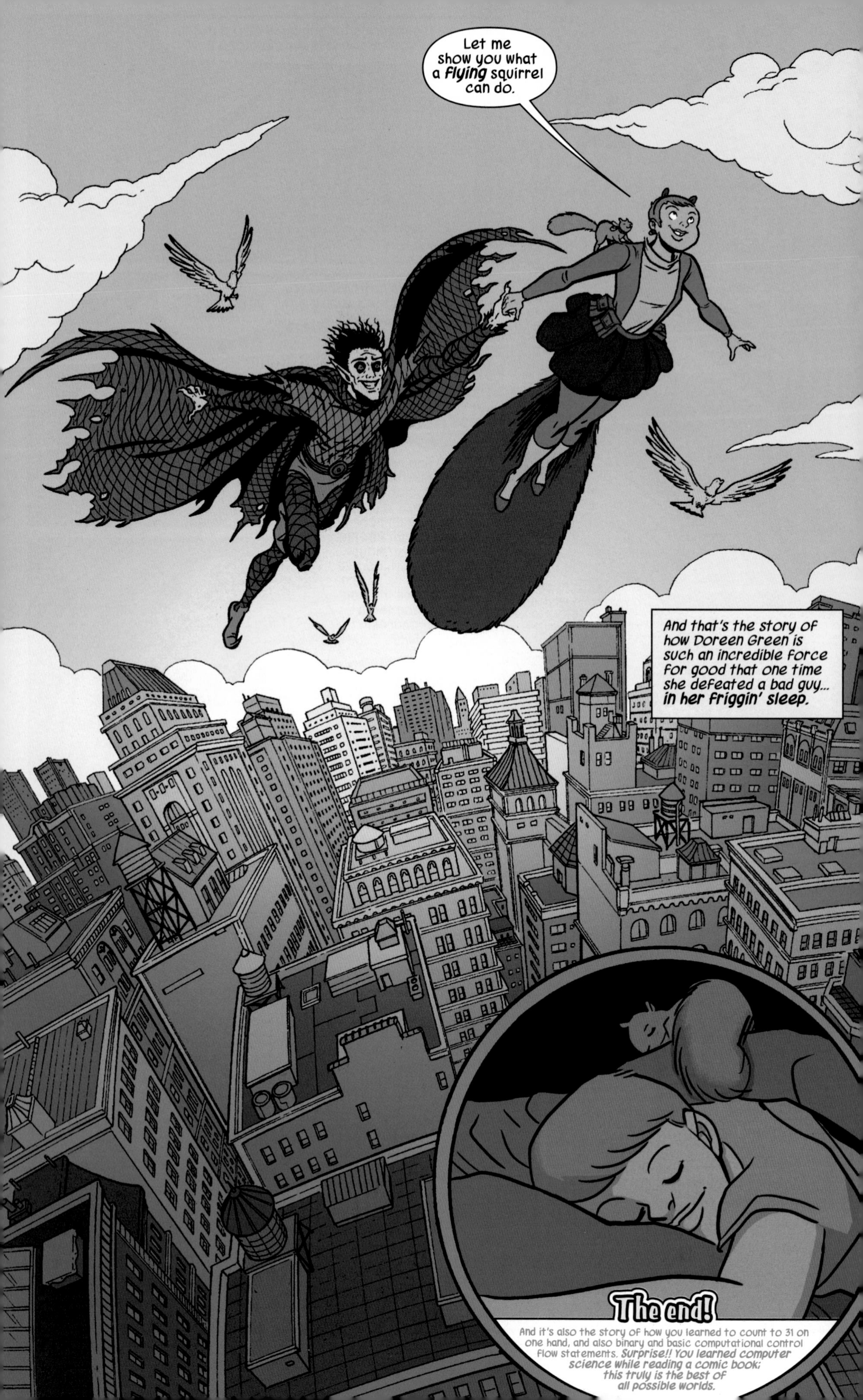
Let me show you what a *flying* squirrel can do.
And that's the story of how Doreen Green is such an incredible force for good that one time she defeated a bad guy... ***in her friggin' sleep.***
The end!
And it's also the story of how you learned to count to 31 on one hand, and also binary and basic computational control flow statements. *Surprise!! You learned computer science while reading a comic book; this truly is the best of all possible worlds.*

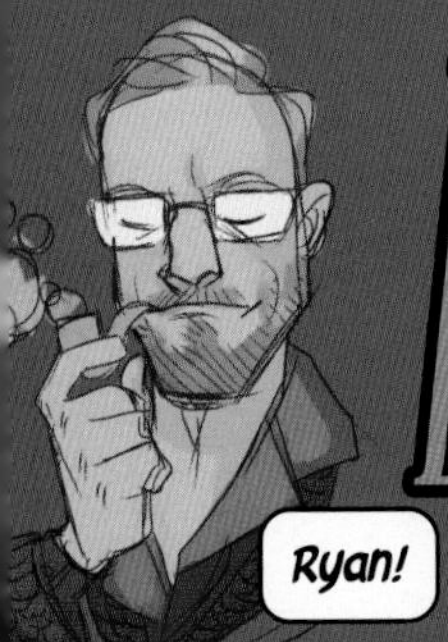
Ryan!

Letters From Nuts

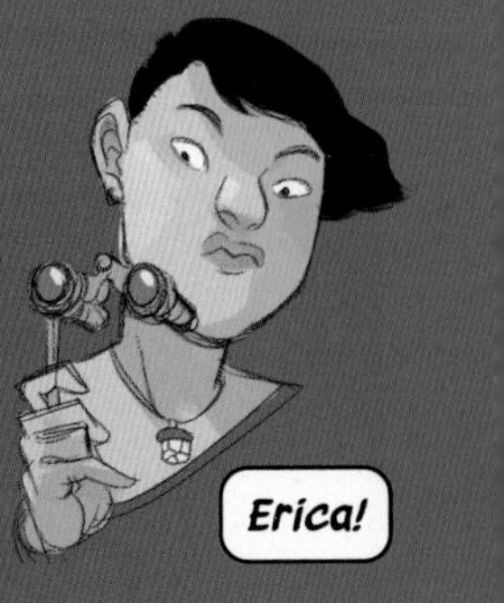
Erica!

Send letters to mheroes@marvel.com or 135 W 50th St, 7th Floor, New York, NY 10020 (Please mark "OKAY TO PRINT")

ica,

I'm totally in love with the proposal page from Squirrel Girl 9. It may be my favorite page in the book to date. Doreen's xpression is so natural and communicative! I really love your ork. Please never stop.

yan,

I have it on good authority that the maddening depths of the ceans will seek their revenge on Tuesday.

Deepest regards,
Gary

RYAN: But which Tuesday, Gary? WHICH TUESDAY??

ERICA: I won't! Because that's when they stop paying you.

oreen,

This is only the 2nd fan letter I've ever written in 40 years of njoying comic books.

I've been rescuing, raising and releasing baby squirrels long efore I had heard of you and Tippy.

The other day I brought Halo to my local comic book store nd she went nuts over your book. She needs a role model like ou to keep her on the good path.

On behalf of all squirrels, we thank you for your service. All ail the unbeatable Squirrel Girl!!!!

Sean D. and Halo
Santa Cruz, CA

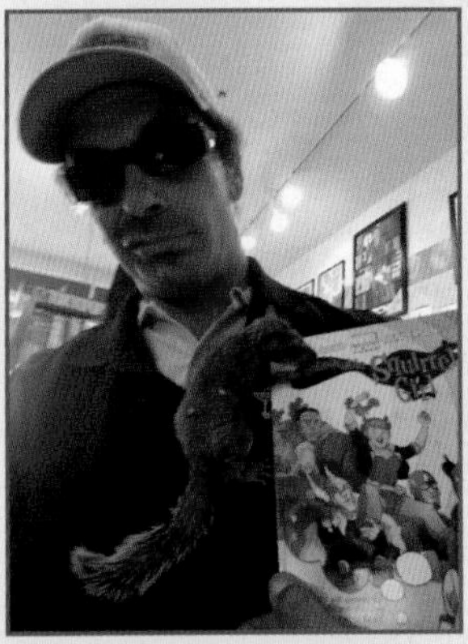

RYAN: This is an amazing photo – the first time I've seen e book and a real squirrel together! – AND you do some pretty mazing things, rescuing baby squirrels for so long! Halo looks dorable and I hope she doesn't try to bury nuts in your hair (I as at San Diego Comic Con and met another squirrel rescuer ho said this happens to her all the time, and I promised I ould work it into the comic).

ERICA: If you ever want to share squirrel facts we're ryanqnorth and @ericafails on twitter. We've read a decent mount on squirrels at this point, but I'm always interested knowing more. Thank you for your important and adorable ork.

ear Squirrel Team,

I have to say, I love that this Mole Man storyline uses the ewspaper Spider-Man version of the character. I guess after he dnapped Aunt May, and she agreed to marry him on the spot, e learned a bit of a bad lesson in how to go about this modern ating thing?

Tim

RYAN: Haha, whoops, I haven't read the Newspaper pider-Man strip! But I have heard from my friend Joshua F. at he's a PRETTY MEMORABLE CHARACTER. But why is Aunt lay going around agreeing to marry everyone? What's your ngle, Aunt May??

ERICA: Aunt May is old, Ryan, and all the guys who want to et with her are in charge of major newspapers (a viable and espected form of news media at the time), or rule underground orlds, or are famous and notable scientists. I say, get some, irl.

ear Ryan and Erica,

My friend Julie gave me the first first 8 issues of SG for my irthday, and I became obsessed! So much so that I found myself oing to a comic book store for the first time in my life at age 30 to buy the second first 7 issues.

While reading the first issue 7, I was struck by the Intro to Databases class. I couldn't figure out why at first, but I realized it was because the issue showed a CS class filled with women and people of color, something I've never seen in real life. As a hapa woman programmer, I really appreciate the diverse representation in SG. Please keep it up!

Thanks,
Nicole

PS: I love the Deadpool cards, but surely SG and Nancy would have created a searchable database by now?

RYAN: Nicole, I am so into this - both the "I started reading comics because of this book" and the "I am a computer science woman of color and it's great to see some representation there"! When I was in school there were just three – THREE! – women in my classes. Ridiculous! That's changing, and it's great, and I hope that when you re-read this comic in a few years that scene WON'T pop out to you for the same reasons, because a wide variety of women doing a wide variety of things (especially in STEM fields) won't seem unusual. Fingers crossed! And thanks so much for writing.

ERICA: My thing is mostly that they're in New York and this isn't an episode of Friends – you're going to see non-white people. Also WOOOO HAPAS REPRESENT.

P.S. I think the cards are more about having the collection rather than convenience, otherwise why flip out at Whiplash instead of just taping your card back together?

Hello Squirrel Girl team!

I'll admit...at first I thought the idea of Squirrel Girl was the stupidest thing Marvel cooked up. However, I am glad to say you guys proved me wrong! She is now my favorite super hero and I collect all things squirrel. You guys have really made an impact on my comic writing (nothing published yet, I'm only 12). I also met Erica at Heroes Con. To wrap up this email I have a question and a suggestion: whose side is Squirrel Girl on in Civil War 2? And can Squirrel Girl meet Deadpool and talk to him about how she collects his trading cards?

Thomas

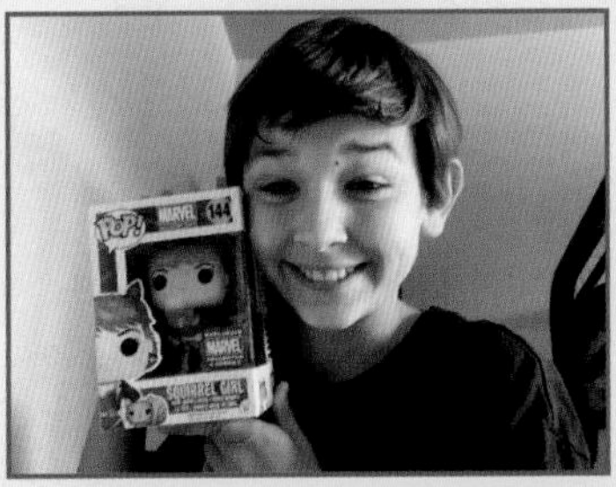

RYAN: Hi Thomas!! Man, I'm super impressed you're writing comics at age 12 – I didn't even start writing comics until I was 23! NICELY DONE. To answer your question: Squirrel Girl is on the side of "HEY MAYBE LET'S TALK ABOUT THIS BEFORE WE START A LITERAL CIVIL WAR," and Squirrel Girl actually WILL meet Deadpool in the upcoming "Squirrel Girl Beats Up The Marvel Universe!" graphic novel, but they don't get a chance to talk about the trading cards on account of how she is so busy beating up the Marvel Universe!

ERICA: Hey! It's nice talking again! I've been drawing for basically all my life so I get it! Keep it up. I can't wait to read your comics when they come out.

Ryan, Erica, and Rico,

Hello there! It's Hazel the Radford University Squirrel here! I just had the best weekend at Heroes Con 2016 with my buddy Professor Scott hanging out with Erica and Rico. I had so much fun meeting all the writers and artists and Erica even drew a sketch of Tippy-Toe that I had made into a button! Best of all: I got to meet Squirrel Girl and Tippy-Toe themselves! (Professor Scott seemed much more excited about some fellow named DMC. He told me he was some sort of musician but the only human group I know is the Squirrel Nut Zippers--- I found the name misleading on two levels.) My only question is, where was Ryan? He sure did miss a fun weekend! I'm attaching a picture of me and Erica so he can see what he missed.

P.S. Professor Scott really enjoyed your crossover with Howard the Duck and, in fact, hasn't enjoyed a crossover that much since he was 12 and Nomad teamed up with Ghost Rider.

Stay nutty, my friends!

Hazel
Squirrel
Nut Gathering Dept.
the trees outside of Young Hall
Radford, Va 24141
hazel@radford.edu

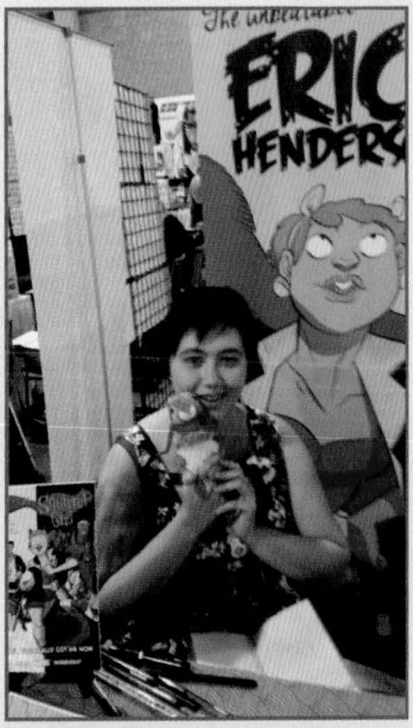

RYAN: I was in scenic Canada, imagining stories that I could ask Erica to draw for me!! But this sounds like an awesome time and I'm sorry I missed it. I really enjoyed the crossover too! I don't know how OTHER crossovers work, but since Chip and I live in the same town, and Erica and Joe live in the same town, we writers just talked about what we could do over dinner and I can only presume the artists did the same thing. It was like an excuse to hang out with friends, only at the end we went home and wrote a comic!

ERICA: That was when Nomad was going through his Lorenzo Lamas phase, right? The BEST Nomad? Anyway, Ryan and I will FINALLY be doing a convention appearance together at this year's New York Comic Con!

Next Issue:

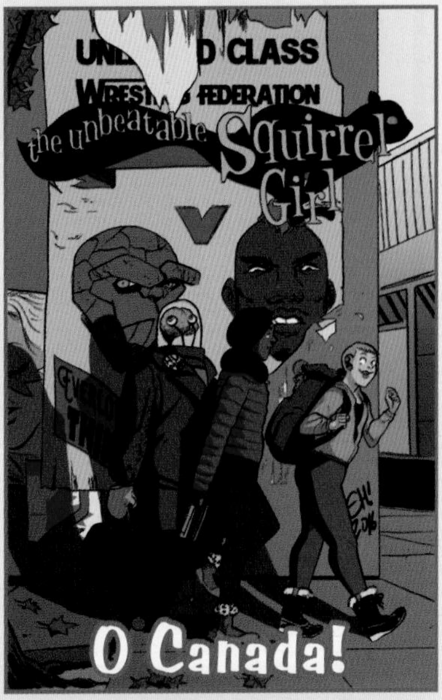

O Canada!

Attention, Squirrel Scouts! Make sure to check out our production blog, **unbeatablesquirrelgirl.tumblr.com**, where we post behind-the-scenes stuff on how the book gets made, along with all sorts of cool things *you* make: fanart, cosplay, whatever!

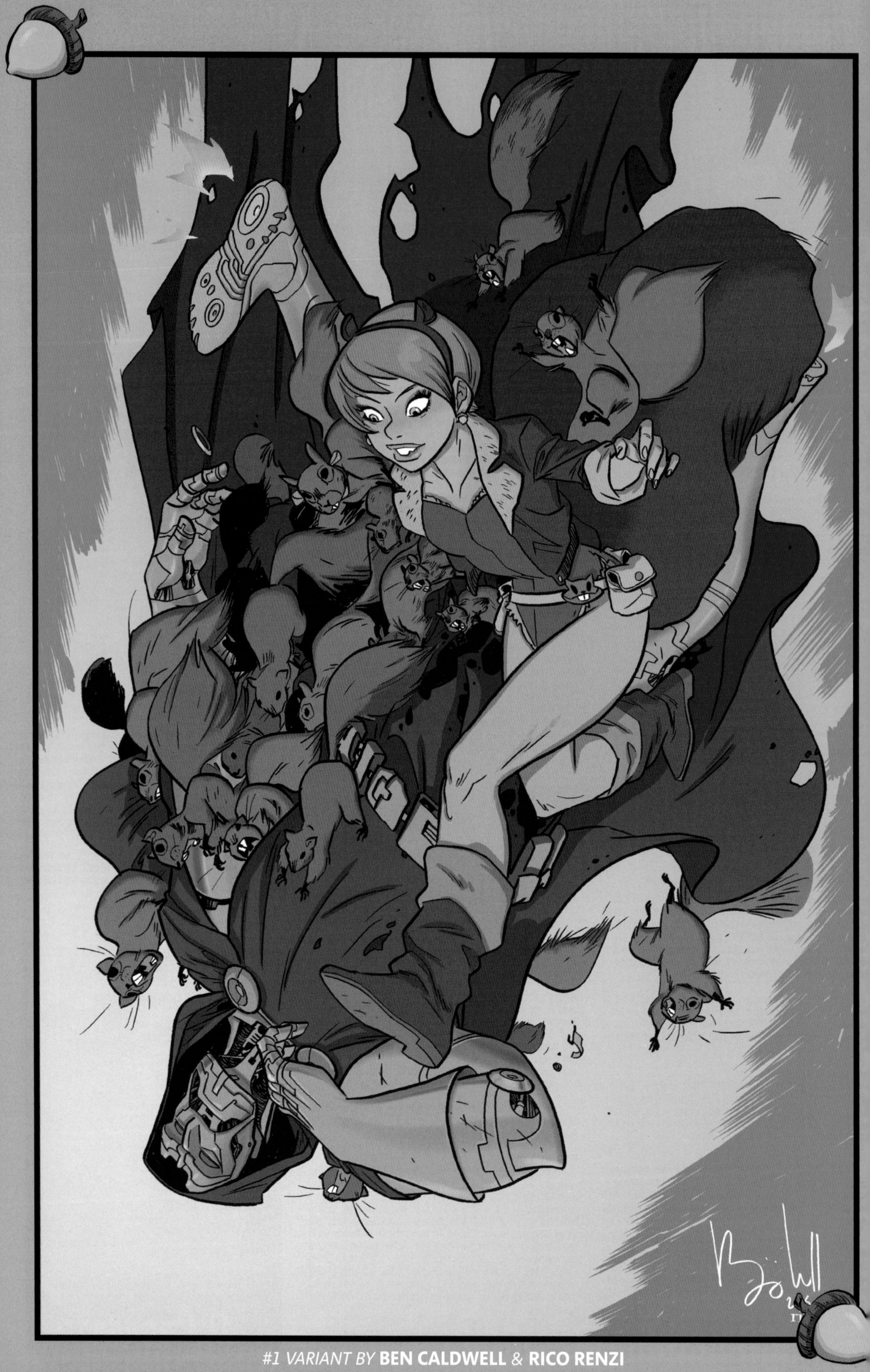

#1 VARIANT BY **BEN CALDWELL** & **RICO RENZI**

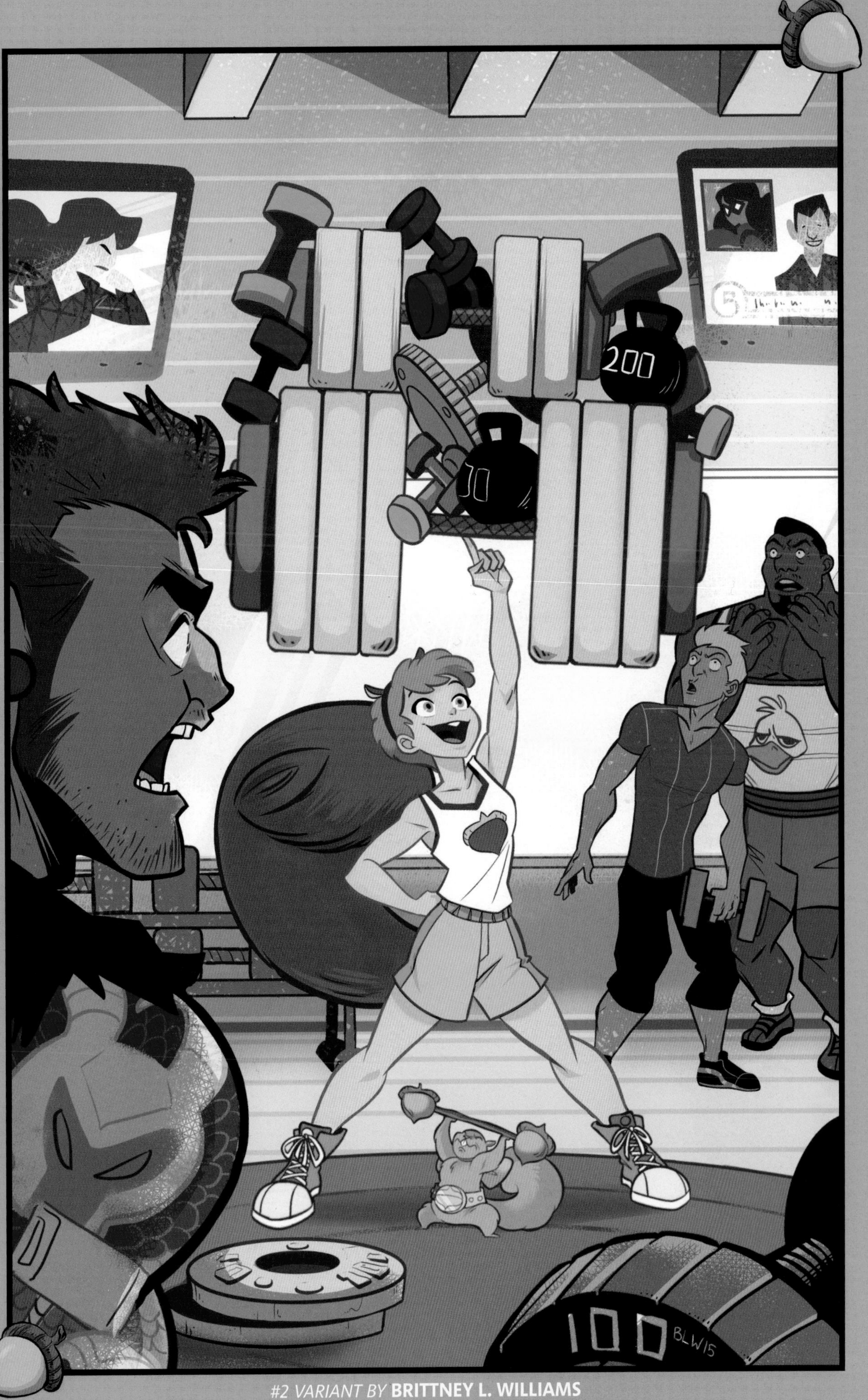
200
100
BLW15

#2 VARIANT BY **BRITTNEY L. WILLIAMS**

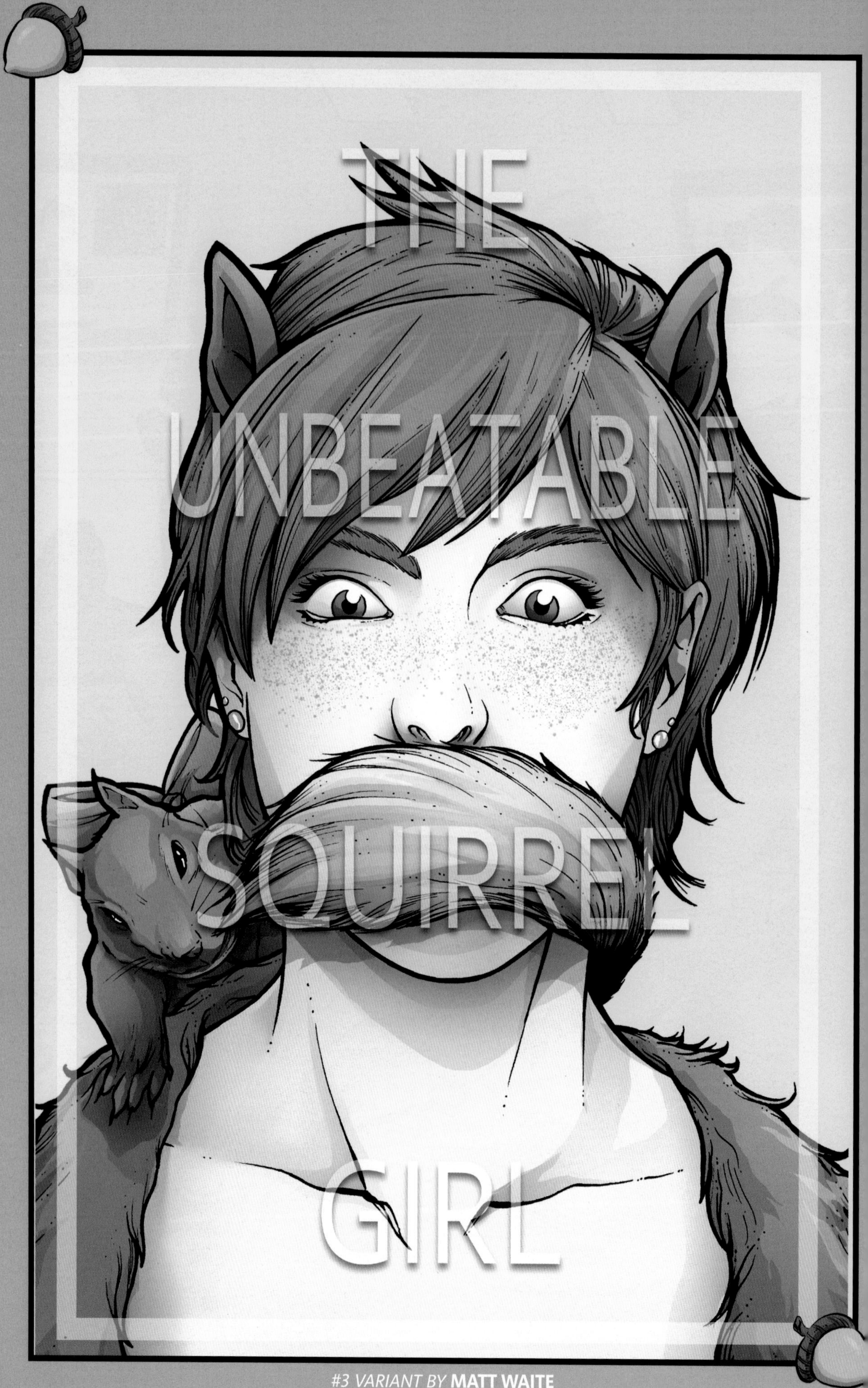
THE
UNBEATABLE
SQUIRREL
GIRL

#3 VARIANT BY **MATT WAITE**

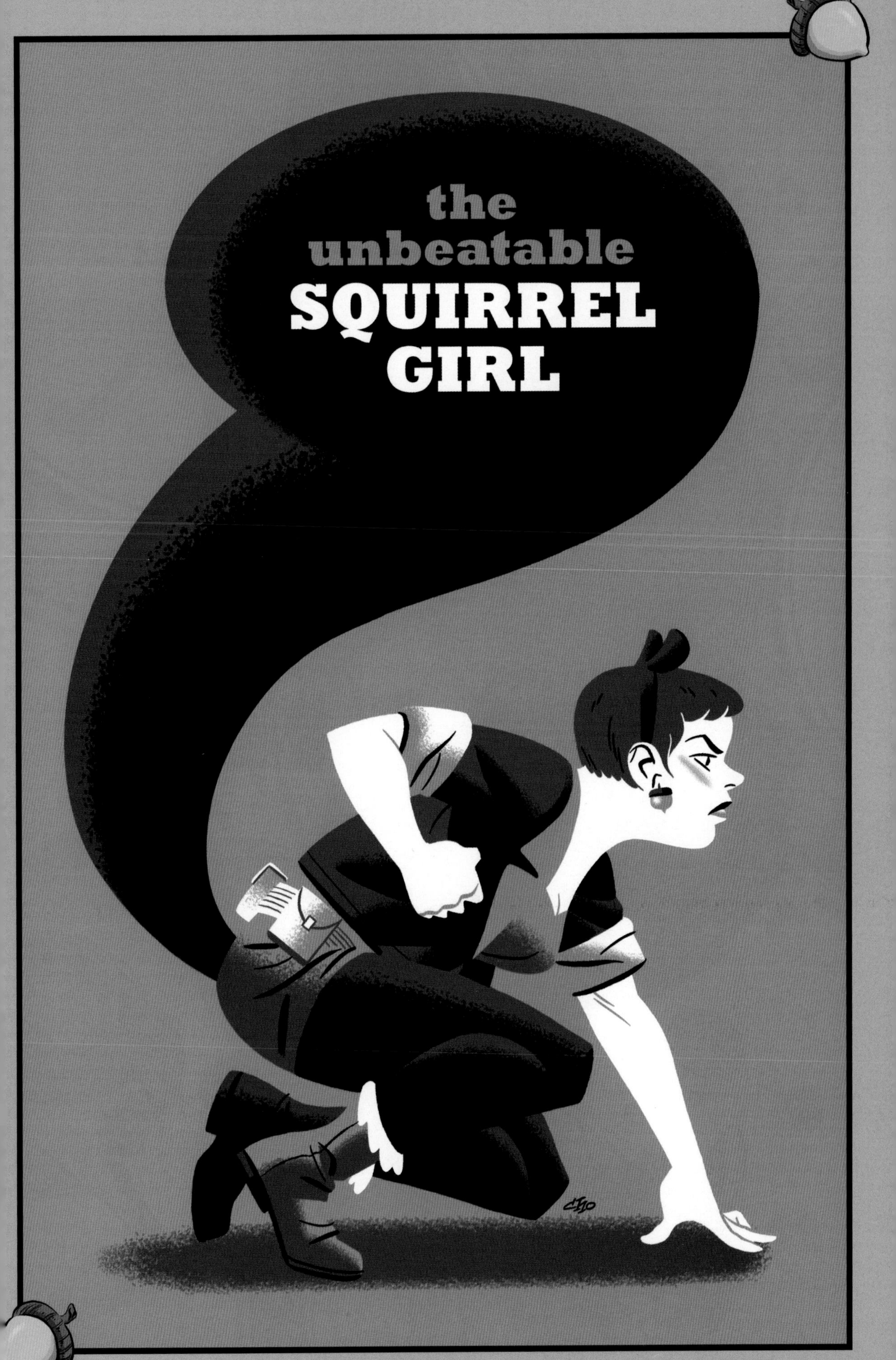

the unbeatable SQUIRREL GIRL
CHO

#5 *VARIANT BY* **MICHAEL CHO**

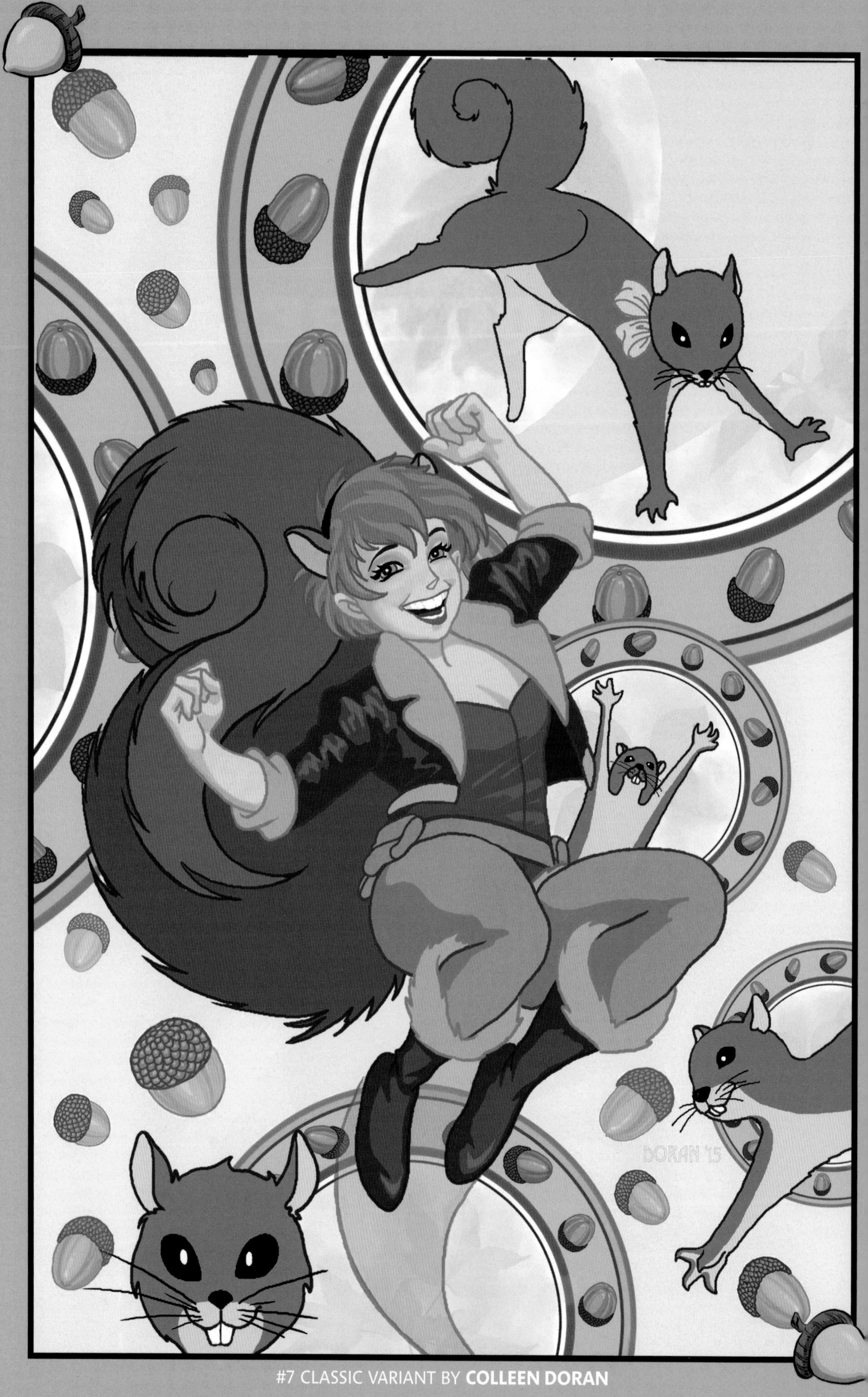
DORAN '15
#7 CLASSIC VARIANT BY **COLLEEN DORAN**

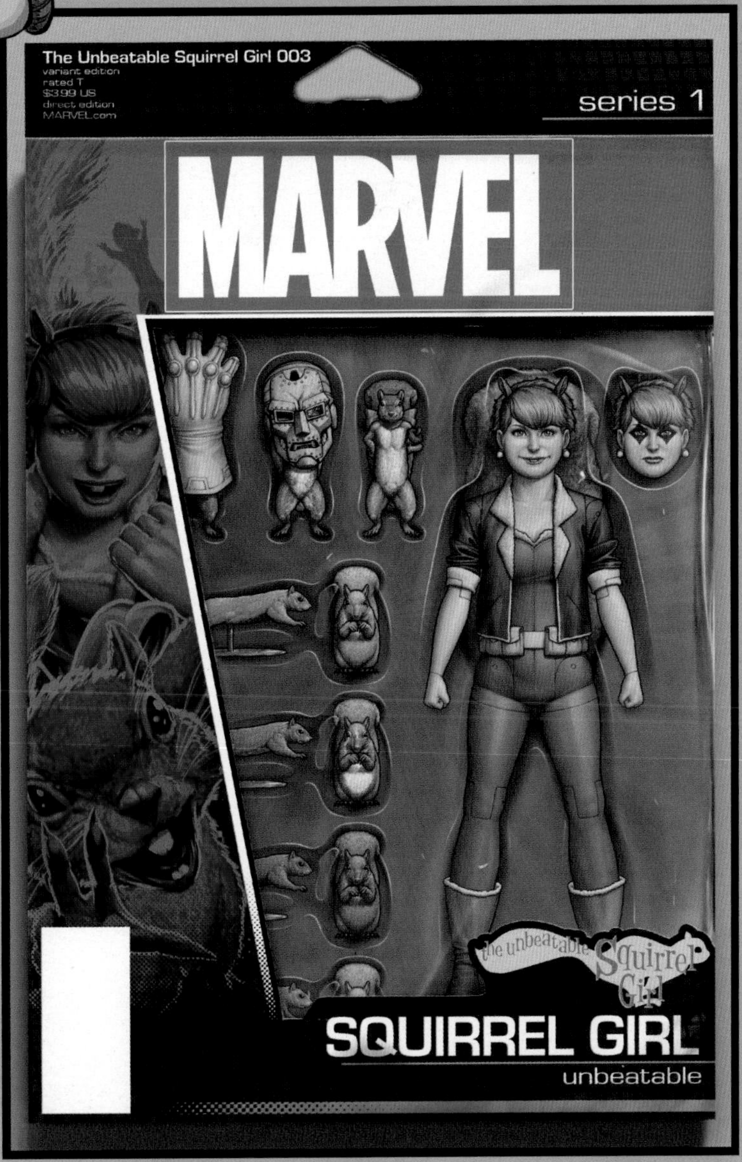
The Unbeatable Squirrel Girl 003
variant edition
rated T
$3.99 US
direct edition
MARVEL.com
series 1
MARVEL
the unbeatable Squirrel Girl
SQUIRREL GIRL
unbeatable

#3 ACTION FIGURE VARIANT
BY **JOHN TYLER CHRISTOPHER**

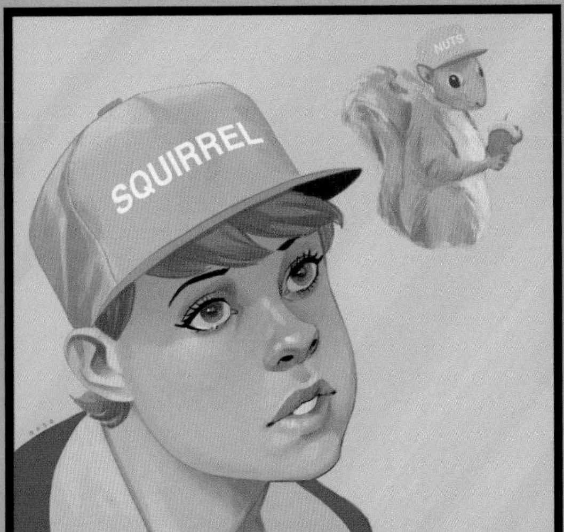
SQUIRREL
NUTS

#1 HIP-HOP VARIANT
BY **PHIL NOTO**

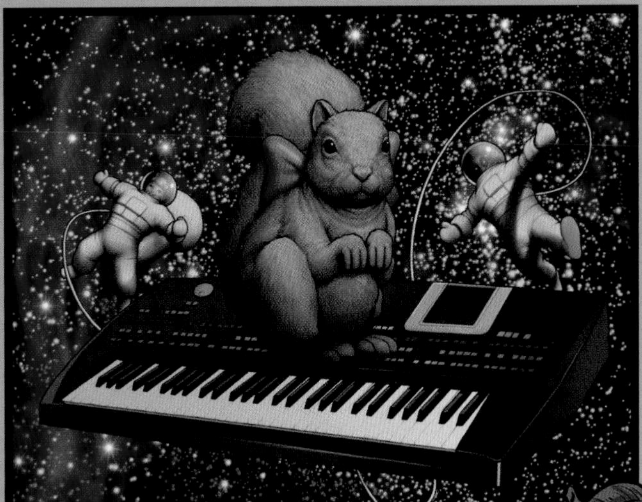

#4 DEADPOOL VARIANT
BY **JOHN TYLER CHRISTOPHER**

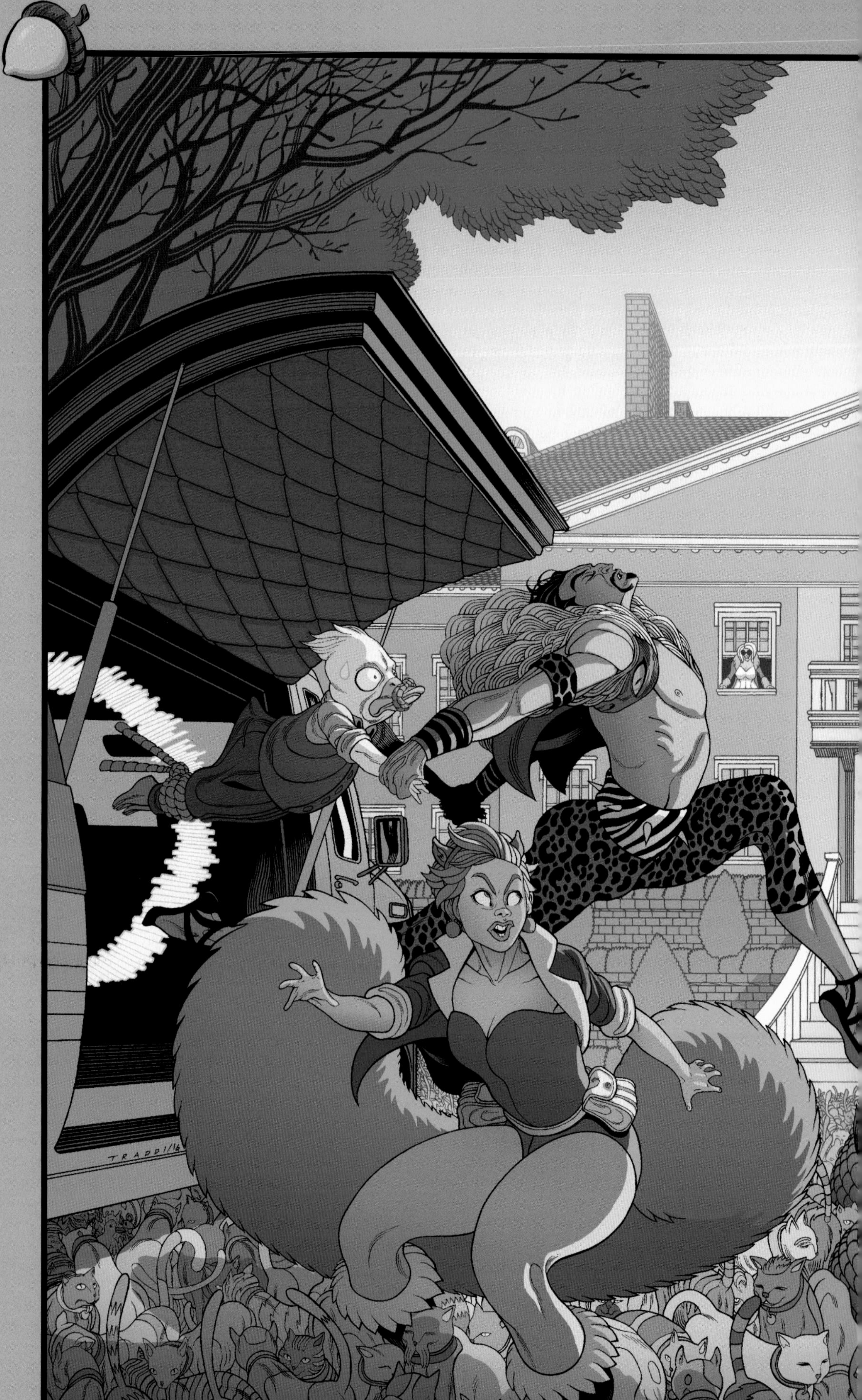
TRADD/16

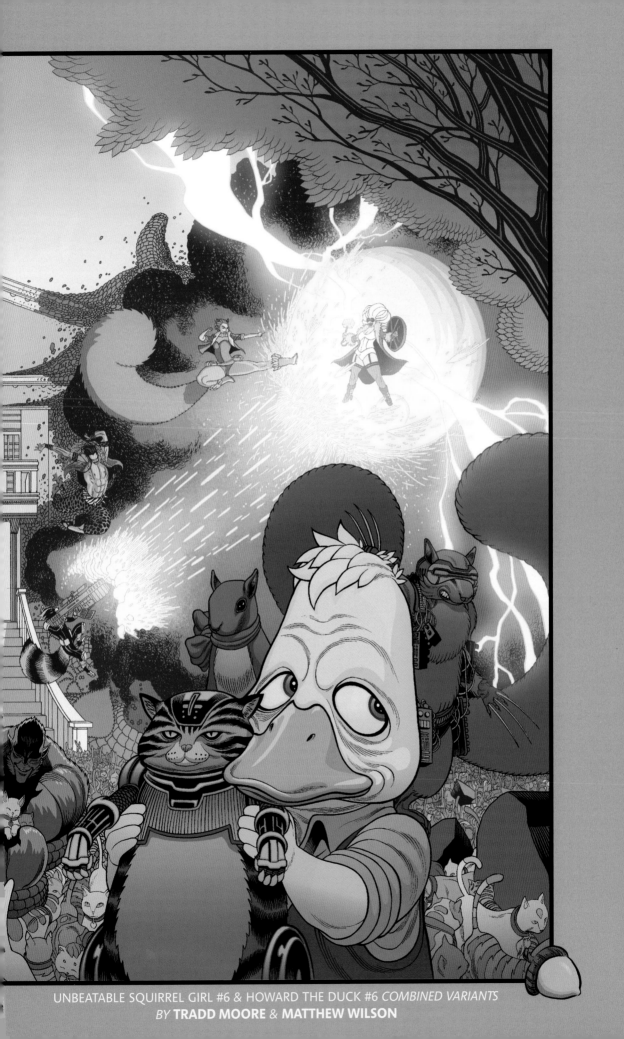

UNBEATABLE SQUIRREL GIRL #6 & HOWARD THE DUCK #6 *COMBINED VARIANTS*
BY **TRADD MOORE** & **MATTHEW WILSON**

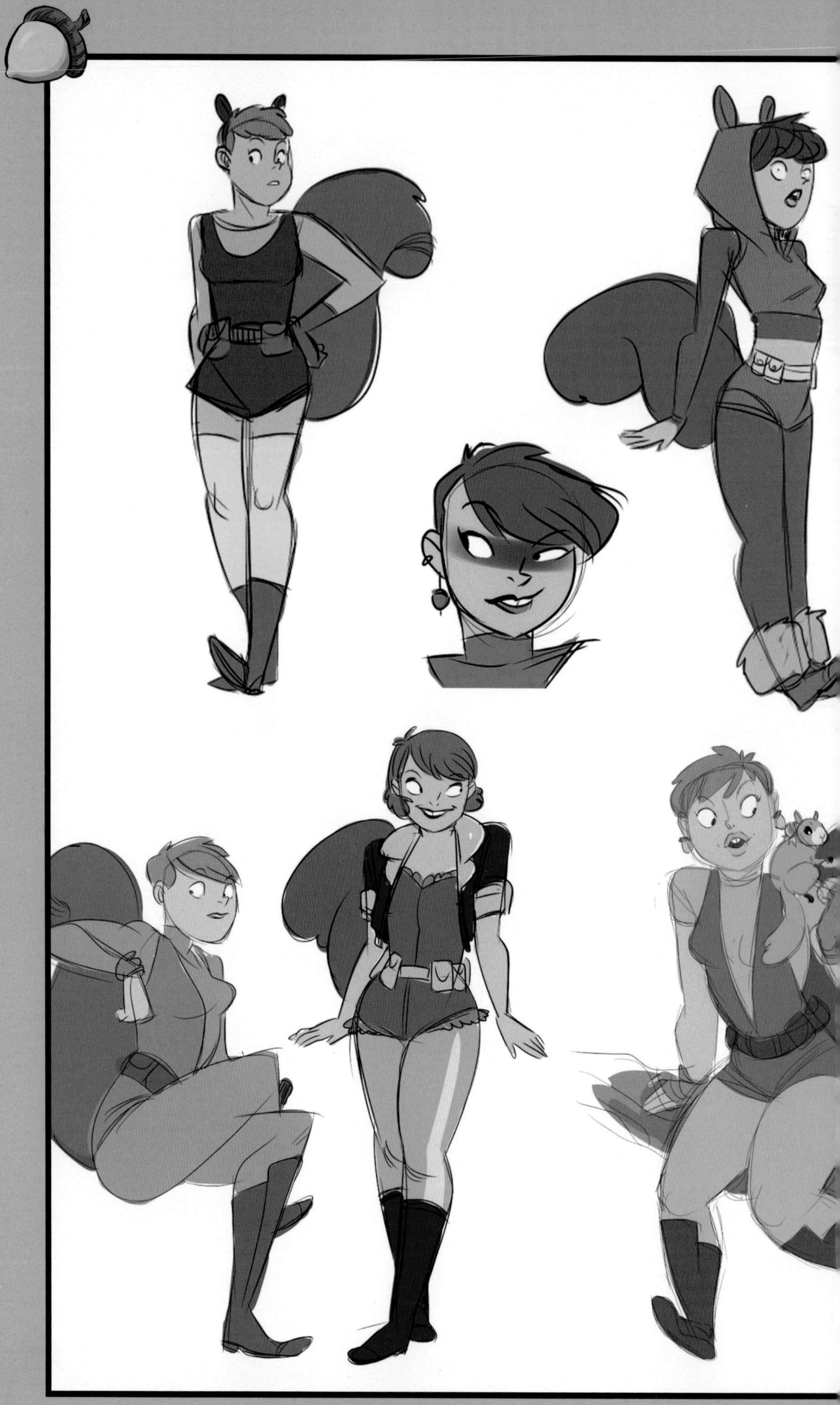

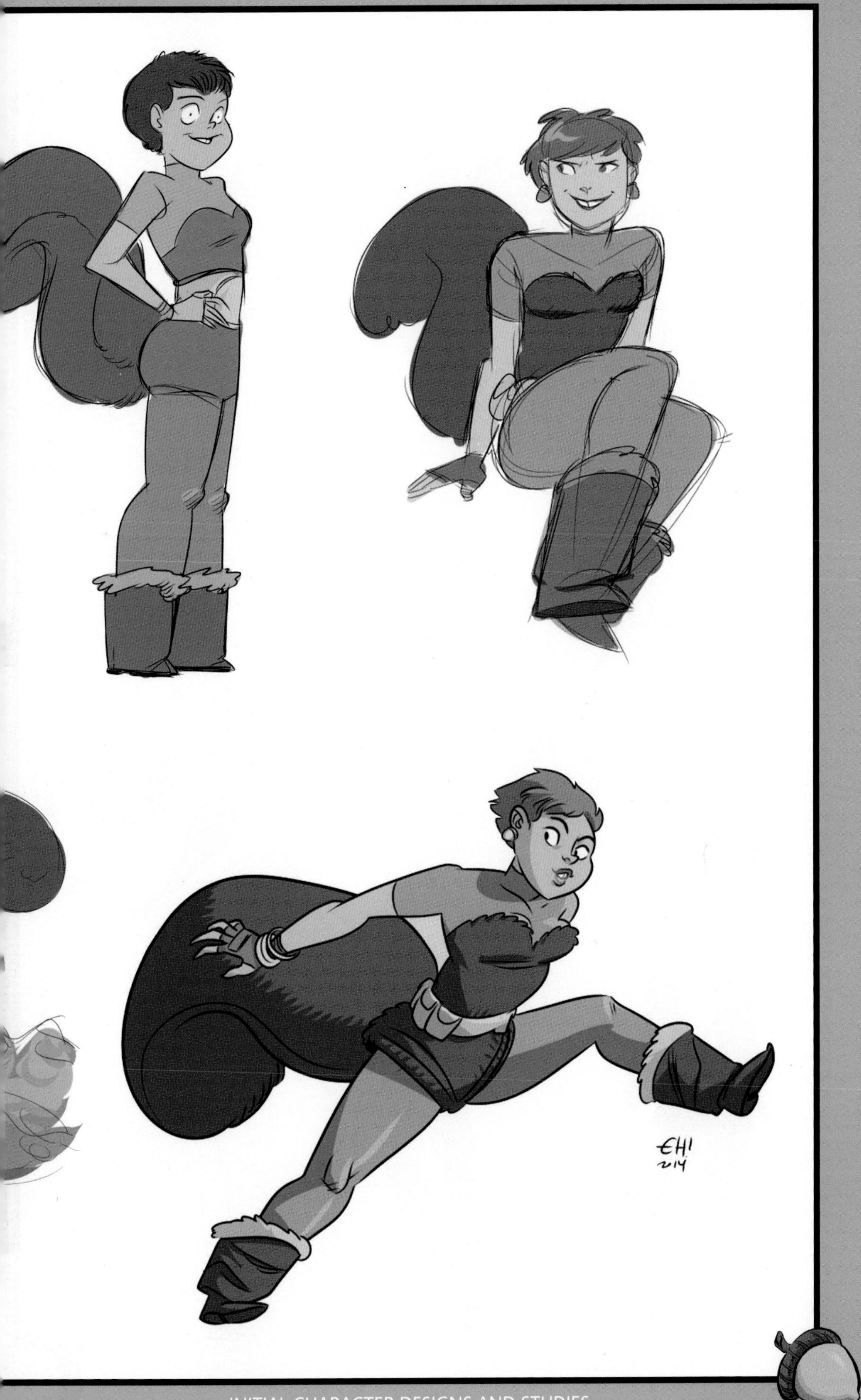
EH!
2014

INITIAL CHARACTER DESIGNS AND STUDIES
BY **ERICA HENDERSON**

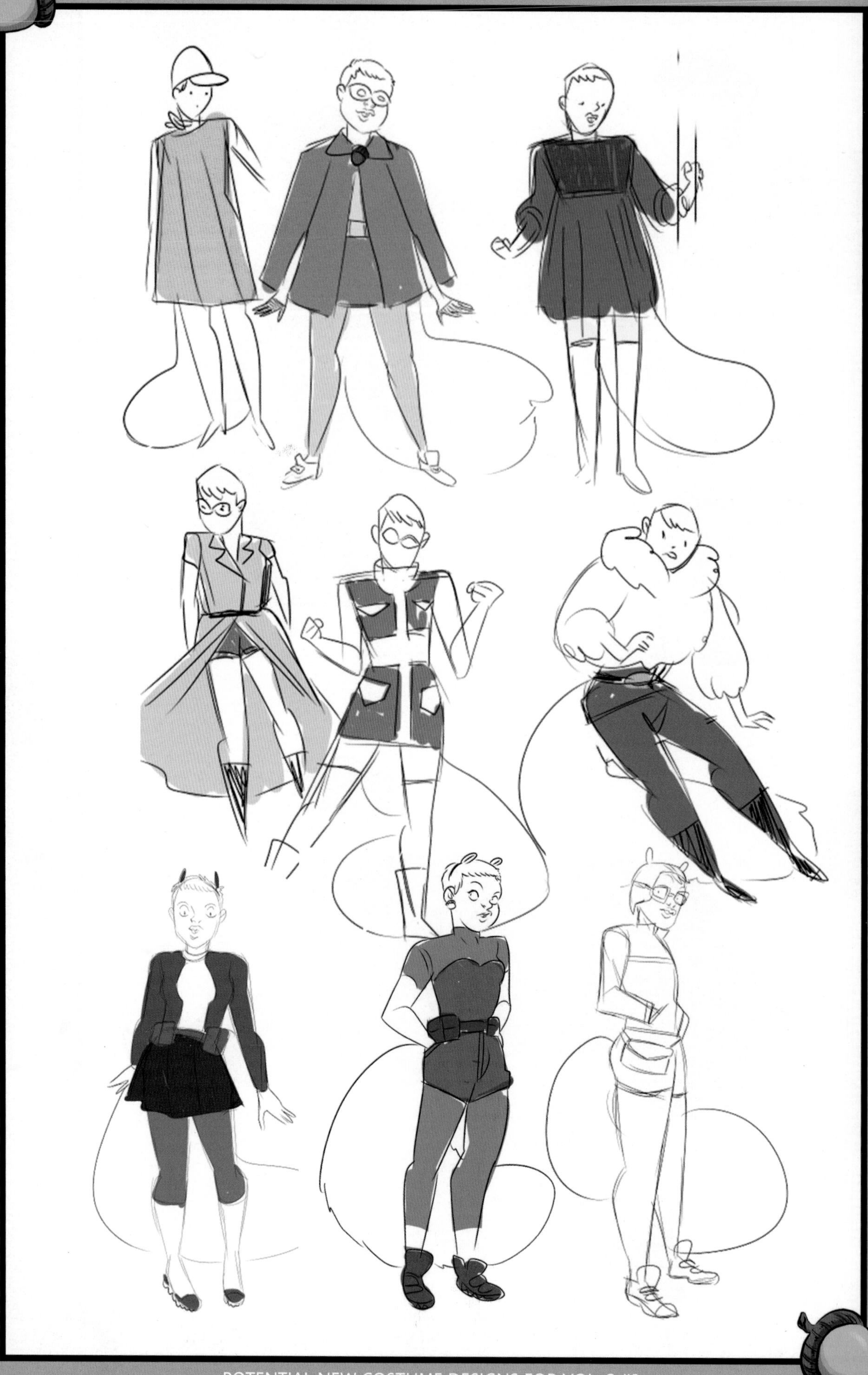

POTENTIAL NEW COSTUME DESIGNS FOR VOL. 2 #1
BY **ERICA HENDERSON**